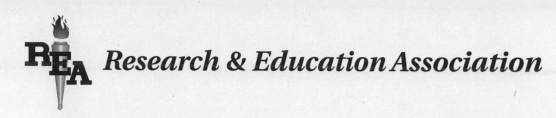

Research & Education Association

The Best Teachers' Test Preparation for the

PRAXIS™

Elementary Education

(Test Codes 0011 and 0014)

 With REA's TEST*ware*® on CD-ROM

Anita Price Davis, Ed.D.
Professor Emerita
Converse College, Spartanburg, S.C.

And the Staff of
Research & Education Association

Visit our Educator Support Center at:
www.REA.com/teacher

Research & Education Association
61 Ethel Road West
Piscataway, New Jersey 08854
E-mail: info@rea.com

The Best Teachers' Test Preparation for the Praxis™ Elementary Education Tests (Test Codes 0011 and 0014) With TEST*ware*® on CD-ROM

Printed in the United States of America

Library of Congress Control Number 2006935113

International Standard Book Number 0-7386-0281-7

Windows® is a registered trademark of Microsoft Corporation.

About the Author

Dr. Anita Price Davis is The Charles A. Dana Professor Emerita of Education and was the Director of Elementary Education at Converse College, Spartanburg, South Carolina. Dr. Davis earned her B.S. and M.A. from Appalachian State University and her doctorate from Duke University. She also received a postdoctoral fellowship to Ohio State University for two additional years of study.

Dr. Davis had worked more than 36 years at Converse College, where she served as the faculty advisor for Kappa Delta Epsilon, a national education honor organization. She also worked 5 years as a public school teacher.

Dr. Davis has received wide recognition for her work, including a letter of appreciation from the U.S. Department of the Interior, inclusion in *Contemporary Authors*, and a citation of appreciation from the Michigan Council of the Social Studies. She has authored/coauthored 23 funded grants for Converse College. She has served as a mentor and was a two-time President of the Spartanburg County Council of the International Reading Association. The state of South Carolina twice named her an outstanding educator, and she was twice a nominee for the CASE U.S. Professor of the Year.

Dr. Davis has authored, co-authored, and edited more than 80 books. She has written two college textbooks titled *Reading Instruction Essentials* and *Children's Literature Essentials*. Dr. Davis has published several history books and is also the author of more than 80 papers, book reviews, journal articles, and encyclopedia entries.

About Research & Education Association

Founded in 1959, Research & Education Association is dedicated to publishing the finest and most effective educational materials—including software, study guides, and test preps—for students in middle school, high school, college, graduate school, and beyond.

REA's Test Preparation series includes books and software for all academic levels in almost all disciplines. Research & Education Association publishes test preps for students who have not yet entered high school, as well as for high school students preparing to enter college. Students from countries around the world seeking to attend college in the United States will find the assistance they need in REA's publications. For college students seeking advanced degrees, REA publishes test preps for many major graduate school admission examinations in a wide variety of disciplines, including engineering, law, and medicine. Students at every level, in every field, with every ambition can find what they are looking for among REA's publications.

REA's practice tests are always based upon the most recently administered exams and include every type of question that you can expect on the actual exams.

REA's publications and educational materials are highly regarded and continually receive an unprecedented amount of praise from professionals, instructors, librarians, parents, and students. Our authors are as diverse as the fields represented in the books we publish. They are well-known in their respective disciplines and serve on the faculties of prestigious high schools, colleges, and universities throughout the United States and Canada.

Today, REA's wide-ranging catalog is a leading resource for teachers, students, and professionals.

We invite you to visit us at *www.rea.com* to find out how "REA is making the world smarter."

Acknowledgments

We would like to thank REA's Larry B. Kling, Vice President, Editorial, for supervising development; Pam Weston, Vice President, Publishing, for setting the quality standards for production integrity and managing the publication to completion; John Cording, Vice President, Technology, for coordinating the design, development, and testing of REA's TEST*ware*® software; Christine Reilley, Senior Editor, for project management and preflight editorial review; Diane Goldschmidt, Senior Editor, for post-production quality assurance; Michelle Boykins and Heena Patel, Technology Project Managers, for their software testing efforts; Christine Saul, Senior Graphic Artist, for cover design; and Jeff LoBalbo, Senior Graphic Artist, for post-production file mapping.

We also gratefully acknowledge Caroline Duffy and Sandra Rush for copyediting the manuscript and the team at Aquent Publishing Services for typesetting and indexing the manuscript.

CONTENTS

Praxis II

Elementary Education
Test Codes 0011 and 0014

Review

About This Book and TEST*ware*®

REA's *Best Teachers' Test Preparation for the PRAXIS Elementary Education Tests (Test Codes 0011 and 0014),* along with our companion software, provides you with an accurate and complete representation of both the PRAXIS II Elementary Education Test: Curriculum, Instruction, and Assessment (Test Code 0011) and the PRAXIS II Elementary Education Test: Content Knowledge (Test Code 0014). To ensure that you have the content information you will need, this volume includes customized reviews of each of the tests; it will help you pinpoint strategies to prepare for, take, and pass the PRAXIS II Elementary Education Examinations. It also provides practice questions based on the most recently administered examinations.

REA's practice tests replicate the actual PRAXIS II exams and carefully capture types of questions—and the level of difficulty—that you can expect to encounter on the PRAXIS II Elementary Education Tests: Curriculum, Instruction, and Assessment (Test Code 0011) and Content Knowledge (Test Code 0014). Following each practice test, you will find an answer key with detailed explanations designed to help you not only to identify the correct answer but also to understand why it is correct. Just as important is the explanation of why the remaining choices are incorrect.

Practice Test 1 for test code 0011 and Practice Test 2 for test code 0014 are also included on the enclosed TEST*ware*® CD-ROM. We strongly recommend that you begin your preparation with the TEST*ware* test. The

software provides timed conditions and instantaneous, accurate scoring, which makes it all the easier to pinpoint your strengths and weaknesses.

Passing the PRAXIS II Elementary Education Tests

About the PRAXIS Series

The PRAXIS Series™ is a group of teacher certification tests that Educational Testing Service (ETS) developed and administers. There are three categories of tests in the series.

PRAXIS I includes the paper-based Pre-Professional Skills Tests (PPST) and the PRAXIS I Computer-Based Tests (CBT). Both versions cover essentially the same subject matter. These exams—which measure reading, mathematics, and writing skills—are often a requirement for admission to a teacher education program.

PRAXIS II includes Subject Assessment/Specialty Area Tests, and the PRAXIS II Elementary Education Tests: Curriculum, Instruction, and Assessment (Test Code 0011) and Content Knowledge (Test Code 0014). In most teacher-training programs, students usually take these tests after having completed their classroom training, the course work, and the practicums.

PRAXIS III is different from the multiple-choice and essay tests typically used for assessment purposes. With this assessment, ETS-trained observers evaluate an instructor's performance in the classroom, using nationally validated criteria. The observers may videotape the lesson, and other teaching experts may critique the resulting tapes.

About the PRAXIS II Elementary Education Tests

Who Takes the PRAXIS II Elementary Education Tests?

Most people who take the PRAXIS II Elementary Education Tests are seeking initial licensure. You should check with your state's education agency to determine which PRAXIS examination(s) you should take; the ETS Web site (*http://www.ets.org/praxis/*) and registration bulletin may also help you determine the test(s) you need to take for certification.

You should also consult your attending institution for its own test requirements. Remember that colleges and universities often require PRAXIS examinations for entry into programs, for graduation, and for the completion of a teacher certification program. These requirements may differ from the requirements the state has for teacher certification. You will want to meet both sets of requirements.

The PRAXIS II examinations cover the subject matter that students typically study in teacher education courses—such content as human growth and development, school curriculum, methods of teaching, and other professional development courses. This book will prepare you to pass the PRAXIS II Elementary Education Tests: Curriculum, Instruction, and Assessment (Test Code 0011) and Content Knowledge (Test Code 0014).

What Are the PRAXIS II Elementary Education Tests?

PRAXIS is ETS's shorthand for Professional Assessments for Beginning Teachers®. The PRAXIS II Elementary Education Tests: Curriculum, Instruction, and Assessment (Test Code 0011) and Content Knowledge (Test

Code 0014) are among several PRAXIS examinations that come under the umbrella of the PRAXIS II: Subject Assessments.

Who Administers the PRAXIS II Elementary Education Tests?

ETS, founded in 1947, develops and administers the PRAXIS examinations. ETS maintains offices in the United States and around the world. Its headquarters, however, are in Princeton, New Jersey.

When Should I Take the PRAXIS II Elementary Education Tests?

The PRAXIS II Elementary Education Tests: Curriculum, Instruction, and Assessment (Test Code 0011) and Content Knowledge (Test Code 0014) are for those who have completed or almost completed their teacher education programs.

Some states may require the tests for initial certification; states may require the tests for beginning teachers during their first months on the job. Each state establishes its own requirements for certification; some states specify the passing of additional or different tests.

Generally, each college and university establishes its own requirements for program admission and for graduation. Some colleges and universities require the test(s) for graduation and/or for completion of a teacher education program.

Check with your college and the state education certification agency for details.

When and Where Does One Take the PRAXIS II Elementary Education Tests?

ETS offers the PRAXIS II Elementary Education Tests six times a year at a number of locations across the nation. The usual testing day is Saturday, but examinees may request an administration on an alternate day if a conflict—such as a religious obligation—exists.

To receive information on upcoming administrations of the tests, consult the ETS registration bulletin or Web site.

Contact ETS at:

Educational Testing Service
Teaching and Learning Division
PO Box 6051
Princeton, NJ 08541-6051
Phone: (609) 771-7395
Web site: *http://www.ets.org/praxis/*
E-mail: *praxis@ets.org*

Special accommodations are available for candidates who are visually impaired, hearing impaired, physically disabled, or specific learning disabled. For questions concerning disability services, contact:

ETS Disability Services: (609) 771-7780
TTY only: (609) 771-7714

Provisions are also available for examinees whose primary language is not English. The ETS registration bulletin and Web site include directions for those requesting such accommodations.

The ETS registration bulletin and Web site also provide information regarding available test sites; reporting test scores; requesting changes in tests, centers, and dates of test; purchasing additional score reports; retaking tests; and other basic facts. In addition, each of these ETS sources lists more than 30 state certification agencies that require or accept PRAXIS tests.

Is There a Registration Fee?

To take a PRAXIS examination, you must pay a registration fee, which is payable by check; money order; or American Express, Discover, MasterCard, or Visa credit cards. In certain cases, ETS offers fee waivers. The registration bulletin and Web site give qualifications for receiving this benefit and describe the application process. Cash is not accepted for payment.

How to Use This Book and TESTware®

What Do I Study First?

To begin your studies, read over the reviews and the suggestions for test-taking, take a practice test in your chosen Elementary Education field on CD-ROM to determine your area(s) of weakness, and then restudy the review material, focusing on your specific problem areas. The course review includes the information you need to know when taking the exam. Make sure to follow up your diagnostic work by taking the printed practice tests in this book to become familiar with the format and feel of the Praxis Elementary Education test you'll be taking.

When Should I Start Studying?

It is never too early to start studying. The earlier you begin, the more time you will have to sharpen your skills. Do not procrastinate! Cramming is not an effective way to study because it does not allow you the time needed to learn the test material. It is important, however, to review the material you need to study one last time the night before you take the test.

Test Format

The PRAXIS II Elementary Education Test: Curriculum, Instruction, and Assessment (Test Code 0011) and the PRAXIS II Elemetary Education Test: Content Knowledge (Test Code 0014) are both two-hour exams composed of all multiple-choice questions. Curriculum, Instruction, and Assessment (Test Code 0011) contains 110 questions; Content Knowledge (Test Code 0014) contains 120 questions. The pace, therefore, is somewhat faster for the Content Knowledge (Test Code 0014) than for the Curriculum, Instruction, and Assessment (Test Code 0011).

The multiple-choice questions assess a beginning teacher's knowledge of certain job-related skills and knowledge. Four choices are available on each multiple-choice question; the options bear the letters A through D. Both the Curriculum, Instruction, and Assessment (Test Code 0011) and the Content Knowledge (Test Code 0014) use four types of multiple-choice questions:

1. The Roman Numeral multiple-choice question

2. The "Which of the Following?" multiple-choice question

3. The "Complete the Statement" multiple-choice question

4. The Multiple-choice Question with Qualifiers

The following sections describe each type of question and suggest some strategies to help you score high.

Roman Numeral Multiple-Choice Questions

Perhaps the most difficult of the types of multiple-choice questions is the Roman numeral question. This format allows you to select more than one correct answer if so desired.

Strategy: Assess each answer before looking at the Roman numeral choices.

Consider the following Roman numeral multiple-choice question designed to test science content information and teaching methodology on the Elementary Education Test:

An experiment is planned to test the effect of microwave radiation on the success of seed germination. One hundred corn seeds will be divided into four sets of 25 each. Seeds in Group 1 will be microwaved for 1 minute, seeds in Group 2 for 2 minutes, and seeds in Group 3 for 10 minutes. Seeds in Group 4 will not be placed in the microwave. Each group of seeds will be soaked overnight and placed between the folds of water-saturated newspaper.

When purchasing the seeds at the store, you find that no single packet contains enough seeds for the entire project; most contain about 30 seeds per packet.

Which of the following is an acceptable approach for testing the hypotheses?

I. Purchase one packet from each of four different brands of seed, one packet for each test group.

II. Purchase one packet from each of four different brands of seed, and divide the seeds from each packet equally among the four test groups.

III. Purchase four packets of the same brand, one packet for each test group.

IV. Purchase four packets of the same brand, and divide the seeds from each packet equally among the four test groups.

    A.   I and II only

    B.   II and IV only

    C.   III and IV only

    D.   IV only

Note: You may choose two answers by selecting A, B, or C. It is possible to choose only one answer by choosing answer D.

Of course, the correct answer is D. The experiment requires a control of all variables other than the one identified in the hypothesis: exposure to microwave radiation. Seeds from different suppliers may be different; for example, one brand may be treated with a fungicide and another not, or the fungicide used may differ from brand to brand. Item III might at first seem acceptable, but unless all the packages are from the same year and production run, the four packages may be significantly different from each other. The best solution is to divide randomly the available seeds equally among the four test groups. Item II allows the experiment to compare also the germination rates of the different brands, but only if (1) the seeds from each packet are isolated within each test group and (2) the number of seeds is large enough to create a statistically significant sample.

This question illustrates that both knowledge of scientific content (curriculum) and instruction (methods)—in addition to assessment—are important on both tests.

"Which of the Following?" Multiple-Choice Questions

In a "Which of the Following?" question, one of the answers is correct among the various choices. **Strategy:** Form a sentence by replacing the first part of the question with each of the answer choices in turn, and then determine which of the created sentences is correct. Consider the following example:

Which of the following is a level of Bloom's Taxonomy?

    A.   Comprehension

    B.   Context

    C.   Accommodation

    D.   Egocentrism

Using the suggested technique, one would read:

    A.   "*Comprehension* is a level of Bloom's Taxonomy."

    B.   "*Context* is a level of Bloom's Taxonomy."

C. "*Accommodation* is a level of Bloom's Taxonomy."

D. "*Egocentrism* is a level of Bloom's Taxonomy."

It is easy to see that A is the correct answer. *Context* refers to the framework of a passage of text; context can include the pictures on the page as well as the words themselves. *Accommodation* refers to adjusting to the environment or the situation; *accommodation* is not a stage in Bloom's Taxonomy and is not an appropriate answer. *Egocentrism* refers to a world view in which the individual or the self is the center. *Egocentrism* is not the correct answer; it does not relate to Bloom's Taxonomy. The best answer is A, which is a level of Bloom's Taxonomy.

The "Which of the Following?" multiple-choice question is not always as straightforward and simple as the previous example. Consider the following "Which of the Following?" multiple-choice question based on the passage (repeated here) that you have already read:

An experiment is planned to test the effect of microwave radiation on the success of seed germination. One hundred corn seeds will be divided into four sets of 25 each. Seeds in Group 1 will be microwaved for 1 minute, seeds in Group 2 for 2 minutes, and seeds in Group 3 for 10 minutes. Seeds in Group 4 will not be placed in the microwave. Each group of seeds will be soaked overnight and placed between the folds of water-saturated newspaper.

During the measurement of seed and root length, students note that many of the roots are not growing straight. Efforts to straighten the roots manually for measurement are only minimally successful as the roots are fragile and susceptible to breakage.

Which of the following approaches is consistent with the stated hypothesis?

A. At the end of the experiment, straighten the roots and measure them.

B. Use a string as a flexible measuring instrument for curved roots.

C. Record the mass instead of length as an indicator of growth.

D. Record only the number of seeds that have sprouted, regardless of length.

The answer to the question is D. The hypothesis is to evaluate seed germination as a function of microwave irradiation. Recording the overall growth or length of the seed root, while interesting, is not the stated hypothesis. Choice C would be a good approach if the hypothesis were to relate seed growth to some variable, as it would more accurately reflect the growth of thicker or multiple roots in a way that root length might not measure.

Sometimes it is helpful to underline key information as you read the question. For instance, as you read the previous question, you might underline the sentence. *An experiment is planned to test the effect of microwave radiation on the success of seed germination.* This sentence will remind you of the stated hypothesis of the experiment and will prevent your having to read the entire question again. The underlining will thus save you time; saving time is helpful when you must answer 110 questions in two hours on the Curriculum, Instruction, and Assessment (Test Code 0011) or when you must answer 120 questions in two hours on the Content Knowledge (Test Code 0014).

"Complete the Statement" Multiple-Choice Questions

The "Complete the Statement" multiple-choice question consists of an incomplete statement for which you must select the answer choice that will complete the statement correctly. Here is an example:

To achieve lasting weight loss, students should

A. enter a commercial diet program.

B. combine permanent dietary changes with exercise.

C. cut calories to below 100 per day.

D. exercise for two hours a day.

The above question relates to health, a curriculum area on the Curriculum, Instruction, and Assessment (Test Code 0011), and addresses information that the average person needs to know.

The best answer to the question is B. Permanent dietary changes and exercise are the only way to produce lasting weight loss. Commercial diets, choice A, do not always include a program of exercise but rather concentrate on diet. Radically reducing calorie intake, choice C, will cause the body to go into starvation mode and slow down digestion to conserve energy. Two hours of daily exercise, choice D, is not practical, and without controlling calorie intake, it would be ineffective.

Multiple-Choice Questions with Qualifiers

Some of the multiple-choice questions may contain *qualifiers*—words like *not*, *least*, and *except*. These added words make the test questions more difficult because rather than having to choose the *best* answer, as is usually the case, you now must select the opposite.

Strategy: Because it is easy to forget to select the negative, a good strategy is to circle the qualifier in the question stem. This will serve as a reminder as you are reading the question and especially if you must re-read or check the answer at a later time.

Consider this question with a qualifier:

Dance can be a mirror of culture. Which of the following is not an illustration of this statement? (You would circle the word *not* to remind you to choose a negative.)

A. Women in the Cook Islands dance with their feet together and sway while the men take a wide stance and flap their knees.

B. Movement basics include body, space, time, and relationship.

C. In Africa, the birth of a child is an occasion for a dance that asks for divine blessings.

D. The court dancers of Bali study for many years to achieve the balance, beauty, and serenity of their dance.

The answer that does *not* illustrate that dance is a mirror of culture is B; it is, therefore, the correct answer to the question. The statement *Movement basics include body, space, time, and relationship* describes only the dimensions of dance movement; in no way does it speak to how dance reflects the culture of which it is part.

Because the Curriculum, Instruction, and Assessment (Test Code 0011) and Content Knowledge (Test Code 0014) tests differ somewhat in the content they cover, this book includes two practice tests for each. Use these practice tests to learn how to pace yourself.

You should spend approximately one minute on each multiple-choice question on the practice tests—and on the real exams, of course.

The practice tests in this book mirror the actual tests. Table 1-1 indicates the differences and the similarities in the two tests.

About the Review Sections

The reviews in this book will help you sharpen the basic skills needed to approach both the PRAXIS II Elementary Education Test: Curriculum, Instruction, and Assessment (Test Code 0011) and the PRAXIS II Elementary Education Test: Content Knowledge (Test Code 0014) and will provide you with strategies for attacking the questions. By using the reviews in conjunction with the pretests and the practice tests, you will better prepare yourself for the actual tests.

This REA study guide covers each content category on both tests. When used in concert, the book's review sections and practice tests will put you in the best possible position to succeed on both of these exams.

You should have learned through your course work and your practical experience in schools most of what you need to know to answer the questions on the test. In your education classes, you should have gained the expertise to make important decisions about situations you will face as a teacher; in your content courses, you should have acquired the knowledge you will need to teach specific content. The reviews in this book will help you fit the information you have acquired into its specific testable category. Reviewing your class notes and textbooks along with systematic use of this book will give you an excellent springboard for passing the tests.

Scoring the Tests

The number of raw points awarded on the tests is based on the number of correct answers given. Your scaled score is computed from your total number of raw points.

Table 1-1. Comparisons and Contrasts Between the PRAXIS 0011 and the PRAXIS 0014

PRAXIS II Elementary Education Test: Curriculum, Instruction, and Assessment (Test Code 0011)	PRAXIS II Elementary Education Test: Content Knowledge (Test Code 0014)
I. Reading and Language Arts Curriculum, Instruction, and Assessment 38 questions, or 35 percent of the test	I. Language Arts 30 questions, or 25 percent of the test
II. Mathematics Curriculum, Instruction, and Assessment 22 questions, or 20 percent of the test	II. Mathematics 30 questions, or 25 percent of the test
III. Science Curriculum, Instruction, and Assessment 11 questions, or 10 percent of the test	III. Social Studies 30 questions, or 25 percent of the test
IV. Social Studies Curriculum, Instruction, and Assessment 11 questions, or 10 percent of the test	IV. Science 30 questions, or 25 percent of the test
V. Arts and Physical Education Curriculum, Instruction, and Assessment 11 questions, or 10 percent of the test	Total number of questions: 120 Time allotted for taking the test: 2 hours
VI. General Information About Curriculum, Instruction, and Assessment 17 questions, or 15 percent of the test	
Total number of questions: 110 Time allotted for taking the test: 2 hours	

The college or university in which you are enrolled may set passing scores for the completion of your teacher education program and for graduation. Be sure to check the requirements in the catalogues or bulletins. You will also want to talk with your advisor.

The passing scores for the PRAXIS II tests vary from state to state. To find out which of the PRAXIS II tests your state requires and what the state's set passing score is, contact your state's education department directly. (See Table 1-2 for contact information.)

Score Reporting

When Will I Receive My Score Report and in What Form Will It Be?

ETS mails test-score reports six weeks after the test date. There is an exception for computer-based tests and for the PRAXIS I examinations. Score reports will list your current score and the highest score you have earned on each test you have taken over the last 10 years.

Along with your score report, ETS will provide you with a booklet that offers details on your scores. For each test date, you may request that ETS send a copy of your scores to as many as three score recipients, provided that each institution or agency is eligible to receive the scores.

Studying for the Tests

It is critical to your success that you study effectively. The following are a few tips to help you do just that:

- Choose a time and place for studying that works best for you. Some people set aside a certain number of hours every morning to study; others may choose to study at night before retiring. Only you know what is most effective for you.

- Be consistent.

- Use your time wisely.

Table 1-2. Contact Information for States' Departments of Education

Alabama	334-242-9700	*http://www.alsde.edu/html/home.asp/*
Alaska	907-465-2800	*http://www.eed.state.ak.us/*
Arizona	602-542-4361	*http://www.ade.az.gov/*
Arkansas	501-682-4202	*http://www.arkedu.state.ar.us/*
California	916-319-0800	*http://www.cde.ca.gov/*
Colorado	303-866-6600	*http://www.cde.state.co.us/*
Connecticut	800-465-4014	*http://www.state.ct.us/sde/*
Delaware	302-739-4601	*http://www.doe.state.de.us/*
District of Columbia	202-724-4222	*http://www.k12.dc.us/dcps/home.html*
Florida	850-245-0505	*http://www.fldoe.org/*
Georgia	404-656-2800	*http://www.doe.k12.ga.us/index.asp/*
Hawaii	808 586-3283	*http://doe.k12.hi.us/*
Idaho	208-332-6800	*http://www.sde.state.id.us/Dept/*
Illinois	217-782-4321	*http://www.isbe.net/*
Indiana	317-232-6610	*http://www.doe.state.in.us/*
Iowa	515-281-3436	*http://www.state.ia.us/educate/*
Kansas	785-296-3201	*http://www.ksde.org/*
Kentucky	502-564-6470	*http://www.education.ky.gov/KDE/Default.htm*
Louisiana	225-342-4411	*http://www.louisianaschools.net/lde/index.html*
Maine	207-624-6600	*http://www.state.me.us/education/homepage.htm*
Maryland	410-767-0100	*http://www.msde.state.md.us/*
Massachusetts	781-338-3395	*http://www.doe.mass.edu/*
Michigan	517-373-3324	*http://www.michigan.gov/mde/*
Minnesota	651-582-8200	*http://www.education.state.mn.us/*
Mississippi	601-359-3513	*http://www.mde.k12.ms.us/*
Missouri	573-751-4212	*http://dese.mo.gov/*
Montana	406-444-2082	*http://www.opi.mt.gov/*
Nebraska	402-471-2295	*http://www.nde.state.ne.us/*
Nevada	775-687-9141	*http://www.doe.nv.gov/*
New Hampshire	603-271-3495	*http://www.ed.state.nh.us/*
New Jersey	609-292-4469	*http://www.state.nj.us/education/*

(Continued)

Table 1-2. (*Continued*)

New Mexico	505-827-5800	*http://www.ped.state.nm.us/*
New York	518-474-5844	*http://www.nysed.gov/*
North Carolina	919-807-3300	*http://www.ncpublicschools.org/*
North Dakota	701-328-2260	*http://www.dpi.state.nd.us/*
Ohio	614-466-4839	*http://www.ode.state.oh.us/*
Oklahoma	405-521-3301	*http://www.sde.state.ok.us/*
Oregon	503-378-3600	*http://www.ode.state.or.us/*
Pennsylvania	717-787-5829	*http://www.pde.state.pa.us/*
Rhode Island	401-222-4600	*http://www.ridoe.net/*
South Carolina	803-734-8493	*http://www.myscschools.com/*
South Dakota	605-773-3553	*http://www.doe.sd.gov/*
Tennessee	615-741-2731	*http://www.state.tn.us/education/*
Texas	512-463-9734	*http://www.tea.state.tx.us/*
Utah	801-538-7521	*http://www.schools.utah.gov/*
Vermont	802-828-3135	*http://www.state.vt.us/educ/*
Virginia	804-786-9412	*http://www.pen.k12.va.us/*
Washington	360-725-6000	*http://www.k12.wa.us/*
West Virginia	304-558-0304	*http://wvde.state.wv.us/*
Wisconsin	608-267-1052	*http://www.dpi.state.wi.us/*
Wyoming	307-777-7675	*http://www.k12.wy.us/*

- Work out a study routine and stick to it; don't let your personal schedule interfere.
- Don't cram the night before the test. You may have heard many amazing tales about effective cramming, but don't kid yourself: most of them are false, and the rest are about exceptional people who, by definition, aren't like most of us.

When you take the practice tests, try to make your testing conditions as much like the actual test as possible. Turn off your television, radio, and telephone. Sit down at a quiet table free from distraction.

As you complete the practice test, score your test and thoroughly review the explanations to the questions you answered incorrectly. Take notes on material you will want to go over again or research further. Keep track of your scores. By doing so, you will be able to gauge your progress and discover your strengths and weaknesses. You should carefully study the material relevant to your areas of difficulty. This will build your test-taking skills and your confidence!

Test-Taking Tips

Although you may not be familiar with tests like the Curriculum, Instruction, and Assessment (Test Code 0011) and Content Knowledge (Test Code 0014), this book will help acquaint you with this type of examination and alleviate your test-taking anxieties. The following are seven specific techniques to help you become accustomed to the PRAXIS II tests:

1. Take the practice tests under the same conditions as you will the actual tests. Stay calm and pace yourself. Wear a (noiseless) watch. After simulating the test only once, you will automatically boost your chances of doing well. You can also get an idea of the subject areas for which you need to study a little more. When you sit down for the actual PRAXIS II tests, you will know what to expect.

2. Read all of the possible answers for the multiple-choice questions. Just because you think you have found the correct response, do not assume that it is truly the best answer. Read through each choice to be sure that you are not making a mistake by jumping to conclusions.

3. Use the process of elimination to select the correct answer to the multiple-choice questions. Read through the answer choices and eliminate as many of them as possible. By eliminating even one answer choice, you will increase your odds of answering the question correctly: you will have a one out of three chance of choosing the correct answer. Without elimination, you would have only a one out of four chance.

4. Remember that you can mark up your test book; you may want to cross out the answer choice(s) that you know are inappropriate. This will save you time if you need to re-read the question. Crossing out the answers you know to be wrong will also increase your chances of selecting the correct one. Do not leave an answer blank on the answer sheet; it is better to guess than to leave an answer space blank.

5. Work quickly and steadily. You will have two hours to complete the test. Avoid focusing on any one problem too long. Taking the practice tests in this book will help you learn to budget your precious time.

6. Study the directions and format of the test. Familiarity breeds confidence. By becoming acquainted with the instructions and with the structure of the test, you can save time when you begin taking the actual test. In addition, you can cut your chances of experiencing any unwanted surprises. When you sit for the test, it should be just as you thought it would be. By studying the directions and format ahead of time, you can avoid both anxiety and the mistakes a case of the jitters causes.

7. Be sure that the answer oval you are marking corresponds to the number of the question in the test booklet. Multiple-choice sections are machine-graded, and machines know nothing of your intention to mark on the line directly above or below. Marking one wrong answer can throw off your entire answer sheet and sink your score. Double-check the numbers on the question and on the answer sheet each time mark your sheet.

The Day of the Test

Before the Test

- Dress comfortably in layers. You do not want to be distracted by being too hot or too cold while you are taking the test.

- Check your registration ticket to verify your arrival time.

- Plan to arrive at the test center early. This will allow you to collect your thoughts and relax before the test; your early arrival will also spare you the anguish that comes with being late.

- Make sure to bring with you your admission ticket and two forms of identification, one of which must contain a recent photograph, your name, and your signature (e.g., a driver's license). You will not gain entry to the test center without proper identification.

- Bring several sharpened No. 2 pencils with erasers for the multiple-choice section and pens if you are taking another test that might have essay or constructed-response questions. You will not want to waste time searching for a replacement pencil or pen if you break a pencil point or run out of ink when you are trying to complete your test. The proctor will not provide pencils or pens at the test center.

- Wear a watch to the test center so you can apportion your testing time wisely. You may not, however, wear one that makes noise or that will otherwise disturb the other test takers.

- Leave all dictionaries, textbooks, notebooks, calculators, briefcases, and packages at home. You may not take these items into the test center.

- Do not eat or drink heavily before the test. The proctor will not allow you to make up time you miss if you have to take a bathroom break. You will not be allowed to take materials with you, and you must secure permission before leaving the room.

During the Test

- Pace yourself. ETS administers the PRAXIS II Elementary Education Test: Curriculum, Instruction, and Assessment (Test Code 0011) and the PRAXIS II Elementary Education Test: Content Knowledge (Test Code 0014) in one two-hour sitting with no breaks.

- Follow all of the rules and instructions that the test proctor gives you. Proctors will enforce these procedures to maintain test security. If you do not abide by the regulations, the proctor may dismiss you from the test and notify ETS to cancel your score.

- Listen closely as the test instructor provides the directions for completing the test. Follow the directions carefully.

- Be sure to mark only one answer per multiple-choice question, erase all unwanted answers and marks completely, and fill in the answers darkly and neatly.

After the Test

- When you finish your test, the proctor will collect your materials and will dismiss the examinees. Go home and relax—you deserve it.

Study Schedule

The following study course schedule allows for thorough preparation to pass the tests. This is a suggested seven-week course of study. However, you can condense this schedule if you have less time to study or expand it if you have more time for preparation. You may decide to use your weekends for study and preparation and go about your other business during the week. You may even want to tape record information and listen to your tape as you travel in your car. However you decide to study, be sure to adhere to the structured schedule you devise.

Week 1: If you're sitting for the Code 0011 Test, take REA's Code 0011 Practice Test on TESTware CD. If you're sitting for the Code 0014 Test, take REA Code 0014 Practice Test on our TEST*ware* CD. Our computerized model tests, which are drawn from the tests we present in our book, will provide a read-out that will enable you to pinpoint your strengths and weaknesses and provide you with instantaneous, accurate scoring. This, in turn, will allow you to customize your review process.

Week 2: Be sure to consult all relevant official materials published by ETS at *www.ets.org/praxis*. Study the PRAXIS II Elementary Education review material in this book. Highlight key terms and information. Take notes on the reviews as you work through them. Writing may aid in your retention of the information. You may also want to make a recording to listen to as you drive.

Week 3: If you're prepping for Code 0011, take Practice Test 2 (0011) in the book. If, after careful review you still need more prep, return to printed Practice Test 1 (0011) in the book. If you're prepping for Code 0014, take Practice Test 1 (0014). If, after careful review you still need more prep, return to printed Practice Test 2 (0014).

Week 4: Condense your notes and findings. You should develop a structured outline detailing specific facts. You may wish to use index cards or audiotapes to aid you in memorizing important facts and concepts.

Week 5: Test yourself using the index cards. You may want to have a friend or colleague quiz you on key facts and items. Take the second full-length exam. Review the explanations for the questions you answered incorrectly. Make notes of additional areas to study and review.

Week 6: Study any areas you consider to be your weaknesses by using your study materials, references, and notes. You may want to retake the tests provided. The study guide in this book provides extra answer sheets for your additional study and practice.

End of Week 6: The night before you take the test, lay out all your materials (pens, pencils, wristwatch, identification, admission ticket, keys, etc.). Review your notes and directions for the test one last time.

Test Day: Take the test! Do your best! Afterward, make notes about the multiple-choice questions you remember. You may not share this information with others, but you may find that the information proves useful on other exams that you take. Relax! Wait for that passing score to arrive.

Test Content

Both tests cover three main categories: (1) curriculum, (2) instruction, and (3) assessment. Curriculum, Instruction, and Assessment (Test Code 0011) separates the questions by category; Content Knowledge (Test Code 0014) integrates the categories into the questions.

Category 1: Curriculum

There are several kinds of curriculum. Leslie Wilson (*http://www.uwsp.edu/education/lwilson/curric/curtyp. htm*) identifies the most important types:

- The *written curriculum* is the formal instruction of the schooling experience. It may refer to the standards set up by learned societies, the texts, the films, and other teaching materials.

- The *hidden curriculum* refers to all the lessons that children acquire in the school. These lessons may include the raising of hands to answer a question, sitting up straight, standing in line, competing for grades, and—of course—ways of learning the content information.

- The *societal curriculum* is that which churches, peer groups, neighborhoods, and so on, teach the students—and us all—through our entire lives.

- The *null curriculum* is that which is not taught. Students get the message from the lack of emphasis on certain topics that this information is not important.

- The *curriculum-in-use* is the curriculum the instructor actually uses and teaches; the school's official written curriculum is the actual curriculum.

- The *phantom curriculum* consists of the messages that are rampant in the media and that serve to acculturate.

- The *concomitant curriculum* refers to the messages emphasized at home, as well as those of the school, the church, and society.

- The *rhetorical curriculum* is that comprised of the ideas and recent information in print.

- The *received curriculum* is that which the students accept and take with them from the school.

- The *internal curriculum* is that unique to each child. The teacher can do little about this curriculum, which is already a part of the individual student's life.

- The *electronic curriculum* refers to the vast amounts of information received from electronic communication. The Internet is vital to this type of curriculum.

Other views of curriculum include

- a body of knowledge that must be transmitted;

- content with the aim of developing reasoning in the students;

- education that must match the student, the student's needs, and the student's patterns of learning;

- the objectives that ensure that the teacher teaches what the standards, state, and community consider important;

- the teachings that will raise a new and better generation.

In simplest form, *curriculum* refers to the set of courses and the content offered by a school or institution. The basic courses and content make up the core *curriculum*. The *extracurricular activities* are those activities that are generally voluntary; many times the students themselves organize these activities with faculty sponsorship. Some examples of extracurricular activities include working on the school newspapers and participating in interschool athletics.

Both the Curriculum, Instruction, and Assessment (Test Code 0011) and the Content Knowledge (Test Code 0014) emphasize the importance of

- **each content area.** For instance, self-expression in reading, awareness of the world in social studies, and the scientific method in science figure into many questions and are topics that are helpful to review.

- **relationships between and among subjects.** For instance, reading skills are essential to all subject areas, and mathematics may be necessary in using the metric system in science. Both tests stress this integration.

- **media and materials for instruction in many subject areas.** For instance, graphs are essential in mathematics, but they may also be used in graphing temperature in countries of the world in social studies or in graphing purchases in economics.

Sources of Data to Determine the Curriculum

Information about what outcomes are important for students comes from several sources. Ralph Tyler in his "Model of Curriculum Design" defines three basic sources of needs: students, society, and content area. (coe.sdsu.edu/people/jmora/MoraModules/TylerCurr-Model.pps; G. F. Madeus and D. L. Stufflebeam. *Educational Evaluation: The Works of Ralph Tyler*. Boston: Kluwer Academic Press). Consideration of these sources leads to a draft of educational outcomes; our philosophy and what we know about educational psychology affect our educational outcomes. Society makes ever-changing demands upon the educational system; for instance, businesses are focusing more on workers who can solve problems. The needs of children and national issues—health problems, environmental concerns, and so on—also provide data for educators.

Thematic Curriculum

Planning thematic curriculum often involves teachers from several areas—such as math, English, history, science, and health—although individual teachers could plan thematic units for their own classes. Using a system developed by Sandra Kaplan, the team of teachers develops a one-word universal theme—for example, survival, conflict, traditions, frontiers, or changes—that applies in all areas. The team lists a series of key words (such as *significance*, *relationships*, *types*, *functions*, *origins*, *value*, or *causes*) that one could associate with the universal theme. The team develops a generalization for the unit, and each teacher plans outcomes for his or her subject area and class. For example, for the theme "Animals," the language arts teacher could assign and discuss with the students the book *Charlotte's Web*. The music teacher could teach them the songs "Animal Fair," "Itsy-Bitsy Spider," and so on. The art teacher could have students work on a collage of a spiderweb with various items woven into the web. The science teacher could have students explore the differences between living and nonliving things. The history teacher could focus on the history of the horse in America. The math teacher could have students graph the life spans of various animals. The health teacher could address animals in the food chain. All teachers would plan learning experiences to lead students to understand the importance of animals in our world. These experiences would be carried out using a wide variety of instructional strategies and resources.

The effective teacher knows how to collaborate with peers to determine content and to plan instruction. Collaboration may be as simple as planning and sharing ideas, or as complex as developing a multidisciplinary thematic unit in which teachers of several subject areas teach around a common theme.

Effective communication is an obvious mark of an effective teacher. Communication occurs only when someone sends a message and another person receives it. Teachers may "teach" and think they're sending a message, but if students aren't listening, there has been no communication because the receivers are not tuned in.

Both tests cover the curriculum, the instruction, and the assessment of the content areas of language arts (reading/language arts on the 0011 exam), mathematics, science, and social studies. This study guide will deal with each content area (the curriculum) and with instruction and assessment in the content chapters to come.

Two additional chapters—vital to the PRAXIS II Elementary Education Test: Curriculum, Instruction, and Assessment (0011)—cover the subject matter areas of arts and physical education as well as general information about curriculum.

The Language Arts

It is important to review the content of the language arts and reading curriculum. Some salient points are worthy of special review:

Section 1: Pedagogy

Topic 1.
What Are the Language Arts?

The language arts include all the subjects related to communication. The school curriculum often gives most attention to reading, writing, literature, and spelling; listening and speaking are other essential parts of the language arts curriculum. A balanced language arts curriculum addresses each topic. Ideally, reading, writing, spelling, listening, speaking, and even the literature are integrated into other content areas.

Topic 2.
Literacy: What Is the First Stage in the Scope and Sequence of Learning to Read?

Marie M. Clay (1966) coined the term *emergent literacy* in her unpublished 1966 doctoral dissertation, *Emergent Reading Behavior* (University of Auckland, New Zealand). She defined *emergent literacy* as the stage during which children begin to receive formal instruction in reading and writing and the point at which educators and adults expect them to begin developing an understanding of print.

Today, educators use the term to describe the gradual development of literacy behavior, or the stage in which students begin learning about print. Educators usually associate emergent literacy with children from birth to about age 5. During the emergent literacy period, children gain an understanding of print as a means of conveying information. It is essential that they develop an interest in reading and writing in this stage (Tompkins 2006).

Some educators suggest that reading readiness or emergent literacy is a **transitional period**, during which a child changes from a nonreader to a beginning reader; others suggest that reading readiness/emergent literacy is a stage (Clay 1979). The Southern Regional Education Board's Health and Human Services Commission (SREB 1994) cautions that children go through emergent literacy at individual rates.

Some **transmission educators** suggest that if a child is not ready to read, the teacher should get the child ready. Others declare that the teacher should not begin formal reading instruction until the child is ready. Most reading readiness advocates take the position that there are certain crucial factors that a teacher or parent should consider in deciding if a child is ready to read (Davis 2004).

Identifying Concepts of Print

An important part of emergent literacy is the skill of identifying print concepts, which involves being able to identify the parts of a book, indicating the directionality of print, and recognizing the connection between spoken and written words.

Parts of Books

Clay (1985) developed a formal procedure for sampling a child's reading vocabulary and determining the extent of a child's print-related concepts. For instance, her assessment checks whether a child can find the title of a book, show where to start reading the book, and locate the last page or end of the book. These components considered essential before children can begin to read may differ from those typically considered essential, such as discriminating between sounds and finding likenesses and differences in print (Finn 1990; Davis 2004). A teacher or parent might hand a book to a child with the back of the book facing the child and in a horizontal position. The adult would then ask questions such as "Where is the name of the book?" "Where does the story start?" "If the book has the words *the end*, where might I find those words?" (Davis 2004).

Directionality of Print

Another part of the skill of identifying concepts of print is being able to indicate the directionality of print. The reader in American society must start at the left side of the page and read to the right. This skill is not an inborn skill but rather one acquired through observation or through direct instruction. Some societies do not write from left to right. For instance, in ancient Greek society, writing followed the same pattern as a person would use when plowing: the reader would start at the top of the page and read to the right until the end of the line, turn, drop down a line, read that line to the left, turn, drop down a line, read that line to the right, and so on. Other languages, such as Hebrew, require the reader to begin at the right and read to the left. Japanese writing is generally vertical (Davis 2004).

To teach left-to-right direction, the teacher can place strips of masking tape on the child's desk, study center, or table area. One strip goes where the left side of the book or writing paper would be and one strip where the right side of the book or writing paper would be. The child colors the left side green and the right side red. The teacher helps the child use this device as a clue to remember on which side to begin reading or writing and reminds the child that *green* means "go" and *red* means "stop." Ideally, the teacher should use similar strips on the chalkboard or poster paper to model writing from left to right (Davis 2004).

Children can also remember on which side to begin reading by holding up their hands with their thumbs parallel to the floor. The left hand makes the shape of the letter *L*, for "left," the side on which to begin reading; the right hand does not make the *L* shape. Another way a teacher can help children who are having trouble distinguishing left from right, or on which side to begin reading and writing, is to point to sentences while reading from a big book or writing on the board; observing the teacher do this can help children master print directionality. Books that are 18 × 12 inches or larger are designed for this purpose and are effective with groups of children. Teachers or parents can also model directionality by passing their hands or fingers under the words or sentences as they read aloud. In fact, reading aloud is an essential activity in the school and at home throughout the school years. (Davis 2004).

Teachers can use games such as Simon Says or songs such as "The Hokey Pokey" to give children practice in the skills of distinguishing left from right. In another instructional game, each child holds a paper plate as if it were a steering wheel, and the teacher calls out directions such as "Turn the wheel to the left" and "Turn your car to the right." As the children "drive" their cars, the teacher observes whether they are turning the wheel in the correct direction (Davis 2004).

Voice-to-Print Match

Being able to recognize the connection between the spoken word and the written word is important to developing reading and writing skills. During the emergent literacy period, children should begin to understand that the printed word is just speech written down. Shared reading (discussed in more detail in the next section, "Identifying Strategies for Developing Concepts of Print") can help children gain this understanding. As the adult reads aloud, the children join in with words, phrases, repetitions, and sentences they recognize. They begin to make the connection between the printed word and the spoken word and between phonemes and graphemes. **Phonemes** are the speech sounds; **graphemes** are the written symbols for the speech sounds. These voice-to-print relationships are important to reading (Davis 2004).

Identifying Strategies for Developing Concepts of Print

Emergent literacy research cautions that in preschool and kindergarten programs, teachers should avoid isolated, abstract instruction and tedious drills. Teachers should avoid programs that tend to ignore and repeat what the children already know. Programs that focus on skills and ignore experiences often place little importance on reading as a pleasurable activity and ignore early writing—important components of whole language (Noyce and Christie 1989).

Developmentally Appropriate Classrooms, Materials, and Curriculum

The SREB (1994) states that the classroom, materials, and curriculum should be developmentally appropriate. **Developmentally appropriate** is a concept with two dimensions: individual appropriateness and age appropriateness. **Individual appropriateness** recognizes that each child is unique. Ideally, schools and teachers respect and accommodate individual differences, which include growth, interest, and styles. **Age appropriateness** implies that there are sequences of growth and change during the first nine years that a teacher must consider when developing the classroom environment and experiences. In general, the age-appropriate skills considered necessary for reading—during the reading readiness period and beyond—are visual discrimination, auditory discrimination, and left-to-right direction (Davis 2004).

Reading Aloud

The U.S. Department of Education recognizes that "parents are their children's first and most influential teachers" (Bennett 1987, 5). The department further notes that "what parents do to help their children learn is more important to academic success than how well-off the family is" (7). After reviewing many studies, the department reports, "The best way for parents [and adults] to help their children become better readers is to read to them—even when they [the children] are very young. Children benefit most from reading aloud when they discuss the stories, learn to identify letters and words, and talk about the meaning of words" (7). The department also finds that "children whose parents simply read to them perform as well as those whose parents use workbooks or have had training in reading. . . . Kindergarten children who know a lot about written language usually have parents who believe that reading is important and who seize every opportunity to act on that conviction by reading to their children" (7).

Jim Trelease (1985) reinforces that parents and teachers should read aloud regularly to children. The reasons Trelease cites for reading aloud include "to reassure, to entertain, to inform or explain, to arouse curiosity, and to inspire" (68). Trelease also explains that reading aloud to a child can strengthen writing, reading, and speaking skills and the child's entire civilizing process. Another important reason for reading to children while they are young is that at that age, children want to imitate what they hear and see adults do. In his book, *The Read-Aloud Handbook*, Trelease suggests stories and books ideal for reading aloud.

The SREB (1994) recommends that schools help parents to become actively involved in their children's education and that schools adopt formal policies to improve communication between parents (or caregivers) and schools.

Shared Reading

At the emergent literacy level, the students and the teacher "share" the tasks involved in reading and writing. Teachers are practicing "shared reading" when they read big books (18 × 12 inches) to their students. Parents are practicing shared reading when they read aloud to their children. At this early stage, the adult is doing most of the reading, but the child follows as the adult reads and chimes in for the reading of familiar words, repeated words, and/or repeated phrases. An upper-grade teacher can also use shared reading when students are reading a difficult book that they may not fully comprehend if they were to read independently; the teacher can read portions aloud, and the students can follow along and read silently (Tompkins 2006).

In 1969, R. G. Heckleman developed his **Neurological-Impress Method (NIM)**, an approach that adults had probably been using with children for generations. He advocates that the teacher sit slightly behind the reader; the teacher and the learner hold (share) the book jointly and read aloud together whenever possible. The teacher should slide a finger along each line and follow the words as the two say the words together. Heckleman reports significant gains in children with whom the method was used. LinguaLinks notes that the method can help 1) develop fluency in reading; 2) impress the words into the memory of the learner; 3) learners to imitate correct phrasing, intonation, fluency, mechanics, and pronunciation; 4) build the learner's confidence; 5) provide immediate success and feedback; and 6) provide a pleasant reading experience. ("Using a Neurological Impress Activity," http:www.sil.org/lingualinks/literacyprogram/Using ANeurologicalImpressActiv.htm) Jimmie Cook and his colleagues (1980) also report on page 473, "The NIM Helps." In 1978, Paul Hollingsworth suggested using a wireless system to make it possible to use the NIM with several students at one time. Marie Carbo (1978) suggests using "talking books" or the recorded book to teach reading. Her method is like NIM, except the child has a recording instead of a one-on-one tutor during the reading. Heckleman, however, emphasizes that human contact is essential to the enjoyment and success of the NIM plan.

Environmental Print

Our environment is rich with words. People see signs advertising everything from fast foods to fast cars. Television shows display many words, and newspapers and magazines depend on words to sell their products and to communicate their messages. Around swimming pools, playgrounds, recreation centers, and movie theaters are printed signs and cautions to help ensure the safety of customers and users. Becoming aware of these environmental words is important to children. They should begin to notice and try to recognize these important words at an early age. Noting the signs and words around them will help children feel comfortable with words and make them aware of the importance of reading in our society.

Anita P. Davis and Thomas R. McDaniel (1998) identify words that they consider essential for physical safety, social acceptability, and the avoidance of embarrassment. Some of these "essential words" are *exit*, *danger*, *high voltage*, *stop*, *beware*, *keep out*, and *no trespassing*. Being able to read these words is vital. Davis and McDaniel advocate that teachers and adults help children notice and master these words in their environment.

Edward Dolch (1960) identifies the most frequently used vocabulary words from preprimer level to grade 3. Listing the words by grade in the Dolch Word List, the author recommends teaching them to primary children to develop their reading vocabulary. Because Dolch advocates teaching the beginning reader to read the words quickly and to "pop" them off immediately, many teachers call the words the "Popper Words."

Language Experience Approach

The language experience approach (LEA) attempts to facilitate students' language development through the use of experiences, rather than with printed material alone. After an event or experience in which the learners in the class participate, the students make a written record of it as a group (with the help of the teacher). In this way, each student can see that

- what I say, I can write;
- what I can write, I can read;
- what others write, I can read.

The LEA can be a part of many levels of teaching. Even high school classes often have the teacher at the board recording information that the class offers about something read or experienced as a group.

Topic 3.
What Are the Next Two Stages in the Scope and Sequence of Learning to Read?

Like Clay (1966), Martha Combs (2006) recognizes the first stage in literacy as the emerging stage but also notes two other stages of development in literacy. Combs's three stages are:

Emerging literacy stage. Children in this stage are making the transition from speaking to writing and reading—with support from others. Reading might involve predictable books; these books will be at the child's frustration reading level initially, but as the children practice, the books are at the instructional level of the children—and eventually at their independent level. Shared reading and interactive writings, which the children compose and the teachers record, provide practice and build confidence.

Developing stage. Children in the developing stage are becoming more independent in their reading, their writing, their speaking. These children are usually on a middle-first to late-second-grade level. Their texts should include many decodable words—these are words that follow a regular pattern and have a predictable sound: *man, tip, me*. The children can practice their decoding skills as they read and gain confidence; they are progressing with their handwriting skills and are becoming more independent in spelling words they need in writing.

Transitional reading stage. Children who are transitional readers usually have an instructional reading level of second grade or beyond. Ideally, these children should spend much of their time with independent-level and instructional-level materials. Their instructors are still there to help them, but the children are able to refine their old skills and practice new skills.

Topic 4.
What Are Important Strategies for Teaching Word Recognition and Language Acquisition, such as Letter-sound Correlations, Phonics, Structural Analysis, Semantics, Syntax, and Scanning?

Again, it is important for teachers, schools, and parents to remember that reading should always be a pleasurable activity. It is best to avoid programs that (1) focus entirely on skills with no connections to reading actual books, (2) ignore the experiences of the children, and (3) repeat what the students already know. Programs that are totally skills-based, nonpleasurable, and unrelated to authentic materials and that neglect the child's needs are nonmotivating (Noyce, 1989). As noted earlier, the programs for teaching word recognition and language acquisition should be developmentally appropriate, individually appropriate, and age appropriate (SREB, 1994).

Phonological Awareness

Increased phonological awareness occurs as children learn to associate the roughly 44 speech sounds in the English language with their visual representation. Children learn to pronounce these 44 sounds as they begin to talk. Because the English language has only 26 letters, it obviously is not a phonetic language; that is, there is no one-to-one correspondence between letters and sounds. The 26 letters are combined in many different ways to reproduce the needed sounds.

When they try to write, children in the early grades create **invented spellings** by applying their understanding of spelling rules. As children progress through the grades, their spellings usually become more conventional.

J. R. Gentry (1981) identifies the stages that students go through in their spelling development. These stages are particularly evident in the writing of students in a whole language classroom. The stages include the **pre-communication stage**, when the student randomly uses letters; the **pre-phonetic stage**, when the student begins to use some letters correctly; the **phonetic stage**, when the student spells the words the way that they sound; the **transitional stage**, during which the student uses both correct spelling and phonetic spelling; and the **correct spelling stage**, when the student spells words correctly (Davis, 2004).

Phonics

The most commonly used method of teaching reading in the United States from colonial times through the 1920s was the phonics method. Other reading methods—the sight word method, modified alphabet approach, and the whole language approach, for example—came into being after the 1920s. However, phonics is still an important part of reading instruction in the United States.

The phonics method of teaching reading emphasizes the association between the grapheme (the written symbol) and the phoneme (the speech sound). The phonics method attempts to relate spelling rules to the process.

William Holmes McGuffey and Rudolf Flesch were proponents of the phonics method. McGuffey produced his series of reading books in 1836. The readers used phonics while teaching morals to students; it was a cultural force, not just a reading textbook. By 1920, sales of McGuffey readers had reached 122 million. In 1955, Flesch wrote *Why Johnny Can't Read—And What You Can Do About It* to warn parents that the reason many children could not read was that the schools were not using the phonics approach.

Phonics is, of course, a skills-based approach. There are several **advantages of the phonics method** that are readily apparent. One important advantage of the phonics method is that it gives children tools for decoding, or figuring out, how to read and pronounce words that they do not know immediately. Because the phonics approach involves phoneme–grapheme associations, auditory learners—those who learn best through the sense of sound—often prefer to read using phonics. Auditory learners can usually hear a sound and associate it easily with its printed symbol. Using phonics with auditory learners is an evident advantage. A third advantage of this method with its emphasis on sound–symbol relationships is that phonics readers can often transfer their skills to spelling. Spelling involves associating sounds with letters; it is the opposite of phonics, which associates symbols with sounds. A final advantage is that phonics readers are often good spellers (Davis 2004).

At its January 1997 meeting, the board of directors of the International Reading Association (IRA) passed a position statement titled "The Rule of Phonics in Teaching Instruction." The key assertions were that phonics is an important aspect in beginning reading instruction, primary teachers value and teach phonics, and effective phonics is integrated into the total language arts program (IRA takes a stand on phonics, 1997).

There are, however, **disadvantages to the phonics method**. A major disadvantage of phonics is that visual learners may not read well by this method. A second disadvantage of the method is that the rules do not hold true all the time. In his now-classic study, Theodore Clymer (1963) reports that he found few phonics generalizations that held true in more than 50 percent of the cases in the primary grades. Four years later, however, Mildred Hart Bailey (1967) found in her study of phonics rules that 27 of the 45 generalizations identified by Clymer held true in 75 percent of the words appearing most often in reading materials for grades 1 through 6.

A third disadvantage of the phonics method is that some students are confused when they learn a phonics rule and then encounter frequent exceptions; inconsistencies pose a problem for them. Some educators, though not all, note a fourth disadvantage to the phonics method: they believe that there is no basis for the view that there are subskills, such as phonics, that students need to read; they see the skills as mythical (Davis 2004).

To help children learn phonics, many teachers find certain techniques for teaching the method helpful. Students should have opportunities to practice the phonics rules and generalizations in context; instructors should make every effort to illustrate the transfer of the phonics rules and generalizations to everyday materials and to other subjects. Analytic phonics (using phonics in context with actual materials), as opposed to synthetic phonics (phonics taught in isolation from meaningful books and materials, often using worksheets), seems to be the more helpful technique. Teachers can introduce a phonics rule or generalization as it appears, but such an incidental approach does not ensure that all students meet and practice the most frequently encountered phonics rules. A structured, systematic, sequential program of phonics helps ensure that readers have at their disposal an arsenal of skills to decode new words and spell the words correctly. Such a plan of presenting the rules and regulations of phonics can help eliminate gaps in students' word-attack skills (Davis 2004).

Marie Carbo (1993), nationally known for her work with reading styles, recognizes the importance of making available phonics instruction in any reading program. She particularly warns, "a good whole language program does include phonics." In *Becoming a Nation of Readers*, the Commission on Reading (1986) stresses that phonics is an essential strategy for beginning reading. Teachers should use a systematic approach and present the skills in meaningful sentences, passages, and materials, not just as words in isolation.

A word of caution for teachers of phonics is that in the beginning, students may read slowly. When students begin to commit high-frequency words to memory, however, reading speed and, in turn, comprehension will increase (Davis 2004). The young child begins recognizing letters and their sounds. These skills will help the child with reading and spelling. Another technique that will help the child in attacking unknown words is analyzing the structure of the words, or structural analysis (Davis 2004).

Word Structure

Breaking a word into its parts, or syllables, is called **structural analysis**. By dividing a word into its syllables and sounding out these smaller parts, students are often able to pronounce longer, unknown words that they previously did not recognize. There are many rules for dividing words into syllables; some of these rules often hold true, but some of the rules do not. As mentioned earlier, Bailey (1967) found in her study of phonics rules that 27 of 45 syllabication rules hold true in 75 percent of the words a child frequently encounters in grades 1 through 6.

Children do not work with all the rules for structural analysis in the early years. Usually, children work mainly with adding word endings to words that are already a part of their sight vocabulary or word families. Some of the endings that children encounter first are the suffixes *-ed*, *-s*, *-es*, and *-ing* (Davis 2004). Fry (1980) says that six suffixes cause a large percentage of the variants: *-ed*, *-s*, *-er*, *-ly*, *-est*, and *-ing*.

However, all the words a beginning reader sees may not be those in the list of sight words the child already knows. Although some texts try to limit the new words a beginning reader (grades K-3) meets at a given time (**controlled vocabulary**), most children do not experience such a protected environment. Young children are constantly encountering new words. It is important, therefore, for the child to have some word-attack skills such as structural analysis to decipher new, unknown words. Separating the prefix and/or the suffix from the root word is an example of structural analysis. After separating these word parts, the child may be able to sound out the word. Examples include *un-tie*, *re-peat*, and *sing-ing* (Davis 2004).

Another important rule for separating words into parts is the compound word rule. With this rule, the child divides a compound word into its parts. The child and the teacher can work together to sound out each part. Examples include *cow-boy* and *foot-ball* (Davis 2004).

Two essential rules for structural analysis are the v/cv and the vc/cv rules. Teachers introduce these rules and encourage the students in the later stages of reading development to employ these attack skills. To use the rules successfully, the child must first determine if each letter in a word is a vowel (v) or a consonant (c). The child can write the label over each letter in the word. Looking for the v/cv or vc/cv pattern, the child separates the word at the appropriate place. Examples of the v/cv rule are *o-ven* and *bo-dy*. Examples of the vc/cv rule are *sum-mer* and *ig-loo* (Davis 2004).

Some rules of structural analysis, such as the following, are complex, useful, and best for older readers (Davis 2004):

1. When *-le* comes at the end of the word and a consonant comes before it, the consonant goes with the *-le*, as in the word *pur-ple* and *bub-ble*. (An exception to this rule is when the word contains a *ck*, one would not separate the *c* and the *k*, as in the word *pick-le*.)

2. The suffix *-ed* forms a separate syllable if *d* or *t* comes before the *-ed*, as in *skidd-ed* and *mist-ed*.

Context Clues

As children progress in their skills and confidence, teachers might encourage them to use picture clues and previously read materials to predict what word would make sense. To help children make their predictions, the teacher can give them a clue, like the first sound of the word. Another way a teacher can provide context clues is to mask words or portions of words with a "magic window"—a sturdy piece of cardboard with a small rectangle cut out of the center. This allows the teacher to single out a letter or syllable for the children to consider. The teacher can also cover up words or parts of words on a transparency sheet on the overhead projector (Combs 2006).

Demonstrating Knowledge of Syntactic, Semantic, and Graphophonemic Cueing Systems

The technique of using all the language cueing systems together is important to comprehension. The following are the three major types of language cues:

Syntactic cues. Attention to syntax can increase **comprehension**, or understanding. These cues include grammatical hints; the order of words; word endings; and the way the words function, or work, in a phrase, sentence, or passage.

Semantic cues. Semantics can include "hints" within the sentence and from the entire passage or text that help the reader determine the meaning. Semantic cues, then, are meaning clues.

Phonemes and graphemes. The phonemes (sounds) and graphemes (written letters) are crucial to reading and writing. A child who does not know the word *phone* but knows that the letters *ph* often sound like the letter *f* and knows that the sound of a phone is a ring may be able to figure out the word in the sentence "I heard the phone ring."

Again, through demonstration, invitation, and discussion, the teacher can help children confirm or correct as they read, monitor understanding during the reading process, and review and retain information after the reading is complete (Davis 2004).

Views about reading and the stages vary from source to source. Most sources agree that it is imperative that teachers **scaffold**, or support, children of all ages. Scaffolding involves demonstrating, guiding, and teaching; the amount of support the teacher provides should depend on the instructional support needed and the individual child. Five stages that mark scaffolding are—moving from greatest to the least as students assume more and more responsibility—the modeled, shared, interactive, guided, and independent levels of support (Tompkins 2006).

Reading Strategies

Looking at strategies used by proficient readers helps teachers make skillful choices of activities to maximize student learning in subject area instruction. Anne Goudvis and Stephanie Harvey (2000) offer the following list:

Activating prior knowledge. Readers pay more attention when they relate to the text. Readers naturally bring their prior knowledge and experience to reading, but they comprehend better when they think about the connections they make between the text, their lives, and the larger world.

Predicting or asking questions. Questioning is the strategy that keeps readers engaged. When readers ask questions, even before they read, they clarify understanding and forge ahead to make meaning. Asking questions is at the heart of thoughtful reading.

Visualizing. Active readers create visual images based on the words they read in the text. These created pictures enhance their understanding.

Drawing inferences. Inferring is when the readers take what they know, garner clues from the text, and think ahead to make a judgment, discern a theme, or speculate about what is to come.

Determining important ideas. Thoughtful readers grasp essential ideas and important information when reading. Readers must differentiate between less important ideas and key ideas that are central to the meaning of the text.

Synthesizing information. Synthesizing involves combining new information with existing knowledge to form an original idea or interpretation. Reviewing, sorting, and sifting important information can lead to new insights that change the way readers think.

Repairing understanding. If confusion disrupts meaning, readers need to stop and clarify their understanding. Readers may use a variety of strategies to "fix up" comprehension when meaning goes awry.

Confirming. As students read and after they read, they can confirm the predictions they originally made. There is no wrong answer. One can confirm negatively or positively. Determining whether a prediction is correct is a goal.

Using parts of a book. Students should use book parts—such as charts, diagrams, indexes, and the table of contents—to improve their understanding of the reading content.

Reflecting. An important strategy is for students to think about, or reflect on, what they have just read. Reflection can be simply thinking, or it can be more formal, such as a discussion or writing in a journal.

While providing instruction in a subject area, the teacher needs to determine if the reading material is at the students' level of reading mastery. If not, the teacher needs to make accommodations either in the material itself or in the manner of presentation.

Teaching the Strategies

An instructor can teach reading strategies explicitly to students in a carefully orchestrated manner. First, the teacher should model the strategy, explain it, and describe how to apply successfully the strategy. It helps if the teacher "thinks aloud" while modeling the strategy for students. Second, the teacher should practice the strategy with the students. It is important to scaffold the students' attempts and support their thinking by giving feedback during conferencing and classroom discussion. In this case, it helps if the students "think aloud" while practicing the strategy. Third, the teacher should encourage the students to apply the strategy and should give them regular feedback. Fourth, once the students clearly understand the strategy, they should apply it on their own in new reading situations. While monitoring students' understanding of the subject matter, the teacher should become aware of students' thinking as they read and as they detect obstacles and confusions that derail their understanding. The teacher can suggest, teach, or implement strategies to help students repair meaning when it breaks down.

Topic 5.
What Is Comprehension and What Are Some Strategies for Teaching It?

Reading is more than calling words. Reading must result in *comprehension*, or understanding.

Comprehension skills include the ability to identify supporting details and facts, the main idea or essential message, the author's purpose, fact and opinion, point of view, inference, and conclusion. To help students develop these skills, teachers can consistently emphasize meaning in the classroom and should focus on the four levels of comprehension: literal, interpretive, critical, and creative.

The **literal level of comprehension**, the lowest level of understanding, involves **reading the lines**, or reading and understanding exactly what is on the page. Students may give back **facts** or **details** directly from the passages as they read. For example, a teacher works with students as they make their own play dough and use the recipe to practice **authentic reading** (Davis 2004). The teacher might question the students on the literal level as they mix their ingredients. Here are some sample questions:

Factual question. How much salt do you add to the mixture?

Sequence question. What is the first step in making the play dough?

Contrast question. Do you add more or less salt than you did flour?

The **interpretive level of comprehension**, the second level of understanding, requires students to **read between the lines**. At this level, students must explain figurative language, define terms, and answer interpretive or inferential questions. **Inferential questions** require the students to **infer**, or figure out, the answers. Asking students to figure out the **author's purpose**, the **main idea** or **essential message**, the **point of view**, and the **conclusion** are examples of inferential questions. Inferential questions may require students to draw conclusions, generalize, derive meaning from the language, speculate, anticipate, predict, and summarize. All such questions are from the interpretive level.

Here are some examples of interpretive questions the teacher could ask at the cooking center while students are making play dough:

Contrast. How is the dry measuring cup different from the liquid measuring cup? Why are they different?

Deriving meaning. What does the term *blend* mean?

Purpose. What is the purpose of making play dough at home? Why would you want to make play dough instead of buying it?

Cause and effect. Why do the directions say to store the play dough in a covered, airtight container?

The **critical level of comprehension** requires a high level of understanding. The students must judge the passage they have read. The critical level is one of the two highest of the levels of understanding; it requires students to **read beyond the lines**. Having students determine whether a passage is true or false, deciding whether a statement is a fact or opinion, detecting propaganda, or judging the qualifications of the author for writing the passage are examples of using the critical level of comprehension. Here are some examples of questions the teacher could ask students as they make play dough to encourage their thinking and understanding at the critical and creative levels:

Checking author's reputation. The recipe for the play dough comes from a book of chemistry experiments. A chemist wrote the book. Do you think that a chemist would be a good person to write about play dough? Why, or why not?

Responding emotionally. Do you prefer to use the play dough we made in class or the play dough that the local stores carry?

Judging. Do you think that the recipe for play dough that is on the recipe card will work? Why, or why not?

The **creative level of comprehension** is at the highest level of understanding. As with the critical level of comprehension, the student must **read beyond the lines**. The student must often make judgments about other actions to take. Answers may vary among the students. The teacher must take care not to stifle creativity by saying one action is better than another. For instance, a teacher might suggest that after making a batch of cookies, a student finds that the baked cookies do not fit in the cookie jar; the teacher asks, "What can the student do?" Answers might include, "Donate the extras to the first-graders," "Give some to the teacher," "Share with my little sister," "Put them in a plastic storage bag." All these answers are creative; the teacher should not judge one as better than another.

Teachers need to be explicit about teaching students to be aware, to check for understanding, and to use reading comprehension strategies to make meaning. To monitor and repair students' understanding, teachers should explicitly teach them to do the following (Goudvis and Harvey 2000):

- Track their thinking through coding with sticky notes, writing, or discussion.

- Notice when they lose focus.

- Stop and go back to clarify thinking.

- Reread to enhance understanding.

- Read ahead to clarify meaning.

- Identify and articulate what is confusing or puzzling about the text.

- Recognize that all of their questions have value. (There is no such thing as a stupid question.)

- Develop the disposition to question the text or author.

- Think critically about the text and be willing to disagree with its information or logic.

- Match the problem with the strategy that will best solve it.

Depending on the situation, instructors may use these strategies across the curriculum in any subject area. In addition, the effective teacher can use graphic organizers such as these:

Double-entry journals. The student enters direct quotes from the text (with page number) in the left column and enters "thinking options"—such as "This is important because," "I am confused because," "I think this means"—in the right column.

Venn diagrams. Venn diagrams consist of two overlapping concentric circles in which the student compares two items or concepts by placing specific criteria or critical attributes for one in the left circle, for the other in the right circle, and attributes or characteristics that are shared by the two in the overlapping section in the center.

Webs or maps. The student charts out a concept or section of text in a graphic outline. The web or map begins with the title or concept often written in the middle of the page and branches out in web fashion; students will note specific bits of information on the branches or strings of the web. Arrows or lines in other formats can make connections from one bit of information to another. The map or web helps the student to think about the reading passage and illustrate its structure; the student is able with the map/web to make a passage more concrete and develop a visual representation of the book or reading section. (Davis, 2004)

Topic 6.
What Are Some Strategies for Developing Critical Thinking Skills?

Benjamin Bloom describes six levels of comprehension in his *Taxonomy* (Bloom 1956). The teacher may wish to develop questions at each level to increase comprehension, develop a series of questions for thought and discussion, or prepare a test.

Bloom's Taxonomy

1. **Knowledge level.** Students give back the information that is on the page.

2. **Comprehension level.** Students show that they can give the meaning of terms, idioms, figurative language, and other elements of written material.

3. **Application level.** After reading a story about how a class raised money for playground equipment, the students discuss some ways that they might improve their own playground.

4. **Analysis level.** Students examine the parts or components of a passage. For example, students might examine a menu and locate food groups, or they might identify terms in a word problem to determine the operations they should use.

5. **Synthesis level.** Students move from specifics to generalities. For instance, the class might develop a solution to the overcrowding problem suggested in a story, or students might construct a platform for the main character to use if she should run for class officer in the school described in another story.

6. **Evaluation level.** Students judge if a passage is fact or opinion, true or false, biased or unbiased.

Assessing Comprehension

A frequent device for assessing comprehension is the use of oral or written questions. A question may be **convergent**, which indicates that only one answer is correct, or **divergent**, which indicates that more than one answer is correct. Most tests, however, include a combination of question types.

Another device for checking comprehension is a **cloze test**, a passage with omitted words the test taker must supply. The test maker must decide whether to require the test taker to supply the exact word or to accept synonyms. Passing scores reflect which type of answer is acceptable. If meaning is the intent of the exercise, the teacher might accept synonyms and not demand the surface-level constructs, or the exact word.

The speed at which a student reads helps determine comprehension, *up to a point*. The faster a student reads, the better that student comprehends, *up to a point*. The slow reader who must analyze each word does not comprehend as well as the fast reader. It is possible, however, to read too fast. Most students have had the experience of having to reread materials. For example, a student reading a physics chapter in preparation for a test might read more slowly than when reading a novel but not slowly enough to note every important detail.

A teacher might ask students to read a passage and record their reading times. Then the teacher might give the students a quiz on the passage. After scoring the quizzes, the teacher could meet with each student to discuss the student's reading speed and its relation to the quiz grade. For students who received low quiz scores, the teacher could assign another passage and attempt to have the student slow down, or perhaps even accelerate, the speed of reading.

Higher-Level Thinking Skills

A teacher might encourage higher-level thinking skills in the classroom through activities such as mapping or webbing; study plans such as the SQ3R (study, question, read, recite, review) discussed later; puzzles, riddles, and "think alouds"; and programs such as the Tactics for Thinking program (which provides activities for all levels of comprehension) adopted by South Carolina.

Mapping and Webbing

Story mapping or webbing helps students think about a reading passage and its structure. Some typical devices in good narrative fiction and that might be useful on a story map include setting, stylistic devices, characters, and plot. A class reading Wilson Rawls's *Where the Red Fern Grows* (1961/1976) created the story map shown here.

Study Plans

The teacher might acquaint students with several plans to help them read content materials. Many of these plans already exist, and the teacher and the students can simply select the plan(s) that works best for them with various subjects. Students may use **mnemonic devices**, or memory-related devices, to help them remember the steps in reading a chapter effectively. Students often use plans like the following SQ3R plan when reading text in content areas:

Survey. Before reading a passage or an entire section of the text, the student should look over the assigned page or chapter and consider some questions. Are there illustrations, charts, or diagrams? What are some of the chapter headings? Are some words in bold type?

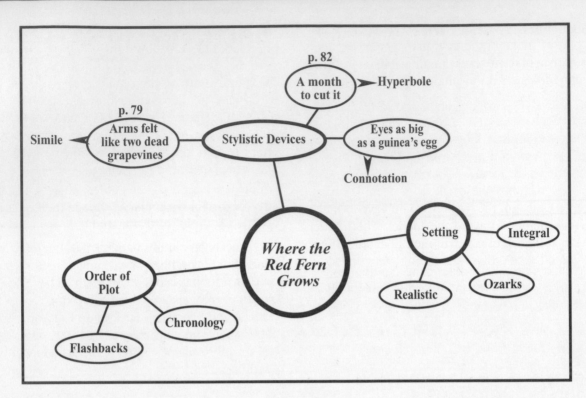

Story Map

Question. The student may wish to devise some questions that the chapter will probably answer. If an assigned chapter has questions at the end, the student can look over the questions before reading the chapter; the questions serve as a guide to the text.

Read. The student now reads the passage to answer the questions at the end of the chapter or to answer the questions that the student developed before reading the chapter.

Recite. The student attempts to answer orally or in writing the student-developed questions or the questions at the end of the chapter.

Review. The student reviews the material to "double-check" the answers given in writing or orally at the previous step.

Richard Vacca and Jo Ann Vacca (1989) express doubt that most students actually use a study plan. Even though an instructor may try to teach the "formula" for reading and studying a passage by having a class memorize the steps, practice the procedure several times, and view the formulas as a lifelong activity, Vacca and Vacca contend that a study system "evolves gradually within each learner" and that the SQ3R plan is difficult even for junior high school

students (227). They suggest that students need to become "text smart" and learn to preview, skim for the main idea, and organize information through mapping or outlining.

Other reading authorities disagree. Judy S. Richardson and Raymond F. Morgan (1990) suggest that students can use the SQ3R plan by fifth or sixth grade. Thomas G. Gunning (1996) reminds teachers that SQ3R has been around since the 1930s; he describes the method as "a widely used and effective study strategy incorporating five steps" (319). John U. Michaelis and Jesus Garcia (1996) suggest that students can create their own self-directed reading strategies. They cite PROVE as an example:

Purpose. Establish a purpose or set up questions to guide your reading.

Read. Read the passage to try to achieve the purpose or answer the questions.

Organize. Outline; place details under main ideas.

Vocabulary. Note any new vocabulary or concepts that you master.

Evaluate. Evaluate to determine if you achieved your purpose.

Puzzles, Riddles, and "Think Alouds"

Students can practice their thinking skills by solving puzzles and riddles alone, in small groups, or as a class with the teacher helping in the modeling process. Here are some puzzles that encourage students to think:

1. A truck heading to Chicago is loaded with ice cream. At a tunnel in a mountain, a sign announces the height of the tunnel is 12 feet, 3 inches. The truck driver knows the truck is 12 feet, 4 inches. To get to Chicago, the trucker would have to make a 75-mile detour to avoid the tunnel. The trucker knows that the ice cream will melt in another hour. How can the truck driver get through the tunnel?

2. Twelve elementary school teachers meet at a party. If each teacher shakes hands with every other teacher, how many handshakes will occur at the party?

3. "As I was going to St. Ives, I met a man with seven wives. Each wife had seven sacks. Each sack had seven cats. Each cat had seven kittens. Sacks, cats, kits, wives. How many were going to St. Ives?" (This is an old nursery rhyme.)

Tactics for Thinking

Developed by Robert J. Marzano and Daisy E. Arredondo (1986) for the South Carolina schools, *Tactics for Thinking* implements the teaching of thinking skills for kindergarten through grade 12. The program asserts that thinking-skills development should be part of the classroom and teacher directed. Components include elaboration, synthesizing, goal seeking, and deep processing.

Summary

Benjamin Bloom gives a taxonomy of six levels of understanding: knowledge, comprehension, application, analysis, synthesis, and evaluation. Tests to indicate the level of comprehension include both cloze tests and tests with convergent and/or divergent questions. A focus on reading speed is often helpful for students to see how fast they read might affect comprehension. A teacher might encourage higher-level thinking skills in the classroom through activities like mapping and webbing; study plans; puzzles, riddles, and "think alouds"; and programs like Tactics for Thinking.

Section 2: Reading

Topic 7.
Vocabulary in Context and Concept Vocabulary

Vocabulary instruction is important to the teaching of the language arts—and other subjects. Teachers identify important vocabulary words in their units and often single out these words for study.

Vocabulary study is more than memorizing definitions, however. Effective teachers employ many strategies to increase the vocabulary of their students. They post new words on the word wall as reminders of the new vocabulary words. The teachers develop lessons about idioms, the use of dictionaries and glossaries, multiple meanings of words, antonyms, synonyms, homonyms, figurative meanings, word parts, and other word-study techniques.

Effective instruction includes making connections to the background of the students. Repetition, meaningful use, and encouraging independent reading also work to enhance vocabulary development (Tompkins 2006, 196–213).

Combs (2006) reminds the educator that children seem to acquire vocabulary when the adult provides explanations of the new words encountered in context. To enhance the learning, the children should have ample opportunities to review and use that knowledge—especially in other contexts. Shared reading especially aids in vocabulary development (190).

Topic 8.
What Are Some Types of Children's Literature?

Literary genres include prose, novels, short stories, poetry, plays or drama, and personal narratives or essays.

Poetry

Poetry is a genre that is difficult to define for children, except as "not prose." Poetry is the use of words to capture something: a sight, a feeling, or perhaps a sound. Poetry needs to be chosen carefully for a child, as poetry ought to elicit from the child a response that connects with the experience of the poem. All children need poetry in their lives. Poetry needs to be celebrated and enjoyed as part of the classroom experience, and a literacy-rich classroom will always include a collection of poetry to read, reread, savor, and enjoy. Some children enjoy the discipline of writing in a poetic format. Reggie Routman has published a series of slim books about teaching children to write poems on their own.

Poetry is perhaps the oldest art and has been a part of people's lives through the centuries. Like the ancient listeners who thrilled to Homer's poetry and the tribes who chanted invocations to their gods, both children and adults in today's generation listen to song lyrics and find themselves, sometimes despite themselves, repeating certain rhythmic lines. An advertisement that listeners chuckle over—or say they hate—has a way of repeating itself as listeners use the catchy phrase or snappy repetition. Both lyricists and advertisers cleverly use language and play on people's ability to pick up on a repeated sound or engaging rhythm or inner rhyme—a part of poetry.

Children love poetry: nursery rhymes, ball-game rhythms, jump-rope patterns. Even with no idea of the meaning of the words (for example, "Little Miss Muffet sat on a tuffet"), a child can respond to their sounds and the pattern they form.

Prose

Prose is another literary type. Students are sometimes confused as to what exactly prose is. Basically, prose is not poetry. Prose is what people write and speak most of the time in everyday intercourse: unmetered, unrhymed language. This does not mean, however, that prose does not have its own rhythms; language, whether written or spoken, has cadence and balance. Certainly prose can have instances of rhyme or assonance, alliteration, or onomatopoeia. Language is, after all, phonic. Furthermore, prose may be either fiction or nonfiction. A novel (like a short story) is fiction; an autobiography is nonfiction. Whereas a novel (or short story) may have some autobiographical elements, an autobiography is, from most readers' point of view, entirely factual.

Textbooks are generally nonfiction prose. Reading textbooks (**basals**) may contain both fiction and nonfiction, poetry and prose.

The **narrative** is a common style of prose that can be fiction or nonfiction. A narrative tells a story or gives an account of an incident or a series of incidents. The account may be autobiographical to make a point, as in George Orwell's essay "Shooting an Elephant."

Narrative fictional children's literature is either traditional or modern in form. **Traditional literature** is composed of ancient stories, and it has a set form. People have passed these stories down through the centuries by word of mouth. Later, others, like Joel Chandler Harris, the Grimm Brothers, and Charles Perrault, recorded the stories for future generations. **Modern literature**, on the other hand, is, as the name suggests, much more recent; its categories can overlap some of the categories of traditional literature and can include additional forms of literature.

Seven Types of Traditional Literature

There are seven types of traditional fiction: parables, fables, fairy tales, folktales, Noodle-head tales, myths, and legends. Each has certain characteristics that set it apart from the others.

Parables. A **parable** is a story that is realistic and has a moral. The story is **didactic**: it teaches a lesson. Unlike the fable, the parable can be, but is not necessarily, true. The Biblical figure Jesus often taught with parables. One of his best known parables is "The Prodigal Son" (Luke 16:11–32 New Revised Standard Edition); others include "The Good Samaritan" (Luke 10:30–36 New Revised Standard Edition), "The Lost Coin" (Luke 15:8–11 New Revised Standard Edition), and "The Parable of the Seeds on Rich and Fallow Ground" (Mark 4:3–8; Luke 8:5–8 New Revised Standard Edition).

Fables. A **fable** is a nonrealistic story with a moral. The fable often has animals as main characters. **Aesop**, a Greek slave supposedly born around 600 BCE, is often credited with having developed the fable; however, whether he actually did so—or ever actually existed—is debatable. Charlotte Huck, the noted children's literature authority and the author of *Children's Literature in the Elementary School* (1968), states that fables were actually in Greek literature as early as 800 BCE (362–64). "The Fox and the Crane," "The Fox and the Crow," and "The Fox and the Grapes" are among the best-known fables. Some scholars use the classification **beast tale** for fables in which animals behave as humans do.

Translators changed Aesop's Fables from Greek to Latin and to English. William Caxton published these fables in England in 1484. It was sometime after the publication of these fables that the Grimm Brothers (1800s) and Charles Perrault (1697) secured the preservation in writing of these fairy tales by publishing them.

Fairy tales. Fairy tales have the element of magic; they do not necessarily have fairies in them. They often have a certain pattern and may present an "ideal" to the listener or the reader. For instance, fairy tales such as "Cinderella," "Snow White," and "Rapunzel" convey a message about the "proper" woman. According to these tales, the ideal woman is beautiful, kind, and long-suffering; she waits for her prince to come and to save her from any disappointment or disaster that may occur.

Charles Perrault first recorded the French fairy tales in the 1600s; they are still in print. It was not until the 1800s that the Grimm Brothers recorded German fairy tales, Joseph Jacobs recorded British fairy tales, Peter Asbjørnsen and Jorgen Moe recorded Scandinavian fairy tales, and Aleksandr Nikolaevich Afanas'ev recorded Russian fairy tales. All these tales are in current editions in English or the language of choice.

Sometimes, writers, such as Nathaniel Hawthorne, use the term **wonder tales** to refer to these fairy tales with their magical elements. The characters of witches, wizards, talking beasts, and other magical animals often possess and demonstrate these magical elements. The use of the **magic three** is another frequent feature of the fairy tale; for instance, the stories often involve three wishes, three attempts at achieving a goal, and three siblings.

Another characteristic of a fairy tale is that the listener or reader knows that good will always win out over evil. A youngster may find frightening witches, wicked ogres, and evil forces, but in the end the protagonist will ". . . live happily ever after."

Stereotyping is another characteristic of the fairy tale. As soon as the storyteller or the reader says the word *stepmother*, for instance, the listener knows that the woman is wicked. Likewise, mere mention of the setting as being in the *woods* conveys a message of fear, impending doom, and evil. The word *prince* causes one to envision a young, handsome man on a white horse! The *princess* is usually the youngest in the family, beautiful, soft-spoken, kind, inactive, and waiting for her prince to come. Such demure fairy-tale female characters stand in direct contrast to the assertive female characters of folktales.

Folktales. Folktales are in the language of the people. The stories do not necessarily have a moral. In fact, entertainment is often the main purpose of folktales. In the 1600s and 1700s, early residents of the Appalachian Mountains, for instance, took many of the fairy tales of England, Scotland, and Ireland with them to the "new" country. The fairy tale "Cinderella" became "Ashpet" in the Appalachians (Chase 1948, 119). The quiet, passive Cinderella became the hard-working, smart, active Ashpet, a character more like the mountain women who had to work and assist their men. "The Bremen Town Musicians" (Grimm, 301–304) became "Jack and the Robbers" in another mountain tale (Chase 1943, 40–46).

Another example of the humorous folktales are the Noodle-head stories. The **Noodle-head stories** are those tales that have a character or characters whom the listener can outsmart. The listener often finds these stories particularly humorous because the characters in these stories make the listener feel superior. "Epaminondas" is an example of the Noodle-head story.

The humor in folktales may be coarse, and the diction is often that of the particular group of people who originated the tales. Richard Chase collected many of the Appalachian folktales and recorded them. He transcribed the tales on paper and told them in personal appearances, on records, and on tapes for the public. He was always careful to use the mountain dialect. His *Jack Tales* (1943) and *Grandfather Tales* (1948) are among his best known works.

Likewise, other cultures around the world have their own unique folktales and fairy tales. For instance, Perrault's French tale of "Cinderella" is "Tattercoats" in Jacobs's collection (1959); in this British version, the prince falls in love with a dirty, ragged girl—not a beautiful, well-dressed figure at the ball. The Norwegian tale *East o' the Sun and West o' the Moon* (Asbjørnsen and Moe 1946) tells the story of Cinderlad, not Cinderella. The Jewish folktale of *Zlateh the Goat* (Singer 1966; illustrated by Maurice Sendak) tells of the survival of a young boy and his goat in a snowstorm.

Myths. Myths are stories to explain things that the teller does not understand. Greeks and Romans used myths and their associated heroes and heroines to explain thunder, fire, and the "movements" of the sun.

Norse myths, too, explain phenomena—especially those associated with the frost, snow, and the cold climate of the north. Likewise, Native American myths explain such phenomena as why the rabbit does not have a tail and why the constellations exist. (Some of these Native American myths have derived the name *legend* instead of the correct name of *myth*.) Another name for these explanations is **pourquoi tales**. Most cultures have their own myths.

Legends. **Legends** are stories—usually exaggerated—about real people, places, and things. George Washington, for instance, was a real person. However, all the stories about him are not true. Because there were no silver dollars minted during the American Revolution, it would have been impossible for him to have tossed a silver dollar across the Potomac. Paul Bunyan may actually have been a logger or lumberjack; it is doubtful that he owned a blue ox or had a pancake griddle large enough that his cook could tie hams on his feet and skate on it. The careful reader of literature realizes that though legends are generally a part of traditional literature, they continue to spring up with modern figures, animals, and places as their central elements.

Four Classifications of Modern Literature

An easy way of classifying modern literature is simply to decide if a book is **realistic or fanciful**. There are times, however, when a more discrete classification method is in order. In this case, modern fiction may be classified into four categories: novels, romance, confession, or Menippean satire.

Novels. **Novels** are realistic stories depicting events that could really happen or could really have happened. A novel has a realistic setting and realistic characters. The setting of a novel could be any planet, any city, or any country—as long as the author can convince the reader that the setting is real. Anyone can serve as a main character as long as the author can convince the reader that the character is believable.

Romance. A **romance**, on the other hand, presents an idealized view of life and even of the setting. The story may—or may not—involve love, but the story does involve fantasy. The characters and the setting are better than real life. An ocean cruise in a romance book might, therefore, involve characters who are young, handsome

or beautiful, and rich; the romantic characters might also possess all the qualities of the elite. The weather would, of course, be clear and pleasant for the entire cruise.

Confession. In a **confession**, one character reveals thoughts and ideas. This particular character is a **round character**, whom the reader knows in detail. In Laura Ingalls Wilder's *Little House in the Big Woods* (1953), for example, the reader knows exactly what the main character (Laura) is thinking; the reader, however, does not know what Mary (Laura's sister) is thinking. In this case, the confession allows the reader to view the thoughts and feelings of only one character.

Menippean satire. A **Menippean satire** allows the reader to see the world through the eyes of another. In Roald Dahl's *Charlie and the Chocolate Factory* (1972), the reader sees the world through Charlie's eyes. The desire for candy becomes almost overpowering for the reader—just as it does for Charlie. The reader has a different outlook on life, candy, and others as a result of experiencing *Charlie and the Chocolate Factory*.

Topic 9.
What Are Some Examples of Figurative Language Students Can Look for in the Literature and Use in Their Own Writing?

One criterion for evaluating juvenile fiction is the writing style of the author. A writer can employ many devices to enhance the flow of the words, to make the writing more appealing, and to clarify the meaning. Figurative language is one such device.

Figurative language includes the use of similes, metaphors, and personification; it is a way of adding information and description to the writing and of encouraging the reader to think about the text. All the details are not "spoon-fed" to the reader.

A **simile** is a comparison between two unlike things that uses *like*, *than*, or *as*. For example, in the memoir *October Sky*, Homer describes Jake Mosby, the new junior engineer, saying, "He's got more money than Carter's got little liver pills" (Hickam 1998, 145). Homer overhears a secretary tell some other women that "he looks just like Henry Fonda" (146). Homer's mother notes that on one occasion Jake is "drunk as Cooter Brown." (146). This figurative language brings imagery to the mind of the reader, requires the reader to think, and adds information to the description.

A **metaphor** is a comparison in which one thing is likened to some other, very dissimilar thing. For example, the character Jake in *October Sky* calls the *McDowell County Banner* "a grocery-store rag" (Hickam 1998, 154). Homer calls the rocket fuel "rocket candy" because of its sweetish odor (181). He also refers to a cord as "a thick electrical umbilical" (199).

Personification is the attribution of human characteristics or behaviors to animals, ideas, inanimate objects, and so on. For instance, Hickam writes that the "big golden moon hovered overhead" (1998, 53). Later he writes that "a shuttle car darted in, its crablike arms sweeping up the coal thrown out" (199).

Topic 10.
Making Sure the Text or Reading Material Is on the Student's Level

To match the reading level of the text to the reading level of the student, the instructor can use a cloze test. As stated earlier in the chapter, a **cloze test** is a reading comprehension test in which the student must supply words that have purposely been omitted from the text. A teacher can create a cloze test by using a selection from the textbook or other material and omitting every *n*th word; the student then must fill in the blanks. The teacher may adjust the percentage of words that the student must fill in correctly on the basis of whether there is an accompanying word bank and whether the teacher will accept synonyms or only the exact words. This test will help to determine if the text is on the student's instructional level, independent level, or frustration level.

The key in Table 2-1 is appropriate *only* if the teacher accepts the exact words—not synonyms—and does not provide a word bank.

Topic 11.
What Are Some Prereading Strategies?

The teacher may guide the student in prereading instruction. The teacher and class together may set up a know-want-learned (K-W-L) chart. The chart may list

Table 2-1. Cloze Test Scoring Guide

Percentage Correct	Reading Level	Difficulty
Above 60%	Independent reading level	This material is easy enough that a child could read it without help.
40%–60%	Instructional reading level	This material is of such a level that a child must have the help of a teacher to complete it successfully.
Below 40%	Frustration reading level	This material is too difficult for the student. Often the child will begin to make excuses to stop the exercise. The child may begin biting his/her nails, twisting her/his hair, fidgeting, and perhaps even asking to go to the bathroom or to get water. The teacher should probably not make the child use material on this level.

what they already *know* about the topic or the story, what they *want* to know and find out as they read, and— after the reading—what they have *learned*.

To ensure that the students master the material, the teacher may even develop **process guides** to help the students as they read. In a process guide, the teacher develops specific helps for a section of the text that the students are going to read and that the teacher believes might cause some problems for specific students. A teacher might include in a process guide to a particular chapter the following information:

- A list of key terms for the students to identify as they read
- A list of key people for the students to identify as they read

- A list of new vocabulary for the students to identify as they read

- A guide to relational words in the passages

- Questions to call the readers' attention to graphic aids in the passage

It is true that process guides are time-consuming to develop, but because schools use most texts and other reading materials for more than one year, the teacher may be able to reuse them from year to year if there are sections of the text that continue to be applicable to the subject and to the students of later years. After the teacher calls the students' attention to certain features of the text and how to read it, the students may be able to develop process guides for themselves or for the person whom they tutor; preparing the guides may serve as a learning/organizing experience (Davis 2000; Karlin 1971).

An important part of helping the students read effectively is helping them to be aware of the **patterns of organization** of various books, the **text structure**, and the use of **book parts**. Because book parts and organization may vary, particularly from one content area to another, the effective teacher will develop methods and/or materials to introduce the students to the texts that they will be using. The teacher will make sure that students know the purpose of bold font, the index, the sideheads, the contents page, and so on.

Before, during, and after instructional input, the students preview, rehearse, or apply what they've learned. In **guided practice**, the teacher watches carefully to make sure that students realize what they are to observe during their reading and that they have grasped the material correctly. Because the teacher is on hand to assess student responses, he or she is able to provide correction or additional input if necessary. During independent practice, students work independently. At the end of each lesson (or at the end of the class), the teacher or students summarize or review what has been learned (Davis 2004).

Topic 12.
Objectives

The education departments of the various states and the professional organizations for each subject have set standards for the curriculum for the grades and subjects; school districts also set objectives that guide the teachers in their instructional planning. Teachers, too, must set objectives for their classes.

The PRAXIS II Elementary Education Test: Content Knowledge (0014) emphasizes learner objectives; the PRAXIS II Elementary Education Test: Curriculum, Instruction, and Assessment (0011) does not. Still, all teachers need to look at these objectives, or guides to instruction.

The name most frequently associated with objectives is Robert F. Mager. He defines an *objective* as being an intent that a statement communicates to the reader (Mager 1962, 3). The statement describes a proposed change in behavior. An objective, then, describes the behavior or outcome that the educator wants the learner to demonstrate.

There are three types of objectives: cognitive (that have to do with thinking and learning), affective (that have to do with valuing and feelings), and psychomotor (that have to do with skills).

The cognitive objectives particularly must be open to few interpretations. The outcomes must be observable. This means that some words (see Table 2-2 for examples) are more acceptable than others in a behavioral objective.

Ideally, the objective will give the criteria for success. The following are some examples:

- The student will be able to list three out of four of the seasons.

- The student will be able to locate the state capital on a map of the state.

- The student will be able to solve 7 out of 10 addition problems correctly.

A complete cognitive behavioral objective will also include the condition under which the students will achieve the criteria and the behavioral outcome desired. The following are examples of some objectives with the condition and the criteria for success:

- In a five-minute time period, the student will be able to solve 50 one-digit addition facts correctly.

- Given a map of their state, all the third-grade students will be able to locate their state capital correctly.

- Given a calendar, the students will be able to locate today's date accurately.

Table 2-2. Unobservable (Unacceptable) and Observable (Acceptable) Words for Behavioral Objectives

Unobservable Words; Words and Phrases Open to Many Interpretations	Observable Words; Words and Phrases Open to Fewer Interpretations
To appreciate	*To construct*
To appreciate fully	*To define*
To comprehend	*To demonstrate*
To enjoy	*To differentiate*
To grasp the significance of	*To draw*
To know	*To identify*
To understand	*To list*
To understand fully	*To locate on a map*
	To match
	To recite
	To solve
	To underline
	To write

Section 3: Writing

Topic 13.
Writing: Its Stages, Process, and Assessment

Demonstrating Knowledge of the Developmental Stages of Writing

For years, educators believed that reading preceded writing in the development of literacy. This belief has recently changed.

Stages in Writing Development

Emerging literacy research indicates that learning to write is an important part in a child's learning to read.

As children begin to name letters and read print, they also begin to write letters and words. Writing development seems to occur at about the same time as reading development—not afterward, as traditional reading readiness assumed. Whole language seeks to integrate the language arts rather than sequencing them. Just as change has marked educators' beliefs about reading instruction and the way that reading develops, change has also marked the methods and philosophies behind the teaching of writing in the schools.

Children seem to progress through certain stages in their writing. Although many authorities have examined the stages in writing development, Alexander Luria presents the most thoroughly elaborated model (Klein 1985; Davis 2004). He cautions, however, that the stages are not entirely a function of age. Luria explains that it is not uncommon to find children from 3 to 6 years old who are the same age but are two to three stages apart in their writing. He also notes that children do not advance systematically through the stages. At times, a child may regress or "zigzag." At other times, the child may appear to remain at one level without progression or regression. Here is a summary of Luria's stages in writing:

Stage 1. The undifferentiated stage from ages 3 to 5 is a period that Luria defines as a prewriting or preinstrumental period. The child does not distinguish between marks written on a page. The marks (writing) seem merely random to the child and do not help the child recall information.

Stage 2. The differentiated stage from about age 4 is when the child intentionally builds a relationship between sounds and written expression. For instance, the child represents short words or short phrases with shorter marks and longer words, phrases, or sentences with longer marks. The child might use dark marks to help remember a sentence such as "The sky was dark." Making such marks is an example of mnemonics, or associating symbols with information.

Stage 3. The pictographic stage from ages 4 to 6 is the period that Robert Klein (1985, 66) says is "the most important stage in the development of the child's perception of writing-as-a-conceptual-act."

The Writing Process

Teachers in the early 1970s were very concerned with spelling and punctuation in students' papers. The teacher did all the "correcting" and watched carefully for grammatical, spelling, and punctuation errors. In the late 1970s, writing "experts" denounced students' compositions as being too dull. The schools began to foster creative writing and encouraged teachers to provide opportunities for creative writing each week. However, many teachers began to view the creative writing as lacking in structure. **Process writing** has since become the buzzword in writing. With process writing, students engage in several activities (Noyce and Christie, 1989):

Prewriting stage. During the first stage in the writing process, the students begin to collect information for the writing that they will do.

Composing or writing stage. The classroom resembles a laboratory. Students may consult with one another and use various books and materials to construct their papers. At this stage, the student-writers do not worry about spelling and mechanics. This is the drafting stage. Some students will use invented spelling as they try to apply their understanding of spelling rules. The students may later edit and revise the words, but on first writing their drafts, they can simply record the word quickly and go on to the next word in the sentence.

Revising stage. Writers polish and improve their compositions.

Editing/evaluation/postwriting stage. Students read and correct their own writing and the works of others. The teacher does not have to do all the evaluating. Students use the dictionary, their thesaurus, their peers, and even the spell-check program on the classroom computers.

Rewrite stage. After their self-evaluations and after their classmates and teachers share praise and constructive criticisms, including spelling and punctuation corrections, the students rewrite their compositions.

In some classes, the students publish their own works and even have an **author's chair** from which the writers can tell some things about themselves, discuss their writing process, and read their compositions aloud (Noyce and Christie 1989). According to research, the most effective writing process includes at least the prewriting, composing, revising, and editing/evaluation/postwriting stages (Bennett 1987).

Topic 14.
Speech

Conventions of Standard American English

The way you speak can vary depending on whom you are speaking to—just as what you wear can vary depending on whom you are going to see. More commonly, language varies according to geographic region, ethnic group, social class, and educational level. The language usually used in U.S. schools is Standard American English. This formal language (dialect) is the language in texts, newspapers, magazines, and the news programs on television.

There are other forms of the English language beside Standard American English. Some variations are the forms spoken in Appalachia, in urban ghettos, and by Mexican Americans, particularly in the Southwest. In all these variations, the syntax, phonology, and semantics differ from Standard American English. When instructing students who do not speak the standard dialect, teachers should not try to replace the culture or the language with Standard American English; the goal of school is to add Standard American English to students' language registers (Tompkins 2006).

Writing Standard American English requires the use of certain mechanics or conventions. Using the conventions in capitalization, punctuation, spellings, and formatting, among others, is a courtesy to readers of the written language (Tompkins 2006). As noted earlier in the chapter, with the language experience approach (LEA), the teacher attempts to facilitate the students' language development through the use of experiences, rather than printed material alone. After the class participates in an experience or event, the students, as a group, record what happened (often with the help of the teacher). The teacher writes exactly what the students say—even if they do not use Standard American English. The idea is to enable each student to see that

- what I say, I can write;
- what I can write, I can read;
- what others write, I can read (Davis 2004).

The teacher may talk at this time about alternative ways to say what the students do not say in Standard American English.

In summary, many forms of language exist, but the school should not try to eradicate the culture or the language of its students.

Characteristics of the Modes of Writing

Writing serves many different functions. The main functions, however, are to narrate, to describe, to explain, and to persuade. Students need to be aware of each of these types of literature. In any event, the four categories are neither exhaustive nor mutually exclusive.

The narrative, as noted earlier in the chapter, is a story or an account of an incident or a series of incidents. The narrative may be nonfiction—autobiographical, for example—or fiction.

The purpose of **descriptive** writing is to provide information about a person, place, or thing. Descriptive writing can be fiction or nonfiction. E. B. White uses description when he relates what the barn is like in *Charlotte's Web* (1952); the book itself, however, is fiction. Realtors use descriptive writing when they advertise a house in a local newspaper; the general public expects the descriptions of events in the local paper to be factual.

The purpose of **expository** writing is to explain and clarify ideas. Students are probably most familiar with this type of writing. While the expository essay may have narrative elements, the storytelling or recounting aspect is minor and subservient to that of the explanation element. Expository writing is typical of many textbooks; for instance, the writing in a textbook on how to operate a computer would likely be expository.

The purpose of **persuasive** writing is to convince the reader of something. Persuasive writing fills current magazines and newspapers and permeates the World Wide Web. The writer may be trying to push a political candidate, to convince someone to vote for a zoning ordinance, or even to promote a diet plan. Persuasive writing usually presents a point, provides evidence, which may be factual or anecdotal, and supports the point. The structure may be very formal, with counterpositions and counterarguments. Whatever the organizational pattern, the writer's intent is to persuade readers of the validity of some claim. Nearly all essays have some element of persuasion.

Authors choose their form of writing not necessarily just to tell a story but to present an idea. Whether writers choose the narrative, descriptive, expository, or persuasive format, they have something on their minds that they want to convey to their readers. When readers analyze writing, they often seek first to determine its form.

There are other types of writing, of course. For instance, **speculative** writing is so named because, as the Latin root suggests, it looks at ideas and explores them rather than merely explaining them, as expository writing does. The speculative essay is often meditative; it often makes one or more points, and the thesis may not be as obvious or clear-cut as that in an expository essay. The writer deals with ideas in an associative manner and plays with ideas in a looser structure than the writer might do in an expository format. This "flow" may even produce intercalary paragraphs, which present alternately a narrative of sorts and thoughtful responses to the recounted events.

Selection of the Appropriate Mode of Writing for a Variety of Occasions, Purposes, and Audiences

The writer must consider the audience, the occasion, and the purpose when choosing the writing mode.

The writer's responsibility is to write clearly, honestly, and cleanly for the reader's sake; the **audience** is very important. After all, writing would be pointless without readers.

Why write? Why add evidence, organize your ideas, or correct bad grammar? The reason to do any of these things is that someone out there—an audience—needs to understand what you mean to say.

The teacher can designate an audience for students' writing. Knowing those who will read their work, students can modify their writing to suit the intended readers. For instance, a fourth-grade teacher might suggest that the class take their compositions about a favorite animal to second-graders and allow the younger children to read or listen to the works. The writers will realize that they need to use manuscript—not cursive—writing, to employ simple vocabulary, and to omit complex sentences when they write for their young audience.

The **occasion** helps to determine the elements of the writing. The language should fit the occasion; particular words may have certain effects: evoke sympathy or raise questions about an opposing point of view, for instance. The students and teacher might try to determine the likely effect on an audience of a writer's choice of a particular word or words.

The **purpose** helps to determine the format (narrative, expository, descriptive, persuasive) and the language of the writer. The students, for instance, might consider the appropriateness of written material for a specific purpose: a business letter, a communication with residents of a retirement center, or a thank-you note to parents. The teacher and students might try to identify persuasive techniques used by a writer in a passage.

In selecting the mode of writing and the content, the writer might ask the following:

- What would the audience need to know to believe you or to accept your position? Imagine someone you know (visualize her or him) listening to you declare your position or opinion and then saying, "Oh yeah? Prove it!"

- What evidence do you need to prove your idea to this skeptic?

- With what might the audience disagree?

- What common knowledge does the audience share with you?

- What information do you need to share with the audience?

The teacher might wish to have the students practice selecting the mode and the language by adapting forms, organizational strategies, and styles for different audiences and purposes.

Topic 15.
Formal and Informal Assessment to Improve Instruction and Enhance Learning

As described earlier in this chapter, the cloze test can help to determine whether a student can read a particular text or other material. Other types of assessment are important in the classroom as well.

Informal Assessment

Evaluation does not have to be expensive and purchased to be useful to the teacher and student alike. For instance, as noted earlier in the chapter, Clay (1985) developed a procedure for sampling the child's reading vocabulary and determining the extent of a child's print-related concepts. Her assessment checks whether children can find the title, show where to start reading a book, and locate the last page or the end of the book. As such, Clay's procedure is an informal way of **determining a child's readiness for reading** (Davis 2004).

Teachers can gain much valuable information by simply observing their students at work. Many school districts use a type of inventory/report card to inform adults in the home of the progress that the kindergartner or first-grader is making. Long-time teachers usually develop, through trial and error, their own means of assessing the skills of students in their classes. Almost every book on teaching reading contains its own informal tests. The SREB's Health and Human Services Commission (1994) cautions that assessment should be **ongoing** and **natural**. The commission has determined that **continual observation of the physical, social, emotional, and cognitive domains of students** by both parents and teachers is the most meaningful approach to assessing young children. To obtain a meaningful, complete view of a young child, the commission endorses portfolios of a child's progress and performance inventories rather than standardized test results. Similarly, letter grades and numeric grades are less likely to give a complete picture than narrative reports on the young child.

Teachers can also develop their own informal reading inventories. The purpose of these assessments is to collect meaningful information about what students can and cannot do. A **running record** is a way to assess students' word-identification skills and fluency in oral reading. As the teacher listens to a student read a page, the teacher uses a copy of the page to mark each word the child mispronounces: the teacher writes the incorrect word over the printed word, draws a line through each word the child skips, and draws an arrow under repeated words.

After determining the words that the child did not read successfully, the teacher can analyze the missed words to determine the reason that the child missed them. This assessment of missed words is **miscue analysis**. The teacher is looking for a pattern in the student's mistakes so that the teacher can provide help to the student.

Edward Fry developed in 1957 a list of "instant words." In 1980, he developed "The New Instant Word List." He explains that the words on the list are the most frequently used words in the English language. He says these words are the ones that young readers need to know. He explains that half of the words in the language are composed of the first 100 words (and their variants) in his list. Using this list is a way to assess how well the students are reading the words instantly (Davis 2004).

Fry also developed a **readability graph**. This mathematical equation gives the relationship between two variables: the number of sentences per 100 words and the number of syllables per 100 words. The result of graphing this information is the grade level of the book (Davis, 2004).

Asking a child to **retell** a story is another type of informal assessment. The ability to retell a story is an informal type of assessment that is useful to the teacher, parent, and—eventually—the child. Informal assessment measures can also include observations, journals, written drafts, and conversations.

The teacher may make **observations** for individual or group work. This method is very suitable for skills or for effective learning. Usually, the teacher makes a **checklist** of competencies, skills, or requirements and then uses the list to check off the ones a student or group displays. A teacher wishing to emphasize interviewing skills could devise a checklist that includes personal appearance, mannerisms, confidence, and addressing the questions asked. A teacher who wants to emphasize careful listening might observe a discussion while using a checklist that includes paying attention, not interrupting, summarizing the ideas of other members of the group, and asking questions of others.

Advantages of checklists include the potential for capturing behaviors—such as shooting free throws on the basketball court, following the correct sequence of steps in a science experiment, or including all important elements in a speech in class—that a paper-and-pencil test may not accurately measure. One characteristic of a checklist that is both an advantage and a disadvantage is its structure, which provides consistency but inflexibility. An open-ended comment section at the end of a checklist can overcome this disadvantage.

Anecdotal records are helpful in some instances, such as capturing the process a group of students uses to solve a problem. This formative data can be useful during feedback to the group. Students can also practice writing explanations of the procedures they use for their projects or science experiments. One advantage of an anecdotal record is that it can include all relevant information. Disadvantages include the amount of time necessary to complete the record and difficulty in assigning a grade. If the purpose of an anecdotal record is solely for feedback, no grade is necessary.

Portfolios are collections of students' best work. They are useful in any subject area when the teacher wants students to take more responsibility for planning, carrying out, and organizing their own learning. Like a portfolio that an artist, model, or performer creates, a student portfolio provides a succinct picture of the child's achievements over a certain period. Portfolios may contain essays or articles written on paper, videotapes, multimedia presentations on computer disks, or a combination. Language arts teachers often use portfolios as a means of collecting the best samples of student writing over an entire year, and some teachers pass on the portfolios to the teacher next year to help in student assessment.

Teachers should provide or assist students in developing guidelines for what materials should go in their portfolios; it would be unrealistic to include every piece of work in one portfolio. Using portfolios requires the students to devise a means of evaluating their own work. A portfolio should not be a scrapbook for collecting handouts or work done by other individuals, but it can certainly include work by a group in which the student was a participant.

Some advantages of portfolios over testing are (a) that they provide a clear picture of students' progress, (b) they are not affected by one inferior test grade, and (c) they help develop students' self-assessment skills. One disadvantage is the amount of time required to teach students how to develop meaningful portfolios. However, the time is valuable if students learn important skills. Another concern is the amount of time necessary for teachers to assess portfolios. However, as students become more proficient at self-assessment, the teacher can spend more time in coaching and advising students during the development of their portfolios. A third concern is that parents may not understand how the teacher will grade the portfolios. The effective teacher devises a system that the students and parents understand before work on the portfolios begins.

Through informal observations and through the use of inventories (formal and informal), teachers should determine the **learning styles** of their students. Student learning styles play an important role in determining classroom structure.

Formal Assessment

Formal measures may include teacher-made tests, district exams, and standardized tests.

Both formative and summative evaluations are part of effective teaching. **Formative evaluation** occurs during the process of learning when the teacher or the students monitor progress in obtaining outcomes and while it is still possible to modify instruction. **Summative evaluation** occurs at the end of a specific time or course of study. Usually, a summative evaluation applies a single grade to represent a student's performance.

The effective teacher uses a **variety of formal assessment techniques**. Ideally, instructors should develop their teacher-made assessment instruments at the same time that they are planning goals and outcomes, rather than after the completion of the lessons. Carefully planned objectives and assessment instruments serve as lesson development guides for the teacher. Paper-and-pencil tests are the most common method for evaluating student progress.

Section 4: Assessment

Assessing Learners

The purpose of both formal and informal assessments in the classroom is to improve the instruction and the learning of the students—all the students. It is important for the teacher (1) to analyze and interpret the information gathered through informal and formal means and (2) to use test results professionally to help all students in the classroom to learn to the best of their ability.

The use of criterion-referenced, norm-referenced, performance-based, classroom, and authentic assessments is essential to giving the child, the teacher, and the parents a complete picture of the child and the child's progress.

Criterion-Referenced Tests

In **criterion-referenced tests (CRTs)**, the teacher attempts to measure each student against uniform objectives or criteria. CRTs allow the possibility that all students can score 100 percent because they understand the concepts being tested. Teacher-made tests should be criterion-referenced because the teacher should develop them to measure the achievement of predetermined outcomes for the course. If teachers have properly prepared lessons based on the outcomes and if students have mastered the outcomes, then scores should be high. This type of test is noncompetitive because students are not in competition with each other for a high score, and there is no limit to the number of students who can score well. Some commercially developed tests are criterion-referenced; however, most are norm-referenced.

Norm-Referenced Tests

The purpose of a **norm-referenced test (NRT)** is to compare the performance of groups of students. This type of test is competitive because a limited number of students can score well. A plot of large numbers of NRT scores resembles a **bell-shaped curve**, with most scores clustering around the center and a few scores at each end. The **midpoint** is an average of data; therefore, by definition, half the population will score above average and half below average. The bell-shaped curve is a mathematical description of the results of tossing coins. As such, it represents the chance or normal distribution of skills, knowledge, or events across the general population. A survey of the height of sixth-grade boys will result in an average height, with half the boys above average and half below. There will be a very small number with heights far above average and a very small number with heights far below average; most heights will cluster around the average.

A **percentile score** (not to be confused with a percentage) is a way of reporting a student's NRT score; the percentile score indicates the percentage of the population whose scores fall at or below the student's score. For example, a group score at the eightieth percentile means that the group scored as well as or better than 80 percent of the students who took the test. A student with a score at the fiftieth percentile has an average score. Percentile scores rank students from highest to lowest. By themselves, percentile scores do not indicate how well the student has mastered the content objectives. **Raw scores** indicate how many questions the student answered correctly and are, therefore, useful in computing a percentage score.

A national test for biology would include objectives for the widest possible biology curriculum, for the broadest use of the test. Reported **normed scores** would enable schools to compare the performance of their students with the performance of students whom the test developers used as its norm group. The test would likely include more objectives than are in a particular school's curriculum; therefore, that school's students might score low in comparison to the norm group. A teacher must be very careful in selecting a norm-referenced test and should look for one with objectives that are the most congruent with the school's curriculum.

The teacher must also consider the test **reliability**, or whether the instrument will give consistent results with repeated measurements. A reliable bathroom scale, for example, will give almost identical weights for the same person measured three times in a morning. An unreliable scale, however, may give weights that differ by six pounds. A teacher evaluates test reliability over time by giving the same, or almost the same, test to different groups of students. However, because many factors can affect reliability, teachers must be careful in evaluating test reliability.

Another aspect of a test that the teacher must carefully assess is the test's **validity**, or whether the test actually measures what it is supposed to measure. If students score low on a test because they could not understand the questions, the test is not valid because it measures reading ability instead of content knowledge. If students score low because the test covered material that was not taught, the test is not valid for that situation. A teacher assesses the validity of his or her own tests by examining the questions to see if they measure what was planned and taught in the classroom. A test must be reliable before it can be valid. However, measurements can be consistent without being valid. A scale can indicate identical weights for three weigh-ins of the same person during one morning but actually be 15 pounds in error. A history test may produce similar results each time the teacher administers it, but the test may not be a valid measure of what the teacher taught and what the students learned.

Tests should be both reliable and valid. If the test does not measure consistently, it cannot be accurate. If it does not measure what it is supposed to measure, then its reliability does not matter. Commercial test producers perform various statistical measures of the reliability and validity of their tests and provide the results in the test administrator's booklet. In addition, the tests should be **objective** so that any bias of the person scoring the test cannot enter into the grading.

The school districts and state may prescribe **standardized tests** as a means of formal assessment. These formal tests should meet the criteria of objectivity, reliability, and validity. Any grouping within the classroom should involve more than just the score on one standardized test. The teacher may wish to use the tests that frequently accompany the reading textbooks or basal readers as another means of assessment; if the tests include scores from previous administrations, the teacher can determine how the student compares with others who have taken the same test.

Performance-Based Assessment

Some states and districts are moving toward performance-based tests, which assess students on how well they perform certain tasks. Students must use higher-level thinking skills to apply, analyze, synthesize, and evaluate ideas and data. For example, a biology performance-based assessment might require students to read a problem, design and carry out a laboratory experiment, and then write summaries of their findings. The performance-based assessment would evaluate both the processes students used and the output they produced. An English performance-based test might ask students to first read a selection of literature and then write a critical analysis. A mathematics performance-based test might state a general problem, require students to invent one or more methods of solving the problem, use one of the methods to arrive at a solution, and write the solution and an explanation of the processes they used.

Performance-based assessment allows students to be creative in solutions to problems or questions, and it requires them to use higher-level skills. Students work on content-related problems and use skills that are useful in various contexts. There are weaknesses, however. This type of assessment can be time consuming. Performance-based assessment often requires multiple resources, which can be expensive. Teachers must receive training in applying the test. Nonetheless, many schools consider performance-based testing to be a more authentic measure of student achievement than are traditional tests.

Classroom Tests

Teachers must consider fundamental professional and technical factors to construct effective classroom tests. One of the first factors to recognize is that test construction is as creative, challenging, and important as any aspect of teaching. The planning and background that contribute to effective teaching are incomplete unless evaluation of student performance provides accurate feedback to the teacher and the student about the learning process.

Good tests are the product of careful planning, creative thinking, hard work, and technical knowledge about the various methods of measuring student knowledge and performance. Classroom tests that accomplish their purpose are the result of the development of a pool of items and refinement of those items based on feedback and constant revision. It is through this process that evaluation of students becomes valid and reliable.

Tests serve as a valuable instructional aid because they help determine pupil progress and also provide feedback to teachers regarding their own effectiveness. Student misunderstandings and problems that the tests reveal can help the teacher understand areas of special concern in providing instruction. This information also becomes the basis for the remediation of students and the revision of teaching procedures. Consequently, the construction, administration, and proper scoring of classroom tests are among the most important activities in teaching.

Essay tests provide another means of evaluating students. There are advantages and disadvantages to essay tests. Advantages of essay questions include the possibility for students to be creative in their answers, the opportunity for students to explain their responses, and the potential to test for higher-level thinking skills. Disadvantages of essay questions include the time students need to formulate meaningful responses and the time teachers need to evaluate the essays. In addition, language difficulties can make essay tests extremely difficult for some students. Consistency in evaluating essays can also be a problem for some teachers, but an outline of the acceptable answers—a scoring rubric—can help a teacher avoid inconsistency. Teachers who write specific questions and know what they are looking for are more likely to be consistent in grading. Also, if there are several essay questions, the effective teacher grades all student responses to the first question, then moves on to all responses to the second, and so on.

Authentic Assessments

Paper-and-pencil tests and essay tests are not the only methods of assessment. Other assessments include projects, observations, checklists, anecdotal records, portfolios, self-assessments, and peer assessments. Although these types of assessments often take more time and effort to plan and administer, they can often provide a more authentic measurement of student progress.

It is essential to note that assessment comes before, during, and after instruction. Preassessment is as important as postassessment

Summary

The two main types of assessment, then, are formal and informal. Both have a place in the classroom, particularly in the reading class. The effective teacher understands the importance of ongoing assessment as an instructional tool for the classroom and uses both informal and formal assessment measures. There is never an occasion to group children permanently on the basis of one assessment—either formal or informal. Any grouping of students should come about after a consideration of *several* assessments, and the grouping should be flexible enough to consider individual differences among the students in each group.

Topic 16.
Activities to Enhance Comprehension During and After Reading

The use of graphic organizers can be helpful to enhancing understanding. Story mapping and webbing, Venn diagrams, double-entry journals, and fishbones discussed earlier in the chapter, are useful graphic organizers.

Another useful graphic organizer is the **fishbone organizer**. This type of graphic can help the reader to illustrate cause and effect. A reader viewing the fishbone chart can immediately see the cause and the direct result of the cause.

Depending on the situation, instructors may use these strategies across the curriculum in any subject area. These and many other graphic organizers can help

Fishbone Map

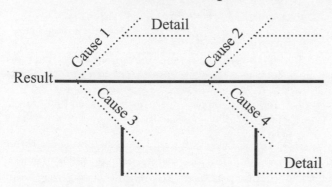

students demonstrate their understanding of a passage by illustrating the structure on paper. (Barry, 182–186)

References

The author consulted the following sources to prepare this chapter. Of particular help was the author's own text on reading, *Reading Instruction Essentials* (Davis 2004).

Aesop. *The Fables of Aesop: Selected, Told Anew, and Their Social History Traced by Joseph Jacobs*. New York: Macmillan, 1950.

Afanas'ev, Aleksandr Nikolaevich. *Russian Fairy Tales*. Translated by Norbert Guterman. New York: Pantheon, 1975.

Alcott, Louisa Mae. *Little Women*. Boston: Little, Brown, 1968. First published 1868 by Roberts Brothers, Boston.

Asbjørnsen, Peter, and Jorgen Moe. *East o' the Sun and West o' the Moon*. Evanston, IL: Row, Peterson, 1946.

Bailey, Mildred Hart. "The Utility of Phonic Generalizations in Grades One Through Six." *Reading Teacher* 20:5 (February 1967): 413–18.

Banks, Lynne Reid. *The Indian in the Cupboard*. Garden City, NY: Doubleday, 1980.

Barry, Leasha M., Betty J. Bennett, Lois Christensen, Alicia Mendoza, Enrique Ortiz, Migdalia Pagan, Sally Robison, Otilia Salmón. *The Best Teacher's Test Preparation for the FTCE*. Piscataway, New Jersey: Research and Education Association, 2005.

Beim, Lorraine, and Jerrold Beim. *Two is a Team*. New York: Harcourt, Brace, 1945.

Bennett, William. *What Works: Research about Teaching and Learning*. Washington, DC: U.S. Department of Education, 1987.

Bloom, Benjamin, Max D. Engelhart, Edward J. Furst, Walker H. Hill, and David R. Krathwohl. *Taxonomy of Educational Objectives: The Classification of Educational Goals. Handbook I: Cognitive Domain*. New York: Longmans, Green, 1956.

Bonham, Frank. *Durango Street*. New York: Dell, 1975. First published 1965 by Dutton, New York.

Bryant, Sara Cone. *Epaminondas and His Auntie*. Boston: Houghton, 1938.

Byars, Betsy. *The Summer of the Swans*. New York: Viking Press, 1970.

Capote, Truman. *Complete Stories of Truman Capote*. New York: Random House, 2004.

Carbo, Marie. "Reading Styles and Whole Language." *Schools of Thought II*. Video. Bloomington, IN: Phi Delta Kappa, 1993.

— "Teaching Reading with Talking Books" *Reading Teacher* 32:3 (December 1978): 267–73.

Chase, Richard. *Jack Tales*. New York: Houghton Mifflin, 1943.

— *Grandfather Tales*. New York: Houghton Mifflin, 1948.

Clay, M. M. "Emergent Reading Behavior." PhD diss., University of Auckland, New Zealand, 1966.

— *Reading: The Patterning of Complex Behavior*. Auckland, New Zealand: Heinemann Educational Books, 1979.

Cleaver, Vera, and Bill Cleaver. *Where the Lilies Bloom*. New York: Lippincott, 1969.

Clymer, Theodore. "The Utility of Phonic Generalizations in the Primary Grades." *The Reading Teacher* 16 (January 1963): 252–58.

Combs, Martha. *Readers and Writers in Primary Grades: A Balanced and Integrated Approach*. Upper Saddle River, NJ: Pearson, 2006.

Commission on Reading. *Becoming a Nation of Readers*. Washington, DC: U.S. Department of Education, September 1986.

Cook, Jimmie E. and Gregory J. Nolan. "Treating Auditory Perception Problems: The NIM Helps." *Academic Therapy* 15:4 (March 1980), 473–81.

Coerr, Eleanor. *Sadako and the Thousand Paper Cranes*. New York: Putnam, 1977.

Cormier, Robert. *The Chocolate War*. New York: Dell, 1977. First published 1974 by Pantheon, New York.

Dahl, Roald. *Charlie and the Chocolate Factory*. New York: Knopf, 1972. First published 1964 by Knopf, New York.

Davis, Anita P. *Children's Literature Essentials*. Boston: American Press, 2000.

Davis, Anita P., and Ed Y. Hall. *Harriet Quimby: First Lady of the Air (An Activity Book for Children)*. Spartanburg, SC: Honoribus Press, 1993.

—*Harriet Quimby: First lady of the Air (An Intermediate Biography)*. Spartanburg, SC: Honoribus Press, 1998.

Davis, Anita P., and Thomas R. McDaniel. "Essential Vocabulary Words." *Reading Teacher*. 52:3. (November 1998), pages 308–309.

Davis, Anita P., and Katharine Preston. *Discoveries*. Hillsborough, ID: Butte Publications, 1996.

Davis, Anita Price. *Reading Instruction Essentials*. 3rd ed. Boston: American Press, 2004.

De Angeli, Marguerite. *Bright April*. Garden City, NY: Doubleday, 1946.

Defoe, Daniel. *Robinson Crusoe*. Boston: Houghton Mifflin, 1972. First published 1719 by W. Taylor Publishers, London.

Dodge, Mary Mapes. *Hans Brinker*. New York: Grosset and Dunlap, 1963. First published 1912 by Thomas Nelson, London

Dolch, Edward William. "Dolch Sight Word List." Champaign, IL: Garrard Press, 1960.

Finn, Patrick J. *Helping Children Learn to Read*. New York: Longman, 1990.

Flesch, Rudolf. *Why Johnny Can't Read-And What You Can Do About It*. New York: Harper and Row, 1955.

Fry, Edward. "Fry's Readability Graph: Clarifications, Validity and Extension to Level 17." *Journal of Reading* 21:3 (December 1977): 242–252.

— "The New Instant Word Lists." *Reading Teacher* 34:3 (December 1980): 264–89.

Garis, Howard. *Uncle Wiggly's Adventures*. New York: Platt and Munk, 1915. First published 1912 by R. F. Fenno, New York.

Gentry, J. R. "Learning to Spell Developmentally." *Reading Teacher* 34:4 (January 1981): 378–81.

Gipson, Fred. *Old Yeller*. New York: Harper, 1956.

Golding, William. *Lord of the Flies*. New York: Perigee, 1954. First published in 1954 by Faber and Faber, Ltd., New York.

Goudvis, Anne, and Stephanie Harvey. *Strategies That Work*. Portland, ME: Stenhouse Publishers, 2000.

Grimm, Jacob, and Wilhelm Grimm. *Grimm's Fairy Tales*. Chicago: Follett, 1968.

Gunning, Thomas G. *Creating Reading Instruction for All Children*. Boston: Allyn and Bacon, 1996.

Heckleman, R. G. "A Neurological-Impress Method of Remedial-reading Instruction." *Academic Therapy* IV (Summer 1969): 277–82.

Henry, Marguerite. *Brighty of the Grand Canyon*. New York: Scholastic, 1967. First published 1953 by Rand McNally and Company, Chicago.

Hesse, Karen. *Out of the Dust*. New York: Scholastic, 1999. First published 1997 by Scholastic, New York.

Hickam, Homer H., Jr. *October Sky*. New York: Dell, 1999. First published 1998 as *Rocket Boys* by Delacorte, New York.

Hinton, S. E. *The Outsiders*. New York: Dell, 1983. First published 1967 by Viking, New York.

Hollingsworth, Paul. "An Experimental Approach to the Impress Method of Teaching Reading," *Reading Teacher* 31 (March, 1978): 624–26.

Huck, Charlotte S. and Doris Young Kuhn. *Children's Literature in the Elementary School*. New York: Holt, Rinehart and Winston, 1968. First published 1961 by Holt, Rinehart and Winston.

"IRA Takes a Stand on Phonics." (Vol. 14:5) *Reading Today* (April/May 1997), 1–4.

Jackson, Jesse. *Call Me Charley*. New York: Harper, 1945.

Jacobs, Joseph. *Favorite Fairy Tales Told in England*. Boston: Little, Brown, 1959.

Karlin, Robert. *Teaching Elementary Reading*. New York: Harcourt Brace Jovanovich, 1971.

Keats, Ezra Jack. *The Snowy Day*. New York: Viking Press, 1962.

Kellogg, Steven. *Paul Bunyan*. New York: Morrow, 1986. First published 1925 by James Stevens, Knopf Publishers, New York.

Klein, Marvin L. *The Development of Writing in Children Pre-K through Grade 8*. Englewood Cliffs, NJ, 1985.

Knight, Eric. *Lassie Come Home*. New York: Scholastic, 1966. First published 1940 by John C. Winston, Philadelphia.

Konigsburg, E. L. *From the Mixed-up Files of Mrs. Basil E. Frankweiler*. New York, Atheneum, 1967.

Lee, Harper. *To Kill a Mockingbird*. New York: Warner Books, 1982. First published 1960 by J. B. Lippincott, Philadelphia.

Lewis, C. S. *The Lion, the Witch, and the Wardrobe*. New York: Macmillan, 1988. First published 1950 by Geoffrey Bles, London.

Mager, Robert F. *Preparing Instructional Objectives*. Palo Alto, California: Fearon Publishers, 1962.

Marzano, Robert J., and Daisy E. Arredondo. *Tactics for Thinking*. Aurora, CO: Mid-Continent Regional Education Laboratories, 1986.

Michaelis, John U., and Jesus Garcia. *Social Studies for Children: A Guide to Basic Instruction*. Boston: Allyn and Bacon, 1996.

Miles, Miska. *Mississippi Possum*. Boston: Little, Brown, 1965.

Montgomery, L. M. *Anne of Green Gables*. New York: Farrar, Straus, and Giroux, 1935. First published 1908 by L. C. Page and Company, Boston

Mowat, Farley. *Never Cry Wolf*. Toronto: Bantam Books, 1984. First published 1963 McClelland and Stewart Limited, Toronto.

Norton, Mary. *The Borrowers*. New York: Harcourt, Brace, 1953.

Noyce, Ruth M., and James F. Christie. *Integrating Reading and Writing Instruction in Grades K–8*. Boston: Allyn and Bacon, 1989.

Chapter 3

Mathematics

Section 1: Critical Thinking, Number Sense, and Numeration

Topic 1.
Critical Thinking and Mathematics

Mathematics is not strictly memorization or literal-level work; thinking and reasoning skills, such as deductive reasoning, inductive reasoning, and adaptive reasoning, are essential. Students must employ upper-level skills from Bloom's Taxonomy (discussed later; see also chapter 2.) to succeed. Refer to Table 3-1.

Deductive reasoning proceeds from general to specific. In deductive lessons, the teacher first teaches the generalizations or rules and then develops examples and elaboration to support the generalizations or rules. For example, a teacher would first instruct students on how to regroup in adding a two-place number and then have the students apply the regrouping rules in the examples they practice.

Using deductive methods, teachers present material through lectures, and students teach each other through presentations. Deductive thinking often requires students to make assessments based on specific criteria that they or others develop.

The **mastery lecture** is a deductive method whereby the teacher presents information to students. New teachers are especially attuned to lecturing because that is the usual mode of instruction in college classes. An advantage of the mastery lecture is that teachers can present large amounts of information in an efficient manner; however, teachers should avoid giving students too much information through lectures. To be most effective, mastery lectures should be short, usually no more than 10 or 15 minutes, and frequently interrupted by questions to and from students. The effective teacher uses both lower- and higher-level questions during lectures.

By contrast, **inductive reasoning** proceeds from specific to general. During inductive lessons, the teacher first introduces a hypothesis or concept, and using inferences from the data, the students develop generalizations. For instance, after seeing the teacher demonstrate several times how to regroup or carry when adding two-place numbers, the students figure out the rule for themselves. With deductive thinking, the teacher gives them the rule first and then the students practice it; with inductive thinking, the students see many applications of the rule and then determine the rule themselves.

Inquiry or discovery lessons are inductive in nature. An **inquiry lesson** starts with a thought-provoking question for which students are interested in finding

Table 3-1. Bloom's Taxonomy

Level of Question	Student Capability	Questioning Verbs
Level 1: Knowledge	Remembers, recalls learned (or memorized) information	*define, describe, enumerate, identify, label, list, match, name, read, record, reproduce, select, state, view*
Level 2: Comprehension	Understands the meaning of information and is able to restate in own words	*cite, classify, convert, describe, discuss, estimate, explain, generalize, give examples, make sense out of, paraphrase, restate (in own words), summarize, trace, understand*
Level 3: Application	Uses the information in new situations	*act, administer, articulate, assess, chart, collect, compute, construct, contribute, control, determine, develop, discover, establish, extend, implement, include, inform, instruct, operationalize, participate, predict, prepare, preserve, produce, project, provide, relate, report, show, solve, teach, transfer, use, utilize*
Level 4: Analysis	Breaks down information into component parts; examines parts for divergent thinking and inferences	*break down, correlate, diagram, differentiate, discriminate, distinguish, focus, illustrate, infer, limit, outline, point out, prioritize, recognize, separate, subdivide*
Level 5: Synthesis	Creates something new by divergently or creatively using information	*adapt, anticipate, categorize, collaborate, combine, communicate, compare, compile, compose, contrast, create, designs, devise, express, facilitate, formulate, generate, incorporate, individualize, initiate, integrate, intervene, model, modify, negotiate, plan, progress, rearrange, reconstruct, reinforce, reorganize, revise, structure, substitute, validate*
Level 6: Evaluation	Judges on the basis of informed criteria	*appraise, compare, and contrast, conclude, criticize, critique, decide, defend, interpret, judge, justify, reframe, support*

an explanation. After posing the question, the teacher guides students in brainstorming a list of what they already know about the topic and then categorizing the information. Students use these categories as topics for group or individual research. The lesson typically ends with students presenting their research to the class (a form of deductive learning, as discussed earlier).

A teacher who uses inquiry strategies takes the role of a facilitator who plans outcomes and provides resources for students as they work. In their role as inquirers, students must take responsibility for their own learning by planning, carrying out, and presenting research and projects.

Some advantages of inductive lessons are that they generally require higher-level thinking by both teacher and students, and they usually result in higher student motivation, interest, and retention than more passive methods. They also provide an interesting change to the teacher, who deals with the same concepts year after year. Disadvantages of inductive lessons include the need for additional preparation by the teacher, access to numerous resources, and additional time for students to conduct research.

Generally, the more planning, predicting, and preparing the teacher does for an inductive lesson, the more successful the students will be. This does not mean that the teacher must use only tightly structured or rigid activities but that the effective teacher tries to predict students' responses and their reactions to them. Fortunately, teachers today do not have to purchase as many additional resources thanks to the variety of information available via the Internet, computerized bibliographic services, interlibrary loans, and CD-ROMs. Because inductive, research-oriented units require more class time, subject-area teachers must work together to determine which concepts are essential for students to understand, which are nonessential, and which ones they can omit.

An effective teacher plays many roles in the classroom. The teacher who uses lecture is in the role of information provider. Students listening to the lecture are usually in the passive, often inattentive, role of listener. The teacher who uses cooperative strategies takes on the roles of a coach, encouraging students to work together, and a facilitator, smoothing students' way through activities and providing resources. Students in a collaborative role must learn social and group roles as well as content to accomplish learning tasks. The teacher who listens to student discussions and presentations and evaluates student papers and projects assumes the role of an audience providing constructive feedback. Students in a discussion role must prepare carefully and think seriously about the topic under discussion.

Adaptive reasoning refers to logical thinking. In mathematics, adaptive reasoning refers to the capacity to think logically about the relationships among concepts and situations. For instance, after solving a subtraction problem, the student should look at the answer to see that it is reasonable. If a child solves the problem $7 - 4$ and finds that the answer is 11, the child might think: "I only had 7 to start with, and then I took 4 away. I could not possibly end up with 11 because that is bigger than 7, not less." Adaptive thinking allows the students who disagree on an answer to check that their reasoning is valid.

The key to converting word problems into mathematical problems is attention to **reasonableness** (adaptive thinking), with the choice of operations being crucial to success. Often, individual words and phrases translate into numbers and operation symbols; making sure that the translations are reasonable is important.

Benjamin Bloom identified six levels of thinking. The fourth stage—analysis—is a vital part of solving mathematical word problems. This level requires the student to break down information into component parts and examine parts for inferences. Effective mathematics teachers, however, must examine each level of Bloom's Taxonomy as they develop objectives for their classrooms.

Topic 2.
Scope and Sequence of Skills

The main topics (scope) in elementary mathematics and the sequence (order) in which the school introduces the topics is essentially the same in all states. Table 3-2 details these main topics and their introduction order.

Topic 3.
Identifying Uses: Calculators, Computers, and Other Technology in Instruction

Calculators, computers, and technology are important instructional and problem-solving tools. Their effectiveness, however, depends on the accuracy

Table 3-2. Scope and Sequence of Skills

Grade Level	Numbers, Order, Values	Addition, Subtraction	Ratios, Measurement, Decimals	Fractions, Comparisons	Equations, Colors, Geometry	Multiplication, Division	Graph, Estimation, Solving
Kindergarten	Count by 1s and 10s to 100 Count by 2s and 5s Write numbers to 10 Write families to 100 Use values of 10s and 1s place	Add single digits with no regrouping	Use dime, nickel, penny, and dollar Tell time on hour and half hour Name days of week and seasons Identify cup and quart Read inches	Recognize ½, ⅓, and ¼ Compare longer, shorter, taller, etc.	Recognize primary and secondary colors and black Recognize square, circle, and triangle Use *up, down, top,* and *next*		Identify what comes next Read pictographs and simple bar graphs
1	Count by 1s, 2s, 5s, and 10s Use place values of 1s, 10s, and 100s place	Write and give addition facts from 1 to 18 Add with regrouping in 1s place Subtract without regrouping	Name months and days Tell time on quarter hour Use nickel, dime, and quarter Identify pint and pound	Recognize ½, ⅓, ¼, ⅕, ⅙, ⅛	Recognize circle, square, oval, diamond, triangle, and cube		Read bar graphs Identify height and length Round numbers using a number line
2	Identify even and odd numbers Use tally marks Use and explain the value of 1,000s place Determine greater than, less than, equal to Identify what comes before and after Use Roman numerals	Add with carrying in 1s, 10s, and 100s place Perform horizontal addition Solve word problems	Name months and their abbreviations Tell time on five minutes Perform operations with money, including $5, $10, and $20 bills Read a Fahrenheit thermometer Identify liquid and dry measures	Compare two numbers Read fraction words Identify fractional parts of groups and sets	Determine area, perimeter, and volume Recognize pyramid, pentagon, and hexagon	Use multiplication facts from 0 to 10	Round numbers, height, and time Read grids and line graphs

3	Read word numbers to 1 million Show expanded numbers Explain the properties of 1 and 0 Use the terms *odd, tally marks, greater than* Be able to tell what comes before, what comes after Use the 1000s place Use Roman numerals	Use sum, estimating, borrowing, word problems Demonstrate carrying or regrouping in the 1s, 10s, and 100s place Use horizontal addition Solve word problems	Use Fahrenheit and Celsius temperature measurements Use tenths Add and subtract dollars and cents Be able to use months and their abbreviations Tell time with accuracy to five minutes Perform operations with money Recognize five, ten- and twenty-dollar bills Use both liquid and dry measures	Identify fractional parts of whole and sets Rename fractions Compare numbers using greater than, less than, and equal signs Use fraction words Demonstrate the use of fractional parts of groups Use sets to illustrate fractions and illustrate fractions with sets	Compute the volume of cube Recognize rays, angles, congruent shapes, and prisms Compute area and perimeter of volume, pyramid, pentagon, hexagon	Use division facts from 1 to 10 Calculate 1- and 2-digit quotients with and without remainders Use multiplication facts 0 to 10	Continue work with graphs and grids Round numbers to the 10,000 place Tell time accurately to the minute
4	Use values to 100 billion Use and recognize prime and composite Determine factors Give ordinal and cardinal numbers	Give addition properties Add and subtract numbers up to 6 digits Subtract with regrouping Subtract money	Use the terms AM and PM Explain the term *century* Compute time in various time zones Use the prefixes *milli-, centi-, deci-, deca-, hecto-, kilo* Convert fractions to decimals Perform operations on decimals and ratios Use equal ratios	Recognize fractional parts of whole and name them correctly Give word fractions Provide equivalent fractions Add and subtract fractions with like and unlike denominators	Recognize shapes and solids Use the terms *obtuse, vertex, ray, diameter, radius* Perform operations on equations	Calculate averages Use zeros in the quotient correctly Multiply 2- to 3-digit numbers	Compare and coordinate graphs

(Continued)

(Continued from previous page)

Grade Level	Numbers, Order, Values	Addition, Subtration	Ratios, Measurement, Decimals	Fractions, Comparisons	Equations, Colors, Geometry	Multiplication, Division	Graph, Estimation, Solving
5	Determine prime factors Use factor trees Use exponents Equal, not equal	Apply addition properties and facts Apply addition operation with 2 to 6 digits Determine missing addends Work with equations Subtract Estimate	Use standard and metric measure Count change Solve problems with ratios and percentages Figure amount of sales tax Determine discounts	Find least common multiples Solve problems with unlike denominators Perform operations on mixed numerals Rename numbers Reduce fractions to lowest terms	Use a compass and a protractor Solve measurement problems using surface area Perform operations on fractions Recognize and use chords Classify polygons	Calculate mean, mode, and median Problem solve by choosing the proper operation Figure probability with one-variable problems Demonstrate ability to apply calculator math	Multiply 3-digit numbers Calculate averages with remainders Divide money Estimate quotients Determine division and multiplication properties
6	Round to 10s, 100s, and 1000s Use scientific notation Use the correct order of operations Use integers Calculate square roots	Continue addition and subtraction Continue to work with equations	Cross products Divide and multiply by 10, 100, 1000 Determine equal ratios Use cross products to solve for *n*	Determine reciprocals Divide by fractions Perform operations on fractions Divide by whole and mixed numbers	Construct a right and equilateral triangle, and a parallelogram and square Bisect an angle	Choose the proper operation Find patterns Set up budgets Apply some business math, such as figuring interest and balancing a check book.	Divide using 4-digit divisors Estimate quotients Supply missing factors

of the input and the ability of the user to operate the devices correctly.

The effective teacher includes resources of all types in the curriculum-planning process. The educator should be very familiar with the school library, the local library, education service center resources, and the libraries of any colleges or universities in the area. Another important set of resources is the audiovisual aids that the teacher can borrow: kits, films, filmstrips, videos, laser disks, and computer software, among others. Audiovisual aids can relate to curricular objectives. Many librarians have keyed their resources to objectives in related subject areas and these keys enable the teacher to incorporate library holdings with ease into the lessons. However, teachers should never use resources with a class unless they have previewed and approved them. The teacher should include the list of resources for a lesson or unit in the curriculum guide or the lesson plan to make use more efficient.

The effective teacher determines the appropriate place in the lesson for audiovisual aids. If the material is especially interesting and thought-provoking, the teacher can use it to introduce a unit. For example, a travel video on coral reefs or snorkeling might be an excellent introduction to the study of ocean depths and how to graph them.

Textbooks do not stay up-to-date on batting averages and stock reports. The Internet; radio and television news reports; local, state and national newspapers and magazines all are important resources for teaching mathematics. Figuring batting averages and watching the stock reports are practical lessons in mathematics. Some newspapers and magazines provide special programs to help teachers use their products in the classroom. Local newspapers may even be willing to send specialists to work with students or act as special resource people.

Technology experts argue that tools such as the Internet make available such a substantial amount of wide-ranging content that today's teachers have a greater role than ever in helping students acquire process skills (such as critical and creative thinking) rather than merely in teaching content skills. Content changes and expands, but thinking processes remain salient and necessary, regardless of the content.

Spreadsheets are especially useful to the math classroom. The reader can see rows and columns of numbers linked to produce totals and averages. Formulas can connect information in one cell (the intersection of a row and column) to another cell. Teachers often keep

grade books on spreadsheets because of the ease in updating information. Once formulas are in place, teachers can enter grades and have completely up-to-date averages for all students. Some spreadsheet programs also include charting functions that enable teachers to display class averages on a bar chart to provide visual comparisons of performance among various classes.

Students can use spreadsheets to collect and analyze numerical data and then sort the data in various orders. For example, students could enter population figures from various countries and then draw various types of graphs—lines, bars, pies, and scatter plots, and so on—to convey information. This type of graphic information can also become a part of multimedia presentations. Various stand-alone graphing and charting software packages are also available.

Graphics or paint programs allow users to draw freehand to produce any type of chart, graph, or picture. In addition, many word-processing programs have some graphic functions. Students can use these programs to produce boxes, circles, or other shapes to illustrate classroom presentations or individual research projects. For teachers, these relatively simple tools make it easy to create handouts and instructional materials with a very professional and polished appearance.

Today's teachers also need to acquire and demonstrate skill in using presentation software (such as Microsoft PowerPoint) to prepare instructional lessons. In many classrooms, the use of presentation software makes the traditional use of transparencies on an overhead projector obsolete. Presentation software also makes it possible to provide students with instructional handouts and outlines to complement classroom instruction. In some situations and in some schools, Web authoring experience and skills will also prove useful.

Teachers must supplement lectures with an array of visual materials that will appeal to both visual and auditory learners. Putting words or outlines on the board or a transparency is very helpful; however, this is still basically a verbal strategy. Drawings, diagrams, cartoons, pictures, caricatures, and graphs are attention-getting visual aids for lectures. Teacher drawings need not be highly artistic, merely memorable. Often a rough or humorous sketch will be more firmly etched in students' minds than elaborate drawings. Using a very simple sketch is a better means of teaching the most critical information than is a complicated drawing. The major points stand out in a simple sketch; the teacher can add details once students understand the basic concepts.

Topic 4.
Sets and Number Concepts

Sets. A basic mathematical concept is that of set. A **set** is a collection of things, real or imagined, related or unrelated. Students may manipulate the objects within the set in various ways.

Classifying objects in a set. Classification allows the students to sort materials according to some specific criteria. A child who is not yet able to count, for example, might sort objects by whether the objects are soft or hard, by whether or not a magnet will attract them, or by other attributes.

Ordering objects in a set. Students may **order** the objects or arrange them in size from smallest to greatest or from largest to smallest.

Patterning objects in a set. Students may try arranging the objects in a set to duplicate **a pattern that they observe**. The students may, for instance, try to replicate a color pattern with beads: red, yellow, red, yellow, and so on. Later, they may try to replicate a number pattern using magnetic numbers; the pattern may be 2, 4, 6, etc. They may even match the correct number of pennies to the magnetic number for another type of patterning. Making a pattern of geometric shapes would be another example; for instance, square, circle, triangle, square, circle, triangle, etc.

Comparing objects in a set. Students may **compare** objects in a set to objects in another set as a help in preparing for number skills. Is there a chair for each toy bear? Does each child in the set of children in the classroom have a carton of milk? Does each carton of milk have a straw for the child to use? Later, the students will compare each object in a set with a counting number; this will give the total number of objects in the set.

Students may try pairing objects with the numbers that they have memorized through rote; this is **oral counting**. After classifying objects, a student may try counting the objects in the groups. For example, if the teacher asks, "How many objects were soft?" the answer is a number that tells how many, and the student will have to count to find the answer.

Number. **Number** is a concept or idea that indicates how many. Children may memorize the counting numbers from 1 to 10 and be able to count by rote before they start school. Many times, however, there is little understanding in the beginning of what number is. After the students have some idea of the value of the numbers, they may arrange the numbers from largest to smallest, or smallest to largest.

Students may try counting by pairing the objects with a number on the number line; this will give a visual comparison. The set {1, 2, 3, 4, . . . } can represent counting numbers. Study the following number line. Notice that the counting numbers start with 1 and that 0 is not in the set of counting numbers.

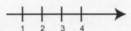

Whole numbers are the counting numbers plus 0: {0, 1, 2, 3, . . . }. Study the following number line below. Notice that 0 is a part of the set of whole numbers.

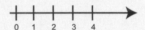

A **number** is a concept; a **numeral** is a symbol used to represent a number. The students must be able to read and to write the numerals. This skill is an important part of a student's early mathematical development. An important part of mathematical learning and of language arts learning is being able to read and to represent the numbers in words: *one, two, three,* and so on.

Students may also try another way of counting: **skip counting**. They may start with 1 and count only the odd numbers: 3, 5, 7, 9, and so on.

Odd numbers are those that cannot be evenly divided by 2. Students may also try skip counting with another beginning point; for instance, they may start with 2 and count only the even numbers: 4, 6, 8, 10, and so on.

Even numbers are those that one can evenly divide by 2.

Topic 5.
Base-10 Numeration System and Place Value

Our numeration system uses the Hindu-Arabic numerals (0, 1, 2, 3, 4, 5, 6, 7, 8, 9) to represent numbers.

Our numeration system follows a **base-10 place-value** scheme. As we move to the left in any number, each place value is 10 times the place value to the right. Similarly, as we move to the right, each place value is one-tenth the place value to the left. For example, in the number 543, the value of the place that the 5 is in (100s) is 10 times the value of the place that the 4 occupies (10s). The place value of the 3 is one-tenth the place value of the 4.

Expanded notation can show the value of each number in its place. Using the same number 543, the values are $(5 \times [10 \times 10]) + (4 \times [10 \times 1]) + (3 \times 1)$.

Exponential notation can show the value of each number. Using the same number 543, the exponential values are $(5 \times 10^2) + (4 \times 10^1) + (3 \times 10^0)$.

Topic 6.
The Four Basic Operations

Operations indicate what one is to do with numbers. There are four main operations: addition, subtraction, multiplication, and division. Multiplication is repeated addition. Division is repeated subtraction.

Addition is an operation that, when performed on numbers of disjoint sets (sets with different members), results in a **sum**. One can show addition on a number line by counting forward. Addition is also a **binary operation**, meaning it combines only two numbers at a time to produce a third, unique number. Adding two whole numbers always results in a whole number.

The **algorithm** of addition is the form in which we write and solve an addition example. Familiar short forms are

$$2 \text{ (addend)} + 3 \text{ (addend)} = 5 \text{ (sum) and}$$

$$2 \text{ (addend)}$$
$$+ 3 \text{ (addend)}$$
$$\overline{5 \text{ (sum)}}$$

The operation of **subtraction** is the **inverse** of addition: what addition does, subtraction undoes. Like addition, subtraction is a binary operation; that is, we work on only two numbers at a time. The result is a third, unique number called the **difference**. Given two whole numbers, subtracting the smaller number from the larger one results in a whole number. However, subtraction of whole numbers does not result in a whole number if the larger whole number is subtracted from the smaller one.

The algorithm of subtraction is the form in which we write and solve a subtraction example. Familiar short forms are

$$5 - 3 = 2 \text{ and}$$

$$5$$
$$- 3$$
$$\overline{2.}$$

Addition problems with a missing addend are solved with the operation of subtraction. For example, $\square$ (addend) + 3 (addend) = 5 (sum).

Multiplication, like addition and subtraction, is a binary operation. The result of the operation of multiplication is the **product**. The product of multiplying two whole numbers is always a whole number.

The operation of **division** has the same inverse relation to multiplication as subtraction has to addition: what multiplication does, division undoes. For example, multiplying 4 by 9 results in a product of 36; dividing 36 by 9 "gives back" a **quotient** of 4. Teaching division should parallel teaching multiplication.

Topic 7.
Modeling the Operations

There are four ways to model the operations:

Concrete method. With the concrete method, the teacher allows the students to use real objects. The students can represent a set and take away objects from it (subtraction), or they can combine two sets with no common objects (addition).

Semiconcrete method. With the semiconcrete method, the students work with visual representations (pictures) instead of actual objects.

Semiabstract method. With the semiabstract method, the students work with one symbol (tally marks, *x*s, *y*s, etc.) to represent objects; instead of actual objects, pictures, or abstract (numerical) representations, the students use one symbol. The semiabstract method can be used to represent, for instance, a multiplication problem. If there are three rabbits and if each rabbit eats four carrots each day, how many carrots will the rabbits eat in one day?

Rabbit 1	////
Rabbit 2	////
Rabbit 3	////

Abstract method. With the abstract level, the student matches the elements of a given group with abstract numbers. To represent three rabbits eating four carrots daily using the abstract method, the student would set up the problem as 3×4.

Topic 8.
Regrouping in Addition and Subtraction

Regrouping in addition, a process that teachers and students once called *carrying*, is evident in addition problems, such $16 + 7$ and $26 + 6$. To begin working with students on this process, the teacher would ideally drop back to the concrete level. For example, to work on the problem $16 + 7$, the teacher would have the students make one bundle of 10 straws and lay 6 straws to the side; when the students see 7 straws added to the 6 straws, they realize that they need to make another bundle of 10 straws. When they make that second bundle, they have the answer: two groups of 10 and 3 extra straws, or 23.

Regrouping in subtraction, a process that teachers and students once called *borrowing*, is evident in problems such as $23 - 7$. The students can readily see that they cannot subtract the big number 7 from the small number 3; to accomplish this process, the students again can use concrete objects to begin the process. With two bundles of 10 straws and one group of 3 straws on the table, the students should count out 7 straws; when the students see that they cannot subtract 7 from 3, they can unbundle one packet of 10 straws and place the 10 straws with the 3 straws. The students can pull 7 straws from the 13; 6 straws will be left along with one bundle of 10—the answer: 16.

Topic 9.
Modeling Multiplication

As noted earlier, pairs of operations that "undo" each other are **inverse**. Multiplication and division are inverse, or "undo," one another.

An **array** can model a multiplication problem. The first number in a multiplication problem is the vertical number in an array; the second number is the horizontal number. The following is the array for $2 \times 3 = 6$.

x	x	x
x	x	x

Topic 10.
Multiplication Properties and Algorithms

The **multiples** of any whole number are the results of multiplying that whole number by the counting numbers. For example, the multiples of 7 are 7, 14, 21, 28, and so on. Every whole number has an infinite number of multiples.

Terms related to multiplication and key properties of the multiplication operation include the following:

Multiplicative identity property of 1. Any number multiplied by 1 remains the same. For instance, $34 \times 1 = 34$. The number 1 is called the **multiplicative identity**.

Property of reciprocals. The product of any number (except 0) multiplied by its reciprocal is 1. The **reciprocal** of a number is 1 divided by that number. Remember that dividing by 0 has no meaning; avoid dividing by 0 when computing or solving equations and inequalities.

Commutative property for addition and multiplication. The order of adding addends or multiplying factors does not determine the sum or product. For example, 6×9 gives the same product as 9×6. Division and subtraction are not commutative.

Associative property for addition and multiplication. Associating, or grouping, three or more addends or factors in a different way does not change the sum or product. For example, $(3 + 7) + 5$ results in the same sum as $3 + (7 + 5)$. Division and subtraction are not associative.

Distributive property of multiplication over addition. A number multiplied by the sum of two other numbers can be handed out, or distributed, to both numbers, multiplied by each of them separately, and the products added together. For example, multiplying 6 by 47 gives the same result as multiplying 6 by 40, multiplying 6 by 7, and then adding the products. That is, $6 \times 47 = (6 \times 40) + (6 \times 7)$. The definition of the distributive property of multiplication over addition can be stated simply: the product of a number and a sum can be expressed as a sum of two products. The simple notation form of the distributive property is

$$a(b + c) = (a \times b) + (a \times c)$$

Another major concept in multiplication is **regrouping**, or carrying. The term *regrouping* indicates the renaming of a number from one place value to another. The short algorithm we are most familiar with does not show the steps that illustrate the regrouping. Students must be able to use the multiplication facts, multiply by 0, and apply regrouping to solve problems such as 268×26.

Topic 11.
Special Properties of 0 and 1

The **natural numbers** include the set of counting numbers (1, 2, 3, 4, 5 . . .) and the set of whole numbers (0, 1, 2, 3, 4, 5 . . .). The natural number 0 has special mathematical significance with respect to the operation of addition. The number 0 added to any natural number yields a sum that is the same as the other natural number; 0 is, therefore, the **additive identity,** or the **identity element of addition**.

Because multiplication is repeated addition, 0 holds a special property with both multiplication and addition. The **multiplication property of 0** states that when a factor is multiplied by 0, then the product is 0. The **identity element of multiplication** is 1; the identity element of multiplication means that any factor multiplied by 1 gives that factor.

Zero is not an identity element for subtraction or for division. Subtraction does not have an identity element. Even though $4 - 0 = 4$, it is not true that $0 - 4 = 4$. Division by 0 is not possible, so 0 is not an identity element for division.

Topic 12.
Factors, Primes, Composites, and Multiples

Factors are any of the numbers or symbols in mathematics that, when multiplied together, form a product. For example, the whole-number factors of 12 are 1, 2, 3, 4, 6, and 12. A number with only two whole-number factors—1 and the number itself—is a **prime number**. The first few primes are 2, 3, 5, 7, 11, 13, and 17. Most other whole numbers are **composite numbers** because they are *composed* of several whole-number factors. The number 1 is neither prime nor composite; it has only one whole-number factor: 1.

As noted earlier, the **multiples** of any whole number are the results of multiplying that whole number by the counting numbers. For example, the multiples of 7 are 7, 14, 21, 28, and so on. Every whole number has an infinite number of multiples.

Topic 13.
Modeling Division

Division, the inverse of multiplication, can be represented in two ways: measurement and partition. With **measurement division**, the students know how many in each group (set) but do not know how many sets. Here is an example: A homeowner has a group of 400 pennies. He plans to give each trick-or-treater 5 pennies. How many trick-or-treaters can receive a treat before the homeowner has to turn out the porch light? In this case, the students know the number of pennies (measurement) each child will receive; they need to find the number of children.

In **partitive division**, students know the number of groups (sets), but they do not know the number of objects in each set. Here is an example: There is a plate of eight cookies on the table. There are four children at the table. How many cookies does each child get if they divide the cookies evenly? The question asks the students to determine how many are in each group.

No properties of division—commutative, associative, and so on—hold true at all times.

Division is the most difficult of the algorithms for students to use. Division begins at the left, rather than at the right. Also, to solve a division problem, students must not only divide but subtract and multiply as well. Students must use estimation with the trial quotients; sometimes it takes several trials before the trial is successful.

Topic 14.
Rational Numbers, Fractions, Decimals, and Percents

Rational numbers are all the numbers that can be expressed as the quotient of two integers; **integers** are counting numbers, the opposite of counting numbers, and zero. Rational numbers can be expressed as fractions, percents, or decimals.

Common **fractions** are in the form a/b, where a and b are whole numbers. Integers can be expressed as fractions, but not all fractions can be expressed as integers. For example, the number 4 can be expressed as $4/1$. However, the fraction $1/4$ cannot be expressed as an integer, or as a whole number. There are more fractions than whole numbers; between every integer is a fraction. Between the fraction and the whole number is another fraction; between the fraction and the other fraction is another fraction, and so on. Negative and positive fractions are not integers unless they are equivalent to whole numbers or their negative counterparts.

Decimal numbers are fractions written in special notation. For instance, 0.25 can be thought of as the fraction $1/4$. All decimal numbers are actually fractions. When expressed as decimals, some fractions terminate and some do not. For instance, 0.315 is a terminating decimal; 0.0575757 . . . is a repeating (nonterminating) decimal. All fractions, however, can be written as decimals. There are more decimals than integers.

Fractions, decimal numbers, and percents are different ways of representing values. It is useful to be able to convert from one to the other. The following paragraphs provide some conversion tips.

The practical method for changing a fraction into a decimal is by **dividing the numerator by the denominator**. For example, $1/4$ becomes 0.25 when 1 is divided by 4, as follows:

$$4 \overline{)1.00} \quad .25$$

Naturally, this can be done longhand or with a calculator. (If the fraction includes a whole number, as in $2\frac{3}{5}$, the whole number is not included in the division.) The decimal number may terminate or repeat. Converting a simple fraction to a decimal number never results in an irrational number. **Irrational numbers** are all the real numbers that are not rational; irrational numbers include $\sqrt{2}$, $\sqrt{3}$, pi, etc. **Rational numbers** are all numbers that can be expressed as the quotient of two integers. (A number cannot be expressed with 0 in the denominator.) **Real numbers** are all the numbers that can be represented by points on the number lines. The set of real numbers includes all the rational numbers (positive numbers, negative numbers, and zero) and all the irrational numbers ($\sqrt{2}$, $\sqrt{3}$, pi, etc.).

To convert a nonrepeating (terminating) decimal number to a fraction in lowest terms, write the decimal as a fraction with the denominator a power of 10, and then reduce to lowest terms. For example, 0.125 can be written as $125/1,000$, which reduces to $1/8$.

Any decimal number can be converted to a **percent** by shifting the decimal point two places to the right and adding the percent symbol (%). For instance, 0.135 becomes 13.5%. (If the number before the percent symbol is a whole number, there is no need to show the decimal point.)

A percent can be converted to a decimal number by shifting the decimal point two places to the left and dropping the percent symbol. For example, 98% becomes 0.98 as a decimal.

A percent can be converted to a fraction by putting the percent (without the percent symbol) over 100 and then reducing. In this way, 20% can be shown as $20/100$, which reduces to $1/5$.

Topic 15.
Ratio, Percents, Proportion

Ratio notation is an alternative method for showing fractions. For example, 2/5 can be expressed as "the ratio of 2 to 5." The use of ratio notation emphasizes the relationship of one number to another. To show ratios, one may use numbers with a colon between them; 2:5 is the same ratio as 2 to 5 and $2/5$.

To illustrate the equivalencies and conversions just described, consider the fraction $19/20$. As a decimal, it is 0.95. As a percent, it is 95%. As a ratio, it is 19 to 20, or 19:20.

Proportion is an equation of two equivalent ratios. For example, 2/5 = N/10 asks the problem solver to supply the missing numerator to make the two fractions equivalent.

Topic 16.
Function Machine

Teachers often use the function machine to encourage the students to find the missing addend, the missing factor, the missing operation, and so on. The function machine can also be used as an introduction to algebra.

If one inserts the number 4 into the 3-times function machine pictured in the figure, the output would be 12.

The following function machine is a subtraction machine. If the output is 12 and the input is 15, what is the value of the function machine?

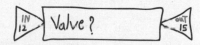

The function machine above is, of course, a plus-3 function machine.

Section 2: Informal Geometry and Measurement

Topic 1.
Identifying Angles or Pairs of Angles as Adjacent, Complementary, Supplementary, Vertical, Corresponding, Alternate Interior, Alternate Exterior, Acute, Obtuse, or Right

An **angle** consists of all the points in two noncollinear rays that have the same vertex. More simply, an angle is commonly thought of as two "arrows" joined at their bases; the point at which they join is called the **vertex**. Two angles are **adjacent** if they share a common vertex, they share only one side, and one angle does not lie in the interior of the other.

Angles are usually measured in **degrees** (°). A circle has a measure of 360°, a half circle 180°, a quarter circle 90°, and so forth. If the sum of the measures of two angles is 90°, the two angles are **complementary**. If the sum of the measures of the two angles is 180°, the two angles are **supplementary**. If two lines intersect, they form two pairs of **vertical angles**.

If a third line intersects two intersecting lines at the same point of intersection, the third intersecting line is called a **transversal**. In the following drawing, *t* is the transversal.

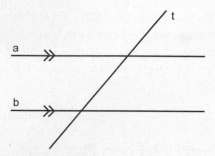

Two lines crossed by a transversal form eight angles. The four angles that lie between the two lines are called **interior angles**. The interior angles that lie on the same side of the transversal are called **consecutive interior angles**. The interior angles that lie on opposite sides of the transversal are called **alternate interior angles**. In the previous figure, angles *A* and *D* are alternate interior angles, as are angles *B* and *C*.

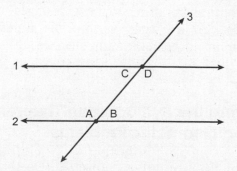

Consider the following drawing. The four angles that lie outside the two lines are the **exterior angles**. Exterior angles that lie on the same side of the transversal are the **consecutive exterior angles**, and those that lie on opposite sides of the transversal are the **alternate**

exterior angles. Angles *A* and *D* are alternate exterior angles; they have the same degree measurement. Angles *B* and *C* are also alternate exterior angles. An interior angle and an exterior angle that have different vertices and have sides on the same side of the transversal are the **corresponding angles**.

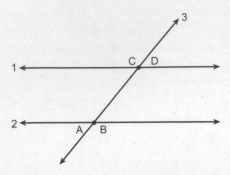

If the measures of two angles are the same, the angles are **congruent**. An angle with a measure of 90° is a **right angle**. An angle measuring less than 90° is an **acute angle**. An angle measuring more than 90° is an **obtuse angle**.

Topic 2.
Identifying Lines and Planes as Intersecting, Perpendicular, or Parallel

If lines have a point or points in common, they are said to **intersect**. Lines are **perpendicular** if they contain the sides of a right angle. Lines are **parallel** if they do not intersect.

Through any two points, there is exactly one straight **line**; straight lines are one-dimensional. A **plane** is two-dimensional (think of a surface without elevations or depressions). These concepts form the foundation of other important geometric terms and ideas.

Topic 3.
Applying the Pythagorean Theorem in Solving Geometric Problems

Triangles have various properties. One is that the sum of the measures of the three angles of any triangle is 180°. If students know the measures of two angles, they can deduce the third using first addition and then subtraction. The **Pythagorean theorem** states that in any right triangle with legs (shorter sides) *a* and *b* and a hypotenuse (longest side) *c*, the sum of the squares of the sides equals the square of the hypotenuse. In algebraic notation, the Pythagorean theorem is given as $a^2 + b^2 = c^2$.

Topic 4.
Identifying the Basic Characteristics of, and Relationships Pertaining to, Regular and Irregular Geometric Shapes in Two and Three Dimensions

Point

Students in the elementary grades typically solve problems involving two- and three-dimensional geometric figures (for example, perimeter and area problems, volume and surface-area problems). A fundamental concept of geometry is the notion of a point. A **point** is a specific location, taking up no space, having no area, and frequently represented by a dot. A point is considered one-dimensional. Through any two points, there is exactly one straight line; straight lines are one-dimensional.

Plane

A **plane** is two dimensional (think of a surface without elevations or depressions). That definition forms the foundation for other important geometric terms and ideas. The **perimeter** of a two-dimensional (flat) shape or object is the distance around the object. **Volume** refers to how much space is inside a three-dimensional, closed container. **Area** is a measure that expresses the size of a plane region; it is expressed in square units. It is useful to think of volume as how many cubic units fit into a solid. If the container is a rectangular solid, the volume is the product of width times length times height. If all six faces (sides) of a rectangular solid are squares, the object is a cube.

Polygons

A **polygon** is a simple closed curve formed by the union of three or more straight sides; a **regular polygon** is one whose angles are equal in measure. Every polygon that is not regular is irregular.

In an *n*-sided regular polygon, the sides are all the same length (**congruent**) and are symmetrically placed about a common center (that is, the polygon is both equiangular and equilateral). Only certain regular polygons are "constructable" using the classical Greek tools of the compass and straightedge.

The terms *equilateral triangle* and *square* refer to regular polygons with three and four sides, respectively. The words for polygons with more than five sides (for example, *pentagon, hexagon, heptagon*, etc.) can refer to either regular or nonregular polygons, although the terms generally refer to regular polygons unless otherwise specified.

Regular Rectangle

A **regular rectangle** is a quadrilateral (four-sided figure) in which sides opposite each other are both of equal length and parallel. A square is the special case of a regular rectangle whose angles are equal (90°) and all sides are of equal length and parallel. If each side of a regular rectangle is of length *s*, the area (*A*) and perimeter (*P*) would be given as follows:

$$A = s^2$$

$$P = 4s \text{ (square)}$$

$$P = l + l + w + w \text{ (quadrilateral)}$$

Regular Triangle

The area of a triangle is the product of half its base multiplied by its height. Using either the Pythagorean theorem or trigonometric functions, one can assign each side a length of *b* and can describe the height of a **regular triangle** (an equilateral triangle) in terms of the length of its sides. The length is equal to *b* multiplied by the square root of ¾, so that the area and perimeter are as follows:

$$A = b^2 \sqrt{3/4}$$

$$P = 3b$$

Polygons in a Plane

In a plane, three-sided polygons are *triangles*, four-sided polygons are *quadrilaterals*, five sides make *pentagons*, six sides are *hexagons*, and eight-sided polygons are *octagons*. (Note that not all quadrilaterals are squares.) If two polygons (or any figures) have exactly the same size and shape, they are *congruent*. If they are the same shape, but different sizes, they are *similar*.

Topic 5.
Applying the Geometric Concepts of Symmetry, Similarity, Congruency, Tessellations, Scaling, and Transformations

Symmetry can be thought of as an imaginary fold line producing two congruent, mirror-image figures. Some geometric figures do not have symmetry.

Polygons may have lines of symmetry, which can be thought of as imaginary fold lines that produce two congruent, mirror-image figures. Squares have four lines of symmetry, and non-square rectangles have two, as shown later. Circles have an infinite number of lines of symmetry; a few are shown on the circle.

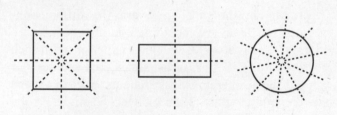

Geometric figures are **similar** if they have exactly the same shape, even if they are not the same size. In the following figure, triangles *A* and *B* are similar:

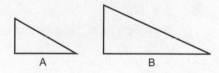

Corresponding angles of similar figures have the same measure, and the lengths of corresponding sides are proportional. In the following figure of similar triangles, $\angle A \cong \angle D$ (meaning "angle *A* is congruent to angle *D*"), $\angle B \cong \angle E$, and $\angle C \cong \angle F$. The corresponding sides of the triangles are proportional, meaning that

$$\frac{AB}{DE} = \frac{BC}{EF} = \frac{CA}{FD}$$

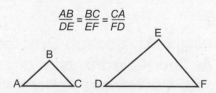

A **tessellation** is a collection of plane figures that fill the plane with no overlaps and no gaps. The following chart provides some examples:

A tessellation of triangles

A tessellation of squares

A tessellation of hexagons

Scaling that is uniform is a linear transformation that enlarges or reduces an object; the scale factor is the same in all directions. The result of uniform scaling is an object that is similar (in the geometric sense) to the original. Scaling may be directional or may have a separate scale factor for each axis direction. This type of scaling may result in a change in shape.

Transformations include a variety of different operations from geometry, including rotations, reflections, and translations. Students will have experiences in such transformations as flips, turns, slides, and scaling. For example, the teacher might ask students to select a shape that is a parallelogram. Then the teacher might ask the students to do the following:

- Describe the original position and size of the parallelogram. Students can use labeled sketches if necessary.

- Translate (or slide) the parallelogram several times. (A **translation** of a figure occurs if it is possible to give an object a straight shove for a certain distance and in a certain direction.) Rotate the parallelogram two times. Students should list the steps they followed.

- Challenge a friend to return the parallelogram to its original position.

- Determine if the friend used a reversal of the original steps or a different set of steps.

Topic 6.
Determining and Locating Ordered Pairs in All Four Quadrants of a Rectangular Coordinate System

The **coordinate plane** is useful for graphing individual ordered pairs and relationships. The coordinate

plane is divided into four quadrants by an *x*-axis (horizontal) and a *y*-axis (vertical). The upper-right quadrant is quadrant I, and the others (moving counterclockwise from quadrant I) are quadrants II, III, and IV.

Ordered pairs indicate the locations of points on the plane. For instance, the ordered pair (−3, 4) describes a point that is three units *left* from the center of the plane (the **origin**) and four units *up*, as shown in the following diagram:

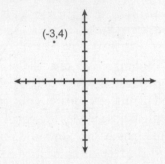

Ordered pairs are sets of data that one can display in a chart and graph on the coordinate plane. For example, the following set of data demonstrates four ordered pairs:

x	*Y*
3	5
4	6
5	7
6	8

Topic 7.
Using Networks to Construct Three-Dimensional Geometric Shapes

A **network** (or net) is a union of points (its vertices or nodes) and the segments (its arcs) connecting them. The nets are, in effect, patterns for building three-dimensional triangles, cubes, and other geometric figures. The teacher may distribute the nets and the students may construct the figures by cutting, folding, and taping. Using the concrete level is an excellent way to develop geometric understanding in students; following the levels of learning mentioned earlier (concrete, semiconcrete, semiabstract, and abstract), the concrete level should come before using drawings alone to solve problems. Nets can help make this understanding possible. Below is a net for a tetrahedron—a tetranet.

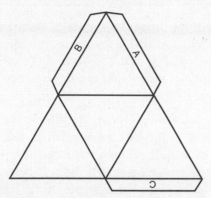

Topic 8.
Standard Units of Measurement

Customary units of measurement are generally the same as **U.S. units**. Customary units of length include inches, feet, yards, and miles. Customary units of weight include ounces, pounds, and tons. Customary units of capacity (or volume) include teaspoons, tablespoons, cups, pints, quarts, and gallons.

The **metric system of measurement** relates to the base-10 place-value scheme. The following chart lists the common metric prefixes:

Prefix	Meaning
Kilo-	Thousand (1,000)
Deci-	Tenth (0.1)
Centi-	Hundredth (0.01)
Milli-	Thousandth (0.001)

The basic unit of linear measure in the metric system is the **meter**, abbreviated as **m**. The relationships among the commonly used linear units of measurement in the metric system are

1 kilometer (km) = 1,000 m

1 meter (m) = 1.0 m

1 decimeter (dm) = 0.1 m

1 centimeter (cm) = 0.01 m

1 millimeter (mm) = 0.001 m

The centimeter is the metric unit of length used for short distances; about 2.5 centimeters equals 1 inch. The kilometer is a metric unit of length used for longer distances; slightly more than 1.5 kilometers equals a mile. A very fast adult runner could run a kilometer in about three minutes.

The basic unit of measurement for mass (or weight) in the metric system is the **gram**, abbreviated as **g**. The relationships among the commonly used units of measurement for mass in the metric system include

1 kilogram (kg) = 1,000 g

1 gram (g) = 1.0 g

1 milligram (mg) = 0.001 g

A large paper clip weighs about 1 gram; it takes about 28 grams to make 1 ounce.

The basic unit of measurement for capacity (or volume) in the metric system is the **liter**, represented by **L** or **l**. The relationships among the most common metric units of capacity include

1 liter (l) = 1,000 milliliters (ml)

1 deciliter (dl) = 100 ml; 10 cl

1 centiliter (cl) = 10 ml

A liter is slightly smaller than a quart; it takes more than four liters to make a gallon.

Here are some frequently used customary-to-metric ratios. (Values are approximate.)

1 inch = 2.54 centimeters

1 yard = 0.91 meter

1 mile = 1.61 kilometers

1 ounce = 28.35 grams

1 pound = 2.2 kilograms

1 quart = 0.94 liter

One can determine the metric-to-customary conversions by taking the reciprocals of each of the factors just listed. For instance, 1 kilometer = 0.62 mile (computed by dividing 1 by 1.61).

An important step in solving problems involving measurement is to decide what is being measured. Generally, such problems will fall under one of these categories: length, area, angles, volume, mass, time, money, and temperature. Solving measurement problems will likely require knowledge in several other areas of mathematics, especially algebra.

The following is one example of a measurement problem that requires knowledge of several math topics (geometry, multiplication, conversions, estimation, measurement, etc.):

> Sophie's Carpet Store charges $19.40 per square yard for the type of carpeting Tony would like in his bedroom (padding and labor included). How much would Tony pay to carpet his 9 × 12-foot room?

> One way to find the solution is to convert the room dimensions to yards (3 × 4 yards) and multiply to get 12 square yards. The final step is to multiply 12 by the price of $19.40 per square yard, for a total price of $232.80.

Section 3: Probability and Statistics

Topic 1.
Applying the Concepts of Central Tendency and Range

Measures of central tendency of a set of values include the mean, median, and mode. The **mean** is found by adding all the values and then dividing the sum by the number of values. The **median** of a set is the middle number when the values are in numerical order. (If the set comprises an even number of values, and therefore no middle value, the mean of the middle two values gives the median.) The **mode** of a set is the value occurring most often. (Not all sets of values have a single mode; some sets have more than one.) Consider the following set:

6, 8, 14, 5, 6, 5, 5

The mean, median, and mode of the set are 7, 6, and 5, respectively. (Note that the mean is often referred to as the average, but all three measures are averages of sorts.)

The **range** of a set of numbers is a measure of the spread of, or variation in, the numbers.

Topic 2.
Determining the Mean, Median, Mode, and Range

To determine the mean of a set of numbers, add the set of numbers and divide by the total number of elements in the set. For example, to find the mean of 15, 10, 25, 5, and 40, you would use the equation $(15 + 10 + 25 + 5 + 40) \div 5 = 19$.

To find the median, order a given set of numbers from smallest to largest; the median is the "middle" number. That is, half the numbers in the set of numbers are below the median and half the numbers in the set are above the median. For example, to find the median of the set of whole numbers 15, 10, 25, 5, and 40, the first step is to order the set of numbers: 5, 10, 15, 25, 40. Because 15 is the middle number (half of the numbers are below 15, half are above 15), 15 is the median of this set of whole numbers. If a set has an even number of numbers, the median is the mean of the middle two numbers. For instance, in the set of numbers 2, 4, 6, and 8, the median is the mean of 4 and 6, or 5.

The mode of the set of numbers 15, 10, 25, 10, 5, 40, 10, and 15 is the number 10 because it appears most frequently (three times).

The **range** of a set of numbers is obtained by subtracting the smallest number in the set from the largest number in the set. For example, to determine the range of the set 15, 10, 25, 5, and 40, you would use the equation $40 - 5 = 35$.

Topic 3.
Determining Probabilities of Dependent or Independent Events

Probability theory provides models for chance variations. The likelihood or chance that an event will take place is called the **probability** of the event. The probability of any event occurring is equal to the number of desired outcomes divided by the number of all possible events. Thus, the probability of blindly pulling a green ball out of a hat (in this case the desired outcome) if the hat contains two green and five yellow balls is 2/7 (about 29%).

The probability of 2/7 can also be expressed as the ratio of 2:7. We can also write the mathematical sentence with words:

Probability of a particular event occurring =

Number of ways the event can occur
Total number of possible events

Topic 4.
Determining Odds For and Against a Given Situation

Odds are related to but different from probability. The odds that any given event *will* occur can be expressed as the ratio of the probability that the event will occur to the probability that the event *will not* occur. In the example from the previous section, the odds that a green ball will be drawn are two to five (2:5) because two balls are green and five balls are not green.

If there are four marbles — three red and one blue--in a jar, the probability of drawing the blue is ¼. There is one chance of a blue marble, and there are four total chances (marbles). Odds describe the number of chances for (or against) versus the number of chances against (or for). Since there is one chance of picking the blue and three chances of picking red, the odds are three to one *against* picking the blue. For odds in favor, just reverse the numbers: the odds are one to three *in favor* of picking the blue.

To repeat, if you express odds as *against*, you put the number of chances against first, versus the number of chances for. If you express odds as *in favor of*, you put the number of chances for first.

Note that the odds in the marbles example do not mean that the probability is ⅓ for or against. To convert odds to probability, one must add the chances. So, for example, if the odds against a horse winning are four to one, this means that, out of five (4 + 1) chances, the horse has one chance in favor of winning; the probability of the horse winning is ⅕ or 20% (*http://www.math-forum.org/library/drmath/view/56495.html*).

Topic 5.
Applying Fundamental Counting Principles Such as Combinations to Solve Probability Problems

As noted earlier, probability is calculated as follows:

Probability of a Particular Event Occurring =

Number of Ways the Event Can Occur
Total Number of Possible Events

Human sex type is determined by the genetic material in the sperm and egg. The genetic sex code for human females is *XX*. The genetic sex code for human males is *XY*. Eggs carry only *X* genes. Sperm carry both *X* and *Y* genes; the *Y* gene is the absence of the *X* gene. The following chart illustrates the probability of a fertilized human egg being male or female:

		Female	
		X	X
Male			
	X	*XX*	*XX*
	Y	*XY*	*XY*

The chart shows that the probability of a female (*XX*) is 2 out of 4, and the probability of a male (*XY*) is 2 out of 4. Therefore, there is a 50% chance of a boy and a 50% chance of a girl.

Section 4: Problem Solving

Topic 1.
Selecting the Appropriate Operation(s) to Solve Problems Involving Ratios, Proportions, and Percents, and the Addition, Subtraction, Multiplication, and Division of Rational Numbers

The key to converting word problems into mathematical problems is attention to **reasonableness**, with the choice of operations being crucial to success. Often, individual words and phrases translate into numbers and operation symbols; making sure that the translations are reasonable is important. Consider this word problem:

Each word problem requires an individual approach, but keeping in mind the reasonableness of the computational setup should be helpful.

Most modern math programs introduce the concept of ratio and use ratio to solve various problems. Consider this example:

Pencils are two for 25 cents. How many pencils can Teresa buy for 50 cents?

"Two pencils for 25 cents" suggests the fixed constant of $\frac{2}{25}$:

$$\frac{2 \text{ (pencils)}}{25 \text{ (cents)}}$$

With a fixed ratio, it should be possible to figure out how many pencils Teresa can buy for 50 cents by setting up an equivalent ratio:

$$\frac{x \text{ (number of pencils)}}{50 \text{ (cents)}}$$

The relationship between the two ratios is one of equality; that is, they are equivalent ratios. As noted earlier in the chapter, an equation of two equivalent ratios is one of proportion. There are several ways to solve the equivalent ratios problem with the pencils, but one way to do it is to use **cross multiplication**:

$$\frac{x}{50} \times \frac{2}{25}$$

Cross multiplication gives $25x = 100$. Solving for x requires dividing 100 by 25 to get 4. Thus, Teresa can buy four pencils for 50 cents.

Another way to solve the problem is to set up a chart. You might even try extending the chart for several rows to be sure the values increase appropriately.

Pencils	Cost
2	25 cents
4	50 cents
6	75 cents

In solving problems involving percents, students must always consider reasonableness in their thinking and estimating. Mathematical reasoning includes analyzing problem situations, making conjectures, organizing information, and selecting strategies to solve

problems. Students must rely on both formal and informal **reasoning processes**. A key informal process relies on reasonableness. Consider this problem:

Center Town Middle School has an enrollment of 640 students. One day, 28 students were absent. What percent of the total number of students was absent?

A.   28%

B.   1%

C.   18%

D.   4%

Even a student who has forgotten how to compute percents would be able to reject some of the answer choices instantly: 28% is more than one-fourth, a "small-but-not-tiny" chunk of 640; answers like 1% and 18% are *unreasonable*.

Look for **key words** in solving problems. The words may provide a clue as to which operation to use. The following chart gives some examples:

Operation	Key Words
Addition	*Added to* *Combined* *Increased by* *More than* *Sum* *Together* *Total of*
Subtraction	*Decreased by* *Difference between* *Difference of* *Fewer than* *Less* *Less than* *Minus*
Multiplication	*Decreased by a factor of* *Increased by a factor of* *Multiplied by* *Of* *Product of* *Times*

Operation	Key Words
Division	*Divide* *Equal groups* *How many groups* *How many to each* *Quotient* *Separate* *Share*

Topic 2.

Using Estimation and Other Problem-Solving Strategies

Estimation is a useful tool in predicting and in checking the answer to a problem. Estimation is at the second level in Bloom's *Taxonomy*—the comprehension level. Thinking at the comprehension level requires students not only to recall or remember information but also to understand the meaning of information and to restate it in their own words.

The ability to render some real-life quandaries into mathematical or logical problems—workable using established procedures—is an important part of finding solutions. Because each quandary will be unique, so too will be students' problem-solving plans of attack. Still, many real-world problems that lend themselves to mathematical solutions are likely to require one of the following strategies:

Guess and check. This is not the same as "wild guessing." With this problem-solving strategy, students make their best guess and then check the answer to see whether it is right. Even if the guess does not immediately provide the solution, it may help students get closer to it so that they can continue to work on it. Here's an example:

The ages of three people add up to 72, and each person is one year older than the last person. What are their ages?

Because the three ages must add up to 72, it is reasonable to take one-third of 72 (24) as the starting point. Of course, even though 24 + 24 + 24 gives a sum of 72, those numbers do not match the information ("each person is one year older").

So, students might guess that the ages are 24, 25, and 26. Checking that guess by addition, students would see that the sum of 75 is too high. Lowering their guesses by one each, they then would try 23, 24, and 25, which indeed add up to 72, giving the students the solution. There are many variations of the guess-and-check method.

Make a sketch or a picture. Being able to visualize a problem can help to clarify it. Consider this problem:

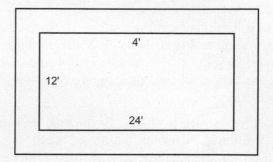

Mr. Rosenberg plans to put a 4-foot-wide concrete sidewalk around his backyard pool. The pool is rectangular, measuring 12 feet by 24 feet. The cost of the concrete is $1.28 per square foot. How much concrete is required for the job?

Students with exceptional visualization abilities will not need a sketch. For most, however, a drawing like the one shown here may be helpful in solving this and many other real-life problems.

Make a table or a chart. Sometimes organizing the information from a problem into a table or chart makes it easier to find the solution.

Make a list. Like a table or chart, a list can help organize information and perhaps provide or at least hint at a solution. The list-making strategy would work well for solving this problem:

How many different outcomes are there if you roll two regular six-sided dice?

Act it out. Sometimes literally "doing" a problem—with physical objects or even their bodies—can help students produce a solution. A class problem that could be solved in this manner is the following:

If five strangers meet and everyone shakes everyone else's hand once, how many total handshakes will there be?

Look for patterns. This technique encourages students to ask, "What's happening here?" Spotting a pattern would be helpful in solving a problem such as this:

> Nevin's weekly savings-account balances for 15 weeks are as follows: $125, $135, $148, $72, $85, $96, $105, $50, $64, $74, $87, $42, $51, $60, $70. If the pattern holds, what might Nevin's balance be the next week?

It appears that Nevin saves for 2–3 weeks; the following week he spends about half the accumulation. Because the total is $70, the observer would probably find about $35 in the savings account after Nevin's typical withdrawal.

Work a simpler problem. By finding the solution to a different but simpler problem, students might spot a way to solve the harder one. Estimating can be thought of as working a simpler problem. To find the product of 23×184 when no calculator or pencil and paper are handy, students could estimate the product by getting the exact answer to the simpler problem, 20×200.

Writing an open math sentence (an equation with one or more variables, or "unknowns") and then solving it. This is sometimes called "translating" a problem into mathematics. Here is a sample problem:

> Tiana earned grades of 77%, 86%, 90%, and 83% on her first four weekly science quizzes. Assuming all grades are equally weighted, what score will she need on the fifth week's quiz to have an average (or mean) score of 88%?

Using the given information, students could set up and solve the following equation to answer the question:

$$\frac{(77 + 86 + 90 + 83 + x)}{5} = 88$$

Work backward. Consider this problem:

> If you add 12 to some number and then multiply the sum by 4, you will get 60. What is the number?

Students could find a solution by *starting at the end*, with 60. The problem states that the 60 came from multiplying a sum by 4. When 15 is multiplied by 4, the result is 60. The sum must be 15; if 15 is the sum of 12 and something else, the "something else" can only be 3.

Topic 3.
Selecting Appropriate Units to Solve Problems

Solving measurement problems requires first determining whether to use customary units or metric units. The next decision is whether the problem involves measurements of length, volume, mass, or temperature. Using the metric system requires choosing the appropriate prefix for *meter*.

There are of course hybrid approaches to problem solving. Students can mix and match strategies wherever they think they are appropriate. In general, attention to reasonableness may be most crucial to problem-solving success, especially in real-life situations.

Social Sciences

Section 1: The Scope and Sequence of the Social Studies Curriculum

Topic 1.
Scope and Sequence of Social Studies

There is a typical scope and sequence for teaching the social studies in U.S. schools. Although the schools do not rigorously follow it because the United States does not have a national system of education, the pattern that frequently emerges and that has been in use since the 1920s is the **expanding horizon approach**, or the **widening horizon curriculum**. Based on the original belief that children learn about their environment in gradually expanding concentric circles, this type of curriculum begins with what the children supposedly already know and moves outward. The typical topics are

Kindergarten–Grade 1: Family, home, school

Grade 2: Community

Grade 3: State history and geography and/or holidays and history of the United States

Grade 4: Regions of the world or state history and geography

Grade 5: American history and American geography

Grade 6: World history and geography

Grade 7: State history and/or U.S. History

Grade 8: Civics, American history

In addition, the national learned societies and state curriculum guidelines also influence the scope and sequence of the curriculum.

Section 2: Geography in the Social Studies Curriculum

Topic 1.
Identifying the Five Themes of Geography, Including the Specific Terms for Each Theme

The five themes of geography are place; location; human-environmental interaction; movement and connections; and regions, patterns, and processes. An understanding of these themes would include the ability to use them to analyze regions, states, countries, and the world to gain a perspective about interrelationships among those areas. When a teacher uses the five themes, students should gain the ability to compare regions:

1. In this world of fast-breaking news from throughout the globe, students must be able to recognize the **place** names of continents, countries, and even cities. In addition to geography, the theme of place encompasses the fields of political science.

2. An understanding of the theme of **location** requires knowledge of both absolute and relative location. **Absolute location** is determined by longitude and latitude. **Relative location** deals with the interactions that occur between and among places. Relative location involves the interconnectedness among people because of land, water, and technology. For example, the Silver River brought commerce and steamboats to the Silver Springs area of Florida; the 99.8 percent pure artesian spring waters in one of the largest artesian spring formations in the world offered respite and beauty to settlers and tourists alike. Hullam Jones invented the glass-bottom boat there in 1878 and enabled visitors to view the underwater world of fish, turtles, crustaceans, and fossils more than 10,000 years old. The location of Silver Springs has contributed to the area's economic development and vitality. In addition to geography, the theme of location encompasses the fields of technology, history, and economics.

3. An understanding of the theme of **human-environmental interaction** involves consideration of how people rely on the environment, how people alter it, and how the environment may limit what people are able to do. For example, Silver Springs is at the headwaters of the Silver River. In the 1850s barges carried cotton, lumber, and nonperishables up the Silver River to the area's growing population. The development of a stagecoach line and the bringing of conventional steamboats to Silver Springs in 1860 aided in the development of Silver Springs and the nearby areas. In addition to geography, the theme of human-environmental interaction encompasses the field of ecology.

4. An understanding of the theme of **movement and connections** requires identifying how people are connected through different forms of transportation and communication networks and how those networks have changed over time. This would include identifying channels of the movement of people, goods, and information. For example, the automobile industry had a profound impact on the number of visitors to Silver Springs, Florida, and on the movement patterns of ideas, fashion, and people. In addition to geography, the theme of movement and connections encompasses the fields of communications, history, anthropology, economics, and sociology.

5. An understanding of the theme of **regions, patterns, and processes** involves identifying climatic, economic, political, and cultural patterns within regions. To comprehend why these patterns were created, students need to understand how climatic systems, communication networks, international trade, political systems, and population changes contributed to a region's development. With an understanding of a particular region, students can study its uniqueness and relationship to other regions. In addition to geography, the theme of regions, patterns, and processes encompasses the fields of economics, sociology, and politics.

The study of global issues and events includes comprehending the interconnectedness of peoples throughout the world (sociology and political science). For example, knowing the relationship between world oil consumption and oil production helps students understand the impact that increased demand for oil in China would have on the price of a barrel of oil, which in turn could affect the decisions of consumers of new vehicles in the United States.

Topic 2.
Interpreting Maps and Other Graphic Representations and Identifying Tools and Technologies to Acquire, Process, and Report Information from a Spatial Perspective

Any study of maps should begin with a study of the globe—a model of the earth with a map on its surface. The globe is more accurate than a flat map. Constantly using the globe helps bring understanding of the earth's shape and structure.

Some of the points on the globe that students should be able to locate include the equator, Antarctic Circle, Arctic Circle, prime meridian, international date line, North Pole, South Pole, meridians, parallels, the Great Circle Route, and time zones.

The use of maps requires students to identify four main types of map projections: conic, cylindrical, interrupted, and plane. Additional graphics that students use in geography include charts, graphs, and picture maps.

Topic 3.
Interpreting Geologic Maps, Including Topographic and Weather Maps That Contain Symbols, Scales, Legends, Directions, Latitudes, and Longitudes

Geologic maps provide much information about the earth and present a perfect opportunity to integrate social studies and science. By reading a **topographical map**, a student can find out about **altitudes** (heights above and below sea level) and landforms. **Symbols** on the map may represent rivers, lakes, rapids, and forests. **Map scales** allow the student to determine distances. The **legends** of a map furnish additional information, including the locations of mineral deposits and quarries, dams and boat ramps, fire and ranger stations, and more. Often a map displays a **compass rose**, which gives the cardinal directions: north, south, east, and west.

Parallels and meridians grid the earth. **Meridians** run from pole to pole, and 360 of them surround the earth in 1-degree increments. Every hour, a given location on the earth's surface rotates through 15 degrees of longitude. Meridians help measure longitude, the distance east and west of the prime meridian, which has a measurement of 0° east-west. **Parallels** are the lines that run in an east-west direction; parallels help measure **latitude**, the distance north and south of the equator.

Geologic maps often contain all this information. A geologic map usually differs from a political map, which shows political boundaries, counties, cities, towns, churches, schools, and other representations of government and people.

Topic 4.
Identifying the Factors That Influence the Selection of a Location for a Specific Activity

Factors that influence the selection of a location for a specific activity include the area's population density, government, latitude (distance from the equator), altitude (height above sea level), distance from bodies of water, culture, economics, landforms, sociology, vegetation, and climate (temperature, rainfall, etc.)

The human development of the area also affects selection. For instance, methods of transportation, highways, airports, communication, waterways, water travel, buildings, industries, and facilities are only a few of the factors that influence location for a specific activity. For some industries, nearness to sources of raw materials for production and ways of transporting the goods after production may be important in selecting an area in which to locate.

Two types of location—absolute and relative— describe the positions of people and places on the earth's surface. Determining **absolute location** requires the use of longitude and latitude on a grid system. The longitude and latitude coordinates identify exact (absolute) location. **Relative location**, on the other hand, recognizes the interdependence of people and places. Places do not exist in isolation. Geographers attempt to identify relationships between or among places and to determine the factors that might encourage those relationships.

Topic 5.
Identifying the Relationship Between Natural Physical Processes and the Environment

One can approach geography—the study of places on the earth's surface—from various perspectives. One study approach is **physical geography**—locating and describing places according to physical features (climate, soils, landforms, vegetation, etc.). Physical geography must take into account how the earth's movements around the sun, the tilt of the earth, the sea, weather patterns, the distance from the equator, the altitude, nd the air affect the earth's surface. The physical approach alone, however, is a narrow methodology from the social science point of view because it ignores the human factor.

Topic 6.
Interpreting Statistics That Show How Places Differ in Their Human and Physical Characteristics

For geography (the study of the earth) to be a true social science, it must take into account the human factor. Some notice of the interaction of the humans and animals that live on the earth—whether the interaction is deliberate or incidental—is an important part of the social sciences. The relationship between a place and the humans and animals that inhabit it is **cultural geography**.

Location affects both plant and animal life. The physical environment—climate, resources, and terrain, and so on—impinges on the life of people by affecting diet, shelter, clothing, accessibility, inventions, religion, resources, and prosperity. In fact, in prehistoric times— even before history, government, or economics—the earth (geography) was the most important element in human life. Geography is still important in society today.

Studying a map of the rivers and the fall line (a physical feature that indicates the navigability of rivers) in North Carolina, for example, reveals why many people decided to settle there. In the late 1800s, textile mills were often built near the fall line so they could use water as a power source. Many people who needed employment and were not highly skilled sought work in the textile mills. This example shows how the physical characteristics of a place can affect the people who move there.

Topic 7.
Identifying How Conditions of the Past, Such As Wealth and Poverty, Land Tenure, Exploitation, Colonialism, and Independence, Affect Present Human Characteristics of Places

Three generalizations of geography relate the past to human characteristics of places:

1. Physical factors and cultural factors are related. For instance, the types of houses that families build reflect the available materials and climates. Therefore, physical differences can arise among houses in various places. The richness of the physical environment can affect the wealth of the people.

2. Change is a constant. The effects of change on people are both physical and cultural. For example, the people themselves bring about some changes; they may modify the environment by cutting trees and affecting the landscape now and in days to come.

3. People modify the environment to suit their changing needs and wants. For example, when tenant farmers lived on another person's land, they had little say over the use of the land; planting gardens for their own families' uses may have been out of the question. Once they were able to purchase land, their use of the land changed; many began planting gardens and fruit trees for their families. Today, people living in an area damaged by a storm may be able to repair the damages caused by the storm and even change the place to suit their current needs and wants.

Topic 8.
Identifying Ways in Which People Adapt to an Environment through the Production and Use of Clothing, Food, and Shelter

Although the environment can affect the way people live, people can change the environment to meet their wants and needs. For example, the jobs that people hold enable them to get money for food, clothing, and shelter. Some jobs—farming, logging, and mining, for example—have a profound effect on the environment. In parts of the world without adequate rainfall, farmers have to use irrigation to grow their crops. Through their adaptation of the environment, the farmers acquire the things they need to survive but, in the process, may damage their environment and ultimately threaten the survival of future generations.

Ideally, people will explore a damaged environment to determine the causes of water and air pollution. They will also determine whether there is any harm to local plants and animals and will ascertain the cause if there is damage. The people will ideally work to change damages to the environment and prevent further harm.

Topic 9.
Identifying How Tools and Technology Affect the Environment

The period from the emergence of the first-known hominids, or humans, around 2.5 million years ago until approximately 10,000 BCE has been designated as the Paleolithic period, or the Old Stone Age. During that period, human beings lived in very small groups of perhaps 10 to 20 nomadic people who were constantly moving from place to place. Human beings had the ability to make tools and weapons from stone and the bones of animals they killed. Hunting large game such as mammoths, which the hunters sometimes drove off cliffs in large numbers, was crucial to the survival of early humans. The meat, fur, and bones of the hunted animals were essential to the survival of prehistoric people, who supplemented their diets by foraging for food.

Early human beings found shelter in caves and other natural formations and took the time to paint and draw on the walls of their shelters. Created during the prehistoric period, cave paintings in France and northern Spain depict scenes of animals, such as lions, owls, and oxen. Around 500,000 years ago, humans developed the means of creating fire and used it to provide light and warmth in shelters and to cook meat and other foods. They also developed improved techniques of producing tools and weapons.

Tools and technology can improve the lives of people; needless to say, tools and technology can also harm the lives of people. Likewise, people can use tools and technology both to improve their environment and to harm or even destroy their immediate areas or even the world. For example, as Alfred Nobel learned after he developed dynamite, escalating the power of weapons has never successfully prevented war. As weapons become more powerful, the danger from the technology increases.

Topic 10.
Identifying Physical, Cultural, Economic, and Political Reasons for the Movement of People in the World, Nation, or State

The people living in a particular area determine the characteristics of that area. The physical characteristics, the cultural characteristics, the economic characteristics, and the political characteristics are important to most area residents and may affect their original decision to settle there.

If the characteristics of an area become unacceptable to residents, the inhabitants may consider moving to a different location. With the ease of transportation today, most people can move more easily than they could have a generation ago. The move may be to another region of their state, the nation, or the world.

Economic reasons for moving include the finances of an individual considering relocating and the economic level required to live comfortably in the area. Some residents may move to a more expensive area, but others may decide to go to a less expensive area. Many change their places of residence, therefore, to get ahead economically or to raise their standard of living.

Some people decide to relocate for **cultural reasons**. These people might consider their neighbors too similar to them and decide to move to an area with more diversity. On the other hand, some people would rather live with others who are similar to them.

Physical reasons can also affect a person's decision to relocate. An understanding of the theme of human-environmental interaction involves considering how people rely on the environment, how they alter it, and how the environment can limit what people are able to do. Sometimes people move to a place where they can satisfy their physical wants or needs. In some cases, people can modify their environment or bring the needed goods to their area without having to relocate. For example, an adaptation of the environment that aided the Illinois shipping industry was the development of the lock and dam system on the Mississippi River.

An understanding of the theme of location, movement, and connections involves identifying how people are connected through different forms of transportation and communication networks and how those networks have changed over time. This would include identifying the channels of movement of people, goods, and information. For example, the textile industry in North Carolina in the 1930s had a profound impact on the movement patterns of ideas and people; many of those without work came to the textile regions seeking jobs. When the textile mills began closing in the 1990s, many people began to leave the area in search of other employment.

Political reasons also compel the movement of people. Many people equate the political system with government. There is a distinction, however. Government carries out the decisions of the political system. The organizations and processes that contribute to the decision-making process make up the political system. Individuals may move to another region or area if they are unhappy with the government and/or political systems in their area and are unable to bring about change. On the other hand, an attractive system of government may bring people to an area.

Topic 11.
Comparing and Contrasting Major Regions of the World

There are many ways of dividing the world into regions. Perhaps the simplest is to consider the equator as a dividing line between the Northern Hemisphere and the Southern Hemisphere. Another way of dividing the world in regions is to draw a line from pole to pole. Such a line may separate the globe into the Eastern Hemisphere and Western Hemisphere. Another way geographers might divide the world into regions is by landmasses, or continents, specifically Africa, Asia, Australia, Europe, North America, and South America; some geographers also include Antarctica as a separate continent. Other geographers prefer to group the regions according to political characteristics. Still others prefer to designate regions by latitudes: low, middle, and high.

Two important higher-order thinking skills that teachers should encourage among their students are comparing and contrasting. The use of regions is an ideal place to work with these skills of comparing and contrasting two (or more) things (or concepts). The process of finding similarities between or among the things or concepts that appear dissimilar on the surface requires deeper thought. W. J. J. Gordon describes a process of synectics, which forces students to make an analogy between two concepts, one familiar and the other new. At first, the concepts might seem completely different, but through a series of steps the students discover underlying similarities. By comparing something new with something familiar, students have a "hook" that will help them remember and understand the new information (Huitt 1998; Gordon 1961).

For example, a biology teacher might ask students to draw an analogy between a cell (new concept) and a city government (familiar concept). Although they seem impossibly different, both concepts involve systems for transportation, systems for disposing of unwanted materials, and parts that govern those systems. After discussion of this analogy, students trying to remember the functions of a cell would find help by relating the functions of the cell to the systems of city government.

Section 3: Prehistory and Early Civilization

Topic 1.
Identifying Major Leaders and Events That Have Influenced Eastern and Western Civilizations

The earth is estimated to be approximately 6 billion years old. The earliest known humans, called **hominids**, lived in Africa 3 to 4 million years ago. Of the several species of hominids that developed, all modern humans descended from just one group, the **Homo sapiens sapiens**. Homo sapiens sapiens is a subspecies of Homo sapiens (along with Neanderthals, who became extinct) and appeared in Africa between 200,000 and 150,000 years ago.

Historians divide prehistory into three periods. The period when people first appeared (around 2.5 million years ago until approximately 10,000 BCE) is the **Paleolithic period,** or **Old Stone Age**. These nomads lived in groups of 10 to 20 and **made tools and weapons** from stone and from the bones of animals they killed. Large animals were crucial to their survival; they sometimes drove the animals off cliffs. The early people foraged for food and took shelter in caves and other natural formations. About 500,000, years ago humans began to use fire for light, cooking, and warmth. They developed improved way to make tools and weapons and developed way to create fire.

The **Mesolithic period,** or **Middle Stone Age**, from 10,000 to 7000 BCE, marks the beginning of a major transformation known as the Neolithic Revolution. Previously, historians and archeologists thought this change occurred later. Thus, they called it the Neolithic Revolution because they thought it took place entirely within the Neolithic period, or New Stone Age. Beginning in the Mesolithic period, humans domesticated plants and began to shift away from a reliance on hunting large game and foraging. Human beings had previously relied on gathering food where they found it and had moved almost constantly in search of game and wild berries and other vegetation. During the Mesolithic period, humans were able to **plant and harvest** some crops and began to stay in one place for longer periods. Early humans also improved their tool-making techniques and developed various kinds of tools and weapons.

During the **Neolithic period**, or **New Stone Age**, this "revolution" was complete, and humans engaged in systematic agriculture and began domesticating animals. Although humans continued to hunt animals to supplement their diet with **meat** and to use the skins and bones to make clothing and weapons, major changes in society occurred. Human beings became settled and lived in farming villages or towns, the population increased, and people began to live in much larger communities. A more settled way of life led to a **more structured social system**; a higher level of organization within societies; the development of **crafts**, such as the production of **pottery**; and a rise in **trade** or exchange of goods among groups.

Between 4000 and 3000 BCE, **writing** developed, and the towns and villages settled during the Neolithic period developed a more complex pattern of existence. The existence of written records marks the **end of the prehistoric period**. The beginning of history coincides with the emergence of the earliest societies that exhibit characteristics that enable them to be considered as civilizations. The first civilizations emerged in Mesopotamia and Egypt.

Ancient and Medieval Times

Appearance of Civilization and Related Cultural and Technological Developments. Between 6000 and 3000 BCE, humans invented the **plow**, developed the **wheel**, harnessed the **wind**, discovered how to smelt **copper ores**, and began to develop accurate **solar calendars**. Small villages gradually grew into populous cities. The **invention of writing** in 3500 BCE in Mesopotamia marks the beginning of civilization and divides prehistoric from historic times.

Mesopotamia. Sumer (4000–2000 BCE) included the city of Ur. The Sumerians constructed **dikes and reservoirs** and established a loose confederation of **city-states**. They probably invented writing (called **cuneiform** because of its wedge-shaped letters). After 538 BCE, the peoples of Mesopotamia, whose natural boundaries were insufficient to thwart invaders, were absorbed into other empires and dynasties.

Egypt. During the end of the Middle Archaic Period (6000–3000 BC), in about 3200 BCE, Menes, or Narmer, probably unified upper and lower Egypt. The capital moved to Memphis during the Third Dynasty (ca. 2650 BCE). The **pyramids** were built during the Fourth Dynasty (ca. 2613–2494 BCE). After 1085 BCE, in the Post-Empire period, Egypt came under the successive control of the Assyrians, the Persians, Alexander the Great, and finally, in 30 BCE, the Roman Empire. The Egyptians developed papyrus and made many medical advances.

Palestine and the Hebrews. Phoenicians settled along the present-day Lebanon coast (Sidon, Tyre, Beirut, Byblos) and established colonies at Carthage and in Spain. They spread **Mesopotamian culture** through their trade networks. The Hebrews probably moved to Egypt in about 1700 BCE and suffered enslavement in about 1500 BCE. The Hebrews fled Egypt under Moses and, around 1200 BCE, returned to Palestine. King David (reigned ca. 1012–972 BCE) defeated the Philistines and established Jerusalem as a capital. The poor and less attractive state of Judah continued until 586 BCE, when the Chaldeans transported the Jews ("the people of Judah" or, in some translations, "the people of God") to Chaldea as advisors and slaves (Babylonian captivity). The Persians conquered Babylon in 539 BCE and allowed the Jews to return to Palestine.

Greece. In the period from about 800–500 BCE, the Greeks organized around the *polis*, or city-state. Oligarchs controlled most of the *polis* until near the end of the sixth century, when individuals holding absolute power (tyrants) replaced them. By the end of the sixth century, **democratic governments** in turn replaced many tyrants.

The Classical Age. The fifth century BCE was the high point of Greek civilization. It opened with the Persian Wars (560–479 BCE), after which Athens organized the Delian League. **Pericles** (ca. 495–429 BCE) used money from the league to rebuild Athens, including construction of the Parthenon and other buildings on the Acropolis hill. Athens's dominance spurred war with Sparta. At the same time, a revolution in philosophy occurred in classical Athens. The **Sophists** emphasized the individual and the attainment of excellence through rhetoric, grammar, music, and mathematics. **Socrates** (ca. 470–399 BCE) criticized the Sophists' emphasis on rhetoric and emphasized a process of questioning, or dialogues, with his students. Like Socrates, **Plato** (ca. 428–348 BCE) emphasized ethics. Aristotle (ca. 384–322 BCE) was Plato's pupil. He criticized Plato and argued that ideas or forms did not exist outside of things. He contended that in treating any object it was necessary to examine four factors: its matter, its form, its cause of origin, and its end or purpose.

Rome. The traditional founding date for Rome is 753 BCE. Between 800 and 500 BCE, Greek tribes colonized southern Italy, bringing their alphabet and religious practices to Roman tribes. In the sixth and seventh centuries BCE, the Etruscans expanded southward and conquered Rome. In the early Republic, power was in the hands of the patricians (wealthy landowners). During the 70s and 60s, **Pompey** (106–48 BCE) and **Julius Caesar** (100–44 BCE) emerged as the most powerful men.

In 60 BCE, Caesar convinced Pompey and Crassus (ca. 115–53 BCE) to form the First Triumvirate. When Crassus died, Caesar and Pompey fought for leadership. In 47 BCE, the Senate proclaimed Caesar dictator and later named him consul for life. **Brutus** and **Cassius** believed that Caesar had destroyed the Republic. They formed a conspiracy, and on March 15, 44 BCE (the Ides of March), Brutus and Cassius assassinated Caesar in the Roman forum. Caesar's 18-year-old nephew and adopted son, Octavian, succeeded him.

The Roman Empire. After a period of struggle, Octavian (reigned 27 BCE–14 CE), named as Caesar's heir, gained absolute control while maintaining the appearance of a republic. When he offered to relinquish his power in 27 BCE, the Senate gave him a vote of confidence and a new title, Augustus. He introduced many reforms, including new coinage, new tax collection, fire and police protection, and land for settlers in the provinces. By the first century CE, Christianity had spread throughout the Empire. Around 312 CE, Emperor Constantine converted to Christianity and ordered toleration in the Edict of Milan (ca. 313 CE). In 391 CE, Emperor Theodosius I (reigned 371–395 CE) proclaimed Christianity the empire's official religion.

The Byzantine Empire. Emperor Theodosius II (reigned 408–450 CE) divided his empire between his two sons, one ruling the East and the other ruling the West. After the Vandals sacked Rome in 455 CE, Constantinople was the undisputed leading city of the Byzantine Empire. In 1453 CE, Constantinople fell to the Ottoman Turks.

Islamic Civilization in the Middle Ages. Mohammed was born about 570 CE. In 630 CE, he marched into Mecca. The Sharia (code of law and theology) outlines five pillars of faith for Muslims to observe. The beliefs that there is one God and that Mohammed is his prophet form the first pillar. Second, the faithful must pray five times a day. Third, they must perform charitable acts. Fourth, they must fast from sunrise to sunset during the holy month of Ramadan. Finally, they must make a *haj*, or pilgrimage, to Mecca. The Koran, which consists of 114 *suras* (verses), contains Mohammed's teachings.

The Omayyad caliphs, with their base in Damascus, governed from 661–750 CE. They called themselves **Shiites** and believed they were Mohammed's true successors. (Most Muslims were **Sunnis**, from the word *sunna*, meaning "oral traditions about the prophet.")

The Abbasid caliphs ruled from 750–1258 CE. They moved the capital to Baghdad and treated Arab and non-Arab Muslims as equals. Genghis (or Chingis) Khan (reigned 1206–1227 CE) and his army invaded the Abbasids. In 1258 CE, they seized Baghdad and murdered the last caliph.

Feudalism in Japan. Feudalism in Japan began with the arrival of mounted nomadic warriors from throughout Asia during the Kofun Era (300–710 CE). Some members of the nomadic groups formed an elite class and became part of the court aristocracy in the capital city of Kyoto, in western Japan. During the Heian Era (794–1185 CE), a hereditary military aristocracy arose in the Japanese provinces; by the late Heian Era, many of these formerly nomadic warriors had established themselves as independent landowners, or as managers of landed estates, or *shoen* owned by Kyoto aristocrats. These aristocrats depended on the warriors to defend their *shoen,* and in response to this need, the warriors organized into small groups called *bushidan.*

After victory in the Taira-Minamoto War (1180–1185 CE), Minamoto no Yorimoto forced the emperor to award him the title of *shogun*, which is short for "barbarian-subduing generalissimo." Yorimoto used this power to found the Kamakura Shogunate, a feudal military dictatorship that survived for 148 years.

By the fourteenth century CE, the great military governors (*shugo*) had augmented their power enough to become a threat to the Kamakura, and in 1333 CE they led a rebellion that overthrew the shogunate. The Tokugawa shogunate was the final and most unified of the three shogunates. Under the Tokugawa, the *daimyo* were direct vassals of the shoguns and were under strict control. The warriors gradually became scholars and bureaucrats under the *bushido*, or code of chivalry, and the principles of neo-Confucianism. Under the Meji Restoration of 1868, the emperor again received power and the samurai class lost its special privileges.

Chinese and Indian Empires. In the third century BCE, the Indian kingdoms fell under the Mauryan Empire. The grandson of the founder of this empire, named Ashoka, opened a new era in the cultural history of India by believing in the Buddhist religion.

Buddha had disregarded the Vedic gods and the institutions of caste and had preached a relatively simple ethical religion that advocated two levels of aspiration—a monastic life of renunciation of the world and a high, but not too difficult, morality for the layman. Although the two religions of Hinduism and Buddhism flourished together for centuries in a tolerant rivalry, Buddhism virtually disappeared from India by the thirteenth century CE.

Chinese civilization originated in the Yellow River Valley, only gradually extending to the southern regions. Three dynasties ruled early China: the Xia or Hsia, the Shang (ca. 1500 to 1122 BCE), and the Zhou (ca. 1122 to 211 BCE). After the Zhou Dynasty fell, China welcomed the teachings of **Confucius**; warfare between states and philosophical speculation created circumstances ripe for such teachings. Confucius made the good order of society depend on an ethical ruler, who would receive advice from scholar-moralists like Confucius himself. In contrast to the Confucians, the Chinese Taoists professed a kind of anarchism; the best kind of government was none at all. The wise man did not concern himself with political affairs but with mystical contemplation that identified him with the forces of nature.

African Kingdoms and Cultures. The **Bantu** peoples lived across large sections of Africa. Bantu societies lived in tiny chiefdoms, starting in the third millennium

BCE, and each group developed its own version of the original Bantu language.

The **Nok** people lived in the area now known as Nigeria. Artifacts indicate that they were peaceful farmers who built small communities consisting of houses of wattle and daub (poles and sticks). The **Ghanaians** lived about 500 miles from what is now Ghana. Their kingdom fell to a Berber group in the late eleventh century CE, and Mali emerged as the next great kingdom in the thirteenth century. The Malians lived in a huge kingdom that lay mostly on the savanna bordering the Sahara Desert. Timbuktu, built in the thirteenth century CE, was a thriving city of culture where traders visited **stone houses**, **shops**, **libraries**, **and mosques**.

The Songhai lived near the Niger River and gained their independence from the Mali in the early 1400s. The major growth of the empire came after 1464 CE, under the leadership of Sunni Ali, who devoted his reign to warfare and expansion of the empire.

Civilizations of the Americas. The great civilizations of early America were agricultural, and the foremost civilization was the Mayan in Yucatan, Guatemala, and eastern Honduras. Farther north in Mexico, a series of advanced cultures arose that derived much of their substance from the Maya. Peoples, such as the Zapotecs, Totonacs, Olmecs, and Toltecs, evolved into a high level of civilization. By 500 BCE, agricultural peoples had begun to use a **ceremonial calendar** and had built **stone pyramids** on which they held religious observances.

The Aztecs then took over Mexican culture, and a major feature of their culture was human sacrifice in repeated propitiation of their chief god. Aztec government was centralized, with an elective king and a large army. Andean civilization was characterized by the evolution of **beautifully made pottery**, **intricate fabrics**, **and flat-topped mounds**, or *huacas*.

In the interior of South America, the Inca, who called themselves "Children of the Sun," controlled an area stretching from Ecuador to central Chile. Sun worshippers, they believed that they were the sun god's vice regents on earth and were more powerful than any other humans. They believed that every person's place in society was fixed and immutable and that the state and the army were supreme. They were at the apex of their power just before the Spanish conquest.

In the present-day southwestern United States and northern Mexico, two varieties of ancient culture are still identifiable. The Anasazi developed **adobe architecture**, worked the land extensively, had a highly developed system of **irrigation**, and made cloth and baskets. The Hohokam built separate stone and timber houses around a central plaza.

Europe in Antiquity. The Frankish Kingdom was the most important medieval Germanic state. Under Clovis I (reigned 481–511 CE), the Franks finished conquering France and the Gauls in 486 CE. Clovis converted to Christianity and founded the Merovingian dynasty.

Charles the Great, or **Charlemagne** (reigned 768–814 CE), founded the Carolingian dynasty. In 800 CE, Pope Leo III named Charlemagne Emperor of the Holy Roman Empire. In the Treaty of Aix-la-Chapelle (812 CE), the Byzantine emperor recognized Charles's authority in the West. The purpose of the Holy Roman Empire was to reestablish the Roman Empire in the West. Charles's son, Louis the Pious (reigned 814–840 CE), succeeded him. On Louis's death, his three sons vied for control of the Empire. The three eventually signed the Treaty of Verdun in 843 CE. This gave Charles the Western Kingdom (France), Louis the Eastern Kingdom (Germany), and Lothair the Middle Kingdom, a narrow strip of land running from the North Sea to the Mediterranean.

In this period, **manorialism** developed as an economic system in which large estates, granted by the king to nobles, strove for self-sufficiency. The lord and his serfs (also called villeins) divided the ownership.

The church was the only institution to survive the Germanic invasions intact. The power of the popes grew in this period. **Gregory I** (reigned 590–604 CE) was the first member of a monastic order to rise to the papacy. He advanced the ideas of penance and purgatory. He centralized church administration and was the first pope to rule as the secular head of Rome. Monasteries preserved the few remnants that survived the decline of antiquity.

The year 1050 marked the beginning of the High Middle Ages. Europe was poised to emerge from five centuries of decline. Between 1000 and 1350, the population of Europe grew from 38 million to 75 million. New technologies, such as **heavy plows**, and a slight temperature rise produced a longer growing season and contributed to agricultural productivity.

The Holy Roman Empire. Charlemagne's grandson, Louis the German, became Holy Roman Emperor under the Treaty of Verdun. Otto became Holy Roman Emperor in 962. His descendants governed the empire until 1024, when the Franconian dynasty assumed power, reigning until 1125. Under the leadership of **William the Conqueror** (reigned 1066–1087), the Normans conquered England in 1066. William stripped the Anglo-Saxon nobility of its privileges and instituted feudalism. He ordered a survey of all property of the realm; the Domesday Book (1086) records the findings.

William introduced feudalism to England. **Feudalism** was the decentralized political system of personal ties and obligations that bound vassals to their lords. Serfs were peasants who were bound to the land. They worked on the *demesne*, or lord's property, three or four days a week in return for the right to work their own land.

In 1215, the English barons forced King John I to sign the **Magna Carta Libertatum**, acknowledging their "ancient" privileges. The Magna Carta established the principle of a limited English monarchy.

In 710 to 711, the Moors conquered Spain from the Visigoths. Under the Moors, Spain enjoyed a stable, prosperous government. The caliphate of Córdoba became a center of scientific and intellectual activity. The Reconquista (1085–1340) wrested control from the Moors. The fall of Córdoba in 1234 completed the Reconquista, except for the small state of Granada.

Most of eastern Europe and Russia was never under Rome's control; Germanic invasions separated the areas from Western influence. In Russia, Vladimir I converted to Orthodox Christianity in 988. He established the basis of Kievian Russia. After 1054, Russia broke into competing principalities. The **Mongols (Tartars)** invaded in 1221. They completed their conquest in 1245 and cut Russia's contact with the West for almost a century.

The **Crusades** attempted to liberate the Holy Land from infidels. Seven major crusades occurred between 1096 and 1300. Urban II called Christians to the First Crusade (1096–1099) with the promise of a plenary indulgence (exemption from punishment in purgatory). Younger sons who would not inherit their fathers' lands were also attracted. The Crusades helped to renew interest in the ancient world. However, the Crusaders massacred thousands of Jews and Muslims, and relations between Europe and the Byzantine Empire collapsed.

Scholasticism. Scholasticism was an effort to reconcile reason and faith and to instruct Christians on how to make sense of the pagan tradition. The most influential proponent of this effort was Thomas Aquinas (ca. 1225–1274), who believed that there were two orders of truth. The lower level, reason, could demonstrate propositions such as the existence of God, but the higher level necessitated that some of God's mysteries, such as the nature of the Trinity, be accepted on faith. Aquinas viewed the universe as a great chain of being, with humans midway on the chain, between the material and the spiritual.

Late Middle Ages and the Renaissance

The Black Death. Conditions in Europe encouraged the quick spread of disease. Refuse, excrement, and dead animals filled the streets of the cities, which lacked any form of urban sanitation. Living conditions were overcrowded, with families often sleeping in one room or one bed; poor nutrition was rampant; and there was often little personal cleanliness. Merchants helped bring the plague to Asia; carried by fleas on rats, the disease arrived in Europe in 1347. By 1350, the disease had killed 25 percent to 40 percent of the European population.

Literature, Art, and Scholarship. Humanists, as both orators and poets, often imitated the classical works that inspired them. The literature of the period was more secular and wide ranging than that of the Middle Ages. **Dante Alighieri** (1265–1321) was a Florentine writer whose *Divine Comedy*, describing a journey through hell, purgatory, and heaven, shows that reason can take people only so far, and that attaining heaven requires God's grace and revelation. Francesco Petrarch (1304–1374) encouraged the study of ancient Rome, collected and preserved works of ancient writers, and produced a large body of work in the classical literary style.

Giovanni Boccaccio (1313–1375) wrote *The Decameron*, a collection of short stories that the Italian author meant to amuse, not edify, the reader. Artists also broke with the medieval past, in both technique and content. Renaissance art sometimes used religious topics but often dealt with secular themes or portraits of individuals. Oil paints, chiaroscuro, and linear perspectives produced works of energy in three dimensions.

Leonardo da Vinci (1452–1519) produced numerous works, including *The Last Supper* and *Mona Lisa*.

Raphael Santi (1483–1520), a master of Renaissance grace and style, theory, and technique, brought all his skills to his painting *The School of Athens*. Michelangelo Buonarroti (1475–1564) produced masterpieces in architecture, sculpture (*David*), and painting (the Sistine Chapel ceiling). His work was a bridge to a new, non-Renaissance style: mannerism.

Renaissance scholars were more practical and secular than medieval ones. **Manuscript collections** enabled scholars to study the primary sources and to reject traditions established since classical times. Also, scholars participated in the lives of their cities as active politicians. Leonardo Bruni (1370–1444), a civic humanist, served as chancellor of Florence, where he used his rhetorical skills to rouse the citizens against external enemies. Niccolo **Machiavelli** (1469–1527) wrote *The Prince*, which analyzed politics from the standpoint of expedience rising above morality in the name of maintaining political power.

The Reformation. The Reformation destroyed western Europe's religious unity and introduced new ideas about the relationships among God, the individual, and society. Politics greatly influenced the course of the Reformation and led, in most areas, to the subjection of the church to the political rulers.

Martin Luther (1483–1546), to his personal distress, could not reconcile the sinfulness of humans with the justice of God. During his studies of the Bible, Luther came to believe that personal efforts—good works such as a Christian life and attention to the sacraments of the church—could not "earn" the sinner salvation but that belief and faith were the only way to obtain grace. By 1515, Luther believed that "justification by faith alone" was the road to salvation.

On October 31, 1517, Luther nailed 95 theses, or statements, about **indulgences** (the cancellation of a sin in return for money) to the door of the Wittenberg church and challenged the practice of selling them. At this time he was seeking to reform the church, not divide it. In 1519, Luther presented various criticisms of the church and declared that only the Bible, not religious traditions or papal statements, could determine correct religious practices and beliefs. In 1521, Pope Leo X excommunicated Luther for his beliefs.

In 1536 **John Calvin** (1509–1564), a Frenchman, arrived in Geneva, a Swiss city-state that had adopted an anti-Catholic position. In 1540, Geneva became the center of the Reformation. Calvin's *Institutes of the Christian Religion* (1536), a strictly logical analysis of Christianity, had a universal appeal. Calvin emphasized the doctrine of **predestination**, which indicated that God knew who would obtain salvation before those people were born. Calvin believed that church and state should unite. Calvinism triumphed as the majority religion in Scotland, under the leadership of John Knox (ca. 1514–1572), and in the United Provinces of the Netherlands. Puritans in England and New England also accepted Calvinism.

The Thirty Years' War. Between 1618 and 1648, the European powers fought a series of wars. The reasons for the wars varied; religious, dynastic, commercial, and territorial rivalries all played a part. The battles were fought over most of Europe and ended with the Treaty of Westphalia in 1648. The Thirty Years' War changed the boundaries of most European countries.

Explorations and Conquests. Between 1394 and 1460 (Prince Henry the Navigator's lifespan) and afterward, a period of exploration and conquests characterized European history. "Section 5: Causes and Consequences of Exploration, Settlement, and Growth" includes more information on the people and the explorations of the period.

Section 4: Revolution and the New World Order

The Scientific Revolution

For the first time in human history, the eighteenth century saw the appearance of a secular worldview: the Age of Enlightenment. The philosophical starting point for the Enlightenment was the belief in the autonomy of man's intellect apart from God. The most basic assumption was faith in reason rather than faith in revelation. René Descartes (1596–1650) sought a basis for logic and believed he found it in man's ability to think. "I think; therefore, I am" was his most famous statement.

Benedict de Spinoza (1632–1677) developed a rational pantheism in which he equated God and nature.

He denied all free will and ended up with an impersonal, mechanical universe. Gottfried Wilhelm Leibniz (1646–1716) worked on symbolic logic and calculus and invented a calculating machine. He, too, had a mechanistic view of the world and life and thought of God as a hypothetical abstraction rather than a persona.

John Locke (1632–1704) pioneered the empiricist approach to knowledge; he stressed the importance of the environment in human development. Locke classified knowledge as either (1) according to reason, (2) contrary to reason, or (3) above reason. Locke thought reason and revelation were complementary and from God.

The Enlightenment's Effect on Society

The Enlightenment affected more than science and religion. New political and economic theories originated as well. John Locke and **Jean-Jacques Rousseau** (1712–1778) believed that people were capable of governing themselves, either through a political (Locke) or social (Rousseau) contract forming the basis of society.

Most philosophers opposed democracy, preferring a limited monarchy that shared power with the nobility. The assault on mercantilist economic theory was begun by the physiocrats in France; the physiocrats proposed a laissez-faire (minimal governmental interference) attitude toward land usage. The culmination of their beliefs was the theory of economic capitalism associated with Adam Smith (1723–1790) and his notions of free trade, free enterprise, and the law of supply and demand.

The French Revolution

The increased criticism directed toward governmental inefficiency and corruption and toward the privileged classes demonstrated the rising expectations of "enlightened" society in France. The remainder of the population (called the Third Estate) consisted of the middle class, urban workers, and the mass of peasants, who bore the entire burden of taxation and the imposition of feudal obligations.

The most notorious event of the French Revolution was the so-called Reign of Terror (1793–1794), the government's campaign against its internal enemies and counterrevolutionaries. **Louis XVI** faced charges of treason, declared guilty, and suffered execution on January 21, 1793. Later the same year, the queen, **Marie Antoinette**, met the same fate.

The middle class controlled the Directory (1795–1799). Members of the Directory believed that through peace they would gain more wealth and establish a society in which money and property would become the only requirements for prestige and power. Rising inflation and mass public dissatisfaction led to the downfall of the Directory.

The Era of Napoleon

On December 25, 1799, a new government and constitution concentrated supreme power in the hands of **Napoleon**. Napoleon's domestic reforms and policies affected every aspect of society.

French-ruled peoples viewed Napoleon as a tyrant who repressed and exploited them for France's glory and advantage. Enlightened reformers believed Napoleon had betrayed the ideals of the Revolution. The downfall of Napoleon resulted from his inability to conquer England, economic distress caused by the Continental System (boycott of British goods), the Peninsular War with Spain, the German War of Liberation, and the invasion of Russia. The actual defeat of Napoleon occurred at the **Battle of Waterloo** in 1815.

The Industrial Revolution

The term *Industrial Revolution* describes a period of transition, when machines began to significantly displace human and animal power in methods of producing and distributing goods and when an agricultural and commercial society became an industrial one.

Roots of the Industrial Revolution are evident in

- the Commercial Revolution (1500–1700) that spurred the great economic growth of Europe and brought about the Age of Discovery and Exploration, which in turn helped to solidify the economic doctrines of mercantilism;

- the effect of the Scientific Revolution, which produced the first wave of mechanical inventions and technological advances;

- the increase in population in Europe from 140 million people in 1750 to 266 million people by the mid-nineteenth century (more producers, more consumers);

- the nineteenth century political and social revolutions that began the rise to power of the middle class and that provided leadership for the economic revolution.

A transportation revolution ensued to distribute the productivity of machinery and to deliver raw materials to the eager factories. This led to the growth of canal systems; the construction of hard-surfaced **"macadam" roads**; the commercial use of the **steamboat**, which **Robert Fulton** (1765–1815) demonstrated; and the **railway locomotive**, which **George Stephenson** (1781–1848) made commercially successful.

The Industrial Revolution created a unique new category of people who depended on their jobs for income and who needed job security. Until 1850, workers as a whole did not share in the general wealth produced by the Industrial Revolution. Conditions improved as the century neared an end. Union action combined with general prosperity and a developing social conscience to improve the working conditions, wages, and hours of skilled labor first and unskilled labor later.

Socialism

The Utopian Socialists were the earliest writers to propose an equitable solution to improve the distribution of society's wealth. The name of this group comes from *Utopia*, **Saint Thomas More's** (1478–1535) book on a fictional ideal society. While they endorsed the productive capacity of industrialism, the Utopian Socialists denounced its mismanagement. Human society was ideally a community rather than a mixture of competing, selfish individuals. All the goods a person needed could be produced in one community.

Scientific socialism, or **Marxism**, was the creation of **Karl Marx** (1818–1883), a German scholar who, with the help of **Friedrich Engels** (1820–1895), intended to replace utopian hopes and dreams with a militant blueprint for socialist working-class success. The principal works of this revolutionary school of socialism were *The Communist Manifesto* and *Das Kapital*.

Marxism has four key propositions:

1. An economic interpretation of history that asserts that economic factors (mainly centered on who controls the means of production and distribution) determines all human history

2. The belief that there has always been a class struggle between the rich and the poor (or the exploiters and the exploited)

3. The theory of surplus value, which holds that the true value of a product is labor; because workers receive a small portion of their just labor price, the difference is surplus value "stolen" from workers by capitalists

4. The belief that socialism is inevitable because capitalism contains the seeds of its own destruction (overproduction, unemployment, etc.). The rich grow richer and the poor grow poorer until the gap between each class (proletariat and bourgeoisie) becomes so great that the working classes rise up in revolution and overthrow the elite bourgeoisie to install a "dictatorship of the proletariat." The creation of a classless society guided by the principle "from each according to his abilities, to each according to his needs" will be the result from dismantling capitalism.

Section 5: Causes and Consequences of Exploration, Settlement, and Growth

Beginnings of European Exploration

Europeans were largely unaware of the existence of the American continent, even though a Norse seaman, **Leif Eriksson**, had sailed within sight of the continent in the eleventh century. Few other explorers ventured nearly as far as America. Before the fifteenth century, Europeans had little desire to explore and were not ready to face the many challenges of a long sea voyage. Just as developments led to changes and conflict in North America and produced an increasing number of distinct cultures and systems, developments in Europe were about to make possible the great voyages that led to contact between Europe and the Americas. In the fifteenth and sixteenth centuries, technological devices such as the **compass** and **astrolabe** freed explorers from some of the constraints that had limited early voyages. Three primary factors—God, gold, and glory—led to increased interest in exploration and eventually to a desire to settle in the newly discovered lands.

Although Europeans, such as Italians, participated in overland trade with the East and sailed through the Mediterranean and beyond, it was the Arabs who played the largest part in such trade and who benefited the most economically. **Prince Henry the Navigator**, ruler of Portugal, sponsored voyages aimed at adding territory and gaining control of trading routes to increase the power and wealth of Portugal. Prince Henry also wanted to spread Christianity and prevent the further expansion of Islam in Africa. Henry the Navigator brought a number of Italian merchant traders to his court at Cape St. Vincent, and subsequently they sailed in Portuguese ships down the western coast of Africa. These initial voyages were extremely difficult because they lacked navigational instruments and any kind of maps or charts. Europeans had charted the entire Mediterranean Sea, including harbors and the coastline, but they had no knowledge or maps of the African coast.

The first task of the explorers was to create accurate charts of the African shoreline. The crews on these initial voyages did not encounter horrible monsters or boiling water, which rumors had said existed in the ocean beyond Cape Bojador, the farthest point Europeans had previously reached. They did discover, however, that strong southward winds made it easy to sail out of the Mediterranean but difficult to return.

Most people believed that Africa and China were joined by a southern continent, eliminating any possibility of an eastern maritime route to the Indian Ocean. Prince Henry, however, sent ships along the coast of Africa because he believed it was possible to sail east through the Atlantic and reach the Indian Ocean.

Technical Innovations Aiding Exploration

One of the reasons that the explorers sailing from Portugal traveled along the coast was to avoid losing sight of land. By the thirteenth century, explorers were using the compass, borrowed from China, to determine direction; it was more difficult to determine the relative position from the North and South Poles and from landmasses or anything else. In the Northern Hemisphere, a navigator could determine the relative north-south position, or latitude, by calculating the height of the **Pole Star** from the horizon. South of the equator, one cannot see the Pole Star; until around 1460, captains had no way to determine their position if they sailed too far south. Although longitude (relative east-west position) remained unknown until the eighteenth century, the introduction of the astrolabe allowed sailors to calculate their latitude south of the equator.

Along with navigational aids, improvements in ship-building and in weaponry also facilitated exploration. Unlike the Mediterranean, it was not possible to use ships propelled only by oarsmen in the Atlantic because the waves were high and the currents and winds were strong. Europeans had initially used very broad sails on ships that went out into the Atlantic; the ships were heavy and often became stranded by the absence of the favorable tailwinds upon which the ships and sailors depended.

The Portuguese borrowed techniques from Arab and European shipbuilding and developed the Caravela Redondo. This ship proved to be more worthy of long voyages because it combined square rigging for speed with lateen sails that were more responsive and easier to handle. Other European states adopted the ship and also the practice of mounting artillery and other weapons on exploration vessels.

Main Elements of European Exploration

As the Portuguese began to trade and explore along the coast of Africa, they brought back slaves, ivory, gold, and knowledge of the African coast. It looked as though the Portuguese might find a route to the Indian Ocean, and it was clear that the voyages sponsored by Prince Henry were benefiting Portugal in many ways.

Other European states wanted to increase their territory and wealth and to establish trade routes to the East. Although the desire for control of trade routes and wealth was a primary motive in launching voyages of exploration, it was not the only incentive.

Europe in the fifteenth and sixteenth centuries, despite the increase in dissenting views, was still extremely religious. The Catholic Church continued to exert a tremendous influence, and some Christians were motivated to go on voyages of discovery to conduct missionary activities and spread the word of God. In addition, after the beginning of the Reformation, many Lutherans, Calvinists, and other groups who had left the Catholic Church emigrated from Europe in the hopes of settling where they would be free from religious persecution or violent conflicts.

Other individuals sponsored or participated in voyages in the hope of gaining wealth or increased opportunities. For example, younger sons of families in Europe were able to secure prominent positions in the church, but they were often not able to find lucrative opportunities at home because the eldest son usually inherited lands and wealth. The voyages of exploration were a means of securing fame and fortune and of obtaining opportunities that would not be available otherwise.

Although the motivation of fame and fortune was often secondary to God and glory, many individuals were attracted to exploration by the possibility of adventure and by their desire to explore uncharted territory. These three factors—gold, God, and glory—operated on both individual and state levels; kings and heads of states were as interested as the seamen were in spreading their faith and increasing the wealth and prestige of their states.

Portugal was the first European state to establish sugar plantations on an island off the west coast of Africa and to import slaves from Africa to labor there. This marked the beginning of the slave trade. The level of trading was initially far less extensive and intense than during the later period of slave trade when Spain and England became involved. In an attempt to maintain control of the slave trade and of the eastern routes to India, the Portuguese appealed to the pope; he ruled in their favor and forbade the Spanish and others to sail south and east in an attempt to reach India or Asia.

When **Ferdinand and Isabella** married and united Spain's two largest provinces (Castile and Aragon), they not only began the process of uniting all of Spain but also agreed to sponsor **Christopher Columbus** in his voyage of exploration. Only the heads of states had the necessary resources and could afford the risk involved in sponsoring a major voyage across the oceans of the world, but most monarchs were unwilling to take such a risk. Columbus was an Italian explorer looking for a sponsor and had approached Ferdinand and Isabella after being turned down by the English government. He convinced the Spanish monarchs that a western route to the Indian Ocean existed and that it would be possible to make the voyage.

However, Columbus had miscalculated the distance of the voyage from Europe to Asia. His estimate of the circumference of the earth was much less than it should have been for an accurate calculation, and no Europeans were aware of the existence of the American continents. One of the reasons that Ferdinand and Isabella were willing to support Columbus was that the previous agreements prevented all states but Portugal from sailing east to reach India. Therefore, the only chance for Spain to launch an expedition to India and to participate in trade and exploration was in the discovery of a western route to India.

European Contact with the Americas

In 1492, Columbus sailed from Spain with 90 men on three ships, the *Niña*, the *Pinta*, and the *Santa María*. After a 10-week voyage, they landed in the Bahamas. On his second trip, Columbus reached Cuba, and then in 1498, during his third trip, he reached the mainland and sailed along the northern coast of South America. Columbus originally thought he had reached India; he referred to the people he encountered in the Bahamas and on his second landing in Cuba as Indians.

There is considerable debate over whether Columbus realized, either during his third voyage or just before his death, that he had landed not in India but on an entirely unknown continent between Europe and Asia. Another question is whether Columbus, who died in obscurity despite his fame for having discovered America, should receive credit for this discovery; earlier explorers had reached the American continent.

However, because Columbus's voyages prompted extensive exploration and settlement of the Americas, it is accurate to state that he was responsible for the discovery of the New World by Europeans. Another result of Columbus's voyages was the increased focus of Spain on exploration and conquest. Nevertheless, the New World took its name from the Florentine merchant **Amerigo Vespucci**—not Columbus. Vespucci took part in several voyages to the New World and wrote a series of descriptions that not only gave Europeans an image of this "New World" but also spread the idea that the discovered lands were not a part of Asia or India. Vespucci, then, popularized the image of the Americas and the idea that the Americas were continents separate from those previously known.

It was a Portuguese navigator, **Vasco da Gama**, who crossed the Isthmus of Panama and came to another ocean, which separates the American continents from China. The Spanish sponsored another Portuguese sailor, **Ferdinand Magellan**, who discovered at the southern end of South America a strait that provided access to the ocean west of the Americas. Magellan named this ocean the Pacific because it was much calmer than the strait through which he had sailed to reach it. Later, he reached the Philippines and met his death in a conflict with the natives. Magellan's voyage, nevertheless, was the final stage of the process whereby Europeans completed the first-known circumnavigation of the globe. Although initially the Spanish were eager to find a route around the Americas that would enable them to sail on toward their original goal, the treasures of the Far East, they began to consider the Americas as a possible source of untapped wealth.

The Spanish claimed all the New World except Brazil, which papal decree gave to the Portuguese. The first Spanish settlements were on the islands of the Caribbean Sea. It was not until 1518 that Spain appointed **Hernando Cortez** as a government official in Cuba; Cortez led a small military expedition against the Aztecs in Mexico. Cortez and his men failed in their first attack on the Aztec capital city, Tenochtitlan, but were ultimately successful.

A combination of factors allowed the small force of approximately 600 Spanish soldiers to overcome the extensive Aztec Empire. The Spanish were armed with rifles and bows, which provided an advantage over Aztec fighters armed only with spears. However, weapons and armor were not the main reason that the Spanish were able to overcome the military forces of the natives.

The Aztec ruler, Montezuma, allowed a delegation, which included Cortez, into the capital city because the description of the Spanish soldiers in their armor and with feathers in their helmets was similar to the description in Aztec legend of messengers who would be sent by the chief Aztec god, Quetzcoatl. The members of Cortez's expedition exposed the natives to smallpox and other diseases that devastated the native population. Finally, the Spanish expedition was able to form alliances with other native tribes that the Aztecs had conquered; these tribes were willing to cooperate to defeat the Aztecs and thus break up their empire.

Twenty years after Cortez defeated the Aztecs, another conquistador, Francisco Pizarro, defeated the Incas in Peru. Pizarro's expedition enabled the Spanish to begin to explore and settle South America. Spain funded the conquistadors, or conquerors, who were the first Europeans to explore some areas of the Americas. However, the sole purpose of the conquistadors' explorations was defeating the natives to gain access to gold, silver, and other wealth. Spain established mines in the territory it claimed and produced a tremendous amount of gold and silver. In the 300 years after the Spanish conquest of the Americas in the sixteenth century, those mines produced 10 times more gold and silver than the total produced by all the mines in the rest of the world.

Spain had come to view the New World as more than an obstacle to voyages toward India; over time, Spain began to think that it might be possible to exploit this territory for more than just mining. It was the conquistadors who made it possible for the Spanish to settle the New World, but they were not responsible for forming settlements or for overseeing Spanish colonies in the New World. Instead, Spain sent officials and administrators from Spain to oversee settlements after their initial formation.

Spanish settlers came to the New World for various reasons: some went in search of land to settle or buy, others went looking for opportunities that were not available to them in Europe, and priests and missionaries went to spread Christianity to the natives. By the end of the sixteenth century, Spain had established firm control over not only the several islands in the Caribbean, Mexico, and southern North America but also in the territory currently within the modern states of Chile, Argentina, and Peru.

Spanish Settlements in the New World

The first permanent settlement established by the Spanish was the predominantly military fort of St. Augustine, located in Florida. In 1598, Don Juan de Onate led a group of 500 settlers north from Mexico and established a colony in what is now New Mexico.

Onate granted *encomiendas* to the most prominent Spaniards who had accompanied him. Under the *encomienda* system, which the Spanish in Mexico and parts of North America established, these distinguished individuals had the right to exact tribute and/or labor from the native population, which continued to live on the land in exchange for the services it provided.

Spanish colonists founded Santa Fe in 1609, and by 1680 about 2,000 Spaniards were living in New Mexico. Most of the colonists raised sheep and cattle on large ranches and lived among approximately 30,000 Pueblo Indians. The Spanish crushed a major revolt that threatened to destroy Santa Fe in 1680. Attempts to prevent the natives—both those who had converted to Catholicism and those who had not—from performing religious rituals that predated the Spaniards' arrival provoked the revolt. The natives drove the Spanish from Santa Fe, but they returned in 1696, crushed the Pueblos, and seized the land. Although the Spanish ultimately quelled the revolt, they began to change their policies toward the natives, who still greatly outnumbered the Spanish settlers.

The Spanish continued to try to Christianize and "civilize" the native population, but they also began to allow the Pueblos to own land. In addition, the Spanish unofficially tolerated native religious rituals although Catholicism officially condemned all such practices. By 1700, the Spanish population in New Mexico had increased and reached about 4,000; the native population had decreased to about 13,000 and intermarriage between natives and Spaniards increased.

Nevertheless, disease, war, and migration resulted in the steady decline in the Pueblo population. New Mexico had become a prosperous and stable region, but it was still relatively weak and, as the only major Spanish settlement in northern Mexico, was isolated.

Effects of European-American Contact

One cannot underestimate the impact of Europeans on the New World, both before and after the arrival of the English and French. The most immediate effect was the spread of disease, which decimated the native population. In some areas of Mexico, for example, 95 percent of the native population died as a result of contact with Europeans and the subsequent outbreaks of diseases like smallpox. In South America, the native population was devastated not only by disease but also by deliberate policies instituted to control and in some cases eliminate native peoples.

Although Europeans passed most diseases to the natives, the natives passed syphilis to the Europeans, who carried it back to Europe.

The European and American continents exchanged plants and animals. Europeans brought over animals to the New World, and they took plants, such as potatoes, corn, and squash, back to Europe, where introduction of these crops led to an explosion of the European population. The decimation of the native population and the establishment of large plantations led to a shortage of workers, and Europeans began to transport slaves from Africa to the New World to fill the shortage.

Section 6: Continued Exploration, Settlement, and Revolution in the "New World."

Topic 1.
Identifying Individuals and Events That Have Influenced Economic, Social, and Political Institutions in the United States

European Settlement and Development in North America

In 1497, King Henry VIII of England sponsored a voyage by **John Cabot** to try to discover a northwest passage through the New World to the Orient. However, the English made no real attempt to settle in the New World until nearly a century later. By the 1600s, the English became interested in colonizing the New World for several reasons.

Many people in England emigrated overseas because the country's population was increasing and because much of the land was being used for raising sheep for wool rather than for growing foodstuffs for survival. Scarce opportunities, like those for buying land, were primary motivators for emigration from England.

Some people in England left their homeland because of the religious turmoil that engulfed England after the beginning of the Protestant Reformation. In addition to converts to Lutheranism and Calvinism, a major emigrating group was the Puritans, who called for reforms to "purify" the church.

Mercantilism also provided a motive for exploration and for the establishment of colonies. According to mercantile theories, an industrialized nation needed an inexpensive source of raw materials and markets for finished products. Colonies provided a way to obtain raw materials and to guarantee a market for industrial goods.

Economic reasons, among others, motivated the French and the Dutch to explore and establish colonies in the New World. In 1609, the year after the first English settlement, the French established a colony in Quebec. Overall, far fewer French settlers traveled to the New World than did English settlers, but the French were able to exercise a tremendous influence through the establishment of strong ties with the natives. The French created trading partnerships and a vast trading network; they often intermarried with the local native population.

The Dutch financed an English explorer, **Henry Hudson**, who claimed for Holland the territory that is now New York. The Dutch settlements along the Hudson, Delaware, and Connecticut rivers developed into the colony of New Netherlands and established a vast trading network that effectively separated the English colonies of Jamestown and Plymouth.

One reason that English settlements began to become more prominent after 1600 was the defeat of the Spanish fleet, the supposedly invincible Armada, by the English in 1588. The changing power balance on the seas encouraged the English to increase their exploration and to attempt colonization of the Americas. The first few colonies founded by the English in America did not flourish.

Sir Humphrey Gilbert, who had obtained a six-year grant giving him the exclusive rights to settle any unclaimed land in America, was planning to establish a colony in Newfoundland, but a storm sank his ship. Instead, **Sir Walter Raleigh** received the six-year grant. Raleigh explored the North American coast and named the territory through which he traveled Virginia, in honor of the "Virgin Queen" Elizabeth I of England. In addition, Raleigh convinced his cousin Sir Grenville to establish a colony on the island of Roanoke.

Roanoke was off the coast of what later became North Carolina. The first settlers lived there for a year while Sir Grenville returned to England for supplies and additional settlers. However, when Sir Francis Drake arrived in Roanoke nearly a year later and found that Sir Grenville had not yet returned, the colonists left on his ship and abandoned the settlement. In 1587, Raleigh sent another group of colonists to Roanoke, but a war with Spain broke out in 1588 and kept him from returning until 1590. When Raleigh returned to Roanoke, the colonists had vanished and had left only one clue: a single word, *Croatan*, carved into a tree. This word could have referred to a nearby settlement of natives whom they might have joined or who might have attacked them. This suggested a number of possibilities in regard to the missing settlers; conclusive proof of their fate was never found.

Colonization: The Jamestown Settlement

In 1606, King James I of England granted to the Virginia Company a charter for exploration and colonization. This charter marked the beginning of ventures sponsored by merchants rather than directly by the Crown. The charter of the Virginia Company had two branches. James I gave one branch to the English city of Plymouth, which had the right to the northern portion of territory on the eastern coast of North America, and he granted the London branch of the company the right to the southern portion.

Considerable difficulties prevented the English from founding and maintaining a permanent settlement in North America. The Plymouth Company failed to establish a lasting settlement. The company itself ran out of money, and the settlers who had gone to the New World gave up and abandoned their established Sagadahoc Colony in Maine.

Having decided to colonize the Chesapeake Bay area, the London Company sent three ships with about 104 sailors to that area in 1607. The company's ships sailed up a river, which they named the James in honor of the English king, and they established the fort and permanent settlement of Jamestown. The London Company and the men who settled Jamestown were hoping to find a northwest passage to Asia, gold, and silver or to be able to find lands capable of producing valuable goods, such as grapes, oranges, or silk.

The colony at Jamestown did not allow the settlers to accomplish any of those things. Its location on the river, which became contaminated every spring, led to the outbreak of diseases such as typhoid, dysentery, and malaria. Over half the colonists died the first year, and by the spring of 1609, only one-third of the total number of colonists who had joined the colony were still alive.

The survival of the colony initially was largely accomplished through the efforts of **Captain John Smith**. Smith was a soldier who turned the colony's focus from exploration to obtaining food. Initially, Smith was able to obtain corn from the local Indians led by **Powhatan** and his 12-year-old daughter, **Pocahontas**. Smith also forced all able men in the colony to work four hours a day in the wheat fields. Attempts by the London Company to send additional settlers and supplies encountered troubles and delays.

Thomas Gates and some 600 settlers, who left for Jamestown in 1609, ran aground on Bermuda and had to build a new ship. Although some new settlers did arrive in Jamestown, disease continued to shrink the population. When a seriously injured Smith had to return to England, his departure deprived the colony of its most effective and resourceful leader.

It was not long after Smith left that the colonists provoked a war with Powhatan, who was beginning to tire of the colonists' demands for corn. Powhatan realized that the settlers intended to stay indefinitely and might challenge the Indians for control of the surrounding territory.

Gates finally arrived in June 1610 with only 175 of the original 600 settlers. He found only 60 colonists who had survived the war with the Indians and the harsh winter of 1610, during which they had minimal food and other resources. Gates decided to abandon Jamestown and was sailing down the river with the surviving colonists on board when he encountered the new governor from England, **Thomas West**, Baron de la Warr. Gates and West returned to Jamestown, imposed martial law, responded to Indian attacks, and survived a five-year war with the Indians. Although the war did not end until 1614, when the colonists were able to negotiate a settlement by holding Pocahontas hostage, the situation in Jamestown began to improve in 1610.

Some of the settlers went to healthier locations, and in 1613 one of them, **John Rolfe**, married Pocahontas. In 1614, the settlers planted a mild strain of tobacco, which gave them a crop they could sell for cash. The Crown issued two new charters that allowed Virginia to extend its borders all the way to the Pacific and made the London Company a joint-stock company. Changes in the company led to a new treasurer, **Sir Edwin Sandy**, who tried to reform Virginia.

Sandy encouraged settlers in Virginia to try to produce grapes and silkworms and to diversify the colony's economy in other ways. Sandy also replaced martial law with English common law. The colonists established a council to make laws, and settlers now had the right to own land. By 1623, about 4,000 additional settlers had arrived in Virginia. Attempts to produce and sell crops other than tobacco, however, failed, and the arrival of large numbers of new colonists provoked renewed conflict with the Indians. A major Indian attack launched in March 1622 killed 347 colonists.

Investors in the London Company withdrew their capital and appealed to the king, and a royal commission visited the colony. As a result of this investigation, the king declared the London Company bankrupt and assumed direct control of Virginia in 1624. Virginia became the first royal colony, and the Crown appointed a governor and a council to oversee its administration. Three trends continued after the Crown assumed control. The first was unrelenting conflict with the Indians. Through war and raids, by 1632 the colonists had killed or driven out most of the Indians in the area immediately around Jamestown. The other two trends were the yearly influx of thousands of new settlers and the high death rate in the colony.

Despite the high mortality rate, the population of the colony began gradually to increase. The expansion of tobacco production led to a demand for labor, and thousands of the young men who came were indentured servants. In exchange for their passage to America and food and shelter during their terms of service, these men were bound to work for their masters for four or five years. After that time, they gained their freedom and often a small payment to help them become established. Most of these men were not able to participate in the running of the colony even after they became free, but some were able to acquire land.

In 1634, the Crown divided Virginia into counties, each with appointed justices and the right to fill all other positions. Under this type of system, individuals from a few wealthy families tended to dominate the government. Most of the counties became Anglican, and the colony continued to elect representatives to its House of Burgesses, an assembly that met with the governor to discuss issues of common law. The king, however, refused to recognize the colony's House of Burgesses. After 1660, the colony became even more dominated by the wealthiest 15 percent of the population, and these individuals and their sons continued to be the only colonists to serve as justices and burgesses. Settlement of the colonies continued, primarily for religious and economic reasons. Conflict between the colonists and the natives was a constant.

Growth of the Slave Trade

The shortage of labor in the southern colonies and a drop in the number of people coming to the colonies as indentured servants forced the colonists to search for other sources of labor. Although the colonists began using African servants and slaves almost immediately after settling in the New World, the slave trade and the slave population in British North America remained small in the first half of the seventeenth century. Toward the end of the seventeenth century, increasing numbers of slaves from Africa became available, and the demand for them in North America further stimulated the growth of the transatlantic slave trade.

By the nineteenth century, millions of Africans had been forcibly taken from their native lands and sold into perpetual slavery. The Europeans sold slaves at forts the slave traders had established on the African coast; the Europeans packed the slaves as closely as possible into the lower regions of ships for the long journey to the Americas. Chained slaves traveled in deplorably unsanitary conditions and received only enough food and water to keep them alive.

Many slaves died during this Middle Passage voyage. Plantation owners in the Caribbean, Brazil, or North America bought the slaves to do the work. It was only after 1697 that English colonists began to buy large numbers of slaves. By 1760, the slave population had reached approximately a quarter of a million with most of the slaves concentrated in the southern colonies. Slave labor replaced indentured servitude, and a race-based system of perpetual slavery developed. Colonial assemblies began to pass "slave codes" in the eighteenth century. These codes identified all non-whites or dark-skinned people as slaves, made their condition permanent, and legalized slavery in British North America.

Salem Witch Trials

During this period of increasing tensions brought about by fears of the occult, intolerance, and conflicts between the religious community and some less-understood individuals, several areas held witchcraft trials. In Salem, Massachusetts, a group of young girls accused servants from West India and older white members of the community, mostly women, of exercising powers that Satan had given to them. Other towns also experienced turmoil and charged residents with witchcraft. In Salem alone, the juries pronounced 19 people guilty; in 1692, after the execution of all 19 victims, the girls admitted their stories were not true.

The witchcraft trials illustrate the highly religious nature of the New England society, but they also suggest that individuals who did not conform to societal expectations were at risk. Most of the accused were outspoken women who were often critical of their communities, were older, and were either widows or unmarried. Some of these women had acquired property despite the accepted views and limitations regarding women's role in society.

Religion in the Colonies and the Great Awakening

The religious nature of colonial settlers did not lead to the kind of intolerance or persecution that had plagued Europe since the Reformation. Conflict among various religious groups did break out occasionally, but British North America enjoyed a far greater degree of religious toleration than anywhere else. Among the reasons this toleration existed were that several religious groups had immigrated to North America and that every colony, except Virginia and Maryland, ignored the laws establishing the Church of England as the official faith of the colony. Even among the Puritans, differences in religious opinion led to the establishment of different denominations.

Although there was some religious toleration, Protestants still tended to view Roman Catholics as a threatening rival. In Maryland, Catholics numbered about 3,000, the largest population of all the colonies, and were the victims of persecution. Jews were often victims of persecution; they could not vote or hold office in any of the colonies, and only in Rhode Island could they practice the Jewish religion openly.

The other main trends in addition to toleration were the westward spread of communities, the rise of cities, and a decline in religious piousness. This sense of the weakening of religious authority and faithfulness led to the Great Awakening.

The Great Awakening refers to a period beginning in the 1730s in which several well-known preachers traveled through British North America giving speeches and arguing for the need to revive religious piety and closer relationships with God. The main message of the preachers was that everyone has the potential, regardless of past behavior, to reestablish their relationship with God. This message appealed to many women and younger sons of landowners who stood to inherit very little. The best-known preacher during this period was **Jonathan Edwards**. Edwards denounced some current beliefs as doctrines of easy salvation. At his church in Northampton, Massachusetts, Edwards sermonized about the absolute sovereignty of God, predestination, and salvation by grace alone.

The Great Awakening further divided religion in America by creating distinctions among New Light groups (revivalists), Old Light groups (traditionalists), and new groups that incorporated elements of both. The various revivalists, or New Light groups, did not agree on every issue. Some revivalists denounced education and learning from books while others founded schools in the belief that education was a means of furthering religion. While some individuals were stressing a need for renewed spiritual focus, others were beginning to embrace the ideas of the Enlightenment.

As discussed earlier, the Scientific Revolution had demonstrated the existence of natural laws that operated in nature, and enlightened thinkers began to argue that man had the ability to improve his own situation through the use of rational thought and acquired knowledge. Intellectuals of the **Enlightenment** shifted the focus from God to man, introduced the idea of progress, and argued that people could improve their own situations and make decisions on how to live rather than just having faith in God and waiting for a better life after death and salvation.

Enlightenment thought had a tremendous impact on the North American colonists, who began to establish more schools, encourage the acquisition of knowledge, and become more interested in gaining scientific knowledge. The colleges founded in North America taught the scientific theories held by **Copernicus**, who argued that planets rotated around the sun not the earth, and **Sir Isaac Newton**, who introduced the key principles of physics, including gravity.

The colonists did not just learn European theories. **Benjamin Franklin** was among the colonists who began to carry out their own experiments and form their own theories. Franklin experimented with electricity and was able to demonstrate in 1752, by using a kite, that electricity and lightning were the same.

Scientific theories also led to inoculations against smallpox. The Puritan theologian **Cotton Mather** convinced the population of Boston that injections with a small amount of the smallpox virus would build up their resistance to the disease and reduce the likelihood of reinfection. Leading theologians and scientists spread European scientific ideas and developed their own theories and applications using their acquired knowledge.

The American Revolution

The Coming of the American Revolution. In 1764, George Grenville pushed through Parliament the **Sugar Act** (the Revenue Act), which aimed to raise revenue by taxing goods imported by Americans. The **Stamp Act** (1765) imposed a direct tax on the colonists for the first time. By requiring Americans to purchase revenue stamps on everything from newspapers to legal documents, the Stamp Act would have created an impossible drain on hard currency in the colonies.

Americans reacted first with restrained and respectful petitions and pamphlets in which they pointed out that "taxation without representation is tyranny." The colonists began to limit their purchase of imported goods. From there, resistance progressed to stronger protests that eventually became violent. In October 1765, delegates from nine colonies met as the Stamp Act Congress and passed moderate resolutions against the act and asserted that Americans could not be taxed without the consent of their representatives. The colonists now ceased all importation.

In March 1766, Parliament repealed the Stamp Act. At the same time, however, it passed the **Declaratory Act**, which claimed for Parliament the power to tax or make laws for the Americans "in all cases whatsoever." In 1766, Parliament passed a program of taxes on items imported into the colonies. The taxes came to be known as the Townsend duties, a name that came from Britain's chancellor of the exchequer, Charles Townsend. American reaction was at first slow, but the sending of troops aroused them to resistance.

Again the colonies halted importation, and soon British merchants were calling on Parliament to repeal the Townsend duties. In March 1770, Parliament repealed all the taxes except that on tea; Parliament wanted to prove that it had the right to tax the colonies if it so desired. When Parliament ended the **Tea Act** in 1773, a relative peace ensued.

In desperate financial condition—partially because the Americans were buying smuggled Dutch tea rather than the taxed British product—the British East India Company sought and obtained from Parliament concessions that allowed it to ship tea directly to the colonies rather than only by way of Britain. The result would be that the East India Company tea, even with the tax, would be cheaper than smuggled Dutch tea. The company hoped that the colonists would thus buy the tea—tax and all—save the East India Company, and tacitly accept Parliament's right to tax them.

The Americans, however, proved resistant to this approach. Rather than acknowledge Parliament's right to tax, they refused to buy the cheaper tea and resorted to various methods, including tar and feathers, to prevent the collection of the tax on tea. In most ports, Americans did not allow ships carrying the tea to land.

In Boston, however, the pro-British governor **Thomas Hutchinson** forced a confrontation by ordering Royal Navy vessels to prevent the tea ships from leaving the harbor. After 20 days, this would, by law, result in selling the cargoes at auction and paying the tax. The night before the time was to expire, December 16, 1773, Bostonians thinly disguised as Native Americans boarded the ships and threw the tea into the harbor. This was the **Boston Tea Party**.

The British responded with four acts collectively titled the **Coercive Acts** (1774), in which they strengthened their control over the colonists. The **First Continental Congress** (1774) met in response to the acts. The Congress called for strict nonimportation and rigorous preparation of local militia companies.

The War for Independence. British troops went to Massachusetts, which the Crown had officially declared to be in a state of rebellion. General Thomas Gage received orders to arrest the leaders of the resistance or, failing that, to provoke any sort of confrontation that would allow him to turn British military might loose on the Americans. Americans, however, detected the movement of Gage's troops toward Concord, and dispatch riders, like **Paul Revere** and **William Dawes**, spread the news throughout the countryside.

In Lexington, about 70 **minutemen** (trained militiamen who would respond at a moment's notice) awaited the British on the village green. A shot was fired; it is unknown which side fired first. This became "**the shot heard 'round the world**."

The British opened fire and charged. Casualties occurred on both sides. The following month, the Americans tightened the noose around Boston by fortifying Breed's Hill (a spur of Bunker Hill). The British determined to remove them by a frontal attack. Twice thrown back, the British finally succeeded when the Americans ran out of ammunition. There were more than 1,000 British casualties in what turned out to be the bloodiest battle of the war (June 17, 1775), yet the British had gained very little and remained "bottled up" in Boston.

Congress put **George Washington** (1732–1799) in charge of the army, called for more troops, and adopted the Olive Branch Petition, which pleaded with **King George III** to intercede with Parliament to restore peace. However, the king gave his approval to the Prohibitory Act, declaring the colonies in rebellion and no longer under his protection. Preparations began for full-scale war against America.

In 1776, the colonists formed two committees to establish independence and a national government. One was to work out a framework for a national government. The other was to draft a statement of the reasons for declaring independence. The statement, called the **Declaration of Independence**, was primarily the work of Thomas Jefferson (1743–1826) of Virginia. It was a restatement of political ideas by then commonplace in America and showed why the former colonists felt justified in separating from Great Britain. Congress formally adopted the Declaration of Independence on **July 4, 1776**.

The British landed that summer at New York City. Washington, who had anticipated the move, was waiting for them. However, the undertrained, underequipped, and badly outnumbered American army was no match for the British and had to retreat. By December, what was left of Washington's army had made it into Pennsylvania.

With his small army melting away as demoralized soldiers deserted, Washington decided on a bold stroke. On Christmas night 1776, his army crossed the **Delaware River** and struck the Hessians (German mercenaries who often served with the British) at **Trenton, New Jersey**. Washington's troops easily defeated the Hessians, still groggy from their hard-drinking Christmas party.

A few days later, Washington defeated a British force at **Princeton, New Jersey**. The Americans regained much of New Jersey from the British and saved the American army from disintegration.

Hoping to weaken Britain, France began making covert shipments of arms to the Americans early in the war. These French shipments were vital for the Americans. The American victory at Saratoga, New York, convinced the French to join openly in the war against England. Eventually, the Spanish (1779) and the Dutch (1780) joined as well.

The final peace agreement between the new United States and Great Britain became known as the Treaty of Paris of 1783. Its terms stipulated the following:

1. The recognition by the major European powers, including Britain, of the United States as an independent nation.

2. The establishment of America's western boundary at the Mississippi River.

3. The establishment of America's southern boundary at latitude 31° north (the northern boundary of Florida).

4. The surrender of Florida to Spain and the retainment of Canada by Britain.

5. The enablement of private British creditors to collect any debts owed by United States citizens.

6. The recommendation of Congress that the states restore confiscated loyalist property.

New Politicians, New Governments, and Social Change

After the adoption and failure of the Articles of Confederation, Congress adopted a new constitution and the Americans elected George Washington as president under its guidelines.

The Federalist Era. George Washington received virtually all the votes of the presidential electors.

John Adams (1735–1826) received the next highest number and became the vice president. After a triumphant journey from his home at Mount Vernon in Virginia, Washington attended his inauguration in New York City, the temporary seat of government.

To oppose the antifederalists, the states ratified 10 amendments—the Bill of Rights—by the end of 1791. The first 9 spelled out specific guarantees of personal freedoms, and the Tenth Amendment reserved to the states all powers not specifically withheld or granted to the federal government.

Alexander Hamilton (1757–1804) interpreted the Constitution as having vested extensive powers in the federal government. This "implied powers" stance claimed that the government had all powers that the Constitution had not expressly denied it. Hamilton's was the "broad" interpretation of the Constitution.

By contrast, Thomas Jefferson and **James Madison** (1751–1836) held the view that the Constitution prohibited any action not specifically permitted in the Constitution. Based on this view of government, adherents of this "strict" interpretation opposed the establishment of Hamilton's national bank. The Jeffersonian supporters, primarily under the guidance of Madison, began to organize political groups in opposition to Hamilton's program. The groups opposing Hamilton's view called themselves Democratic-Republicans or Jeffersonians.

The Federalists, Hamilton's supporters, received their strongest confirmation from the business and financial groups in the commercial centers of the Northeast and from the port cities of the South. The strength of the Democratic-Republicans lay primarily in the rural and frontier areas of the South and West. Federalist candidate John Adams won the election of 1796. The elections in 1798 increased the Federalists' majorities in both houses of Congress that used their "mandate" to enact legislation to stifle foreign influences.

The **Alien Act** raised new hurdles in the path of immigrants trying to obtain citizenship, and the **Sedition Act** widened the powers of the Adams administration to muzzle its newspaper critics. Democratic-Republicans were convinced that the Alien and Sedition Acts were unconstitutional, but the process of deciding on the constitutionality of federal laws was as yet undefined.

The Jeffersonian Era. Thomas Jefferson and **Aaron Burr** ran for the presidency on the Democratic-Republican ticket, though not together, against John Adams and Charles Pinckney for the Federalists. Both Jefferson and Burr received the same number of votes in the Electoral College, so the election went to the House of Representatives. After a lengthy deadlock, Alexander Hamilton threw his support to Jefferson. Burr had to accept the vice presidency, the result obviously intended by the electorate.

The adoption and ratification of the Twelfth Amendment in 1804 ensured that a tie vote between candidates of the same party could not again cause the confusion of the Jefferson-Burr affair. Following the constitutional mandate, an 1808 law prevented the importation of slaves. An American delegation purchased the trans-Mississippi territory from Napoleon for $15 million in April 1803 (the Louisiana Purchase), even though they had no authority to buy more than the city of New Orleans.

The War of 1812. Democratic-Republican **James Madison** won the election of 1808 over Federalist Charles Pinckney, but the Federalists gained seats in both houses of Congress.

The Native American tribes of the Northwest and the **Mississippi Valley** were resentful of the government's policy of pressured removal to the West, and the British authorities in Canada exploited their discontent by encouraging border raids against the American settlements. At the same time, the British interfered with American transatlantic shipping, including impressing sailors and capturing ships. On June 1, 1812, President Madison asked for a declaration of war, and Congress complied. After three years of inconclusive war, the British and Americans signed the Treaty of Ghent (1815). It provided for the acceptance of the status quo that had existed at the beginning of hostilities, and both sides restored their wartime conquests to the other.

The Monroe Doctrine. As Latin American nations began declaring independence, British and American leaders feared that European governments would try to restore the former New World colonies to their erstwhile royal owners. In December 1823, **President James Monroe** (1758–1831) included in his annual message to Congress a statement that the peoples of the American hemisphere were "henceforth not to be considered as subjects for future colonization by any European powers."

The Marshall Court. Chief Justice **John Marshall** (1755–1835) delivered the majority opinions in several critical decisions in the formative years of the U.S. Supreme Court. These decisions served to strengthen the power of the federal government (and of the court itself) and restrict the powers of state governments. Here are two key examples:

- *Marbury v. Madison* (1803) established the Supreme Court's power of judicial review over federal legislation.
- In *Gibbons v. Ogden* (1824), a case involving competing steamboat companies, Marshall ruled that commerce includes navigation and that only Congress has the right to regulate commerce among states. Marshall's ruling voided the state-granted monopoly.

The Missouri Compromise. The Missouri Territory, the first territory organized from the Louisiana Purchase, applied for statehood in 1819. Because the Senate membership was evenly divided between slaveholding and free states at that time, the admission of a new state would give the voting advantage to either the North or the South. As the debate dragged on, the northern territory of Massachusetts applied for admission as the state of Maine. By combining the two admission bills, the Senate hoped to reach a compromise by admitting Maine as a free state and Missouri as a slave state. To make the Missouri Compromise palatable for the House of Representatives, the Senate added a provision prohibiting slavery in the remainder of the Louisiana Territory north of the southern boundary of Missouri (latitude 36°30′).

Jacksonian Democracy. Andrew Jackson (1767–1845), the candidate of a faction of the emerging Democratic Party, won the election of 1828. Jackson was popular with the common man. He seemed to be the prototype of the self-made westerner: rough-hewn, violent, vindictive, with few ideas but strong convictions. He ignored his appointed cabinet officers and relied instead on the counsel of his "Kitchen Cabinet," a group of partisan supporters. He exercised his veto power more than any other president before him.

Jackson supported the removal of all Native American tribes to an area west of the Mississippi River. The **Indian Removal Act** of 1830 provided for the federal enforcement of that process. One of the results of this policy was the **Trail of Tears**, the forced march under U.S. Army escort of thousands of Cherokee Indians to the West. One-quarter or more of them, mostly women and children, perished on the journey.

The National Bank. The Bank of the United States had operated under the direction of Nicholas Biddle since 1823. He was a cautious man, and his conservative economic policy enforced conservatism among state and private banks—which many bankers resented. In 1832, Jackson vetoed the national bank's renewal, and it ceased being a federal institution in 1836.

The Antislavery Movement. In 1831, **William Lloyd Garrison** started his newspaper the *Liberator* and began to advocate total and immediate emancipation. He founded the New England Antislavery Society in 1832 and the American Antislavery Society in 1833. Theodore Weld pursued the same goals but advocated more gradual means.

The movement split into two wings: Garrison's radical followers and the moderates who favored "moral suasion" and petitions to Congress. In 1840, the Liberty Party, the first national antislavery party, fielded a presidential candidate on the platform of "free soil" (preventing the expansion of slavery into the new western territories).

The Role of Minorities. The women's rights movement focused on social and legal discrimination, and women like Lucretia Mott and Sojourner Truth became well-known figures on the speakers' circuit. By 1850, roughly 200,000 free blacks lived in the North and West. Prejudice restricted their lives, and "Jim Crow" laws separated the races.

Manifest Destiny and Westward Expansion. The coining of the term *Manifest Destiny* did not occur until 1844, but the belief that the destiny of the American nation was expansion all the way to the Pacific Ocean—and possibly even to Canada and Mexico—was older than that. A common conviction was that Americans should share American liberty and ideals with everyone possible, by force if necessary. In the 1830s, American missionaries followed the traders and trappers to the Oregon country and began to publicize the richness and beauty of the land. The result was the Oregon Fever of the 1840s, as thousands of settlers trekked across the Great Plains and the Rocky Mountains to settle the new Shangri-la.

Texas had been a state in the Republic of Mexico since 1822, following the Mexican revolution against Spanish control. The new Mexican government invited immigration from the North by offering land grants to Stephen Austin and other Americans. By 1835, approximately 35,000 "gringos" were homesteading on Texas land. When the Mexican officials saw their power base eroding as the foreigners flooded in, they moved to tighten control through restrictions on immigration and through tax increases. The Texans responded in 1836 by proclaiming independence and establishing a new republic. Texas requested that the United States annex it. Many American citizens protested this annexation; they feared retaliation from Mexico and expressed concern about the annexation of such a large area with slavery. Congress learned that Great Britain might serve as protector for Texas, and this was a major reason for changing its vote. In 1845, after a series of failed attempts at annexation, the U.S. Congress admitted Texas to the Union.

The Mexican War

Though Mexico broke diplomatic relations with the United States immediately after Texas's admission to the Union, there was still hope of a peaceful settlement. In the fall of 1845, President **James K. Polk** (1795–1849) sent **John Slidell** to Mexico City with a proposal for a peaceful settlement, but like other attempts at negotiation, nothing came of it. Racked by coup and counter-coup, the Mexican government refused even to receive Slidell. Polk responded by sending U.S. troops into the disputed territory. On April 5, 1846, Mexican troops attacked an American patrol. When news of the clash reached Washington, Polk sought and received from Congress a declaration of war against Mexico.

Negotiated peace came about with the signing of the Treaty of Guadalupe Hidalgo on February 2, 1848. Under the terms of the treaty, Mexico ceded to the United States the southwestern territory from Texas to the California coast.

Sectional Conflict and the Causes of the Civil War

The Crisis of 1850. The Mexican War had barely started when, on August 8, 1846, a freshman Democratic congressman, **David Wilmot** of Pennsylvania, introduced his **Wilmot Proviso** as a proposed amendment to a war appropriations bill. It stipulated that "neither slavery nor involuntary servitude shall ever exist" in any territory to be acquired from Mexico. The House passed the proviso, but the Senate did not; Wilmot introduced his provision again amidst increasingly acrimonious debate.

One compromise proposal called for the extension of the 36°30′ line of the Missouri Compromise westward through the Mexican cession to the Pacific, with territory north of the line closed to slavery. Another compromise solution was *popular sovereignty*, which held that the residents of each territory should decide for themselves whether to allow slavery.

Having more than the requisite population and being in need of better government, California petitioned in September 1849 for admission to the Union as a free state. Southerners were furious. Long outnumbered in the House of Representatives, the South would find itself, should Congress admit California as a free state, similarly outnumbered in the Senate. At this point, the aged **Henry Clay** proposed a compromise. For the North, Congress would admit California as a free state; the land in dispute between Texas and New Mexico would go to New Mexico; popular sovereignty would decide the issue of slavery in the New Mexico and Utah territories (all of the Mexican cession outside of California); and there would be no slave trade in the District of Columbia. For the South, Congress would enact a tougher fugitive slave law, promise not to abolish slavery in the District of Columbia, and declare that it did not have jurisdiction over the interstate slave trade; the federal government would pay Texas's $10 million pre-annexation debt.

The Kansas-Nebraska Act. All illusion of sectional peace ended abruptly in 1854 when Senator **Stephen A. Douglas** of Illinois introduced a bill in Congress to organize the area west of Missouri and Iowa as the territories of Kansas and Nebraska on the basis of popular sovereignty. The **Kansas-Nebraska Act** aroused a storm of outrage in the North, which viewed the repeal of the Missouri Compromise as the breaking of a solemn agreement, hastened the disintegration of the Whig Party, and divided the Democratic Party along North-South lines.

Springing to life almost overnight as a result of northern fury at the Kansas-Nebraska Act was the Republican Party. This party included diverse elements whose sole unifying principle was banning slavery from all the nation's territories, confining slavery to the states where it already existed, and preventing the further spread of slavery.

The Dred Scott Decision. In *Dred Scott v. Sanford* (1857), the Supreme Court attempted to settle the slavery question. The case involved a Missouri slave, **Dred Scott**, whom the abolitionists had encouraged to sue for his freedom on the basis that his owner had taken him to a free state, Illinois, for several years and then to a free territory, Wisconsin.

The Court attempted to read the extreme southern position on slavery into the Constitution, ruling not only that Scott had no standing to sue in federal court but also that temporary residence in a free state, even for several years, did not make a slave free. In addition, the Court ruling signified that the Missouri Compromise (already a dead letter by that time) had been unconstitutional all along because Congress did not have the authority to exclude slavery from a territory, nor did territorial governments have the right to prohibit slavery.

The Election of 1860. As the 1860 presidential election approached, the Republicans met in Chicago, confident of victory and determined to do nothing to jeopardize their favorable position. Accordingly, they rejected as too radical the front-running candidate, New York Senator **William H. Seward**, in favor of Illinois's favorite son **Abraham Lincoln** (1809–1865). The platform called for federal support of a transcontinental railroad and for the containment of slavery. On election day, the voting went along strictly sectional lines. Lincoln led in popular votes; though he was short of a majority of popular votes, he did have the needed majority in Electoral College votes and received election.

The Secession Crisis. On December 20, 1860, South Carolina, by vote of a special convention, seceded from the Union. By February 1, 1861, six more states (Alabama, Georgia, Florida, Mississippi, Louisiana, and Texas) had followed suit.

Representatives of the seceded states met in Montgomery, Alabama, in February 1861 and declared themselves to be the Confederate States of America. They elected former secretary of war and United States senator **Jefferson Davis** (1808–1889) of Mississippi as president and Alexander Stephens (1812–1883) of Georgia as vice president.

Civil War and Reconstruction

Hostilities Begin. In his inaugural address, Lincoln urged Southerners to reconsider their actions but warned that the Union was perpetual, that states could not secede, and that he would, therefore, hold the federal forts and installations in the South. Only two remained in federal hands: Fort Pickens, off Pensacola, Florida; and Fort Sumter, in the harbor of Charleston, South Carolina.

From **Major Robert Anderson**, commander of the small garrison at Sumter, Lincoln soon received word that supplies were running low. Desiring to send in the needed supplies, Lincoln informed the governor of South Carolina of his intention but promised that no attempt would be made to send arms, ammunition, or reinforcements unless Southerners initiated hostilities.

Confederate **General P. G. T. Beauregard**, acting on orders from President Davis, demanded Anderson's surrender. Anderson said he would surrender if not resupplied. Knowing supplies were on the way, the Confederates opened fire at 4:30 AM on April 12, 1861. The next day, the fort surrendered. The day following Sumter's surrender, Lincoln declared an insurrection and called for the states to provide 75,000 volunteers to put it down. In response, Virginia, Tennessee, North Carolina, and Arkansas declared their secession. The remaining slave states—Delaware, Kentucky, Maryland, and Missouri—wavered but stayed with the Union.

The North enjoyed many advantages over the South. It had the majority of wealth and was vastly superior in industry. The North also had an advantage of almost three to one in manpower; over one-third of the South's population was slaves, whom Southerners would not use as soldiers. Unlike the South, the North received large numbers of **immigrants** during the war. The North retained control of the U.S. Navy; it could command the sea and blockade the South. Finally, the North enjoyed a much superior system of railroads.

The South did, however, have some advantages. It was vast in size and difficult to conquer. In addition, its troops would be fighting on their own ground, a fact that would give them the advantage of familiarity with the terrain and the added motivation of defending their homes and families.

The Homestead Act and the Morrill Land Grant Act. In 1862, Congress passed two highly important acts dealing with domestic affairs in the North. The Homestead Act granted 160 acres of government land free of charge to any person who would farm it for at least five years. Many of the settlers of the West used the provisions of this act. The Morrill Land Grant Act offered large amounts of the federal government's land to states that would establish "agricultural and mechanical" colleges. The founding of many of the nation's large state universities was under the provisions of this act.

The Emancipation Proclamation. By mid-1862, Lincoln, acting under pressure from radical elements of his own party and hoping to make a favorable impression on foreign public opinion, determined to issue the **Emancipation Proclamation**, which declared free all slaves in areas still in rebellion as of January 1, 1863. At the recommendation of William Seward, former New York Senator and now his secretary of state, Lincoln waited to announce the proclamation until the North won some sort of victory. The Battle of Antietam (September 17, 1862) provided this victory.

Northern Victory

Lincoln ran on the ticket of the National Union Party—essentially, the Republican Party with the addition of loyal or "war" Democrats. His vice presidential candidate was **Andrew Johnson** (1808–1875), a loyal Democrat from Tennessee.

In September 1864, word came that **General William Sherman** (1820–1891) had taken Atlanta. The capture of this vital southern rail and manufacturing center brought an enormous boost to northern morale. Along with other northern victories that summer and fall, it ensured a resounding election victory for Lincoln and the continuation of the war to complete victory for the North.

General Robert E. Lee (1807–1870) abandoned Richmond, Virginia, on April 3, 1865, and attempted to escape with what was left of his army. Under the command of **Ulysses S. Grant** (1822–1885), Northern forces cornered Lee's troops and forced his surrender at Appomattox, Virginia, on April 9, 1865. Other Confederate troops still holding out in various parts of the South surrendered over the next few weeks.

Lincoln did not live to receive news of the final surrenders. On April 14, 1865, **John Wilkes Booth** shot Lincoln in the back of the head while the president was watching a play in Ford's Theater in Washington, D.C.

Reconstruction. In 1865, Congress created the **Freedman's Bureau** to provide food, clothing, and education and generally to look after the interests of former slaves.

To restore legal governments in the seceded states, Lincoln had developed a policy that made it relatively easy for southern states to enter the collateral process.

Congress passed a **Civil Rights Act** in 1866, declaring that all citizens born in the United States are, regardless of race, equal citizens under the law. This act became the model of the Fourteenth Amendment to the Constitution.

President Andrew Johnson obeyed the letter but not the spirit of the Reconstruction acts. Congress, angry at his refusal to cooperate, sought in vain for grounds to impeach him. In August 1867, Johnson violated the Tenure of Office Act, which forbade the president from removing from office those officials who had been approved by the Senate. This test of the act's constitutionality took place not in the courts but in Congress. The House of Representatives impeached Johnson, who came within one vote of being removed from office by the Senate.

The Fifteenth Amendment. In 1868, the Republicans nominated Ulysses S. Grant for president. His narrow victory prompted Republican leaders to decide that it would be politically expedient to give the vote to all blacks, Northern as well as Southern. For this purpose, leaders of the North drew up and submitted to the states the Fifteenth Amendment. Ironically, the idea was so unpopular in the North that it won the necessary three-fourths approval only because Congress required the southern states to ratify it.

Industrialism, War, and the Progressive Era

The Economy. Captains of industry—such as **John D. Rockefeller** in oil, **J. P. Morgan** in banking, **Gustavus Swift** in meat processing, **Andrew Carnegie** in steel, and **E. H. Harriman** in railroads—created major industrial empires. In 1886, **Samuel Gompers** and **Adolph Strasser** put together a combination of national craft unions, the **American Federation of Labor (AFL)**, to represent labor's concerns about wages, hours, and safety conditions. Although militant in its use of the strike and in its demand for collective bargaining in labor contracts with large corporations, the AFL did not promote violence or radicalism.

The Spanish-American War. The Cuban revolt against Spain in 1895 threatened American business interests in

Cuba. Sensational "yellow" journalism and nationalistic statements from officials such as Assistant Secretary of the Navy **Theodore Roosevelt** (1858–1919) encouraged popular support for direct American military intervention on behalf of Cuban independence.

On March 27, 1897, President **William McKinley** (1843–1901) asked Spain to call an armistice, accept American mediation to end the war, and stop using concentration camps in Cuba. Spain refused to comply. On April 21, Congress declared war on Spain with the objective of establishing Cuban independence (Teller Amendment). The first U.S. forces landed in Cuba on June 22, 1898, and by July 17 had defeated the Spanish forces. Spain ceded the Philippines, Puerto Rico, and Guam to the United States in return for a payment of $20 million to Spain for the Philippines.

Theodore Roosevelt and Progressive Reforms. On September 6, 1901, while attending the Pan American Exposition in Buffalo, New York, President McKinley was shot by Leon Czolgosz, an anarchist. The president died on September 14. Theodore Roosevelt, at age 42, became the nation's twenty-fifth president and its youngest president to date.

In accordance with the Antitrust Policy (1902), Roosevelt ordered the Justice Department to prosecute corporations pursuing monopolistic practices. Attorney General P. C. Knox first brought suit against the Northern Securities Company, a railroad holding corporation put together by J. P. Morgan, and then moved against John D. Rockefeller's Standard Oil Company. By the time he left office in 1909, Roosevelt had indictments against 25 monopolies.

Roosevelt engineered the separation of Panama from Colombia and the recognition of Panama as an independent country. The **Hay-Bunau-Varilla Treaty** of 1903 granted the United States control of the Canal Zone in Panama for $10 million and an annual fee of $250,000; the control would begin nine years after ratification of the treaty by both parties. Construction of the **Panama Canal** began in 1904 and was completed in 1914.

In 1905, the African American intellectual and militant **W. E. B. DuBois** founded the **Niagara Movement**, which called for federal legislation to protect racial equality and to grant full citizenship rights. Formed in 1909, the **National Association for the Advancement of Colored People** pressed actively for the rights of African Americans. A third organization of the time, the radical labor organization called the **Industrial Workers of the World** (IWW, or Wobblies; 1905–1924) promoted violence and revolution. The IWW organized effective strikes in the textile industry (1912) and among a few western miners' groups , but it had little appeal to the average American worker. After the Red Scare of 1919, the government worked to smash the IWW and deported many of its immigrant leaders and members.

The Wilson Presidency. The nation elected Democratic candidate **Woodrow Wilson** (1856–1924) as president in 1912. Before the outbreak of World War I in 1914, Wilson, working with cooperative majorities in both houses of Congress, achieved much of the remaining progressive agenda, including lower tariff reform (Underwood-Simmons Act, 1913); the Sixteenth Amendment (graduated income tax, 1913); the Seventeenth Amendment (direct election of senators, 1913); the Federal Reserve banking system (that provided regulation and flexibility to monetary policy, 1913); the Federal Trade Commission (to investigate unfair business practices, 1914); and the Clayton Antitrust Act (improving the old Sherman Act and protecting labor unions and farm cooperatives from prosecution, 1914).

Wilson's Fourteen Points. When America entered World War I in 1917, President Wilson maintained that the war would make the world safe for democracy. In an address to Congress on January 8, 1918, he presented his specific peace plan in the form of the Fourteen Points. The first five points called for open rather than secret peace treaties, freedom of the seas, free trade, arms reduction, and a fair adjustment of colonial claims. The next eight points addressed national aspirations of various European peoples and the adjustment of boundaries. The fourteenth point, which he considered the most important and which he had espoused as early as 1916, called for a "general association of nations" to preserve the peace.

Social Conflicts. Although many Americans had called for immigration restriction since the late nineteenth century, the only major restriction imposed on immigration by 1920 had been the Chinese Exclusion Act of 1882. Labor leaders believed that immigrants depressed wages and impeded unionization. Some progressives believed that they created social problems. In June 1917, Congress, over Wilson's veto, imposed a **literacy test for immigrants** and **excluded many Asian nationalities**.

In 1921, Congress passed the **Emergency Quota Act.** In practice, the law admitted almost as many immigrants as the nation wanted from such nations as Britain, Ireland, and Germany but severely restricted Italians, Greeks, Poles, and eastern European Jews hoping to enter the country. The law became effective in 1922 and reduced the number of immigrants annually to about 40 percent of the 1921 total. Congress then passed the National Origins Act of 1924, which further reduced the number of southern and eastern European immigrants and cut the annual immigration total to 20 percent of the 1921 figure. In 1927, the nation set the annual maximum number of immigrants allowed into the United States to 150,000.

On Thanksgiving Day in 1915, **William J. Simmons** founded the **Knights of the Ku Klux Klan**. Its purpose was to intimidate African Americans, who were experiencing an apparent rise in status during World War I. The Klan's methods of repression included cross burnings, tar and featherings, kidnappings, lynchings, and burnings. The Klan was not a political party, but it endorsed and opposed candidates and exerted considerable control over elections and politicians in at least nine states.

Fundamentalist Protestants, under the leadership of **William Jennings Bryan**, began a campaign in 1921 to prohibit the teaching of evolution in the schools and protect the belief in the literal biblical account of creation. The South especially received the idea well.

The Great Depression and the New Deal

The Crash. Signs of recession were apparent before the market crash in 1929. The farm economy, which involved almost 25 percent of the population, coal, railroads, and New England textiles had not been prosperous during the 1920s.

After 1927, new construction declined and auto sales began to sag. Many workers lost their jobs before the crash of 1929. Stock prices increased throughout the decade. The boom in prices and volume of sales was especially active after 1925 and was intensive from 1928 to 1929. Careful investors recognized the overpricing of stocks and began to sell to take their profits.

During October 1929, prices declined as more people began to sell their stock. **Black Thursday**, October 24, 1929, saw the trading of almost 13 million shares; this was a large number for that time, and prices fell precipitously. Investment banks tried to boost the market by buying, but on October 29, **Black Tuesday**, the market fell about 40 points, with 16.5 million shares traded.

Hoover's Depression Policies. The nation had elected **Herbert Hoover** (1874–1964) to the presidency in 1928. In June 1929, Congress passed the Agricultural Marketing Act, which created the Federal Farm Board. The board had a revolving fund of $500 million to lend agricultural cooperatives to buy commodities, such as wheat and cotton, and hold them for higher prices.

The Hawley-Smoot Tariff of June 1930 raised duties on both agricultural and manufactured imports. Chartered by Congress in 1932, the Reconstruction Finance Corporation loaned money to railroads, banks, and other financial institutions. It prevented the failure of basic firms, on which many other elements of the economy depended, but many people criticized it as relief for the rich.

The Federal Home Loan Bank Act, passed in July 1932, created home loan banks, which made loans to building and loan associations, savings banks, and insurance companies. Its purpose was to help avoid foreclosures on homes.

The First New Deal. Franklin D. Roosevelt (1882–1945), governor of New York, easily defeated Hoover in the election of 1932. By the time of Roosevelt's inauguration on March 4, 1933, the American economic system seemed to be on the verge of collapse. In his inaugural address, Roosevelt assured the nation that "the only thing we have to fear is fear itself," called for a special session of Congress to convene on March 9, and asked for "broad executive powers to wage war against the emergency." Two days later, he closed all banks for a brief time and forbade the export of gold or the redemption of currency in gold. A special session of Congress from March 9 to June 16, 1933 ("The Hundred Days") passed a great body of legislation that has left a lasting mark on the nation. Historians have divided Roosevelt's legislation into the First New Deal (1933–1935) and a new wave of programs beginning in 1935 called the Second New Deal.

Passed on March 9, the first day of the special session, the Emergency Banking Relief Act provided additional funds for banks from the Reconstruction Finance

Corporation and the Federal Reserve, allowed the Treasury to open sound banks after 10 days and to merge or liquidate unsound ones, and forbade the hoarding or exporting of gold. Roosevelt, on March 12, assured the public of the soundness of the banks in the first of many "fireside chats," or radio addresses. People believed him. Most banks were soon open, and their deposits were outnumbering withdrawals.

The **Banking Act of 1933**, or the Glass-Steagall Act, established the Federal Deposit Insurance Corporation to insure individual deposits in commercial banks and to separate commercial banking from the more speculative activity of investment banking. The Federal Emergency Relief Act appropriated $500 million for state and local governments to distribute to aid the poor. The act also established the Federal Emergency Relief Administration under **Harry Hopkins** (1890–1946).

The **Civilian Conservation Corps** enrolled 250,000 young men aged 18 to 24 from families on relief to go to camps where they worked on flood control, soil conservation, and forest projects under the direction of the War Department. The **Public Works Administration** had $3.3 billion to distribute to state and local governments for building projects such as schools, highways, and hospitals. The Agricultural Adjustment Act of 1933 created the **Agricultural Adjustment Administration**. Farmers agreed to reduce production of principal farm commodities and received subsidies in return. Farm prices increased; when owners took land out of cultivation, however, tenants and sharecroppers suffered. The repeal of the law came in January 1936 on the grounds that the processing tax was not constitutional.

The **National Industrial Recovery Act** was the cornerstone of the recovery program. In June 1933, Congress passed the National Industrial Recovery Act. In executing the provisions of the code, President Roosevelt established the National Recovery Administration (NRA); the goal was the self-regulation of business and the development of fair prices, wages, hours, and working conditions. Section 7-a of the NRA permitted collective bargaining for workers; laborers would test the federal support for their bargaining in the days to come. The slogan of the NRA was, "We do our part." The economy improved but did not recover.

The Second New Deal. The **Works Progress Administration (WPA)** began in May 1935, following the passage of the Emergency Relief Appropriations Act of April 1935. The WPA employed people from the relief rolls for 30 hours of work a week at pay double that of the relief payment but less than private employment.

Created in May 1935, the **Rural Electrification Administration** provided loans and WPA labor to electric cooperatives so they could build lines into rural areas that the private companies did not serve. Passed in August of 1935, the **Social Security Act** established for persons over age 65 a retirement plan to be funded by a tax on wages paid equally by employee and employer. The government paid the first benefits, ranging from $10 to $85 per month in 1942. Another provision of the act forced states to initiate unemployment insurance programs.

Labor Unions. The 1935 passage of the National Labor Relations Act, or the **Wagner Act**, resulted in a massive growth of union membership but at the expense of bitter conflict within the labor movement. Primarily craft unions made up the **American Federation of Labor (AFL)**, formed in 1886. Some leaders wanted to unionize mass-production industries, such as automobile and rubber manufacturing, with industrial unions.

In November 1935, **John L. Lewis** formed the **Committee for Industrial Organization (CIO)** to unionize basic industries, presumably within the AFL. **President William Green** of the AFL ordered the CIO to disband in January 1936. When the rebels refused, the AFL expelled them. The insurgents then reorganized the CIO as the independent Congress of Industrial Organizations. Labor strikes, particularly in the textile mills, marked the end of the 1930s. Soon the nation would receive another test.

World War II

The American Response to the War in Europe. In August 1939, Roosevelt created the War Resources Board to develop a plan for industrial mobilization in the event of war. The next month, he established the Office of Emergency Management in the White House to centralize mobilization activities.

Roosevelt officially proclaimed the neutrality of the United States on September 5, 1939. The Democratic Congress, in a vote that followed party lines, passed a new Neutrality Act in November. It allowed the cash-and-carry sale of arms and short-term loans to belligerents but forbade American ships to trade with belligerents or Americans to travel on belligerent ships.

Roosevelt determined that to aid Britain in every way possible was the best way to avoid war with Germany. In September 1940, he signed an agreement to give Britain 50 American destroyers in return for a 99-year lease on air and naval bases in British territories in Newfoundland, Bermuda, and the Caribbean.

The Road to Pearl Harbor. In late July 1941, the United States placed an embargo on the export of aviation gasoline, lubricants, and scrap iron and steel to Japan and granted an additional loan to China. In December, additional articles—iron ore and pig iron, some chemicals, machine tools, and other products—fell under the embargo.

In October 1941, a new military cabinet headed by **General Hideki Tojo** took control of Japan. The Japanese secretly decided to make a final effort to negotiate with the United States and to go to war if there was no solution by November 25. A new round of talks followed in Washington, but neither side would make a substantive change in its position. The Japanese secretly gave final approval on December 1 for a surprise attack on the United States.

The Japanese planned a major offensive to take the Dutch East Indies, Malaya, and the Philippines and to obtain the oil, metals, and other raw materials they needed. At the same time, they would attack Pearl Harbor in Hawaii to destroy the American Pacific fleet to keep it from interfering with their plans.

At 7:55 AM on Sunday, December 7, 1941, the first wave of Japanese carrier-based planes unexpectedly attacked the American fleet in **Pearl Harbor**. A second wave followed at 8:50 AM. The United States suffered the loss of two battleships sunk, six damaged and out of action, three cruisers and three destroyers sunk or damaged, several lesser vessels destroyed or damaged, and the destruction of all the 150 aircraft on the ground at Pearl Harbor. Worst of all, 2,323 American servicemen were killed and about 1,100 were wounded. The Japanese lost 29 planes, five midget submarines, and one fleet submarine.

Declared War Begins. On December 8, 1941, Congress declared war on Japan, with one dissenting vote—Representative Jeanette Rankin of Montana. On December 11, Germany and Italy declared war on the United States. Great Britain and the United States established the Combined Chiefs of Staff, headquartered in Washington, to direct Anglo-American military operations.

On January 1, 1942, representatives of 26 nations met in Washington, D.C., and signed the Declaration of the United Nations, pledged themselves to the principles of the Atlantic Charter, and promised not to make a separate peace with their common enemies.

The Home Front. In *Korematsu v. United States* (1944), the Supreme Court upheld sending the Issei (Japanese Americans from Japan) and Nisei (native-born Japanese Americans) to concentration camps. The camps did not close until March 1946 until after the end of World War II.

President Roosevelt died on April 12, 1945, at Warm Springs, Georgia. **Harry S Truman** (1884–1972), formerly a senator from Missouri and vice president of the United States, became president on April 12, 1945. (Harry Truman did not have a middle name; he used only the letter *S*, which he did not follow with a period.)

The Atomic Bomb. The Army Corps of Engineers established the Manhattan Engineering District in August 1942 for the purpose of developing an atomic bomb; the program eventually took the name the **Manhattan Project**. **J. Robert Oppenheimer** directed the design and construction of a transportable atomic bomb at Los Alamos, New Mexico. On July 16, 1945, the Manhattan Project exploded the first atomic bomb at Alamogordo, New Mexico.

The *Enola Gay* dropped an atomic bomb on Hiroshima, Japan, on August 6, 1945, killed about 78,000 people, and injured 100,000 more. On August 9, the United States dropped a second bomb on Nagasaki, Japan. Japan surrendered on August 14, 1945, and signed the formal surrender on September 2.

The Postwar Era

The Cold War and Containment. In February 1947, Great Britain notified the United States that it could no longer aid the Greek government in its war against Communist insurgents. The next month, President Truman asked Congress for $400 million in military and economic aid for Greece and Turkey. In his **Truman Doctrine**, Truman argued that the United States must support free peoples who were resisting Communist domination.

Secretary of State George C. Marshall proposed in June 1947 that the United States provide economic aid to help rebuild Europe. The following March, Congress passed the European Recovery Program; popularly known as the **Marshall Plan**, the program provided more than $12 billion in aid.

Anticommunism. On February 9, 1950, Senator **Joseph R. McCarthy** of Wisconsin stated that he had a list of known Communists who were working in the State Department. He later expanded his attacks. After making charges against the army, the Senate censured and discredited him in 1954.

Korean War. On June 25, 1950, North Korea invaded South Korea. President Truman committed U.S. forces to the United Nations (UN) auspices; **General Douglas MacArthur** would command the troops. By October, UN forces (mostly American) had driven north of the thirty-eighth parallel, which divided North and South Korea.

Chinese troops attacked MacArthur's forces on November 26, pushing them south of the thirty-eighth parallel, but by spring 1951, UN forces had recovered their offensive. The armistice of June 1953 left Korea divided along virtually the same boundary that had existed before the war.

Eisenhower-Dulles Foreign Policy. Dwight D. Eisenhower (1890–1969), elected president in 1952, chose **John Foster Dulles** as secretary of state. Dulles talked of a more aggressive foreign policy, calling for "massive retaliation" and "liberation" rather than containment. He wished to emphasize nuclear deterrents rather than conventional armed forces.

After several years of nationalist war against French occupation, in July 1954 France, Great Britain, the Soviet Union, and China signed the Geneva Accords, which divided Vietnam along the seventeenth parallel. The North would be under the leadership of **Ho Chi Minh** and the South under **Emperor Bao Dai**. The purpose of the scheduled elections was to unify the country, but **Ngo Dinh Diem** overthrew Bao Dai and prevented the elections from taking place. The United States supplied economic aid to **South Vietnam**.

In January 1959, **Fidel Castro** overthrew the dictator of Cuba. Castro criticized the United States, moved closer to the Soviet Union, and signed a trade agreement with the Soviets in February 1960. The United States prohibited the importation of Cuban sugar in October 1960 and broke off diplomatic relations in January 1961.

Space Exploration. The launching of the Soviet space satellite *Sputnik* on October 4, 1957, created fear that America was falling behind technologically. Although the United States launched *Explorer I* on January 31, 1958, the concern continued. In 1958, Congress established the **National Aeronautics and Space Administration** to coordinate research and development and passed the National Defense Education Act to provide grants and loans for education.

Civil Rights. Eisenhower completed the formal integration of the armed forces; desegregated public services in Washington, D.C., naval yards, and veterans' hospitals; and appointed a civil rights commission. In *Brown v. Board of Education of Topeka* (1954), **Thurgood Marshall**, lawyer for the National Association for the Advancement of Colored People, challenged the doctrine of "separate but equal" (*Plessy v. Ferguson*, **1896**). The Court declared that separate educational facilities were inherently unequal. In 1955, the Court ordered states to integrate "with all deliberate speed."

On December 11, 1955, in Montgomery, Alabama, **Rosa Parks** refused to give up her seat on a city bus to a white man and faced arrest. Under the leadership of **Martin Luther King Jr.** (1929–1968), an African American pastor, African Americans of Montgomery organized a bus boycott that lasted for a year until, in December 1956, the Supreme Court refused to review a lower-court ruling that stated that separate but equal was no longer legal.

In February 1960, a segregated lunch counter in Greensboro, North Carolina, denied four African American students service; the students staged a sit-in. This inspired sit-ins elsewhere in the South and led to the formation of the Student Nonviolent Coordinating Committee, which had a chief aim of ending segregation in public accommodations.

The New Frontier, Vietnam, and Social Upheaval

Kennedy's New Frontier. Democratic Senator **John F. Kennedy** (1917–1963) won the presidential election of 1960. The Justice Department, under Attorney General **Robert F. Kennedy**, began to push for civil rights, including desegregation of interstate transportation in the South, integration of schools, and supervision of elections. President Kennedy presented a comprehensive civil rights bill to Congress in 1963. With the bill held up in Congress, 200,000 people marched and demonstrated on its behalf, and Martin Luther King Jr. gave his "I Have a Dream" speech.

Cuban Missile Crisis. Under Eisenhower, the **Central Intelligence Agency** had begun training some 2,000 men to invade Cuba and to overthrow Fidel Castro. On April 19, 1961, this force invaded at the **Bay of Pigs**; opposing forces pinned them down, demanded their surrender, and captured some 1,200 men.

On October 14, 1962, a U-2 reconnaissance plane brought photographic evidence of the construction of missile sites in Cuba. Kennedy, on October 22, announced a blockade of Cuba and called on the Soviet premier, **Nikita Khrushchev** (1894–1971), to dismantle the missile bases and remove all weapons capable of attacking the United States from Cuba. Six days later, Khrushchev backed down and withdrew the missiles. Kennedy lifted the blockade.

Johnson and the Great Society. On November 22, 1963, **Lee Harvey Oswald** assassinated President Kennedy in Dallas, Texas; **Jack Ruby** killed Oswald two days later. Debate still continues as to whether the assassination was a conspiracy. **Lyndon B. Johnson** (1908–1973) succeeded John Kennedy as president of the United States.

The **1964 Civil Rights Act** outlawed racial discrimination by employers and unions, created the Equal Employment Opportunity Commission to enforce the law, and eliminated the remaining restrictions on black voting.

Michael Harrington's *The Other America: Poverty in the United States* (1962) showed that 20 to 25 percent of American families were living below the governmentally defined poverty line. The Economic Opportunity Act of 1964 sought to address the problem by establishing a job corps, community action programs, education programs, work-study programs, job training, loans for small businesses and farmers, and a "domestic peace corps" called Volunteers in Service to America. The Office of Economic Opportunity administered many of these programs.

Emergence of Black Power. In 1965, Dr. Martin Luther King Jr. announced a voter registration drive. With help from the federal courts, he dramatized his effort by leading a march from Selma, Alabama, to Montgomery,

Alabama, between March 21 and 25. The Voting Rights Act of 1965 authorized the attorney general to appoint officials to register voters.

Seventy percent of African Americans lived in city ghettos. In 1966, New York and Chicago experienced riots, and the following year there were riots in Newark and Detroit. The Kerner Commission, appointed to investigate the riots, concluded that the focus of the riots was a social system that prevented African Americans from getting good jobs and crowded them into ghettos.

On April 4, 1968, **James Earl Ray** assassinated King in Memphis, Tennessee. Ray was an escaped convict; he pled guilty to the murder and received a sentence of 99 years in prison. Riots in more than 100 cities followed.

Vietnam. After the defeat of the French in Vietnam in 1954, the United States sent military advisors to South Vietnam to aid the government of **Ngo Dinh Diem**. The pro-Communist Vietcong forces gradually grew in strength because Diem failed to follow through on promised reforms and because of the support from North Vietnam, the Soviet Union, and China.

"Hawks" in Congress defended President Johnson's policy and, drawing on the containment theory, said that the nation had the responsibility to resist aggression. The claim was if Vietnam should fall, all Southeast Asia would eventually go. Antiwar demonstrations were attracting large crowds by 1967. "Doves" argued that the war was a civil war in which the United States should not meddle.

On January 31, 1968, the first day of the Vietnamese new year (Tet), the Vietcong attacked numerous cities and towns, American bases, and even Saigon. Although they suffered large losses, the Vietcong won a psychological victory as American opinion began turning against the war.

The Nixon Conservative Reaction. Republican **Richard M. Nixon** (1913–1994), emphasizing stability and order, defeated Democratic nominee Hubert Humphrey by a margin of one percentage point. The Nixon administration sought to block renewal of the Voting Rights Act and delay implementation of court-ordered school desegregation in Mississippi. In 1969, Nixon appointed **Warren E. Burger**, a conservative, as chief justice. Although more conservative than the Warren court, the Burger court did declare in 1972 that the death penalty in use at the time was unconstitutional in 1972; it struck down state antiabortion legislation in 1973.

The president turned to "Vietnamization," the effort to build up South Vietnamese forces while withdrawing American troops. In 1969, Nixon reduced American troop strength by 60,000 but at the same time ordered the bombing of Cambodia, a neutral country. In the summer of 1972, negotiations between the United States and North Vietnam began in Paris. A few days before the 1972 presidential election, **Henry Kissinger**, the president's national security advisor, announced that "peace was at hand."

Nixon resumed the bombing of North Vietnam in December 1972; he claimed that the North Vietnamese were not bargaining in good faith. In January 1973, the two sides reached a settlement in which the North Vietnamese retained control over large areas of the South and agreed to release American prisoners of war within 60 days. Nearly 60,000 Americans had been killed and 300,000 more wounded, and the war had cost American taxpayers $109 billion. On March 29, 1973, the last American combat troops left South Vietnam. The North Vietnamese forces continued to push back the South Vietnamese, and in April 1975, Saigon fell to the North.

Watergate, Carter, and the New Conservatism

Watergate. The Republicans renominated Nixon, who won a landslide victory over the Democratic nominee, Senator **George McGovern**. What became known as the Watergate crisis began during the 1972 presidential campaign. Early on the morning of June 17, a security officer for the Committee for the Reelection of the President, along with four other men, broke into Democratic headquarters at the Watergate apartment complex in Washington, D.C. The authorities caught the men going through files and installing electronic eavesdropping devices.

In March 1974, a grand jury indicted some of Nixon's top aides and named Nixon an unindicted co-conspirator. Meanwhile, the House Judiciary Committee televised its debate over impeachment. The committee charged the president with obstructing justice, misusing presidential power, and failing to obey the committee's

subpoenas. Before the House began to debate impeachment, Nixon announced his resignation on August 8, 1974, to take effect at noon the following day.

Gerald Ford (1913–) then became president. Ford was in many respects the opposite of Nixon. Although a partisan Republican, he was well liked and free of any hint of scandal. Ford almost immediately encountered controversy when in September 1974 he offered to pardon Nixon. Nixon accepted the offer although he admitted no wrongdoing and had not yet received any charges of crime.

Carter's Moderate Liberalism. In 1976, the Democrats nominated **James Earl Carter** (1924–), formerly governor of Georgia, who ran on the basis of his integrity and lack of Washington connections. Carter narrowly defeated Ford in the election.

Carter offered amnesty to Americans who had fled the draft and gone to other countries during the Vietnam War. He established the departments of energy and education and placed the civil service on a merit basis. He created a "superfund" for cleanup of chemical waste dumps, established controls over strip mining, and protected 100 million acres of Alaskan wilderness from development.

Carter's Foreign Policy. Carter negotiated a controversial treaty with Panama, affirmed by the Senate in 1978, that provided for the transfer of ownership of the canal to Panama in 1999 and guaranteed its neutrality. In 1978, Carter negotiated the Camp David Accords between Israel and Egypt. Israel promised to return occupied land in the Sinai to Egypt in exchange for Egyptian recognition, a process completed in 1982. An agreement to negotiate the Palestinian refugee problem proved ineffective.

The Iranian Crisis. In 1978, a revolution forced the **shah of Iran** to flee the country and replaced him with a religious leader, **Ayatollah Ruhollah Khomeini** (ca. 1900–1989). Because the United States had supported the shah with arms and money, the revolutionaries were strongly anti-American, calling the United States the "Great Satan."

After Carter allowed the exiled shah to come to the United States for medical treatment in October 1979, some 400 Iranians broke into the American embassy in Teheran on November 4 and took the occupants captive.

They demanded the return of the shah to Iran for trial, the confiscation of his wealth, and the presentation of his wealth to Iran. Carter rejected these demands; instead, he froze Iranian assets in the United States and established a trade embargo against Iran. After extensive negotiations with Iran, in which Algeria acted as an intermediary, the Iranians freed the American hostages on January 20, 1981.

Attacking Big Government. Republican **Ronald Reagan** (1911–2004) defeated Carter by a large electoral majority in 1980. Reagan placed priority on cutting taxes. He based his approach on "supply-side" economics, the idea that if government left more money in the hands of the people, they would invest rather then spend the excess on consumer goods. The results would be greater production, more jobs, and greater prosperity, resulting in more income for the government despite lower tax rates. However, the federal budget deficit ballooned from $59 billion in 1980 to $195 billion by 1983. Reagan ended ongoing antitrust suits against IBM and AT&T and fulfilled his promise to reduce government interference with business.

Iran-Contra. In 1985 and 1986, several Reagan officials sold arms to the Iranians in hopes of encouraging them to use their influence in obtaining the release of American hostages being held in Lebanon. Profits from these sales went to the Nicaraguan *contras*—a militant group opposed to the left-leaning elected government—thus circumventing congressional restrictions on funding the *contras*. The attorney general appointed a special prosecutor, and Congress held hearings on the affair in May 1987.

The Election of 1988. Vice President George H. W. Bush (1924–) won the Republican nomination. Bush defeated Democrat **Michael Dukakis**, but the Republicans were unable to make any inroads in Congress.

Operation Just Cause. Since coming to office, the Bush administration had been concerned that Panamanian dictator **Manuel Noriega** was providing an important link in the drug traffic between South America and the United States. After economic sanctions, diplomatic efforts, and an October 1989 coup failed to oust Noriega, Bush ordered 12,000 troops into Panama on December 20 for what became known as Operation Just Cause.

On January 3, 1990, Noriega surrendered to the Americans and faced drug-trafficking charges in the United States. Found guilty in 1992, his sentence was 40 years.

Persian Gulf Crisis. On August 2, 1990, Iraq invaded Kuwait, an act that Bush denounced as "naked aggression." The United States quickly banned most trade with Iraq, froze Iraq's and Kuwait's assets in the United States, and sent aircraft carriers to the Persian Gulf. On August 6, after the UN Security Council condemned the invasion, Bush ordered the deployment of air, sea, and land forces to Saudi Arabia and dubbed the operation Desert Shield.

On February 23, the allied air assault began. Four days later, Bush announced the liberation of Kuwait and ordered offensive operations to cease. The UN established the terms for the cease-fire, which Iraq accepted on April 6.

The Road to the Twenty-First Century

The Election of 1992. William Jefferson Clinton (1946–) won 43 percent of the popular vote and 370 electoral votes, while President Bush won 37 percent of the popular vote and 168 electoral votes. Although he won no electoral votes, the Independent Party candidate Ross Perot (1930–) gained 19 percent of the popular vote.

Domestic Affairs. The **North American Free Trade Agreement (NAFTA)**, negotiated by the Bush administration, eliminated most tariffs and other trade barriers between the United States, Canada, and Mexico. Passed by Congress and signed by Clinton in 1993, NAFTA became law in January 1994.

In October 1993, the Clinton administration proposed legislation to reform the health care system, which included universal coverage with a guaranteed benefits package, managed competition through health care alliances that would bargain with insurance companies, and employer mandates to provide health insurance for employees. With most Republicans and small business, insurance, and medical business interests opposed to the legislation, the Democrats dropped their attempt at a compromise package in September 1994.

Impeachment and Acquittal. Clinton received criticism for alleged wrongdoing in connection with a real estate development called Whitewater. While governor of Arkansas, Clinton had invested in Whitewater, along with **James B. and Susan McDougal**, owners of a failed savings and loan institution. After Congress renewed the independent counsel law, a three-judge panel appointed **Kenneth W. Starr** to the new role of independent prosecutor.

The Starr investigation yielded massive findings in late 1998, roughly midway into Clinton's second term, including information on an adulterous affair that Clinton had had with Monica Lewinsky while she was an intern at the White House. It was on charges stemming from this report that the House of Representatives impeached Clinton in December 1998 for perjury and obstruction of justice. The Senate acquitted him of all charges in February 1999.

Continuing Crisis in the Balkans. During Clinton's second term, continued political unrest abroad and civil war in the Balkans continued to be a major foreign policy challenge. In 1999, the Serbian government attacked ethnic Albanians in Kosovo, a province of Serbia. In response, North Atlantic Treaty Organization (NATO) forces, led by the United States, bombed Serbia. Several weeks of bombing forced Serbian forces to withdraw from Kosovo.

The Election of 2000. Preelection polls indicated that the election would be close, and few ventured to predict the outcome. Indeed, the election outcome was much in doubt for several weeks after the election. Though Clinton's vice president, **Al Gore** (1948–), won the popular vote, the Electoral College was very close, and Florida (the state governed by George W. Bush's brother) was pivotal in deciding the election.

George W. Bush (1946–), son of the former president **George H. W. Bush**, appeared to win Florida, but by a very small margin; a recount began. Then, controversy over how to conduct the recount led to a series of court challenges, with the matter ultimately decided by the U.S. Supreme Court, which ruled in favor of Bush. George W. Bush thus became the forty-third president of the United States.

Terrorism Hits Home. The new president would soon face the grim task of dealing with a massive terrorist attack on major symbols of U.S. economic and military might. On the morning of September 11, 2001, hijackers deliberately crashed U.S. commercial jetliners into the World Trade Center in New York—toppling its 110-story twin towers, commandeered an airliner, and crashed a plane into the Pentagon, just outside Washington, D.C. Passengers on the hijacked airplane took over the plane; by

crashing it in Pennsylvania they saved many lives. Thousands died in the destruction of the World Trade Center, the deadliest act of terrorism in American history.

Though the person behind the attacks was not immediately known, Bush cast prime suspicion on the Saudi exile Osama bin Laden, the alleged mastermind of the bombings of two U.S. embassies in 1998 and of a U.S. naval destroyer in 2000. The United States had earlier seen terrorism on its home soil carried out by Islamic militants in the 1993 bombing of the World Trade Center and by a member of the American militia movement in the bombing of the Oklahoma City federal building in 1995.

In supposed retaliation for the terrorism brought against the United States, U.S. forces attacked Afghanistan. Many of these forces remain in the country of Afghanistan to this day. The final outcome of the troop invasion is still uncertain.

Disputes with Iraq continued when the United States reported that the country held "weapons of mass destruction." Bush declared war (a disputed option) with Iraq. The outcome of sending troops to Iraq is undetermined.

Topic 2.
Identifying Immigration and Settlement Patterns That Have Shaped the History of the United States

"The United States is a nation of immigrants" is a frequently quoted remark. The quotation, however, may cause some to forget that the Europeans came to a country already occupied by Native Americans.

The New World that Columbus and other explorers discovered in the late fifteenth and early sixteenth centuries was neither recently formed nor recently settled. It had actually been settled between 15,000 and 35,000 years before. As in other areas of the world, the native peoples of the so-called New World formed communities but did not immediately develop written languages. The lack of any kind of written record makes interpreting the prehistorical past more difficult. Archeologists and anthropologists working in North and South America have unearthed the remains of these early communities, and it is on this evidence that anthropologists base the earliest theories about the origins, movements, and lifestyles of native people.

It is important to remember that there is not one universally accepted theory regarding the earliest history of the people who settled North and South America. It is also important to remember that by the time Europeans came into contact with the indigenous peoples of the Americas, more than 2,000 distinct cultures and hundreds of distinct languages existed. It is therefore necessary to trace not just the origins but also the developments, affected by various factors such as the environment, that took place before the Europeans arrived. This will provide an understanding of the various Indian cultures and societies and the impact that contact with Europeans had on them.

Previous sections and topics relate to the topic, "Identifying Immigration and Settlement Patterns That Have Shaped the History of the United States." The reader may wish to review the earlier sections/topics, such as "Section 3: Prehistory and Early Civilization," "Section 5: Causes and Consequences of Exploration, Settlement, and Growth," and "Section 6: The Continued Exploration, Settlement, and Revolution in the 'New World'" to review some of the groups that came to America, their reasons for being here, and where they settled. The previous passages also give some attention to the legislation surrounding these immigrants, the Native Americans, human rights, and calls for immigration restriction.

Calls for immigration restriction had begun in the late nineteenth century, but the only major restriction imposed on immigration had been the Chinese Exclusion Act of 1882. Labor leaders believed that immigrants depressed wages and impeded unionization. Some progressives believed that they created social problems.

In June 1917, Congress, over President Wilson's veto, had imposed a literacy test for immigrants and excluded many Asian nationalities. In 1921, Congress passed the Emergency Quota Act. In practice, the law admitted almost as many immigrants as wanted to come from such nations as Britain, Ireland, and Germany but severely restricted Italians, Greeks, Poles, and eastern European Jews wanting to enter the country. The law became effective in 1922 and reduced the number of immigrants annually to about 40 percent of the 1921 total. Congress then passed the National Origins Act of 1924, which further reduced the number of southern and eastern European immigrants and cut the annual immigration total to 20 percent of the 1921 figure. In 1927,

the annual maximum number of immigrants allowed into the United States was reduced to 150,000.

On Thanksgiving Day in 1915, the William J. Simmons founded the Knights of the Ku Klux Klan to intimidate African Americans, who were experiencing an apparent rise in status during World War I. The Klan's methods of repression included cross burnings, tar and featherings, kidnappings, lynchings, and burnings. The Klan was not a political party, but it endorsed and opposed candidates and exerted considerable control over elections and politicians in at least nine states. As a result of KKK activity, many of the immigrants—especially those from African nations—moved to sections of the North.

In *Korematsu v. United States* (1944), the Supreme Court upheld sending the Issei (Japanese Americans from Japan) and Nisei (native-born Japanese Americans) to concentration camps. The camps closed in March 1946. Some of the concentration camp victims remained on the West Coast although some did return to their previous area of residence in the United States; some elected to relocate in Japan.

Since the United States first began tracking the arrival of immigrants within its boundaries in 1820, the United States has accepted 66 million legal immigrants, with 11 percent arriving from Germany and 10 percent from Mexico . However, two centuries of immigration and integration have not yielded consensus on the three major immigration questions: how many, from where, and in what status newcomers should arrive.

The U.S. immigration system in the early twenty-first century recognizes 800,000 to 900,000 foreigners a year as legal immigrants, admits 35 million nonimmigrant tourist and business visitors a year, and knows of another 300,000 to 400,000 unauthorized foreigners who settle in the country annually. Recent decades have witnessed contentious debates over the place of immigrants and their children in the educational, welfare, and political systems of the United States, or more broadly, whether the immigration system serves U.S. national interests (Martin 2002). Restrictions have been more frequently proposed after the 9/11 attack, the war in Iraq, health care concerns for the population, and increased controversy surrounding illegal immigrants.

Table 4-1 ranks the ten leading countries of birth of the foreign-born resident population from 1850 to 1960.

Table 4-1. 10 Countries of Birth of the Foreign-Born Population, 1850–2000 (resident population)

Ten leading countries	1850	1880	1900	1930	1960	1970	1980	1990	2000
1	Ireland 962,000	Germany 1,967,000	Germany 2,663,000	Italy 1,790,000	Italy 1,257,000	Italy 1,009,000	Mexico 2,199,000	Mexico 4,298,000	Mexico 7,841,000
2	Germany 584,000	Ireland 1,855,000	Ireland 1,615,000	Germany 1,609,000	Germany 990,000	Germany 833,000	Germany 849,000	China 921,000	China 1,391,000
3	Great Britain 379,000	Great Britain 918,000	Canada 1,180,000	United Kingdom 1,403,000	Canada 953,000	Canada 812,000	Canada 843,000	Philippines 913,000	Philippines 1,222,000
4	Canada 148,000	Canada 717,000	Great Britain 1,168,000	Canada 1,310,000	United Kingdom 833,000	Mexico 760,000	Italy 832,000	Canada 745,000	India 1,007,000
5	France 54,000	Sweden 194,000	Sweden 582,000	Poland 1,269,000	Poland 748,000	United Kingdom 686,000	United Kingdom 669,000	Cuba 737,000	Cuba 952,000
6	Switzerland 13,000	Norway 182,000	Italy 484,000	Soviet Union 1,154,000	Soviet Union 691,000	Poland 548,000	Cuba 608,000	Germany 712,000	Vietnam 863,000
7	Mexico 13,000	France 107,000	Russia 424,000	Ireland 745,000	Mexico 576,000	Soviet Union 463,000	Philippines 501,000	United Kingdom 640,000	El Salvador 765,000
8	Norway 13,000	China 104,000	Poland 383,000	Mexico 641,000	Ireland 339,000	Cuba 439,000	Poland 418,000	Italy 581,000	Korea 701,000
9	Holland 10,000	Switzerland 89,000	Norway 336,000	Sweden 595,000	Austria 305,000	Ireland 251,000	Soviet Union 406,000	Korea 568,000	Dominican Republic 692,000
10	Italy 4,000	Bohemia 85,000	Austria 276,000	Czechoslovakia 492,000	Hungary 245,000	Austria 214,000	Korea 290,000	Vietnam 543,000	Canada 678,000

Source: U.S. Census Bureau. "Countries of Birth of the Foreign-Born Population, 1850–2000." *Profile of the Foreign-Born Population in the United States: 2000.*

In the year 2000 the U. S. Census Bureau in its Current Population Survey indicated the regions of birth of foreign-born residents. Of the 28,000,000 foreign-born residents in the United States in 2000, almost 40% (11,327,000) resided in the West. The South had the second highest percentage with almost 27% (7,596,000). The region with the third highest number of foreign-born residents (6,420,000) was the Northeast, which had almost 23%. About 10% (3,036,000) of the foreign-born residents lived in the Midwest. (U.S. Census Bureau, *Current Population Survey*, March 2000. *http://www.census.gov/population/socdemo/foreign/ p20-534/tab0314.txt*)

Martin (2002) predicts that immigration is likely to continue at current levels of 900,000 legal and 300,000 unauthorized a year. In the words of Kenneth Prewitt, a former director of the U.S. Census Bureau, America is "the first country in world history which is literally made up of every part of the world" (Alvarez 2001).

Setting limits on numbers of immigrants, providing services for those who are illegal immigrants in the United States, locating the immigrants who come to the United States, and finding work for those who are newly-arrived without taking jobs from those who are already settled are some of the debatable issues that concern legislators and citizens of the country.

Section 7: Economics

Topic 1.
Identifying Ways That Limited Resources Affect the Choices Made by Government and Individuals

A basic understanding relating to economics is that wants are unlimited while resources are limited. When resources are limited, it affects prices (the amount of money needed to buy goods, services, or resources). Individuals and institutions must, therefore, make choices when making purchases. These seemingly local decisions may affect other people and even other nations.

A true sense of global interdependence results from an understanding of the relationship between local decisions and global issues. For example, individual or community actions regarding waste disposal or recycling can affect the availability of resources worldwide. A country's fuel standards can affect air pollution, oil supplies, and gas prices. The government can provide the legal structure and help needed to maintain competition, redistribute income, reallocate resources, and promote stability.

There are two main types of resources:

Economic resources. The land (natural), labor (human), capital, and entrepreneurial ability used in the production of goods and services; productive agents; factors of production.

Human resources. The physical and mental talents and efforts of people; these resources are necessary to help produce goods and services.

The result of combining resources may be entrepreneurship. As a human resource that also takes advantage of economic resources to create a product, **entrepreneurship** is characterized by nonroutine decisions, innovation, and the willingness to take risks.

Topic 2.
Comparing and Contrasting the Characteristics of Different Economic Institutions

Two important higher-order thinking skills that teachers should encourage in their students are comparing and contrasting. The study of various economic institutions is an ideal place to work with these two skills. The following are the main economic institutions of the United States:

Banks. Serve anyone in the general public. Small groups of investors who expect a certain return on their investments own the banks. Only the investors have voting privileges; customers do not have voting rights, cannot be elected board members, and do not participate in governing the institution. The Federal Deposit Insurance Corporation insures the banks. Typically, banks do not share information, ideas, or resources.

Credit unions. Owned by members. Each person who deposits money is a member, not a customer. Surplus earnings go to the members in higher dividends, low-cost or free services, and lower loan rates. The National Credit Union Share Insurance Fund insures credit unions. All credit unions share ideas, information, and resources.

Federal Reserve System. The central banking system of the United States. It has a central board of governors in Washington, D.C. There 12 Federal Reserve Bank districts in major cities throughout the nation. The district banks issue bank notes, lend money to member banks, maintain reserves, supervise member banks, and help set the national monetary policy. Alan Greenspan served as the chairman of the board of governors for 18 years. On Greenspan's retirement on January 31, 2005, Ben Bernanke succeeded him.

Stock market. An abstract concept. It is the mechanism that enables the trading of company stocks. It is different from the **stock exchange**, which is a corporation in the business of bringing together stock buyers and sellers.

Topic 3.
Identifying the Role of Markets from Production, through Distribution, to Consumption

A **market** is the interaction between potential buyers and sellers of goods and services. Money is the usual medium of exchange. **Market economies** have no central authority; custom plays a very small role. Every consumer makes buying decisions based on his or her own needs, desires, and income; individual self-interest rules. Every producer decides personally what goods or services to produce, what price to charge, what resources to employ, and what production methods to use. Profits motivate the producers. There is vigorous competition in a market economy. **Supply and demand** may affect the availability of resources needed for production, distribution, and consumption.

After production, the producer ideally distributes the product to the places where consumers need or want the product—and have the money to pay for the goods or services. In the United States, there is a large and active government (command) sector, but there is a greater emphasis on the market economy.

The following are the major types of economies in world today:

Command economies. Rely on a central authority to make decisions. The central authority may be a dictator or a democratically constituted government. Although a command economy relies mainly on the government to direct economic activity, there is a small market sector as well.

Traditional economies. Largely rely on custom to determine production and distribution issues. While not static, traditional systems are slow to change and are not well-equipped to propel a society into sustained growth. Many of the poorer countries of the developing world have traditional systems.

Mixed economies. Contains elements of each of the two previously defined systems. All real-world economies are mixed economies, but the proportions of the mixture can vary greatly.

Capitalist economies. Produce resources owned by individuals.

Socialist economies. Produce resources owned collectively by society. In other words, resources are under the control of the government.

Efficiency occurs when a society produces the types and quantities of goods and services that most satisfy its people. Failure to do so wastes resources. **Technical efficiency** occurs when a society is able to use its resources to best advantage in order to produce the most types and the largest quantity of goods and services. Again, failure to do so wastes resources. **Equity** occurs when the distribution of goods and services conforms to a society's notions of "fairness." These goals often determine the type of economic system that a country has.

Topic 4.
Identifying Factors to Consider When Making Consumer Decisions

Adam Smith (1723–1790) was a Scottish economist whose writing may have inaugurated the modern era of economic analysis. Published in 1776, *The Wealth of Nations* is an analysis of a market economy.

Smith believed that a market economy was a superior form of organization from the standpoint of both economic progress and human liberty. Smith acknowledged that **self-interest** was a dominant motivating force in a market economy; this self-interest, he said, was ultimately consistent with the **public interest**. An "invisible hand" guided market participants to act in ways that promoted the public interest. **Profits** may be the main concern of firms, but only firms that **satisfy** consumer demand and offer **suitable prices** earn profits.

Goods and services refer to things that satisfy human **needs**, **wants**, or **desires**. **Goods** are tangible items, such as food, cars, and clothing; **services** are intangible items such as education and health care. A market is the interaction between potential buyers and sellers of goods and services. **Money** is usually the medium of exchange. The **supply** of a good is the quantity of that good that producers offer at a certain price. The collection of all such points for every price is the **supply curve**. **Demand** for a good is the quantity of a good that consumers are willing and able to purchase at a certain price. The **demand curve** is the combination of quantity and price, at all price levels.

Topic 5.
Identifying the Economic Interdependence among Nations

Understanding global interdependence begins with recognizing that world regions include economic, political, historical, ecological, linguistic, and cultural regions. This understanding should include knowledge of military and economic alliances such as NATO, of cartels, and of the ways in which their existence affects political and economic policies within regions. Knowledge of world regions and alliances leads to identification of issues that affect people worldwide. Common issues that affect people everywhere include **finances**, **movement of labor**, **trade**, food production, human rights, use of natural resource, prejudice, and poverty.

A true sense of global interdependence results from an understanding of the relationship between local decisions and global issues; for example, how individual or community actions regarding waste disposal or recycling can affect the availability of resources worldwide. Fuel emission standards, for example, can affect air pollution, oil supplies, and gas prices.

Microeconomics focuses on problems specific to a household, firm, or industry, rather than national or global issues. Microeconomics gives particular emphasis to how these units make decisions and the consequences of those decisions.

Macroeconomics is the study of the economy as a whole. Some of the topics considered include inflation, unemployment, and economic growth. **Economic theory** is an explanation of why certain economic phenomena occur. For example, there are theories explaining the rate of inflation, how many hours people choose to work, and the amount of goods and services a specific country will import. Economic theory is essentially a set of statements about cause-and-effect relationships in the economy.

Topic 6.
Identifying Human, Natural, and Capital Resources and How These Resources Are Used in the Production of Goods and Services

Necessary for the production of goods and services are human resources, natural resources, and capital resources. **Human resources** are the people employed in a business or organization; in other words, a firm's human resources are its personnel. Originally, the term for human resources was *labor*. **Natural resources** are the material sources of wealth. Examples of natural or material resources are timber, fresh water, and mineral deposits that occur in a natural state and have economic value.

The word *capital* comes from the Latin word *caput*, which means "head." In economics, capital originally meant the profit that one made; the measure of profit was probably heads (caput) of cattle. In finance and economics today, **capital** means how much real, usable money a person or a company has.

Topic 7.
Identifying How Transportation and Communication Networks Contribute to the Level of Economic Development in Different Regions

Economics is the study of society's choices among a limited amount of resources to attain the highest practical satisfaction. It is the allocation of scarce resources among competing ends.

Because people across the globe can now interact with each other almost instantly, the choices available to them throughout the world are more readily apparent today than they have been in the past. For example, advances in communication—especially through the satellites—made it possible for someone in Los Angeles to witness the devastation Hurricane Katrina wrought on the Gulf Coast in August 2005 and to become aware of the wants and needs there. Similarly, a person in Tokyo can see the goods and products readily available to American consumers in the newscasts and movies shown in Japan. People in New York can pick up the phone and call a person in London without delay to discuss the latest automobile styles. It is evident that people can see and hear about the goods and services available in other parts of the world; such knowledge affects the needs and wants of the world's people.

Convenient transportation and even world travel is now possible for a large number of people throughout the world. Around the globe, people are becoming more aware of the world's products, services, and even clothing styles (blue jeans) as they see people who live an ocean away using the products, service, and clothing. Even fast-food chains are familiar throughout the globe.

As people become aware of lifestyles in other places, their wants and needs may change. People may aspire to what they perceive as a higher economic level. Transportation and communication networks, therefore, have helped initiate many changes in people's needs and wants and have ultimately contributed to the economic development of many regions.

Section 8: Political Science

Topic 1.
Identifying the Structure, Functions, and Purposes of Government

Many people equate the terms *political system* and *government*, but the two concepts are distinct.

Definitions

Government is the agency for regulating the activities of people. It is the system that carries out the decisions of the political system or, in some countries, the decisions of the ruler. The organizations and processes that contribute to the decision-making process comprise the **political system**.

Structure

The distribution of power within the various **structures** of government is a key variable. Separation of powers among branches of the federal government is another aspect of structure useful in comparing political systems. The following are among the most important structures of government:

Confederation. A weak central government delegates principal authority to smaller units, such as states. The United States had this structure under the Articles of Confederation, before the Constitution was ratified in 1789.

Federal. Sovereignty is divided between a central government and a group of states. Contemporary examples of federal republics are the United States, Brazil, and India.

Unitary. The centralized government holds the concentration of power and authority. Examples include France and Japan.

Authoritarian. A government's central power is in a single or collective executive, with the legislative and judicial bodies having little input. Some examples of this include the former Soviet Union, the People's Republic of China, and Nazi Germany.

Parliamentary. The legislative and executive branches are combined, with a prime minister and cabinet selected from within the legislative body. They maintain control so long as the legislative assembly supports their major policies. Great Britain is an example of this form of government.

Presidential. The executive branch is clearly separate from the legislative and judicial branches. However, all three (particularly the executive and legislative branches) must cooperate for policy to be consistent and for smooth government operation. An example of this is the United States.

As just noted, the government of the United States is both a federal system, which divides the sovereignty between the central government and the states, and a presidential system, which has the executive branch clearly separated from the legislative and judicial branches. All countries, of course, do not have a division of power.

Functions

The *Merit Students Encyclopedia* (Halsey and Johnston 1991) notes that the **functions** of a government include (1) political functions, to maintain order within its territories and to protect its borders; (2) legal functions (in fact the word *anarchy*—meaning "lack of government"—has come to mean lawlessness); (3) economic functions, or those concerned with the economic activity of citizens; and/or (4) social functions, which may include civil rights, religion, and education.

Purposes

The question of how to define the purpose of government has been puzzling scholars from Plato's time to the present day. Although some say that government's purpose is to protect all people's rights and preserve justice, others contend that its purpose is to preserve and protect the rights of the few. From these diverging definitions, myriad ideologies—such as communism, liberalism, conservatism, and many others—have evolved. Although most thinkers agree that government is morally justified, they disagree on the role and form of government. News commentator Bob Schieffer stated boldly in 2005, following Hurricane Katrina, "There is no purpose for government except to improve the lives of its citizens."

Topic 2.
Demonstrating Knowledge of the Rights and Responsibilities of a Citizen in the World, Nation, State, and/or Community

Essential democratic principles include those fundamental to the American judicial system, such as the right to due process of law, the right to a fair and speedy trial, protection from unlawful search and seizure, and the right to avoid self-incrimination. The democratic values include life, liberty, the pursuit of happiness, the common good, justice, equality, truth, diversity, popular sovereignty, and patriotism. Furthermore, the ideals

of American democracy include the following essential constitutional principles: the rule of law, separation of powers, representative government, checks and balances, individual rights, freedom of religion, federalism, limited government, and civilian control of the military.

It is essential—indeed, a responsibility—for citizens to be active in maintaining a democratic society. Active citizens participate in the political process by voting, providing services to their communities, and regulating themselves in accordance with the law. Citizens of the United States need also to assume responsibilities to their communities, their states, the nation, and the world.

Topic 3.
Identifying Major Concepts of the U.S. Constitution and Other Historical Documents

Historical Documents

The **Articles of Confederation**, adopted in 1777 after the quarrel with Great Britain, provided for a **unicameral** Congress, in which each state would have one vote, as had been the case in the Continental Congress. Executive authority under the articles would be vested in a committee of 13, with one member from each state. Amending the articles required the unanimous consent of all the states. Under the Articles of Confederation, the government could declare war, make treaties, determine the number of troops and amount of money each state should contribute to a war effort, settle disputes between states, admit new states to the Union, and borrow money. It could not levy taxes, raise troops, or regulate commerce.

As time went on, the inadequacy of the Articles of Confederation became increasingly apparent. In 1787 there was a call for a convention of all the states in Philadelphia for the purpose of revising the Articles of Confederation. The assembly unanimously elected George Washington to preside, and the enormous respect that he commanded helped hold the convention together through difficult times.

The 55 delegates who met in Philadelphia in 1787 to draft a constitution drew on a variety of sources to shape the government that would be outlined in the document. Three British documents were important to the delegates' work: the **Magna Carta (1215)**, the **Petition of Right**

(1628), and the **Bill of Rights (1689)**. These three documents promoted the concept of limited government and were influential in shaping the fundamental principles embodied in the Constitution. The British philosopher John Locke, who wrote about the social contract concept of government and the right of people to alter or abolish a government that did not protect their interests, was another guiding force in the drafting of the Constitution.

Crises in Establishing the U.S. Constitution

One major problem that the delegates faced involved the number of state representatives. With George Washington presiding over the discussions, the delegates finally adopted a proposal known as the **Great Compromise**, which provided for a president, two senators per state, and representatives elected to the House according to their states' populations.

Another major crisis involved disagreement between the North and the South over slavery. To reach a compromise this time, the delegates decided that each slave was to count as three-fifths of a person for purposes of apportioning representation and direct taxation on the states (the Three-Fifths Compromise). Before 1808, the federal government could not stop the importation of slaves.

The delegates had to compromise on the nature of the presidency. The result was a strong presidency with control over foreign policy and the power to veto Congress's legislation. Should the president commit an actual crime, Congress would have the power of impeachment. Otherwise, the president would serve for a term of four years and was eligible for reelection without limit. As a check to the possible excesses of democracy, an Electoral College elected the president; each state would have the same number of electors as it did senators and representatives combined.

The U.S. Constitution

The new Constitution was to take effect when nine states, through special state conventions, had ratified it. By June 21, 1788, the required nine states had ratified, but the crucial states of New York and Virginia still held out. Ultimately, the promise of the addition of a bill of rights helped win the final states. At his inauguration in March 1789, George Washington became the nation's first president.

One of the most significant principles embodied in the Constitution is the concept of a federal system that divides the powers of government between the states and the national government. The local level handles local matters; those issues that affect all citizens are the responsibility of the federal government. Such a system was a natural outgrowth of the colonial relationship between the Americans and the mother country of England.

The Tenth Amendment declares: "Those powers not delegated to the United States by the Constitution, nor prohibited by it to the States, are reserved to the States respectively, or to the people." The federal government and those of the separate states have powers that may in practice overlap, but in cases where they conflict, the federal government is supreme.

In 1920, the passage of the Eighteenth Amendment prohibited the manufacture, transportation, and sale of alcoholic beverages in the United States. Speakeasies became popular, and bootlegging became a profitable underground business. The ratification of the Twenty-first Amendment repealed Prohibition in 1933.

Congress approved the Nineteenth Amendment, providing for women's suffrage in 1919; the Senate had defeated women's suffrage earlier in 1918. The states ratified the Nineteenth Amendment in time for the election of 1920.

Topic 4.
Identifying How the Legislative, Executive, and Judicial Branches Share Powers and Responsibility

A key principle of the U.S. Constitution is separation of powers. The national government is divided into three branches—legislative, executive, and judicial—each with separate functions, but they are not entirely independent. Articles I, II, and III of the main body of the Constitution outline these functions.

The Legislative Branch

Legislative power is vested in a bicameral (two houses) Congress, which is the subject of Article I of the Constitution. The expressed or delegated powers are set forth in Section 8 and can be divided into several broad categories.

Economic powers are as follows:

1. Lay and collect taxes.
2. Borrow money.
3. Regulate foreign and interstate commerce.
4. Coin money and regulate its value.
5. Establish rules concerning bankruptcy.

Judicial powers comprise the following:

1. Establish courts inferior to the Supreme Court.
2. Provide punishment for counterfeiting.
3. Define and punish piracies and felonies committed on the high seas.

War powers of Congress include the following:

1. Declare war.
2. Raise and support armies.
3. Provide and maintain a navy.
4. Provide for organizing, arming, and calling forth the militia.

Other **general peace powers** include the following:

1. Establish uniform rules on naturalization.
2. Establish post offices and post roads.
3. Promote science and the arts by issuing patents and copyrights.
4. Exercise jurisdiction over the seat of the federal government (District of Columbia).

The Constitution also grants Congress the power to discipline federal officials through impeachment and removal from office. The House of Representatives has the power to charge officials (impeach), and the Senate has the power to conduct the trials. The first impeachment of a president was that of Andrew Johnson.

Significant also is the Senate's power to confirm presidential appointments (to the cabinet, federal judiciary, and major bureaucracies) and to ratify treaties. Both houses are involved in choosing a president and vice president if there is no majority in the Electoral College. The House of Representatives votes for the president from among the top three electoral candidates, with each state delegation casting one vote. The Senate votes for the vice president. The Senate has exercised this power only twice, in the disputed elections of 1800 and 1824.

The Executive Branch

Article II of the Constitution deals with the powers and duties of the president. The chief executive's constitutional responsibilities include the following:

1. Serve as commander in chief.
2. Negotiate treaties (with the approval of two-thirds of the Senate).
3. Appoint ambassadors, judges, and other high officials (with the consent of the Senate).
4. Grant pardons and reprieves for those convicted of federal crimes (except in impeachment cases).
5. Seek counsel of department heads (cabinet secretaries).
6. Recommend legislation.
7. Meet with representatives of foreign states.
8. See that federal laws are "faithfully executed."

The president's powers with respect to foreign policy are paramount. Civilian control of the military is a fundamental concept embodied in the naming of the president as commander in chief. In essence, the president is the nation's leading general. As such, the president can make battlefield decisions and shape the military policy.

The president also has broad powers in domestic policy. The most significant domestic policy tool is the president's budget, which the president must submit to Congress. Though Congress must approve all spending, the president has a great deal of power in budget negotiations. The president can use considerable resources in persuading Congress to enact legislation, and the president also has opportunities, such as in the annual State of the Union address, to reach out directly to the American people to convince them to support presidential policies.

The Judicial Branch

Article III of the Constitution states that "the judicial power of the United States shall be vested in one Supreme Court and in such inferior courts as the Congress may from time to time ordain and establish."

The Constitution makes two references to a trial by jury in criminal cases (in Article III and in the Sixth Amendment).

Topic 5.
Demonstrating Knowledge of the U.S. Electoral System and the Election Process

To become president, a candidate must be (1) a natural-born United States citizen, (2) a resident of the United States for at least 14 years, and (3) at least 35 years old. Each political party must select a candidate as its representative in an upcoming election. At the end of the primaries and caucuses, each party holds a national convention and finalizes its selection of its presidential nominee. Each presidential candidate chooses a vice presidential candidate.

The candidates usually begin their campaign tours once they have the nomination of their parties. In November, U.S. citizens cast their votes, but they are not actually voting directly for the presidential candidate of their choice in the general election. Instead, voters cast their votes for **electors**, who are part of the Electoral College and who are supposed to vote for the candidate that their state prefers.

The 55 delegates who met in Philadelphia in 1787 to draft a constitution established the Electoral College originally as a compromise between electing the president by popular vote and by Congressional election. At first the legislators in some states chose the electors; some states had the people elect the electors.

In 1796, political parties started to operate. Each state would have the same number of electors as the state had senators and representatives. Each elector voted for two candidates. The person receiving the largest number of votes became the president, and the person receiving the second-highest number of votes became the vice president (as specified in Article II).

The Twelfth Amendment to the U.S. Constitution specifies that the electors must meet in their respective states and cast their votes for president and vice president. The slates of electors pledge to vote for the candidates of the parties that the people select. Each elector must have his or her vote signed and certified. The electors send the votes to the president of the Senate for counting in front of Congress. The person having the majority (two-thirds of the votes cast) is declared president. The House chooses the president from the top three if there is no majority. The Twentieth Amendment dictates the process that takes place if no president has qualified by the third day of January.

The president and vice president are the only two nationally elected officials. (State elections determine senators and representatives.) As discussed earlier, if no majority is achieved in the Electoral College, the House of Representatives votes for the president, and the Senate for the vice president.

Topic 6.
Identifying the Structures and Functions of U.S. Federal, State, and Local Governments

Structures

According to the Constitution, all governmental powers ultimately stem from the people. As mentioned earlier, local governments generally handle local matters, and those issues that affect all citizens are the responsibility of the federal government. This system was a natural outgrowth of the colonial relationship between the Americans and the mother country of England.

The Tenth Amendment gives to the States those powers that the Constitution does not deny to the States and that the Constitution does not give to the Federal Government; if there is overlapping between the state government and the federal government, the federal government is supreme.

Functions

The following powers are reserved for the federal government:

1. Regulate foreign commerce.
3. Regulate interstate commerce.
4. Mint money.
5. Regulate naturalization and immigration.
6. Grant copyrights and patents.
7. Declare and wage war and declare peace.
8. Admit new states.

9. Fix standards for weights and measures.

10. Raise and maintain an army and a navy.

11. Govern Washington, D.C.

12. Conduct relations with foreign powers.

13. Universalize bankruptcy laws.

The state governments have the following powers:

1. Conduct and monitor elections.

2. Establish voter qualifications within the guidelines established by the Constitution.

3. Provide for local governments.

4. Ratify proposed amendments to the Constitution.

5. Regulate contracts and wills.

6. Regulate intrastate commerce.

7. Provide for education for its citizens.

8. Levy direct taxes.

Topic 7.
Identifying the Relationships between Social, Economic, and Political Rights and the Historical Documents That Secure These Rights

Throughout the summer and fall of 1787, the Constitutional Convention worked on the new Constitution. Of the 55 delegates, only 39 signed. George Mason of Virginia objected to the fact that the Constitution contained no bill of rights. Eventually, the Bill of Rights became the first 10 amendments to the Constitution. As time passed, Congress ratified several other amendments. Various portions of the Constitution provided for social, economic, and political rights.

Articles I, II, and II provide for the legislative, executive, and judicial powers. Article IV guarantees citizens of each state the privileges and immunities of the other states; this was to help prevent discrimination against visitors. It also ensures criminal extradition between states: if a person commits a crime in one state and escapes to another state, the state in which that person is hiding must give the person up to the state from which the criminal escaped. In addition, Article IV provides to the states federal protection against invasion and domestic unrest.

The Bill of Rights

When the first Congress met in 1789, it had on its agenda the consideration of 12 amendments to the Constitution written by James Madison. The states approved 10 of the 12 on December 15, 1791. Those 10 amendments make up the Bill of Rights (*Congress for Kids*):

First Amendment. Right to freedom of worship, speech, press, and assembly

Second Amendment. Right to keep and bear arms

Third Amendment. Right against quartering of troops

Fourth Amendment. Right against unreasonable searches and seizures

Fifth Amendment. Rights of accused person: grand jury, due process, just compensation

Sixth Amendment. Right to jury trial

Seventh Amendment. Rights in suits; decisions of facts in case decided by jury; judge's role limited to questions about the law

Eighth Amendment. Prohibition of cruel and unusual punishment

Ninth Amendment. Rights retained by people

Tenth Amendment. Rights retained by states

Other Amendments to the Constitution

An amendment is either an addition to the Constitution or a change in the original text. Making additions or revisions to the Constitution is no small feat. Since 1787, more than 9,000 amendments have been proposed, but only 27 have been approved (*Congress for Kids*):

Eleventh Amendment. A citizen of one state may sue a citizen of another state only if that person has the state's permission

Twelfth Amendment. Election of the president

Thirteenth Amendment. Abolishment of slavery

Fourteenth Amendment. Definition of *citizen*; protection of the citizen against states' abridging rights

Fifteenth Amendment. Suffrage rights not denied or abridged by "race, color, or previous condition of servitude"

Sixteenth Amendment. Income tax

Seventeenth Amendment. Senators elected by popular vote

Eighteenth Amendment. Prohibition of intoxicating liquors

Nineteenth Amendment. Women's suffrage

Twentieth Amendment. Beginning and ending of terms of elected officials (members of Congress, vice president, president); presidential succession

Twenty-first Amendment. Repeal of Eighteenth Amendment

Twenty-second Amendment. Limitation of president to two terms in office

Twenty-third Amendment. District of Columbia given vote in presidential elections

Twenty-fourth Amendment. Repeal of poll tax in federal elections

Twenty-fifth Amendment. Appointment of vice president if vacancy in that office occurs; procedure in case of presidential disability

Twenty-sixth Amendment. Establishment of voting age at 18

Twenty-seventh Amendment. No change in compensation for representatives and senators can take effect until an intervening election of representatives.

Topic 8.
Demonstrating Knowledge of the Processes of the U.S. Legal System

The contemporary judicial branch consists of thousands of courts and is, in essence, a dual system, with each state having its own judicial structure functioning simultaneously with a complete set of federal courts. The most significant piece of legislation with reference to establishing a federal court network was the Judiciary Act of 1789. That law organized the Supreme Court and set up the federal district courts (13) and the circuit (appeal) courts (3).

The Supreme Court today is made up of a chief justice and eight associate justices. The president with the approval of the Senate appoints the justices for life; the justices often come from the ranks of the federal judiciary. In recent years, the public has viewed the appointment of Supreme Court justices with intense scrutiny,

and in some cases, heated political controversy has accompanied the choices for appointment.

Understanding of the role of law in a democratic society results from a knowledge of the nature of civil, criminal, and constitutional law and how the organization of the judicial system serves to interpret and apply such laws. Essential judicial principles include comprehension of rights, such as the right of due process, the right to a fair and speedy trial, and the right to a hearing before a jury of one's peers. Additional judicial principles include an understanding of the protections granted in the Constitution, which include protection from self-incrimination and unlawful searches and seizures.

The U.S. Constitution makes two references to trials by jury (Article III and the Sixth Amendment). The accused seems to benefit by the provision because a jury consists of 12 persons; the accused cannot receive a conviction unless all 12 agree that the defendant is guilty. There is mention of a speedy trial to prevent incarceration indefinitely unless the jury finds the accused guilty and the person receives such a sentence. The public trial statement ensures that the defendant receives just treatment. In 1968, the Supreme Court ruled that jury trials in criminal courts extended to the state courts as well as the federal courts. The Sixth Amendment uses the phrase "compulsory process for obtaining witnesses." This means that it is compulsory for witnesses for the defendant to appear in court.

Topic 9.
Identifying the Roles of the United States in International Relations

The United States is not an island either geographically or politically. The United States demonstrates its leadership and participation in global interdependence economically, politically, historically, ecologically, linguistically, and culturally. The United States belonged to a group of nations (the Allied Powers) during World War II, but historian Chitwood says that when the United States ratified the treaty of the military alliance of the North Atlantic Treaty Organization (NATO) on April 4, 1949, it reached a far point in its departure from global isolation (Chitwood 867); the treaty of NATO states that each member will come to the aid of any other member that becomes a victim of outside attack. Twenty-six countries from North America and Europe entered into the treaty. NATO both safeguards and promotes the values of law, individual liberty, democracy, and the peaceful resolution of disputes; it provides a forum in which the United States, Canada, and European countries can consult about security issues and take appropriate, joint action on them. The alliance considers an attack against one member as being an attack against all. NATO-led forces are helping to bring stability to Iraq, Afghanistan, Kosovo, and Darfur. NATO protects its members through military and political means. (*NATO Official Homepage*)

The United States participates in other alliances also. For example, the United States supports the United Nations Educational, Scientific and Cultural Organization (UNESCO), a specialized United Nations agency to build peace in the minds of people, publish scientific breakthroughs, educate, build classrooms in devastated countries, encourage communication, respect diverse cultures, and promote the natural and social sciences. ("United Nations Educational, Scientific, and Cultural Organization," *http://portal.unesco.org*)

The United States is aware that there are common issues—like food production, human rights, use of natural resources, prejudice, poverty, and trade—that affect regions and nations worldwide. It also realizes that military and economic alliances and cartels can affect nations, regions, and the world.

A country with a true sense of global interdependence realizes that its actions can affect the world. For instance, continuing to allow the use of certain sprays in a country can damage the ozone layer and affect the entire world.

Section 9: Anthropology, Sociology, and Psychology

Anthropology is the study of human culture. Anthropologists study both modern-day and prehistoric culture. There are several types of anthropologists:

1. Archaeologists excavate and scientifically analyze the remains of extinct people to attempt reconstruction of their way of life. Richard Leakey is an archaeologist.

2. Primatologists study the group behavior of primates (nonhuman) such as gorillas, baboons, and chimpanzees. Jane Goodall is a primatologist.

3. Ethnographers gather information about culture through fieldwork done on site. Margaret Mead was an ethnographer.

4. Linguistic anthropologists study languages, particularly language in a social context.

5. Physical (or biological) anthropologists study living and fossil human beings and primates, such as chimpanzees and monkeys.

Sociology is the study of the social behavior of humans within a group. The groups studied can include families, mobs, workers in large organizations, criminals, medical groups, men, women, and so on; of particular concern is how the groups and the institutions interact. The sociologist and Nobel Prize Winner Gunnar Myrdal was a prominent sociologist; his *An American Dilemma* of 1949 dealt with the "Negro in America [which] represents nothing more and nothing less than a century-long lag of public morals." (Myrdal, 24) He saw the problem as being "an integral part of, or a special phase of, the whole complex of problems in the larger civilization. It cannot be treated in isolation." (Myrdal, xlix)

Psychology is the study of human behavior—individuals and small groups of people. Educators are perhaps most familiar with psychologists Jean Piaget (a developmental psychologist who studies individuals over a lifespan) and B. F. Skinner (a behavioral or experimental psychologist). Social psychologists study the behavior of people in groups . Cognitive psychologists are interested in how people think and learn. Clinical psychologists study abnormal behavior. It is interesting, however, that some people do not classify psychology as a social studies subject.

Section 10: Instruction and Assessment of the Social Sciences

Topic 1.
Identifying Appropriate Resources for Teaching Social Studies Concepts

The ability to understand and apply skills and procedures related to the study of social sciences involves knowledge of the use of **systematic inquiry**. Inquiry is essential for use in examining single social sciences topics or integrated social sciences. Being able to engage in inquiry involves the ability to acquire information from a variety of resources and to organize and interpret that information. The process of inquiry begins with **designing and conducting investigations** that lead to the identification and analysis of social sciences issues.

Systematic social science inquiry uses various resources. Among the most commonly used resources **primary sources** are diaries, ledgers, oral histories, artifacts, and census reports; **secondary sources** include textbooks and **encyclopedias.**

The effective teacher uses a variety of educational resources (including people and technology) to enhance both individual and group learning. Resources of all types are also key elements of the **curriculum planning process**. The effective teacher should be very familiar with the school library, the local public library, education service center resources, and the library of any college or university in the area. Another important set of resources is the audiovisual aids the teacher can borrow: kits, films, filmstrips, videos, laser discs, and computer software, among others. All used audiovisual aids should relate to curricular objectives.

Many librarians have keyed their resources to objectives in related subject areas and have thus enabled the teacher to incorporate them with ease into the lessons. However, teachers should never use resources with a class without previewing the resources and approving their use with the class. The curriculum guide or the lesson plan should ideally include the list of resources the teacher might use.

The effective teacher determines the appropriate place in the lesson for audiovisual aids. If the material is especially interesting and thought provoking, the teacher can use it to introduce a unit or to summarize it. Throughout the unit, the teacher and students may use the Internet for research.

Print Resources

The most common print material is the textbook, which teachers usually select from a list of books approved by the state. The use of textbooks has some disadvantages. The cost of textbooks has increased drastically in recent years, and some do not match curriculum guidelines. The adoption process is a long one, and textbooks (particularly for history) can become out-of-date quickly; therefore, the teacher must use additional resources with recent dates.

Another limitation of textbooks is their tendency to provide sketchy or minimal information, partly because publishers must include such a broad range of topics. An ineffective teacher may use the "chapter a week" theory of "covering" a textbook. This method gives no consideration to the importance of information in each chapter or its relevance to the overall district curriculum. Merely covering the material does not promote critical thinking on the part of the teacher or the student. Students tend to believe the textbook is something they must endure and not necessarily employ as a tool for learning. The effective teacher chooses sections from the textbook that are relevant to the learning goals and omits the rest. The teacher may supplement the sketchy textbook treatments by using an abundance of other resources.

Local, state, and national newspapers and magazines are important sources of up-to-date information not available in textbooks. Some newspapers and magazines have special programs to help teachers use their products in the classroom as sources of information and for reading and writing opportunities. Local newspapers may even be willing to send specialists to work with students or act as special resource people.

Visual Materials

The most available visual tools in classrooms are the chalkboard and the overhead projector. Several principles apply to both. The teacher must write clearly and in large letters. Overhead transparencies should never be typed on a regular typewriter because the print is too small. Computers allow type sizes of at least 18 points, which is the minimum readable size. Also, both boards and transparencies should be free of clutter. Teachers must remove old information from the board or screen before adding new information. These tools work more effectively if the teacher plans their use ahead of time. Using different colors emphasizes relationships or differences.

Posters and charts can complement lessons, but they should not clutter the walls so that students are unable to focus on what's important for the current lesson. Teachers may display posters and charts on a rotating basis.

A multimedia production can include images, text, and sound from a videodisc, CD, graphics software, word processing software, and a sound effects program. Teachers can develop classroom presentations, but students can also develop learning units as part of a research or inquiry project. The cost of a multimedia system remains relatively high, but students can use it to develop high-level thought processes, collaborative work, research skills, content knowledge, and understanding.

The Internet is essential to the students and the teachers in gathering information. Computer programs, filmstrips, films, and videos are appealing to students because visual images on television, computers, and video games already surround them. Films, computer displays, and filmstrips have the advantage of large-screen projection so all students can see clearly, but many projection devices are expensive.

Teachers may stop videos, films, and filmstrips for discussion. Students comprehend better and remember longer if the teacher introduces a video or film appropriately and stops it frequently to discuss it with the students. This method also helps keep students' attention focused and assists them in learning note-taking skills.

Some of the best graphic aids are those that individual students or groups of students develop. While learning about subject-area concepts, students become familiar with the design and presentation of information. Students can take pictures of their products to put in a portfolio or scrapbook.

Compact Discs and Interactive Video

Compact discs (CDs) provide a sturdy, condensed system of storage for pictures and sound. These discs can store many separate frames of still images, up to two hours of music, or two hours of motion pictures with sound. An advantage of a CD rather than videotape is that one can assess each frame separately and quickly by inputting its number. The simplest level of use involves commands to play, pause, forward, or reverse.

A CD or video program can become interactive with a computer link. The teacher can then access individual images, sequence images, and pace the information from the interactive system. A social studies teacher with a collection of pictures of the world's art treasures can choose which pictures to use, order the images, and design custom-made lessons for repeated use or for easy revision. The teacher can develop numerous lessons from one CD or videotape. More comprehensive interactive programs use the computer to present information, access a disc to illustrate main points, and ask for responses from the student.

Human Resources

Parents and other members of the community can be excellent local experts from whom students can learn about any subject: economics from bankers, history from veterans, music from a specific period from local musicians or recording collectors, community history from local historians or librarians, business from owners of companies—the list of possibilities is endless. Effective teachers make sure that any invited guest understands the purpose of the visit and the goals or objectives of the presentation. Preparation can make the class period more focused and meaningful.

Field trips are excellent sources of information, especially about careers and current issues like pollution control. One field trip can yield assignments in mathematics, history, science, English, art, architecture, music, or health. Teachers can collaborate with each other to produce thematic assignments for the field trip or simply to coordinate the students' assignments. Often a history report can serve as an English paper as well. Data can be analyzed in math classes and presented with the aid of computers.

Topic 2.
Evaluating Examples of Primary Source Documents for Historical Perspective

Evaluating primary source documents to gain a historical perspective involves the ability to analyze and interpret the past. Analysis and interpretation result from an understanding that history is logically constructed; this conclusion results from careful analysis of documents, eyewitness accounts, letters, diaries, artifacts, photos, historical sites, and other primary sources. It is through these primary source documents that history can come alive.

The Library of Congress has on-line a wide range of primary source documents, from the Declaration of Independence and the Constitution to recordings and photographs made during the Great Depression. Students can even conduct interviews with veterans and examine the diaries, letters, and discharge papers that veterans or members of their families or communities may possess. Visits to local museums, libraries, and courthouses can also uncover primary source documents.

Topic 3.
Identifying Appropriate Assessment Methods in Teaching Social Science Concepts

The basic goals of assessment are to enhance teachers' knowledge of learners and their needs, to monitor students' progress toward goals and outcomes, and to modify instruction when progress is not sufficient.

Purposes of Assessment

The effective teacher understands the importance of ongoing assessment as an instructional tool for the classroom and uses both informal and formal assessment measures. Informal measures can include observation, journals, written drafts, and conversations. Formal measures can include teacher-made tests, district exams, and standardized tests.

Both formative and summative evaluations are part of effective teaching. **Formative** evaluation occurs during the process of learning, when the teacher or the students monitor progress in obtaining outcomes and while it is still possible to modify instruction. **Summative** evaluation occurs at the end of a specific time or course of study. Usually, a summative evaluation applies a single grade to represent a student's performance.

Teacher-Made Tests

Teachers should develop assessments at the same time that they plan goals and outcomes; teachers should not wait to prepare assessments until after they have taught all the lessons. Carefully planned objectives and assessment instruments serve as lesson development guides for the teacher.

Paper-and-pencil tests are the most common method for evaluation of student progress. Among the various types of questions are multiple-choice, true/false, matching, fill-in-the-blank, short answer, and essay questions. The first five types tend to test students' knowledge or comprehension levels; teachers can, however, with some forethought develop objective tests which cover all levels of Bloom's Taxonomy. Essays may test at the lower levels also, but they can be suitable for assessing learning at higher levels. **Projects**, **papers**, **and portfolios** (authentic assessments) can assess higher-level thinking skills.

To test students' recall of factual information, a short objective test (with multiple-choice, true/false, matching, fill-in-the blank questions) might be most effective and efficient. Students can answer the first three types of questions on machine-scorable scan sheets for quick and accurate scoring. Again, the teacher does not have to limit the objective test questions to the lower levels of knowledge and can even provide an opportunity for an explanation of answers.

To test students' ability to analyze an event, compare and contrast two concepts, make predictions about an experiment, or evaluate a character's actions, an **essay** question may provide the best opportunity for the students to show what they can do. The teacher should make the question explicit enough for students to know exactly what is expected. For example, "Explain the results of World War II" is too broad; students do not know the teacher's expectations. A more explicit question is, "Explain the three results of World War II that you think had the most impact on participating nations. Explain the criteria you used in selecting these results."

Advantages of an essay include the possibility for students to be creative in their answers, the opportunity for students to explain their responses, and the potential to test for higher-level thinking skills. Disadvantages of essay questions include the time needed for students to formulate meaningful responses, language difficulties of some students, and the time needed to evaluate the essays.

Consistency in evaluating essays can also be a problem for some teachers, but an outline of the acceptable answers—a scoring *rubric*—can help a teacher avoid inconsistency. Teachers who write specific questions and know what they are looking for are more likely to be consistent in grading. Also, if there are several essay questions, the effective teacher grades all student responses to the first question, then moves on to all responses to the second, and so on.

Authentic Assessments

Paper-and-pencil tests or essays are not the only methods of assessment. Others include projects, observation, checklists, anecdotal records, portfolios, self-assessments, and peer assessments. Although these types of assessment often take more time and effort to plan and administer, they can often provide a more authentic assessment of student progress.

Projects are common in almost all subject areas. Projects promote student control of learning experiences and provide opportunities for research into various topics and the chance to use visuals, graphics, videos, or multimedia presentations in place of, or in addition to, written reports. Projects also promote student self-assessment because students must evaluate their progress at each step of the project. Many schools have history fairs for which students plan and develop projects to display. Projects can also be part of economics and other areas of the social sciences.

Effective teachers must make clear the requirements and the criteria for evaluation of projects before students begin work. Teachers must also assist students in selecting projects that are feasible, for which the school has learning resources, and that do not require an exorbitant investment of time and expense.

The advantages of projects are that students can use visuals, graphics, art, or even music abilities; students can be creative in their topics and research; and the projects can appeal to various learning styles. The primary disadvantage is difficulty with grading, although this can be overcome by devising a checklist for required elements and a rating scale for quality.

Observation is another assessment method for individual or group work. Observation is very suitable for skills or for effective learning. Usually, the teacher makes a **checklist** of competencies, skills, or requirements and checks off the ones the student or group displays. A teacher who wants to emphasize careful listening might observe a discussion while using a checklist that includes paying attention, not interrupting, summarizing the ideas of other members of the group, and asking questions of others.

Advantages of checklists include the potential for capturing behavior—such as important elements in a speech in class—that a paper-and-pencil test cannot accurately measure. One characteristic of a checklist that is both an advantage and a disadvantage is its structure, which provides consistency but inflexibility. An open-ended comment section at the end of a checklist can overcome this disadvantage.

Anecdotal records are helpful in some instances, such as capturing the process a group of students uses to solve a problem. This formative data can be useful during feedback to the group. Students can also write explanations of the procedures they use for their projects. One advantage of an anecdotal record is that it can include all relevant information. Disadvantages include the amount of time necessary to complete the record and the difficulty in assigning a grade. If the anecdotal record is solely for feedback, no grade is necessary.

Portfolios are collections of students' best work and can be useful in any subject area where the teacher wants students to take more responsibility for planning, carrying out, and organizing their own learning. Like a portfolio that an artist, model, or performer creates, a student portfolio provides a succinct picture of the child's achievements over a certain period. Portfolios may contain essays or articles written on paper, videotapes, multimedia presentations on computer disks, or a combination. Teachers often use portfolios as a means of collecting the best samples of student writing over an entire year, and some teachers pass on the portfolios to the next teacher to help in student assessment.

Teachers should provide or assist students in developing guidelines for what materials should go in their portfolios because it would be unrealistic to include every piece of work in one portfolio. Using portfolios requires the students to devise a means of evaluating their own work. A portfolio should not be a scrapbook for collecting handouts or work done by other individuals, although it can certainly include work by a group in which the student was a participant.

Some advantages of portfolios over testing are that they provide a clear picture of a student's progress, they are not affected by one inferior test grade, and they help develop students' self-assessment skills. One disadvantage is the amount of time required to teach students how to develop meaningful portfolios. However, the time is well spent if students learn valuable skills. Another concern is the amount of time teachers must spend to assess portfolios. As students become more proficient at self-assessment, however, the teacher can spend more time in coaching and advising students throughout the development of their portfolios. Another concern is that parents may not understand the grading of portfolios. The effective teacher devises a system that the students and parents understand before work on the portfolio begins.

Self-Assessment and Peer Assessment

One goal of an assessment system is to promote student self-assessment. Because most careers require employees or managers to evaluate their own productivity as well as that of others, self-assessment and peer assessment are important lifelong skills. Effective teachers use a structured approach to teach self-assessment, help students set standards at first by making recommendations about standards, and then have students gradually move toward developing their own criteria and applying those criteria to their work.

One method of developing self-assessment is to ask students to apply the teacher's own standards to a product. For example, a history teacher who uses a rating scale for essays might have students use that scale on their own papers and compare their evaluations with those of the teacher. A science teacher who uses a checklist while observing an experiment might ask students to use the same checklist; students can compare their scores with the teacher's. The class can set standards for evaluating group work and individual work. Collaborative groups are effective vehicles for practicing the skills involved in self-assessment and peer assessment.

Performance-Based Assessment

Some states and districts are moving toward performance-based tests, which assess students on how well they perform certain tasks. Performance-based tests allow students to use higher-level thinking skills to apply, analyze, synthesize, and evaluate ideas and data. Performance-based testing evaluates process and output. A history performance-based assessment might require students to research a specific topic over a period of several days, make presentations of their findings to the rest of the class, and write a response that uses what they have learned from their own research and from that of their classmates.

Testing Measurements

There are primarily two types of testing measurements. In **criterion-referenced** tests, the teacher measures each student against uniform objectives or criteria. Teacher-made tests should be criterion-referenced because the teacher should develop them to measure the achievement of predetermined outcomes for the course.

The purpose of a **norm-referenced test (NRT)** is to compare the performance of groups of students. This type of test is competitive because a limited number of students can score well. A plot of large numbers of NRT scores resembles a bell-shaped curve. Interpretation involves using terms like **percentile scores** (which rank students from highest to lowest), **normed scores** (which can help compare the performance of test-takers with the performance of a norm group), **reliability** (whether the instrument will give consistent results with the repetition of the measurement), and **validity** (whether the test actually measures what it is supposed to measure). Chapter 2 also includes a discussion of assessment and measurement, particularly as related to norm-referenced and criterion-referenced assessment.

References

Alvarez, Lizette. "Census Director Marvels at the New Portrait of America." *New York Times*, January 1, 2001.

Cayne, Bernard S., ed. *Merit Students Encyclopedia*. Chicago: Crowell-Collier, 1969.

Chitwood, Oliver Perry and Frank Lawrence Owsley, and H. C. Nixon. *The United States: From Colony to World Power*. New York: D. Van Nostrand, 1949.

Congress for Kids. "Constitution: Amendments." *http://congressforkids.net/Constitution_amendments.htm*.

Davis, Anita Price. *North Carolina during the Great Depression: A Documentary Portrait of a Decade*. Jefferson, NC: McFarland, 2003.

Florida Smart. "Florida Population and Demographics." *http://www.floridasmart.com/facts/demographics.htm*.

Gordon, W. J. J. *Synectics*. New York: Harper and Row, 1961.

Halsey, William D., and Bernard Johnston, eds. *Merit Students Encyclopedia*. New York: Macmillan, 1991.

Harrington, Michael. *The Other America: Poverty in the United States*. New York: Macmillan, 1962.

Huitt, W. "Critical Thinking: An Overview." *Educational Psychology Interactive*. *http://chiron.valdosta.edu/whuitt/col/cogsys/critthnk.html*.

Martin, Philip L. "Immigration in the United States." Institute of European Studies, University of California, Berkeley. *http://ies.berkeley.edu/pubs/workingpapers/ay0102.html*.

Myrdal, Gunnar with the assistance of Richard Sterner and Arnold Rose. *An American Dilemma: The Negro Problem and Modern Democracy*. New York: Harper and Brothers Publishers, 1944.

NATO Official Homepage. *http://www.nato.int*.

Schieffer, Bob. "Government Failed the People." *CBS News* (September 4, 2005). *http://www.cbsnews.com/stories/2005/09/06/opinion/schieffer/main818486.html.*

Schug, Mark C., and R. Beery. *Teaching Social Studies in the Elementary*. Prospect Heights, IL: Waveland Press, 1987.

Schuncke, George M. *Elementary Social Studies: Knowing, Doing, Caring*. New York: Macmillan, 1988.

"United Nations Educational, Scientific, and Cultural Organization," *http://portal.unesco.org.*

U.S. Census Bureau, *Current Population Survey, March 2000.* *http://www.census.gov/population/socdemo/foreign/p20-534/tab0314.txt.*

U. S. Census Bureau. "Countries of Birth of the Foreign-Born Population, 1850–2000." *Profile of the Foreign-Born Population in the United States: 2000.* as cited by Information Please® Database, ©2006 Pearson Education, Inc. *http://www.Infoplease.com/ipa/A0900547.html.*

U.S. Census Bureau. "State and County Quickfacts: Florida." *http://quickfacts.census.gov/qfd/states/12000.html.*

Woolever, Roberta and Kathryn P. Scott. *Active Learning in Social Studies: Promoting Cognitive and Social Growth*. Glenview, IL: Scott, Foresman, 1988.

Section 1: Earth Science

Topic 1.
Revolution of the Earth

Earth revolves around the sun. The axis of Earth is tilted at a 23.5-degree angle, and the axis always points toward the North Star (Polaris). The tilt and the revolution about the sun cause the seasons. **Earth's distance from the sun does not cause the seasons**. In fact, the Northern Hemisphere is closer to the sun in the winter—not in the summer. This closeness of the Earth to the sun in the winter is because of the elliptical pattern that the Earth follows as it revolves about the sun.

The Northern Hemisphere experiences **summer** when it is tilted toward the sun. Summer begins in the Northern Hemisphere on June 21, when the rays of the sun shine directly on the area. The hours of daylight are longer in the summer in the Northern Hemisphere, and the rays of the sun cover a smaller part of the surface of Earth in the summer. At that time of year, therefore, the Northern Hemisphere has hot surface temperatures and, because of the tilt of Earth, more hours of sunlight than darkness. This means that the longer direct rays of the sun last longer in the summer.

When the Northern Hemisphere is tilted away from the sun, it experiences **winter**. Winter begins in the Northern Hemisphere on December 22. During this season, the days are shorter, fewer direct rays from the sun reach the Northern Hemisphere, and the hours of night are longer than in the summer.

When it is summer in the Northern Hemisphere, it is winter in the Southern Hemisphere. When it is winter in the Northern Hemisphere, it is summer in the Southern Hemisphere. In the **fall** and **spring**, Earth is not tilted toward or away from the sun; it is somewhere between. The days and nights have an almost equal number of hours in the spring and fall. The Northern Hemisphere has equal days and nights at the **vernal equinox** (March 21) and at the **autumnal equinox** (September 23).

Topic 2.
Identifying the Components of Earth's Solar System and Comparing Their Individual Characteristics

The solar system is the sun and its nine orbiting planets. The sun, composed of hydrogen, has a mass 750 times that of all the planets combined. The names of the planets in order from the sun are Mercury, Venus, Earth, Mars, Jupiter, Saturn, Uranus, Neptune, and Pluto. Rocky, metallic materials primarily compose the innermost planets of Mercury, Venus, Earth, and Mars; hydrogen, helium, and ices of ammonia and methane compose the outermost planets of Neptune, Saturn, Uranus, and Pluto. Composed largely of hydrogen gas, Jupiter—a giant, half-formed sun—is an exception among the planets.

Many of the planets have satellite moons, including Earth, Mars, and Pluto, each of which has two, and Jupiter, which has eight. Uranus has more than twenty moons than Saturn has the distinguishing feature of rings. Both Earth and Venus have significant atmospheres. Jupiter has a giant red spot.

The accepted unit of measurement for expressing distances from the sun is the **astronomical unit (AU)**, with 1 AU equal to the distance from the sun to Earth. The planet closest to the sun is Mercury at 0.39 AU, and the planet farthest from the sun is Pluto at 39.4 AU.

Topic 3.
Identifying the Phases of the Moon and the Moon's Effect on Earth

The moon is a satellite of Earth that orbits the Earth at the rate of one revolution every 29.5 days. Although it is the second brightest heavenly body, the moon does not give off its own light. Rather, it reflects the sun's light. The amount of lighted moon we see on Earth changes, however. Depending on where the moon is in its orbit, more or less of its lighted surface is visible from Earth. When the amount of visible lighted surface of the moon is increasing, the moon is *waxing*; when the amount of visible light is decreasing, the moon is *waning*. These changes in the amount of visible lighted surface are the **phases** of the moon:

New moon. The moon is between Earth and the sun. When the dark side of the moon is turned toward Earth, it is difficult to see the moon from Earth.

Crescent moon. As the moon continues to revolve around Earth (west to east), a crescent-shaped slice of the moon becomes visible from Earth.

Half moon (first quarter). About a week after the crescent moon, roughly one-half of the moon is visible.

Gibbous moon. Almost all the moon is visible a few days after the half moon.

Full moon. About two weeks after the new moon, the Earth is between the sun and the moon. Almost all the lighted side of the moon is visible from Earth.

Half moon (last quarter). After the full-moon phase, the moon moves to another half-moon phase. The phases begin again.

When Earth blocks sunlight from reaching the moon, it creates a shadow on the moon's surface. This shadow on the moon's surface is the **lunar eclipse**. When the moon blocks sunlight from hitting Earth, the result is a **solar eclipse**.

The moon exerts a **gravitational pull** on Earth. This pull causes **tides**, or periodic changes in the ocean water surfaces or sea level.

Section 2: Earth History

Topic 1.
Knowledge of Processes That Shape the Earth, Identifying Characteristics of Geologic Formations, the Mechanisms by Which They Were Formed, and Their Relationship to the Movement of Tectonic Plates

Geology is the study of the structure and composition of the earth. The three layers that compose the earth are the core, mantle, and crust. Solid iron and nickel make up the core, which is about 7,000 kilometers in diameter. The **mantle** is the semimolten layer between the crust and the core. It is about 3,000 kilometers thick. The **crust** is the solid outermost layer, composed of bedrock overlaid with mineral and/or organic sediment (soil) and ranging from 5 to 40 kilometers thick.

At times, large sections of the earth's crust move and create faults, earthquakes, volcanoes, and mountains. These moving sections of the earth are **plates**, and the study of their movements is **plate tectonics**.

Faults are cracks in the crust and are the results of the movements of plates. **Earthquakes** occur when plates slide past one another quickly. Volcanoes may also cause earthquakes. A seismograph measures earthquakes and uses the Richter scale.

Volcanoes are mountains that form when two plates move away from one another to let magma reach the crust. **Magma** is molten rock beneath the earth's crust.

Lava is molten rock on the earth's surface. A volcano shoots out magma, which eventually hardens into lava, and releases ash. Sometimes the erupting volcano forms rivers of lava.

Volcanoes exist all over the world—for example, the Pacific Ocean, the Hawaiian Islands, and the southeastern border of Asia. The composition of volcanoes is fiery igneous rock, ash, and many layers of dirt and mud that have hardened from previous eruptions. Volcanic activity causes the crust of the earth to buckle upward and form mountains.

Plate tectonics is a relatively new theory that has revolutionized the way geologists think about the earth. According to the theory, large lithospheric plates form the surface of the earth. The size and position of these plates change over time. The edges of the plates, where they move against each other, are sites of intense geologic activity such as earthquakes, volcanoes, and mountain building. Plate tectonics is a combination of two earlier ideas: continental drift and seafloor spreading. **Continental drift** is the movement of continents over the earth's surface and their change in position relative to each other. **Seafloor spreading** is the creation of new oceanic crust at midocean ridges and movement of the crust away from the midocean ridges.

The following are some of the evidence of continental drift and the underlying plate tectonics:

- The shapes of many continents are such that they look as though they are separate pieces of a jigsaw puzzle. For example, the east coasts of North America and South America and the west coasts of Africa and Europe appear to fit together.
- Many fossil comparisons along the edges of continents that look as if they fit together suggest species similarities that would make sense only if the two continents were joined at some point in the past.
- Much seismic, volcanic, and geothermal activity occurs more frequently along plate boundaries than in sites far from boundaries.
- Ridges, such as the Mid-Atlantic Ridge, occur where plates are separating because of lava welling up from between them as they pull apart. Likewise, mountain ranges are forming where plates are pushing against each other (for example, the Himalayas, which are still growing).

Topic 2.
Identifying Fossil Formation and Its Use in Interpreting the Past and Extrapolating to the Future

Fossils are preserved remnants of or marks made by plants and animals that were once alive. As such, fossils are one source of information about changes in the environment over time. Finding fossils of marine organisms in what is now a desert is an opportunity to discuss scientific ways of knowing, how science forms and tests hypotheses, and how theories develop to explain the reasons behind observations.

Fossils formed in several ways. In some cases, sediment covered some animals and then hardened into rock, preserving the hard parts of the animals' bodies. Other animals fell into tar pits, swamps, or quicksand, which ultimately hardened and preserved the animals' bones and teeth. Ice and mud preserved some animals in their entirety. The sticky sap from trees trapped some insects and later hardened; when oceans and sediment eventually covered the trees and sap, the sap turned to amber, in which some parts of the insects remained preserved as fossils. Some animals became petrified; others left casts of their remains. Some plants and animals left prints; for example, coal retained the prints of plants and animals pressed into it.

Scientifically literate individuals understand the concepts of uncertainty in measurement and the basis of scientific theories. Such an understanding may lead the teacher in an elementary classroom to refer to fossils and rocks simply as "very old," to say that dinosaurs "lived long ago," and to preface statements of scientific theory with the observation, "Many scientists believe."

Section 3: Physical Science

Topic 1.
Identifying the Physical and Chemical Properties of Matter

Matter is everything that has mass and volume. **Mass** is the amount of matter in an object; one way to measure mass is by using a lever arm balance. **Volume** is the amount of space an object occupies. Water is matter because it takes up space (that is, it has volume); light is not matter because it does not take up space.

Weight, although sometimes incorrectly interchanged with mass, is a measure of the force of gravity on an object; a spring scale can determine weight. An electronic scale may display an object's mass in grams, but the scale is dependent on gravity for its operation. An electronic scale, such as some butchers use, is accurate only when an expert (usually with the state trade agency) has adjusted the electronics for the local gravitational force. Although an object appears "weightless" as it floats inside the space shuttle, it is not; gravitational forces from both the earth and the sun keep it in orbit and affect the object. The force of gravity is proportional to the product of the masses of the two objects under consideration divided by the square of the distance between them. Earth, being larger and more massive than Mars, has proportionally higher gravitational forces. This is the basis of the observation in H. G. Wells's *The War of the Worlds,* in which he describes the Martian invaders as "the most sluggish things I ever saw crawl."(Wells, Chapter 7, page 3)

Density is the ratio of mass to volume. An intrinsic property, density depends on the type of matter but not the amount of matter. Thus, the density of a five-ton cube of pure copper is the same as that of a small copper penny. However, the modern penny is a thin shell of copper over a zinc plug, and the density of the coin may be significantly lower than that of the older pure copper coin.

Density is related to **buoyancy**. Objects sink in liquids or gases alike if they are denser than the material that surrounds them. Archimedes's principle, also related to density, states that an object is buoyed up by a force equal to the mass of the material the object displaces. Thus, a 160-pound concrete canoe will easily float in water if the volume of the submerged portion of the canoe is equal to the volume of 20 gallons of water. (The weight of water is approximately 8 pounds per gallon; therefore, 8 lbs/gal × 20 gal = 160 lbs.)

Density is not the same as **viscosity**, a measure of thickness or flowability. The strength of intermolecular forces between molecules determines, for example, that molasses will be slow in January or that hydrogen bromide is a gas in any season.

Matter can undergo chemical and physical changes. A **physical change** affects the size, form, or appearance of a material. These changes can include melting, bending, or cracking. Physical changes do not alter the molecular structure of a material. **Chemical changes** do alter the molecular structure of matter. Examples of chemical changes are burning, rusting, and digestion. Under the right conditions, compounds can break apart, combine, or recombine to form new compounds; this process is called a **chemical reaction**. Chemical equations can describe chemical reactions. For instance, sodium hydroxide and hydrochloride combine to form sodium chloride and water. The chemical equation for that reaction is

$$NaOH + HCl \rightarrow NaCl + H_2O$$

The materials to the left of the arrow are **reactants**, and materials to the right of the arrow are **products**.

Topic 2.
Identifying the Characteristics of Elements, Compounds, and Mixtures and Distinguishing Among the Three Main States of Matter

Classifications of matter also include elements, compounds, mixtures, or solutions. An **element** consists of only one type of atom. An example is iron. A symbol of one or two letters, such as Fe (iron) or C (carbon), represents an element. A **compound** is matter that comprises atoms chemically combined in definite weight proportions. An example of a compound is water, which is oxygen and hydrogen combined in the ratio of two hydrogen molecules to one oxygen molecule.

A **mixture** is made up of one or more types of molecules, not chemically combined and without any definite weight proportions. For example, milk is a mixture of water and butterfat particles. Mixtures can be separated by either physical or chemical means. An example of a physical means would be straining the butterfat from milk to make skim milk. **Solutions** are **homogeneous** mixtures—that is, mixtures with evenly distributed substances. An example of a solution is seawater. Separating the salt from seawater requires the process of evaporation.

The three main **states of matter** are solids, liquids, and gases. A **solid** has a definite volume and a definite shape; an example is ice. A **liquid** has a definite volume but has no definite shape; an example is water. A **gas** has no definite volume or shape; an example is water vapor or steam.

Topic 3.
Identifying the Basic Components of the Atom

Atoms are the basic building blocks of matter. Three types of subatomic particles, which have mass and charge, make up atoms. The three components of atoms are protons, neutrons, and electrons. **Protons** and **neutrons** are in the **nucleus**, or solid center of an atom. **Electrons** are in the outer portion of an atom.

Under most conditions, atoms are indivisible. However, atoms may split or combine to form new atoms during atomic reactions. Atomic reactions occur deep inside the sun, in nuclear power reactors, in nuclear bombs, and in radioactive decay.

As mentioned earlier, a unique symbol of one or two letters, such as K (potassium) or Na (sodium), represents each element. Atoms of the same element have the same number of protons in their nuclei. An atom is the smallest particle of an element that retains the characteristics of that element. Each element has an atomic number, which is equal to the number of protons in an atom of that element. The **periodic table** is an arrangement of all the elements in order according to their atomic number; this table is a reference tool; summarizes the atomic structure, mass, and reactive tendencies of elements; and groups elements vertically according to their chemical properties. Two or more atoms may combine to form molecules.

Topic 4.
Applying Knowledge of Energy, Temperature, and Heat

Energy is the ability of matter to move other matter or to produce a chemical change in other matter; scientists also define energy as the ability to do work. There are two main forms of energy: kinetic or potential.

Kinetic energy is the energy of motion; the energy is contained in the movement inside of the object. The formula for kinetic energy is

$$KE = \frac{1}{2} mv^2$$

where m is the mass and v is the velocity of an object.

Potential energy is the storage of energy. An icicle hanging off the roof is an example of potential energy. The formula for potential energy is

$$PE = mgh$$

where m is mass, g is the gravitational force constant, and h is the height. The icicle's potential energy converts to kinetic energy as it falls, to sound energy as it hits the pavement, and to kinetic energy again as the fragments skitter off.

Heat is the energy of moving molecules. **Temperature** describes how hot or cold a material is. Temperature has nothing to do with the amount of heat a material has; it has to do only with the degree of "hotness" or "coldness" of the material. Temperature depends on the speed at which the molecules in a material are moving. The faster the molecules are moving, the hotter the temperature becomes.

A **thermometer** measures temperature. There are several types of thermometers, but the most common ones are glass tubes containing mercury or a liquid, such as colored alcohol. Thermometers usually use the Fahrenheit scale or the Celsius scale.

Topic 5.
Identifying Types of Energy

Within the kinetic and potential forms of energy, there are six main groups of energy: (1) heat energy, (2) chemical energy, (3) electrical energy, (4) nuclear energy, (5) mechanical energy, (6) magnetic energy, and (6) radiant energy, a form of wave energy.

Heat energy, as discussed above, is the energy of moving molecules.

Our food stores **chemical energy** for later conversion to kinetic energy and heat in our bodies.

Electrical energy is the energy that moving electrons produce. A stream of electrons moving through a substance is an **electric current**. Electrical energy enables us to light our homes and operate our telephones, televisions, and computers.

Nuclear energy results when the nucleus of an atom splits in two or when the nuclei of atoms become fused together; both cases produce great amounts of energy.

Mechanical energy is the form of energy most evident in the world. All moving bodies produce mechanical energy. The energy that machines create is mechanical energy.

Magnetic energy is the force (pull or push) of a magnet. The poles of two magnets placed near each other will repel one another if they are alike and will attract each other if they are different. The space around a magnet can also act like a magnet; this is the magnetic field.

Radiant energy is a form of wave energy. X-rays, infrared rays, radio waves, and ultraviolet rays are a few of the many types of radiant energy. The sun produces **solar energy**. All heat on the earth—except that from the interior of atoms—comes from the sun. The sun warms the earth, and energy from the sun enables plants to synthesize the food for their own needs and for the animals that eat them. The heat from the sun allows for evaporation. The sun is vital to survival.

Section 4: Knowledge of the Processes of Life

Topic 1.
Comparing and Contrasting Living and Nonliving Things

Biology is the study of living things. Living things are differentiated from nonliving things by the ability to perform a specific set of life activities at some point in a normal life span. Table 5-1 describes the activities that define life.

It is important to note that living things *must*, during a typical life span, be able to perform *all* these activities. It is quite common for nonliving things to perform one or more of these activities. For example, robots can move, respond, and repair, and crystals can grow: neither robots nor crystals, of course, are living things.

A **cell** is the basic structural unit of living things. In a living thing, a cell is the smallest component that can, by itself, be considered living. Plant cells and animal cells, though generally similar, are distinctly different;

Table 5-1. Required Activities of Living Things

Activity	Description
Food getting	Procuring the food needed to sustain life by eating, absorption, or photosynthesis
Respiration	Exchanging of gases
Excretion	Eliminating wastes
Growth	Increasing in size over part or all of a life span
Repair	Repairing damaged tissue
Movement	Willfully moving a portion of a living thing's body, or channeling growth in a particular direction
Response	Reacting to events or things in the environment
Secretion	Producing and distributing chemicals that aid digestion, growth, metabolism, etc.
Reproduction	Making new living things similar to the parent

for example, plant cells have unique plant structures, cell walls, and vacuoles that animal cells do not have.

Topic 2.
Distinguishing Among Microorganisms

Bacteria are single-celled living organisms. They reproduce themselves by duplicating. They do not need a host for survival. Bacteria are responsive to antibiotics.

A **virus** is smaller than one cell. It lives and multiplies within a host cell for survival; therefore, a virus is **intracellular** and not a living thing. Antibiotics, which are intended to kill living things, are not effective against viruses. The only way to treat a person with a virus is to provide supportive therapy that may help the body fight off the virus. The only way to protect a person against viruses is through vaccines. Vaccines help the body build up antibodies against viruses. Vaccines are not available for every virus, however, and do not cure viruses. Some biologists believe that a virus is a living organism; they believe that the virus can be described as a protein coat surrounding strands of nuclear material.

Protozoans are one-celled living organisms that live inside or outside a cell. Only some protozoans are susceptible to antibiotics.

Topic 3.
Differentiating Structures and Functions of Plant and Animal Cells

As discussed earlier, a cell is the basic structural unit of living things and the smallest unit that can, by itself, be considered living. Plant cells and animal cells, though generally similar, are distinctly different. Figure 5-1 illustrates the structures of animal and plant cells.

Cells are made of several smaller structures called **organelles**, which are surrounded by cell fluid, or cytoplasm. The functions of several cell structures are listed in Table 5-2.

Topic 4.
Identifying the Major Steps of the Plant Physiological Processes of Photosynthesis, Respiration, Reproduction, and Transpiration

Cells perform several chemical processes to maintain essential life activities. The sum of these necessary chemical processes is called **metabolism**. Table 5-3 lists the processes related to metabolism and the organelles involved.

Cells need to move materials into their structures to get energy and to grow. The **cell membrane** allows certain small molecules to flow freely across it. This flow of chemicals from areas of high concentration to areas of low concentration is called **diffusion**. **Osmosis** is diffusion of water across a semipermeable membrane. Particles too large to pass through the cell membrane may be engulfed by the cell membrane and stored in vacuoles until they can be digested. This engulfing process is called **phagocytosis**.

All cells need energy to survive. Sunlight energy is made biologically available when plant cells convert it to chemical energy during **photosynthesis**. Photosynthesis is carried out in the **chloroplasts** of green cells. **Chlorophyll**, the pigment found in chloroplasts, catalyzes (causes or accelerates) the photosynthetic reaction that turns carbon dioxide and water into glucose (sugar) and oxygen. Sunlight and chlorophyll are needed for the reaction to occur. Chlorophyll, because it is a catalyst, is not consumed in the reaction and may be used repeatedly.

The term *respiration* has two distinct meanings in the field of biology. As a life activity, respiration is the exchange of gases in living things. As a metabolic process, respiration is the release of energy from sugars for use in life activities. All living things get their energy from the digestion (respiration) of glucose (sugar).

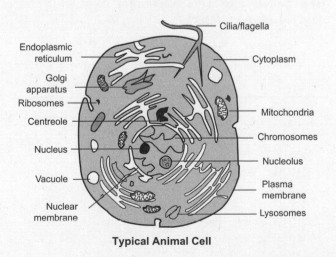

Typical Animal Cell

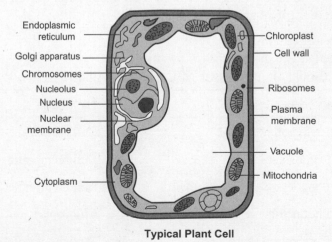

Typical Plant Cell

Figure 5-1. Typical Animal and Plant Cells

Table 5-2. Cell Structures and Their Functions

Organelle	Function
Cell membrane	Controls movement of materials into and out of cells
Cell wall	Gives rigid structure to plant cells
Chloroplast	Contains chlorophyll, which enables green plants to make their own food
Cytoplasm	Jellylike substance inside a cell; comprises the cytosol and organelles but not the nucleus
Mitochondrion	Liberates energy from glucose in cells for use in cellular activities
Nucleus	Directs cell activities; holds DNA (genetic material)
Ribosome	Makes proteins from amino acids
Vacuole	Stores materials in a cell

Respiration may occur with oxygen (aerobic respiration) or without oxygen (anaerobic respiration, or fermentation). Most often the term *respiration* is used to refer to aerobic respiration. Aerobic respiration occurs in most plant and animal cells.

Fermentation occurs in yeast cells and other cells in the absence of oxygen. Fermentation by yeast produces the alcohol in alcoholic beverages and the gases that make yeast breads rise and have a light texture.

Reproduction is a process whereby living plant or animal cells or organisms produce offspring. Individual plants have growth limitations imposed by inherited characteristics and environmental conditions. If the plant grows excessively, any number of reproductive processes may be simulated. However, in plants, reproduction may be either sexual or asexual.

Asexual plant propagation, also known as vegetative reproduction, is the method by which plants reproduce without the union of cells or nuclei of cells. The product of asexual plant propagation is genetically identical to the parent. Asexual propagation takes place either by **fragmentation** or by special asexual structures. An example of fragmentation is growing new plants from cuttings.

Sexual plant propagation almost always involves seeds produced by two individuals, male and female. Most plant propagation is, in fact, from seed, including all annual and biennial plants. Seed **germination** begins when a sufficient amount of water is absorbed by the seed, precipitating biochemical changes that initiate cell division.

Water is essential for plant life. The plant needs the water to make food, among other uses. A plant usually takes in more water than it needs. To get rid of excess water, the stomata of the leaves allow the water to pass out as water vapor. This evaporation of water from the plant is **transpiration**.

Table 5-3. Processes of Cell Metabolism

Process	Organelle	Life Activity
Diffusion	Cell membrane	Food getting, respiration, excretion
Osmosis	Cell membrane	Food getting, excretion
Phagocytosis	Cell membrane	Food getting
Photosynthesis	Chloroplasts	Food getting
Respiration (aerobic)	Mitochondrion	Provides energy
Fermentation	Mitochondrion	Provides energy

Topic 5.
Identifying the Structures and Functions of Organs and Systems of Animals, Including Humans

Not all cells are alike. Cells that perform different functions differ in size and shape. A group of the same kind of cells is called a **tissue**. A group of the same kind of tissues working together is an **organ**. Examples of animal organs are the brain, stomach, heart, liver, and kidneys. A group of organs that work together to accomplish a special activity is a **system**. The complex organism known as the human body is made up of several organ systems.

The **skeletal system** is composed of bones, cartilage, and ligaments. The area where two or more bones come together is called a **joint**. Bone surfaces in a joint are often covered with **cartilage**, which reduces friction in the joint. **Ligaments** are connective tissues that hold bones together. The human skeleton consists of more than 200 bones connected at joints by ligaments. Movements are effected by contractions of the skeletal muscles, to which the bones are attached by tendons. Muscular contractions are controlled by the nervous system.

The **muscular system** controls movement of the skeleton and movement within organs. Three types of muscle exist: striated (voluntary), smooth (involuntary), and cardiac. Tendons attach muscles to bone. Skeletal muscles work in pairs. The alternating contractions of muscles within a pair causes movement in joints.

The **nervous system** has two divisions: the somatic, allowing voluntary control over skeletal muscle, and the autonomic, or involuntary, controlling cardiac and glandular functions. Voluntary movement is caused by nerve impulses arising in the brain, carried by cranial or spinal chord nerves connecting to skeletal muscles. Involuntary movement occurs in direct response to outside stimulus. Involuntary responses are called reflexes. Various nerve terminals called receptors constantly send impulses to the central nervous system. There are three types of receptors:

Exteroceptors. Pain, temperature, touch, and pressure receptors

Interoceptors. Internal environment receptors

Proprioceptors. Movement, position, and tension receptors

Each receptor routes nerve impulses to specialized areas of the brain for processing.

The energy required for sustenance of the human body is supplied by food. The **digestive system** receives and processes food. The digestive system includes the mouth, esophagus, stomach, large intestine, and small intestine.

The **excretory system** eliminates wastes from the body. Excretory organs include the lungs, kidneys, bladder, large intestine, rectum, and skin. The lungs excrete gaseous waste. The kidneys filter blood and excrete wastes, mostly in the form of urea. The bladder holds liquid wastes until they can be eliminated through the urethra. The large intestine absorbs water from solid food waste, and the rectum stores solid waste until it can be eliminated. The skin excretes waste through perspiration.

The **circulatory system** is responsible for internal transport in the body. It is composed of the heart, blood vessels, lymph vessels, blood, and lymph. The **immune system** is important for health and indeed life. The body defends itself against foreign proteins and infectious microorganisms by means of a complex dual system that depends on recognizing a portion of the surface pattern of the invader. Lymphocytes and antibody molecules are generated to destroy the invader molecules.

The **respiratory system** performs the essential process of respiration. In humans, respiration involves the expansion and contraction of the lungs. Some animals, however, make use of gills and other means of respiration. The **reproductive system** is essential for the continuance of life in animals and in humans.

Topic 6.
Identifying the Major Steps of the Animal Physiological Processes

The essential process of **respiration** in humans is effected by the expansion and contraction of the lungs. In the lungs, oxygen enters tiny capillaries, where it combines with hemoglobin in the red blood cells and is carried to the tissues through circulation of the blood. At the same time, carbon dioxide passes through capillaries into the air contained within the lungs. Inhaling draws air that is higher in oxygen and lower in carbon dioxide into the lungs; exhaling forces air from the lungs that is high in carbon dioxide and low in oxygen.

Reproduction is the process whereby living plant or animal cells or organisms produce offspring. In almost all animal organisms, reproduction occurs during or after the period of maximum growth. Reproduction in animals can be further subdivided into asexual and sexual.

Asexual animal propagation occurs primarily in single-celled organisms. Through a process known as **fission**, the parent organism splits into two or more daughter organisms and loses its original identity. In some instances, cell division results in the production of buds that arise from the body of the parent and then later separate to develop into new organisms identical to the parent. Reproductive processes in which only one parent gives rise to the offspring are scientifically classified as asexual reproduction. The offspring produced are identical to the parent.

Sexual animal propagation is a result of sperm uniting with ova for fertilization. The primary means of this kind of reproduction are insemination (copulation between a male and female vertebrate) and cross-fertilization (the depositing of ova and sperm in water at some distance from each other, most commonly by fish).

Digestion is the process of receiving and processing food; food supplies the energy required for sustenance of the human body. The digestive system includes the mouth, stomach, large intestine, and small intestine. Digestion begins when food is physically broken down by mastication, or chewing, and then mixed with saliva. Food is chemically broken down in the stomach, where the gastric and intestinal juices continue the process. Thereafter, the mixture of food and secretions makes its way down the alimentary canal by peristalsis, rhythmic contractions of the smooth muscle of the gastrointestinal system. The small intestine absorbs nutrients from food, and the large intestine absorbs water from solid food waste.

Circulation is the internal transportation system of the body. The circulatory system is composed of the heart, blood vessels, lymph vessels, blood, and lymph. The heart is a muscular four-chambered pump. The upper chambers are the **atria** and the lower chambers are the ventricles. Blood flows throughout the body. The heart pumps the blood, which first passes through the right chambers of the heart and through the lungs, where it acquires oxygen. From there, it is pumped back into the left chambers of the heart. Next, it is pumped into the main artery, the aorta, which branches into increasingly smaller arteries. Beyond that, blood passes through tiny, thin-walled structures called capillaries. In the capillaries, the blood gives up oxygen and nutrients to tissues and absorbs a metabolic waste product containing carbon dioxide. Finally, blood completes the circuit by passing through small veins, which join to form increasingly larger vessels; finally the blood reaches the largest veins that return the blood to the right side of the heart.

Section 5: Personal Health; Science in Personal and Social Perspectives

Topic 1.
Identifying Parts and Sequences of Biogeochemical Cycles of Common Elements in the Environment

The amount of oxygen and carbon dioxide in the air remains the same as a result of the **carbon dioxide–oxygen cycle**. To make food, green plants take in carbon dioxide from the air. The waste product that plants give off in the process is oxygen. When animals breathe in oxygen to digest their food, they give off carbon dioxide as a waste product.

The amount of nitrogen in the air remains constant as a result of the **nitrogen cycle**. Nitrogen-fixing bacteria live in the soil and in the roots of legumes (for example, beans, peas, and clover). Bacteria change the nitrogen in the air (that plants cannot use) into nitrogen materials that plants can use. After animals eat plants, they give off waste materials that contain nitrogen. Bacteria in the soil act on the animals' waste materials and on dead plants and animals and break them down and making the remaining nitrogen available. **Nitrifying bacteria** return the nitrogen to the soil for plants to use. **Denitrifying bacteria** change some of the nitrogen in the materials and the dead plants and animals to free nitrogen, which returns to the air and continues the nitrogen cycle.

The air today is different in composition from what it was when the earth was formed. Large amounts of hydrogen and helium characterized the composition of air millions of years ago. As the earth cooled, water vapor, carbon dioxide, and nitrogen became components of the air. When the water vapor condensed, carbon dioxide and nitrogen remained. The plants reduced the amount of carbon dioxide in the air and increased the amount of oxygen in the air. Today pollution is changing the composition of the air.

Topic 2.
Identifying Causes and Effects of Pollution

Pollution is any material added to an ecosystem that disrupts its normal functioning. Typical pollutants are excess fertilizer that remains in the soil or runs off into water sources, waste materials that factories and manufacturing plants dump into the water or onto the ground, and industrial emissions into the air. Pollution generates large quantities of gases and solids every day. Smokestacks, chimneys, and car exhaust pipes are some sources of air pollutants. Some pollutants are simply annoying, but others are dangerous to the health of those exposed. Continuous exposure to polluting materials discharged into the air can cause lung diseases or aggravate existing health conditions. Bomb tests (hydrogen and atom) add radioactive particles to the air, and if more testing occurs, the particles may accumulate and become increasingly dangerous.

If weather conditions prevent the distribution of polluting materials, air pollution can become increasingly severe. When cold air is next to the ground with warm air lying on top, polluting materials remain concentrated in one area. The warm air acts as a blanket, and the cold air remains stationary. This is a **temperature inversion**.

A recent phenomenon (since 1950) is **acid rain**—a form of precipitation that contains high levels of sulfuric or nitric acid. Acid rain occurs when sulfur dioxide and nitrogen oxide combine with atmospheric moisture. Acid rain can pollute drinking water, damage plant and animal life, and even erode monuments and buildings. Among the primary causes of acid rain are the burning of certain fuels—including the gas used to power automobiles.

Topic 3.
Identifying the Living and Nonliving Factors That Influence Population Density

Our surroundings form a complex, interconnected system in which living organisms exist in relationship with the soil, water, and air. Because they are linked through chemical and physical processes, Earth's inhabitants are in states of continual change or dynamic equilibrium.

Ecosystem is the term for all the living and nonliving things in a given environment and how they interact. Scientifically literate individuals are aware of their surroundings, the interdependence of every aspect of those surroundings, and the impact of human activities. Mutualistic and competitive relationships also exist among the organisms in an ecosystem, determining how organisms rely on each other and how they exist in competition and conflict with each other.

Energy transformations are the driving force within an ecosystem. Many organisms obtain energy from light. For example, light drives the process of photosynthesis in green plants. Solar energy also provides the heat that cold-blooded animals require. Another source of energy for organisms is other organisms, including other plants and animals.

When one source of energy is depleted in an ecosystem, many organisms must shift their attention to other sources of energy. For example, a bear derives energy primarily from berries, fish, or nuts, depending on the season. The **energy pyramid** for an ecosystem illustrates these relationships and identifies the organisms most dependent on the other organisms in the system. Higher-order organisms cannot survive for long without the other organisms beneath them in the energy pyramid.

The availability of adequate food within an ecosystem can explain the system's functioning, the size of an animal's territory, or the effects of a single species preying too heavily on organisms above it in the food chain.

Over time, ecosystems change, both from natural processes and from human activities. Scientifically literate individuals can identify how the environment changes, how those changes impact the organisms that live there, and what the differences are between long-term and short-term variation. Natural succession occurs when one community replaces another. For example, the colonies of fungus grow and thrive on rodent droppings under ideal conditions; then different colonies replace the ones currently thriving on the rodent droppings.

Ecology is the study of the relationship between living things and their environment. An **environment** is all the living and nonliving things surrounding an organism. A **population** is a group of similar organisms, such as a herd of deer. A **community** is a group of populations that interact with one another. A pond community, for example, is made up of all the plants and animals in the pond. An **ecosystem** is a group of populations that share a common pool of resources and a common physical or geographical area.

Each population lives in a particular area and serves a special role in the community. This combination of defined role and living areas is the concept of **niche**. The niche of a pond snail, for example, is to decompose materials in ponds. The niche of a field mouse is to eat seeds in fields. When two populations try to fill the same niche, **competition** occurs. If one population replaces another in a niche, **succession** occurs. Succession is the orderly and predictable change of communities as a result of population replacement in niches.

Topic 4.
Analyzing Various Conservation Methods and Their Effectiveness in Relation to Renewable and Nonrenewable Natural Resources

Conservation is the practice of using natural areas without disrupting their ecosystems. This definition suggests **interdependence** among people and the world and **practices** or actions to improve or maintain the world. These practices must recognize that there are both renewable and nonrenewable resources. **Renewable resources** are those that can endure indefinitely under wise practices; examples of renewable resources are soil, vegetation, animals, and fresh water. **Nonrenewable natural resources** can be depleted; examples of nonrenewable resources are copper, coal, oil, and metals.

Laws to manage the mining and drilling of natural resources and laws on the use and recycling of natural resources are among the efforts to conserve nonrenewable resources. A major component of conservation is

educating people on the importance of managing nonrenewable natural resources.

Renewable resources are dependent on each other—they are **interdependent**. Crops cannot grow in the soil without water. Bees play a part in the life cycle of many plants, and animals help provide carbon dioxide for photosynthesis. Managed forests ensure a supply of wood, a steady flow of water, and protection of the soil against wind and water damage. Laws governing hunting and fishing are effective—when enforced—in ensuring that game and other animals can renew themselves and continue their role in the web of life.

In the 1930s, the Civilian Conservation Corps enrolled 250,000 men aged 18 to 24 from families on relief to go to camps where they worked on flood control, soil conservation, park development, and forest projects under the direction of the federal government. Conservation is not a new concept, but it is still not as effective as it could be. Again, education is the key.

Section 6: History and Nature of Science and Inquiry

Topic 1.
Demonstrating Knowledge of Basic Science Processes

The **scientific method** is *not* a specific set of steps that is rigorously followed whenever a question arises that can be answered using the knowledge and techniques of science. Rather, it is a process of observation and analysis used to develop a reliable, consistent, and objective representation and understanding of our world. The scientific method is useful for answering many but not all questions. The processes that make up the scientific method are identifying a problem or question, observing and describing, formulating hypotheses, making predictions based on the hypotheses and testing those predictions (experimenting), interpreting results, and deriving conclusions.

Scientists—and students—must carefully observe their surroundings and consider the data available.

The scientific method is best applied to situations in which the experimenter can control the variables, eliminating or accounting for all extraneous factors, and can perform repeated independent tests that change only one variable at a time. Scientists and students must be able to find similarities and differences and to classify the information, objects, plants, and animals accordingly.

Scientists and students must be able to communicate to share their observations and their questions. This communication can be either written or oral. To communicate data clearly enough to foster sound interpretation, the scientists or students can present the information in various formats: graphs, diagrams, maps, concrete models, role playing, and charts, among others.

Quantifying the results of observing and classifying is part of effective communication. Effective quantifying requires the selection of appropriate tools for observing, describing, measuring, comparing, and computing. The **microscope** and **telescope** extend the range of human observation beyond human physiology. The **spectroscope** separates visible light into its component colors, and the **spectrophotometer** measures the selective absorption of those colors as a function of some property of a solution, solid, or gas. **Mathematics** is a tool to evaluate the results of our observations, to organize large quantities of data into averages, ranges, and statistical probabilities. The fundamental uncertainty of the measuring device limits quantifying and measurements.

The concept of **significant figures** derives from the simple assumption that calculations on measurements cannot generate results that are more precise than the measurements themselves. For example, if you divide one pie into three pieces, a calculator might report that each piece represents 0.33333333 (depending on the number of digits on the calculator display). You know from experience that there will be crumbs left in the pan and that no amount of care in dividing the pieces will result in the level of accuracy the calculation suggests. Most of us assume every measuring device to be accurate to the smallest of the subdivisions marked, and every measurement with such a device should include one additional estimated digit. For example, when you use a ruler with one centimeter as its smallest division, you should record your measurements to the tenth of a centimeter, the smallest measured digit plus one estimated digit.

The following terms form an indispensable part of the vocabulary used in scientific experimentation:

Observation. The act of sensing some measurable phenomenon.

Organization. Relating parts to a coherent whole.

Experimental. Testing the effect of an independent variable on a dependent variable in a controlled environment.

Inference. Deducing a conclusion from a measurement or observation that is not explicit to either. For example, you can infer that a classroom of 30 students has 16 girls if you know that there are 14 boys. Here the inference is done by subtracting 14 from 30.

Prediction. Stating the outcome of an experiment in advance of doing it. An example would be predicting that a plot of velocity versus time for a freely falling object will be a straight line.

Topic 2.
Applying Knowledge of the Integrated Science Processes of Manipulating Variables, Defining Operationally, Forming Hypotheses, Measuring (Metric), Graphing, and Interpreting Data

As noted in the previous section, the processes that make up the scientific method are observing and describing, formulating hypotheses, making predictions based on the hypotheses and testing those predictions (experimenting), and deriving conclusions.

In planning experiments, the scientist or student is generally attempting to test a hypothesis. A **hypothesis** is an educated guess about the relationship between two variables that is subject to testing and verification. The outcome of the test in a well-designed experiment answers questions suggested by the hypothesis in a clear and unambiguous way.

In planning and conducting an experiment, the scientist or student must (1) identify relevant variables, (2) identify equipment and apparatus to be used to measure and record the variables, (3) eliminate or suppress any other factors that could influence measured variables, and (4) decide on a means of analyzing the data obtained. In conducting experiments, it is imperative that questions raised by the hypotheses be testable and that the data recorded be sufficiently accurate and repeatable.

Testable Questions

An example of a testable question might be, "Does mass have an influence on acceleration for bodies subjected to unbalanced forces?" This question is testable because it identifies specific variables (force, mass, and acceleration) one can measure and control in any experiment that seeks to establish a connection. Thus, testable questions must specify variables that are subject to both measurement and control.

Data Representation

Data is often represented in graphical form, where raw data is plotted. The independent (controlled) variable is usually displayed on the x-axis of a graph (horizontal), and the dependent variable is usually displayed on the y-axis (vertical). Graphs can either be linear (a straight line) or nonlinear. Often equations can be fitted to graphs obtained for purposes of finder analyses. Use of a graphing calculator and specialized software can facilitate both the data collection and data representation in graphical form. Note that x-y plots are not the only means of data representation. Charts, diagrams, and tables are also often used to display results.

Interpreting Experimental Results

Sometimes experimental work involves measurements that do not directly yield the desired variable value but can be interpreted or reduced to provide the desired value. The experimental approach in that case is indirect.

An example is the measurement of acceleration of gravity, or g, a fundamental gravitational constant. One common method is to measure displacement over time for a falling body. The resulting graph is then reduced (interpreted) to yield a plot of velocity versus time. This plot in turn is then reduced (interpreted) to yield a plot of acceleration versus time, from which the acceleration of gravity, g, can be read. Inherent to each of the reductions was finding the slope (the rise divided by the run) at various points, which is a mathematical technique that enables interpretation of the results.

Variables

The science fair project is a common tool for instruction in the scientific method. Many formal and informal sources, often Web based, provide lists of suggested science fair topics, but not all are experiments. For the youngest students, it is appropriate and useful for the focus to be on models and demonstrations—for example, a model of the solar system or a volcano, or a clay cross section of an egg. Older students should move to true experiments that focus on identifying a testable hypothesis and controlling all experimental variables but the one of interest.

Many projects that begin as models or demonstrations can be elevated to experiments. A proposal to demonstrate how windmills work can be made an experiment when the student adds quantitative measurements of one variable against variations in one other variable; the student must hold all other variables constant. For example, using an electric fan, the student could measure the number of rotations per minute as a function of the fan setting (low, medium, or high). Then, while keeping the fan setting constant, the student could conduct several experiments that vary the number of fans, the sizes of fans, or the shapes of fans, measuring the rotational speed at each variation.

Collecting and Presenting Data

Scientifically literate individuals have detailed and accurate content knowledge that is the basis of their scientific knowledge. They do not try to recall every detail of that knowledge but build conceptual frameworks on which they can add both prior knowledge and new learning. From this framework of facts, concepts, and theories, scientifically literate individuals can reconstruct forgotten facts and use them to answer new questions not previously considered. Scientifically literate individuals are lifelong learners who ask questions that can be answered using scientific knowledge and techniques.

Scientific information is communicated to nonscientific audiences to inform, guide policy, and influence the practices that affect all of society. This information is presented through text, tables, charts, figures, pictures, models, and other representations that require interpretation and analysis. Scientifically literate individuals can (1) read and interpret these representations and (2) select appropriate tools to present the information they gather.

Science is based on experimentation, but not all knowledge is derived daily from first principles. Scientifically literate individuals are informed by existing knowledge and are aware of the sources, accuracy, and value of each source. Not every source is equally reliable, accurate, or valid. Classroom teachers are advised to use trusted educational sites.

Scientifically literate individuals can evaluate critically the information and evidence they collect and the conclusions or theories to which that information and evidence leads. Such analysis incorporates an understanding of the limitations of knowledge in general and, more specifically, the limitations of all measurements and information based on the quality of the experimental design. Scientifically literate individuals can evaluate claims for scientific merit, identify conflicting evidence, and weigh the value and credibility of conflicting information. They can also recognize that not every question can be answered using scientific knowledge. They should value the contributions of other cultures and other ways of knowing, including art, philosophy, and theology.

Measurement

Measurement includes (1) estimating and converting measurements within the customary and metric systems; (2) applying procedures for using measurement to describe and compare phenomena; (3) identifying appropriate measurement instruments, units, and procedures for problems involving length, area, angles, volume, mass, time, money, and temperature; and (4) using a variety of materials, models, and methods to explore concepts and solve problems involving measurement.

Topic 3.
Applying Knowledge of Inquiry Approaches to Learning Science Concepts

Effective teachers use not one but many methods and strategies to enhance student learning. Teachers choose various strategies to meet both content- and student-driven purposes. If the purpose is to investigate current problems without specific answers, the teacher might choose an inquiry lesson.

To engage in **inquiry**, a student must be able to acquire information from a variety of resources and organize and interpret that information. Inquiry may involve designing and conducting investigations that lead to the identification of issues to analyze. Inquiry is essential for examining single topics or integrated sciences.

Scientists and students should understand the principles and processes of scientific investigation and how to promote the development of scientific knowledge and skills, including the use of scientific thinking, inquiry, reasoning, and investigation. Effective science-teaching methods include the following:

- Determining the type of scientific investigation (for example, experimentation, systematic observation) that best addresses a given question or hypothesis.
- Demonstrating a knowledge of considerations and procedures, including safety practices, related to designing and conducting experiments (for example, formulation of hypotheses; use of control and experimental groups; and recognition of variables being held constant, those being manipulated, and those responding in an experiment).
- Recognizing how to use methods, tools, technologies, and measurement units to gather and organize data, compare and evaluate data, and describe and communicate the results of investigations in various formats.
- Understanding concepts, skills, and processes of inquiry in the social sciences (for example, locating, gathering, organizing, formulating hypotheses) and how to promote students' development of knowledge and skills in this area

Teaching methods can be divided into two categories: inductive and deductive. Using **inductive** methods, teachers encourage students to study, conduct research, collect and analyze data, and then develop generalizations and rules based on their findings. During inductive lessons, first a hypothesis or concept is introduced, and then generalizations are developed based on inferences from data.

Inquiry or discovery lessons are inductive in nature. An inquiry lesson starts with a thought-provoking question for which students are interested in finding an explanation. After posing the question, the teacher guides students in brainstorming a list of what they already know about the topic and then categorizing the information. Students use these categories as topics for group or individual research. The lesson typically ends with students presenting their research to the class (a form of deductive learning, as discussed later).

A teacher who uses inquiry strategies takes the role of a facilitator who plans outcomes and provides resources for students as they work. In their role as inquirers, students must take responsibility for their own learning by planning, carrying out, and presenting research and projects.

Some advantages of inductive lessons are that they generally require higher-level thinking by both teacher and students, and they usually result in higher student motivation, interest, and retention. They are also more interesting to the teacher, who deals with the same concepts year after year. Disadvantages of inductive lessons include the need for additional preparation by the teacher, access to numerous resources, and additional time for students to conduct research.

Generally, the more planning, predicting, and preparing the teacher does for an inductive lesson, the more successful the students will be. This does not mean that the activity must be tightly structured or set in concrete, but the effective teacher tries to predict students' responses and their reactions to them. The need to purchase additional resources has been moderated by computerized bibliographic services, interlibrary loans, and CD-ROMs with all types of information. Because inductive, research-oriented units require more class time, subject-area teachers must work together to determine which concepts are essential for students to understand and which are nonessential.

An effective teacher plays many roles in the classroom. The teacher who uses lecture is in the role of information provider. Students listening to the lecture are usually in the passive, often inattentive, role of listener. The teacher who uses cooperative strategies takes on the roles of a coach, encouraging students to work together, and a facilitator, smoothing students' way through activities and providing resources. Students in a collaborative role must learn social and group roles as well as content to accomplish learning tasks. The teacher who listens to student discussions and presentations and evaluates student papers and projects assumes the role of an audience providing constructive feedback. Students in a discussion role must prepare carefully and think seriously about the topic under discussion.

Using **deductive** methods, teachers present material through lectures and students teach each other through presentations. In deductive lessons, the generalizations or rules are taught first, and then examples and elaboration are developed to support the generalizations or rules. Deductive thinking often requires students to make assessments based on specific criteria that they or others develop.

The **mastery lecture** is a deductive method whereby information is presented to students by the teacher. New teachers are especially attuned to lecturing because that is the usual mode of instruction in college classes. An advantage of the mastery lecture is that large amounts of information can be presented in an efficient manner; however, teachers should avoid giving students too much information through lectures. To be most effective, mastery lectures should be short, usually no more than 10 or 15 minutes, and frequently interrupted by questions to and from students. The effective teacher uses both lower- and higher-level questions during lectures.

Lectures must also be supplemented with an array of visual materials that will appeal to both visual and auditory learners. Putting words or outlines on the board or a transparency is very helpful; however, this is still basically a verbal strategy. Drawings, diagrams, cartoons, pictures, caricatures, and graphs are attention-getting visual aids for lectures. Teacher drawings need not be highly artistic, merely memorable. Often a rough or humorous sketch will be more firmly etched in students' minds than elaborate drawings. Using a very simple sketch is a better means of teaching the most critical information than is a complicated drawing. The major points stand out in a simple sketch; details can be added once students understand the basic concepts.

Teachers should also be careful to instruct students on how to take notes while listening to a speaker. Note-taking is a skill that will be useful during every student's career, whether educational or professional. One way teachers can teach note-taking skills is to show students notes or an outline from the lecture they are about to hear or to write notes or an outline on the board or on a transparency while they are presenting the information. This activity requires careful planning by the teacher and will result in a more organized lecture. A well-structured lecture is especially helpful for sequential learners, who like organization. It also helps random learners develop organizational skills. A web, map, or fishbone is a more creative method of connecting important points in a lecture or a chapter; Chapter 2 includes more about these graphic organizers of wcbs, maps, fishbones, etc. The effective teacher will use both systems and teach both to students, so they have a choice of strategies.

Section 7: Content-Specific Pedagogy

Topic 1.
Identifying the Appropriate Laboratory Equipment for Specific Activities

A variety of tools or instruments are used in scientific experimentation. These include microscopes, scales, graduated cylinders, meter sticks, micrometers, voltmeters, and ammeters. In general, these devices measure mass, volume, length, and voltage.

Inherent to the proper use of measuring devices is a recognition of their limitations in accuracy and precision. Precision concerns the number of places that one can reliably read from any measurement device. For example, a meter stick is generally good to three-place precision, the first two places being determined by scale markings and the third place determined by the estimated position between scale markings.

Scientific process skills, including the proper and accurate use of laboratory equipment, are an important component of science education. Instruction is necessary to guide the effective use of each measurement or observation tool: rulers, microscopes, balances, laboratory glassware, and so forth. As students develop their measuring skills, they move from simple observations and conformist activities to using these tools to find answers to questions that they develop themselves.

Topic 2.
Identifying Safety Procedures for Teaching Science, Including the Care of Living Organisms and the Accepted Procedures for the Safe

Preparation, Use, Storage, and Disposal of Chemicals and Other Materials

Rules and regulations on safety procedures for teaching science may change. It is important to review the current rules and regulations. Some general rules are listed here:

Handling Living Organisms Safely

- Live vertebrates are not appropriate for elementary students, except for observation.
- Students should not touch or handle reptiles; the animals may carry *Salmonella* bacteria.
- Some plants may be toxic and should not be used in the classroom.
- Wash hands after handling plants and animals.
- Use gloves when handling animals that might bite or scratch.
- Generally, children should not bring pets to class. If they are brought, only the owner should handle the animals.
- Treat animals with care and respect.
- Remember that animal hair, scales, and waste can cause allergic reactions.
- Plant and animal specimens from ponds, ditches, canals, and other bodies of water may contain microorganism that can cause disease. Suppliers can provide cultures that are safer.
- Set aquariums on stable furniture out of traffic ways. Be sure electrical accessories are plugged into a ground fault circuit interrupter (GFCI) outlet. Ensure that thermostats and heating elements are working correctly.

Safety Equipment and Fire-Prevention Measures for Classrooms

- Teachers and students must wear eye-protective devices when using hazardous materials in activities such as heating of materials, tempering a metal, working with caustic or explosive materials, and working with hot liquids or solids.
- School boards should give out or sell plano (safety) glasses to students, teachers, and visitors.
- Fire extinguishers must be available to classrooms.
- Fire blankets must be available in each classroom where a fire hazard exists.

- Fire alarms, detector systems, lighting, and electrical outlets should be in operating condition, even in storage rooms.
- Outlets should be grounded.
- Outlets within two feet (six feet for new constructions) of water supplies must have a GFCI protection device.
- All buildings must have GFCI-protected outlets.
- Extension cords must not be stapled.
- Extension cords must not be run through or over doors, windows or walls.
- Extension cords must not be spliced or taped.
- Extension cords must be in only continuous lengths.
- Adapters must be approved by the Underwriters Laboratories (UL).
- Adapters must have overcurrent protection with a total rating of no more than 15 amperes.
- Every classroom with electrical receptacles at student workstations should have an emergency shut-off switch that is unobstructed within 15 feet of the teacher's workstation.

Preparation, Use, Storage, and Disposal of Chemicals and Other Materials

An elementary classroom usually does not contain hazardous chemicals or equipment, but the following rules are necessary for classrooms where they are present:

- Rooms where students handle materials or chemicals that are harmful to human tissue must have a dousing shower, a floor drain, and an eye-washing facility.
- Rooms where students handle materials or chemicals that are harmful should have emergency exhaust systems, fume hoods, and fume hood supply fans that shut down when emergency exhaust fans are operating.
- Lockable cabinets are required for hazardous materials or hazardous chemicals.

Monitoring Guide for Chemical Storage

- Chemical storage areas must be secured with lock and key and have limited student access.
- Signs prohibiting access to students must be clearly posted.
- Chemical storage areas must be well lighted to avoid mix-ups.
- The floor space must not be cluttered.

- The area must be inventoried at least once a year. The chemical labels and the inventory list must have the name, supplier, date of purchase of mix, the concentration, and the amount available.
- Chemicals must be purged at least once a year.
- Chemical storage must use recognized storage patterns; chemicals should be stored in compatible groups—not in alphabetical order.
- Chemical storage areas must include materials to dilute and absorb a large-volume (one-gallon) chemical spill.
- Certain chemicals that present a potential for explosion are not allowed in science classrooms or chemical storage areas. These include benzoyl peroxide, phosphorus, carbon disulfide, ethyl ether, disopropyl ether, picric acid, perchloric acid, potassium chlorate, and potassium metal.
- Some chemicals present a danger as a human carcinogen and are not allowed in science classrooms or chemical storage areas. These include arsenic compounds, benzene, chloroform, nickel powder, asbestos, acrylonitrile, benzidine, chromium compound, ortho-toluidine, cadmium compounds, and ethylene oxide.

Tables 5-4 and 5-5 are checklists for teachers to use to ensure that their classrooms are safe places for students to learn science.

Through active, hands-on activities, science instruction is made a richer and more meaningful experience.

From simple observations and activities at early grades to detailed controlled experiments at higher grades, students who do science to learn science understand science better. While students are engaged in the process of discovery and exploration, the teacher must be engaged in protecting students' health and safety. The hazards vary with the discipline; thoughtful planning and management of the activities will significantly reduce the risks to students. In all cases, students must use appropriate personal hygiene (hand washing) and wear personal protective equipment (goggles, gloves) while engaged in laboratory or field activities.

Substitution of less hazardous materials whenever possible is a high priority. For example, in the physical sciences, teachers can (1) replace mercury thermometers with alcohol or electronic ones, (2) replace glass beakers and graduated cylinders with ones made of

Table 5-4. Checklist for Chemical Storage in Schools

Ventilation

Temperature

Heat detector

Secured

Well illuminated

Uncluttered floor

Chemical inventory

Chemicals purged annually

Chemicals grouped correctly

Labels on chemical containers

Flammables cabinet

Spill protection

No explosives

No carcinogens

Table 5-5. Checklist for Science Classroom

Fire extinguisher

Fire blanket

Gas cut-off (present and labeled)

Water cut-off (present and labeled)

Electrical cut-off (present and labeled)

Dousing shower

Floor drain

Eye-washing facility

Room ventilation adequate

Fume hood

Grounded receptacles

Ground fault circuit interrupters within 2 inches of water

No flammable storage

Face protection meet standards

Face protection in sufficient numbers

Face protection sanitized

durable polyethylene, and (3) eliminate or reduce the use of hazardous chemicals. In the earth sciences, (1) rocks and minerals used in class should not contain inherently hazardous materials, (2) students should not be allowed to taste the minerals, and (3) reagents like hydrochloric acid used for identification of carbonate minerals should be dispensed from spill-proof plastic containers. In the life sciences, special care should be given to (1) safe practices with sharp objects, (2) the safe handling of living organisms, and (3) the care and use of microscopes. Experiments or activities involving the collection or culture of human cells or fluids should be discouraged and proper sterilization procedures followed to prevent the growth or spread of disease agents. When possible, field activities like visiting nature centers or other outdoor facilities or museums can bring valuable enrichment to the science curriculum in all disciplines. However, the teacher must assume responsibility for planning and implementing activities that not only increase students' learning but also maintain their health and safety.

Section 8: Science and Technology

Topic 1.
Identifying the Interrelationship of Science and Technology

Technology can be loosely defined as the application of science for the benefit of people. For political, geographic, and economic reasons, not all people have the same ready access to clean, safe water supplies or to adequate food supplies, despite the technological capabilities that basic science has provided. Science certainly can be beneficial, but arguably it can also harm humankind and the environment.

Science gives us the knowledge and tools to understand nature's principles; that knowledge can often be applied for some useful purpose. Few would debate the benefits of the wheel and axle, the electric light, the polio vaccine, and plastic. The benefits of science and technology become more complicated to evaluate when discussing the applications of gene splicing for genetically modified foods, of cloning, of nuclear energy to replace fossil fuels, or of atomic energy to prepare weapons of mass destruction. Science can tell us how to do something, not whether we should.

Scientific literacy helps us participate in the decision-making process of our society as well-informed and contributing members. Real-world decisions have social, political, and economic dimensions; scientific information can often support or refute those decisions. Understanding that the inherent nature of scientific information is unbiased and based on experimental evidence that can be reproduced by any laboratory under the same conditions can help us all make better decisions, recognize false arguments, and participate fully as active and responsible citizens.

The science teacher should incorporate the effective use of technology to plan, organize, deliver, and evaluate instruction for all students. Moreover, the effective teacher includes resources of all types in the curriculum-planning process. Among the resources educators should be very familiar with are (1) the school library, (2) the city or county library, (3) education service center resources, and (4) the library of any college or university in the area.

Teachers should have lists of all audiovisual aids that they can borrow, such as kits, films, filmstrips, videos, laser discs, and computer software. All audiovisual aids should be related to curricular objectives. Many librarians have keyed their resources to objectives in related subject areas, making it easy for teachers to incorporate them into their lessons. However, the teacher should be sure to preview and approve all resources before using them with a class. The list of resources to accompany a lesson or unit should ideally be a part of the curriculum guide or the lesson plan.

Presentations

Although it is very likely that prospective teachers have had some background in instructional design, some basic guidelines for creating and presenting effective slide presentations are worth repeating (Truehaft 1995). First, it is important that teachers consider the purpose of the presentation: what is the message? Teachers should avoid the temptation to include "bells and whistles" or any advanced technology so dazzling that it detracts from the message.

Second, it is important for the presentation to be consistent; that is, the transitions from slide to slide should, in general, be the same. The backgrounds (or templates) should remain the same. Typefaces and font sizes should be consistent. The use of color to highlight or separate text should also be consistent.

Third, students must be able to see clearly and read easily. The type size must be large enough. Projecting a presentation onto a television screen causes the images to appear smaller than when an LCD projector is used. To ensure that the presentation is easy to read, the teacher should limit the amount of text on each slide. Students may find it difficult to read a slide with more than six or eight lines of type on it. Lots of "white space" gives a presentation a clean, easy-to-read appearance. The teacher should use just one or two kinds of fonts. For small pieces of text (titles or labels, for example), a sans serif typeface may be best (such as Arial or Helvetica); however, if you have long passages of text, a serif typeface (such as Times New Roman or Bookman) is easier to read.

Just as it is desirable to limit the amount of text on a slide and to limit the fonts used, it is also important to limit the number of graphic elements used. Each slide should include only one or two graphics and one message or main point.

Visibility is a primary consideration. Whether the text is readable depends on the contrast between the text color and the background. It is best to use dark text on a light background or vice versa (such as black on white or white on black). An accent color (such as red) can emphasize important points.

Before making a presentation, the teacher must ensure that all equipment is functioning and that he or she knows how to use the computer and the projection device controls. If using sound, the teacher should check the volume. To maintain students' attention, the teacher must be fully in charge of the presentation.

Computers

When computers first appeared in classrooms, they were primarily used to give students drill and practice in simple skills like arithmetic operations. As the technology advanced, elaborate systems of practice and testing with management capabilities enabled teachers to track student achievement.

Drill-and-practice software is useful for students who need considerable practice in certain skills because it gives students immediate feedback; they need not wait for the teacher to correct their papers to know if they chose the correct answers. Many of these programs have game formats to make the practice more interesting. One disadvantage of drill-and-practice software is that they generally employ lower-level learning.

Topic 2.
Identifying the Tools and Technology Used for Data Collection and Problem Solving

Reliability of data obtained in any experiment is always a concern. At issue is reproducibility and accuracy. In general, data must be **reproducible** by the experimenter and others using the same apparatus. Results that cannot be reproduced are suspect. **Accuracy** is often limited by the measurement instruments used in the experiment. Any reported numerical result must always be qualified by the uncertainty in its value. A typical example might be a voltage meter readout of 3.0 volts. If the meter has a full-scale reading of 10 volts and accuracy of 3 percent, the actual value could be anywhere between 2.7 volts and 3.3 volts.

Computer programs and on-line resources make data collection and problem solving easier and more accurate. Compared to the goose quill, the modern ballpoint pen is a dramatic advancement in the technology of written communication. However, neither replaces the critical, analytical, and creative act of authorship. Likewise, although many tools are available to assist in observation,

data collection, analysis, and the presentation of scientific information, no technology can replace the role of the investigator who must formulate meaningful questions, perform critical analyses, reach meaningful conclusions, and recognize how to use scientific tools effectively. Technology provides the tools on which all of modern science is based. By making some of these tools available in their classrooms, teachers give students the opportunity to participate firsthand in the process of inquiry and discovery.

Technology used in the classroom must facilitate student learning, remove barriers to understanding, and prevent the creation of new barriers that might delay or obscure the scientific concepts being taught. Scientific process skills, including the proper and accurate use of laboratory equipment, are an important component of science education. Instruction is necessary to guide the effective use of each measurement or observational tool: rulers, microscopes, balances, laboratory glassware, and so forth. As students develop these skills, they move from simple observations to using these tools to find answers to questions that they develop themselves.

Section 9: Technology in the Classroom

Topic 1.
Identifying the Purposes and Functions of Common Computer Software

Many software tools are extremely useful for teachers and students. **Word-processing programs** allow students to write, edit, and polish written assignments, such as term papers and research reports. Most programs include spelling and grammar checkers that enable students to enhance the quality of their written assignments. With most word processors, students can put the text into columns topped by headlines of varying sizes to produce periodic newsletters. For example, a class could write a series of reviews of scientific articles and add information about class activities in science. **Desktop publishing programs** allow students to integrate text and graphics to produce more complex publications like a school newspaper or yearbook.

Databases are like electronic file cards; they allow students to input data and then retrieve it in various formats and arrangements. For example, science students can input data about an experiment on temperature, volume, or time, for instance, and then manipulate the data to call out information in a variety of ways. The most important step in learning about databases is dealing with huge quantities of information. Students need to learn how to analyze and interpret the data to discover connections among isolated facts and figures and how to eliminate unnecessary information.

On-line databases are essential tools for research. Students can access databases related to science as well as many other subject areas. Through electronic mail (e-mail), students can communicate over the computer with scientific associations and scientists from around the world. Massive bibliographic databases are also available to help students and teachers find the resources they need. One can usually obtain many of the print materials through interlibrary loan. The use of electronic systems can geometrically increase the materials available to students.

Spreadsheets are similar to teacher grade books. One can link rows and columns of numbers to produce totals and averages. Formulas can connect information in one cell (the intersection of a row and column) to another cell. Teachers often keep grade books on a spreadsheet because of the ease in updating information. Once formulas are in place, teachers can enter grades and have completely up-to-date averages for all students. Some spreadsheet programs also include charting functions that enable teachers to display class averages on a bar chart and thus provide a visual comparisons of performance among various classes. Several stand-alone graphing and charting software packages are also available.

Students can use spreadsheets to collect and analyze numerical data, sort the data in various orders, and create various types of graphs, bars, columns, scatters, histograms, and pies to convey information. Students can use the graphics they produce to enhance written reports or in multimedia presentations.

Topic 2.
Computer-Assisted Instruction

In the past, teachers used computers strictly for **drill-and-practice** lessons, giving students an alternative to printed worksheets to practice simple skills like arithmetic operations. Publishers developed many elaborate systems of practice and testing with management systems that enabled teachers to keep track of students' progress. As mentioned earlier, drill-and-practice software is useful for students who need to hone basic skills. One advantage of these programs is the immediate feedback they provide to students; they know if they chose the correct answer without having to wait for the teacher to correct their papers. Many drill-and-practice programs have game formats to make students' practice sessions more interesting. One disadvantage of the programs is they generally require low-level thinking skills.

Tutorials are a step above drill-and-practice programs because they also include explanations and information. A student makes a response, and then the program branches to the most appropriate section based on the student's answer. Tutorials often help with remedial work but are also useful for instruction in any topic—for instance, the metric system. Improved graphics and sound allow non-English-speaking students to listen to correct pronunciation while viewing pictures of words. Tutorials can supplement, not supplant, teacher instruction.

Topic 3.
Selection and Evaluation Criteria

The effective teacher uses criteria to evaluate audiovisual, multimedia, and computer resources. The first thing to look for is congruence with lesson goals. If the software does not reinforce student outcomes, the teacher should not use it, no matter how flashy or well-crafted it is. A checklist for instructional computer software could include appropriate sequence of instruction, meaningful student interaction with the software, learner control of screens and pacing, and motivation. Other factors to consider are the ability to control sound and progress, effective use of color, clarity of text and graphics, and potential as an individual or group assignment.

In addition to congruence with curriculum goals, the teacher needs to consider students' strengths and needs, their learning styles or preferred modalities, and their interests. Students' needs can be determined through formal or informal assessment. Most standardized tests include an indication of which objectives the student did not master. Students can receive help in mastering these objectives from computer or multimedia aids.

Topic 4.
Identifying Ways Technology Can Be Used by Students to Represent Understanding of Science Concepts

Graphics or paint programs allow students to produce freehand drawings of cells viewed under a microscope, plants or animals observed outdoors, or other images. Students can use these programs to illustrate classroom presentations, individual research projects, or multimedia presentations. Many word-processing programs have some graphic functions.

Simulations or **problem-solving programs** provide opportunities for students to have experiences that otherwise could not take place in the classroom because of time or cost constraints or simply because the classroom setting does not allow for such experiences. For example, several simulation programs available give students the opportunity to "dissect" animals. Using the program rather than attempting to perform real dissections saves time and materials, is less messy, and allows students who might be reluctant to dissect real animals to learn about them. Other software might explore the effects of weightlessness on plant growth, a situation that would be impossible to set up in the classroom lab.

Students may even teach each other through multimedia presentations. Students in an inquirer role often take responsibility for their own learning by planning, carrying out, and presenting research and projects.

Topic 5.
Identifying Telecommunications Terminology, Processes, and Procedures

Communication across long distances is **telecommunication**. Telecommunications can include computer networking, telephones, telegraphy, radio, television, and data communications. These forms of communication can play an important role in science classroom instruction.

A telecommunication system has several components. The **transmitter** changes or encodes the message into a physical result called the **signal**. The transmission **channel** is the medium the message travels through and may modify or degrade the signal while it is on its way from the transmitter to the receiver. The **receiver** recovers and decodes the message within certain limits. The human eye, ear, and brain are examples of receivers.

Telecommunications can be in point-to-point, point-to-multipoint, or broadcast form. Broadcast telecommunications is a particular form of point-to-multipoint telecommunication that goes directly from the transmitter to the receivers without passing through intermediaries. A telecommunications engineer analyzes both the statistical properties of the message and the physical properties of the transmission medium or the line. The engineer must design effective encoding and decoding mechanisms.

When designing a system, a telecommunications engineer must consider the human sensory organs (especially the eyes and ears) and both the physiological and psychological characteristics of human perception. The engineer must research what defects the user can tolerate in the signal and decide which ones will not significantly impair the hearing or the viewing of the message. Economics also plays an important role in establishing a telecommunications system.

In a conversation between two people, the message is the information that one person wants to communicate to the other. The sender's brain, vocal cords, larynx, and mouth produce the sounds (speech). The spoken result—the sound waves or the pressure fluctuations in the air—is the signal.

The channel is composed of the air carrying sound waves and all the properties of the sound, including echoes, reverberations, and ambient noise. All channels have noise. An important aspect to consider in the channel is the **bandwidth**. A telephone, with its low bandwidth channel, cannot carry all the audio information that the sender transmits in the conversation. Some distortion and irregularities in the speaker's voice that would not be as evident in normal speech can occur in a telephone conversation.

The receiver is the listener's auditory system, including the ear and the auditory nerve, and the brain, which receives and decodes auditory signals. The receiver must also filter out background noise. Devices like radios and telephones that come between the speaker and the listener can distort the original vocal signal.

Topic 6.
Demonstrating Knowledge of Legal and Ethical Practices as They Relate to Information and Technological Systems

Computer technology is becoming a larger focus of the classroom. In addition to being part of the curriculum, educators frequently use computers as aids in storing information and developing lesson materials. Computer software programs and databases fall under the domain of copyright law. As defined by federal law, computer programs, such as a word-processing software or graphic design programs, are "a set of statements or instructions to be used directly in a computer in order to bring about a certain result" (Public Law 96-517, Section 117).

Often a teacher will make a backup, or copy of a computer program, in case the original disk containing the program becomes damaged. A backup copy is not considered an infringement of the copyright law as long as the teacher follows these rules when creating the backup:

1. The teacher must make the new copy or adaptation only to facilitate use of the program in conjunction with the machine.

2. The new copy or adaptation must be for archival purposes only, and all archival copies must be destroyed in the event that continued possession of the computer program should cease to be rightful.

3. Any copies prepared or adapted may not be leased, sold, or otherwise transferred without the authorization of the software copyright owner. Copies of a computer program cannot be shared or borrowed. The original disk should not be used to install a program on more than one machine unless the owner has a license to do so from the computer software company. If unsure about the licensing status of a computer program, the teacher can check with the media specialist or school administrator.

Teachers are role models for their communities; therefore, all educators must be aware of the software copyright law and be in complete compliance.

Topic 7.
Protecting Children Accessing the Internet

As teachers discover more ways to use the Internet as an instructing tool, they must also be mindful of the Children's Internet Protection Act (CIPA) and the Neighborhood Children's Internet Protection Act (N-CIPA), which passed Congress in December 2000. Both were part of a large federal appropriations measure (Public Law 106-554).

The legislation established three basic requirements that schools and libraries using the Internet must meet, or be "undertaking actions" to meet:

1. The school or library must use blocking or filtering technology on all computers with Internet access. The blocking or filtering must protect against access to certain visual depictions, including obscenity, child pornography, and materials harmful to minors. The law does not require the filtering of text.

2. The school or library must adopt and implement an Internet safety policy that addresses the key criteria, including

   a. access by minors to inappropriate matter on the Internet and the Web;

   b. the safety and security of minors when using electronic mail, chat rooms, and other forms of direct electronic communications;

   c. unauthorized access, including so-called hacking, and other unlawful activities by minors online;

   d. unauthorized disclosure, use, and dissemination of personal identification information regarding minors;

   e. measures designed to restrict minors' access to materials harmful to minors.

3. The school or library must hold a public meeting to discuss the Internet safety policy; specifically, the law requires that the school or library "provide reasonable public notice and hold at least one public hearing or meeting to address the proposed Internet safety policy."

Topic 8.
Technology and Copyright Issues

Copyright is a form of protection provided by the laws of the United States (U.S. Code, Title 17) to the authors of "original works of authorship," including literary, dramatic, musical, artistic, and certain other intellectual works. The protection applies to both published and unpublished works. It is illegal for anyone to violate any of the rights provided by copyright law to the owner of the copyright. These rights, however, are not unlimited. Sections 107 through 121 of the **1976 Copyright Act** establish limitations on the rights of copyright holders. In some cases, these limitations are specified exemptions from copyright liability. One major limitation is the doctrine of fair use, which is given a statutory basis in Section 107 of the 1976 Copyright Act.

The **fair use doctrine** allows limited reproduction of copyrighted works for educational and research purposes. In general, a teacher can copy a chapter from a book; an article from a periodical or newspaper; a short story, short essay, or short poem, whether or not from a collective work; and/or a chart, graph, diagram, drawing, cartoon, or picture from a book, periodical, or newspaper. For a classroom, a teacher can make multiple copies (not to exceed the number of students in the class) as long as the copying meets the following tests of brevity, spontaneity, and cumulative effect, and as long as each copy includes a notice of copyright.

Brevity generally refers to a poem of 250 words or less or a prose passage less than 2,500 words. **Spontaneity** refers to the need for a teacher to use a work without undertaking the normal time to obtain copyright permission. Finally, the **cumulative effect** test refers to copying material for only one class, from a single author, and no more than nine times during a term. Suggested guidelines for fair use can be found at the University of Texas System Web site at http://www.utsystem.edu/OGC/IntellectualProperty/copypol2.htm.

Regarding the fair use of multimedia materials, it is generally acceptable for teachers and students to incorporate others' work into a multimedia presentation and display or perform it as long as the presentation is for a class assignment. It is suggested that educators be conservative in the use of such materials, using only small amounts of others' works and not making unnecessary copies of such works. Complete information about copyright can be found at the official Web site of the U.S. Library of Congress Copyright Office: *http://www.loc.gov/copyright/*.

Teachers must monitor student performance to ensure that the highest standards of academic integrity are upheld and that cheating is not allowed. In addition, teachers should make students aware of the consequences and penalties for academic dishonesty (including plagiarism).

Topic 9.
The Internet

The Internet and the World Wide Web are having a profound effect on students and teachers alike. This very powerful learning tool is best viewed as a source of information. By linking computers around the world, the Internet serves as a network of networks. From 500 hosts in 1983, the Internet had rapidly grown to about 30 million hosts in 1998, and the number continues to mount at a dramatic rate. At the start of the twenty-first century, an estimated 360 million people had access to the Internet.

Oscar Wilde once argued that there is no such thing as a good or bad book and that a work of literature exists apart from issues of morality. The same logic could be applied to the Internet. Like any source of information, the Internet can be used well or badly. The amount of information available is so enormous that people often have difficulty finding the exact information they are seeking. Moreover, because no form of quality control exists to filter the massive amounts of information posted on the Internet, much of what is available is inaccurate, misleading, or false. Consequently, teachers must instruct students in using critical thinking skills to judge the accuracy of information, look for evidence and substantiation of claims, and separate facts from opinions. Educators and parents alike must also be concerned about the appropriateness of the information accessed by students; a wide range of material is available and some of it is unsuitable for children.

To safeguard children and provide some kind of quality control, federal law requires public schools to use Internet filters. These tools are designed to limit access to unsuitable material; however, some of the filters do not discriminate adequately, so that questionable material may still be accessed while some acceptable material may be blocked. Thus, teachers must carefully supervise students' use of this powerful resource.

The Internet offers many tools that classroom teachers will find valuable. Basically, teachers should be familiar with common Internet browsers (such as Microsoft Explorer and Netscape) and popular search engines (such as Yahoo, Excite, Lycos, and Google) that make it possible to research any topic. Many Web sites offer teaching tips and tools, so teachers will want to investigate these and bookmark the ones that are most pertinent and reliable. Communicating with colleagues, parents, and even students is made convenient through e-mail.

The Internet, then, is a common tool of the twenty-first century, used by both teachers and students. Internet sites are constantly being developed and renovated, so sites that are popular today may be gone tomorrow. However, the following sites have been popular with teachers for many years:

- U.S. Department of Education: *http://www.ed.gov/*
- Texas Education Agency: *http://www.tea.state.tx.us/*
- Education World: *http://www.education-world.com/*
- National Education Association: *http://www.nea.org/*

- Discovery Channel/Education: *http://school.discovery.com/teachingtools/teachingtools.html*
- TeachersFirst: *http://www.teachersfirst.com/*

References

Blough, Glenn O., and Julius Schwartz. *Elementary School Science and How to Teach It.* New York: Rhinehart and Winston, 1969.

Children's Internet Protection Act (CIPA), Public Law No. 106-554 (2000) (codified at 20 U.S.C. § § 6801, 6777, 9134 [2003]; 47 U. S. C. § 254 [2003]).

Computer Software Copyright Act, Public Law Number 96-517, § 10(b), 94 Stat.3028 (1980) (codified at 17 U. S. C. § 117 [1988]).

Copyright. U.S. Code, Title 17. Enacted July 30, 1947, Ch. 391, 61 Stat. 652. Revised in its entirety by Public Law 94-553, Title I, Section 101, October 19, 1976, 90 Stat. 2541.

Digital Performance Right in Sound Recordings Act of 1995 amended section 106 by adding paragraph (6). Public Law No. 104-39, 109 Stat. 336. In 1999, a technical amendment substituted "121" for "120." Public Law No. 106-44, 113 Stat. 221, 222. The Intellectual Property and High Technology Technical Amendments Act of 2002 amended section 106 by substituting section "107 through 122" for "107 through 121" Public Law No. 107-273, 116 Stat. 1758, 1909.

Truehaft, J. "Multimedia Design Considerations." Using Technology in Education. Algonquin College, 1995. *http://www.algonquinc.on.ca/edtech/mmdesign.html.*

U.S. Congress. Children's Internet Protection Act. 106th Congress *http://www.cybertelecom.org/cda/cipatext.htm.*

U.S. Copyright Law. U.S. Copyright Office, Library of Congress *http://www.copyright.gov/title17/.*

Victor, Edward. *Science for the Elementary School.* New York: Macmillan, 1975.

Wells, H. G. *The War of the Worlds: Book 1.* Web edition edited by John Walker. *www.fiyrnukab.cg/etexts/www/warworlds/blc7.html.*

Planning, Learning, and the Role of the Learner

Section 1: Planning

The effective teacher realizes that having an interesting, carefully planned curriculum is one of the best ways to bring about student learning, promote desired student behavior, and prevent most discipline problems. The teacher knows how to plan and conduct lessons in a variety of learning environments that lead to student outcomes consistent with state and district standards:

- The teacher determines instructional long-term goals and short-term objectives appropriate to student needs.

- The teacher identifies activities that support the knowledge, skills, and attitudes students must learn in a given subject area.

- The teacher identifies materials based on instructional objectives and student learning needs and performance levels.

Topic 1.
Goals

All successful teachers begin the term with a clear idea of what they expect students to learn in a given course. Establishing long-range goals for a course—goals that are age-appropriate and reflect student ability and needs—help to clarify the knowledge and skills that teachers and students will work toward during the school year.

The local board of education can establish long-range goals as can knowledgeable curriculum specialists, a single teacher, or a group of teachers. Stated in clear, concise language, these goals define the knowledge that students will achieve or the skills that they will acquire through specific instructional activities. For example, a language arts instructor might state the following long-range goals for high school students:

- The student is able to identify major American poets and authors of the twentieth century.

- The student is able to write narrative, informative, and persuasive essays.

- The student is able to properly cite research references.

- The student is able to identify important themes in literature.

- The student is able to identify with multicultural perspectives on the American experience.

After developing a list of potential goals for a course, the teacher should evaluate those goals against the following criteria:

Importance. The resulting learning must be significant and relevant enough for students to want to achieve them.

Instruction. Appropriate classroom activities must be able to support the learning of the stated goal.

Evaluation. Students must be able to demonstrate the achievement of the goal.

Suitability. The goal must be challenging, as well as reachable, for all students.

Topic 2.
Importance of Goals

There are many ways to evaluate the importance of selected goals. Teachers can judge goals on the basis of whether the stated outcome is necessary to gain advanced knowledge of a particular field of study, as in the following goals: Students will memorize the letters of the alphabet; students will master the use of punctuation. Goals can be evaluated on the basis of whether their achievement will lead students to become better citizens, as in this goal: Students will apply their knowledge of the constitution to judge a contemporary court case. Goals can also be judged on the basis of whether their achievement will lead students to become well-adapted members of society or competitive in the workforce, as in the following: Students will be able to demonstrate their ability to use the Internet to locate information. Finally, goals can be selected on the basis of whether their achievement will help prepare students for college admissions standards.

Topic 3.
One-minute Goal-setting

Kenneth Blanchard and Spencer Johnson (1981), the authors of *The One Minute Manager*, a best-selling book for those wanting to achieve success, describe one-minute goal-setting as (1) deciding on goals, (2) identifying what good behaviors are, (3) writing out goals, (4) reading and rereading goals, (5) reviewing goals every day, and (6) determining if behaviors match goals. This list is applicable to the classroom teacher who needs to decide on behavioral goals and identify behaviors both expected and unacceptable.

Topic 4.
Outcome-oriented Learning

Effective teachers plan carefully so that outcome-oriented activities will produce students who are self-directed learners, in group or individual environments. Effective teachers know how to plan so that the curriculum guides, lesson plans, actual lessons, tests, and assessments are correlated. They plan in advance, explain the unit's goals and objectives to the students, then choose activities that will help the class reach the desired outcomes.

In outcome-oriented learning, teachers define outcomes, or what they want students to know, do, and be when they complete a required course of study. The teachers set high but realistic goals and objectives for their students and plan instructional activities that will assist students in achieving these goals. The key to effective outcome-oriented planning is to consider the desired outcomes and determine the teacher and student behaviors that will improve the probability that students will achieve the outcomes.

Outcome-based planning starts with the end product—what must the students learn or accomplish in a particular course or grade level. For example, a third-grade math teacher may decide that one final outcome of the math class is for the students to be able to complete 100 basic addition facts in five minutes with 100 percent accuracy. He or she then works "backward" to determine prerequisite knowledge and skills students need to have to accomplish this outcome. By continuing to ask these questions about each set of prerequisites, the teacher finds a starting point for the subject or course and develops goals and objectives. The outcomes should be important enough for the teacher to require them of all students. An outcome-oriented system means that the teacher supplies the students with sufficient time and practice to acquire the knowledge and skills. It also means that the teacher takes into account students' various learning styles and time required for learning, and makes adaptations by providing a variety of educational opportunities.

Section 2: Instruction

To ensure that students achieve the stated goal, teachers must choose appropriate classroom activities support its learning. When students have completed these activities, they should be able to demonstrate successfully the knowledge or skills that they have achieved.

Topic 1.
Evaluation

Through the successful completion of writing assignments, tests, projects, or activities, students must be able to demonstrate that they have achieved the stated long-range goals.

More about evaluation is available in Chapter 4 under Topic 3. Identifying Appropriate Assessment Methods in Teaching Social Science Concepts and in Chapter 2 under Topic 15. Formal and Informal Assessment to Improve Instruction and Enhance Learning.

Topic 2.
Suitability

All goals for a given course must be achievable for the entire class, while leaving room to challenge students to master new skills. To determine if long-range goals are appropriate, teachers can refer to a number of resources, including student files, which may include the results of basic skills tests, reading level evaluations, and writing samples.

The teacher has knowledge of strategies to create and sustain a safe, efficient, supportive learning enviroment:

- The teacher evaluates the appropriateness of the physical environment for facilitating student learning and promoting safety.

- The teacher identifies a repertoire of techniques for establishing smooth, efficient, and well-paced routines.

- The teacher identifies strategies to involve students in establishing rules and standards for behavior.

- The teacher identifies emergency procedures for student and campus safety.

Topic 3.
Physical Environment

While certain physical aspects of the classroom cannot be changed (size, shape, number of windows, type of lighting, etc.), others can be. Windows can have shades or blinds that distribute light correctly and permit darkening the room for video or computer viewing. If the light switches do not allow part of the lights to remain on, sometimes schools will change the wiring system. If not, teachers can use a lamp to provide minimum lighting for monitoring students during videos or films. Schools often schedule maintenance, such as painting and floor cleaning, during the summer. Often school administrators will accede to teachers' requests for a specific color of paint, given sufficient time for planning.

All classrooms should have a bulletin board used by the teacher and by the students. The effective teacher has plans for changing the board according to units of study. Space should be reserved for display of student work and projects, either on the bulletin board, the wall, or in the hallway. (Secondary teachers who need creative ideas can visit elementary classrooms.)

Bare walls can be depressing; however, covering the wall with too many posters can be visually distracting. Posters with sayings that promote cooperation, study skills, and content ideas should be displayed, but teachers should change them several times during the school year because students will ignore the displays when they become too familiar.

Most classrooms have movable desks, which allow for varied seating arrangements. If students are accustomed to sitting in rows, this is sometimes a good way to start the year. Harry K. Wong (2004) describes his method of assigning seats on the first day of school, which is to assign each desk a column and row number, then give students assignment cards as they come into the room. Another method is to put seating assignments on an overhead, visible when students enter the room. Once students are comfortable with classroom rules and procedures, the teacher can explain to students how to quickly move their desks into different formations for special activities, then return them to their original positions in the last 60 seconds of class.

The best place for the teacher's desk is often at the back of a room, so there are few barriers between the teacher and the students and between the students and the chalkboards. This arrangement encourages the teacher to walk around the classroom for better monitoring of students.

Topic 4.
Social and Emotional Climate

The effective teacher maintains a climate that promotes the lifelong pursuit of learning. One way to do this is to have students practice research skills that will be helpful throughout life. All subject areas can promote the skills of searching for information to answer a question, filtering it to determine what is appropriate, and using what is helpful to solve a problem.

The effective teacher also facilitates a positive social and emotional atmosphere and promotes a risk-taking environment for students. The teacher should set up classroom rules and guidelines for how he or she will treat students, how students will treat him or her, and how students will treat each other; students should be a part of developing the rules. In part, this means that the teacher does not ridicule or put down students or tolerate such behavior among the students. It also means that the teacher has an accepting attitude toward student ideas, especially when the idea is not what he or she was expecting to hear. Sometimes students can invent excellent ideas that are not always clear until they are asked to explain how they arrived at them.

Students should feel free to answer and ask any questions that are relevant to the class, without fear of sarcasm or ridicule. Teachers should always avoid sarcasm. Sometimes teachers consider sarcasm to be mere teasing, but because some students often interpret it negatively, effective teachers avoid all types and levels of sarcasm.

Topic 5.
Academic Learning Time

The effective teacher maximizes the amount of time spent for instruction. A teacher who loses 5 minutes at the beginning of class and 5 minutes at the end of class wastes 10 minutes a day that could have been spent at educational activities. Ten minutes may not seem like a lot of time to lose. However, this is equivalent to a whole period a week, four classes a month, and 25 periods a year.

Academic learning time is the amount of allocated time that students spend in an activity at the appropriate level of difficulty with the appropriate level of success. The appropriate level of difficulty is one which challenges students without frustrating them. Students who have typically been lower achievers need a higher rate of success than those who have typically been higher achievers. One way to increase academic learning time is to teach procedures to students so they will make transitions quickly. Another way to increase academic

learning time is to have materials and resources ready for quick distribution and use. In addition, teachers can give students a time limit for a transition or an activity. To encourage time on task and to prevent off-task behavior and discipline problems, time limits for group work should be slightly shorter than the amount students need. It is also essential for the teacher to have additional activities planned should the class finish activities sooner than anticipated. As students complete group work, they should have other group or individual activities so they can work up until the last minute before the end of class.

Topic 6.
"With It"-ness in the Classroom

Teachers must be "with it" in a classroom to prevent misbehavior that will interrupt the flow of learning. The level of "with it"-ness must extend beyond the obvious events of the classroom. A teacher needs to understand the dynamics behind the actions that occur in the classroom, and then proceed accordingly.

Many factors influence student behavior. Young children will generally follow the rules of the classroom out of a desire to please their teachers. Misbehavior that occurs in a classroom may be the result of a conflict that is occurring elsewhere. Teachers should be aware that these conflicts can occur between peers, between students and the teacher, or as a result of events in the student's family or out-of-classroom experiences.

The goal of "with it"-ness is to prevent misconduct in the classroom. Through everyday interactions, the teacher develops a sense of an individual student's normal behavior and general mental state. The "with it" teacher also develops a sense of the relations between the students in a class and within the school. Noticing the beginning of a conflict between individuals in a class enables the "with it" teacher to mediate the students to a resolution that avoids the disruption of class time. The teacher should explain well and clearly display the desired behavior for the students in a classroom. Posted rules provide a constant guide and reminder of classroom rules. Teachers can also use these displays as a reference when discussing expected behavior, either individually or with the class as a whole.

Teachers should self-monitor their interactions with misbehaving students. Children may act out if they feel they are threatened, disliked, or treated unfairly. A "with it" teacher knows which particular students are causing the class disruption and works to curb this behavior without punishing the class as a whole. The teacher's response to the behavior or the teacher's allowing the misbehavior to persist can disrupt the learning momentum.

Both the individual student and the class as a whole are affected by how the teacher handles classroom misconduct. The effective approach is when the teacher compliments the positive behavior modeled by other students in the classroom, rather than individually reprimanding student misbehavior. If certain students are not properly addressing the task at hand, the teacher can say, "I like the way Glen is working in his math book" or "Belinda, I like the way you are quietly raising your hand and waiting your turn." By doing so, the teacher is reinforcing the desired behavior for the class without directly addressing and calling attention to the misbehavior. The individual student has an opportunity to monitor his or her own behavior, and class momentum is not lost.

Teachers can also guide a student toward appropriate behavior by stating the student's name or explaining on what task he or she should currently be working. Nonverbal cues include walking toward the student, making eye contact, or gently touching the student's desk or shoulder. These techniques will not disrupt the flow of the classroom. Teachers must clearly voice their expectations without yelling or becoming angry. Quiet and controlled reprimands are very effective. Maintaining control without involving punitive measures lowers the tension in the entire classroom. Students should not feel uncomfortable because the teacher is angry. This is especially important when teachers are working with small groups or when working on simultaneous tasks. Individualized instruction should not suffer when the teacher must reprimand another student. When a teacher demonstrates "with it"-ness, students do not feel that they have an opportunity to misbehave just because the teacher is not focusing attention directly on them.

Topic 7.
Procedures for Learning Success

One of the most challenging and important synthesizing activities of the teaching professional is determining how to match what needs to be taught with the specifications of those who need to learn it. The successful teacher spends considerable time becoming familiar with required instructional objectives, curriculum, and texts; the teacher should do this well in advance of the start of the school year. In addition to general knowledge about the intellectual and social developmental levels of students, the particular needs that characterize any specific group of students, including their individual learning styles, are more apparent to the teacher after the first few days and weeks of school. The effective teacher must be organized enough to choose and sequence learning activities before the school year begins but flexible enough to adapt these activities after becoming acquainted with the special needs and learning styles of specific students.

There are several steps the teacher should follow to ensure success for student learning:

1. Know and start teaching at the proper level of the students.

2. Share with students learning objectives and the processes chosen to attain them.

3. Prepare for the successive steps in the learning process—from instruction, through guidance and support, to feedback.

4. Choose relatively small steps in which to progress, and include regular assessments of these progressions.

5. Distinguish between the learning a student can do independently and that which is best facilitated and monitored by the teacher; choose methods appropriate to content and skills.

6. Include a variety of activities and methods that appeal to the full range of student learning styles and preferences.

Topic 8.
Organizing Activities

Instructional objectives necessitate that the skill or knowledge to be taught should be valuable on its own or should clearly lead to something else that is valuable. When the class begins, the teacher should share these long-range objectives with students as part of the teacher's planned "idea scaffolding," to acknowledge learning as a mutual enterprise. Sharing these objectives is the first important learning activity because this serves as the basis for the communal task of "making sense" of the learning in progress. Because teachers are expected to be professionally prepared to recognize the cognitive and social levels of students, they may need to review the generally accepted theories of Jean Piaget, Erik Erikson, and other research theorists to recall specific characteristics appropriate to various developmental levels. Familiarity with the learning objectives and material to be mastered and the level of the students enables the teacher to choose and develop a wide range of appropriate activities and tentatively to sequence them in ways that facilitate learning.

Careful, incremental goal-setting allows for considerable flexibility in pace and methods and leads to further valuable sequencing of strategies. For example, a variety of activities may enhance close reading: the teacher may model close reading of a very short story; the teacher may assign small-group work with close reading of paragraphs where one student identifies an important detail, and another student suggests its relevance to the details; the teacher can show the class an overhead color-marking of important descriptive words from one page of a short story or poem; students can work on individual in-class color-marking for the next page, followed by a group discussion of student results; the teacher can assign homework to color-mark a short story or poem; and students can work on group assignments graphing elements of literary text.

A perceptive teacher's growing awareness of individual student learning styles can enhance preliminary planning for any specific group of students. Because students do not fall precisely into theoretical stages, activities must reflect a range of developmental levels and learning styles. This includes concrete as well as abstract dimensions, opportunities for instruction by the teacher, and exploration and discovery by individual students and groups. Once the teacher launches the learning enterprise, the teacher's continued instruction, support, regular assessment, and feedback help maximize the potential of learning opportunities.

Topic 9.
Wait Time for Questions

Students need adequate time to respond to questions. Teachers must not allow outbursts, or choral responses of answers to their questions. Allowing students to answer questions without first being specifically called on for their response generates a faction of students who are always answering the questions. In addition, providing a wait time—or an appropriate time to think about the answer—of three to five seconds is necessary for students to formulate their responses. The proper way to ask a question is to (1) ask the question, (2) provide adequate wait time, (3) call on the student, and (4) tell the student if the response was correct. If it is correct, it is appropriate to give specific praise. However, overuse of specific praise devalues the praise mechanism within the classroom. Students who constantly receive praise do not know when to be proud of their good answers. The only time a teacher should call a student's name *before* asking the question is when the teacher needs to bring a student back into the discussion for disciplinary reasons. Then, it is appropriate to call the name first to ensure that the student is aware of the question being asked. This technique not only brings back a disruptive or off-task student but also gives the student a nonverbal message that his or her attention is necessary.

Topic 10.
Effective Use of Time

Idle hands generate a variety of discipline issues. The teacher should keep a steady pace throughout the entire class from the beginning of the lesson to the independent practice or homework time. A mere minute wasted each day adds up to well over three hours of lost instruction during a single year. Smooth transitions from topic to topic, class to class, and subject to subject are necessary so there is no wasted time, a minimal amount of interruptions, and almost nonexistent downtime.

Topic 11.
Organizing Instruction

First, a teacher should have prepared all materials and be ready to go before beginning any classroom lesson. When class begins, the teacher should immediately start with an initiating or motivational activity that has the students working and interested from the beginning. This activity could begin with a "hook" that draws student interest, states the objective for the lesson, or reviews concepts that will help lead to lesson success. During this time, the teacher may choose to take attendance or complete other required administrative activities. The teacher should use a smooth transition into the instructional part of the lesson and follow it by a short assessment, also referred to as a *guided practice activity* that determines the students' level of understanding. Last, the closure of the lesson should remind the students of the key components of the lesson.

The transition from initiation to lesson presentation to closure follows the rules for giving a good speech. First, the teacher tells the students what he or she is going to say (motivational hook); second, the teacher tells the students (instructional section); last, the teachers reviews what was just taught (closure). Keep in mind that the instructional section can use a variety of approaches including a guided discovery lesson, a free exploration lesson, cooperative projects, or a teacher-directed lesson. Instructional variety is a surefire way of maintaining student interest and improving achievement. Good instruction may include providing clear directions, asking open-ended questions, addressing questions, modeling approaches, encouraging discourse, and assessing student understanding to monitor their progress and to provide them feedback. The conclusion of most lessons will have students practicing the skills they learned in class.

This momentum ensures a smooth transition and a natural routine that encourage learning, provide a consistent pattern that students will anticipate, and assist the teacher in moving smoothly from one activity to another. Routines help students anticipate the next move. However, varied routines help in minimizing the boredom that can exist within a regulated, highly routine environment.

One experienced teacher of upper elementary students has suggested the following guidelines for teachers in managing their classes:

- Let students have input whenever you can, and when you cannot, let them think they are giving input.

- Listen to students; they have surprising insights and viewpoints.

- Be consistent with expectations and consequences.

- Do not make exceptions to school rules, even if you do not agree with them.

- Do not correct or reprimand a student in front of a class. Quickly establish that your classroom is a safe place and can be a fun place, but that disrespect for learning, others, or property is not appropriate and there will be no warnings.

- Do not begin teaching until everyone is ready to learn.

- Do consult with colleagues and administrators for advice.

- Make sure that students know their rights and their responsibilities.

Topic 12.
Technology in Instruction

The effective teacher has knowledge of strategies for the implementation of technology in the teaching and learning process:

- The teacher identifies appropriate software to prepare materials, deliver instruction, assess student achievement, and manage classroom tasks.

- The teacher identifies appropriate classroom procedures for student use of available technology.

- The teacher identifies appropriate policies and procedures for the safe and ethical use of the Internet, networks, and other electronic media.

- The teacher identifies strategies for instructing students in the use of search techniques, the evaluation of data collected, and the preparation of presentations.

Topic 13.
Educational Technology in the Primary Classroom

Technology is an important part of the world and, therefore, must be an important part of the educational environment. Students should be exposed as early as possible to computer literacy so that they will be prepared for a technologically advanced society. Teachers can use appropriate software to meet content standards and curriculum goals. Teachers must be able to integrate their existing curriculum to meet these standards.

Section 3: The Role of the Learner

Jaime Escalante, called "America's greatest teacher" (Barry, 198–199; Pipes) and the subject of the motion picture *Stand and Deliver,* tells a story about having two students named Johnny in his class. He says that one, "good Johnny," was a dedicated and responsible student, courteous, polite, and high achieving. The other Johnny, "bad Johnny," seldom came to class, and when he did, he created discipline problems. "Bad Johnny" wouldn't listen, wouldn't do his work, and wouldn't cooperate.

On the night of the annual open house, a very nice woman came to Mr. Escalante's classroom and introduced herself, saying, "I am Johnny's mother." Mr. Escalante assumed she was "good Johnny's" mother. He said, "Oh, I am so glad to meet you. You must be very proud of your son. He is an exceptional student, and I am pleased to have him in my class."

The next day, "bad Johnny" came to class. After class, he approached Mr. Escalante and asked, "Hey, why did you tell my mother those things last night? No one has ever said anything like that about me." It was then that Mr. Escalante realized his mistake. He did not admit his error to Johnny, and the strangest thing happened next. "Bad Johnny" stopped being bad. He started coming to class. He started doing his work. He started making good grades. Mr. Escalante concludes his story by saying, "I ended up with two 'good Johnnys' in my class."

This anecdote emphasizes an important aspect of teaching: teacher perception is ultimately significant. Students may be what their teachers think them to be. What's more, students may become what their teachers believe them to be. Teachers report that when they treat their students as responsible young adults, most students rise to the occasion. (Barry and others, 198–199; Pipes)

Topic 1.
Cognitive Development and Moral Decision Making

Of course, teachers of young children may have to contend with some different issues, but all teachers should be aware of age and maturational differences among students. Jean Piaget, whose ideas on cognitive development have greatly influenced American education, thought that children younger than eight years of age (because of their egocentric thought) were unable to take the perspective of another individual. Thus, Piaget concluded that children under the age of eight made decisions about right and wrong on the basis of how much

harm was caused. For example, children might say that a child who ate two forbidden cookies was less guilty than the child who ate six forbidden cookies. Children over the age of eight, however, were able to take into consideration whether the individual acted purposely or accidentally. For example, a child who broke a toy by accident was not as guilty of misbehavior as the child who broke the toy on purpose. Researchers who have tested Piaget's ideas have found that children younger than age eight are able to engage in moral reasoning at much more complex levels than Piaget thought possible.

The term *standards*, when used with regard to behavior, evokes issues of right and wrong, sometimes referred to as *ethical or moral decisions*. With regard to moral development, teachers should be familiar with the concepts of Lawrence Kohlberg. Kohlberg (1984), following the example of Piaget, developed a scenario to quiz children and teens.

Kohlberg told a story about a man whose wife was so seriously ill that she would die without medication, yet her husband had no money to buy her medicine. After trying various legal means to get the medicine, her husband considered stealing it. Kohlberg asked if it was wrong or right to steal the drug and to explain why it was either wrong or right. Kohlberg did not evaluate whether the respondent said it was wrong or right to steal the drug; he was interested in the reasons given to justify the actions. On the basis of the responses he received, Kohlberg proposed six stages of moral development.

Stage 1, punishment and obedience, describes children who simply follow the rules so as to escape punishment. If kindergarten-age children, for example, are told not to talk or they'll lose their chance to go outside for recess, they will not want to lose their playground privileges, and so they will not talk. On the other hand, stage 2, individualism and change, refers to children who follow the rules, not only to escape punishment but also when they think there is some reward in following the rules. These older primary-grade children, for example, seek not only to escape punishment but also to receive a reward or benefit for their good behavior.

Kohlberg's stage 3 has mutual interpersonal expectations and interpersonal conformity; at this stage, children want to please the people who are important to them. Junior high students, for example, may behave in a manner that gains the approval of their peers or their idols.

At stage 4, Kohlberg said, adolescents become oriented to conscience, and they recognize the importance of established social order. Teens at this stage obey the rules unless those rules contradict higher social responsibilities. In other words, most high school students realize that rules are necessary, and they will obey most rules if the rules reflect basic social values, such as honesty, mutual respect, courtesy, and so forth.

Post-conventional morality was the term Kohlberg gave to stages 5 and 6. At stage 5, individuals recognize the importance of both individual rights and social contracts but believe that people should generally abide by the rules to bring the greatest good to the majority. Kohlberg believed that about one-fifth of adolescents reach stage 5. Therefore, Kohlberg would have expected that few high school students would be operating at this level.

Finally, Kohlberg would not have expected high school students to reach stage 6; he believed that very few individuals ever reached this stage. The person in stage 6 recognizes principles of justice. Individuals at this stage believe that individuals should obey most rules because most rules reflect just principles; however, if rules violate ethical principles, individuals have a greater obligation to follow their conscience even if that means breaking the rules. Social reformers, such as Martin Luther King Jr., would be examples of those who attain stage 6 moral reasoning.

Kohlberg's theory describes the progression of children's moral reasoning from school entry at kindergarten (stage 1) to graduation from high school (stages 4 and 5, for some). Kohlberg's theory is widely taught and applied in school settings but not without controversy. Some have contended that Kohlberg's theory is limited and biased because of his research techniques (getting reactions to a scenario) and because a study of white, middle-class males under the age of 17 was the basis of his theory. Many would say that his ideas have limited application to other ethnic groups, socioeconomic groups, or females.

One theorist interested in applying Kohlberg's theory to women is Carol Gilligan, a student of Kohlberg's, who developed an alternative theory of moral development in women. Gilligan (1982) found that women, unlike the men at Kohlberg's stages 5 and 6, tend to value caring and compassion for others above abstract, rational principles. Therefore, when women make decisions, they base their conclusions on how their choices and actions will affect others. Gilligan posited that women pass through three levels of moral reasoning although, as in Kohlberg's theory of development, not all reach the third level. At the first level, the individual has concerns only about herself. At the second level, the individual sacrifices her own interests for the sake of others. Finally, at the third level, the individual synthesizes responsibilities to both herself and to others.

Effective teachers may want to consider the implications of these theories for the behavior of students in their classes, in particular, how students will respond to rules of behavior. Although those taking the PRAXIS exams will not be tested on these specific theorists, their theories are, nonetheless, a valuable resource for assessing student behavior. For example, according to Kohlberg, younger students are more concerned about punishments and rewards; older students are more concerned about reasonable rules based on principles of fairness and equality. According to Gilligan, female students may be thinking about how rules affect their friendships. To illustrate, according to these theorists, a male student might be offended by someone cheating (because cheating is wrong) and report the individual to the teacher. Female students, on the other hand, might value their friendship with the cheater more than the principle of honesty; therefore, female students might be less likely to report cheating to the teacher.

Topic 2.
Learning Styles and Personality Types

Information about learning styles and personality types essential to effective teaching can also shed light on how individuals make ethical and moral decisions. For example, research indicates that the population is fairly evenly distributed between people who make decisions based on rational, logical, and objective data—thinking types—and those who make decisions based on feelings—feeling types. Slightly more males than females are thinking types. The feeling half of the population tends to make decisions based on how those decisions may affect others, avoiding conflict and promoting harmony; slightly more females than males are feeling types.

Most people (approximately 76 percent) are the sensing type, those who learn through sensory experiences;

they are linear learners who enjoy facts and details. They like sequential organization and memory tasks. They often work slowly and methodically and take great care to finish each project before beginning another one.

On the other hand, the minority (approximately 24 percent) are the intuitive type. This type learns not through experience but by insight and inspiration. Facts and details bore these students, who prefer global concepts and theories. They dislike memory work. Generally, they are quick to grasp ideas and catch on to the gist of things; this means they can be disruptive because they have already learned their lesson or finished their assignment. While they generally perform well on tests, they also daydream and lose interest quickly in the things that they deem uninteresting or dull. They like to do several things at once and find it tedious to have to slow down or wait for others to finish.

Section 4: Classroom Management

Teachers who understand the differences among the learners and ways of thinking, whether it is in regard to information processing or moral decision making, can use this information to establish standards for classroom behavior. Standards should reflect community values and norms and should take into consideration students' ethnicity (that is, what language they speak at home), socioeconomic status, and religious beliefs. These factors are important when formulating a dress code, determining how to address authority figures, defining the use of appropriate language, examining interactions between males and females, or developing school safety procedures. An important part of the teacher's role is to educate the students about school policies and/or district and state policies with regard to these issues.

What are common values across cultural, ethnic, religious, and social strata? Honesty, mutual respect, consideration, and courtesy are among those virtues that have widespread acceptance. Students (and their parents) should know about standards for attendance, grades, and student behavior. Students should know how to dress for school, how to address their teachers and other school employees, and what is appropriate language for school (limiting the use of slang or vulgarities). They

should know rules for turning in homework, for making up missed assignments, and for handing in work late (if it is accepted). They should know what they can and cannot bring to school (certain kinds of materials and tools). They should know what will happen if they break the rules.

Psychological research on behavior modification and reducing aggression shows that modeling acceptable and nonaggressive behaviors is more effective than catharsis and punishment. Teachers are most effective when they follow the rules and exemplify the standards of conduct themselves. Teachers who are courteous, prompt, enthusiastic, in control, patient, and organized provide examples for students through their own behavior. Teachers should (1) make reasonable efforts to protect students from conditions that would harm learning or mental and physical health and safety; (2) not restrain students from independent action in pursuit of learning; (3) not deny students' access to diverse points of view; (4) not intentionally suppress or distort information regarding students' academic program; (5) not expose a student to unnecessary embarrassment or disparagement; (6) not violate or deny students' legal rights; (7) not harass or discriminate against students on the basis of race, color, religion, sex, age, national or ethnic origin, political beliefs, marital status, handicapping condition, sexual orientation, or social and family background; (8) make reasonable efforts to assure that students are protected from harassment and discrimination; (9) not exploit a relationship with a student for personal gain or advantage; and (10) keep information in confidence or as required by law. Teachers who honor this code will be modeling the appropriate standards of behavior for their students.

In addition to modeling appropriate behaviors, another effective way of treating misbehavior (that is, more effective than catharsis and punishment) is the use of incompatible responses. Effective teachers learn how to employ these responses. Some studies even suggest that teachers use open body language (arms open, not crossed) and positive facial expressions (smiling) to diffuse student anger.

Topic 1.
Rules and the Student's Role in Decision Making

Some educational experts have suggested that standards and rules are most effective if students play a role in formulating them. This does not mean that students make all the rules; it means that they can contribute ideas. Stephen Covey, author of the best-selling *The Seven Habits of Highly Effective People* (1989), suggests that people who desire to be effective or successful should be proactive. He explains that being *proactive* means anticipating everything that can go awry before it does; teachers should think about what could go wrong in class concerning a student's conduct and be prepared in case it ever happens. Of course, a teacher may not be able to predict everything that a student may attempt, but trying to analyze many possibilities may provide a teacher some level of comfort in dealing with misbehaviors. Covey also uses the term *proactive* to stress the importance of self-direction, not only for teachers but also for students.

Allowing students to have a voice in establishing standards and formulating codes provides students with an excellent opportunity to exercise their problem-solving skills and critical-thinking abilities. Although one key purpose of education is often graduating students who are responsible citizens capable of participating thoughtfully in a democratic society, educational practices have had a tendency to foster dependency, passivity, and a "tell me what to think and do" complacency. Older students especially can benefit from participating in the decision-making process.

Many of the principles of total quality management (TQM)—a technique American industries and businesses have used to attain greater success, efficiency, and effectiveness—have been successfully applied to American education. One of the key ingredients of TQM is information sharing so that all partners in an endeavor are aware of goals and objectives. If education is the endeavor, then applying TQM principles means that teachers and students, parents and principals, and other supporting players are all partners in the endeavor. Following TQM principles also means that if all partners have information concerning goals and objectives, then they can form a team to work cooperatively with greater efficiency and effectiveness to achieve goals and objectives.

These ideas require teachers to share authority with students and allow students a voice in decision making. For some teachers, learning to share control with students may be difficult. Helping students to make some of their own decisions will conflict with some teachers' training and with their own ideas and expectations about being

in charge; however, the many benefits of shared decision making, already described, are worth the struggle to adjust.

Although this may not sound like the perfect classroom to every teacher, Covey describes what is, for him, the most exciting learning experience:

> As a teacher, I have come to believe that many great classes teeter on the very edge of chaos. . . . There are times when neither the teacher nor the student knows for sure what's going to happen. In the beginning, there is a safe environment that enables people to be open, to learn, and to listen to each other's ideas. Then comes the brainstorming, where the spirit of evaluation is subordinated to the spirit of creativity, imagining, and intellectual networking. Then an absolutely unusual phenomenon begins to take place. The excitement transforms the entire class.

Covey describes a dynamic classroom, not one in stasis; however, there are important requirements for the classroom. First, the students have to feel safe, safe not only from physical harm but also from mental harm—from mockery, intimidation, unfair criticisms, threats—from teachers, or, especially, other classmates. These features describe a classroom where mutual respect and trust exists between teacher and students and among the students themselves.

Topic 2.
Rules and School Safety

The importance of a safe school environment for promoting good behavior has been mentioned already; however, statistics indicate that school safety is a vital concern for all educators. More than 100,000 students bring weapons to school each day. Every day, these weapons kill or wound 40 students. One out of every 5 students is afraid to go the restroom at school for fear of victimization. In addition to student fears, more than 6,000 teachers receive threats by students each year.

The following factors contribute to school violence and antisocial behaviors: overcrowding, poor design and use of school space, lack of disciplinary procedures, student alienation, multicultural insensitivity, rejection of at-risk students by teachers and peers, and anger or resentment at school routines. On the other hand, the following characteristics contribute to school safety: positive school climate and atmosphere, clear and high performance expectations for all students, practices and values that promote inclusion, student bonding to school, high levels of student participation and parent involvement in school activities, and opportunities to acquire academic skills and develop socially.

Effective teachers need to be alert to the signs of potentially violent behavior but recognize that they can easily misinterpreted and misunderstand these signs. Warning signs should be the impetus for getting children help, not for excluding, punishing, or isolating them. Experts also emphasize that teachers should not regard warning signs as a checklist for identifying, labeling, or stereotyping children; teacher must keep referrals to outside agencies confidential. Except for suspected child abuse or neglect cases teachers must have parental consent for referral.

The American Psychological Association has identified four "accelerating factors" that increase the risk of violence. These four factors are (1) early involvement with drugs and alcohol; (2) easy access to weapons, especially handguns; (3) association with antisocial, deviant peer groups; and (4) pervasive exposure to media violence. Longitudinal studies (studies following groups over time) show youth violence and delinquency seem linked with situations in which (1) one or more parents have been arrested; (2) the child has been the client of a child-protection agency; (3) the child's family has experienced death, divorce, or another serious transition; (4) the child has received special-education services; and/or 5) the youth exhibits severe antisocial behavior.

Along somewhat analogous lines, the U.S. Departments of Education and Justice (1998) have compiled a long list of possible early warning signs. These signs include (1) social withdrawal (often associated with feelings of depression, rejection, persecution, unworthiness, and lack of confidence); (2) excessive feelings of isolation and being alone; (3) excessive feelings of rejection; (4) being a victim of violence—including physical or sexual abuse; (5) feelings of being picked on and persecuted; (6) low school interest and poor academic performance; (7) expression of violence in writings and drawings; (8) uncontrolled anger; (9) patterns of impulsive and chronic hitting, intimidating, and bullying behaviors; (10) history of discipline problems; (11) history of violent and aggressive behaviors; (12) intolerance for

differences and prejudicial attitudes; (13) drug use and alcohol use; (14) affiliation with gangs; (15) inappropriate access to, possession of, and use of firearms; and (16) serious threats of violence.

In addition to these early warning signs, the Departments of Education and Justice list what they call *imminent* warning signs, requiring an immediate response. These are (1) serious physical fighting with peers or family members; (2) serious destruction of property; (3) rage for seemingly minor reasons; (4) detailed threats of lethal violence; (5) possession and/or use of firearms and weapons; and (6) other self-injurious behaviors or threats of suicide. School authorities and possibly law enforcement officials must intervene immediately if a child has presented a detailed plan to harm or kill others or is carrying a weapon, particularly a firearm, and has threatened to use it. In situations where students present other threatening behaviors, the school must inform parents immediately.

Violence prevention strategies at school range from adding social-skills training to the curriculum to installing metal detectors at the entrances to buildings. Educational experts recommend that schools teach all students procedures in conflict resolution and anger management and explain the school rules, expectations, and disciplinary policies.

The federal Gun-Free Schools Act of 1994 requires every state to pass zero-tolerance laws on weapons at school or face the loss of federal funds. Every state has complied with this law and requires school districts to expel students for at least a year if they bring weapons to school.

The U.S. Departments of Education and Justice (1998) have produced a joint report *Early Warning. Timely Response.* Recommending actions to promote school safety. First, an open discussion of safety issues is essential:

> Schools can reduce the risk of violence by teaching children about the dangers of firearms, as well as appropriate strategies for dealing with feelings, expressing anger in appropriate ways, and resolving conflicts. Schools also should teach children that they are responsible for their actions and that the choices they make have consequences for which they will be held accountable. *(Early Warning. Timely Response., p. 4.)*

Teachers should treat students with equal respect, create ways for students to share their concerns, and help children to feel safe when expressing their feelings.

In review, effective and safe schools develop and enforce consistent rules that are clear, broad-based, and fair. Effective schoolwide disciplinary policies include a code of conduct, specific rules, and consequences that can accommodate student differences on a case-by-case basis when needed. School policies need to include anti-harassment and antiviolence policies and due process rights. Rules should reflect the cultural values and educational goals of the community. School staff, students, and families should be involved in the development, discussion, and implementation of fair rules, written and applied in a nondiscriminatory manner, and accommodating cultural diversity. Consequences for violating rules must be commensurate with the offenses, and negative consequences must accompany positive teaching for socially appropriate behaviors. Finally, there must be zero-tolerance for illegal possession of weapons, drugs, or alcohol.

Topic 3.
"One-minute Praise"

Blanchard and Johnson (1981) offer a "one-minute praise" method by which they encourage catching people (in this case, students) doing something right. Blanchard and Johnson suggest that teachers should praise people immediately and tell them what they did right. In applying this principle to students, the teacher would tell students how he or she feels about their behavior, how it has helped others in class, and how it has helped the success of the class. The teacher would stop for a moment after the praise to let the student feel good about the praise. Finally, the teacher would encourage the student to continue behaving in this manner, shaking hands with the student.

Likewise, the one-minute reprimand could also be useful. However, the teacher should reprimand the student after class, avoiding interruptions to a lesson whenever possible. Specifically, the teacher should tell the student what was done wrong. After correcting the student, the teacher should stop and let the student think about the situation for a moment. Then, the teacher should shake hands with the student and remind the student that he or she is important as a person, even though

his or her behavior was inappropriate. It is important to distinguish between the individual student (who deserves respect) and the individual's actions (which may be disrespectful and/or unacceptable).

As final advice, Blanchard and Johnson admonish, "When it's over, it's over." After correcting the student, the teacher should not harbor a grudge or ill-will toward the student or dwell on the infraction but move on to the next task at hand. The authors conclude their book by stating, "Goals begin behaviors, [sic] Consequences maintain behaviors." (Blanchard, cited by Barry, 283–284.)

Topic 4.
The Honor Level System

Budd Churchward, creator of Discipline by Design: The Honor Level System (School Discipline Consulting) describes a system of discipline with four stages. Step 1 is a reminder. He explains that a reminder is not a reprimand. A reminder can address an individual or the entire class. Churchward stresses that many students will learn quickly to respond to reminders, but he points out, "Some teachers may complain that they should not have to remind children over and over. We remind the children because they are children."

Step 2 is a reprimand, approaching a student and issuing a verbal or written reprimand. The teacher does not give a verbal warning across the room but delivers it personally to the student. The teacher comes close to the student and tells him or her what to do and then asks the student to identify the next step (step 3). Written warnings, however, are even more effective. The teacher approaches the student and gives the student an infraction slip. The teacher has checked an item on the slip and tells the student that if no further problem occurs, the student can throw the slip away at the end of the class or period. If the misbehavior continues, the teacher will collect the slip and turn it in (to the principal's office). Churchward emphasizes that it is important that the child have possession of the slip and know that he or she is in control of the slip and what happens to it next (fostering and encouraging internal locus of control, or a feeling of being in charge, being self-directed, or proactive, as Covey would say).

Step 3 is collecting the infraction slip. If the teachers must again approach the student about the misbehavior, he or she reminds the student of the warning that the student previously received. If the student received a verbal warning, the teacher now sends an infraction slip to the office. If the student has the infraction slip, the teacher takes it. The teacher then asks the student to identify the next step.

The fourth and final step is to send the offender to the office; this will remove the student from class. Churchward advises that if the teacher follows the first three steps faithfully, the teacher will rarely have to use the last step. However, if things do go this far, Churchward insists that the teacher can stay calm and unemotional, perhaps saying something such as, "Tomorrow we will try again. I'm sure that we can work this out."

Churchward recommends that the teacher post these steps in several places in the classroom and also post three to five selected classroom rules important to teaching. The list should be short and positive. For example, instead of writing, "Students will not ask for repeated directions," the teacher should write, "Students will follow directions the first time they hear them." By taking time to go over the rules and the steps with students, the teacher ensures that the students will know that they can always look on the wall if the teacher asks them what the next step will be. Churchward says it is important to let students know that they may be asked to identify the next step if they get in trouble; also, students should know that the teacher has the right to skip steps in extreme cases if there are certain behaviors that cannot be tolerated. Teachers should be specific about unacceptable behaviors and give students exact examples of acceptable behavior.

Topic 5.
Other Practices to Encourage Good Classroom Behaviors

Some other practices that may encourage good classroom behaviors are monitoring, low-key interventions, "I" messages, and positive teaching.

Briefly, *monitoring* refers to the teacher's walking around the room to monitor what students are doing. After a teacher gives an assignment, he or she should wait a few minutes to give students time to get started, move around the room, and check to make sure that all students have begun their work. The teacher can also give individualized instruction as needed. The teacher's

presence can perhaps motivate the students who are not working. The teacher should not interrupt the class during monitoring but should use a quiet voice to show personal attention.

Low-key interventions are quiet and calm. Effective teachers are careful that students are not rewarded for misbehavior by becoming the focus of attention. By being proactive, teachers have anticipated problems before they occur. When correcting misbehaving students, the teachers are inconspicuous, making sure not to distract others in the class. When they lecture, effective teachers know to frequently mention students by name to bring the students' attention back to class.

"I" messages are an effective communication technique for the classroom. The message begins with the word *I* and conveys feelings. For example, a teacher might say, "I am very frustrated about the way you are ignoring instruction. When you talk while I am talking, I have to stop teaching and that is very frustrating."

Positive discipline refers to the use of language to express what the teacher wants instead of the things that students cannot do. Instead of saying, "No fighting," a teacher might say, "Settle conflicts using your words." Taking a positive approach with language also means praising students frequently. An effective teacher is quick to praise students for their good behavior and to use smiles, positive body language, and laudatory words.

Topic 6.
Classroom Misbehavior

Teachers should maintain a system of classroom rules, consequences, and rewards to guide students toward proper classroom behavior; the goal of the teacher is keeping students engaged and on task. Inevitably, students will misbehave and test the techniques and procedures that teachers use to guide students back on task. Some students will not respond to the effective teacher's standard procedures. If a student continues to misbehave frequently or in a disturbing manner, the effective teacher observes the student with the intent of determining if any external influences are causing the misbehavior that may require additional intervention from the student's teacher and family.

When under stress, students may be inclined to act out or to behave differently for the duration of the stress-inducing event. Students may react to events in the classroom or in their homes in a manner that violates the established policies of the classroom. For example, nervousness caused by a test or a school play audition may cause a student to speak out of turn or appear skittish. The loss of a loved one may cause a student to become depressed. Such behaviors are normal reactions to stress. However, teachers must pay attention to these situations and observe if the misbehavior occurs for an extended period of time. Unusual and/or aggressive student behavior may indicate that the student is suffering from severe emotional distress. Teachers must be careful to note the frequency, duration, and intensity of the student's misconduct.

Teachers should note frequent, atypical behaviors, such as lying, stealing, and fighting. The teacher should attempt to determine the motivation behind the behavior. Is the child lying to avoid a reprimand? Is the student telling false stories to hide feelings of insecurity? Does the student cry during a particular subject or at random moments during the school day? These are some of the many questions the teacher needs to consider.

Misbehaving may be a sign that a student is losing control of his or her actions and is looking for help. The role of the teacher in these situations is to help determine if the student is acting out as a reaction to a particular issue or if there is a deeper emotional problem. Some students may require various forms of therapy to treat the emotional disturbances that cause the misbehavior. Therapy can examine the possibilities of a more severe cause for the student's behavior.

If concerned that a student is suffering from emotional stress, the teacher should contact, and remain in constant discussion with, the student's parents. It is particularly important in these situations to establish an open dialogue with the student's family to facilitate the student's treatment. Parents and teachers working together will be able to provide important and unique insights into the student's situation.

School professionals are another valuable resource for advice, assistance, and support when dealing with students' emotional disturbances. Guidance counselors, school psychiatrists, and other specialists are able to aid in the counseling of these students and make recommendations for the parents and teacher. Together with the student's family, these professionals may develop or recommend a particular program or therapy for treatment.

When working with a class of students with emotional disorders, the teacher might have to be flexible. While the goal of any management system is to prevent misbehavior, the teacher must be prepared to provide an area or opportunity for the student to regain control if an emotional episode occur.

Teachers should also be aware that drug therapy is often a form of treatment. Prescribed by medical doctors, the drug treatments that are available can help students gain independence from their disorder. However, these drugs treat the symptoms rather than the cause of the disorder, and can have severe side effects. No one should take drug treatments lightly; adults should make sure to monitor the use of the drugs.

References

Further reading of these references may enhance understanding and may also increase performance on the examination.

Barry, Leasha M.; Bennett, Betty J.; Christensen, Lois; Mendoza, Alicia; Ortiz, Enrique; Pagan, Migdalia; Robison, Sally; Salmón Otilia, Ph.D. *The Best Teacher's Test Preparation for the Florida Teacher Certification Examination Professional Education Test*. Piscataway, New Jersey: Research & Education Association, 2005.

Blanchard, K., and S. Johnson. *The One Minute Manager*. New York: Berkley Books, 1981.

Border, L. "Morphing: A Quintessential Human Capability." *National Teaching and Learning Forum* Volume 7, Number 4 (May 1998), 8–11.

Churchward, Budd. *Discipline by Design, The Honor Level System*. http://www.honorlevel.com/x83.xml.

Covey, Stephen. *The Seven Habits of Highly Effective People*. New York: Simon and Schuster, 1989.

Gilligan, C. *In a Different Voice: Psychological Theory and Women's Development*. Cambridge, MA: Harvard University Press, 1982.

Education Resources Information Clearinghouse on Educational Policy and Management. "Trends and Issues: School Safety." http://www.eric.uoregon.edu/trends_issues/safety/index.html.

Kohlberg, L. *The Psychology of Moral Development: The Nature and Validity of Moral Stages*. Vol. 2, *Essays on Moral Development*. 1984.

Myers, I. B. *Gifts Differing*. Palo Alto, CA: Consulting Psychologists Press, 1980.

Piaget, Jean. *Intelligence and Affectivity: Their Relationship during Child Development*. Palo Alto, CA: Annual Review, 1981. First published 1954.

Pipes, Sally. "Celebrating Private Initiative in Criminal Justice." Fifth Annual Privatization Competition Awards Dinner,

Ritz-Carlton, San Francisco, California, May 6, 1998. *http://www.pacificresearch.org/resources/awards/privatiz/bennett.html.*

Piaget, Jean. *The Origins of Intelligence in Children.* New York: Norton and Company, 1963. First published 1936.

Piaget, Jean. T*he Psychology of Intelligence.* New York: Routledge, 2001. First published 1963.

School Discipline Consulting. "Discipline by Design: The Honor Level System." *http://www.honorlevel.com/x83.xml.*

Sternberg, R. *In Search of the Human Mind.* Ft. Worth, TX: Harcourt Brace, 1995.

U.S. Departments of Education and Justice. *Early Warning, Timely Response.* Washington, DC: U.S. Government Printing Office, 1998.

Wong, Harry K. *First Days of School: How to Be an Effective Teacher.* Mountain View, CA: Harry K. Wong Publications, 2004.

Arts and Physical Education

The topics of arts and physical education are on the PRAXIS II Elementary Education Test: Curriculum, Instruction, and Assessment (Test Code 0011) but not on the PRAXIS II Elementary Education Test: Content Knowledge (Test Code 0014). For this reason, this study guide includes tests for each. Students preparing for the PRAXIS II Elementary Education Test: Content Knowledge (0014) can skip this chapter—although any knowledge about the subjects and teaching is never wasted.

Section 1: Basic Concepts in Art

Topic 1.
Identifying the Elements of Art and Principles of Design and Ways They Express Text, Ideas, Meanings, and Emotions

Ideas, meanings, and human emotions are varied and numerous. To respond to these many stimulations, students must have knowledge of and be able to use many of the elements of art (the things that make up a painting, drawing, or design) and the basic principles of design (what one does with the elements of design). These are the basic principles:

Line. A linear mark from a pen or brush; the edge created where two shapes meet.

Color. Hue. There are three primary colors (red, yellow, blue) and three secondary colors (green, orange, violet); tertiary colors are colors that fall between primary and secondary colors, and compound colors are those containing a mixture of the three primary colors. In addition, complimentary colors are those that lie opposite each other on the color wheel, and saturated colors are those that lie around the outside of the color wheel.

Shape. A self-contained, defined area of a form (geometric or organic). A positive shape in a painting automatically results in a negative shape. Whenever you put any kind of mark or image on the page, you create two shapes: the named shape is the positive shape and the leftover shape is the negative shape. If you make the letter *A* on a page, the letter is the positive shape and the rest of the page is the negative shape. We become so accustomed to seeing the positive image that it is difficult to focus on the negative image.

Form. A total structure; a synthesis of all the visible aspects of a structure or design; all the elements of a work of art independent of their meaning.

Texture. The surface quality of a shape. These qualities include rough, smooth, soft, hard, and glossy. Texture can be physical (felt with the hand; e.g., a buildup of paint, layering, etc.) or visual (giving the illusion of texture; e.g., the paint gives the impression of texture, but the surface remains smooth and flat).

Balance. Similar to balance in physics. For example, a large shape close to the center can be balanced by a smaller shape that is close to the edge; a large light-toned shape can be balanced on the surface by a small dark-toned shape.

Movement. A way of combining elements of art to produce the appearance of action; a representation of or suggestion of motion; implied motion.

Topic 2.
Demonstrating Knowledge of Strategies to Develop Creative Responses through Art to Ideas Drawn from Text, Music, Speech, Movement, and Visual Images

To respond creatively through art to text images, music and visual suggestions, and speech and movement ideas, students need a variety of techniques and media. This means that they must work with many art forms. Ideally, even the child in the earliest grades engages in drawing, painting, designing, constructing, crafts, sculpting, weaving, finger painting, and—to a limited extent—Styrofoam carving. In grades 3 through 5, students should work further with drawing, painting, designing, constructing crafts, and sculpting and should start new techniques like printmaking, sponge painting, graphics, film animation, and environmental design. In the upper-elementary grades, students should continue with the earlier activities, media, and techniques and add jewelry making and intaglio.

Topic 3.
Identifying Appropriate Uses of Art Materials and Tools for Developing Basic Processes and Motor Skills

Both large and small motor skills are involved in art activities. For example, students might use larger motor skills in painting a mural on a cement-block fence than in painting a small clay figure.

Art materials for the elementary art program include scissors, wet and dry brushes, fabrics, wrapping papers, film, computers, clay, glue, Styrofoam, construction paper, crayons, beads, and much more (South Carolina Visual and Performing Arts Curriculum Framework Writing Team 1993).

Topic 4.
Identifying a Variety of Developmentally Appropriate Strategies and Materials to Assess Skills, Techniques, Creativity, and Communication in Art

The overall goals of art education include

- developing aesthetic perception;

- providing opportunities to examine many art forms of both natural and human in form;

- providing opportunities to reflect on and discuss observations and reactions;

- providing opportunities to develop and extend their own art abilities;

- providing opportunities to identify symbols and characteristics of art, objects of arts, and natural art forms;

- increasing awareness of tactile art;

- fostering the ability to select and enjoy arts (natural and human made); and

- promoting the ability to analyze and enjoy forms based on informed judgments.

Topic 5.
Critiquing a Work of Art Using Vocabulary Appropriate for Description, Analysis, Interpretation, and Evaluation

Students should be able to describe a work of art using terms like *line*, *color*, *value*, *shape*, *balance*, *texture*, *repetition*, and *rhythm*. Students should be able to discuss some of the major periods in the history of the visual arts. It is important that students be able to confront a work and judge its aesthetic merits, regardless of their ability to recognize it from memory. Analytical questions a teacher might ask include the following:

- What is the purpose of the work? Religious? Entertainment? Philosophical? Emotional? Didactic? Pure form? Social or political commentary?

- To what culture does it belong, and to what geographical region and period? How does it reflect that context?

- Is its origin and/or function popular or commercial?

- Does it derive organically from the needs or celebratory functions of a community, or is it a self-conscious artistic creation of one individual?

- What style is it in? For example, is the music baroque, classical, or romantic? Is it influenced by ethnic or popular music?

Often after answering such questions, some students might be able to determine the specific artist by putting all the clues together, as in a detective story.

Table 7-1 summarizes an elementary school art curriculum.

Topic 6.
Identifying Characteristics of Style in Works of Art

A **style** is an artist's manner of expression. When a group of artists during a specific period (usually a few months, years, or decades) have a common style, it is called an **art movement**. Art movements seem to occur only in the West and may occur in both visual art and architecture.

Topic 7.
Identifying Strategies for Developing Students' Analytical Skills to Evaluate Works of Art

To judge the quality of a work of visual art—whether it is or is not good art—students need to consider the following questions:

1. Does the work achieve its purpose?

2. Has the artist spoken with a unique voice, regardless of style, or could this artwork just as easily be the work of someone else?

3. Is the style appropriate to the expressed purpose of the work?

4. Is the work memorable and distinctive?

5. Has the artist used all the technical elements available to the particular discipline with accomplished skill?

Any activity that encourages children to use their thinking skills can help students develop the analytical skills needed to evaluate visual arts. The thinking skills, according to Benjamin Bloom's Taxonomy (Krathwohl, Bloom, and Masia 1964), proceed from knowledge, comprehension, application, analysis, and synthesis to evaluation. The skill of **analysis** requires looking at the parts that make up the whole. Viewing many types of art, examining the works of many artists, and experimenting with various media themselves help students to analyze art forms. Using the vocabulary associated with art helps them form and express their opinions.

Section 2: Basic Concepts of Music

Music is the arrangement of sounds for voice and musical instruments and, like dance and visual art, requires training and repetitive practice. For most of history, music has been an outgrowth of a community's or an ethnic group's need to celebrate; it is often linked to storytelling or poetry. In Europe, a system of musical notation developed during the Middle Ages, and the use of notation (written symbolic indications of pitch and duration of tones) is a convenient way to distinguish "art" (or classical, or complexly composed) music from folk and ethnic music.

Traditional instruments have been indigenous variations on drums, horns, pipes (such as flutes), and hollow boxes fitted with vibrating strings (such as lyres or lutes). Since the seventeenth century, orchestral instruments of the West have multiplied to include pianos, saxophones, clarinets, cellos, and, in our own era, electronic synthesizers.

Topic 1.
Identifying the Elements of Music

There are several elements of music:

Rhythm. The contrast among the various lengths of musical tones. For instance, in "The Star-Spangled

Table 7-1. Art Strategies, Materials, Skills, Techniques, Creativity, and Communication

Grades	Strategies	Materials	Skills	Techniques	Creativity	Communication
Kindergarten–2	Provide a wide variety of art: natural and human-made forms	Use art materials in the art room and classroom	Use terms such as *line, color, value, shape, balance, texture, repetition,* and *rhythm*	Try various art media and produce art forms	Experiment with various art supplies	Create feelings, ideas, and impressions through art products
	Experiment with art materials	Use art forms from nature and humans, slides, art shows, visiting guests, trips, the computer, etc.	Respond to art	Behave as a responsible member of an audience	Create simple art projects	Use art terms and concepts to express thoughts about art
	Provide opportunities to view art in the classroom, the art room, and elsewhere		Describe feelings and ideas while viewing art	Use an art program to locate exhibits at an art show	Respond to art in an individual way	
			Use various art materials to produce art in the art room and classroom			
			Use a program from an art exhibit			
			Practice acceptable behavior at an art exhibit or as a member of an audience			
3–5	Provide occasions to experience art of many periods and many cultures through art exhibits, computer, slides, speakers, etc.	Use actual art materials in the classroom and art room	Continue to use terms such as *line, color, value, shape, balance, texture, repetition,* and *rhythm*	Try various art media and produce art forms	Encouraged to express self through art	Create art using various materials to express self
		Use actual art forms from speakers and teacher	Continue to respond to art	Behave as a responsible member of an audience	Encouraged to create art	Create original art
					Encouraged to improvise	Hear, read, and learn about careers in art

Continued

Table 7-1. Art Strategies, Materials, Skills, Techniques, Creativity, and Communication *(Continued)*

Grades	Strategies	Materials	Skills	Techniques	Creativity	Communication
	Experiment with ways to produce art using many media	View slides; use computer programs, etc. Attend programs and study written programs	Become more adept at describing feelings and ideas while producing and viewing art Continue to use various art materials to produce art in the art room and classroom Use a program from an art exhibit Practice acceptable behavior at an art exhibit or as a member of an audience Distinguish between classical and popular art	Use an art program to locate exhibits at an art show Describe feelings about own arts and the art of others	Encouraged to respond to art	Practice basic etiquette for showing own art and as a member of an audience Read art programs Express ideas about origin, culture, etc., of art
6–8	Provide occasions to view art of many cultures and many periods through exhibits, slides, books, computer searches, speakers, etc. Encouraged to respond to art and create own art Communicate orally and in written form about art Use a range of types of art	Use many art media, including those for weaving, film, crafts, etc. Reseach and access art through compact discs (CDs), Internet searches, slides, books, etc. Study programs for art shows Attend exhibits and guest speaker lectures	Use art to express self Use many different art media to produce many art forms Identify major artists, media, and periods	Produce simple art products Demonstrate understanding of terms when others use them Use correct terminology Read about art	Create some simple art Explain the art and the feelings it produces	Realize that art can be a career Produce an original art piece for display Express a feeling for an event by producing art Analyze art Talk about ways that art can be used as a career

Banner," the rhythm is short, short, medium, medium, medium, long.

Harmony. The vertical aspect of the groups of notes. The sheet music uses simultaneous combinations of musical tones to indicate harmony.

Melody. The succession of the notes. Melody is the horizontal aspect of the notes. Sometimes the teacher may refer to the melody as the *tune*.

Form. The structure of the song, or the way that it is put together. Sometimes there is a refrain that is repeated; sometimes there is a chorus that is used after each verse.

Texture. The context in which simultaneous sounds occur. The sounds can be chords (harmony) or even counterpoint (concurrent melodies of equal importance).

Timbre or tone. The quality of the musical sound.

Dynamics. The volume or the loudness of the sound or the note. The two basic dynamic indications are *p* (for *piano*, meaning softly or quietly) and *f* (for *forte*, meaning loudly or strong).

These elements work together to express a text, ideas, certain emotions, settings, time, and place through music.

Topic 2.
Identifying Appropriate Vocal Literature for Children

Children's **vocal ranges** vary from one child to the next. However, in a 1979 study, Sylvesta ("Sally") Wassum found that first-grade children had a vocal range on one octave, 64 percent were able to sing as high as C_5 (C_4 is middle C), and 90 percent could sing as low as C_4. Of the singers in sixth grade, 98 percent had a vocal range of an octave or more; 52 percent could vocalize two octaves or more.

The voice ranges of girls and boys remain about the same until the boys' voices begin to change—usually, sometime during junior high. When selecting vocal literature (music for singing), the teacher must consider the age-appropriate range of the students and their vocal abilities.

The materials used for a quality music program in any grade should reflect various musical periods and styles, cultural and ethnic diversity, and a gender balance. The goal of a quality music program is to make students aware that music is both a part of and a reflection of many cultures and many ethnic groups. The teacher should provide and encourage students to sing, play, and listen to music of many cultural and ethnic groups. The teacher should include diverse **styles** (basic musical languages) and **genres** (categories); the main musical styles are discussed later in the chapter.

Topic 3.
Developmentally Appropriate Singing Techniques

The voices of singing children should sound as if they are "floating out" rather than forced. To help students achieve the preferred sound, the teacher might ask students to imagine trying to support a feather fluttering a few inches from their mouths.

Posture is an important part of good singing. Children should not slouch when they are singing; they should stand or sit erectly as they sing. An excellent way to attain the desired straight spine is to have the students stand. Standing helps to allow for sufficient breath.

Inhaling the **breath** should mimic directing it to the area just below the rib cage; as the child takes in a breath, the wall of the child's abdomen should move out. The expansion that is necessary for the inhalation should not come from raising the shoulders or from puffing up the chest; instead, the inhalation should result from the diaphragm moving toward the waistline. Because the flow of air should be steady, the child's mouth should remain open. The child should not try to manipulate the voice box; the idea is not to sing *with* the larynx but to sing *through* the larynx (Hoffer 1982). Whether standing or sitting, children should make sure that both feet are flat on the floor. When standing, children should be certain that their hands are down at their sides or clasped loosely in front; children should not clasp their hands tightly in the back or place their hands in their pockets.

The **tone** is the musical sound of the voice; it may describe the quality of the musical sound. For instance, one might say that someone sings with a "nasal tone," a "thin tone," or a "full tone." A synonym for *tone* is *timbre*.

The voice of the average child is similar to the voice of the adult in terms of range but not quality. The teacher should not encourage children to imitate the heavier and fuller quality of the mature adult voice. Children can sing high, but as in an adult, tension results when the pitch is too high. The average voice range is from around middle C to F (fifth line); D and E-flat (fourth line and space) are, however, far more comfortable. For the beginner, a very comfortable range is from E-flat (first line) to B-flat or C.

Topic 4.
Identifying Correct Performance Techniques for Rhythmic and Melodic Classroom Instruments

As defined earlier, *music* is the arrangement of sounds for voice and musical instruments and, like dance, requires training and repetitive practice. Making music is a basic experience. Mothers sing to their babies. Children beat sticks together, make drums, and sing during their play. Adults whistle or sing along with tunes on the radio. Sound and music naturally draw people; music is an important part of culture, religious practice, and personal experience for all people. Some people become professional musicians, whereas others whistle, sing, or play for their own enjoyment and nothing more.

It is important that students have the opportunity to experience as many ways to make music as possible. It is through the acquisition of basic skills in singing and playing instruments that people grow in their ability to express themselves through music. As students develop skills, they are also exposed to basic musical concepts such as melody, harmony, rhythm, pitch, and timbre (tone). With experience, students come to make decisions about what is acceptable or not acceptable within a given cultural or historical context and thereby develop their own aesthetic awareness. Only a very small segment of society does not make music. These people would likely choose to make music if they could but are unable as a result of a physical impairment or personal choice (e.g., a vow of silence). Music making is a natural part of human experience.

There is a distinction between the study of simple instruments and the study of orchestral instruments. The child does not usually begin the study of orchestral instruments until the fourth or fifth grade; a music teacher—not the classroom teacher—gives instruction in orchestral instruments. The instruments that the classroom teacher normally teaches include the **rhythmic instruments** (e.g., triangle, tambourine, blocks, and sticks), **melodic instruments** (e.g., melody bells and simple flutes), and **harmonic instruments** (e.g., chording instruments, such as the autoharp).

Rhythmic Instruments

After the students have a chance to move with the music in the manner that the music suggests and after singing games and action songs, they may be ready to try rhythmic instruments. The students will need opportunities to experiment with triangles, tambourines, sticks, and blocks, among others, to experience the sounds they make; students might try striking the tambourine with the hand to get one sound and with the knee to get another, for instance. After this experimentation, the teacher and class will be ready to try something new.

If the teacher decides on which instruments the class will use, who will use them, and when, music instruction becomes a teacher-directed activity that can stifle the children's creativity. Allowing the students to make decisions about what and when to play is a more engaging technique than the teacher-directed approach. For example, the teacher might write out a piece of music on a large sheet of paper and allow the students to draw pictures where they should play their instruments. Another student-directed approach to music instruction is first having students listen to a piece of music and then allowing them to decide on the instruments they want to play and when it seems right to play them. This more creative approach is appropriate for young children who cannot read music or even for music readers who want to produce their own performance techniques. Upper-grade students can even try making their own instruments.

Melodic Instruments

Melodic bells are melodic instruments that the child strikes with a mallet. The child may use the bells before the flutes. The simple flutes include the trade names of Flutophone, Song Flute, and Tonette. Teachers usually include these melodic instruments with the music instruction at about the fifth grade. For most of these instruments, the child supports the flute using the right thumb; to play the notes, the child covers the various holes with the fingers. The use of the fingers to help attain the sounds varies from one instrument to the other. The melodic instruments are helpful to use as the children are learning to read music.

Harmonic Instruments

The wooden base of an autoharp (which is approximately rectangular in shape) has wire strings stretched across it. The child can press the wooden bars attached at right angles; when the child presses the bars and strums the wires, the instrument produces chords. Students can experiment with harmony using the autoharp. They will find that sometimes a variety of choices of chords "sound right" but that at other times only one choice works.

Topic 5.
Reading and Interpreting Simple, Traditional, and Nontraditional Music Notation

Music notation is a way of writing music. Teaching students to use, read, and interpret music notation will heighten their enjoyment of music. Students can begin with **simple music notation**. For example, students might try listening to a simple melody and making dashes on the board or on their papers to indicate the length the notes are held. As they sing "Three Blind Mice," for instance, they would mark dashes of similar length for the words/notes *three* and *blind*.

With **traditional music notation**, the students use the lines and spaces on the staff. They observe that there are four spaces and five lines, for instance. They also notice that the appearance of the notes indicates the length, and the placement of the notes on the staff indicates the various tones.

Nontraditional music notation is something that many students in the upper grades may have noticed in their books. In the South, for example, many of the hymnals use a nontraditional type of music notation called shape notes. Instead of the elliptical note head in the traditional notation, the heads of the notes are in various shapes to show the position of the notes on the major scale. Another nontraditional music notation is Braille notation.

Topic 6.
Identifying Characteristics of Style in Musical Selections

Often, after listening to a piece of music, a person might be able to determine the specific artist by putting several clues together, as in a detective story. To help students reach this level of discernment, the teacher should expose them to diverse styles (basic musical languages) and genres (categories). Dividing music into categories is difficult. Styles are constantly emerging. Many songs include multiple genres. Nevertheless, the main groupings are as follows:

- Classical
- Gospel
- Jazz
- Latin American
- Blues
- Rhythm and blues
- Rock
- Country
- Electronic
- Electronic dance
- Electronica
- Melodic
- Hip hop
- Rap
- Contemporary African
- Punk
- Reggae
- Dub

Because music often reflects the events of the time, the technology, the composer and performer(s), the beliefs, and the cultures, music changes over time. The ancient Greeks accompanied the recitation of poetry with the stringed lyre, and choral songs were heard between recited passages. In the early Christian era, plainsong, or unaccompanied religious chant, was codified and arranged with early forms of music notation by Pope Gregory the Great (late sixth century). This is the origin of Gregorian chant. By the twelfth and thirteenth centuries, the important form of polyphony, upon which the distinctive art music of the West is based, enabled supportive melodies to be added to the main chant. Throughout the later Middle Ages, both religious and secular polyphonic music was composed and melodies and rhythms became more diversified.

During the Renaissance, the spirit of humanism and rationalism pervaded polyphonic music, and music began to be seen as a mark of culture. Emphasis was placed upon secular music and dance and instrumental music ensembles.

Baroque music of the seventeenth and early eighteenth centuries employed a greater complexity of contrapuntal, or multimelodic, form, and the beginnings of harmony, the use of colorful instrumental ensembles, and great drama and emotion. Other innovative forms included the oratorio, the cantata, the sonata, the suite, the concerto, and the fugue. The great works of baroque music were composed by Antonio Vivaldi and Johann Sebastian Bach.

The greatest composers of the classical period of the latter half of the eighteenth century, marked by clarity of form, logical thematic development, and strict adherence to sonata form, were Franz Joseph Haydn and Wolfgang Amadeus Mozart. Mozart's structurally exquisite works approach perfection of form while adding to music inventive melodic diversity. The German composer Ludwig van Beethoven ushered in the romantic school of symphonic music. His symphonies and piano sonatas, concertos, and string quartets explode with dramatic passion, expressive melodies and harmonies, and complex thematic development.

Romantic composers included Frédéric Chopin, Hector Berlioz, Franz Liszt, Richard Strauss, and Felix Mendelssohn. Other important symphonic composers of the nineteenth century were Robert Schumann, Johannes Brahms, Peter Ilyich Tchaikovsky, and Gustav Mahler. Other important influences in nineteenth-century music include the use of ethnic influences or folk melodies and music of a nationalistic vein, as well as of popular song (often linked to composers who were outstanding melodists and harmonic innovators).

The concert music of the twentieth century increasingly endeavored to enlarge the boundaries of rhythm, form, and harmony, seemingly parallel to the direction in the visual arts away from traditional structure and melodic-harmonic connections with listeners and toward more personal or intellectual experiments in abstraction. Ethnic and popular influences continued to exert an important pull in the creation of twentieth-century music. Ragtime, blues, jazz, and other popular folk, dance, and commercial music provided material for some of the most innovative and exciting work in twentieth-century music. Composers after World War II experimented with tape-recorded sound (Edgard Varese) and conceptual music based on indeterminacy or chance (John Cage).

Topic 7.
Identifying Strategies for Developing Students' Analytical Skills to Evaluate Musical Performance

As with analyzing visual arts, any work that encourages children to use their thinking skills can help develop the analytical skills needed to evaluate musical performance. For example, a teacher might ask young children, after they played "Here We Go 'Round the Mulberry Bush," some questions requiring them to perform some very basic analysis of the music. A simple question might be, "Do you think this song would be good to march to on the playground?" Upper-elementary students might listen to *Peter and the Wolf*, by Sergei Prokofiev, and try to identify the instruments in the recording. The students might talk about why the composer used certain instruments for a character, suggest other instrument sounds for the characters, and give their justifications for the new instrument. Because these activities involve analysis, they help develop the upper-level thinking skills needed to evaluate musical performance.

Topic 8.
Identifying a Variety of Developmentally Appropriate Strategies and Materials to Assess Skills, Techniques, Creativity, and Communication in Music

The overall goals of music education include

*   encouraging responsiveness to music,
*   increasing involvement in music,

- aiding in music discrimination,

- promoting understanding of music and music structure,

- increasing listening awareness, and

- developing sensitivity to the expressive qualities of music.

Table 7-2 describes the elements of an elementary school music curriculum.

Topic 9.
Critiquing Musical Performance Using Vocabulary Appropriate for Description, Analysis, Interpretation, and Evaluation

Although students can experience music and find it satisfying, challenging, or beautiful without prior knowledge of a piece or an understanding of its form, cultural significance, and so forth, some knowledge can enrich the experience. People respond to music naturally. They do not need prompting or help to respond. However, to share their thoughts and feelings about music, students must learn how to put their responses into musical terminology. Some people call music a language, but it does not function as a spoken language. It does not provide specific information, instructions, or reactions. Rather, music sparks thoughts, feelings, and emotions. To put their experiences into words, musicians and artists have developed vocabularies and approaches to discussing music and art. This does not mean there is only one way to respond to or talk about music or art. However, students will more easily understand music and musicians, art and artists, if they first understand and can use the kind of vocabulary and approaches that musicians or artists use to discuss their work. This includes terms as basic as *melody* and *harmony* and as profound as *the aesthetic experience*.

People cannot express themselves or effectively communicate if they do not understand the structures and rules that underlie the "language" that they are trying to use. Although music does not provide the kind of specific communication that spoken language does, it has structures. When students are able to think about and discuss music, they gain a deeper understanding of the music and can better express their responses to the music.

The aesthetic experience is what draws people to music. The experience is one that most people have had but one that some people cannot describe. In fact, words seem clumsy when it comes to something that can be so profound and wonderful. The type of music, the period, or the performer does not necessarily limit the aesthetic experience. It is equally as possible to have an aesthetic experience when listening to a child sing a simple melody as it is when listening to a professional orchestra performing a symphony by Beethoven. The important thing is to share that aesthetic experience. It is part of what makes music and art special.

There are many ways to encourage exploration of and growth through aesthetic responsiveness. A common experience is a crucial starting point. After students listen attentively to several pieces of music, the teacher might ask them to describe how each piece made them feel. It is often best for students to write their responses down before starting a discussion. Then, the teacher might ask them to explain why each piece of music made them feel the way they indicated. To the music, young students will likely provide simple, straightforward emotional responses (e.g., "It made me feel happy!"). Older students should explore why the music affected the feelings that it did and use both musical concepts (e.g., "It made me feel happy because it was in a major key") and nonmusical associations (e.g., "It made me feel happy because it sounded like a circus, and I like to go to the circus"). Through this kind of sharing, along with teacher insights and readings about how other people have responded to music, students can explore and come to a deeper understanding of their personal responses to music, other art forms, and possibly the world. In addition, it should provide them with practical ways to express their responses or reactions to what they experience in life.

In addition to having aesthetic experiences, recognizing their value, and being able to grapple with discussing or sharing those experiences, teachers and students must attempt to foster an appreciation for the arts and their ability to create meaning. The arts provide an opportunity to explore and express ideas and emotions through a unique view of life experiences. It is through the experience of

Table 7-2. Music Strategies, Materials, Skills, Techniques, Creativity, and Communication

Grades	Strategies	Materials	Skills	Techniques	Creativity	Communication
Kindergarten–2	Provide exposure to a wide variety of sounds: recorded music, sheet music, live performances	Play simple instruments	Classify sounds as high and low; use body to show high and low	Play simple rhythm instruments	Walk, run, jump to music	Create symbols to notate sounds of music
	Experiment with ways to change sounds	Use CDs, tapes, records	Play simple rhythm instruments	Sing, especially rote songs	Create simple songs	Use musical terms and concepts to express thoughts about music
	Use simple instruments in the classroom	Attend programs		Move in time with the music		
3–5	Provide experiences with music of many periods and many cultures	Play simple instruments	Sing rounds	Play music	Encourage students to express themselves through music	Sing and play instruments from written notation
	Experiment with ways to change sounds	Use CDs, tapes, records	Sing two-part songs by rote	Dance to music	Encourage students to create sounds	Create own notation system
	Use simple instruments in the classroom	Attend programs and study written programs	Conduct simple songs	Conduct duple and triple meter	Encourage students to improvise	Hear, read, and learn about careers in music
	Move to music		Move to music			Notate a simple phrase
			Distinguish between classical and popular music			Create a simple phrase
						Practice basic etiquette for performing and listening as part of an audience
						Read music notation

(*Continued*)

Table 7-2. (Continued)

Grades	Strategies	Materials	Skills	Techniques	Creativity	Communication
						Express ideas about origin, culture, etc., of music listened to in class
6–8	Provide occasions to listen to music of many cultures and many periods	Play simple instruments	Sing rounds	Play simple accompaniment on autoharp, guitar, etc.	Create some simple songs	Write notation for original song
	Encourage students to respond to music and create their own music	Use CDs, tapes, records	Sing three-part songs by rote	Read some music	Create an accompaniment	Write own idea of notation for song heard
		Attend programs and study written programs	Conduct simple songs	Use correct terminology	Create a dance	Read notation
	Provide opportunities for students to communicate with notation	Use the autoharp and/or guitar	Move to music	Perform dance steps		
			Identify major and minor scales			
	Use a range of instruments and types of music		Dance			

music, or any art form, that people begin to transcend the mundane day-to-day experience and reach beyond to a richer life experience.

When preparing for this part of the exam, you must understand that the primary objectives of music education are teaching the contexts of music, the concepts and skills involved in experiencing music, and the aesthetic and personal dimensions of music. These constitute a broad overview of the field of music and the musical experience.

Music does not exist in a vacuum. The historical or cultural context of a piece of music is very important. Students should know and be able to discuss the context of music by making connections among social studies, reading or language arts, and the fine arts. For example, when students are reading stories about the American Revolution, they should be aware that it occurred during the period known as the classical period in music history. Listening to a piece by Haydn or Mozart, talking about how they reacted to the Old World, and comparing their works to a colonial American tune by Billings is an effective way to understand the historical, cultural, and societal contexts of music.

Similarly, the visual art of Andy Warhol, the music of the Beatles, the assassination of John F. Kennedy, and the war in Vietnam all took place within the same approximate time frame. The teacher can ask students to find contrasts and similarities among these artistic and social events; students can attempt to find ways that the historical context affected music and ways that music affected and reflected history.

These examples from American history are easy for most to grasp quickly. However, the objective seeks to have teachers and students consider the role of music in history and culture beyond the American experience. By having students listen to music from China, Japan, Germany, Australia, or Africa when they are studying these cultures, the teacher enriches the students' learning experience and makes it more memorable for them. It is even more valuable for students to view live or videotaped performances of the music and dance of these cultures because often the music is performed in traditional costume with traditional instruments (sometimes very different from modern instruments). Seeing the costumes and the movement are an important part of understanding the culture.

Section 3: Basic Concepts in Physical Education

Topic 1.
Demonstrating Knowledge of the Interrelatedness of Physical Activity, Fitness, and Health

The axiom "Use it or lose it" certainly holds for the human body. Our bodies thrive on **physical activity**, which is any bodily movement produced by skeletal muscles and resulting in energy expenditure. Unfortunately, Americans tend to be relatively inactive. In a recent survey, 25 percent of adult Americans had not participated in any leisure-time physical activities in the past month; in 2003, 38 percent of students in grades 9 through 12 viewed television three hours or more per day. (Centers for Disease Control and Prevention)

Physical fitness enables a person to meet the physical demands of work and leisure comfortably. It is a multicomponent trait related to the ability to perform physical activity. A person with a high level of physical fitness is also at lower risk of developing chronic disease.

Lack of activity can cause many problems, including flabby muscles, a weak heart, poor circulation, shortness of breath, obesity, coronary artery disease, hypertension, type 2 diabetes, osteoporosis, and certain types of cancer. Overall, mortality rates from all causes are lower in physically active people than in sedentary people. In addition, physical activity can help people manage mild-to-moderate depression, control anxiety, and prevent weakening of the skeletal system.

By **increasing physical activity**, a person may improve heart function and circulation, respiratory function, and overall strength and endurance. All of these lead to improved vigor and vitality. Exercise also lowers the risk of heart disease by strengthening the heart muscle, lowering pulse and blood pressure, and lowering the concentration of fat in both the body and the blood. It can also improve appearance, increase range of motion, and lessen the risk of back problems associated with weak bones and osteoporosis.

Each person should engage in regular physical activity and reduce sedentary activities to promote health, psychological well-being, and a healthy body weight. On most days of the week, children should engage in at least 60 minutes of physical activity.

Proper hydration is important during physical activity. Two steps that help prevent dehydration during prolonged physical activity or when it is hot are (1) consuming fluid regularly during the activity and (2) drinking several glasses of water or other fluid after the physical activity is completed (U.S. Department of Agriculture).

Topic 2.
Demonstrating Basic Knowledge of Nutrition and Its Role in Promoting Health

Along with exercise, a knowledge of and a participation in a healthy lifestyle are vital to good health and longevity. The elements of good nutrition, the role of vitamins, elimination of risk factors, and strategies to control weight are all part of a healthy lifestyle.

In the spring of 2005, the U.S. Department of Agriculture (USDA) changed the food pyramid to guide Americans in how to eat healthily. As shown in the Figure 7-1, the food pyramid has six rainbow-colored divisions. The climbing figure reminds us all to be active.

The food groups indicated on the pyramid are as follows:

Figure 7-1. USDA Food Pyramid

Source: U.S. Department of Agriculture, Steps to a Healthier You, http://www.mypyramid.gov/.

1. Grains (orange).
2. Vegetables (green).
3. Fruits (red).
4. Fats and oils (yellow, the smallest group).
5. Milk and dairy products (blue).
6. Meat, beans, fish, and nuts (purple).

Complex carbohydrates—vegetables, fruits, high-fiber breads, and cereals—should comprise at least one-half of the diet. These foods provide fiber, which helps digestion, reduces constipation, and reduces the risk of colon cancer. Complex carbohydrates also provide water, which is vital to the entire body.

Proteins should make up about one-fifth of the diet. Proteins build and repair the body. Protein sources include fish, beans, peas, lentils, peanuts, and other pod plants; red meat contains protein, but because it is high in saturated fat, one should eat it less often. **Saturated fat** is present also in cocoa butter, palm oil, and coconut oil.

There is a link between high-fat diets and many types of cancer. Diets high in saturated fats cause the body to produce too much **low-density lipoprotein (LDL)**, which is one type of **cholesterol**. The other type of cholesterol is **high-density lipoprotein (HDL)**. Some cholesterol is essential to the brain functions and to the production of certain hormones, but too much LDL cholesterol encourages the buildup of plaque in the arteries. LDL cholesterol can be controlled through proper diet, and HDL cholesterol levels can be raised by exercise. **Triglycerides** are other types of fat in the blood that are important to monitor; triglycerides seem to be inversely proportional to HDLs.

Unsaturated vegetable fats are preferable to saturated fats. Unsaturated fats appear to offset the rise in blood pressure that accompanies too much saturated fat and may lower cholesterol and help with weight loss. Unsaturated fats are present in vegetable products. Although whole milk products contain saturated fat, the calcium they contain is vital to health. For this reason, weight-loss diets still recommend dairy products but in the form of skim milk and low-fat cheese.

Vitamins are essential to good health; however, a person must be careful not to take too much of certain vitamins. The fat-soluble vitamins, A, D, E, and K, are stored in the body, and excessive amounts will cause some dangerous side effects. All other vitamins are water-soluble and are generally excreted through the urinary system and the skin when taken in excess. Here is a brief synopsis of the vitamins and minerals needed by the body:

Vitamin A. Needed for normal vision, prevention of night blindness, healthy skin, resistance to disease, and tissue growth and repair. Found in spinach, carrots, broccoli, and other dark green or yellow-orange fruits and vegetables; also found in liver and plums.

Vitamin D. Promotes absorption of calcium and phosphorous and the normal growth of healthy bones, teeth, and nails. Formed by the action of the sun on the skin. Present in halibut liver oil, herring, cod liver oil, mackerel, salmon, and tuna and is an additive to many milk products.

Vitamin E. Protects cell membranes, seems to improve elasticity in blood vessels and may prevent the formation of blood clots and protect red blood cells from damage by oxidation. Found in wheat germ oil, sunflower seeds, raw wheat germ, almonds, pecans, peanut oil, and cod liver oil.

Vitamin B$_1$ (thiamin). Helps with the functioning of nerves, muscle growth, and fertility. Also aids in the production of energy, appetite, and digestion. Found in pork, legumes, nuts, enriched and fortified whole grains, and liver.

Vitamin B$_2$ (riboflavin). Aids in the production of red blood cells, good vision, healthy skin, mouth tissue, and energy. Found in lean meat, dairy products, liver, eggs, enriched and fortified whole grains, and green leafy vegetables.

Vitamin B$_3$ (niacin). Promotes the production of energy and appetite, aids the functioning of the digestive and nervous systems, and promotes healthy skin and tongue. Present in beef liver, peanuts, chicken, salmon, and tuna.

Vitamin B$_6$ (pyridoxine). Promotes red blood cell formation and growth. Found in liver, beans, pork, fish, legumes, enriched and fortified whole grains, and green leafy vegetables.

Vitamin B$_{12}$. Promotes healthy nerve tissue, production of energy, and utilization of folic acid. Aids in the formation of healthy red blood cells. Found in dairy products, liver, meat, poultry, fish, and eggs.

Vitamin C. Promotes healing and growth, resists infection, increases iron absorption, and aids in bone and tooth formation and repair. Found in citrus fruits, cantaloupe, potatoes, strawberries, tomatoes, and green vegetables.

Minerals are essential to good health. Several are necessary:

Sodium. Maintains normal water balance inside and outside cells, regulates blood pressure, and balances electrolytes and chemicals. Found in salt, processed foods, bread, and bakery products.

Potassium. Maintains the volume and balance of body fluids, prevents muscle weakness and cramping, and is important for normal heart rhythm and electrolyte balance in the blood. Found in citrus fruits, leafy green vegetables, potatoes, and tomatoes.

Zinc. Promotes taste, appetite, healthy skin, and wound healing. Found in lean meat, liver, milk, fish, poultry, whole grain cereals, and shellfish.

Iron. Promotes red blood cell formation and oxygen transport to the cells, and prevents nutritional anemia. Found in liver, lean meats, dried beans, peas, eggs, dark green leafy vegetables, and whole grain cereals.

Calcium. Promotes strong bones, teeth, and nails. Helps maintain muscle tone, prevents osteoporosis and muscle cramping, and promotes sound nerve function and heartbeat. Found in milk, yogurt, and other dairy products, and dark leafy vegetables.

Phosphorus. Regulates blood chemistry and internal processes; promotes strong bones and teeth. Found in meat, fish, poultry, and dairy products.

Magnesium. Promotes energy production, helps maintain normal heart rhythm, ensures nerve and muscle function, and prevents muscle cramps. Found in dried beans, nuts, whole grains, bananas, and leafy green vegetables.

Topic 3.
Identifying the Process of Decision Making and Goal Setting in Promoting Individual Health and Wellness

One of the primary reasons for the teaching of physical education is to instill in students a willingness to exercise and to encourage students to make good decisions about their health. To that end, it is important that students understand the benefits of participating in a lifelong program of exercise and physical fitness and of avoiding the risks of choosing an unhealthy lifestyle.

Reaping the Benefits, Avoiding the Risks

Fortunately, it is not difficult to find justification for exercising and maintaining a consistently high level of fitness. The benefits of a consistent program of diet and exercise are many. Improvements in cardiac output, maximum oxygen intake, and enhancing the blood's ability to carry oxygen are just a few of these benefits.

Another aspect of physical education concerns awareness and avoidance of the risks that are present in our everyday lives. Some risk factors include being overweight, smoking, using drugs, having unprotected sex, and not eliminating excessive stress. Education is the key to minimizing the presence of these risk factors. Unfortunately, because of the presence of peer pressure and the lack of parental control, the education is sometimes not enough.

Weight Control Strategies

Statistics show that Americans get fatter every year. Even though countless books and magazine articles are available on the subject of weight control, often the only place a student gets reliable information about diet is in a classroom. The unfortunate reality is that people who are fat do not live as long, on average, as those who are thin. Being overweight has been isolated as a risk factor in various cancers, heart disease, gall bladder problems, and kidney disease. Chronic diseases such as diabetes and high blood pressure are also aggravated by, or caused by, being overweight.

Conversely, being underweight presents a great many problems. Our society often places too much emphasis on losing weight. Women are especially prone to measuring their self-worth by the numbers they read on the bathroom scale. Ideal weight and a good body fat ratio are the goals when losing weight. A correlation may exist between body fat and high cholesterol. Exercise is the key to a good body fat ratio. Exercise helps keep the ratio low, improve cholesterol levels, and prevent heart disease.

To lose weight, calories burned must exceed calories consumed. No matter what kind of diet is tried, that principle applies. There is no easy way to maintain a healthy weight. Again, the key is exercise. If calorie intake is restricted too much, the body goes into starvation mode and operates by burning fewer calories. Just a 250-calorie drop a day combined with a 250-calorie burn will result in a loss of one pound a week. Crash diets, which bring about rapid weight loss, are not only unhealthy but also ineffective. Slower weight loss is more lasting. Aerobic exercise is the key to successful weight loss. Exercise speeds up metabolism and causes the body to burn calories. Timing of exercise will improve the benefits. Exercise before meals speeds up metabolism and helps suppress appetite. Losing and maintaining weight is not easy. Through education, people will be better able to realize that maintaining a healthy weight is crucial to a healthy life and should be a constant consideration.

Topic 4.
Demonstrating Knowledge of Common Health Problems and Risk Behaviors Associated with Them

The health of students and their families depends not only on individual and family decisions about diet and exercise but also on various social factors. For example, advertising often encourages children to make unhealthy decisions. Students as young as kindergarten and first grade can learn how to recognize advertisements (e.g., for candy or sugar-laden cereal) that might lead them to unhealthy behavior. By third or fourth grade, children should be able to demonstrate that they are able to make health-related decisions regarding advertisements in various media. Teachers can encourage students to (1) avoid alcohol, tobacco, stimulants, and narcotics; (2) get plenty of sleep and exercise; (3) eat a well-balanced diet; (4) receive the proper immunizations; and (5) avoid sharing toothbrushes, combs, hats, beverages, and food with others. In addition, any study of the physical environment—in science, social studies, or other subjects—should relate to health whenever possible. Examples include

- the effects of pollution on health;

- occupational-related disease (e.g., "black lung" disease and the effects of chemicals on soldiers);

- the different health care options available to people in different parts of the world and in different economic circumstances;

- differentiation between communicable and non-communicable diseases; and

- the importance of even very young children washing their hands frequently.

Older children should be able to explain the transmission and prevention of communicable diseases, and all children should learn which diseases cannot be transmitted through casual contact.

Topic 5.
Distinguishing between Developmentally Appropriate and Inappropriate Instructional Practices That Consider the Interaction of Cognitive, Affective, and Psychomotor Domains

There are three areas or domains of learning:

Psychomotor domain. Pertains especially to physical activities or skills that the individual masters. For example, playing basketball demands many physical skills, including dribbling, making free throws from the free-throw line, and doing a lay-up shot.

Affective domain. Pertains to feelings and attitudes. A basketball player who enjoys playing with the other team members feels more positive about the practices and games than the player who does not enjoy playing with team members. The coach certainly wants the players to feel joy in the game they are playing.

Cognitive domain. Pertains to thinking. Some basketball coaches administer paper-and-pencil tests to be certain that the players understand the rules.

Of course, physical activities or instructional activities in the elementary school must be developmentally appropriate. The characteristics of children in grades 1 through 3 suggest that throwing the ball is easier than catching a ball; therefore, dodge ball is popular. Other characteristics of children age 6 through 8 indicate that they like large-muscle activities, games in which they can shout and chase each other, repetition of favorite games, and free play. Children in the upper-elementary grades are ready for increasing skill development, more

games with rules, and activities involving tossing and catching balls.

Topic 6.
Identifying Various Factors to Consider When Planning Physical Activities

When planning physical activities—or any classroom activity, for that matter—the teacher should attempt to

- create and sustain a safe, efficient, supportive learning environment;

- evaluate the appropriateness of the physical environment for facilitating student learning and promoting safety;

- identify a repertoire of techniques for establishing smooth, efficient, and well-paced routines;

- involve students in establishing rules and standards for behavior;

- identify emergency procedures for student and campus safety.

While certain physical aspects of the classroom are permanent (e.g., size and shape of the room, number of windows, type of lighting, etc.), others are changeable. Windows can have shades or blinds that distribute light correctly and allow for a darkened room for video or computer viewing. If the light switches do not allow some of the lights to remain on, sometimes schools will change the wiring system. If not, teachers can use a lamp to provide minimum lighting for monitoring students during videos or films. Schools often schedule maintenance, such as painting and floor cleaning, during the summer. Often school administrators will comply with teachers' requests for specific colors of paint if they have sufficient time for ordering a different color.

Most classrooms have movable desks, which allow for varied seating arrangements and for opening up areas of the classroom for group games or activities. However, the teacher should ensure that students cannot fall over or bump against furniture and be injured.

The equipment used in physical activities should vary according to the age of the students. For instance, large sports balls are better for young children than are small balls.

Topic 7.
Analyzing the Influence of Culture, Media, Technology, and Other Factors When Planning Health and Wellness Instruction

All classrooms should have a bulletin board for the teacher and the students. The effective teacher has plans for changing the board according to units of study. Space for displaying students' work, either on the bulletin board, the wall, or in the hallway, is necessary.

Bare walls can be depressing; however, covering the walls with too many posters can be visually distracting. Posters with sayings that promote cooperation, rules for games, diagrams for warm-up drills, study skills, and content ideas are helpful. Teachers should change the displays several times during the school year because students will ignore them when they become too familiar.

Some physical activities require technological equipment. For instance, a dance class might need a compact disc (CD) player to play music and a video player to watch a film of a finished dance; a softball team might need a computer to check the rules of the game. Technology contributes to effective instruction.

Physical education—on the playground or in the classroom—has definite association with almost every subject in the curriculum. The opportunities for integrating physical education with other subjects in the curriculum are many. For example, students may develop an appreciation for other cultures and for other ways of life if teachers include games and dances from other cultures and other nations in their lesson plans. Teachers can integrate these activities into the curriculum or employ them in isolation during the physical education periods.

Using advertisements, public health brochures, and Web sites can help teachers when planning wellness and health instruction. Students, too, may receive or be able to locate pertinent materials; the teacher can use them as a springboard to instruction.

Topic 8.
Scoring Team, Dual, and Individual Sports

Team, dual, and individual sports all have a prominent place in a successful physical education curriculum.

Since one of the attributes of a quality physical education program is its carryover value, it is easy to justify the inclusion of these activities in a curriculum. Learning the rules and keeping score supplies students with a framework for goals and for learning how to deal with both victory and defeat. Here are examples of some sports and games that are useful to achieve the aforementioned goals:

Team Sports

- Volleyball: 6 players, two out of three games. Winner scores 25 points with a margin of 2.

- Basketball: 5 players. Most points at the end of the game wins.

- Softball: 9 or 10 players. Most runs at the end of seven innings wins.

- Field hockey: 11 players. Most goals wins.

- Soccer: 11 players. Most goals wins.

- Flag football: 9 or 11 players. Six points for a touchdown, one or two for a point after, and two for a safety. (The number per team can change to accommodate the ability and size of the class).

Dual and Individual Sports

- Tennis: Either doubles or singles. Four points: 15, 30, 40, and game. Tie at 40 (*deuce*). Winner must win by a margin of 2. Remember, *love* means 0 points in tennis.

- Badminton: Either doubles or singles. For doubles, 15 points wins; for singles, 21 points wins. Winner must win by a margin of 2.

- Table tennis: Either doubles or singles. In either case, 21 points by a margin of 2 wins.

- Shuffleboard: Either singles or doubles. Participants determine the winning score—50, 75, or 100 points—before the game begins.

Section 4: Arts and Physical Education Teaching Strategies

Motivational Factors

Students often say that they like teachers who motivate them. Although teachers can be highly motivated themselves and demonstrate interest in the subject matter and in their students, in fact, teachers are not responsible for students' motivation. Motivation is a student's responsibility and must come from within the student. However, effective teachers will help students develop self-discipline, self-control, and self-motivation. These skills of self-management can be taught, yet the skills require a great deal of effort and practice for students to gain true proficiency in using them.

When students say that they like or want teachers who motivate them, they are probably referring to some characteristics that teachers possess that are attractive and interesting to learners. So, while it is true that teachers are not responsible for students' motivation, it is also true that teachers can influence motivation, that teachers can promote and/or inhibit motivation in the classroom by their attitudes and their actions.

Three Motivational Principles

Marcia Baxter-Magolda (1992) offers three principles to guide teachers and to lead to greater effectiveness in the classroom. Interestingly, each of these principles leads to empowering students and, thus, is motivational in nature.

Validating Students as Knowers

The first principle is to *validate students as knowers*. The basis of this principle is the idea of the active learner who brings much to the classroom (the dynamic view of human development). How can teachers validate students? Baxter-Magolda suggests that teachers display a caring attitude toward students. This means that it is appropriate for teachers to take an interest in students, to learn about their likes and dislikes. and to find out about their interests and hobbies, both in school and outside school. This also means that it is okay for teachers to show enthusiasm and excitement for their classes, for the subject matter they teach, and for the students they teach. It also means, as Carol Tavris (1994) notes, that it is good for teachers to show empathy for students' emotional needs.

Baxter-Magolda recommends that teachers appropriately question authority by example and that they allow students to ask questions of them. This means that teachers model critical thinking skills in the classroom. Teachers can question authority when they examine and evaluate readings—whether from textbooks or other sources. Teachers can question authorities when they teach propaganda techniques, exposing advertising claims and gimmicks. Teachers can question authority when they discuss the media and how so-called news sources shape and form public opinion. There are numerous opportunities for teachers in dealing with current affairs and public opinion to question authority and inculcate in their students' critical thinking and higher-ordered reasoning skills. Also, when teachers allow students to question them, teachers are acknowledging that everyone is a learner. Everyone should participate in a lifelong process of continuous learning. It is no shame or disgrace for the teacher to admit that sometimes he or she does not know the answer to a question. This gives the teacher the opportunity to show students how adults think, how they have a level of awareness (metacognition) when they do not know something, and how they go about finding answers to their questions. Teachers who admit that they do not have all the answers have the opportunity to show students how answers can be found and/or to reveal to students that there are no easy answers to some of life's most difficult questions.

To validate students as knowers, teachers must also value students' opinions, ideas, and comments. Teachers' affirmations include smiles and nods of approval, positive comments (such as, "That's a good answer"), and encouraging cues (such as, "That may seem like a reasonable answer, but can you think of a better answer?" or "Can you explain what you mean by that answer?"). Validating students as knowers also means supporting students' voices, giving them ample opportunity to express their own ideas, to share their opinions, and to make their own contributions to the classroom. These opportunities can include times of oral discussion as well as written assignments.

Jointly Constructed Meaning

Another principle in Baxter-Magolda's guidelines for teaching effectiveness is for teachers and students to recognize that learning is *a process of jointly constructing meaning*. To explain, Baxter-Magolda says, teachers should create a dialogue with students (also an important concept in Piagetian theory) and emphasize mutual learning. Also in agreement with Piagetian principles, Baxter-Magolda recommends that teachers reveal their own thinking processes as they approach subjects, as they analyze and understand new subjects, and as they solve problems and reach decisions. She further advises that teachers share leadership and promote collegial learning (group work), acknowledging that individual achievement is not the sole purpose or focus for learning. Through the process of collaborating, students will learn significant lessons directly applicable to work situations where most accomplishments are the result of team efforts, not the sole efforts of individuals.

Situating Learning in the Students' Own Experiences

Baxter-Magolda's final principle for teachers is to *situate learning in the students' own experiences.* She suggests that for a teacher to do this, they must let students know that the teacher wants them in class; using inclusive language (avoiding ethnic and cultural bias and stereotyping and instead using gender-neutral and inclusive language), and focusing on activities will convey the importance of the student.

Activities are important for motivation because they give learners things to do, to become involved in, to arouse their attention and interest, and to provide an outlet for their physical and mental energy. Activities can have an additional positive benefit in that they can serve to connect students to each other, especially when students have opportunities to participate in collaborative learning (the way things happen in the "real world") and to work in groups. Finally, in situating learning in students' own experiences, teachers should consider the use of personal stories in class, as appropriate. (These stories must not violate anyone's right to privacy and confidentiality.) Moreover, teachers can share personal stories that allow them to connect with students in a deeper and more personal way.

In 1993, Robert Coles, the child psychologist, Harvard professor, and author of numerous scholarly and popular books, wrote of his experiences teaching in a Boston inner-city high school. He told of his disillusionment and his struggle to claim students' respect and attention so that he could teach them. Finally, there was a classroom confrontation, followed by a self-revelation (the realization that he had to show his students what he was like as a person). He shared some of his thoughts and feelings about loneliness. He told about his own boyhood experiences of visiting museums with his mother and what she taught him about art. In the end, he, too, had a revelation; he concluded that when teachers share what they have learned about themselves with their students,

they often can transcend the barriers of class and race. A teacher can change a "me" and a "them" (the students) into an "us." Building camaraderie this way becomes an optimal starting point for teaching and learning (Coles 1993). Dr. Coles' experience was that telling his story to the class was a step toward helping his students claim some motivation of their own.

When students assume responsibility for their own motivation, they are learning a lesson of personal empowerment. Unfortunately, although personal empowerment is probably one of the most important lessons anyone ever learns, it is a lesson infrequently taught in classrooms across the country. Empowerment has at least four components, one of which is self-esteem. A good definition of *self-esteem* is "my opinion of me, your opinion of you." It is what we think and believe to be true about ourselves, not what we think about others and not what they think about us. Self-esteem appears to be a combination of self-efficacy and self-respect as seen against a background of self-knowledge.

Self-efficacy, simply stated, is one's confidence in one's own ability to cope with life's challenges. Self-efficacy refers to having a sense of control over life or, better, over one's responses to life. Experts say that ideas about self-efficacy get established by the time children reach the age of 4. Because of this early establishment of either a feeling of control or no control, classroom teachers may find that even primary grade students believe that they have no control over their life, that it makes no difference what they do or how they act. Therefore, it is all the more important that teachers attempt to help all students achieve coping skills and a sense of self-efficacy.

Control, in this definition of self-efficacy, appears to have both external or internal motivators. For example, external motivators include such things as luck and the roles played by others in influencing outcomes. Internal motivators are variables within the individual. If a student who relies on external motivators does well on a test and is asked, "How did you do so well on that test?," he or she might reply, "Well, I just got lucky," or "The teacher likes me." If that same student failed the test and is asked why, he or she might answer, "Well, it wasn't my lucky day," "The teacher doesn't like me," or "My friends caused me to goof off and not pay attention so I didn't know the answers on the test." A student who relies on internal motivators and who does well on a test may explain, "I am smart and always do well on tests," or "I studied hard and that's why I did well." On the other hand, even the student who relies on internal motivators can do poorly on tests and then may explain, "I'm dumb, and that's why I don't do well," or "I didn't think the test was important, and I didn't try very hard." Even though students have similar experiences regarding issues of control, what is important is how students explain their experiences. If students have external motivators, they are likely to either dismiss their performance (success or failure) as matters of luck, or to credit or blame the influence of others. If students have internal motivators, then they are likely to attribute their performance to either their intelligence and skills (ability) or their effort.

Students who have external motivators need help understanding how their behavior contributes to and influences outcomes in school. These students need clarification as to how the teacher will determine their grades and precise information about how the instructor will evaluate their work. Students who have internal motivators but low self-esteem (such as thinking, "I'm dumb") need help identifying their strengths and assets; when students receive information about learning styles and determine their own ways of learning, they may learn more about themselves.

Another factor in empowerment is self-respect. Self-respect is believing that one deserves happiness, achievement, and love. Self-respect is treating one's self at least as nicely as one treats other people. Many students are not aware of their internal voices (which are established at an early age). Internal voices are constantly sending messages, either positive or negative. Psychologists say that most of us have either a generally positive outlook on life, and our inner voice sends generally positive messages ("You're okay," "People like you," "Things will be all right," and so forth), or a generally negative outlook on life, and an inner voice sending negative messages ("You're not okay," "You're too fat, skinny, ugly, stupid," and so forth). Many students need to become aware of their inner voice and how it can be setting them up for failure. They need to learn that they can tell their inner voice to stop sending negative messages and that they can reprogram their inner voice to be kinder and gentler and to send positive messages. However, it does require effort, practice, and time to reprogram the inner voice.

Two tools that can help students in the reprogramming process are affirmations and visualizations (Ellis 1991). Affirmations are statements describing what students want. Affirmations must be personal, positive, and written in the present tense. What makes affirmations effective are details. For example, instead of saying, "I am stupid," students should say, "I am capable. I do well in school because I am organized, I study daily, I get all my work completed on time, and I take my school work seriously." Students should repeat these affirmations until they can say them with total conviction. Visualizations are images students can create whereby they see themselves the way they want to be. For example, if a student wants to improve his or her typing skills, then the student evaluates what it would look like, sound like, and feel like to be a better typist. Once the student identifies the image, then the student has to rehearse that image in her or his mind, including as many details and sensations as possible. Both visualization and affirmation can restructure attitudes and behaviors. They can be tools for students to use to increase their motivation.

Finally, the fourth component of empowerment is self-knowledge. Self-knowledge refers to an individual's strengths and weaknesses, assets and liabilities; self-knowledge comes about as a result of a realistic self-appraisal, including a determination and an examination of learning styles. Achieving self-knowledge also requires that students have opportunities to explore their goals and values. Students who have determined their goals and values can more easily see how education will enable them to achieve those goals and values. Conversely, students are not motivated when they do not have goals and values or when they do not know what their goals and values are. In other words, without self-knowledge, motivation is impossible. Therefore, teachers who follow Baxter-Magolda's guidelines for effective instruction and who teach their students about personal empowerment are teachers who realize the importance of motivation and who set the stage for students to claim responsibility for their own successes and failures. Such teachers help students to become motivated to make changes and accomplish more.

References

Barry, Leasha M.; Bennett, Betty J.; Christensen, Lois; Mendoza, Alicia; Ortiz, Enrique; Pagan, Migdalia; Robison, Sally; Otilia, Salmón. *The Best Teacher's Test Preparation for the Florida Teacher Certification Examination Professional*

Education Test. Piscataway, New Jersey: Research & Education Association, 2005.

Baxter-Magolda, M. B. *Knowing and Reasoning in College: Gender-Based Patterns in Students' Intellectual Development.* San Francisco: Jossey-Bass, 1992.

Califano, Joseph A. Jr. "Teen Tipplers: America's Underage Drinking Epidemic." Statement, National Press Club, Washington, DC, February 26, 2002. *http://www.casacolumbia.org/absolutenm/templates/articles.asp?articleid=247&zoneid=31*

Centers for Disease Control and Prevention. "Physical Activity for Everyone: Physical Activity Terms." *http://www.cdc.gov/nccdphp/dnpa/physical/terms/index.htm.*

Coles, Robert. "Point of View: When Earnest Volunteers Are Sorely Tested." *Chronicle of Higher Education.* Volume XXXIX: 35 (May 5, 1993), page A52.

Cummins, James Patrick. "The Role of Primary Language Development in Promoting Educational Success for Language Minority Students." In *Schooling and Language Minority Students: A Theoretical Rationale*, edited by California State Department of Education Los Angeles: California State University, 1981, pages 3–49.

———. "Tests, Achievement, and Bilingual Students." *Focus* Volume IX (February 1, 1982), 1–5.

Elliott, Raymond. *Teaching Music.* Columbus, OH: Charles E. Merrill, 1960.

Ellis, D. *Becoming a Master Student.* Rapid City, SD: College Survival, 1991.

Erikson, E. *Childhood and Society.* New York: Horton, 1963.

Florida State Law, chap. 232.277. *http://www.firn.edu/~doe/besss/pdf/law_update.pdf#search='florida%20chapter%20232.277.*

Goplerud, E. N., ed. *Breaking New Ground for Youth at Risk: Program Summaries.* Rockville, MD: Alcohol, Drug Abuse, and Mental Health Administration, Office for Substance Abuse Prevention, 1990. Rep. No. DHHS-ADM-89-1658 (OSAP Technical Rep. 1).

Hoffer, Charles R. *Teaching Music in the Elementary Classroom.* New York: Harcourt Brace Jovanovich, 1982.

Johnson, Elaine M. *Making Prevention Work.* Rockville, MD: Center for Substance Abuse Prevention, 1998.

Kaufman, P., X. Chen, S. P. Choy, S. A. Ruddy, A. K. Miller, K. A. Chandler, C. D. Chapman, M. R. Rand, and P. Klaus. *Indicators of School Crime and Safety, 1999.* Washington, DC: U.S. Departments of Education and Justice, National Center for Education Statistics and Bureau of Justice Statistics, 1999.

Kohlberg, Lawrence. *The Psychology of Moral Development: The Nature and Validity of Moral Stages (Essays on Moral Development).* Vol. 2. New York: Harpercollins, 1984.

Krathwohl, David R., Benjamin S. Bloom, and Bertram B. Masia. *Taxonomy of Educational Objectives.* New York: David McKay, 1964.

National Clearinghouse for Alcohol and Drug Information. *Straight Facts about Drugs and Alcohol.* Rockville, MD: National Clearinghouse for Alcohol and Drug Information, 1998.

National Organization for Fetal Alcohol Syndrome. *http://www.nofas.org/faqs.aspx?id=9.*

Piaget, J. *The Psychology of Intelligence.* London: Routledge and Kegan Paul, 1950.

Prevention Institute. "What Factors Increase the Risk of Being Involved in Violence?" *http://www.preventioninstitute.org/schoolvio14.html.*

South Carolina Visual and Performing Arts Curriculum Framework Writing Team. *South Carolina Visual and Performing Arts Framework.* Columbia: South Carolina State Board of Education, 1993.

Tavris, C. "Coping with Student Conflict Inside and Outside the Classroom." Paper presented at Texas Junior College Teachers' Conference, San Antonio, TX, February 25, 1994.

U.S. Department of Agriculture. "Steps to a Healthier You." *http://www.mypyramid.gov.*

U.S. Department of Education. "Creating Safe and Drug-Free Schools: An Action Guide." September 1996. *http://www.ncjrs.org/pdffiles/safescho.pdf.*

U.S. Departments of Education and Justice. *Early Warning, Timely Response.* Washington, DC: U.S. Government Printing Office, 1998.

Wassum, Sylvesta "Sally." "Elementary school children's vocal range." *Journal of Research in Music Education,* 27:4 (Winter 1979), 214–226.

Praxis II

Elementary Education
Test Code 0011

Practice Test 1

This test is also on CD-ROM in our special interactive Praxis Elementary Education (0011) TEST*ware*®. It is highly recommended that you first take this exam on computer. You will then have the additional study features and benefits of enforced timed conditions and instantaneous, accurate scoring. See page 3 for guidance on how to get the most out of our Praxis Elementary Education software.

Answer Sheet

1. Ⓐ Ⓑ Ⓒ Ⓓ
2. Ⓐ Ⓑ Ⓒ Ⓓ
3. Ⓐ Ⓑ Ⓒ Ⓓ
4. Ⓐ Ⓑ Ⓒ Ⓓ
5. Ⓐ Ⓑ Ⓒ Ⓓ
6. Ⓐ Ⓑ Ⓒ Ⓓ
7. Ⓐ Ⓑ Ⓒ Ⓓ
8. Ⓐ Ⓑ Ⓒ Ⓓ
9. Ⓐ Ⓑ Ⓒ Ⓓ
10. Ⓐ Ⓑ Ⓒ Ⓓ
11. Ⓐ Ⓑ Ⓒ Ⓓ
12. Ⓐ Ⓑ Ⓒ Ⓓ
13. Ⓐ Ⓑ Ⓒ Ⓓ
14. Ⓐ Ⓑ Ⓒ Ⓓ
15. Ⓐ Ⓑ Ⓒ Ⓓ
16. Ⓐ Ⓑ Ⓒ Ⓓ
17. Ⓐ Ⓑ Ⓒ Ⓓ
18. Ⓐ Ⓑ Ⓒ Ⓓ
19. Ⓐ Ⓑ Ⓒ Ⓓ
20. Ⓐ Ⓑ Ⓒ Ⓓ
21. Ⓐ Ⓑ Ⓒ Ⓓ
22. Ⓐ Ⓑ Ⓒ Ⓓ
23. Ⓐ Ⓑ Ⓒ Ⓓ
24. Ⓐ Ⓑ Ⓒ Ⓓ
25. Ⓐ Ⓑ Ⓒ Ⓓ
26. Ⓐ Ⓑ Ⓒ Ⓓ
27. Ⓐ Ⓑ Ⓒ Ⓓ
28. Ⓐ Ⓑ Ⓒ Ⓓ

29. Ⓐ Ⓑ Ⓒ Ⓓ
30. Ⓐ Ⓑ Ⓒ Ⓓ
31. Ⓐ Ⓑ Ⓒ Ⓓ
32. Ⓐ Ⓑ Ⓒ Ⓓ
33. Ⓐ Ⓑ Ⓒ Ⓓ
34. Ⓐ Ⓑ Ⓒ Ⓓ
35. Ⓐ Ⓑ Ⓒ Ⓓ
36. Ⓐ Ⓑ Ⓒ Ⓓ
37. Ⓐ Ⓑ Ⓒ Ⓓ
38. Ⓐ Ⓑ Ⓒ Ⓓ
39. Ⓐ Ⓑ Ⓒ Ⓓ
40. Ⓐ Ⓑ Ⓒ Ⓓ
41. Ⓐ Ⓑ Ⓒ Ⓓ
42. Ⓐ Ⓑ Ⓒ Ⓓ
43. Ⓐ Ⓑ Ⓒ Ⓓ
44. Ⓐ Ⓑ Ⓒ Ⓓ
45. Ⓐ Ⓑ Ⓒ Ⓓ
46. Ⓐ Ⓑ Ⓒ Ⓓ
47. Ⓐ Ⓑ Ⓒ Ⓓ
48. Ⓐ Ⓑ Ⓒ Ⓓ
49. Ⓐ Ⓑ Ⓒ Ⓓ
50. Ⓐ Ⓑ Ⓒ Ⓓ
51. Ⓐ Ⓑ Ⓒ Ⓓ
52. Ⓐ Ⓑ Ⓒ Ⓓ
53. Ⓐ Ⓑ Ⓒ Ⓓ
54. Ⓐ Ⓑ Ⓒ Ⓓ
55. Ⓐ Ⓑ Ⓒ Ⓓ
56. Ⓐ Ⓑ Ⓒ Ⓓ

57. Ⓐ Ⓑ Ⓒ Ⓓ
58. Ⓐ Ⓑ Ⓒ Ⓓ
59. Ⓐ Ⓑ Ⓒ Ⓓ
60. Ⓐ Ⓑ Ⓒ Ⓓ
61. Ⓐ Ⓑ Ⓒ Ⓓ
62. Ⓐ Ⓑ Ⓒ Ⓓ
63. Ⓐ Ⓑ Ⓒ Ⓓ
64. Ⓐ Ⓑ Ⓒ Ⓓ
65. Ⓐ Ⓑ Ⓒ Ⓓ
66. Ⓐ Ⓑ Ⓒ Ⓓ
67. Ⓐ Ⓑ Ⓒ Ⓓ
68. Ⓐ Ⓑ Ⓒ Ⓓ
69. Ⓐ Ⓑ Ⓒ Ⓓ
70. Ⓐ Ⓑ Ⓒ Ⓓ
71. Ⓐ Ⓑ Ⓒ Ⓓ
72. Ⓐ Ⓑ Ⓒ Ⓓ
73. Ⓐ Ⓑ Ⓒ Ⓓ
74. Ⓐ Ⓑ Ⓒ Ⓓ
75. Ⓐ Ⓑ Ⓒ Ⓓ
76. Ⓐ Ⓑ Ⓒ Ⓓ
77. Ⓐ Ⓑ Ⓒ Ⓓ
78. Ⓐ Ⓑ Ⓒ Ⓓ
79. Ⓐ Ⓑ Ⓒ Ⓓ
80. Ⓐ Ⓑ Ⓒ Ⓓ
81. Ⓐ Ⓑ Ⓒ Ⓓ
82. Ⓐ Ⓑ Ⓒ Ⓓ
83. Ⓐ Ⓑ Ⓒ Ⓓ
84. Ⓐ Ⓑ Ⓒ Ⓓ

85. Ⓐ Ⓑ Ⓒ Ⓓ
86. Ⓐ Ⓑ Ⓒ Ⓓ
87. Ⓐ Ⓑ Ⓒ Ⓓ
88. Ⓐ Ⓑ Ⓒ Ⓓ
89. Ⓐ Ⓑ Ⓒ Ⓓ
90. Ⓐ Ⓑ Ⓒ Ⓓ
91. Ⓐ Ⓑ Ⓒ Ⓓ
92. Ⓐ Ⓑ Ⓒ Ⓓ
93. Ⓐ Ⓑ Ⓒ Ⓓ
94. Ⓐ Ⓑ Ⓒ Ⓓ
95. Ⓐ Ⓑ Ⓒ Ⓓ
96. Ⓐ Ⓑ Ⓒ Ⓓ
97. Ⓐ Ⓑ Ⓒ Ⓓ
98. Ⓐ Ⓑ Ⓒ Ⓓ
99. Ⓐ Ⓑ Ⓒ Ⓓ
100. Ⓐ Ⓑ Ⓒ Ⓓ
101. Ⓐ Ⓑ Ⓒ Ⓓ
102. Ⓐ Ⓑ Ⓒ Ⓓ
103. Ⓐ Ⓑ Ⓒ Ⓓ
104. Ⓐ Ⓑ Ⓒ Ⓓ
105. Ⓐ Ⓑ Ⓒ Ⓓ
106. Ⓐ Ⓑ Ⓒ Ⓓ
107. Ⓐ Ⓑ Ⓒ Ⓓ
108. Ⓐ Ⓑ Ⓒ Ⓓ
109. Ⓐ Ⓑ Ⓒ Ⓓ
110. Ⓐ Ⓑ Ⓒ Ⓓ

Elementary Education: Curriculum, Instruction, and Assessment (0011) Practice Test 1

TIME: 120 Minutes
110 Questions

1. Teachers can provide a positive testing environment by

   (A) encouraging students to be anxious about a test.
   (B) providing a comfortable physical setting.
   (C) surprising students with disruptions and distractions.
   (D) emphasizing the consequences for poor performance.

2. If the mastery level for a skill is set at 75 percent, what does the student need to accomplish to exhibit mastery?

   (A) A grade of C or higher
   (B) A grade of B or higher
   (C) answer 75 percent of all of the particular skill questions correctly
   (D) answer 75 percent of all of the skills correctly

3. When a teacher asks the class if they agree or disagree with a student's response, the teacher is using

   (A) redirect.
   (B) corrective.
   (C) positive feedback.
   (D) direct response.

4. Written academic feedback is most productive when it

   (A) is delayed by a day.
   (B) is uniform.
   (C) includes at least one positive remark.
   (D) is not specific.

5. As the decades change, so do the labels the school systems use to identify students who differ from the mainstream—and may have difficulty with mathematics and other subjects. The school systems of the 21st Century identify these "differing" students as

   (A) at risk.
   (B) culturally deprived.
   (C) culturally different.
   (D) slow learners.

6. Goals for individual students

   (A) should be based upon the student's academic record.
   (B) should be the same for all students.
   (C) are created from individual observations only.
   (D) are developed after considering the student's history and motivation.

7. Feedback sessions for a test are most effective

    (A) when they are immediate.
    (B) when they are delayed by a day or so.
    (C) when they are delayed for a few weeks.
    (D) when the feedback is written on paper only.

8. Good and Gouws found that effective teachers reviewed

    (A) verbally.
    (B) at the end of a lesson.
    (C) as students showed weaknesses in specific areas.
    (D) daily, weekly, and monthly.

9. An important goal of the inclusion of students with disabilities in the least restrictive environment

    (A) is a focus on disability and a decreased focus on ability.
    (B) is a focus on inability.
    (C) is the use of the neighborhood school as the first option for the child with a disability.
    (D) is an educational placement of students with disabilities in the neighborhood school only if there is compelling evidence to do so.

10. Effective praise should be

    (A) authentic and low-key.
    (B) used sparingly.
    (C) composed of simple, positive responses.
    (D) used to encourage high-achieving students.

11. While waiting for students to formulate their responses to a question, a student blurts out an answer. The teacher should

    (A) ignore the answer entirely.
    (B) respond immediately to the student's answer.
    (C) silently acknowledge the student's response, and then address the response after the question has been answered by someone else.
    (D) move on to another question without comment.

12. Teachers/tutors who work with students pulled for a short time from a general-education classroom

with inclusion have had most satisfactory results with certain techniques of literacy instruction. The most satisfactory method is

    (A) de-emphasizing skills.
    (B) using only basic texts.
    (C) increased positive reinforcement.
    (D) whole language instruction.

13. Teaching reading through literature is a prevalent method today. Instructors who seek to teach reading through literature should have as a main concern

    (A) the factual aspects of a passage.
    (B) what the words may suggest, for instance an image, a sound, an association, or a feeling.
    (C) neither factual information nor aesthetic purposes.
    (D) the situation, the passages, and the students.

14. Students who speak English as a Second Language (ESL) can be successful in the classroom in the presence of certain conditions. Which of the following attributes characterizes ESL students who are least successful in the classroom? Least successful ESL students

    (A) make many mistakes initially.
    (B) take many risks.
    (C) have teachers and fellow classmates who are accepting of mistakes and do not correct the ESL student's mistakes every time that they occur.
    (D) listen more than they participate.

15. Inside a barn were lambs and people. If we counted 30 heads and 104 legs in the barn, how many lambs and how many people were in the barn?

    (A) 10 lambs and 20 people
    (B) 16 lambs and 14 people
    (C) 18 lambs and 16 people
    (D) 22 lambs and 8 people

16. According to the operant model in behavioral theory, negative reinforcement is

    (A) operant behavior.
    (B) stimulus for operant behavior.
    (C) unknowingly strengthening negative behavior.
    (D) removing a stimulus that causes a behavior to increase.

17. The first kindergarten was started by

    (A) Benjamin Franklin.
    (B) Friedrich Froebel.
    (C) Maria Montessori.
    (D) Johann Pestalozzi.

18. The atmospheres of the Moon and other celestial bodies were studied by using telescopes and spectrophotometers long before the deployment of interplanetary space probes. In these studies, scientists used the spectral patterns of sunlight that passed through the atmosphere of distant objects to learn what elements make up those atmospheres. Which of the following explains the source of the black-line spectral patterns?

    (A) When an element is excited, it gives off light in a characteristic spectral pattern.
    (B) When light strikes an object, some wavelengths of light are absorbed by the surface and others are reflected to give the object its color.
    (C) When light passes through a gas, light is absorbed at wavelengths characteristic of the elements in the gas.
    (D) The black lines are the spectra of ultraviolet light, which is called black light because it cannot be seen with human eyes.

19. Mr. Dobson wants to use a variety of grouping strategies during the year. Sometimes he groups students with others of similar ability; sometimes he groups students with varying ability. Sometimes he permits students to choose their own groupings. Sometimes he suggests that students work with a particular partner; sometimes he assigns a partner. Sometimes he allows students to elect to work individually. This flexibility in grouping strategies indicates Mr. Dobson recognizes that

    (A) fifth graders like surprises and unpredictable teacher behavior.
    (B) grouping patterns affect students' perceptions of self-esteem and competence.
    (C) frequent changes in the classroom keep students alert and interested.
    (D) it is not fair to place the worst students in the same group consistently.

20. The social studies teachers of an inner city school wanted to change to a more relevant curriculum. The department wanted to have units on economics throughout the world instead of only regions of the United States. Mrs. Dunn was asked to submit a proposal for the new curriculum, related activities, sequencing, themes, and materials. In consultation with the other teachers in the department, a needs assessment was planned. The group felt that the needs assessment would

    (A) help the students make a connection between their current skills and those that will be new to them.
    (B) reveal community problems that may affect the students' lives and their performance in school.
    (C) foster a view of learning as a purposeful pursuit, promoting a sense of responsibility for one's own learning.
    (D) engage students in learning activities and help them to develop the motivation to achieve.

21. When the needs assessment was evaluated, it revealed an ethnically diverse community. Student interests and parental expectations varied, different language backgrounds existed, student exceptionalities were common, and academic motivation was low. The question confronting the teachers was how to bridge the gap from where the students were to where they should be. The available choices were to

    (A) change the text only.
    (B) relate the lessons to the students' personal interests.
    (C) create a positive environment to minimize the effects of the negative external factors.
    (D) help students to learn and to monitor their own performance.

The following scenario is to be used for questions 22 and 23.

During the period of community-involvement field experiences, Ms. Parks continually directs her students' attention to the fact that science is a way of solving problems. Following this field experience period, Ms. Parks asks her students to identify a problem in their school and to devise a scientific way of studying and solving that problem. The students work in groups for two class periods and select the following problem for investigation: It is late spring, and the classroom gets so hot during the afternoon that the majority of the students are uncomfortable. Their research question becomes, "Why is it hotter in our classroom than in the music room, art room, or library? How can we make our classroom cooler?"

22. Of the following choices, what is the most important benefit of allowing the students to select their own problem to investigate, rather than having the teacher assign a problem?

    (A) Students become self-directed problem-solvers who can structure their own learning experiences.
    (B) The teacher can best assess each student's academic and affective needs in a naturalistic setting.
    (C) Students will have the opportunity to work with a wide variety of instructional materials.
    (D) Students will learn to appreciate opposing viewpoints.

23. Which of the following is the most important force at work when students are allowed to select their own problem for investigation?

    (A) Increased student motivation
    (B) Increased student diversity
    (C) Increased structure of student groups
    (D) Increased use of self-assessment

24. Mrs. Jones has been using bar graphs on the overhead projector to a) provide salaries of various occupations/professions and b) to indicate the required education and skills for each occupation/profession. At the end of the question-and-answer/discussion period, the goal was for students to have an awareness of the correlation between their skills or lack of skills and their salaries. A parent/guardian support group would be established to enhance the students'

motivation to master new skills. Strategies for use at home and in the classroom would be developed. Mrs. Dunn felt that with the aid of parents

    (A) she could promote her own professional growth as she worked cooperatively with professionals to create a school culture that would enhance learning and result in positive change.
    (B) she would be meeting the expectations associated with teaching.
    (C) she would be fostering strong home relationships that support student achievement of desired outcomes.
    (D) she would be exhibiting her understanding of the principles of conferences, trust, and cooperation.

The following scenario is to be used for questions 25–28.

Mr. Brown feels very uncomfortable when he has to make decisions about the assessment of students. He has had some difficulty with various types of assessment. He decides it is time to talk to Mr. Williams, the principal.

25. Which of the following would be the most effective way for Mr. Brown to document his teaching in an authentic setting and to be aware of students' efforts, progress, and achievements in one or more areas?

    (A) Standardized tests
    (B) Teacher-made tests
    (C) Observation
    (D) Portfolio

26. Which would be the most effective way to evaluate specific objectives and specific content in Mr. Brown's course?

    (A) Self and peer evaluation
    (B) Portfolio
    (C) Teacher-made test
    (D) Observation

27. Mr. Williams asks Mr. Brown what type of test scores are rated against the performance of other

students and are reported in terms of percentiles, stanines, and scaled scores. Mr. Brown should give which response?

(A) Portfolio
(B) Teacher-made test
(C) Observation
(D) Standardized test

28. When the teacher's role is that of a facilitator who utilizes students' knowledge and understanding of specific evaluation criteria, what type of assessment is being used?

(A) Portfolio
(B) Teacher-made test
(C) Self and peer assessment
(D) Observation

Question 29 refers to the following passage.

Tom Jones was asked to improve the remedial reading curriculum for upper elementary-grade students. He found that the students were continually tested and evaluated on reading, that the current objectives were unclear, and that the teaching materials were inappropriate. Following a lengthy observation of Mrs. Ratu's teaching strategies, Mr. Jones concluded that she was teaching basic reading skills in the same manner as did the lower elementary teachers. The teaching materials used a controlled vocabulary and simple sentences. The students were being taught to rely heavily upon pictures and illustrations for the story. Most of the material was fictional in genre. Rote was Mrs. Ratu's preference for learning. Mr. Jones analyzed the test results and found that many of the students in Mrs. Ratu's class had average scores in the areas of art, math, and music. He concluded that, with the exception of reading, most were normal students and would be successful when their remediation was complete. Mr. Jones made several decisions: (1) the students would be evaluated annually with an achievement test; (2) reading materials of interest to upper elementary students would be substituted for elementary materials; (3)

each student would be encouraged to read about the subject of his or her choice; and (4) roundtable discussions would be developed for each "favorite subject."

29. Mrs. Ratu's method of teaching remedial reading focused upon

I. the level at which the students should have learned the basic reading skills.
II. her own minimal competency in instructional design and evaluation.
III. her lack of understanding of the learners in her class.
IV. her desire to make remedial reading easy for the students.

(A) I only.
(B) I and IV only.
(C) II and III only.
(D) II only.

30. Language-minority students who speak their native language instead of English in the classroom

(A) do not have the right to do so.
(B) have the responsibility to do so.
(C) have the obligation to do so.
(D) are a challenge to educators.

31. To help a language-minority student most, recent research (Elley and Mangubhai) suggests that

(A) listening and speaking proficiency should precede literacy instruction.
(B) the teacher should help the student develop reading skills coincidentally with speaking skills but independently from writing skills.
(C) the teacher should help the student develop writing skills before reading skills since motor skills precede reading.
(D) the teacher should seek to help the students to develop reading and writing concomitantly.

32. Dominique Woods has two years of teaching experience at a large urban high school. This is her first year teaching at a small, suburban, ethnically mixed high school. She wants to take advantage of the week of faculty meetings before school opens to become better acquainted with the school

grounds, faculty, curriculum, and available materials. How could she best utilize her time?

(A) Tour the school while noting the teacher's room, materials room, and other important rooms.

(B) Talk to the principal about what is expected of her.

(C) Talk with a willing teacher who has spent several years at the school about community characteristics and available materials as they apply to the curriculum.

(D) Obtain a copy of the curriculum to take to the materials room where it can be determined what materials are available for classroom use.

33. The probability of parents' offspring showing particular traits can be predicted by using

(A) the Linnaean System.

(B) DNA tests.

(C) the Punnett Square.

(D) None of the above.

34. An acidic solution can have a pH of

(A) 20.

(B) 10.

(C) 8.

(D) 5.

35. A material with definite volume but no definite shape is called

(A) titanium.

(B) gas.

(C) liquid.

(D) solid

36. The intensity of an earthquake is measured by

(A) a thermograph.

(B) a seismograph.

(C) a telegraph.

(D) an odometer.

37. _____ is defined as the ability to do work.

(A) Force

(B) Energy

(C) Speed

(D) Distance

Question 38 refers to the following passage.

Creating an English garden on a mountainside in the Ouachita Mountains in central Arkansas may sound like an impossible endeavor, but after two years, this dream is becoming reality. By digging up the rocks and replacing them with bags of top soil, humus, and peat, the persistent gardener now has sprouts that are not all weeds. Gravel paths meander through the beds of shasta daisies, marigolds, lavender, valerian, iris, day lilies, Mexican heather, and other flowers. Ornamental grasses, dogwood trees, and shrubs back up the flowers. Along the periodic waterway created by an underground spring, swamp hibiscus, helenium, hosta, and umbrella plants display their colorful and seasonal blooms. The flower beds are outlined by large rocks dug up by a pickax. Blistered hands are worth the effort when people stop by to view the mountainside beauty.

38. This essay can be described as being

(A) speculative.

(B) argumentative.

(C) narrative.

(D) expository.

39. New research (Goodman) and alternative views (Flores) about all children—including the at-risk—challenge the status quo and ask teachers to revalue their habitudes and practices related to traditional ways of teaching. These assumptions for math teachers and language arts teachers indicate

(A) that at-risk children bring very few experiences to the classroom.

(B) that many children cannot be successful in a regular classroom program.

(C) that observing children and their language in authentic settings is not as helpful as standardized testing to determine literacy.

(D) that families of at-risk children are interested in their children and in their school experiences.

Use the figure below and the following facts to answer question 40:

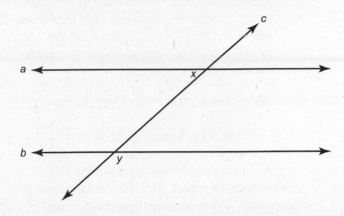

Lines *a* and *b* are parallel,

c is a line, and

the measure of angle *x* is 50°.

40. What is the measure of angle *y*?

   (A) 50°
   (B) 100°
   (C) 130°
   (D) 80°

41. In the given figure, assume that AD is a line. What is the measure of angle AXB?

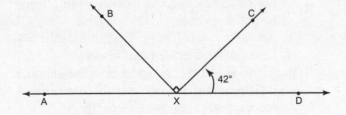

   (A) 48°
   (B) 90°
   (C) 42°
   (D) There is not enough information given to answer the question.

42. Which formula can be used to find the area of the triangle shown below?

   (A) $A = (l \times h)/2$
   (B) $A = (l + h)/2$
   (C) $A = 2(l + h)$
   (D) $A = 2(l \times h)$

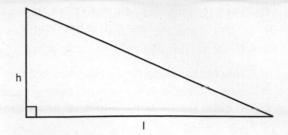

43. Which formula can be used to find the area of the figure below? (Assume the curve is *half* of a circle.)

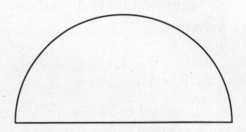

   (A) $A = \pi r$
   (B) $A = 2\pi r^2$
   (C) $A = \pi r^2$
   (D) $A = \pi r^2/2$

Use the figure below to answer question 44. Assume the following:

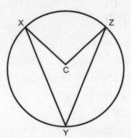

Point C is the center of the circle.

Angles XYZ and XCZ intercept minor arc XZ.

The measure of angle XYZ is 40°.

44. What is the measure of the major arc XYZ?

   (A) 140°
   (B) 280°
   (C) 160°
   (D) 320°

45. Why should children be encouraged to figure out the structure and the features of the text they are attempting to comprehend and remember?

   I. It helps the students to understand the way the author organized the material to be presented.

   II. It helps the students to look at the features of the text.

   III. Talking about the structure of the text provides an opportunity for the teacher to point out the most salient features to the students.

   IV. The discussions may help the child make connections between the new material in the chapter and what is already known about the topic.

(A) I and III
(B) II and IV
(C) I and IV
(D) I, II, III, and IV

46. Ms. Smith decided to stage three different versions of *Cinderella* with her students. Knowing that this is one of the world's most famous fairy tales, she located Chinese, Native American, and Russian versions of the story. She found age-appropriate plays of each that could be staged in her classroom. In addition to acting in these plays, her students are creating scenery, costumes, and props to use in their performances. Which of the following best describes what Ms. Smith primarily expects her students to achieve through these activities?

   I. Understanding cultural similarities and differences through dramatic literature

   II. Understanding theatrical practices

   III. Gaining experience with creative drama practices

   IV. Gaining experience with adapting stories into plays

(A) I only
(B) I and II
(C) III and IV
(D) I, II, and IV

47. In order to extend the literacy of others, teachers must engage in some self-reflection to meet the needs of the learners. Teachers will find that

(A) comparing their own literacy history to that of their students is futile.

(B) considering how a school setting helped them and making such comparisons with the students they teach is probably inapplicable.

(C) school experiences have no effect on the self identity of most of the diverse learners.

(D) self-evaluation of their own values, attitudes, and dispositions is helpful.

Question 48 refers to the following passage.

   Mrs. Gettler teaches 26 third graders in a large inner city school. About one-third of her students participate in the ESL program at the school. Mrs. Gettler suspects that some of the students' parents are unable to read or write in English. Four of the students receive services from the learning resource teacher. At the beginning of the year, none of the students read above 2.0 grade level, and some of the students did not know all the letters of the alphabet.

48. Which of the following describes the instructional strategy that is most likely to improve the reading levels of Mrs. Gettler's students?

(A) An intensive phonics program that includes drill and practice work on basic sight words.

(B) An emergent literacy program emphasizing pattern books and journal writing using invented spelling.

(C) An instructional program that closely follows the third-grade basal reader.

(D) Participation by all students in the school's ESL program so they can receive services from the learning resource center.

The following scenario is to be used for questions 49 through 52.

   Mrs. Doe began planning a two-week unit of study of the Native Americans for her fifth-grade class. To begin the unit, she chose a movie on the twenty-first century Native Americans. As Mrs. Doe reflectively listened, the students asked key questions.

   The following day, Mrs. Doe reviewed the use of encyclopedias, indexes, and atlases. She then divided the students into groups and took them to the library. Each group was responsible for locating information on a particular topic. The topics were maps showing the topography of the land, charts illustrating the climate, plants and animals, a map showing migration routes, and a map showing the general areas where the Native Americans settled.

49. The students' involvement in the unit of study is a result of

   I. the teacher's reflective listening during the discussion.
  II. the available resources and materials.
 III. careful planning and its relationship to success in the classroom.
 IV. the students' personal acquaintance with Native Americans.

  (A) I only
  (B) I and II only
  (C) II and III only
  (D) I and IV only

50. Days 3 and 4 of this unit were spent with each group being involved in library research. They wrote information on index cards. Each group prepared a presentation that included a written explanation of an assigned topic, a shadow box, and a sawdust map or models of Native American clothing. A pictograph was to be used in the telling of a legend or folk story. The presentation concluded with a collage depicting the Native American way of life. Multiple strategies and techniques were used for

   I. motivation of the group and its effects on individual behavior and learning.
  II. allowing each student regardless of ability to participate in the project.
 III. integrating the project with other subjects.
 IV. developing a foundation for teaching American history.

  (A) I, II, and III only
  (B) I and II only
  (C) III only
  (D) IV only

51. Day 10 of the unit was Field Trip Day, which involved visiting museums. The students were given a choice of museums. Each student was expected to take notes of what was seen, heard, and experienced to share with the remainder of the class on the following day. Field Trip Day and its experiences

   I. allowed the students to make connections between their current skills and those that were new to them.
  II. allowed external factors to create a learning environment that would take advantage of positive factors.
 III. allowed a sense of community to be nurtured.
 IV. allowed the students to take responsibility for their own learning.

  (A) I and II only
  (B) III only
  (C) IV only
  (D) III and IV only

52. Giving the students a choice of field trip locations

   I. was meant to enhance the students' self-concept.
  II. was meant to respect differences and enhance the students' understanding of the society in which they live.
 III. was meant to foster the view of learning as a purposeful pursuit.
 IV. was meant as an example of using an array of instructional strategies.

  (A) II only
  (B) II and IV only
  (C) I and II only
  (D) III only

53. Troubled by what seems to be an increase in gang-type activity among younger children, Mr. Billings wants to find out what his students think and know about gangs. He wants to learn the most he can about the students' thinking about this topic in the least amount of time. Additionally, he wants to give all students the chance to share what they think and know while maximizing interaction among students. The students will spend the entire morning reading, talking, and writing a group report about this subject. Which of the following

seating arrangements would best help Mr. Billings meet his objectives?

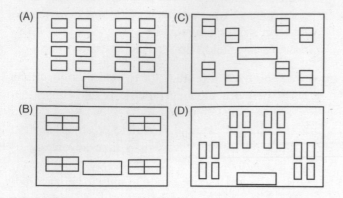

54. The strength of requiring a cognitive objective and a performance objective is that

   (A) some students are not test takers and do poorly on paper and pencil tests.
   (B) the score for one objective could offset the score for the other objective.
   (C) the developmental level in one domain may affect performance in another domain.
   (D) the teacher is matching the students' learning styles to her teaching style.

55. When developing a unit about the Erie Canal for elementary-age students, how would you handle assessment of the students?

   (A) Explain to the students that the unit will cover a variety of projects; therefore, you will be using different assessment tools.
   (B) Explain to the students each project in the unit, then describe what they will be asked to do.
   (C) Give to the students a list of new vocabulary words that they will need to know for the final test.
   (D) Explain to the students that they will need to hand in their notebooks at the end of the unit.

56. Rubrics are used by many teachers in elementary schools for the purposes of assessment. What criteria should be used when creating a rubric?

   I. Set clearly defined criteria for each assessment.
   II. Include a rating scale.

   III. Use only one idea at a time so that students are not confused.
   IV. Tell students that they can rate themselves.

   (A) IV and III
   (B) III and II
   (C) I and II
   (D) None of these

57. Mr. O'Brien ends class by telling students that over the next few weeks they will be required to keep a communications journal. Every time they have an eventful exchange—either positive or negative, they are to record the details of the exchange in their journal. This assignment is given as

   (A) a way to help students improve their composition and rhetorical skills.
   (B) a way of understanding individual students, monitoring instructional effectiveness, and shaping instruction.
   (C) a way of helping students become more accountable for the way they manage their time.
   (D) the basis for giving daily grades to students.

The following scenario is to be used for questions 58 through 60.

Scenario: It is the first day of class. Ms. Johnson, the language arts teacher, tells the students a little bit about herself. She tells them that she wants to know about each individual in the class. She asks them to write about themselves and hand their papers to her as they leave the class to go to lunch.

58. By requiring that students write about themselves, Ms. Johnson is

   (A) fulfilling her responsibilities as an English teacher.
   (B) preparing her class to create autobiographies.
   (C) relying on the Language-Experience-Approach (LEA) for instruction.
   (D) preparing her class to read biographies about great Americans from diverse cultural backgrounds.

59. Ms. Johnson collects the students' papers at the end of class. As she reads the papers, she decides

that the best way to give her students positive feedback is

(A) not to mark errors on the paper so as not to discourage or inhibit their creativity.
(B) to make at least one positive comment about each paragraph.
(C) begin with one or two positive comments about the paper and then suggest how students could improve their writing.
(D) give everyone a high grade on the paper for participating in the assignment.

60. After Ms. Johnson finishes reading all the students' papers, she observes that some of the students had difficulty identifying and describing their strengths, whether in class or outside class. She believes that all of her students have strengths and she wants to help them see the assets they possess. She decides that in the next class, students will

(A) take a learning style assessment to uncover their particular learning strengths and characteristics.
(B) listen to a lecture about how everyone possesses special skills and strengths.
(C) read a chapter from a book about Guilford's Structure of Intellect, as a precursor to a discussion about how intelligence is specialized and diverse.
(D) rewrite their papers, correcting their errors and revising their paragraphs to name at least two additional classroom strengths they possess and at least two additional interpersonal skills they possess.

61. Mr. Swenson teaches mathematics in high school. He is planning a unit for his advanced math students on fractal geometry, using the computer lab for demonstrations and exploration. The students have used various computer programs to solve algebra and calculus problems. As Mr. Swenson plans a unit of study, he determines that a cognitive outcome will be that students will design and produce fractals by using a computer program. An effective outcome is that students will become excited about investigating a new field of mathematics and will show this interest by choosing to develop a math project relating to fractals. The most appropriate strategy to use first would be

(A) explaining the exciting development of fractal geometry over the past 10 to 15 years.
(B) demonstrating on the computer the way to input values into formulas to produce fractal designs.
(C) giving students a few simple fractal designs and asking them to figure out the formulas for producing them.
(D) showing students color pictures of complex fractals and asking them for ideas about how they could be drawn mathematically.

62. Which teacher action works best to reduce racial problems in a classroom? A teacher should

(A) work to make all students think, talk, and act as he or she does to foster harmony.
(B) seek to be conscious of differences among students.
(C) treat all students in the same way.
(D) seek to be color blind.

63. The characteristics of fascism include all of the following EXCEPT:

(A) totalitarianism.
(B) democracy.
(C) romanticism.
(D) militarism.

64. The industrial economy of the nineteenth century was based upon all of the following EXCEPT:

(A) the availability of raw materials.
(B) an equitable distribution of profits among those involved in production.
(C) the availability of capital.
(D) a distribution system to market finished products.

65. "Jim Crow" laws were laws that

(A) effectively prohibited blacks from voting in state and local elections.
(B) restricted American Indians to U.S. government reservations.
(C) restricted open-range ranching in the Great Plains.
(D) established separate segregated facilities for blacks and whites.

66. Which of the following is used to effect the release of a person from improper imprisonment?

    (A) A writ of mandamus.
    (B) A writ of habeas corpus.
    (C) The Fourth Amendment requirement that police have probable cause in order to obtain a search warrant.
    (D) The Supreme Court's decision in *Roe v Wade*.

67. Which of the following defines a salt?

    (A) One of the reactant products of an acid and base
    (B) One of the reactant products of a base and water
    (C) One of the reactant products of an acid and water
    (D) A reactant product of a phase transformation.

68. The atomic number for neutral (unionized) atoms as listed in the periodic table refers to

    (A) the number of neutrons in an atom.
    (B) the number of protons in an atom.
    (C) the number of electrons in an atom.
    (D) Both (B) and (C).

69. Which of the following is a phenomenon involving the physical properties of a substance?

    (A) Corrosion of iron
    (B) Burning of wood
    (C) Rocket engine ignition
    (D) Melting of ice

70. Isotopes of a given element contain

    (A) more electrons than protons with equal numbers of neutrons.
    (B) more protons than electrons with equal numbers of neutrons.
    (C) equal numbers of protons and electrons with differing numbers of neutrons.
    (D) unequal numbers of protons and electrons with differing numbers of neutrons.

71. Newton's second law of motion states that "the net force acting on a body is equal to the product of its mass and its acceleration." Which of the following is a good example of the law's application?

    (A) Decreased friction between surfaces by means of lubrication.
    (B) Potential energy stored in a compressed spring.
    (C) A rocket lifting off at Cape Canaveral with increasing speed.
    (D) Using a claw hammer to pull a nail out with multiplied force.

72. Which of the following is most likely to contain the greatest thermal energy?

    (A) The Pacific Ocean with an average temperature of ~5°F.
    (B) A 1 g sample of molten metal at 2,000°F.
    (C) A bucket of water at 75°F.
    (D) Lake Michigan at an average temperature of ~5°F.

73. Which cellular component is responsible for the regulation of exchanges of substances between a cell and its environment?

    (A) The endoplasmic reticulum
    (B) The cell nucleus
    (C) The cytoplasm
    (D) The cell membrane

74. Humans have 46 chromosomes in their body cells. How many chromosomes are found in the zygote?

    (A) 2
    (B) 10
    (C) 23
    (D) 46

75. Human body temperature regulation via the skin involves

    (A) respiration.
    (B) transpiration.
    (C) perspiration.
    (D) sensation.

76. Darwin's original theory of natural selection asserts that

    (A) all organisms have descended with modification from a common ancestor.
    (B) random genetic drift plays a major role in speciation.

(C) species characteristics are inherited by means of genes.

(D) speciation is usually due to gradual accumulation of small genetic changes.

77. The lunar period is nearest in length to

(A) 24 hours.
(B) 30 days.
(C) 365 days.
(D) 1 week.

78. A supernova normally occurs when

(A) a star first initiates fusion.
(B) galaxies collide.
(C) the end of a star's lifetime nears, with its nuclear fuel exhausted.
(D) a wandering comet plunges into the a star's interior.

79. The most important factor in Earth's seasonal patterns is the

(A) distance from the Sun to Earth.
(B) Earth's rotation period of 24 hours.
(C) tilting of the Earth's axis.
(D) the Moon and associated tides.

80. Metamorphic rocks are

(A) derived from igneous rocks.
(B) unrelated to igneous rocks.
(C) a type of sedimentary rock.
(D) a type of rock not found on this planet.

81. Which of the following is considered to be evidence for plate tectonics?

(A) Continental coastline "fit"
(B) Identical fossil evidence at "fit" locations
(C) Intense geological activity in mountainous regions
(D) All of the above

82. Seafloor spreading is characterized as

(A) plate spreading with upwelling magma forming ridges.
(B) plate collisions with associated ridge formation.
(C) plate spreading with no ridge formation.
(D) plate collisions with no ridge formation.

83. Igneous rocks are formed by

(A) magma cooling in underground cells and pockets.
(B) magma ejected aboveground as lava, which cools.
(C) layers of sediment collecting and compacting at the bottom of lakes and seas.
(D) both (A) and (B).

84. In descending order of abundance, what is the composition of the Earth's atmosphere?

(A) Oxygen, nitrogen, carbon dioxide, trace gases
(B) Nitrogen, oxygen, carbon dioxide, trace gases
(C) Nitrogen, carbon dioxide, oxygen, trace gases
(D) Carbon dioxide, oxygen, nitrogen, trace gases

85. What is the greatest common divisor of 120 and 252?

(A) 2
(B) 3
(C) 6
(D) 12

86. How many odd prime numbers are there between 1 and 20?

(A) 7
(B) 8
(C) 9
(D) 10

87. Mrs. Tyler has observed that two children are regularly excluding others from their group of playmates on the playground. On numerous occasions, she has overheard name calling and taunting of these two children by the group. What criteria should guide her decision-making as she determines how to respond?

(A) Children are resilient and will find playmates they get along with on their own.
(B) There is no place in a classroom for disrespectful or hurtful behavior because it is known to negatively impact the learning environment.
(C) Some people just don't like other people.
(D) It is the parents' job to teach children to accept others.

88. Mr. Bates is a second-year early childhood teacher in an urban school. Because so many of his students have language deficits, he uses songs and gestures to call them together, line them up, and accomplish other organizational procedures. This practice indicates that Mr. Bates understands the

    (A) importance of continuous monitoring of instructional effectiveness.
    (B) developmental characteristics of young children.
    (C) importance of communicating enthusiasm for learning.
    (D) importance of adjusting communication to ensure that directions and explanations are understood.

89. At the end of each week, Ms. Axtel takes a few minutes to write in her journal. She makes written comments about the lessons she taught that week, as well as the students' responses to those lessons. She also includes comments about how to change or revise the lessons in the future. This practice indicates that Ms. Axtel is

    (A) concerned about process writing.
    (B) a reflective practitioner.
    (C) keeping notes for her formal evaluation.
    (D) is a habitual journal writer.

90. One Monday morning, Ms. Axtel arrives early for school. She notices that Angela, a second-grade student in her class, is waiting outside the front door even though it is at least an hour before the earliest bus should arrive. When Ms. Axtel stops to ask Angela if she is all right, Angela begins to cry. Ms. Axtel notices several large bruises on Angela's legs and arms. It is Ms. Axtel's responsibility to

    (A) follow the protocol for the school district for notifying law enforcement authorities as soon as possible that she suspects that Angela may have been beaten or abused.
    (B) comfort Angela and call her mother later in the day to learn what happened.
    (C) recognize that Angela must have misbehaved and was punished by her parents.
    (D) learn more about Angela's family before making any other decisions.

91. Students in Pygmalion Primary School have studied the home and family, the school and community, and the state and nation, and are now studying regions of the world. The approach being used is probably which of the following?

    (A) Expanding horizon approach
    (B) Spiral curriculum
    (C) Learning centers
    (D) Open classroom

92. If a teacher is considered to be "with it," that teacher

    (A) is always aware of what is going on in the classroom.
    (B) wears modern clothes.
    (C) understands student trends.
    (D) uses language that the students relate to easily.

93. Mrs. Gerig, a second-grade teacher, is worried about a new student, Roseanna Jimenez, who will probably be tested for Limited English Proficiency (LEP) soon. Roseanna does not speak in class. She watches what the other children do and follows suit. She nods for "yes" and shakes her head for "no." She laughs at silly things she sees, but she rarely utters a word at school. When she is asked to read with Mrs. Gerig, she hunches over and cries. When she is asked to write, she copies words from the word wall or writes her ABC's. After a few days, Mrs. Gerig checks the student records and sees that the parents have listed English as the home language. What should Mrs. Gerig do?

    (A) Demand that Roseanne speak, read, and write in English.
    (B) Request a meeting with the parents, the campus designee for LEP, and a campus administrator as soon as possible to discuss Roseanne's academic progress and the benefits of the LEP program.
    (C) File a concern with the district office regarding the likelihood of the inaccuracy of the parent information reported on the home language survey.
    (D) Say nothing and do the best she can to teach Roseanne to read and write in English.

94. Mrs. Gettler realizes that a student's preferred learning style contributes to his or her success as a student. Mrs. Gettler wants to accommodate as many of her students' individual learning styles as possible. Which of the following describes the way to identify baseline information about the students' learning styles?

(A) Mrs. Gettler should record her observations of individual student's behaviors over a period of several weeks.
(B) Each of the students should be tested by the school psychologist.
(C) Mrs. Gettler should administer a group screening test for identifying learning styles.
(D) Mrs. Gettler should review the permanent file of each student and compare the individual's previous test scores with classroom performance.

95. As the school year progresses, Mrs. Gettler includes discussions of holidays of many cultures. She introduces each holiday prior to the actual day of celebration. The children prepare decorations, learn songs, and read stories about children in the countries where the holiday is celebrated. Which of the following best describes the most likely purpose of this activity?

(A) Celebrating holidays of many cultures is one way to teach appreciation of human diversity.
(B) Celebrating holidays of many cultures is one way to satisfy the demands of political action groups.
(C) Celebrating holidays is one way to encourage students to read aloud to one another.
(D) Celebrating holidays is one way to encourage students to participate in class activities.

96. The students in a dual-grade class have written stories following the "Brown Bear, Brown Bear" format. The stories have been revised and edited by the teacher, Ms. Sanchez. For the next several days, students will enter their stories into the computer using a special software package that allows the addition of graphics and animation. Based on student need, Ms. Sanchez scaffolds each student's work on an as-needed basis. Which of the following criteria should guide her decision-making as she designs an evaluation rubric for the publishing task?

(A) The local/state/national standards and the prior experience of her students regarding technology use
(B) Information from the parent survey regarding student interests
(C) Roles and responsibilities of support staff in the building
(D) The stages of play development in young children and the correlation to computer readiness.

97. The homeroom mother wants to create a phone list of all the students in the class. She distributes the list to the parents to facilitate communication while planning and preparing for parties, field trips, and other special projects during the year. Ms. Sanchez must

(A) make sure that all students are included on the list so that no one is left out.
(B) determine that only students whose parents have approved the release of this information are included on the list.
(C) prepare the list herself to ensure accuracy.
(D) tell the homeroom mother that the campus leadership must approve the idea and the release of this information.

98. The Council of Exceptional Children issued a policy statement in 1993. The policy statement of the Council of Exceptional Children concerning the education of children with disabilities (1993)

(A) acknowledges that a continuum of service can never be available to all children.
(B) recognizes that inclusion is not a realistic goal for schools and communities.
(C) recommends that trained personnel and support practices strengthen general education classrooms which service students with disabilities.
(D) concludes that general education classrooms cannot serve students with disabilities.

99. Two children are fighting. The best approach for the teacher to take first is which of the following?

(A) Send another person for an administrator, separate the two, turn the aggressor over to the administrator, and then deal personally with the victim.

(B) Separate the two and take both to the guidance counselor for a conference.

(C) Separate the two and attend first to the victim.

(D) A teacher of young children should not attempt to separate the two unless an adult witness is present.

100. Which of the following vitamins is not fat soluble?

(A) Vitamin D
(B) Vitamin C
(C) Vitamin E
(D) Vitamin K

101. Of the following, which test does NOT measure muscular strength and endurance in children?

(A) Pull-ups
(B) Flexed arm hang
(C) Grip strength test
(D) Sit-and-reach test

102. Dance can reflect the religion of a culture by

I. offering adoration and worship to the deity.
II. appealing to the deity for survival in war.
III. asking the deity for success in the hunt.
IV. miming the actions of planting and harvesting crops.

(A) I and II only
(B) I and III only
(C) II, III, and IV only
(D) I, II, III, and IV

103. Which of the following is NOT a characteristic of cholesterol?

(A) Cholesterol plays a role in the function of the brain.
(B) Cholesterol is a component in the creation of certain hormones.
(C) Cholesterol is produced in the liver.
(D) Excess cholesterol found in the blood of many people usually comes from internal production.

104. A table tennis game is scored to

(A) 15 points.
(B) 15 points, with a margin of two.

(C) 21 points, with a margin of two.
(D) 21 points.

105. Harmony results when a melody is accompanied by

I. a rhythm instrument.
II. a guitar.
III. another instrument or singer playing or singing the melody.
IV. another instrument playing chords.

(A) I and II only
(B) I and III only
(C) II and III only
(D) II and IV only

106. Reading and then dramatizing a story, using that story as the basis of a puppet play, scripting that story and performing it in the classroom, and then attending a performance of that story done as a play by a theatre company illustrates which of the following concepts?

(A) Teachers should work with material until they find the correct way to use it with students.
(B) There are multiple ways to express and interpret the same material.
(C) Plays are more interesting than classroom dramatizations.
(D) Students learn less as audience members than as participants in drama activities.

107. Which one of the following statements is most true regarding the materials of visual art?

(A) Industrial innovations in art-making materials have improved art in the past 150 years.
(B) The use of uncommon materials in art-making has improved art in the past 150 years.
(C) The use of unusual materials in art-making has changed the standards by which we view art.
(D) Industrial innovations in art-making materials have had little influence on visual art.

108. Which of the following is an important reason why music should be included in every child's daily classroom activities?

(A) The imagination, creativity, and aesthetic awareness of a child can be developed through music for more creative living in our mechanized society.

(B) Students need an opportunity to stay current with today's popular music culture.

(C) Making and listening to music is part of our cultural experience and provides opportunities for personal aesthetic growth.

(D) Participating in creatively planned musical activities helps build a child's self-esteem and understanding of others.

109. Which of the following is true for both jazz dance and tap dance?

(A) The technique is based upon isolation of body parts.

(B) The technique is primarily based upon intricate rhythms in the feet.

(C) The technique is based upon lightness and denial of gravity.

(D) The technique emerged from a blending of African and European cultures.

110. Which of the following is NOT true about the act of creating dances?

(A) It involves creative problem solving.

(B) It must happen outside of the classroom within a special time.

(C) It can express ideas and explore feelings.

(D) It can teach math or science.

Praxis II

Elementary Education
Test Code 0011

Answers: Practice Test 1

Answer Key

1. (B)	23. (A)	45. (D)	67. (A)	89. (B)
2. (C)	24. (C)	46. (B)	68. (D)	90. (A)
3. (A)	25. (D)	47. (D)	69. (D)	91. (A)
4. (C)	26. (C)	48. (B)	70. (C)	92. (A)
5. (A)	27. (D)	49. (C)	71. (C)	93. (B)
6. (D)	28. (C)	50. (B)	72. (A)	94. (A)
7. (B)	29. (C)	51. (A)	73. (D)	95. (A)
8. (D)	30. (D)	52. (B)	74. (D)	96. (A)
9. (C)	31. (D)	53. (B)	75. (C)	97. (B)
10. (A)	32. (C)	54. (C)	76. (A)	98. (C)
11. (C)	33. (C)	55. (B)	77. (B)	99. (C)
12. (C)	34. (D)	56. (C)	78. (C)	100. (B)
13. (D)	35. (C)	57. (B)	79. (C)	101. (D)
14. (D)	36. (B)	58. (C)	80. (A)	102. (D)
15. (D)	37. (B)	59. (C)	81. (D)	103. (D)
16. (D)	38. (C)	60. (A)	82. (A)	104. (C)
17. (B)	39. (D)	61. (D)	83. (D)	105. (D)
18. (C)	40. (C)	62. (B)	84. (B)	106. (B)
19. (B)	41. (A)	63. (B)	85. (D)	107. (C)
20. (A)	42. (A)	64. (B)	86. (A)	108. (C)
21. (C)	43. (D)	65. (D)	87. (B)	109. (D)
22. (A)	44. (B)	66. (B)	88. (D)	110. (B)

Elementary Education: Curriculum, Instruction, and Assessment (0011) Practice Test 1

Detailed Explanations of Answers

1. (B)

Students are able to perform better on tests when their physical setting, which includes lighting, temperature, and seating, is favorable. When students feel anxious over a test (A), or when teachers threaten against poor performances (D), students do not perform as well. Outside disruptions (C) can break a student's concentration; this is especially true for younger children.

2. (C)

When a teacher sets a mastery level at a certain percentage, students who reach that percentage are considered to have mastered that skill and receive a grade of "A" for their efforts. Therefore, (A) and (B) are incorrect. Answering 75 percent of all of the skills correctly (D) is also incorrect because in order to master a particular skill, the student does not need to master all of the skills.

3. (A)

A redirect (A) occurs when a teacher asks one student to react to the response of another student. A corrective (B) occurs when a teacher responds to a student error by explaining why it is an error and then provides a correct answer. When teachers are redirecting, they are neither giving any feedback (C) nor directly responding (D) to the student comments.

4. (C)

Written academic feedback should contain specific comments on errors and how to improve them. It should also contain a positive remark that notes an aspect of the assignment that was done well. Therefore, delaying feedback by a day (A), specifying uniform guidelines (B), and presenting feedback in a vague manner (D) are not the correct answer choices.

5. (A)

As the decades change, so do the labels the school systems use to identify children who differ from the mainstream—and may have difficulty with mathematics and other subjects; the school systems of the 21st century tend to label children who differ from the mainstream as "at-risk (A)," not "culturally different (C)," "slow learners (D)," "semi-lingual," "culturally deprived (B)," or "limited-English speaking."

6. (D)

Individual goals for a student should be developed after reviewing both the student's history and assessing the student's motivation. This will ensure that the goals can be met by the student. Goals should not be based solely on the student's academic record (A) or created only from individual observations (C). They should also not be the same for all students (B) because students learn at different levels and aim for different goals.

7. (B)

Research has shown that it is favorable to provide feedback in test situations when the feedback is delayed by a day or so, rather than giving immediate feedback (A). Delaying the feedback session for a few weeks is not beneficial to the students because too much time has elapsed (C). A class review of the test has been shown to be more beneficial in clearing up misunderstandings than handwritten notations (D).

8.   (D)

Good and Gouws found that effective teachers conducted reviews as part of their daily, weekly, and monthly routines. Therefore, (A), (B), and (C) are incorrect because they were not findings in the Good and Gouws study.

9.   (C)

Inclusion places the focus on ability and decreases the focus on disability and inability; A and B are incorrect. With inclusion, the neighborhood school accepts children as the first option and considers other educational placements only if that child, even with substantial support, cannot succeed in the class with age-appropriate peers. (C) is the best option. The neighborhood school should not be the last option; (D) is not the best choice.

10.   (A)

Praise has been shown to be the most effective when it is authentic and low-key (A). It should be used frequently; therefore (B) is incorrect. It should consist of complex responses that provide information about the reasons for the quality of the student response; therefore, (C) is incorrect. It should be used to provide all students with positive experiences; therefore, (D) is incorrect.

11.   (C)

If the teacher ignores the answer entirely (A) or moves on to another question (D), it devalues the student response. If the teacher responds immediately to the digression (B), the disruptive behavior has been rewarded. The correct answer is (C).

12.   (C)

Teachers/tutors who have "pulled out" students from an inclusive classroom situation for short term

instruction have found that these diverse learners seem to learn best with increased positive instruction (C). Skills should be emphasized; A, therefore, is incorrect. The use of ONLY basic texts is not highly effective; (B) is not the best choice. Whole language instruction (D) does not work with everyone; (D) is not the best choice.

13.   (D)

Teachers and students must clarify the purposes for reading. These purposes—which may vary from passage to passage, student to student, and situation to situation—include aesthetics, fact attainment (efference), and a combination of factual and aesthetic purposes. (D) is, therefore the best answer. Neither the factual aspects (A) nor what the words suggest (B) is important alone. Both factual information and aesthetic purposes are important; (C) is not an adequate answer.

14.   (D)

To master a second language, one must participate. Those students who listen instead of participating are least successful. (D) is the correct choice. All students—successful and unsuccessful—will make many mistakes; (A) is not appropriate. The students who are going to be successful will take risks—not vice versa; (B) is a poor choice. Teachers and fellow classmates do not need to focus on mistakes ESL students make; reinforcement is crucial. (C) is not a good answer. The classroom should be a supportive classroom environment that allows English-as-Second-Language (ESL) students to take risks since 1) writing and reading develop through social interactions, not merely listening; 2) literacy develops through relationships between English learners and English speakers; 3) ESL students will risk interactions only if fully supported; and 4) mistakes often precede success.

15.   (D)

Let x be the number of lambs in the barn. Then, because each person and lamb has only one head, the number of people must be $30 - x$. Since lambs have four legs, the number of lamb legs equals $4x$. Similarly, the number of human legs equals $2(30 - x)$. Thus, the equation for the total number of legs (104) is:

$$4x + 2(30 - x) = 104.$$

Use the distributive property, $a(b - c) = ab - ac$, to get

$$4x + 60 - 2x = 104,$$

which reduces to

$$2x + 60 = 104.$$

Subtract 60 from each side to get

$$2x = 44, \text{ or } x = 22.$$

So the number of lambs is 22, and the number of people is $30 - 22 = 8$.

16. (D)

According to the operant model in behavioral theory, negative reinforcement is removing a stimulus, which causes a behavior to increase. Reinforcement can be positive or negative in that is it applied or removed. All reinforcement, positive or negative, increases the likelihood that the behavior will occur again. Likewise, punishment can be positive or negative, but all punishment decreases the likelihood that the behavior will occur again.

17. (B)

Friedrich Wilhelm Froebel, a German philosopher and educator, was the founder of the modern kindergarten. Benjamin Franklin (A) was a political leader, philosopher, and scientist who developed the structure of the modern high school. Maria Montessori (C) was an Italian physician who developed an early childhood curriculum based on a structured environment. Johann Pestalozzi (D) established the first training schools for teachers in Prussia.

18. (C)

Black line spectra are formed when the continuous spectra of the Sun passes through the atmosphere. The elements in the atmosphere absorb wavelengths of light characteristic of their spectra (these are the same wavelengths given off when the element is excited; for example, the red color of a neon light). By examining the line spectral gaps scientists can deduce the elements that make up the distant atmosphere. Item (A) is true, but it explains the source of a line spectrum. Item (B) is true, but it explains why a blue shirt is blue when placed under a white or blue light source. Recall that a blue shirt under a red light source will appear black because there are no blue wavelengths to be reflected. Item (D) is a partial truth, black lights do give off ultraviolet light that the human eye cannot see.

19. (B)

Grouping patterns affect a student's perceptions of self-esteem and competence. Maintaining the same groups throughout the year encourages students in the average group to view themselves as average, students in the above average group to view themselves as above average, and students in the below average group to view themselves as below average. Choice (A) is incorrect because most students do not like unpredictable teacher behavior. Response (C) is incorrect because changes in the classroom often create an atmosphere of mistrust and uneasiness, and do not cause students to be more alert. Choice (D) is incorrect because although the explanation is correct, it is incomplete when compared to the answer (B).

20. (A)

A needs assessment will help students make the connection between their current skills and those that will be new to them. (B) is wrong because a needs assessment focuses on the skills a student currently possesses. (C) is incorrect because the needs assessment is designed to determine what needs to be taught that is not currently in the curriculum. (D) is a false statement. A needs assessment is not designed to motivate students.

21. (C)

A positive environment must be created to minimize the effects of negative external factors. (A) is inappropriate because changing the text but allowing the environment to remain the same only results in maintaining the status quo. (B) is incorrect because relating the students' personal interests to the new material is only a part of creating a positive environment. (D) is wrong because, again, it is only a small part of maximizing the effects of a positive learning environment.

22. (A)

When students are allowed to select their own problems for study, they become self-directed problem-solvers. As such, they have the opportunity to structure their own learning experiences. Assessing students' needs in a naturalistic setting (B) is highly time-consuming and not an important benefit of having students select their own problem to investigate. There may not be a wide variety of instructional materials available to the students (C) as they engage in studying the temperature problem, so this is not likely to be a major benefit. Learning to appreciate opposing viewpoints (D) is a competency that would be better addressed in social studies and language arts rather than in an activity that deals with a natural empirical science.

23. (A)

People are more highly motivated to solve problems that they choose, rather than problems that are chosen for them. Choosing a problem for investigation does not increase student diversity (B). Problem selection has nothing to do with the structure of student groups (C). Although students may engage in more self-assessment, this is not the most important force at work (D).

24. (C)

The teacher would be fostering strong home relationships that support student achievement of desired outcomes. Choice (A) is the result of (C). As the teacher interacts with professionals in the community, her own professional growth is promoted. (B) is also the result of (C). All teachers are expected to interact with the community to help meet the expectations associated with teaching. (D) is incomplete because strong home relationships are developed through the principles of conferences, trust, and cooperation.

25. (D)

This question relates to enabling teachers to document their teaching and to be aware of students' efforts, progress, and achievements. A portfolio is a purposeful collection of work that exhibits efforts, progress, and achievement of students and enables teachers to document teaching in an authentic setting. Standardized tests are commercially developed and are used for specific events (A). A teacher-made test is used to evaluate specific objectives of the course, so (B) is not the best choice. Observation is used only to explain what students do in classrooms and to indicate some of their capabilities; therefore, (C) is incorrect.

26. (C)

This question relates to evaluating specific objectives and content. Teacher-made tests are designed to evaluate the specific objectives and specific content of a course. (A) is incorrect because self and peer evaluation utilizes students' knowledge according to evaluation criteria that is understood by the students. A portfolio (B) is a purposeful collection of work that exhibits effort, progress, and achievement of students and enables teachers to document teaching in an authentic setting. Observation (D) is used to explain what students do in classrooms and to indicate to some degree their capabilities.

27. (D)

Standardized tests rate student performance against the performance of other students and report the scores in terms of percentiles, stanines, and scaled scores. A portfolio (A) is a collection of student effort, progress, and achievement. Teacher-made tests evaluate specific objectives and content, so (B) is incorrect. Students' classroom behaviors and capabilities are evaluated through observation, making (C) incorrect.

28. (C)

Self and peer assessment requires that the students be aware of and understand the evaluation criteria. A collection of work that exhibits students' success and enables teachers to document teaching is a portfolio

(A). A teacher-made test (B) evaluates specific objectives and content. Observation (D) is used to indicate capabilities and actions of students.

29. (C)

Mrs. Ratu's lack of competency is exhibited in her lack of understanding of her students and in her teaching at the elementary level. Mrs. Ratu was not teaching her students at the appropriate level (A). Although she may have desired to make reading easy for her students (B), she was not going about it correctly. When appropriate techniques are used, teaching ninth graders to read is no more difficult than teaching third graders to read.

30. (D)

Students who speak English as a Second Language are a challenge to educators. Guidelines, however, are available to help both specialized and mainstream teachers who have not worked with ESL students in the past. (D) is the best answer. Language-minority students have the right and the responsibility to learn to read and write in English. (B), which indicates that ESL students do not have the right to speak their native language, is incorrect and should not be a selection. ESL students do not have the obligation to speak their native language; (C) is not a good choice. ESL students do have the right in our country to speak their native language; (A) is not, therefore, a good choice.

31. (D)

Activities that tend to combine reading, writing, listening, and speaking are more likely to enhance literacy and the development of orality for the language-minority student. (D) suggests that this integration is advantageous. (D) is the best answer. (A), (B), and (C) indicate a sequence in literacy instruction; none of these answers is appropriate.

32. (C)

The most efficient way to gain information about a new setting is to speak with someone who is familiar with the circumstances. Orienting oneself with the physical layout (A) would be helpful but cannot tell her about the student population or materials. Although communication with the principal (B) is always a good idea, the principal usually will have little time to have an in-depth discussion and will not be able to tell specifically which books are available. Eventually, Ms. Woods will need to match curriculum guidelines to the material available (D), but sitting in a closet will not introduce her to staff and student characteristics.

33. (C)

All known living things are grouped in categories according to shared physical traits. The process of grouping organisms is called classification. Carl Linné, also known as Linnaeus, devised the classification system used in biology today. In the Linnaean system (A), all organisms are given a two-word name (binomial). The name consists of a genus (e.g., *Canis*) and a species (e.g., *lupus*) designation. The DNA holds the genetic materials of a cell, so (B) could not be the correct answer. Because there is a correct answer, (D) is not a correct choice.

When the genetic type of parents is known, the probability of the offspring showing particular traits can be predicted by using the Punnett Square (C). A Punnett Square is a large square divided into four small boxes. The genetic symbol of each parent for a particular trait is written alongside the square, for one parent along the top and for the other parent along the left side, as shown in the figure.

Parent Aa

	Ⓐ	ⓐ
Ⓐ	AA	Aa
ⓐ	Aa	aa

(Parent Aa along the left side)

Each gene symbol is written in the boxes below or to the right of it. This results in each box having two gene symbols in it. The genetic symbols in the boxes are all the possible genetic combinations for a particular trait of the offspring of these parents. Each box has a 25 percent probability of being the actual genetic representation for a given child.

34. (D)

"Acid" and "base" are terms used to describe solutions of differing pH. The concentration of hydrogen ions in a solution determines its pH. Solutions having a pH of 0 to 7 are called acids and have hydrogen ions (H+) present. Common acids include lemon juice, vinegar, and battery acid; acids are corrosive and taste sour. Solutions having a pH of 7 to 14 are called bases (or alkaline) and have hydroxide ions (OH–) present; bases are caustic and feel slippery in solution. Common bases include baking soda and lye. Solutions of pH 7 are called neutral and have both ions present in equal but small amounts. Coice (D) is the correct answer because 5 is the only number between 0 and 7 (acids).

35. (C)

A liquid has a definite volume, but it molds to the shape of the container holding it. Titanium (A) is a solid (D), and solids have a definite shape and volume, so (A) and (D) are not the best answers. A gas will expand to fit the container in both volume and shape, so (B) is not the correct answer.

36. (B)

The instrument for measuring the intensity of an earthquake is a seismograph. A thermograph (A) measures temperature, a telegraph (C) is a communication device, and an odometer (D) measures distance traveled, so (A), (C), and (D) are not correct.

37. (B)

Energy is defined as the ability to do work. Work occurs when a force (push or pull) is applied to an object, resulting in movement. Work = force × distance. The greater the force (A) applied, or the longer the distance traveled (D), or interval between two points, the greater the work done, but they are not the ability to do the work. Speed is rate of movement, so (C) is not the best answer.

38. (C)

Essays fall into four rough categories: speculative, argumentative, narrative, and expository. The purpose of this essay is narrative (C). The narrative essay may recount an incident or a series of incidents and is almost always autobiographical, in order to make a point. The informality of the storytelling makes the narrative essay less insistent than the argumentative essay, but more directed than the speculative essay. But the thesis may not be as obvious or clear-cut as that in an expository or argumentative essay. This essay is not speculative (A).

The speculative essay (A) is so named because, as its Latin root suggests, it looks at ideas and explores them rather than explains them. The purposes of the argumentative essay (B) are always clear: to present a point and provide evidence, which may be factual or anecdotal, and to support it. The structure is usually very formal, as in a debate, with counterpositions and counterarguments. An expository essay (D) may have narrative elements, but that aspect is minor and subservient to that of explanation.

39. (D)

New research (K. Goodman) challenges the status quo literacy and asks teachers to revalue their habitudes and practices related to the traditional way of teaching language and literacy. Flores, Cousin, and Diaz propose alternative views about *all* children. These assumptions show that even the at-risk are proficient in some communication skills; bring many experiences into the classroom; need opportunities to learn language in rich, integrated settings; can be successful in regular classroom programs; can be monitored by observing their language use in authentic settings; and the at-risk, also, have families interested in the school setting and are potential partners in the educational experience. For these reasons, it is evident that (D) is the right answer; families of at-risk students still have an interest in their children and are potential partners. Because at-risk children can bring many experiences to the classroom and can be successful in a classroom, (A) and (B) are incorrect. Standardized literacy tests may not be as helpful to a teacher as observing the students in authentic settings; (C) is incorrect.

40. (C)

When two parallel lines are crossed by another line (called a transversal), eight angles are formed. However, there are only two angle measures among the eight angles, and the sum of the two measures is 180°. All the smaller angles will have the same measure, and all the larger angles will have the same measure. In this case, the smaller angles all measure 50°, so the larger angles (including angle *y*) all measure 130°.

41. (A)

One must know two things to answer the question. One is the meaning of the small square at the vertex of angle BXC. That symbol means that angle BXC is a *right angle* (one with 90°). The second is that a straight line, such as AXD, can be thought of as a *straight angle*, which measures 180°. Therefore, since the sum of the angles DXC (42°) and BXC (90°) is 132°, the remaining angle on the line must measure 48° (= 180° − 132°).

42. (A)

The area of any rectangle is equal to the measure of its length times the measure of its width (or, to say it differently, the measure of its base times the measure of its height). A right triangle can be seen as half of a rectangle (sliced diagonally). Answer (A) represents, in effect, half of a rectangle's area (i.e., the area divided by 2).

43. (D)

The formula for finding the area of any circle is $A = \pi r^2$ (about 3.14 times the length of the radius times itself). In this case, take half of πr^2; hence, answer (D) is correct.

44. (B)

Angle XYZ is an inscribed angle (its vertex is on the circle). Angle XCZ is a central angle (its vertex is at the circle's center). When two such angles intercept (or cut off) the same arc of the circle, there exists a specific size relationship between the two angles. The measure of the central angle will always be double the measure of the inscribed angle. In this case, that means that the measure of angle XCZ must be 80°. That means that minor arc XZ also has measure 80°. Every circle (considered an arc) has measure 360°. That means that major arc XYZ has measure 280° (360°−80°).

45. (D)

Children learn more from a text if the teacher helps them figure out how the book was put together. It makes the text more understandable. It also helps them read the text critically, as part of the conversation can address the issue of what is missing in the text.

46. (B)

In using three different versions of this well-known story, Ms. Smith is creating an opportunity to bring a multicultural perspective to the drama activity (I). In versions of *Cinderella* from around the world, the story of the mistreated but kindhearted protagonist is basically the same, but the characters, settings, and ways in which the plot unfolds are culturally centered. Furthermore, because Ms. Smith is using scripted versions of the story and staging these plays with costumes, scenery, and props, she is making theatrical elements integral to the performances (II). The students are engaging in formal dramatic activity that will result in a theatrical product, rather than informal, process-centered drama, so III is incorrect. Choice IV is incorrect because the students are not the ones who have adapted the story and, therefore, they are not having firsthand experience with that process. So the correct answer is (B), which includes only I and II.

47. (D)

Teachers must engage in ongoing self-evaluation of their own values, attitudes, disposition, and belief systems to teach diverse learners effectively and to invite and extend literacy forms, skills, and interests; these teachers must reflect on how their 1) literacy histories compare to those of other teachers and students; 2) peer experiences may have been privileged in school settings, and 3) literacy experiences are tied to their identities in order to extend literacy. (D) is the best answer. For this reason, choice (A) is incorrect because remembering one's past can help. Thinking back on one's school setting may be applicable—not inapplicable; (B) is a poor choice. Answer (C) suggests that school experiences have no effect on the learner's self identity; this is false and (C) is not a correct answer.

Formative assessment is continuous and intended to serve as a guide to future learning and instruction. Summative evaluation (A) and summative assessment (B) are both used to put a final critique or grade on an activity or assignment with no real link to the future. Peer assessment would require students to critique each other (D).

48. (B)

The best way to teach children to read, regardless of grade level, is to use a program of emergent literacy that includes pattern books and journal writing with invented spelling. Although an intensive phonics program that includes drill and practice work may be effective with some students, it is not the most effective way to teach all students to read, so (A) is incorrect. Choice (C) is clearly incorrect because none of the students read above 2.0 grade level. An ESL program is intended to provide assistance to only those students who are learning English as a second language, so (D) is incorrect. Additionally, the learning resource teacher should provide assistance to only those students who have been identified as having a learning disability that qualifies them to receive services.

49. (C)

Careful planning (III), which includes checking on the availability of resources and materials (II) resulted in student involvement in the unit (I). Mrs. Doe did reflective thinking during the discussion; however, reflective thinking is only one component of communication and is included in careful planning and its correlation to success in the classroom. Resources and materials were available, but this is a result of careful planning. Personal acquaintance with a Native American (IV) would

have helped shape the students' attitudes, but it is not necessary for student involvement. So the correct answer (C) includes II and III only.

50. (B)

Multiple strategies were planned for the motivation of the students (I), but a result of the strategies was that each student participated in some way regardless of ability (II) and the unit was integrated into other subjects (III) (e.g., reading, writing) through library assignments. Ultimately, the unit will be integrated with the other subjects; however, this is not the only goal, so (A) and (C) are incorrect. Developing a foundation for teaching American history (IV) is not even a long-range goal, although the attitudes and beliefs developed in the project may become the foundation upon which the students will build their philosophy of American history. Therefore, (D) is incorrect.

51. (A)

The external factors of the field trip could create a positive motivation and would allow the students to make the connection between their old skills and the new skills they were learning (I). The external factors involved in a field trip are positive; however, Mrs. Doe gave instructions that each student was to take notes on what he or she saw, heard, and experienced (II). The skill of note taking was founded upon the library assignment that had preceded the field trip, and the students were to make the connection. No mention is made of community involvement in the field trip; the statement III is not relevant. The students did not take responsibility for their own learning (IV); they were given instructions concerning what they were to do before they left for the field trip. Choices (B), (C), and (D), which include incorrect statements (III and IV), are therefore incorrect.

52. (B)

Respect was shown to the children by allowing them a choice of field trips (II). It is an example of the array of instructional strategies (IV) used by Mrs. Doe. (A) is incomplete and therefore incorrect. Enhancing students' self-concept and fostering the view of learning as a purposeful pursuit [(C) and (D)] are both incorporated in II, respecting differences and understanding the society in which we live.

53. (B)

Placing the students in small groups in which they meet face to face will allow Mr. Billings to maximize the students' interaction while giving each student the maximum opportunity to speak. Placing students in the traditional rows facing the front (A) discourages student interaction and minimizes each student's opportunities to speak. Although placing students in pairs (C) maximizes each student's opportunity to speak, it limits the sources of interaction because each student may share thoughts with only one other student. In contrast, a group of four allows the student to interact as part of three dyads, two triads, and a quad. When placing the students in cooperative groups, it is wise to arrange the desks within the physical space of the classroom in such a way that each group's talking does not distract the members of other groups, as it does in (D).

54. (C)

Requiring both a cognitive and a performance objective makes the student show that he or she not only had the knowledge but could apply that knowledge to a life situation, so (C) is the correct response. Although statement (A) is true, it is not the foundation for developing specific objectives. Statement (B), again, is an assumption and not relevant to the setting of certain objectives. Teaching style and learning styles (D) are not relevant to the behavioral objectives.

55. (B)

This question is designed to demonstrate an understanding that the performance objective should directly tie into the assessment. Students need to know what the expectation is for them to complete the necessary assignments. Students do not understand what assessment tools are; they need clear directions and a list of explanations, so (A) is incorrect. Although the unit may have many new vocabulary words, students need to learn them within the context of the unit rather than from a random list; they should not feel threatened when learning to prepare for a test, so (C) is incorrect. There is no connection between notebooks and learning, so (D) is incorrect.

56. (C)

Rubrics are designed to help teachers assess each student's achievement and the quality of his/her responses (I). Therefore, each criterion needs to have quality points (II), such as outstanding (5–4), good (3–2), and/or fair (1–0). Rubrics need to cover a number of subject areas to allow for a fair assessment of the student's work, in contrast to option III. Students may rate themselves (IV); however, the teacher needs to work with them as they complete the ratings. Therefore, only I and II, or option (C) is correct.

57. (B)

Students often disclose more personal information in journals than when speaking in class. The teacher can also check for comprehension of content and the success or failure of class objectives. Journals typically are not graded with consideration to standard usage or grammatical constructions; therefore, (A) is incorrect. The assignment has no direct bearing on time-management skills; therefore, (C) is incorrect. Choice (D) is irrelevant: no mention is made of giving daily grades on the journal writing.

58. (C)

The Language-Experience-Approach (LEA) is a proven method of increasing students' reading and writing proficiency and their overall language competency. It requires that students write about what they know. Choices (A), (B), and (D) are irrelevant. Choice (A) superficially addresses that Ms. Johnson is an English teacher and choice (B) refers to autobiographies, something that is not mentioned in the preceding information. Choice (D) foreshadows the library project, but it has not yet been introduced into the context of these questions.

59. (C)

A basic principle in providing students with appropriate feedback is to first note the student's strengths (or positive aspects of the student's work and/ or performance) and then to note specific ways the student can improve his or her work and/or performance. Therefore, the best approach for a teacher to take in providing students with feedback on written work is to first note the good things about students' writing and then to suggest ways to improve. Choices (A) and (B) are in essence the same; both choices indicate that only students' strengths would be acknowledged, omitting the important aspect of addressing ways students can improve. Neither action would enhance students' cognitive skills or their metacognitive skills (or self-awareness). Choice (D) is unacceptable because it denigrates the teacher's responsibility to evaluate students' performance on the basis of individual merit against the standards established by particular disciplines.

60. (A)

Option (A) is the best answer of the four options for the following reasons. First, learning style information acknowledges that although learners acquire knowledge in different ways, those differences can lead to effective learning when students are taught cognitive strategies that complement their natural learning tendencies; basically, teaching students about learning styles (and especially about their own learning styles) is a recognition of human diversity. Second, beyond mere recognition of human diversity is the legitimacy of different approaches to learning. Every student can perform at a level of proficiency, although not every student will attain that level in the same manner; in other words, learning styles validate students as learners and promote high standards for academic achievement. Third, when students are taught not only about learning styles in general, but specifically about their own learning styles, they are empowered to take responsibility for their own learning. Fourth, of the four options, only choices (A) and (D) are tasks actively engaging the student. Choices (B) and (C) are both passive activities, and are therefore poor choices. Choice (D) requires that students perform a task without any help (direct instruction) for accomplishing the task; simply asking students to name additional strengths without giving them an opportunity to self-examine, to self-assess, and to explore their strengths will not produce the desired outcome. Only choice (A) gives students the information they need to accomplish the task the teacher has identified as being important.

61. (D)

The question relates to appropriate sequencing of activities. Choice (D) is the best introductory activity in order to generate student interest in this new field of mathematics and to get students thinking about how to produce fractals. It would stimulate students to use higher-level thinking skills to make predictions by drawing on their knowledge of how to solve problems mathematically. Choice (A) would be the least appropriate to begin the study. Students who want to learn more could research this topic after they have developed an interest in fractals. Choice (B) would be appropriate as a later step, after students are interested in the process and are ready to learn how to produce fractals. Choice (C) would be appropriate as a subsequent step in the process of learning how to produce fractals. Choice (B) requires students to use preplanned formulas; Choice (C) allows them to develop their own formulas, a very high-level activity.

62. (B)

Teachers can contribute to racial problems if they (C) treat all students the same, (D) ignore individual differences, and (A) work to make students act as the teacher does. Instead, teachers must be aware of individual differences in the classroom (B) to improve relations.

63. (B)

Democracy is the correct response because it is the antithesis of the authoritarianism of fascism. Indeed, the totalitarian, romantic, militaristic, and nationalistic characteristics were, in large part, a reaction against the perceived inadequacies of democracy.

64. (B)

The industrial economy of the nineteenth century was not based upon an equitable distribution of profits among all those who were involved in production. Marxists and other critics of capitalism condemned the creed of capitalists and the abhorrent conditions of the industrial proletariat. Raw materials, a constant labor supply, capital, and an expanding marketplace were critical elements in the development of the industrial economy.

65. (D)

In the 1880s and 1890s, the U.S. Supreme Court struck down desegregation laws and upheld the doctrine of segregated "separate but equal" facilities for blacks and whites. These laws became known as "Jim Crow" laws. Their impact was to allow racist governments in the South to set up "separate but unequal" facilities in which blacks were forced to sit in the rear of streetcars and buses and to eat in the back rooms of restaurants, were excluded completely from white businesses, and had to use separate and usually inferior public restroom facilities. These laws allowed white supremacists to "put blacks in their place" and effectively kept blacks from achieving anything near equal status. It wasn't until the 1950s and 1960s that new Supreme Court decisions finally forced the repeal of these laws.

66. (B)

A writ of habeas corpus (B) is a court order that directs an official who is detaining someone to produce the person before the court so that the legality of the detention may be determined. The primary function of the writ is to effect the release of someone who has been imprisoned without due process of law. For example, if the police detained a suspect for an unreasonable time without officially charging the person with a crime, the person could seek relief from a court in the form of a writ of habeas corpus. (A) is incorrect because a writ of mandamus is a court order commanding an official to perform a legal duty of his or her office. It is not used to prevent persons from being improperly imprisoned. The Fourth Amendment requirement that police have probable cause in order to obtain a search warrant regulates police procedure. It is not itself a mechanism for affecting release of a person for improper imprisonment, so (C) is incorrect. Answer (D) is incorrect because the decision in *Roe v Wade* dealt with a woman's right to have an abortion; it had nothing to do with improper imprisonment.

67. (A)

By definition, acids and bases combine to produce a salt and water. An example would be HCI (hydrochloric acid) and NaOH (sodium hydroxide) reacting to form NaCI (salt) and water.

68. (D)

Atoms are neutral, so the net charge must be zero, requiring that the number of negative particles (electrons) equals the number of positive particles (protons).

69. (D)

(A), (B), and (C) all involve chemical changes in which iron, wood, and rocket fuel, respectively, are reacted with other substances to produce a reactant product with different chemical properties. Melted ice in the form of water still has the same chemical formula, so the correct answer is (D).

70. (C)

Isotopes for a given element all have the same chemical properties, differing only in their atomic weight, or number of neutrons.

71. (C)

Newton's second law states that an unbalanced force acting on a mass will cause the mass to accelerate. In equation form, $F = ma$, where F is force, m is mass, and a is acceleration. Only (C) involves a mass that is being accelerated by an unbalanced force.

72. (A)

Thermal energy is the total amount of internal energy of a given body, whereas temperature is a measure of the vibrational activity of atoms or molecules within the material. Therefore, thermal energy involves both the mass and temperature of a given body. Thus, (A) is the most likely answer, as its mass far exceeds 1 g, a bucket of water, and Lake Michigan. (B) is ruled out because even though its temperature is very high, its mass is extremely small.

73. **(D)**

The cell membrane (D) is a selectively permeable barrier that permits some substances to pass through while forming a barrier for others. None of the other choices have this property.

74. **(D)**

(D) is correct because the zygote of a human is a cell derived from a sperm containing 23 chromosomes and an egg containing 23 chromosomes. (A) cannot be the correct answer because it represents too few chromosome for either a haploid sex cell or a diploid body cell. (B) cannot be the correct answer because it also represents too few chromosome for either a haploid sex cell or a diploid body cell. (C) cannot be the correct answer because it represents the number of chromosomes in a sperm or an egg.

75. **(C)**

The body regulates water and heat through perspiration. Transpiration describes a process not involving humans; thus (B) is not correct. Respiration (A) is breathing in humans and will cause some water loss, but the question asks how the body regulates substances through the skin. (D), sensation, is the ability to process or perceive. Although the skin does have nerve endings that can sense, this does not involve temperature or water regulation.

76. **(A)**

Choices (B), (C), and (D) are ruled out because Darwin was unaware of the genetic work that was later done by Mendel. Darwin and most other nineteenth-century biologists never knew of Mendel and his research. It was not until the beginning of the twentieth century that Mendel's pioneer research into genetic inheritance was rediscovered.

77. **(B)**

The lunar period is about 30 days, or one month, which is the time it takes for the Moon to orbit Earth one time.

78. **(C)**

A star "going nova" is presumed to be at the end of its life. As hydrogen (or sometimes helium) is depleted, the fusion reaction becomes incapable of sustaining the pressures required to push the star's mass outward against the pull of gravity. The star then collapses, resulting in a gigantic explosion known as a supernova. Choice (A) is neither observed nor possible; (B) is not observed; and (D), although occasionally observed, does not trigger nova-sized explosions.

79. **(C)**

The tilting of Earth's axis causes the Northern Hemisphere to point more sunward in the summer months and more antisunward in the winter months (with the reverse being true for the Southern Hemisphere), so (C) is the correct answer. (B) is ruled out because the rotation period is the same from season to season. (A) is ruled out because Earth is actually somewhat closer to the sun in December through January than it is in June through July, which is winter for the Northern Hemisphere. (D) is ruled out because this is a daily, not seasonal, phenomenon.

80. **(A)**

Igneous rocks are transformed or "metamorphed" into metamorphic rocks. Thus, they are related to igneous, not sedimentary, and are found on this planet.

81. **(D)**

The east coast of South America and the west coast of Africa fit together like pieces of a jig-saw puzzle. Fossil remains in locations where "fit" is observed are too well matched to be coincidental. Earthquakes and volcanism are more prevalent in mountainous regions, where plates collided, than in other regions. Thus, all support the theory of plate tectonics.

82. **(A)**

According to the theory of plate tectonics, plate spreading is associated with magma upwelling to fill the vacated space, which forms ridges at these locations. This is true also under the oceans.

83. (D)

The raw material for igneous rock formation is magma, which—when cooled either above or below ground—becomes igneous rock.

84. (B)

Multiple investigators have confirmed the order given in (B): Nitrogen, oxygen, carbon dioxide, trace gases.

85. (D)

To find the greatest common divisor (GCD), factor both numbers and look for common factors. The product of these common factors is the GCD. The GCD here is the greatest integer that divides both 120 and 252.

$$120 = 2^3 \times 3 \times 5 \text{ and } 252 = 2^2 \times 3^2 \times 7,$$

so the GCD $= 2^2 \times 3 = 12$.

86. (A)

A prime number is an integer that is greater than one and that has no integer divisors other than 1 and itself. So, the prime numbers between 1 and 20 (not including 1 and 20) are: 2, 3, 5, 7, 11, 13, 17, 19. But 2 is not an odd number, so the odd primes between 1 and 20 are: 3, 5, 7, 11, 13, 17, 19. Hence, there are seven odd primes between 1 and 20.

87. (B)

Teachers must be vigilant in establishing and maintaining a safe, nurturing, and respectful learning environment. It must be made clear from the beginning that cruelty and disrespect will not be tolerated. Even though children are resilient (A), their early social experiences impact their future learning both positively and negatively. Children must be taught that they must be

kind to everyone in the class, even if they are not close friends, so (C) is incorrect. Although it is the parents' responsibility to model good behavior (D), this unfortunately often does not occur, and therefore good behavior must be explicitly taught in schools.

88. (D)

Songs, rhymes, and hand and arm signals resonate with young children as play. When procedural instructions are prompted in this way, young children have connections on cognitive, emotional, and physical levels. (A), (B), and (C) are incorrect because they do not focus on communicating directions for organizational procedures.

89. (B)

Maintaining a written journal about events in the classroom as well as student responses is a technique used by reflective practitioners to review and evaluate their personal growth as professionals. (A) is incorrect because journal writing may or may not indicate a concern about process writing. Additionally, journal writing alone is not the same as process writing. (C) is incorrect because the purpose of the journal is much broader, even though the instructor may use some of her journal entries in her formal evaluation. (D) is incorrect because it is too simplistic. If Ms. Axtel were a habitual journal writer, she would be writing about a variety of topics, not just emphasizing those related to teaching.

90. (A)

Teachers are responsible to report any suspected cases of child abuse to the appropriate authorities; the teacher must follow the protocol of the district because the procedure varies from state-to-state. It is illegal, however, not to share the information appropriately and immediately. (B) is incorrect because regardless of the parent's explanations, if the instructor feels that the child may have been abused, it must be reported. (C) is incorrect because the bruises described would not be consistent with an ordinary spanking for misbehavior. (D) is incorrect because even though further information might be helpful, the instructor still must report the incident.

91. (A)

The scope and sequence of social studies given here is a direct example of the expanding horizon or widening horizon approach developed originally in the 1920s and still used by many textbook companies, school systems, and teachers. The spiral curriculum (B) enables the children to build progressively on information learned previously, and it does not fit the sequence described. Learning centers (C) is a type of classroom organization; however, the sequence described seems to relate more to the vertical organization of the school than to the horizontal organization suggested by learning centers. The open classroom (D) is based on the British primary schools and involves much pupil freedom and choice. Like learning centers, the open classroom relates to horizontal school organization whereas the question concerns vertical organization.

92. (A)

A teacher's "with it"-ness relates to the ability to observe and manage disruptions quickly, quietly, and at all times. For example, a "with-it" teacher who is helping a student with deskwork would be able to detect and distinguish any disruptive behavior in a different part of the room.

93. (B)

Response (B) is respectful of the learner and her parents while providing an opportunity to discuss the student's needs and the teacher's instructional goals. Parents who do not speak English often opt out of the LEP services because they want their children to speak English. They may not understand that the foundation of reading and writing is oral language, and therefore the LEP program would offer the strongest academic program for learning to read and write as well to speak English. (A) is incorrect because it is not centered around the student and would force inappropriate instructional cycles for this student. (C) is incorrect because it dismisses the option of a campus-level solution with the parents and moves it to a policy-level issue. (D) is wrong because it is not student-centered and very likely is out of compliance with district policy and procedure.

94. (A)

One of the most reliable ways to identify individual learning styles is to observe students over a period of time and to make informal notes about their work habits and their choices within the classroom. (B) is incorrect because although a school psychologist could provide information about each student's learning style, teachers can identify this information on their own. (C) is incorrect because although administering a group screening test will identify learning styles, such a test may be difficult to obtain, and the teacher could gain the same knowledge through simple observation. (D) is incorrect because a student's permanent file may not contain this information. An individual student's learning style may have changed over the years, and there is no guarantee that this change will be noted in the permanent record.

95. (A)

Celebrating holidays of different cultures teaches appreciation for human diversity. Even though celebrating different cultures has become a political issue, this should not influence a teacher when planning such a lesson, so (B) is incorrect. (C) is incorrect because although celebrating holidays is one way to encourage students to read, this may or may not be related to encouraging students to read aloud. Celebrating holidays may encourage all students to participate in class activities (D), but teaching an appreciation for human diversity is a more accurate statement of the most significant reason for the activity.

96. (A)

The evaluation rubric should be based on current technology standards. Because this is a multi-aged classroom, the rubric should include competencies from both grade levels. (B) is incorrect because a parent survey will not provide the information needed to design a rubric. (C) is incorrect because knowing the job expectations for colleagues is not relevant to this problem. (D) is incorrect because stages of play development and computer readiness do not relate to the issue of rubric design.

97. (B)

Regulations regarding privacy must be followed at all times. To this end, most districts have adopted policies and procedures that facilitate getting approval from parents to release this information. Teachers must ensure that only the approved information is released. (A) is incorrect because in this case, privacy trumps inclusion. (C) is incorrect because it is not necessary for Ms. Sanchez to prepare the list herself. It would be enough if she checked it for approved release status as well as accuracy. (D) is incorrect because campuses and districts adopt procedures to facilitate and make uniform the release of this information.

98. (C)

It is important that general education classrooms receive trained personnel to help service students with disabilities and that support practices strengthen general education classrooms. Hopefully, a continuum of service will be available to all children; (A) is not a good answer. Inclusion is a goal for schools and communities; (B) should not be selected. General education classrooms can serve students with disabilities in many ways; (D) is not acceptable.

99. (C)

After separating the two, the teacher should attend first to the victim and, if possible, deal with the situation. The guidance counselor may be consulted (B) if it is a school rule, but the teacher may handle the situation more easily himself/herself. If the teacher responds first to the aggressor, it conveys that he or she is more important. The teacher should not wait for a witness before separating the two children (D) because harm could come to either or both. Separating the two by having the aggressor dealt with by the administrator and the victim dealt with by the teacher is not the best approach.

100. (B)

Vitamin C is water soluble—the remaining choices are fat soluble.

101. (D)

The grip strength test (C), pull-ups (for boys) (A), and flexed arm hang (for girls) (B), are all tests to measure muscular strength and endurance. The sit and reach test measures flexibility.

102. (D)

Statements I, II, III, and IV are all true, so (D) is the best choice. Dance can reflect the religion of a culture in many ways due to its deep historical roots in religious tradition.

103. (D)

Excess cholesterol found in the blood typically comes from cholesterol in a diet rather than internal production. Cholesterol, which is produced in the liver (C), plays a vital role in brain function (A) and is important for creating certain hormones (B).

104. (C)

Table tennis is scored to 21 and must be won by a margin of two points. In doubles play for badminton, the winner must score 15 points (A). Singles badminton is also scored to 21 points with a margin of two points needed for victory.

105. (D)

This question focuses on a basic musical concept, "harmony." Harmony is the performance of two or more different pitches simultaneously. Therefore, when looking at the answers provided, it is good to begin by eliminating answers that have nothing to do with pitch. A rhythm instrument is a non-pitched instrument in almost all cases, so choice I is not pitch-related and that means that answers (A) and (B) are eliminated because they both include choice I. Two or more different pitches must be performed simultaneously to have harmony, so choice III can also be eliminated because there are two performers, but not two different pitches. That eliminates answer (C) and leaves answer (D) as the best and correct answer.

106. (B)

One of the virtues of using drama/theatre with young people is that it challenges them to think independently and creatively. Often, there is not one right answer or interpretation. Using the same material in a variety of theatrical formats offers the following advantages: (1) Information is presented through multiple channels, thereby increasing opportunities for knowing; (2) using different types of dramatic activities broadens both the appeal of and the learning opportunities inherent in the material; (3) multiple formats increase opportunities to engage students and to address their learning styles; and (4) students can see that there are various ways of creating meaning and expressing ideas. Answer (A) is incorrect because there may not be only one correct way to use material. As the rationale for the correct answer implies, exploring content is one way to move students beyond the obvious and encourage them to use higher-level thinking skills. Answer (C) is incorrect because it requires a value judgment based upon personal preference; it is not grounded in fact. Likewise, (D) is incorrect because it reflects a value judgment that is without substance. Some students may learn more by directly participating in activities; others may learn more by watching a performance. Both creative drama activities and theatre performances are educationally sound undertakings.

107. (C)

The use of uncommon materials has dramatically changed the criteria by which one assesses visual art.

108. (C)

(C) is the best answer because it covers all three of the objectives in at least a minimal way. (A) is the second best answer because it deals with several of the objectives, but the focus on creativity keeps it from being the best answer. Answers (B) and (D) are not good answers because they do not deal with the objectives.

109. (D)

The technique for both jazz dance and tap dance emerged from a blending of African and European cultures.

110. (B)

It is not true of creating dances that "It must happen outside of the classroom within a special time," so (B) is the correct answer. In fact, dance should have a place in the classroom, where the focus should be placed on creative movement.

Praxis II

Elementary Education
Test Code 0011

Practice Test 2

Answer Sheet

1. Ⓐ Ⓑ Ⓒ Ⓓ
2. Ⓐ Ⓑ Ⓒ Ⓓ
3. Ⓐ Ⓑ Ⓒ Ⓓ
4. Ⓐ Ⓑ Ⓒ Ⓓ
5. Ⓐ Ⓑ Ⓒ Ⓓ
6. Ⓐ Ⓑ Ⓒ Ⓓ
7. Ⓐ Ⓑ Ⓒ Ⓓ
8. Ⓐ Ⓑ Ⓒ Ⓓ
9. Ⓐ Ⓑ Ⓒ Ⓓ
10. Ⓐ Ⓑ Ⓒ Ⓓ
11. Ⓐ Ⓑ Ⓒ Ⓓ
12. Ⓐ Ⓑ Ⓒ Ⓓ
13. Ⓐ Ⓑ Ⓒ Ⓓ
14. Ⓐ Ⓑ Ⓒ Ⓓ
15. Ⓐ Ⓑ Ⓒ Ⓓ
16. Ⓐ Ⓑ Ⓒ Ⓓ
17. Ⓐ Ⓑ Ⓒ Ⓓ
18. Ⓐ Ⓑ Ⓒ Ⓓ
19. Ⓐ Ⓑ Ⓒ Ⓓ
20. Ⓐ Ⓑ Ⓒ Ⓓ
21. Ⓐ Ⓑ Ⓒ Ⓓ
22. Ⓐ Ⓑ Ⓒ Ⓓ
23. Ⓐ Ⓑ Ⓒ Ⓓ
24. Ⓐ Ⓑ Ⓒ Ⓓ
25. Ⓐ Ⓑ Ⓒ Ⓓ
26. Ⓐ Ⓑ Ⓒ Ⓓ
27. Ⓐ Ⓑ Ⓒ Ⓓ
28. Ⓐ Ⓑ Ⓒ Ⓓ

29. Ⓐ Ⓑ Ⓒ Ⓓ
30. Ⓐ Ⓑ Ⓒ Ⓓ
31. Ⓐ Ⓑ Ⓒ Ⓓ
32. Ⓐ Ⓑ Ⓒ Ⓓ
33. Ⓐ Ⓑ Ⓒ Ⓓ
34. Ⓐ Ⓑ Ⓒ Ⓓ
35. Ⓐ Ⓑ Ⓒ Ⓓ
36. Ⓐ Ⓑ Ⓒ Ⓓ
37. Ⓐ Ⓑ Ⓒ Ⓓ
38. Ⓐ Ⓑ Ⓒ Ⓓ
39. Ⓐ Ⓑ Ⓒ Ⓓ
40. Ⓐ Ⓑ Ⓒ Ⓓ
41. Ⓐ Ⓑ Ⓒ Ⓓ
42. Ⓐ Ⓑ Ⓒ Ⓓ
43. Ⓐ Ⓑ Ⓒ Ⓓ
44. Ⓐ Ⓑ Ⓒ Ⓓ
45. Ⓐ Ⓑ Ⓒ Ⓓ
46. Ⓐ Ⓑ Ⓒ Ⓓ
47. Ⓐ Ⓑ Ⓒ Ⓓ
48. Ⓐ Ⓑ Ⓒ Ⓓ
49. Ⓐ Ⓑ Ⓒ Ⓓ
50. Ⓐ Ⓑ Ⓒ Ⓓ
51. Ⓐ Ⓑ Ⓒ Ⓓ
52. Ⓐ Ⓑ Ⓒ Ⓓ
53. Ⓐ Ⓑ Ⓒ Ⓓ
54. Ⓐ Ⓑ Ⓒ Ⓓ
55. Ⓐ Ⓑ Ⓒ Ⓓ
56. Ⓐ Ⓑ Ⓒ Ⓓ

57. Ⓐ Ⓑ Ⓒ Ⓓ
58. Ⓐ Ⓑ Ⓒ Ⓓ
59. Ⓐ Ⓑ Ⓒ Ⓓ
60. Ⓐ Ⓑ Ⓒ Ⓓ
61. Ⓐ Ⓑ Ⓒ Ⓓ
62. Ⓐ Ⓑ Ⓒ Ⓓ
63. Ⓐ Ⓑ Ⓒ Ⓓ
64. Ⓐ Ⓑ Ⓒ Ⓓ
65. Ⓐ Ⓑ Ⓒ Ⓓ
66. Ⓐ Ⓑ Ⓒ Ⓓ
67. Ⓐ Ⓑ Ⓒ Ⓓ
68. Ⓐ Ⓑ Ⓒ Ⓓ
69. Ⓐ Ⓑ Ⓒ Ⓓ
70. Ⓐ Ⓑ Ⓒ Ⓓ
71. Ⓐ Ⓑ Ⓒ Ⓓ
72. Ⓐ Ⓑ Ⓒ Ⓓ
73. Ⓐ Ⓑ Ⓒ Ⓓ
74. Ⓐ Ⓑ Ⓒ Ⓓ
75. Ⓐ Ⓑ Ⓒ Ⓓ
76. Ⓐ Ⓑ Ⓒ Ⓓ
77. Ⓐ Ⓑ Ⓒ Ⓓ
78. Ⓐ Ⓑ Ⓒ Ⓓ
79. Ⓐ Ⓑ Ⓒ Ⓓ
80. Ⓐ Ⓑ Ⓒ Ⓓ
81. Ⓐ Ⓑ Ⓒ Ⓓ
82. Ⓐ Ⓑ Ⓒ Ⓓ
83. Ⓐ Ⓑ Ⓒ Ⓓ
84. Ⓐ Ⓑ Ⓒ Ⓓ

85. Ⓐ Ⓑ Ⓒ Ⓓ
86. Ⓐ Ⓑ Ⓒ Ⓓ
87. Ⓐ Ⓑ Ⓒ Ⓓ
88. Ⓐ Ⓑ Ⓒ Ⓓ
89. Ⓐ Ⓑ Ⓒ Ⓓ
90. Ⓐ Ⓑ Ⓒ Ⓓ
91. Ⓐ Ⓑ Ⓒ Ⓓ
92. Ⓐ Ⓑ Ⓒ Ⓓ
93. Ⓐ Ⓑ Ⓒ Ⓓ
94. Ⓐ Ⓑ Ⓒ Ⓓ
95. Ⓐ Ⓑ Ⓒ Ⓓ
96. Ⓐ Ⓑ Ⓒ Ⓓ
97. Ⓐ Ⓑ Ⓒ Ⓓ
98. Ⓐ Ⓑ Ⓒ Ⓓ
99. Ⓐ Ⓑ Ⓒ Ⓓ
100. Ⓐ Ⓑ Ⓒ Ⓓ
101. Ⓐ Ⓑ Ⓒ Ⓓ
102. Ⓐ Ⓑ Ⓒ Ⓓ
103. Ⓐ Ⓑ Ⓒ Ⓓ
104. Ⓐ Ⓑ Ⓒ Ⓓ
105. Ⓐ Ⓑ Ⓒ Ⓓ
106. Ⓐ Ⓑ Ⓒ Ⓓ
107. Ⓐ Ⓑ Ⓒ Ⓓ
108. Ⓐ Ⓑ Ⓒ Ⓓ
109. Ⓐ Ⓑ Ⓒ Ⓓ
110. Ⓐ Ⓑ Ⓒ Ⓓ

Elementary Education: Curriculum, Instruction, and Assessment (0011) Practice Test 2

TIME: 120 Minutes
110 Questions

1. Before working with mathematical word problems, a teacher needs to determine that

   (A) the student can complete the math unit.
   (B) the student is at a high enough reading level to understand the problems.
   (C) the math textbook mirrors the skills used in the word problems.
   (D) the class will be on-task for the problems.

2. A student describes an analysis of a recent presidential address for the class. The teacher replies, "You have provided us with a most interesting way of looking at this issue!" The teacher is using

   (A) simple positive response.
   (B) negative response.
   (C) redirect.
   (D) academic praise.

3. When a teacher leads choral chants, the teacher is

   (A) practicing aural skills.
   (B) practicing vocal exercises.
   (C) having students repeat basic skills orally.
   (D) repeating what the students answer.

4. A lesson for which students are given a tankful of water and various objects and are asked to order the objects by weight would be considered a(n)

   (A) science lesson.
   (B) discovery-learning lesson.
   (C) inductive-reasoning lesson.
   (D) eg-rule lesson.

5. Mr. Drake is a first-grade teacher who is using the whole language method while teaching about animals. Before reading a story to the students, Mr. Drake tells the students what he is expecting them to learn from reading the story. What is his reason for doing this?

   (A) The students should know why the instructor chose this text over any other.
   (B) It is important for teachers to share personal ideas with their students in order to foster an environment of confidence and understanding.
   (C) Mr. Drake wants to verify that all students are on-task before he begins the story.
   (D) Mr. Drake is modeling a vital prereading skill in order to teach it to the young readers.

6. Mr. Drake wants to ensure that the class will have a quality discussion on the needs of house pets. In response to a student who said that her family abandoned their cat in a field because it ate too much, Mr. Drake asks: "What is one way to save pets that are no longer wanted?" This exercise involves what level of questioning?

   (A) Evaluation
   (B) Analysis
   (C) Comprehension
   (D) Synthesis

7. Mr. Drake has a heterogeneously grouped reading class. He has placed the students in groups of two—one skilled reader and one remedial reader—and asked that they read the selected story and question each other until they feel that they both understand the story. By planning the lesson this way, Mr. Drake has

   (A) set a goal for his students.
   (B) condensed the number of observations necessary, thereby creating more time for class instruction.
   (C) made it possible for another teacher to utilize the limited materials.
   (D) utilized the students' strengths and weaknesses to maximize time, materials, and the learning environment.

8. Mr. Drake is continuing his lesson on the animal kingdom. He wants to ensure that the students learn as much as they can about animals, so he incorporates information familiar to the students into the new information. Knowing that these are first-grade learners, what should Mr. Drake consider when contemplating their learning experience?

   (A) The students will know how much information they can retrieve from memory.
   (B) The students will overestimate how much information they can retrieve from memory.
   (C) The students will be able to pick out the information they need to study and the information they do not need to study due to prior mastery.
   (D) The students will estimate how much they can learn in one time period.

9. Before reading a story about a veterinary hospital, Mr. Drake constructs a semantic map of related words and terms using the students' input. What is his main intention for doing this?

   (A) To demonstrate a meaningful relationship between the concepts of the story and the prior knowledge of the students
   (B) To serve as a visual means of learning
   (C) To determine the level of understanding the students will have at the conclusion of the topic being covered
   (D) To model proper writing using whole words

10. Student data such as scores on tests and assignments would be the best criteria for determining which of the following?

    (A) Only the students' academic grades
    (B) Behavior assessment
    (C) Student grades and the teacher's quality of instruction
    (D) Student grades and behavior assessment

11. Results of a standardized test indicate that a teacher's students did poorly on the mathematics problem-solving section; students in another classroom in the same school did much better. What would be the best action to take for the teacher of the students who did poorly?

    (A) Look at the students' scores from last year to justify their poor achievement.
    (B) Tell future students to study more because that section is more difficult.
    (C) Suggest that parents hire a math tutor.
    (D) Ask the other teacher to share the strategies used to help make the other students successful.

12. Mr. Joseph is a fifth-grade math and science teacher working in a large suburban middle school. At the beginning of each of his classes, he stands outside of his classroom and greets his students as they walk into his classroom. Mr. Joseph notices students coming into his class who appear upset or angry and show signs of poor self-esteem. Sometimes he overhears his students arguing with other students before class. Often, these students seem to "shut down" during class and do not follow

along with the work. He knows this is a problem, but he is not sure what he should do to solve it. He wants to keep these students from getting behind in their learning. To reduce this problem, Mr. Joscph should

(A) inform the school counselor of the problem and send each student with these symptoms to see the counselor as soon as class starts.

(B) call the parents of students who seem upset or angry and try to persuade them to fix the problem.

(C) send students with these kinds of problems out in the hall so they can get themselves together and learn.

(D) create an environment in his classroom where students feel safe and let them know he is aware of their problems and will do all he can to help them learn.

13. The question, "What was the name of Hamlet's father?" is

(A) a high-order question of evaluation.
(B) a low-order question that can be used to begin a discussion.
(C) a transition.
(D) questioning a skill.

14. Mr. Owen, a third-grade teacher, has been teaching in a small rural district for three years. He enjoys the slow pace of the community and the fact that he knows most of his students' families relatively well. He is a member of the Evening Lions Club, plays on the church basketball team, and volunteers at the animal shelter.

His class this year is made up of 21 eight- and nine-year-olds. Most of the students are of average ability, two receive special services for learning disabilities, and one receives speech therapy. Mr. Owen works hard at making his classroom an exciting place to learn, with lots of hands-on, problem-based cooperative group projects. In the past, students have had difficulty grasping relationships between math concepts and economics. Mr. Owen has decided to offer a savings program with the help of local banks. Once a week, students will make deposits into their savings accounts. Periodically, they will use their accounts to figure interest

at different rates, class totals saved, etc. As part of the social studies curriculum, he encourages them to do chores at home and in their neighborhoods to earn the money for their savings. This approach is evidence that Mr. Owen understands the importance of

(A) the relevance and authenticity in planning instructional activities for students.
(B) integrating curriculum concepts across disciplines that support learning.
(C) saving money.
(D) all of the above.

15. Students are presented with the following problem: "Bill is taller than Ann, but Ann is taller than Grace. Is Ann the tallest child or is Bill the tallest?" This question requires students to use

(A) inductive reasoning.
(B) deductive reasoning.
(C) hypothesis formation.
(D) pattern identification.

16. Which of the following is the correct chronological order for the events in history listed below?

I. Puritans arrive in New England.
II. Protestant Reformation begins.
III. Columbus sets sail across the Atlantic.
IV. Magna Carta is signed in England.

(A) IV, III, II, I
(B) IV, III, I, II
(C) III, IV, II, I
(D) III, II, I, IV

17. The intellectual movement that encouraged the use of reason and science and that anticipated human progress was called the

(A) American System.
(B) Mercantilism.
(C) Enlightenment.
(D) Age of Belief.

18. In the U.S. government, the function of "checks and balances" is meant to

(A) regulate the amount of control each branch of government would have.

(B) make each branch of government indepen-dent from one another.
(C) give the president control.
(D) give the Supreme Court control.

19. Which of the following groups did not play a role in the settlement of the English colonies in America?

(A) Roman Catholics.
(B) Puritans.
(C) Mormons.
(D) Quakers.

20. On the following map, which letter represents the Philippines?

(A) K
(B) D
(C) I
(D) M

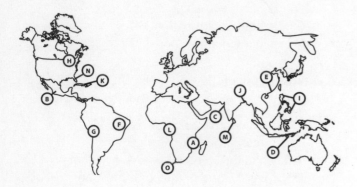

21. The Bill of Rights

(A) listed the grievances of the colonists against the British.
(B) forbade the federal government from en-croaching on the rights of citizens.
(C) gave all white males the right to vote.
(D) specified the rights of slaves.

22. A teacher asks her eighth-grade English students to select a career they would enjoy when they grow up and then to find three sources on the Internet with information about that career. She tells the students that they must find out how much edu-cation is required for this career. If the career re-quires postsecondary education, then the student must find a school or college that provides this education and find out how long it will take to be

educated or trained for this career. Through this assignment, the teacher is helping her students to

(A) explore short-term personal and academic goals.
(B) explore long-term personal and academic goals.
(C) evaluate short-term personal and academic goals.
(D) synthesize long-term personal and academic goals.

23. A teacher asks a student, "When you were study-ing for your spelling test, did you remember a mne-monic we talked about in class for spelling *princi-pal* that 'a principal is your pal'?" The teacher is

(A) leading the student in a divergent thinking exercise.
(B) teaching the student mnemonics, or memory devices.
(C) asking a question to guide the student in cor-recting an error.
(D) modeling inductive reasoning skills for the student.

24. When working with ESL students, the teacher should be aware that

(A) students should speak only English in class.
(B) an accepting classroom and encouraging les-sons will foster learning.
(C) such students should be referred to a special-ist.
(D) limiting the number of resources available is beneficial to the students.

25. Ms. Borders, a second-year third-grade teacher, is preparing a theme study on water and the related concepts of conservation, ecology, and human needs. One of her instructional outcomes deals with students' abilities to demonstrate their new learning in a variety of ways. As she plans her unit of study, Ms. Borders first needs to consider

(A) the strengths and needs of the diverse learn-ers in her classroom.
(B) the amount of reading material she assigns.
(C) how the theme connects to other academic disciplines.
(D) inviting guest speakers to the classroom.

26. Sequential language acquisition occurs when students

    (A) learn a second language after mastery of the first.
    (B) learn a second language at the same time as the first.
    (C) learn two languages in parts.
    (D) develop language skills.

27. Teachers should provide a variety of experiences and concrete examples for children with reading difficulties because some children

    (A) come from environments with limited language exposure.
    (B) have poor learning habits.
    (C) have trouble distinguishing letters.
    (D) can speak well but have difficulty reading.

28. A teacher writes "All men are created equal" on the board and asks each student to explain the meaning of the statement. One student says that it means that all people are equal, but another student says that it just applies to men. A third student says that it is a lie because not all people are equally good at all things, and that, for example, some people can run faster than others and some can sing better than others. The teacher's instructional aim is to

    (A) see whether students can reach consensus on the meaning of the statement.
    (B) see how well students can defend their beliefs.
    (C) provoke the students to disagree with the statement.
    (D) engage the students in critical thinking and to allow them to express their opinions.

29. If the other students laugh when a first-grade girl says, "I want to be a truck driver when I grow up," and tell her, "Girls can't drive big trucks," what should the teacher do?

    (A) Tell the class to quiet down, that the student can be whatever she wants to be when she grows up.
    (B) Tell the class that most truck drivers are men.
    (C) Tell the class that both women and men can be truck drivers, depending on their skills.
    (D) Ask the class to vote on whether women should be truck drivers.

Use the bar graph titled "Unemployment, 1929–1945" to answer the two questions that follow.

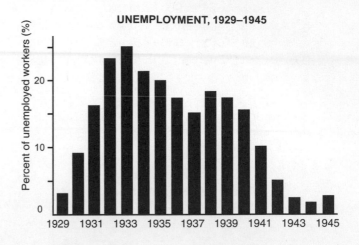

UNEMPLOYMENT, 1929–1945

30. According to the bar graph, the unemployment rate was highest in

    (A) 1929.
    (B) 1933.
    (C) 1938.
    (D) 1944.

31. According to the graph, the unemployment rate was lowest in

    (A) 1929.
    (B) 1933.
    (C) 1938.
    (D) 1944.

32. According to the graph titled "Households by Income Class," which one of the following statements is true?

Households by Income Class

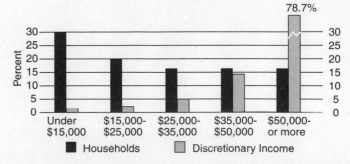

Percentage Distribution of Households and Discretionary Income (Total U.S. = 100 percent)

(A) About 50 percent of households had annual incomes of less than $15,000.

(B) Almost 75 percent of households had annual incomes of $50,000 or more.

(C) About 78 percent of households had annual incomes of $50,000 or more.

(D) About 20 percent of households had annual incomes between $15,000 and $25,000.

33. According to the graph titled "Age of Household Head," which one of the following statements is true?

Age of Household Head

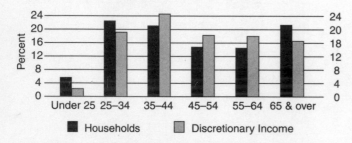

Percentage Distribution of Households and Discretionary Income (Total U.S. = 100%)

(A) Middle-aged households tend to have greater discretionary income.

(B) The youngest have the most discretionary income.

(C) The oldest have the most discretionary income.

(D) The older people get, the less discretionary income they have.

34. An ESOL student is proficient in oral language; however, he continues to experience difficulty with academic language used in science and social studies classes. The teacher believes academic proficiency correlates with oral language proficiency. What has the teacher failed to acknowledge in her analysis of the student's language proficiency?

(A) Both basic interpersonal communication skills and cognitive academic language proficiency are needed for successful academic performance.

(B) Basic interpersonal communication skills develop equally with cognitive academic language proficiency.

(C) Basic interpersonal communication skills are criteria for successful academic performance.

(D) Cognitive academic language proficiency is primary to basic interpersonal communication skills.

35. A student making top grades in class has received a percentile score of 63 on a nationally standardized math test. The best explanation of the student's score is

(A) a percentile score of 63 means that on a scale of 1–100, the student is 37 points from the top.

(B) a percentile score of 63 means that out of a group of 100 students, 37 would score higher and 62 would score lower, and the student has done well by scoring in the top half of all students taking the test.

(C) a percentile score of 63 is just like a grade of 63 on a test; it means that the student made a low D on the test.

(D) a percentile score of 63 means that out of a group of 100 students, 37 would score higher and 62 would score lower, showing a big difference between the student's performance on the standardized test and in class.

36. The launching of *Sputnik* by the Soviet Union in 1957 triggered increased emphasis on all of the following areas of study EXCEPT

(A) world history.
(B) math.
(C) science.
(D) foreign language.

37. Rueben Stein is a middle-school teacher who wants to teach his class about the classification system in the animal kingdom. He decides to introduce this unit to his class by having the students engage in general classification activities. He brings to class a paper bag filled with 30 household items. He dumps the contents of the bag onto a table and then asks the students, in groups of three or four, to put like items into piles and then to justify or explain why they placed certain items into a particular pile. By assigning this task to his students, Mr. Stein is

providing his students with a developmentally appropriate task because

(A) middle-school students like to work in groups.

(B) the items in the bag are household items with which most students will be familiar.

(C) the assignment gives students the opportunity to practice their skills at categorizing.

(D) the assignment will give students a task to perform while the teacher finishes grading papers.

38. Maria Smith is a sixth-grade teacher who is concerned about a student who is failing English class. The student has not turned in any outside assignments, and Ms. Smith has noticed a definite decline in the quality of work the student completes in class. Ms. Smith also has observed that the student has great difficulty staying awake in class and that she seems irritable and distracted most of the time. In her efforts to help the student, Ms. Smith decides to ask the student

(A) if she has been having family problems.

(B) if she realizes that the quality of her classwork is suffering and if she knows of any reasons for the decline.

(C) to work on better time-management skills.

(D) to start coming in early or to stay after class to receive extra help with her work.

39. Elva Rodriguez teaches fourth grade. She has structured her class so that students can spend 30 minutes daily, after lunch, in sustained silent reading activities with books and reading materials of their own choosing. In order to maximize this reading opportunity and to recognize differences among learners, Ms. Rodriguez

(A) allows some students to sit quietly at their desks while others are allowed to move to a reading area where they sit on floor cushions or recline on floor mats.

(B) makes sure that all students have selected appropriate reading materials.

(C) plays classical music on a tape player to enhance student learning.

(D) dims the lights in the classroom in order to increase students' reading comprehension.

40. Karla Dixon is a second-grade teacher who has selected a book to read to her class after lunch. She shows the students the picture on the cover of the book and reads the title of the book to them. She then asks, "What do you think this book is about?" By asking this question, Ms. Dixon is

(A) learning which students are interested in reading strategies.

(B) trying to keep the students awake because she knows they usually get sleepy after lunch.

(C) encouraging students to make a prediction, a precursor of hypothetical thinking.

(D) finding out which students are good readers.

41. Mrs. Johnson teaches sixth-grade reading. She teaches reading skills and comprehension through workbooks and through reading and class discussion of specific plays, short stories, and novels. She also allows students to make some selections according to their own interests. Because she believes there is a strong connection between reading and writing, her students write their responses to literature in a variety of ways. Some of her students have heard their high school brothers and sisters discuss portfolios, and they have asked Mrs. Johnson if they can use them also.

Which of the following statements are appropriate for Mrs. Johnson to consider in deciding whether to agree to the students' request?

I. Portfolios will develop skills her students can use in high school.

II. Portfolios will make Mrs. Johnson's students feel more mature because they would be making the same product as their older brothers and sisters.

III. Portfolios will assist her students in meeting course outcomes relating to reading and writing.

IV. Portfolios will make grading easier because there will be fewer papers and projects to evaluate.

(A) I, II, and IV

(B) I and III only

(C) II and III only

(D) II and IV only

42. The diagram below shows a path for electric flow. As the electrically charged particle flow moves through one complete circuit, it would NOT have to go through

    (A) V to get to W.
    (B) W to get to M.
    (C) Q to get to T.
    (D) T to get to S.

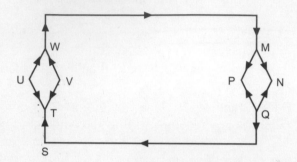

43. The floor of a 9′ × 12′ rectangular room depicted in the diagram is to be covered in two different types of material. The total cost of covering the entire room is $136.00. The cost of covering the inner rectangle is $80.00. The cost of covering the shaded area is $56.00. To compute the cost of material per square foot used to cover the shaded area, which of the following pieces of information is (are) NOT necessary?

    I.   The total cost of covering the entire room
    II. The cost of covering the inner rectangle
    III. The cost of covering the shaded area

    (A) I only
    (B) II only
    (C) I and II
    (D) I and III

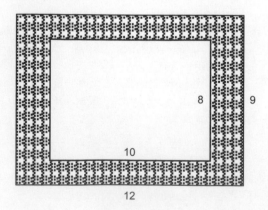

44. The drop in temperature that occurs when sugar is added to coffee is the result of

    I.   sugar passing from a solid to a liquid state.
    II. sugar absorbing calories from the water.
    III. heat becoming latent when it was sensible.

    (A) I only
    (B) I and II
    (C) I, II, and III
    (D) I and III

45. Ms. Thompson wants to teach her students about methods of collecting data in science. This is an important skill for first-graders. Which of the following describes the most appropriate method of teaching students about collecting data in science?

    (A) Ms. Thompson should arrange the students into groups of four. She should then have each group observe the class's pet mouse while she gently touches it with a feather. The students should record how many times out of 10 the pet mouse moves away from the feather. Then, she should gently touch the class's philodendron 10 times with a feather. The students should record how many out of 10 times the philodendron moves away from the feather.
    (B) Ms. Thompson should arrange the students into groups of four. She should give each group five solid balls made of materials that will float and five solid balls made of materials that will not float. She should have the students drop the balls into a bowl of water and record how many float and how many do not.
    (C) Ms. Thompson should show the students a video about scientific methods of gathering data.
    (D) Ms. Thompson should have a scientist come and talk to the class about methods of collecting data. If she cannot get a scientist, she should have a science teacher from the high school come and speak about scientific methods of data collection.

46. A positive condition depending on the absence of cold is

    (A) Fahrenheit.
    (B) intense artificial cold.
    (C) heat.
    (D) Celsius.

Questions 47–49 refer to the following short passages.

(A)   Once upon a time and a very good time it was, there was a moocow coming down along the road and this moocow that was coming down along the road met a nicens little boy named baby tuckoo . . .

(B)   And thus have these naked Nantucketers, these sea hermits, issuing from their anthill in the sea, overrun and conquered the watery world like so many Alexanders . . .

(C)   A large rose tree stood near the entrance of the garden: the roses growing on it were white, but there were three gardeners at it, busily painting them red. Alice thought this a very curious thing, and she went nearer to watch them, and, just as she came up to them, she heard one of them say "Look out now, Five!"

(D)   Emma was not required, by any subsequent discovery, to retract her ill opinion of Mrs. Elton. Her observation had been pretty correct. Such as Mrs. Elton appeared to her on this second interview, such she appeared whenever they met again: self-important, presuming, familiar, ignorant, and ill-bred. She had a little beauty and a little accomplishment, but so little judgment that she thought herself coming with superior knowledge of the world, to enliven and improve a country neighborhood . . .

47.   Which passage makes use of allusion?

   (A)
   (B)
   (C)
   (D)

48.   Which passage employs a distinct voice to imitate the speech of a character?

   (A)
   (B)
   (C)
   (D)

49.   Which passage is most likely taken from a nineteenth-century novel of manners?

   (A)
   (B)
   (C)
   (D)

Questions 50–53 refer to the following passage.

The issue of adult literacy has finally received recognition in the media as a major social problem. It is more important that the politicians themselves recognize the seriousness of the problem and support increased funding for literacy programs.

Literacy education programs need to be directed at two different groups of people with very different needs. The first group is composed of people who have very limited reading and writing skills. These people are complete illiterates. A second group is composed of people who can read and write but whose skills are not sufficient to meet their needs. This second group is called functionally illiterate. Successful literacy programs must meet the needs of both groups.

Instructors in literacy programs have three main responsibilities. First, the educational needs of the illiterates and functional illiterates must be met. Second, the instructors must approach the participants in the program with empathy, not sympathy. Third, all participants must experience success in the program and must perceive their efforts as worthwhile.

50.   What is the difference between illiteracy and functional illiteracy?

   (A)   There is no difference.
   (B)   A functional illiterate is enrolled in a literacy education program, but an illiterate is not.
   (C)   An illiterate cannot read or write, and a functional illiterate can read and write but not at a very high skill level.
   (D)   There are more illiterates than functional illiterates in the United States today.

51.   What is the purpose of the passage?

   (A)   To discuss the characteristics of successful literacy programs
   (B)   To discuss the manner in which literacy programs are viewed by the media

(C) To discuss some of the reasons for increased attention to literacy as a social issue

(D) All of the above

52. According to the passage, which of the following is NOT a characteristic of successful literacy programs?

(A) Participants should receive free transportation.

(B) Participants should experience success in the program.

(C) Instructors must have empathy, not sympathy.

(D) Programs must meet the educational needs of illiterates.

53. What is the author's opinion of the funding for literacy programs?

(A) Too much

(B) Too little

(C) About right

(D) Too much for illiterates and not enough for functional illiterates

Questions 54 and 55 refer to the following passage.

Mr. Dobson teaches fifth-grade mathematics at Valverde Elementary. He encourages students to work in groups of two or three as they begin homework assignments so they can answer questions for each other. Mr. Dobson notices immediately that some of his students choose to work alone even though they had been asked to work in groups. He also notices that some students are easily distracted even though the other members of their group are working on the assignment as directed.

54. Which of the following is the most likely explanation for the students' different types of behavior?

(A) Fifth-grade students are not physically or mentally capable of working in small groups; small groups are more suitable for older students.

(B) Fifth-grade students vary greatly in their physical development and maturity; this

variance influences the students' interests and attitudes.

(C) Fifth-grade students lack the ability for internal control and therefore learn best in structured settings. It is usually best to seat fifth graders in single rows.

(D) Mr. Dobson needs to be more specific in his expectations for student behavior.

55. Mr. Dobson wants to encourage all of his students to participate in discussions related to the use of math in the real world. Five students in one class are very shy and introverted. Which of the following would most likely be the best way to encourage these students to participate in the discussion?

(A) Mr. Dobson should call on these students by name at least once each day and give participation grades.

(B) Mr. Dobson should not be concerned about these students because they will become less shy and introverted as they mature during the year.

(C) Mr. Dobson should divide the class into small groups for discussion so these students will not be overwhelmed by speaking in front of the whole class.

(D) Mr. Dobson should speak with these students individually and encourage them to participate more in class discussions.

Question 56 refers to the following passage.

Mrs. Kresmeier teaches sixth-grade language arts classes. One of her curriculum goals is to help students improve their spelling. As one of her techniques, she has developed a number of special mnemonic devices that she uses with the students, getting the idea from the old teaching rhymes like "I before E except after C or when sounding like A as in neighbor or weigh." Her own memory tricks—"The moose can't get loose from the noose" or "Spell rhyme? Why me?"—have caught the interest of her students. Now, besides Mrs. Kresmeier's memory tricks for better spelling, her students are developing and sharing their own creative ways to memorize more effectively.

56. To improve her students' spelling, Mrs. Kresmeier's method has been successful primarily because of which of the following factors related to student achievement?

    (A) The students are not relying on phonics or sight words to spell difficult words.
    (B) Mrs. Kresmeier has impressed her students with the need to learn to spell.
    (C) The ideas are effective with many students and help to create a learning environment that is open to student interaction.
    (D) Mrs. Kresmeier teaches spelling using only words that can be adapted to mnemonic clues.

Questions 57–59 refers to the following passage.

Mr. Freeman is preparing a year-long unit on process writing for his fifth-grade class. He plans for each student to write about a series of topics over each six-week grading period. At the end of each grading period, students will select three completed writing assignments that reflect their best work. Mr. Freeman will review the assignments and conference with each student. During the conference, Mr. Freeman will assist the students with preparing a list of writing goals for the next grading term.

57. Which of the following best describes Mr. Freeman's plan for reviewing student writing assignments, conferencing with each student, and helping each student set specific goals for writing to be accomplished during the next grading period?

    (A) Summative evaluation.
    (B) Summative assessment.
    (C) Formative assessment.
    (D) Peer evaluation.

58. Mr. Freeman's goal in planning to conference with each student about the student's writing could be described as

    (A) creating a climate of trust and encouraging a positive attitude toward writing.

    (B) an efficient process for grading student writing assignments.
    (C) an opportunity to stress the importance of careful editing of completed writing assignments.
    (D) an opportunity to stress the value of prewriting in producing a final product.

59. Philip, a student in Mr. Freeman's class, receives services from a resource teacher for a learning disability that affects his reading and writing. Which of the following is the most appropriate request that Mr. Freeman should make of the resource teacher to help Philip complete the writing unit?

    (A) Mr. Freeman should ask the resource teacher to provide writing instruction for Philip.
    (B) Mr. Freeman should excuse Philip from writing assignments.
    (C) Mr. Freeman should ask the resource teacher for help in modifying the writing unit to match Philip's needs.
    (D) Mr. Freeman should ask the resource teacher to schedule extra tutoring sessions to help Philip with the writing assignments.

60. Mr. Liu, a math teacher, and Mr. Lowery, a science teacher, are planning a celebration of Galileo's birthday. The students will research Galileo's discoveries, draw posters of those discoveries, and prepare short plays depicting important events in his life. They will present the plays and display the posters for grades 1–4. This is an example of

    (A) an end-of-the-year project.
    (B) problem solving and inquiry teaching.
    (C) working with other teachers to plan instructions.
    (D) teachers preparing to ask the PTA for science lab equipment.

61. The principal asks Mr. Liu and Ms. Gonzalez, another fifth-grade math teacher in the school, to visit the math classes and the computer lab in the middle school that most of the students at Valverde Elementary will attend. By asking Mr. Liu and Ms. Gonzalez to visit the middle school, the principal is most likely encouraging

    (A) collaboration among the math teachers at Valverde and the middle school.

(B) Mr. Liu and Ms. Gonzalez to consider applying for a job at the middle school.

(C) the use of computers in math classes at Valverde.

(D) the use of the middle school math curriculum in the fifth-grade classes.

62. Use the Pythagorean theorem to answer this question: Which of the following comes closest to the actual length of side x in the triangle below?

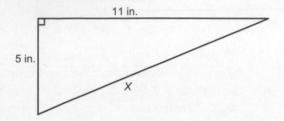

(A) 14 in.

(B) 12 in.

(C) 11 in.

(D) 13 in.

63. If the two triangles, ABC and DEF, shown below are similar, what is the length of side DF?

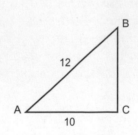 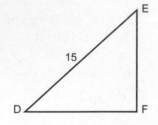

(A) 12.5 units

(B) 13 units

(C) 12 units

(D) 13.5 units

64. Which of the following types of pollution or atmospheric phenomena are correctly matched with their underlying causes?

 I. global warming – carbon dioxide and methane

 II. acid rain – sulfur dioxide and nitrogen dioxide

 III. ozone depletion – chlorofluorocarbons and sunlight

 IV. aurora borealis – solar flares and magnetism

(A) I and II only

(B) II and III only

(C) I and IV only

(D) I, II, III, and IV

65. Which of the following observations best describes the "Ring of Fire"?

(A) Similarities in rock formations and continental coastlines created the "Ring of Fire."

(B) Earth's plates collide at convergent margins, separate at divergent margins, and move laterally at transform-fault boundaries.

(C) Earthquakes produced waves that continue to travel through the Earth in all directions and created the "Ring of Fire."

(D) Volcanoes form when lava accumulates and hardens.

66. Use the pie chart below to answer the following question. If the total number of people voting was 600, which of the following statements are true?

Votes for City Council

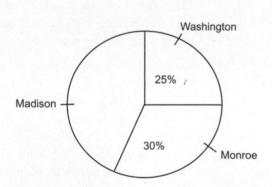

 I. Madison received more votes than Monroe and Washington combined.

 II. Madison received 45 percent of the votes.

 III. Monroe received 180 votes.

 IV. Madison received 180 votes.

(A) I and III only

(B) I and IV only

(C) II and III only

(D) II and IV only

67. Which of the following scenarios could be represented by the graph shown below?

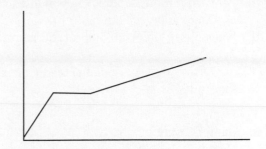

(A) Mr. Cain mowed grass at a steady rate for a while, took a short break, and then finished the job at a steady but slower rate.
(B) Mr. Cain mowed grass at a steady rate for a while, mowed at a steady but slower rate and then took a break.
(C) Mr. Cain mowed grass at a variable rate for a while, took a short break, and then finished the job at a variable rate.
(D) Mr. Cain mowed grass at a steady rate for a while, took a short break, and then finished the job at a steady but faster pace.

68. Only one of the statements below is necessarily true according to the bar graph below. Which one?

Ms. Patton's Earnings, 1998–2002

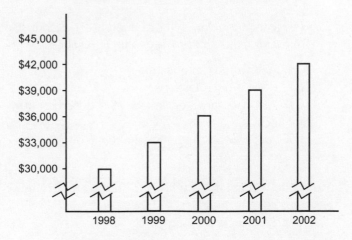

(A) The range of Ms. Patton's earnings for the years shown is $15,000.
(B) Ms. Patton's annual pay increases were consistent over the years shown.
(C) Ms. Patton earned $45,000 in 2003.

(D) Ms. Patton's average income for the years shown was $38,000.

69. Which equation best describes the following graph?

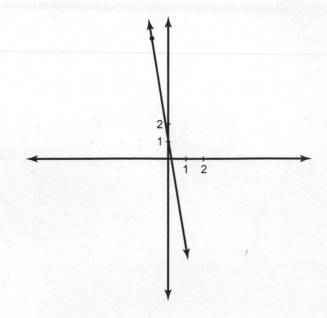

(A) $y = 0x$
(B) $y = x + 0$
(C) $y = -8x$
(D) $y = 8x$

70. What is the solution to the equation $x/3 - 9 = 15$?

(A) 18
(B) 8
(C) 36
(D) 72

71. Translate this problem into a one-variable equation, then solve the equation. What is the solution?

"There are <u>ten</u> vehicles parked in a parking lot. Each is either a car with four tires or a motorcycle with two tires. (Do not count any spare tires.) There are 26 wheels in the lot. How many cars are there in the lot?"

(A) 8
(B) 6
(C) 5
(D) 3

72. Which equation could be used to solve the following problem?

    "Three consecutive odd numbers add up to 117. What are they?"

    (A) $x + (x + 2) + (x + 4) = 117$
    (B) $1x + 3x + 5x = 117$
    (C) $x + x + x = 117$
    (D) $x + (x + 1) + (x + 3) = 177$

Use the following scenario for questions 73 and 74.

Tom Jones was asked to improve the remedial reading curriculum for upper elementary-grade students. He found that the students were continually tested and evaluated on reading, that the current objectives were unclear, and that the teaching materials were inappropriate. Following a lengthy observation of Mrs. Ratu's teaching strategies, Mr. Jones concluded that she was teaching basic reading skills in the same manner as did the lower elementary teachers. The teaching materials used a controlled vocabulary and simple sentences. The students were being taught to rely heavily upon pictures and illustrations for the story. Most of the material was fictional in genre. Rote was Mrs. Ratu's preference for learning. Mr. Jones analyzed the test results and found that many of the students in Mrs. Ratu's class had average scores in the areas of art, math, and music. He concluded that, with the exception of reading, most were normal students and would be successful when their remediation was complete. Mr. Jones made several decisions: (1) the students would be evaluated annually with an achievement test; (2) reading materials of interest to upper elementary students would be substituted for elementary materials; (3) each student would be encouraged to read about the subject of his or her choice; and (4) roundtable discussions would be developed for each "favorite subject."

73. Mrs. Ratu's method of teaching remedial reading focused upon

    I. the level at which the students should have learned the basic reading skills.
    II. her own minimal competency in instructional design and evaluation.
    III. her lack of understanding of the learners in her class.
    IV. her desire to make remedial reading easy for the students.

    (A) I only
    (B) I and IV only
    (C) II and III only
    (D) II only

74. Mr. Jones, having reviewed the students' scores in other classes, knew

    I. that development in one area would lead to development in another area.
    II. how to use a variety of techniques for creating intrinsic and extrinsic motivation.
    III. that allowing students to have choices in their learning would create camaraderie.
    IV. that roundtable discussions would make class more enjoyable but have no effect on students' grades.

    (A) I and II only
    (B) II only
    (C) I, II, and III only
    (D) IV only

75. How can a teacher elicit a high-order response from a student who provides simple responses?

    (A) Ask follow-up questions.
    (B) Repeat the questions.
    (C) Ask the same questions of a different student.
    (D) Ask another student to elaborate on the original response.

76. While waiting for students to formulate their responses to a question, a student blurts out an answer. The teacher should

    (A) ignore the answer entirely.
    (B) respond immediately to the student's answer.
    (C) silently acknowledge the student's response, and then address the response after the question has been answered by someone else.
    (D) move on to another question without comment.

77. What is one way of incorporating non-performers into a discussion?

   (A) Ask a student to respond to a previous student's statement.
   (B) Name a student to answer a question.
   (C) Only call on students with their hands raised.
   (D) Allow off-topic conversations.

78. Teachers, researchers, and policymakers have indicated the greatest challenge to implementing effective professional development is the lack of

   (A) presenters.
   (B) time.
   (C) resources.
   (D) interested teachers.

79. Piaget's theory of cognitive development states that

   (A) children should be able to understand complex directions.
   (B) younger children are unable to understand complex language.
   (C) younger children will be unable to understand directions, even in simple language.
   (D) directions should not be given to young children.

80. Children under the age of eight

   (A) are unable to answer questions.
   (B) process information more slowly than older children.
   (C) can answer the same questions as slightly older children.
   (D) cannot learn in a cooperative environment.

81. Inductive thinking can be fostered through which activity?

   (A) Choral chanting of skill tables
   (B) Computer experience
   (C) Multiple-choice questions
   (D) Personal-discovery activities

82. How can a teacher elicit a high-order response from a student who provides simple responses?

   (A) Ask follow-up questions.
   (B) Repeat the questions.
   (C) Ask the same questions of a different student.
   (D) Ask another student to elaborate on the original response.

83. Bloom divided educational objectives into which of the following domains?

   (A) Knowledge, affective, and evaluation
   (B) Cognitive, affective, and psychomotor
   (C) Affective, value judgments, and psychomotor
   (D) Knowledge, comprehension, and application

84. The pose of the horse in the sculpture pictured below serves to express

   (A) physical aging and decay.
   (B) massiveness and stability.
   (C) lightness and motion.
   (D) military prowess.

Flying Horse. 2nd Century Han. Wuwie Tomb, Gansu.

85. In the lines below, what does the stage direction "(*Aside*)" mean?

King: Take thy fair hour, Laertes; time be thine,

And thy best graces spend it at thy will!

But now, my cousin Hamlet, and my son,—

Hamlet: (*Aside*) A little more than kin, and less than kind.

   (A) The actor steps aside to make room for other action on stage.
   (B) The actor directly addresses only one particular actor on stage.
   (C) The actor directly addresses the audience, while out of hearing of the other actors.
   (D) The previous speaker steps aside to make room for this actor.

86. Who is the central focus in the picture *The Death of Socrates* shown below, and why?

The Death of Socrates, Jacques-Louis David, 1789

Source: Metropolitan Museum of Art, New York

(A) The man on the left, with his hands and face pressed against the wall, because he is separate and thus draws the viewer's attention.

(B) The man sitting at the foot of the bed, because he is at the lowest elevation.

(C) The man standing beside the bed, because he is standing alone.

(D) The man sitting on the bed, because the other men are focused on him.

87. Which of the following seems most true of the sculpture *David* pictured here?

David, Gianlorenzo Bernini, 1623

Source: Galleria Borghese, Rome

(A) The statue is conceived as a decorative work without a narrative function.

(B) The figure seems to be static, passive, and introverted.

(C) The figure is depicted as though frozen in a moment of action.

(D) The figure's garments indicate that he is a soldier or warrior.

Question 88 refers to the following passage.

Kate Tillerson is an art teacher at McGregor High School, where she has taught successfully for several years. She is respected by her students as well as her fellow teachers. This year, the new director of curriculum for the McGregor Independent School District has introduced several curriculum ideas, one of which is the concept of authentic assessment. All curriculum areas have had one or more staff development sessions on this concept. The idea will be incorporated into the curriculum as one of the strategies for assessment in each discipline and at each grade level. Kate has just received a request from the Fine Arts Department chairperson to submit an example of a lesson involving authentic assessment. A central office form on which to complete the example accompanies the request, along with a review of the authentic assessment concept, a model of a completed example, and a deadline for submitting teachers' samples.

Kate's general response to the entire focus on authentic assessment has been that everything she does in her classroom is based upon authentic assessment philosophy. She really sees no need for making any changes in the curriculum guide or for preparing the assignment sent to her. However, Kate is an excellent teacher and generally cooperates in the various curriculum tasks requested of her. She has been a leader of staff development sessions within the district and has shared her innovative ideas with fellow professionals at both regional and state meetings of art educators.

88. Which of the following responses should Kate make to her departmental chairperson's request?

   (A) Kate files the request under "things to do" and forgets about it.
   (B) Kate writes a passionate letter in response to the Fine Arts Department chairperson's request, explaining how she feels about the proposed example of an authentic assessment in art. She sends a copy of this letter to her chairperson and also to the director of curriculum and takes no further action.
   (C) Kate writes a passionate letter in response to the Fine Arts Department chairperson's request, explaining how she feels about the proposed example of an authentic assessment in art. Attached to the letter is a model unit of study Kate has used in her classes, including an authentic assessment project described in detail but not submitted on the form provided by the director of curriculum. Kate sends copies of these items to both her chairperson and the director of curriculum.
   (D) Kate completes an authentic assessment project idea on the form provided by her chairperson. She submits this idea with supplementary photographs of students' projects and a copy of the grading rubric returned to the students for each project photographed. She also sends a videotape of a student discussing the project he has submitted for the unit of study.

89. Physical education goals for children include all of the following EXCEPT:

   (A) aerobic conditioning
   (B) sportsmanship.
   (C) joining a sports team
   (D) strength training

90. Which of the following is the most important artistic device in the example shown below?

**Tawaraya Sotatsu and Hon-Ami Koetsu,
Deer Scroll, Early Edo period**

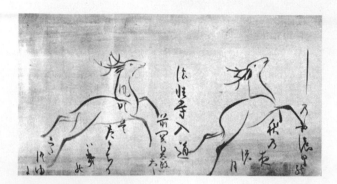

Source: Seattle Art Museum, Seattle

   (A) Line
   (B) Tone
   (C) Color
   (D) Volume

91. Which is the national professional organization that represents teachers of students who speak another language?

   (A) IRA
   (B) NATM
   (C) NASDTEC
   (D) TESOL

92. Until recently, a very quiet, reserved student had completed all her work on time and was making satisfactory progress. Lately, however, she has been erratic in her school attendance, and when she comes to school, she appears distracted. She is having trouble staying on-task and finishing her work. She has failed to turn in several recent assignments. On the last writing assignment, she wrote a very graphic poem about a girl who was sexually assaulted. The level of details used in the poem was shocking to the teacher. Her teacher should

   (A) ignore the topic of the poem, grade it on its poetic merit only, and return it to the student, waiting to see what will happen with the next assignment.
   (B) grade the poem on its poetic merit and return it to the student with a written comment

that she would like to talk to her about the poem.

(C) ask the student to stay after class, return the poem, and ask the student about it.

(D) make a copy of the poem and distribute it to other teachers to solicit their opinions about the poem.

93. If a child in your class suffers from serious emotional disturbances, it is important to

   (A) maintain open communication with the parents.

   (B) keep the child separate from the other students.

   (C) only discuss the student only with other teachers.

   (D) keep an eye on attendance.

94. When a student writes about attempting suicide in a journal, the best way for the teacher to deal with the situation is to

   (A) write encouraging notes to the student in the margins of the journal.

   (B) ask the student to come over to his or her house after school to spend some time together.

   (C) suggest that the student read some inspirational and motivational books.

   (D) take the student's threats of suicide seriously and report the situation to the appropriate school authorities.

95. While the teacher is reading aloud to the class, Linda is telling jokes to get her peers to laugh. According to behavioral theory, what is a possible hypothesis for the function of Linda's behavior?

   (A) Linda tells jokes to make her peers laugh, which may serve to gain attention for Linda or may serve to distract the teacher from the lesson, which allows Linda to escape academic tasks.

   (B) Linda tells jokes to make the teacher angry.

   (C) Linda obviously has trouble at home and therefore this is an issue her parents need to deal with.

   (D) Linda enjoys the performing arts.

96. Listening is a process students use to extract meaning out of oral speech. Activities in which teachers can engage in to assist students in becoming more effective listeners include

   I. clearly setting a purpose for listening.

   II. allowing children to relax by chewing gum during listening.

   III. asking questions about the selection.

   IV. encouraging students to forge links between the new information and knowledge already in place.

   (A) I and II

   (B) II, III, and IV

   (C) I, III, and IV

   (D) I, II, III, and IV

97. For the following graph, which shows the distribution of test scores in Ms. Alvarez's class, which of the following statements do you know to be true?

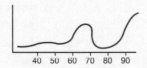

   I. The majority of students scored higher than 60.

   II. The test was a fair measure of ability.

   III. The mean score is probably higher than the median.

   IV. The test divided the class into distinct groups.

   (A) I and II

   (B) I and IV

   (C) I, III, and IV

   (D) IV only

98. Mrs. Johnson, a language arts teacher, is considering having her students use the Internet to help them with their essay writing. The librarian tells her that certain rules and regulations must accompany the use of the Internet in schools and libraries. These rules and regulations do NOT include:

   (A) the use of blocking or filtering technology to protect students against access to certain visual depictions on all school and library computers with Internet access.

   (B) the filtering of text.

(C)   disclosing personal identification about minors.

(D)   unauthorized access, including so-called "hacking," by minors online.

99.   A language arts teacher is considering copying some writings to supplement the textbook. Certain copyright laws govern the use of materials in the classroom. Which of the following is NOT true?

(A)   The "fair use" doctrine prohibits even limited reproduction of copyrighted works for educational and research purposes.

(B)   A teacher can copy a chapter from a book; an article from a periodical or newspaper; and/or a chart, graph, diagram, drawing, cartoon, or picture from a book, periodical, or newspaper.

(C)   A teacher can make copies of a short story, a short essay, or a short poem, whether or not from a collective work.

(D)   For a classroom, a teacher can make multiple copies (not to exceed the number of students in the class) as long as the copying meets the tests of brevity and spontaneity, meets the cumulative effect test, and each copy includes a notice of copyright.

100. Students in a reading class decide that they would like to read about an American they admire. Asking the members of the class to work together in pairs, Ms. Johnson requests that the students select and find a magazine article about the person they have chosen. In order to form pairs so that students can work together in the library, Ms. Johnson decides that the approach that will allow students to be most productive is to assign students to work together so as to ensure that learning preferences and learner characteristics are compatible for the pair of students. In choosing this approach, Ms. Johnson

(A)   avoids having students form their own groups so that the students simply end up working with someone they like.

(B)   takes advantage of the information she has about students' individual learning styles so as to maximize student learning effectiveness and efficiency.

(C)   avoids randomly assigning students to pairs.

(D)   risks having incompatible students working together in pairs.

101. Which of these painters are considered Impressionists?

   I.   Monet
  II.   Rembrandt
 III.   Da Vinci

(A)   I only
(B)   II only
(C)   I and II
(D)   I, II, and III

102. Using student ideas and interests in a lesson

(A)   takes students off-task.
(B)   detracts from the subject content.
(C)   does not allow for evaluation of students' prior knowledge.
(D)   increases learning and student motivation.

103. The tango, samba, cha-cha and bossa nova are all examples of

(A)   African dance
(B)   Mid-eastern dance
(C)   Latin American dance
(D)   Indian dance

104. Ms. Woods has come to the conclusion that her students are having trouble assessing their own writing strengths and weaknesses. Which of the following would be appropriate ways of monitoring and improving the students' writing?

   I.   Have students submit an original work on a topic they choose every day to be graded.
  II.   Have students identify, with the help of the teacher, one area of writing in which they feel they need improvement; they will then focus on this area until they have reached their goal and are ready to identify a new area.
 III.   Keep all draft and final copies in a portfolio; the student will pick a piece to discuss with the teacher at a teacher-student conference.
  IV.   Once a week the teacher will read a quality composition written by a class member.

(A) II and III only
(B) I and III only
(C) I, III, and IV only
(D) II, III, and IV only

105. Andy Warhol's portrait of Marilyn Monroe was done in which genre?

(A) impressionism
(B) cubism
(C) pop art
(D) Dadaism

106. What concepts are always present in cooperative learning?

   I. Team rewards
  II. Individual accountability
 III. Equal opportunities
 IV. Rules

(A) I, III, and IV only
(B) I, II, and III only
(C) II, III, and IV only
(D) I, II, III, and IV only

Question 107 refers to the following passage.

(The veranda of the Voynitzevs' country house. It looks out onto a sunlit garden, with the tall trees of the forest beyond, bisected by a grassy walk. The whoosh of a rocket taking off. The lights come up to reveal YA-KOV in the garden with a large box of assorted fireworks in his arms. Beside him stands DR. TRILETZKY, a match in his hand.

They are gazing up into the sky—DR. TRILETZ-KY with delight, YAKOV with apprehension. There is a smell of sulfur in the air. The rocket bursts, off.)

107. The above passage is most likely taken from

(A) a Victorian novel.
(B) the stage directions of a play.
(C) the critical notes to a literary work.
(D) the rough draft of a literary work.

108. Ms. Eagleton has noticed that during class discussions, many students answer her questions with one or two words or a short phrase. She makes certain that she provides enough time for students to consider the quesstion and prepare an answer before calling on a student to resposnd. Which of the following reasons is probably the cause of the students' short answers?

(A) The students are too intimidated to provide lengthy answers.
(B) The questions usually require factual recall.
(C) The students are uncertain about the answer, so they keep their comments short.
(D) The questions are probably too difficult for these students.

109. This form of exercise emphasizes breathing techniques, stretching, and relaxation:

(A) yoga
(B) pilates
(C) aerobic conditioning
(D) spinning

110. BMI represents

(A) body movement index.
(B) body mass index.
(C) binary motion index.
(D) bilingual maturational index.

Praxis II

**Elementary Education
Test Code 0011**

Answers: Practice Test 2

Answer Key

1. (B)	23. (C)	45. (B)	67. (A)	89. (C)
2. (D)	24. (B)	46. (C)	68. (B)	90. (A)
3. (C)	25. (A)	47. (B)	69. (C)	91. (D)
4. (B)	26. (A)	48. (A)	70. (D)	92. (C)
5. (D)	27. (A)	49. (D)	71. (D)	93. (A)
6. (D)	28. (D)	50. (C)	72. (A)	94. (D)
7. (D)	29. (C)	51. (D)	73. (C)	95. (A)
8. (B)	30. (B)	52. (A)	74. (C)	96. (C)
9. (A)	31. (D)	53. (B)	75. (A)	97. (B)
10. (C)	32. (D)	54. (B)	76. (C)	98. (B)
11. (D)	33. (A)	55. (C)	77. (A)	99. (A)
12. (D)	34. (D)	56. (C)	78. (B)	100. (B)
13. (B)	35. (D)	57. (C)	79. (B)	101. (A)
14. (D)	36. (A)	58. (A)	80. (B)	102. (D)
15. (B)	37. (C)	59. (C)	81. (D)	103. (C)
16. (A)	38. (B)	60. (C)	82. (A)	104. (D)
17. (C)	39. (A)	61. (A)	83. (B)	105. (C)
18. (A)	40. (C)	62. (B)	84. (C)	106. (B)
19. (C)	41. (B)	63. (A)	85. (C)	107. (B)
20. (C)	42. (A)	64. (D)	86. (D)	108. (B)
21. (B)	43. (C)	65. (B)	87. (C)	109. (A)
22. (B)	44. (C)	66. (C)	88. (D)	110. (B)

Elementary Education: Curriculum, Instruction, and Assessment (0011) Practice Test 2

Detailed Explanations of Answers

1. (B)

It is important to ensure that the word problems given to students are at their reading level; otherwise, a teacher will be unable to evaluate their successes with these problems accurately. (A), (C), and (D) are not the best answers to the question.

2. (D)

Academic praise comprises specific statements that give information about the value of the object or about its implications. A simple positive response, such as, "That's a good answer!" (A), does not provide any information other than the praise. There is nothing negative (B) about the teacher's response. A redirect (C) occurs when a teacher asks a student to react to the response of another student.

3. (C)

Choral chant is the term used for students' repeating basic facts, spellings, and laws.

4. (B)

A discovery-learning lesson is one in which the class is organized to learn through the students' own active involvement in the lesson. In inductive-reasoning lessons (C), the students are provided with examples and non-examples and are expected to derive definitions from this information. The eg-rule method (D) moves from specific examples to general rules or definitions. Even though the lesson may take place in a science class (A), the type of learning is discovery.

5. (D)

Comprehension is shown when the reader questions his or her intent for reading. For example, one may be reading a story to find out what terrible things may befall the main character. The rationale for choosing a book may be an interesting bit of information (A), but it is not a major topic of discussion with the students. Sharing personal information (B) creates a certain bond, but this is not directly relevant to the question. It is also important that all students are on-task before the beginning of a lesson (C), but this is a smaller part of the skill modeled in response (D).

6. (D)

A question testing whether a student can synthesize information will include the need to make predictions or solve problems. An evaluation question (A) will require a judgment of the quality of an idea or solution. In order to be real analysis (B), the question would have to ask students to analyze given information to draw a conclusion or find support for a given idea. Comprehension questions (C) may require the rephrasing of an idea in the students' own words, and then using this for comparison.

7. (D)

By having a mixed-level pair read together, the remedial student receives instruction and the skilled student receives reinforcement. This method uses alternate teaching resources, the students themselves, to enhance the learning environment. A certain goal, comprehension, has been set (A), but this is not the most important outcome. The teacher will need to observe fewer groups (B), but it is unlikely that this will change the time needed to work with all groups as long as quality is to be maintained. Even though they are reading in pairs, each student should have a book, and it would be impractical to permit another teacher to utilize the books while one teacher is using them.

8. (B)

Students at this age do not have the cognitive skills to realize how much they have actually learned or how much they will actually be able to retain. For this reason, (A) must be incorrect. At this stage in their intellectual development, students cannot differentiate material that is completely understood from material they have not completely comprehended (C). Students will generally feel that they are capable of learning much more than they will actually retain (D).

9. (A)

By mapping out previous knowledge, information already known can be transferred to support new information. Although words on the board are visual (B), this is not the underlying motive. Semantic mapping done at the beginning of a story tests how much knowledge the students have about the topic at the outset, not the conclusion (C). Although this method does model proper use of words (D), this is not the main intent of the exercise.

10. (C)

Data gathered within the learning environment resulting from day-to-day activities could also provide a means for reflection and discussion. This includes using student scores in class not only for their most recognized use, student academic grades, (A), but also using the success of students to guide a teacher's professional development plan. Looking for inconsistencies in grading can be a basis for teachers to explore their teaching practices while looking for new and more effective methods. In considering answers (B) and (D), student academic grades should never be used in behavior assessment.

11. (D)

All teachers have different strengths and weaknesses. By working collaboratively, they can share their abilities to create more strengths and fewer weaknesses. If a teacher has found a method of teaching a concept that is successful, it is worth trying. Viewing the students' scores from the previous year would assist in seeing if they had made any progress since their last test (omit comma) but should not be used to justify their poor scores (A). This does nothing to assist students in improving their academic achievement. Telling future students to study more (B) or suggesting math tutors (C) may be good advice omit comma but should not be the only course of helping students improve in a certain area.

12. (D)

During late childhood and early adolescence, students often exhibit problems with self-image, physical appearance, eating disorders, feelings of rebelliousness, and other similar problems. Teachers should be aware of these developmental problems and do all they can to minimize them in the classroom. By providing a safe learning environment and letting students know that the teacher is aware of these issues, the teacher can assist in keeping these students on-task. (A) is incorrect. Many students at this age exhibit these kinds of problems. This reaction would cause a major disruption in the learning process, and generally counselors do not have time to address all of the students' problems. (B) is incorrect. Although parents can sometimes help, solution (B) should be used only for the most severe cases. (C) is incorrect because calling other students' attention to any student's problems in this way often only makes the problems worse by isolating and ostracizing individuals.

13. (B)

The question presented here is a low-order question (B) that ensures that a student is focused on the task at hand; it can be used to develop into higher questioning. A high-order question (A) tests the student's ability to apply information, evaluate information, create new information, and so on, rather than to recall simple content. Transitions (C) are used to connect different ideas and tasks. The information that the question is looking for is one of content, not skill (D).

14. (D)

The integrated, real-life nature of this project builds deeper understandings of the economic concept of work and wages, saving versus spending, and banking. While providing the authentic experience of working and saving, the project also builds the class's capacity to complete mathematical functions such as figuring interest rates and compounding interest. In addition, the idea of the value of saving money has been communicated.

15. (B)

The example illustrates a deductive reasoning task (B). Inductive reasoning (A) would be giving the class some information and asking them to form a rule or generalization. Choices (C) and (D) are simply examples of inductive tasks.

16. (A)

The Magna Carta was signed in 1215. Columbus's voyages began in the fifteenth century. The Protestant Reformation occurred in the sixteenth century. The Puritans came to America in the seventeenth century. Therefore, the best choice is (A).

17. (C)

Choice (A), as conceived by Henry Clay, referred to the nationalist policy of uniting the three economic sections of the United States following the War of 1812. Choice (B) is an economic theory whose principal doctrine was the belief that the wealth of nations was based on the possession of gold. Choice (D) is tied to tradition and emotion. Choice (C) is the best possible answer.

18. (A)

Choice (A) is correct; checks and balances provide each of the branches with the ability to limit the actions of the other branches. (B) is incorrect; branches of the federal government do not achieve independence from each other because of checks and balances. Choices (C) and (D) are also incorrect because they deal with only one branch, whereas the system of checks and balances involves the manner in which the three branches are interrelated.

19. (C)

Choices (A), (B), and (D) all played a role in the early settlements of the English colonies in America. The correct response is item (C); Mormonism was founded at Fayette, New York, in 1830, by Joseph Smith. The Book of Mormon was published in 1830; it describes the establishment of an American colony from the Tower of Babel.

20. (C)

The letter *K* represents Cuba, letter *D* represents Indonesia, and letter *M* represents Sri Lanka. The correct answer is (C) because letter *I* represents the Philippine Islands.

21. (B)

The Bill of Rights clearly states that Congress may not make laws abridging citizens' rights and liberties. Choices (C) and (D) are incorrect because the Bill of Rights does not talk about voting rights or slaves. A list of grievances (A) is contained in the Declaration of Independence.

22. (B)

This assignment asks students to gather information or explore long-term goals—goals many years in the future. Short-term goals (A, C) are those that can be achieved in days, weeks, or maybe months. Answer (D), synthesize, is a more complicated process than merely gathering information.

23. (C)

The teacher is asking the student questions to allow the student to correct a spelling error. Spelling does not allow for divergent or creative thinking (A). Although the teacher reminds the student of a mnemonic, the teacher is not teaching the mnemonic (B). Finally, applying spelling rules or guides to improve spelling would be an example of deductive reasoning, not inductive reasoning (D).

24. (B)

It is very important that all students feel welcome, but it is especially effective for ESL students to feel comfortable and welcomed in the classroom. Students should be able to use many resources to help them so (D) is incorrect. Most schools will not have a specialist to whom the teacher can refer the student; (C) is not an acceptable choice. A teacher should never deprive a student of the student's language or culture; (A) is not an appropriate answer.

25. (A)

Ms. Borders must consider the learning preferences and emotional factors of her learners as she constructs learning activities for the study. To consider cooperative group projects versus independent work is one aspect of her preparation. Another would be the range of products deemed acceptable as demonstrations of knowledge (written or spoken, visual or performed art, technology-based, etc.). Choices (B), (C), and (D) might be considered once she plans the study, but they are unrelated to the issue of preparing for the stated instructional outcomes.

26. (A)

Students learn to speak two languages in one of two ways: sequentially, in which one language is mastered before the study of the second language has begun (A), or simultaneously, in which both languages are learned concurrently (B). Sequential language acquisition does not mean a student learns two languages in parts (C) or that the student develops language skills (D).

27. (A)

Some students may not speak English at home or may have limited exposure to the vocabulary of the classroom. It is important to be aware of these factors and provide the materials appropriate to help guide mastery. Answers that say negative things about the students are never the best choice; for that reason, one should not choose answer (B), (C), or (D).

28. (D)

The teacher hopes to engage the students in critical thinking by allowing them to express their opinions; the teacher realizes that students will have different interpretations of the statement. (A), (B), and (C) are possible outcomes, but (D) is the best answer because it relates specifically to the teacher's aim.

29. (C)

The best response (C) is to emphasize that occupations are open to both men and women and that most people make career choices based on their abilities and their preferences. (A) and (B) fail to take advantage of the opportunity to teach the class about equal opportunity in career choices, and (D) implies that popular opinion determines career choices.

30. (B)

The 1933 bar is highest, and the graph measures the percent of unemployment by the height of the bars. The bars for 1929 (A), 1938 (C), and 1944 (D) are all lower than the bar for 1933, the year in which unemployment was the highest.

31. (D)

1944 (the bar between 1943 and 1945) is the lowest bar on the graph. As previously mentioned, the graph measures the percentage of unemployment on the length of the bars. The bars for 1929 (A), 1933 (B), and 1938 (C) are all higher than the bar for 1944.

32. (D)

Choice (A) is wrong because about 30%, not 50%, of households had under $15,000. Choices (B) and (C) are also incorrect because slightly more than 15% fell into this category.

33. (A)

Graph reading and interpretation is the primary focus of this question. Choice (B) is obviously wrong because the youngest have the least discretionary income. The oldest group has less discretionary income than those between 25 and 65; therefore, item (C) is wrong. The discretionary income for all ages over 25 is more than for those under 25; (D) is incorrect.

34. (D)

In general, teachers believe that oral language proficiency correlates with academic proficiency. Research indicates, however, that oral language proficiency is easily acquired through daily living experiences, whereas academic language proficiency requires an academic setting with context-related activities.

35. (D)

Choice (D) is the best answer because it contains information that is technically correct and expresses a concern about the difference in the student's standardized test score and about the usual performance in math

class. (A) is technically correct; however, it does not really provide as complete an answer as (D). (B) tends to provide the student with a false impression; although the student scored in the top half, as one of the best students in class, the student could have been expected to have scored perhaps in the top 10 percent or at least the top quartile. (C) is simply a false statement.

36. (A)

The United States was shocked by the launching of Sputnik by the Soviet Union in 1957. Comparisons between Soviet education and the education available in the public schools of the United States indicated a need to emphasize math (B), science (C), and foreign language (D) for the United States to compete with other countries and to remain a world power.

37. (C)

According to Piaget's theory of cognitive development, students in middle school would be at the stage of concrete operational thought. Students at this stage of cognitive development would be able to categorize items. Choice (A) is a false statement. Although some students do like to work in groups, other students prefer to work alone—at this and at any age group or cognitive stage. Preferring to learn in groups (or socially) or to learn alone (or independently) is a characteristic of learning style or preference, not a characteristic of cognitive or affective development. Choice (B) is irrelevant to the teacher's intent in assigning the task. Students could just as easily work with unfamiliar items, grouping them by observable features independent of their use or function. Choice (D) is not a good choice under any circumstances. Teachers should assiduously avoid giving students any assignments merely to keep them busy while they do something else. All assignments should have an instructional purpose.

38. (B)

This question opens the door for dialogue with the student about a range of possible problems. This response shows that the teacher is concerned about the student and her welfare without making assumptions, jumping to conclusions, and/or intruding into the private affairs of the student. Choice (A) presumes that the source of all problems lies with the family. Although the student may be having family-related difficulties, there are other possibilities to consider as well. The student may have taken on an extra-curricular activity that is taking too much of her time away from her studies, or the student may be having health problems. It is unwise for the teacher to conclude that the student is having family problems. Choice (C) is inappropriate because it too narrowly identifies one possible coping mechanism as the solution to the student's problem. Although the student may benefit from acquiring better time-management skills, it also is possible that the student's present problems have little or nothing to do with time management. Choice (D) is equally inappropriate in that it demands that the student devote even more time to school, even though she currently is having trouble with present demands. If the student is unwell, then certainly spending more time at school is not the solution to her problem. Clearly, choice (B) is the best choice for helping the student identify her problem(s) and find a solution.

39. (A)

Only choice (A) takes into account differences among learners by giving them options as to how and where they will read. Choice (B) violates the students' freedom to select reading materials they find interesting and wish to read. When students are allowed to choose their own reading materials, it may seem that some students select materials beyond their present reading comprehension. However, reading research indicates that students can comprehend more difficult material when their interest level is high. Therefore, any efforts by the teacher to interfere with students' selection of their own reading material would be ill advised (D). Choices (C) and (D) are equally poor in that they both describe a concession to only one group of learners. For example, with choice (C), even though some students may prefer to read with music playing in the background, other students may find the music distracting. The best action for the teacher to take would be to allow some students to listen to music on earphones while others read in quiet. In regard to choice (D), some students will prefer bright illumination just as some students will read better with the lights dimmed. Ms. Rodriguez would do well to

attempt to accommodate various learner needs by having one area of the room more brightly illuminated than the other.

40. (C)

The teacher is encouraging students to become engaged in the learning process by making a prediction based on limited information given in the book title and cover illustration. When students can generate their own predictions or formulate hypotheses about possible outcomes on the basis of available (although limited) data, they are gaining preparatory skills for formal operations (or abstract thinking). Although second-grade students would not be expected to be at the level of cognitive development characterized by formal operations, Piagetian theory would indicate that teachers who model appropriate behaviors and who give students opportunities to reach or stretch for new cognitive skills are fostering students' cognitive growth. Choice (A) is a poor choice because students' responses to this one question posed by the teacher cannot be used to assess adequately their interest in reading activities. Choice (B), likewise, is a poor choice in that it implies no instructional intent for asking the question. Choice (D) is incorrect because students' responses to a single question cannot allow the instructor to determine which students are good readers and which ones are not.

41. (B)

The question asks for appropriate statements for Mrs. Johnson to consider in making an instructional decision. Option I is a valid reason for teaching students how to develop portfolios. Teachers teach students skills that will be useful in school and in their careers. Although Option II may produce positive affective results, feeling mature because students are imitating older siblings is not a sufficient reason to choose portfolios. Option III is the most appropriate reason for using portfolios. Most activities and projects that promote achievement of course outcomes would be considered appropriate strategies. Option IV is not necessarily true; portfolio assessment can result in more written work, which can be more time consuming. Even if option IV were true, emphasizing student achievement is more important than easing the workload of teachers. Options I and III (choice (B)) are appropriate.

42. (A)

Note that the particle flow divides at two points, T and M. At these points the flow has two paths to reach either point W or point Q. Thus, the correct choice is (A). Particle flow can reach point W by going through point U, rather than V. It would have to flow through all other points listed in order to make a complete circuit or total clockwise path.

43. (C)

To find the cost per square foot of material to cover the shaded area, one divides the total cost of covering the shaded area (III) by the square footage of the shaded area. Only option III is necessary; I and II are *not* necessary. The answer is, therefore, (C). The problem would be solved as follows: The total area of the larger rectangle is the base times the height, 12 ft × 9 ft, which equals 108 sq ft. Therefore, the area of the shaded portion surrounding the inner rectangle is

$$108 \text{ sq ft} - 80 \text{ sq ft} = 28 \text{ sq ft}$$

If the total cost of material is $56 to cover the shaded area of 28 sq ft, the cost per square foot is $56/28 sq ft = $2/sq ft.

44. (C)

The best answer is (C) because it includes three correct statements. The sugar does pass from a solid to a liquid state (I), the sugar does absorb calories from the water (II), and the heat does become latent when it is sensible (III). Since I, II, and III are all causes of the drop of temperature when sugar is added to coffee, *all three* must be included when choosing an answer. Although choices (A), (B), and (D) each contain one or more of these causes, none contains all three; subsequently, each of these choices is incorrect.

45. (B)

A hands-on activity will best help the students learn about data collection. (B) is the only choice that employs a hands-on activity, so this is the best answer. The students would learn about direct observation by watching Ms. Thompson tickle the mouse and the philodendron (A); however, this method would not be as effective as allowing the students to conduct their own data collection. Research suggests that viewing a video (C) is an inefficient method of learning. Having a guest speaker tell the students about data collection (D) is not a good choice for first-graders.

46. (C)

Because heat is a positive condition depending on the absence of cold, (C) is the correct answer. Fahrenheit and Celsius are measures of temperature, not conditions; therefore, (A) and (D) are incorrect choices. Heat is the opposite of intense artificial cold; (B) is not acceptable.

47. (B)

This passage from Melville's *Moby-Dick* contains an allusion in the phrase, "like so many Alexanders." Melville is illustrating the strength and power of whalers ("naked Nantucketers") by alluding and comparing them to Alexander the Great, the famous conqueror who died in 323 BCE.

48. (A)

This passage, which opens James Joyce's *A Portrait of the Artist as a Young Man*, is written in "baby talk" ("moocow," "nicens," "baby tuckoo") to convey to readers the age, speech, and mental state of the narrator.

49. (D)

Nineteenth-century novels of manners employed such themes as the importance (or unimportance) of "good breeding," the elation (and suffocation) caused by society, and the interaction of individuals within the confines of a closed country community, to name just a few. This passage, taken from Jane Austen's *Emma*, mentions "opinions" of other characters, the importance of "beauty" and "accomplishment" (note how Emma sees them as almost saving graces for Mrs. Elton), and the "improvement" of a "country neighborhood."

50. (C)

Choice (C) is the definition of illiterate and functional illiterate stated in the second paragraph. Choice (A) cannot be correct because the passage clearly distinguishes between illiterates and functional illiterates. Choice (B) is not correct because the definition stated is not related to participation in a program. The relative number of illiterates and functional illiterates is not discussed,; choice (D) is incorrect.

51. (D)

This passage has several purposes. First, the author presents some complaints concerning the way literacy issues are presented in the media (B). The author also discusses the increased attention given to literacy by society (C). Third, the author discusses many aspects of successful literacy programs (A). Therefore, choice (D), which includes all of these purposes, is correct.

52. (A)

This question must be answered using the process of elimination. You are asked to select a statement that names a possible program component that is *not* characteristic of successful literacy programs. Choice (A) is correct because choices (B), (C), and (D) are specifically mentioned in the passage.

53. (B)

Choice (B) is correct because the author specifically states that politicians should support increased funding for literacy programs. Choices (A) and (C) are incorrect because the author states that funding should be increased. There is no discussion of funding for different programs, so choice (D) is incorrect.

54. (B)

The variance in fifth graders' physical size and development has a direct influence on their interests and attitudes, including their willingness to work with others and a possible preference for working alone. (A) is incorrect because fifth graders do have the physical and mental maturity to work in small groups. (C) is incorrect because not all fifth-grade students lack the ability for internal control. (D) is incorrect; although Mr. Dobson might need to be more specific in his directions to the students, this is not the main reason for their behavior.

55. (C)

Students who are shy are usually more willing to participate in small groups than in discussions involving the entire class. (A) is incorrect because calling on each student once per day will not necessarily assist shy students to participate in class discussions, even if participation grades are assigned. (B) is incorrect because although students may become less shy as the year progresses, the teacher still has a responsibility to encourage students to participate. Choice (D) is incorrect because although speaking to students individually may help some to participate, it is likely more students will participate if the procedure outlined in choice (C) is implemented.

56. (C)

Mrs. Kresmeier uses effective communication strategies to teach students and encourages them to interact for the same purposes. Mnemonic devices are apparently a new technique for most of the students; in addition, the teacher's own creative spelling clues are often new ones matching the age level, interests, and patterns of humor enjoyed by her students. The most success is probably derived from her encouragement to examine the words to find a feature that can be turned into a mnemonic device. (A) is incorrect because there has been no attempt to rule out other techniques of learning to spell. (B) is incorrect because certainly other teachers have also impressed upon the students that spelling is important. The creative methodology is probably the major difference between Mrs. Kresmeier's method and those that students have encountered in the past. (D) is incorrect because no evidence exists to show that Mrs. Kresmeier is especially selective in choosing her spelling lessons.

57. (C)

Formative assessment (C) is continuous and is intended to serve as a guide to future learning and instruction. Summative evaluation (A) and summative assessment (B) are both used to put a final critique or grade on an activity or assignment with no real link to the future. Peer assessment would require students to critique each other (D).

58. (A)

Meeting one-to-one to discuss a student's strengths and weaknesses creates a feeling of trust and confidence between the student and the teacher. Grading papers solely on the content of a conference (B) is not an efficient means of grading. The student/teacher conference should not focus on only one part of the writing process, such as careful editing (C) or pre-writing (D).

59. (C)

The role of the resource teacher is to provide individual instruction for students who qualify for services and, through collaborative consultation, work with the classroom teacher to adapt instruction to match each student's needs. A resource teacher should not be entirely responsible for teaching a learning-disabled student (A) and is also not responsible for tutoring outside of the scheduled class meetings (D). A learning-disabled student should not be totally excused from assignments (B).

60. (C)

This is an example of working with other teachers to plan instruction. Response (A) is incorrect because it is incomplete. This activity may complete the school year, but this activity is not necessarily an end-of-the-year project. (B) is incorrect because problem solving and inquiry teaching are only small components of the activity. Choice (D) is incorrect because asking students to research Galileo and asking the PTA to buy science equipment are not necessarily related.

61. (A)

Visiting other teachers in other schools will promote collaboration and cooperation. Choice (B) is incorrect because there is no reason to believe that the principal is encouraging these teachers to apply for a job in the middle school. Choice (C) is incorrect because, although using computers in science classes may be a topic on which teachers choose to collaborate, choice (A) is more complete. Choice (D) is incorrect because the middle school math curriculum is not intended for use in the fifth grade.

62. (B)

Use the Pythagorean theorem to compute the length of any side of any right triangle, as long as the lengths of the other two sides are known. For any right triangle with side lengths a, b, and c, where c is the length of the hypotenuse (the longest side, and the one opposite the right angle), $a^2 + b^2 = c^2$. Substituting the real values for a and b from the problem gives

$$c^2 = 11^2 + 5^2$$

or

$$c^2 = 146.$$

To complete the work, take the (positive) square root of 146, which is slightly more than 12 ($12 \times 12 = 144$).

63. (A)

If two triangles are similar, they have the exact same shape (although not necessarily the same size). This means that the corresponding angles of the two triangles have the same measure and the corresponding sides are proportional. To find the missing side (side DF) set up the proportion:

$$AB/AC = DE/DF$$

or, by substituting the given values,

$$12/10 = 15/x$$

where x is the length of side DF. This can be read as "12 is to 10 as 15 is to x." The problem can be solved by using cross-multiplication. Thus, $12x = 150$, or $x = 12.5$.

64. (D)

All are correctly matched.

65. (B)

Expansion occurring on the ocean floor creates pressure around the edges of the Pacific Plate and produces geologic instability where the Pacific Plate collides with the continental plates on all sides. Neither earthquakes (C), hardened lava (D), or rock similarities (A) alone are sufficient to account for the "Ring of Fire."

66. (C)

Washington and Monroe together received 55% of the votes. Everyone else voted for Madison; Madison must have received 45% of the votes. (All of the candidates' percents must add up to 100%.) Statement I cannot be true and statement II must be true. Monroe received 30% of the 600 votes. 0.30 times 600 is 180, so statement III is true. Madison received 45% of the vote, and 45% of 600 is 270, so statement IV is false. Therefore, only II and III are true, and the correct answer is (C).

67. (A)

The somewhat steep straight line to the left tells you that Mr. Cain worked at a steady rate for a while. The completely flat line in the middle tells you he stopped for a while—the line does not go up because Mr. Cain did not cut grass then. Finally, the line continues upward (after his break) less steeply (therefore more flatly), indicating that he was working at a slower rate.

68. (B)

Because Ms. Patton's increases were constant ($3,000 annually), and because the directions tell you that only one statement is true, choice (B) must be the correct answer. To be more confident, however, you can examine the other statements. The range of Ms. Patton's earnings is $12,000 (the jump from $30,000 to $42,000), not $15,000, so choice (A) cannot be correct. Although Ms. Patton may have earned $45,000 in 2003, you do not know that because the graph goes only to 2002; choice (C) cannot be correct. Choice (D) gives the incorrect earnings average; it was $36,000, not $38,000.

69. (C)

There are several ways to determine which equation best matches the line. An easy way is to decide first whether the line has a positive or negative slope. Because the line moves from the upper left to the lower right, it has a negative slope. In a linear equation of the form $y = mx + b$ (where y is isolated on the left side of the equation), the coefficient of x is the slope of the line. The only equation with a negative slope (-8) is choice (C), so that is the correct answer. Another clue that choice (C) is correct is that the line appears fairly steep, and a slope of -8 (or 8) is considered fairly steep, too.

70. (D)

Using the rules for solving one-variable equations, the original equation is transformed as follows:

$$x/3 - 9 = 15.$$

Adding 9 to each side of the equation gives

$$x/3 = 24.$$

Multiplying both sides by 3 gives

$$x = 72.$$

71. (D)

One way to solve the problem is by writing a one-variable equation that matches the information given:

$$4x + 2(10 - x) = 26$$

The $4x$ represents four tires for each car. Use x for the number of cars because at first you do not know how many cars there are. Then $(10 - x)$ represents the number of motorcycles in the lot. (If there are 10 vehicles total, and *x* of them are cars, subtract *x* from 10 to get the number of "leftover" motorcycles.) Then $2(10 - x)$ stands for the number of motorcycle tires in the lot. The sum of the values $4x$ and $2(10 - x)$ is 26, which gives the equation above. Using the standard rules for solving a one-variable equation, *x* (the number of cars in the lot) equals 3. Another approach to answering a multiple-choice question is to try substituting each choice for the unknown variable in the problem to see which one makes sense.

72. (A)

The correct equation must show three consecutive odd numbers being added to give 117. Odd numbers (just like even numbers) are each two units apart. Only the three values (x, $x + 2$, $x + 4$) given in choice (A) are each two units apart. Because the numbers being sought are odd, one might be tempted to choose (D). However, the second value in choice (D), ($x + 1$), is not two units apart from the first value (x); it is different by only one.

73. (C)

Mrs. Ratu's lack of competency is exhibited in her lack of understanding of her students and in her teaching at the elementary level. Mrs. Ratu was not teaching her students at the appropriate level (A). Although she may have desired to make reading easy for her students (D), she was not going about it correctly. When appropriate techniques are used, teaching ninth graders to read is no more difficult than teaching third graders to read.

74. (C)

Mr. Jones knew that development in one area leads to development in other areas. He also knew that using a variety of instructional techniques could lead to inquiry, motivation, and even further development in certain areas. Allowing students to have choices in their learning leads to a positive self-concept and can lead to camaraderie. Roundtable discussions lead to questions and often to the solving of problems and, therefore, to the improvement of grades (D).

75. (A)

A teacher can guide a student to a higher-level answer through questioning. Repeating the question (B) would probably elicit the same response, and asking a different student (C, D) would not help the student who provided the simple response.

76. (C)

If the teacher ignores the answer entirely (A) or moves on to another question (D), it devalues the student's response. If the teacher responds immediately to the digression (B), the disruptive behavior has been rewarded. The correct answer is (C).

77. (A)

Nonperformers are students who are not involved in the class discussion at that particular moment. Asking students to respond to student statements (A) is one way of incorporating nonperformers into a class discussion. Therefore, (B), (C), and (D) are incorrect.

78. (B)

School schedules do not usually include time for teachers to engage in professional development activities such as consulting, observing colleagues, engaging in research, learning and practicing new skills, curriculum development, or professional reading. Contributing to this teachers' lack of time for professional development is the prevailing school culture that considers a teacher's proper place during school hours to be in front of the class. This isolates teachers from one another and discourages collaborative work. Presenters (A) for professional developments are plentiful, and creative school administrators can even use their own cache of teachers to deliver very effective in-service opportunities and workshops. Also, there are plenty of interested teachers (D), provided the professional development activities correspond to the needs of the teachers. Finally, although there will generally be a certain lack of resources (C) in education, this problem is not as pronounced as the lack of time.

79. (B)

Piaget identified four stages of cognitive development. As children go through each stage, they will develop new abilities, but they will be unable to exhibit this ability until they reach that particular stage. Children under the age of eight do not have the understanding of language that grasps complexities (A). Accordingly, teachers should use simple language when working with these children (C, D).

80. (B)

When designing learning activities, teachers should be aware that younger students process information more slowly than their older counterparts. Activities for younger children should be simple and short in duration.

81. (D)

In inductive thinking, students derive concepts and definitions based upon the information provided to them, which can be fostered through personal-discovery activities (D), by which students try to determine the relationships among the objects given to them. Choral chanting (A) practices skills; multiple-choice questions (C) usually test objective knowledge; and general computer experience (B) fosters computer knowledge.

82. (A)

A teacher can guide a student to a higher-level answer through questioning. Repeating the question (B) would probably elicit the same response, and asking a different student (C, D) would not help the student who provided the simple response.

83. (B)

Bloom classified educational objectives into a classification system that was divided into three domains—cognitive (memory and reasoning), affective (emotions), and psychomotor (physical abilities).

84. (C)

The horse shows lightness and motion (C). You should notice, for instance, that the tail and feet seem to imply movement. The horse is young and spry; (A) could not be true. The horse does not suggest warlike attitudes; (D) is not appropriate. The horse is light on its feet; massiveness (B) is not acceptable.

85. (C)

An aside is a comment spoken directly to the audience that the other actors on stage are supposedly unable to hear. Thus, the correct answer is choice (C).

86. (D)

This question tests one's ability to determine the central focus in a staged dramatic production and to explain why there is such a focus. The central attraction in this picture is the man on the bed (D). Many eyes are turned to him, and he appears to be speaking. The other men in the picture are turned away from the viewers, and many are directing their attention toward the man on the bed. Since this character is in a full front position, he will draw more attention than those in profile or full back, which are weaker positions.

87. (C)

Gianlorenzo Bernini's *David* of 1623 is a perfect example of the Baroque sculptor's wish to express movement and action and to capture a fleeting moment of time. Here, the figure's twisting posture and intense facial expression create a dynamic, not a static, character, as David begins the violent twisting motion with which he will hurl the stone from his sling; (B) is incorrect. His gaze is directed outward at an unseen adversary, implying interaction with another character and denying any purely ornamental conception behind this work (A). The figure's meager garments, far from identifying him as a warrior (D), emphasize both his physical vulnerability and his idealized, heroic beauty.

88. (D)

Kate, as an effective teacher and respected professional in her school as well as beyond her district, realizes the intent of central office curriculum efforts is to raise the standards of instruction throughout the district. While Kate, as a team player in the educational process, may be performing at the highest level, other teachers need boosting. The work that Kate submits will probably be used as a model for other teachers throughout the district. The thoroughness of her response indicates that she will be invited to make other presentations at area and state professional meetings, perhaps on the topic of authentic assessment.

Choice (A) is an unprofessional action by Kate. It could be because of forgetfulness or laziness, but nonetheless it is certainly expressing rudeness and lack of cooperation by ignoring the request made of her and all teachers in the district. None of these characteristics represents a teacher who is effective in the classroom and highly respected by her students and peers. Choice (B) indicates that Kate, rather than being forgetful or lazy, is unaware of or resentful of the role she plays as a curriculum developer within her teaching assignment. Her decision to write a "passionate letter in response" to the request is somewhat immature. The professional teacher who seriously questions a curricular approach from central office would discuss the situation reasonably, calmly, and privately with the new director of curriculum.

Of course, the very fact that Kate feels she has been incorporating authentic assessment ideas in her teaching for some time indicates that she values the concept. Should her role not be one of support to get other teachers to value authentic assessment as well? Choice (C) is incorrect because Kate, although showing support for the concept of authentic assessment, is still blocking the central office efforts to get some degree of uniformity in preparation of curriculum material. Again, her "passionate letter in response" to the request for an authentic assessment sample indicates poor judgment on Kate's part. The effective professional would find some other way to communicate her concerns if the provided format for the model of authentic assessment could be improved.

89. (C)

The physical education curriculum is designed to promote healthful living in students and to introduce them to a variety of physical activities. Thus aerobic conditioning helps train their hearts, strength training works on muscle groups and sportmanship teaches children how to behave to one another. Joining a team is an optional activity for children, not a goal of physical education

90. (A)

The seventeenth-century Japanese ink-on-paper scroll painting shown in the example relies almost exclusively on the qualities of line to convey the graceful forms of two leaping deer. In this painting, called *Deer Scroll*, both the animals and the scripted characters share the same quality of fluid, rhythmic, spontaneous "writing." Gradations of tone (B) and color (C) are unimportant here because the images are defined by black lines on white. Volume (D), too, is absent because these forms show no shading or modulation of tone.

91. (D)

Among all of the nationally recognized professional organizations, Teachers of English to Speakers of Other Languages, Inc, (TESOL) is identified as the organization that provides professional support for educators; (D) is the best answer. The IRA stands for the International Reading Association; (A) is not the best choice. NATM represents the National Association of Teachers of Mathematics; (B) is incorrect. NASDTEC is the abbreviation for the National Association of State Directors of Teacher Education and Certification; (C) is not the best choice.

92. (C)

There is sufficient evidence to suggest that the student is a victim of sexual abuse. The situation is too serious to delay action (A) or to remain passive (B). In no case would it be appropriate to copy and distribute the poem to other teachers (D).

93. (A)

It is important to keep strong communication lines open with the parents so that the child can get the best possible care and understanding from both the parents and the teacher.

94. (D)

Students' threats of suicide must be taken seriously, and teachers must refer to trained professionals to take action in the face of such threats. (A), (B), and (C) are inadequate responses to threats of suicide.

95. (A)

Linda's behavior serves a purpose or function. To assess the purpose or function of a behavior, teachers can use a functional behavioral assessment. Students normally do not exhibit behaviors for the purpose of making others angry (B). While Linda's behavior is generally not reflective of any specific home problems (C). It is possible that Linda just simply enjoys telling jokes, but it is unlikely that she chooses would choose to do so in the midst of a class lesson for the sheer enjoyment of performing (D). Hypotheses about the functions of behaviors address why the person might be exhibiting the behavior and what they are accomplishing or avoiding by exhibiting it.

96. (C)

Clearly setting a purpose for listening (I), asking questions about the selection (III), and encouraging students to forge links between the new information and knowledge already in place (IV) are all supported by research as effective strategies.

97. (B)

Just from looking at the graph, it is clear that most of the space under the curve is past the 60 mark on the x-axis, and there are clearly two groups. Answer (D) is eliminated because it doesn't include statement I. Statement II cannot be answered by what the graph shows. It appears possible that certain questions were too difficult for many in the class and that there were not enough questions to differentiate students in the 70–90 range, but perhaps the class performed exactly as it should have, given the students' ability and Ms. Alvarez's teaching. The distribution can give Ms. Alvarez many clues about the test and the students and even herself, but by itself tells her nothing about the fairness of the test. Thus, answer (A) can be eliminated. Also, without specific data, we cannot determine whether the mean is higher than the median, so (C) is incorrect.

98. (B)

Rules and regulations for schools and libraries that make the use of the Internet available to students do *not* currently include the filtering of text (B). However, these computers must provide the use of blocking or filtering technology to protect students against access to certain visual depictions (A). The rules also require that personal information about the students must not be disclosed (C) and prohibit the use of the computers for "hacking" (D).

99. (A)

(A) is not true; the "fair use" doctrine *does* allow limited reproduction of copyrighted works for educational and research purposes. Teachers can copy chapters, articles, charts, graphs, diagrams, or cartoons for the classroom, so (B) is legally possible and is *not* the correct answer. Regardless of whether the copy is from a collective work, an educator may make copies of a short story, essay, or poem for the classroom; so (C) is true and is not the answer to the question. Because teachers can make multiple copies for the class (not to exceed the number of students in the class) as long as the copying meets the tests of brevity and spontaneity, (D) is not the best choice.

100. (B)

Although (A), (C), and (D) are possible choices, the best answer to the question is (B). (A), (C), and (D) are basically restatements of the idea that the teacher forms the groups instead of the students; this was specified in the context of the question. The only option which gives a rationale for the teacher's action is answer (B).

101. (A)

The Impressionists were a group of painters who wanted to show their view of reality, not necessarily a photographic image of what appered. They often used a pointillist style of painting, in which the painting consisted of dots of colors. Claude Monet is an acclaimed painter of this style. Remrandt, a 16th century Dutch artist, is famous for his use of chiaroscuro, or light and dark to evoke emotions and scenes. Leonard Da Vinci is the artist famous for, among his many other talents, his painting of the Sistine Chapel in the Vatican.

102. (D)

Students are more likely to be more enthusiastic when something they enjoy is the subject or focus of a lesson; this, in turn, helps to build the academic success of the lesson.

103. (C)

These dances all orginated in South America, although they spread in popularity all over the world.

104. (D)

Choice (D) includes all of the techniques that would be useful in improving and monitoring writing. The students have set goals toward which they will strive (II) bit by bit until they reach them. The teacher and student have an opportunity to discuss good and bad points of the student's writing in a nonthreatening atmosphere (III). It is always helpful to have a model of good writing (IV), and by choosing students' papers, the teacher enhances students' self-esteem. Thus, choice (A), which does not include IV, is incorrect. Forcing a student to write every night (I) will do little to create quality work; therefore, choices (B) and (C) are incorrect.

105. (C)

Andy Warhol made the genre of pop art famous. Pop art uses typical cultural icons, such as Warhol's Campbell Soup cans or Marilyn Monroe to make a statement about popular culture. Impressionism was a nineteenth century art form used by such artists as Monet to create a dreamy, "impressionistic" view of reality. Cubism, which Picasso made famous, separated reality into geometric figures. Dadaism, an early 20th century movement, is exemplified the work of Max Ernst and Marcel Duchamp. It was a rebellion against the times and preached that everyone had a right to his/her own interpretation of reality.

106. (B)

Team rewards (I), individual accountability (II), and equal opportunities for success (III) are always present in cooperative learning. Rules (IV) and specific tasks (V) may be part of the instructions given for cooperative learning groups, but are not required in cooperative learning situations; therefore, choices (A), (C), and (D) are incorrect.

107. (B)

It is obvious that this passage is taken from the stage directions of a play because of the visual and auditory descriptions given. Also, the passage says that "lights come up" and a "rocket bursts, off," meaning "offstage."

108. (B)

Questions that demand recall of factual information usually can be answered in one or two words or in a short phrase. If lengthy answers are desired, the question format must change. There is no information to indicate that students are intimidated, therefore (A) is incorrect. Uncertainty about answers usually causes students to provide long, rambling responses, so (C) is incorrect. Because the students are providing answers, it does not seem reasonable that the questions are too difficult, so (D) is incorrect.

109. (A)

Yoga, a form of exercise brought from the Far East, emphasizes correct breathing, stretching exercises, and relaxation techniques. Pilates is a method of strengthening one's "core," or abdominal and back muscles.

110. (B)

BMI, or body mass index, is a tool for indicating weight status. It is a measure of weight for height and helps determine whether an individual is overweight, underweight, or at a normal weight.

Praxis II

Elementary Education
Test Code 0014

Practice Test 1

Answer Sheet

1. Ⓐ Ⓑ Ⓒ Ⓓ	31. Ⓐ Ⓑ Ⓒ Ⓓ	61. Ⓐ Ⓑ Ⓒ Ⓓ	91. Ⓐ Ⓑ Ⓒ Ⓓ
2. Ⓐ Ⓑ Ⓒ Ⓓ	32. Ⓐ Ⓑ Ⓒ Ⓓ	62. Ⓐ Ⓑ Ⓒ Ⓓ	92. Ⓐ Ⓑ Ⓒ Ⓓ
3. Ⓐ Ⓑ Ⓒ Ⓓ	33. Ⓐ Ⓑ Ⓒ Ⓓ	63. Ⓐ Ⓑ Ⓒ Ⓓ	93. Ⓐ Ⓑ Ⓒ Ⓓ
4. Ⓐ Ⓑ Ⓒ Ⓓ	34. Ⓐ Ⓑ Ⓒ Ⓓ	64. Ⓐ Ⓑ Ⓒ Ⓓ	94. Ⓐ Ⓑ Ⓒ Ⓓ
5. Ⓐ Ⓑ Ⓒ Ⓓ	35. Ⓐ Ⓑ Ⓒ Ⓓ	65. Ⓐ Ⓑ Ⓒ Ⓓ	95. Ⓐ Ⓑ Ⓒ Ⓓ
6. Ⓐ Ⓑ Ⓒ Ⓓ	36. Ⓐ Ⓑ Ⓒ Ⓓ	66. Ⓐ Ⓑ Ⓒ Ⓓ	96. Ⓐ Ⓑ Ⓒ Ⓓ
7. Ⓐ Ⓑ Ⓒ Ⓓ	37. Ⓐ Ⓑ Ⓒ Ⓓ	67. Ⓐ Ⓑ Ⓒ Ⓓ	97. Ⓐ Ⓑ Ⓒ Ⓓ
8. Ⓐ Ⓑ Ⓒ Ⓓ	38. Ⓐ Ⓑ Ⓒ Ⓓ	68. Ⓐ Ⓑ Ⓒ Ⓓ	98. Ⓐ Ⓑ Ⓒ Ⓓ
9. Ⓐ Ⓑ Ⓒ Ⓓ	39. Ⓐ Ⓑ Ⓒ Ⓓ	69. Ⓐ Ⓑ Ⓒ Ⓓ	99. Ⓐ Ⓑ Ⓒ Ⓓ
10. Ⓐ Ⓑ Ⓒ Ⓓ	40. Ⓐ Ⓑ Ⓒ Ⓓ	70. Ⓐ Ⓑ Ⓒ Ⓓ	100. Ⓐ Ⓑ Ⓒ Ⓓ
11. Ⓐ Ⓑ Ⓒ Ⓓ	41. Ⓐ Ⓑ Ⓒ Ⓓ	71. Ⓐ Ⓑ Ⓒ Ⓓ	101. Ⓐ Ⓑ Ⓒ Ⓓ
12. Ⓐ Ⓑ Ⓒ Ⓓ	42. Ⓐ Ⓑ Ⓒ Ⓓ	72. Ⓐ Ⓑ Ⓒ Ⓓ	102. Ⓐ Ⓑ Ⓒ Ⓓ
13. Ⓐ Ⓑ Ⓒ Ⓓ	43. Ⓐ Ⓑ Ⓒ Ⓓ	73. Ⓐ Ⓑ Ⓒ Ⓓ	103. Ⓐ Ⓑ Ⓒ Ⓓ
14. Ⓐ Ⓑ Ⓒ Ⓓ	44. Ⓐ Ⓑ Ⓒ Ⓓ	74. Ⓐ Ⓑ Ⓒ Ⓓ	104. Ⓐ Ⓑ Ⓒ Ⓓ
15. Ⓐ Ⓑ Ⓒ Ⓓ	45. Ⓐ Ⓑ Ⓒ Ⓓ	75. Ⓐ Ⓑ Ⓒ Ⓓ	105. Ⓐ Ⓑ Ⓒ Ⓓ
16. Ⓐ Ⓑ Ⓒ Ⓓ	46. Ⓐ Ⓑ Ⓒ Ⓓ	76. Ⓐ Ⓑ Ⓒ Ⓓ	106. Ⓐ Ⓑ Ⓒ Ⓓ
17. Ⓐ Ⓑ Ⓒ Ⓓ	47. Ⓐ Ⓑ Ⓒ Ⓓ	77. Ⓐ Ⓑ Ⓒ Ⓓ	107. Ⓐ Ⓑ Ⓒ Ⓓ
18. Ⓐ Ⓑ Ⓒ Ⓓ	48. Ⓐ Ⓑ Ⓒ Ⓓ	78. Ⓐ Ⓑ Ⓒ Ⓓ	108. Ⓐ Ⓑ Ⓒ Ⓓ
19. Ⓐ Ⓑ Ⓒ Ⓓ	49. Ⓐ Ⓑ Ⓒ Ⓓ	79. Ⓐ Ⓑ Ⓒ Ⓓ	109. Ⓐ Ⓑ Ⓒ Ⓓ
20. Ⓐ Ⓑ Ⓒ Ⓓ	50. Ⓐ Ⓑ Ⓒ Ⓓ	80. Ⓐ Ⓑ Ⓒ Ⓓ	110. Ⓐ Ⓑ Ⓒ Ⓓ
21. Ⓐ Ⓑ Ⓒ Ⓓ	51. Ⓐ Ⓑ Ⓒ Ⓓ	81. Ⓐ Ⓑ Ⓒ Ⓓ	111. Ⓐ Ⓑ Ⓒ Ⓓ
22. Ⓐ Ⓑ Ⓒ Ⓓ	52. Ⓐ Ⓑ Ⓒ Ⓓ	82. Ⓐ Ⓑ Ⓒ Ⓓ	112. Ⓐ Ⓑ Ⓒ Ⓓ
23. Ⓐ Ⓑ Ⓒ Ⓓ	53. Ⓐ Ⓑ Ⓒ Ⓓ	83. Ⓐ Ⓑ Ⓒ Ⓓ	113. Ⓐ Ⓑ Ⓒ Ⓓ
24. Ⓐ Ⓑ Ⓒ Ⓓ	54. Ⓐ Ⓑ Ⓒ Ⓓ	84. Ⓐ Ⓑ Ⓒ Ⓓ	114. Ⓐ Ⓑ Ⓒ Ⓓ
25. Ⓐ Ⓑ Ⓒ Ⓓ	55. Ⓐ Ⓑ Ⓒ Ⓓ	85. Ⓐ Ⓑ Ⓒ Ⓓ	115. Ⓐ Ⓑ Ⓒ Ⓓ
26. Ⓐ Ⓑ Ⓒ Ⓓ	56. Ⓐ Ⓑ Ⓒ Ⓓ	86. Ⓐ Ⓑ Ⓒ Ⓓ	116. Ⓐ Ⓑ Ⓒ Ⓓ
27. Ⓐ Ⓑ Ⓒ Ⓓ	57. Ⓐ Ⓑ Ⓒ Ⓓ	87. Ⓐ Ⓑ Ⓒ Ⓓ	117. Ⓐ Ⓑ Ⓒ Ⓓ
28. Ⓐ Ⓑ Ⓒ Ⓓ	58. Ⓐ Ⓑ Ⓒ Ⓓ	88. Ⓐ Ⓑ Ⓒ Ⓓ	118. Ⓐ Ⓑ Ⓒ Ⓓ
29. Ⓐ Ⓑ Ⓒ Ⓓ	59. Ⓐ Ⓑ Ⓒ Ⓓ	89. Ⓐ Ⓑ Ⓒ Ⓓ	119. Ⓐ Ⓑ Ⓒ Ⓓ
30. Ⓐ Ⓑ Ⓒ Ⓓ	60. Ⓐ Ⓑ Ⓒ Ⓓ	90. Ⓐ Ⓑ Ⓒ Ⓓ	120. Ⓐ Ⓑ Ⓒ Ⓓ

Elementary Education: Content Knowledge (0014) Practice Test 1

TIME: 120 Minutes
120 Questions

> **Four-Function or Scientific Calculator Permitted**

1. Teachers can provide a positive testing environment by

   (A) encouraging students to be anxious about a test.
   (B) providing a comfortable physical setting.
   (C) surprising students with disruptions and distractions.
   (D) emphasizing the consequences for poor performance.

2. If the mastery level for a skill is set at 75 percent, what does the student need to accomplish to exhibit mastery?

   (A) A grade of C or higher
   (B) A grade of B or higher
   (C) answer 75 percent of all of the particular skill questions correctly
   (D) answer 75 percent of all of the skills correctly

3. When a teacher asks the class if they agree or disagree with a student's response, the teacher is using

   (A) redirect.
   (B) corrective.
   (C) positive feedback.
   (D) direct response.

4. Written academic feedback is most productive when it

   (A) is delayed by a day.
   (B) is uniform.
   (C) includes at least one positive remark.
   (D) is not specific.

5. As the decades change, so do the labels the school systems use to identify students who differ from the mainstream—and may have difficulty with mathematics and other subjects. The school systems of the 21st Century identify these "differing" students as

   (A) at risk.
   (B) culturally deprived.
   (C) culturally different.
   (D) slow learners.

6. Goals for individual students

   (A) should be based upon the student's academic record.
   (B) should be the same for all students.
   (C) are created from individual observations only.
   (D) are developed after considering the student's history and motivation.

7. Feedback sessions for a test are most effective

   (A) when they are immediate.
   (B) when they are delayed by a day or so.
   (C) when they are delayed for a few weeks.
   (D) when the feedback is written on paper only.

8. Good and Gouws found that effective teachers reviewed

   (A) verbally.
   (B) at the end of a lesson.
   (C) as students showed weaknesses in specific areas.
   (D) daily, weekly, and monthly.

9. An important goal of the inclusion of students with disabilities in the least restrictive environment

   (A) is a focus on disability and a decreased focus on ability.
   (B) is a focus on inability.
   (C) is the use of the neighborhood school as the first option for the child with a disability.
   (D) is an educational placement of students with disabilities in the neighborhood school only if there is compelling evidence to do so.

10. Effective praise should be

    (A) authentic and low-key.
    (B) used sparingly.
    (C) composed of simple, positive responses.
    (D) used to encourage high-achieving students.

11. While waiting for students to formulate their responses to a question, a student blurts out an answer. The teacher should

    (A) ignore the answer entirely.
    (B) respond immediately to the student's answer.
    (C) silently acknowledge the student's response, and then address the response after the question has been answered by someone else.
    (D) move on to another question without comment.

12. Teachers/tutors who work with students pulled for a short time from a general education classroom with inclusion have had most satisfactory results with certain techniques of literacy instruction. The most satisfactory method is

    (A) de-emphasizing skills.
    (B) using only basic texts.
    (C) increased positive reinforcement.
    (D) whole language instruction.

13. Teaching reading through literature is a prevalent method today. Instructors who seek to teach reading through literature should have as a main concern

    (A) the factual aspects of a passage.
    (B) what the words may suggest, for instance an image, a sound, an association, or a feeling.
    (C) neither factual information nor aesthetic purposes.
    (D) the situation, the passages, and the students.

14. Students who speak English as a Second Language (ESL) can be successful in the classroom in the presence of certain conditions. Which of the following attributes characterizes ESL students who are least successful in the classroom? Least successful ESL students

    (A) make many mistakes initially.
    (B) take many risks.
    (C) have teachers and fellow classmates who are accepting of mistakes and do not correct the ESL student's mistakes every time that they occur.
    (D) listen more than they participate.

15. Inside a barn were lambs and people. If we counted 30 heads and 104 legs in the barn, how many lambs and how many people were in the barn?

    (A) 10 lambs and 20 people.
    (B) 16 lambs and 14 people.
    (C) 18 lambs and 16 people.
    (D) 22 lambs and 8 people.

16. According to the operant model in behavioral theory, negative reinforcement is

    (A) operant behavior.
    (B) stimulus for operant behavior.
    (C) unknowingly strengthening negative behavior.
    (D) removing a stimulus that causes a behavior to increase.

17. The first kindergarten was started by

    (A) Benjamin Franklin.
    (B) Friedrich Froebel.
    (C) Maria Montessori.
    (D) Johann Pestalozzi.

18. The atmospheres of the Moon and other celestial bodies were studied by using telescopes and spectrophotometers long before the deployment of interplanetary space probes. In these studies, scientists used the spectral patterns of sunlight that passed through the atmosphere of distant objects to learn what elements make up those atmospheres. Which of the following explains the source of the black-line spectral patterns?

    (A) When an element is excited, it gives off light in a characteristic spectral pattern.
    (B) When light strikes an object, some wavelengths of light are absorbed by the surface and others are reflected to give the object its color.
    (C) When light passes through a gas, light is absorbed at wavelengths characteristic of the elements in the gas.
    (D) The black lines are the spectra of ultraviolet light, which is called black light because it cannot be seen with human eyes.

19. Mr. Dobson wants to use a variety of grouping strategies during the year. Sometimes he groups students with others of similar ability; sometimes he groups students with varying ability. Sometimes he permits students to choose their own groupings. Sometimes he suggests that students work with a particular partner; sometimes he assigns a partner. Sometimes he allows students to elect to work individually. This flexibility in grouping strategies indicates Mr. Dobson recognizes that

    (A) fifth graders like surprises and unpredictable teacher behavior.
    (B) grouping patterns affect students' perceptions of self-esteem and competence.
    (C) frequent changes in the classroom keep students alert and interested.
    (D) it is not fair to place the worst students in the same group consistently.

20. The social studies teachers of an inner city school wanted to change to a more relevant curriculum. The department wanted to have units on economics throughout the world instead of only regions of the United States. Mrs. Dunn was asked to submit a proposal for the new curriculum, related activities, sequencing, themes, and materials. In consultation with the other teachers in the department, a needs assessment was planned. The group felt that the needs assessment would

    (A) help the students make a connection between their current skills and those that will be new to them.
    (B) reveal community problems that may affect the students' lives and their performance in school.
    (C) foster a view of learning as a purposeful pursuit, promoting a sense of responsibility for one's own learning.
    (D) engage students in learning activities and help them to develop the motivation to achieve.

21. When the needs assessment was evaluated, it revealed an ethnically diverse community. Student interests and parental expectations varied, different language backgrounds existed, student exceptionalities were common, and academic motivation was low. The question confronting the teachers was how to bridge the gap from where the students were to where they should be. The available choices were to

    (A) change the text only.
    (B) relate the lessons to the students' personal interests.
    (C) create a positive environment to minimize the effects of the negative external factors.
    (D) help students to learn and to monitor their own performance.

The following scenario is to be used for questions 22 and 23.

During the period of community-involvement field experiences, Ms. Parks continually directs her students' attention to the fact that science is a way of solving problems. Following this field experience period, Ms. Parks asks her students to identify a problem in their school and to devise a scientific way of studying and solving that problem. The students work in groups for two class periods and select the following problem for investigation: It is late spring, and the classroom gets so hot during the afternoon that the majority of the students are uncomfortable. Their research question becomes, "Why is it hotter in our classroom than in the music room, art room, or library? How can we make our classroom cooler?"

22. Of the following choices, what is the most important benefit of allowing the students to select their own problem to investigate, rather than having the teacher assign a problem?

(A) Students become self-directed problem-solvers who can structure their own learning experiences.

(B) The teacher can best assess each student's academic and affective needs in a naturalistic setting.

(C) Students will have the opportunity to work with a wide variety of instructional materials.

(D) Students will learn to appreciate opposing viewpoints.

23. Which of the following is the most important force at work when students are allowed to select their own problem for investigation?

(A) Increased student motivation
(B) Increased student diversity
(C) Increased structure of student groups
(D) Increased use of self-assessment

24. Mrs. Jones has been using bar graphs on the overhead projector to a) provide salaries of various occupations/professions and b) to indicate the required education and skills for each occupation/profession. At the end of the question-and-answer/discussion period, the goal was for students to have an awareness of the correlation between their skills or lack of skills and their salaries. A parent/guardian support group would be established to enhance the students' motivation to master new

skills. Strategies for use at home and in the classroom would be developed. Mrs. Dunn felt that with the aid of parents

(A) she could promote her own professional growth as she worked cooperatively with professionals to create a school culture that would enhance learning and result in positive change.

(B) she would be meeting the expectations associated with teaching.

(C) she would be fostering strong home relationships that support student achievement of desired outcomes.

(D) she would be exhibiting her understanding of the principles of conferences, trust, and cooperation.

The following scenario is to be used for questions 25–28.

Mr. Brown feels very uncomfortable when he has to make decisions about the assessment of students. He has had some difficulty with various types of assessment. He decides it is time to talk to Mr. Williams, the principal.

25. Which of the following would be the most effective way for Mr. Brown to document his teaching in an authentic setting and to be aware of students' efforts, progress, and achievements in one or more areas?

(A) Standardized tests
(B) Teacher-made tests
(C) Observation
(D) Portfolio

26. Which would be the most effective way to evaluate specific objectives and specific content in Mr. Brown's course?

(A) Self and peer evaluation
(B) Portfolio
(C) Teacher-made test
(D) Observation

27. Mr. Williams asks Mr. Brown what type of test scores are rated against the performance of other students and are reported in terms of percentiles,

stanines, and scaled scores. Mr. Brown should give which response?

(A) Portfolio
(B) Teacher-made test
(C) Observation
(D) Standardized test

28. When the teacher's role is that of a facilitator who utilizes students' knowledge and understanding of specific evaluation criteria, what type of assessment is being used?

(A) Portfolio
(B) Teacher-made test
(C) Self and peer assessment
(D) Observation

Question 29 refers to the following passage.

Tom Jones was asked to improve the remedial reading curriculum for upper elementary-grade students. He found that the students were continually tested and evaluated on reading, that the current objectives were unclear, and that the teaching materials were inappropriate. Following a lengthy observation of Mrs. Ratu's teaching strategies, Mr. Jones concluded that she was teaching basic reading skills in the same manner as did the lower elementary teachers. The teaching materials used a controlled vocabulary and simple sentences. The students were being taught to rely heavily upon pictures and illustrations for the story. Most of the material was fictional in genre. Rote was Mrs. Ratu's preference for learning. Mr. Jones analyzed the test results and found that many of the students in Mrs. Ratu's class had average scores in the areas of art, math, and music. He concluded that, with the exception of reading, most were normal students and would be successful when their remediation was complete. Mr. Jones made several decisions: (1) the students would be evaluated annually with an achievement test; (2) reading materials of interest to upper elementary students would be substituted for elementary materials; (3) each student

would be encouraged to read about the subject of his or her choice; and (4) round-table discussions would be developed for each "favorite subject."

29. Mrs. Ratu's method of teaching remedial reading focused upon

I. the level at which the students should have learned the basic reading skills.
II. her own minimal competency in instructional design and evaluation.
III. her lack of understanding of the learners in her class.
IV. her desire to make remedial reading easy for the students.

(A) I only
(B) I and IV only
(C) II and III only
(D) II only

30. Language-minority students who speak their native language instead of English in the classroom

(A) do not have the right to do so.
(B) have the responsibility to do so.
(C) have the obligation to do so.
(D) are a challenge to educators.

31. To help a language-minority student most, recent research (Elley and Mangubhai) suggests that

(A) listening and speaking proficiency should precede literacy instruction.
(B) the teacher should help the student develop reading skills coincidentally with speaking skills but independently from writing skills.
(C) the teacher should help the student develop writing skills before reading skills since motor skills precede reading.
(D) the teacher should seek to help the students to develop reading and writing concomitantly.

32. Dominique Woods has two years of teaching experience at a large urban high school. This is her first year teaching at a small, suburban, ethnically mixed high school. She wants to take advantage of the week of faculty meetings before school opens to become better acquainted with the school

grounds, faculty, curriculum, and available materials. How could she best utilize her time?

(A) Tour the school while noting the teacher's room, materials room, and other important rooms.
(B) Talk to the principal about what is expected of her.
(C) Talk with a willing teacher who has spent several years at the school about community characteristics and available materials as they apply to the curriculum.
(D) Obtain a copy of the curriculum to take to the materials room where it can be determined what materials are available for classroom use.

33. The probability of parents' offspring showing particular traits can be predicted by using

(A) the Linnaean System.
(B) DNA tests.
(C) the Punnett Square.
(D) None of the above.

34. An acidic solution can have a pH of

(A) 20
(B) 10
(C) 8
(D) 5

35. A material with definite volume but no definite shape is called

(A) titanium.
(B) gas.
(C) liquid.
(D) solid

36. The intensity of an earthquake is measured by

(A) a thermograph.
(B) a seismograph.
(C) a telegraph.
(D) an odometer.

37. _____ is defined as the ability to do work.

(A) Force
(B) Energy
(C) Speed
(D) Distance

Creating an English garden on a mountainside in the Ouachita Mountains in central Arkansas may sound like an impossible endeavor, but after two years, this dream is becoming reality. By digging up the rocks and replacing them with bags of top soil, humus, and peat, the persistent gardener now has sprouts that are not all weeds. Gravel paths meander through the beds of shasta daisies, marigolds, lavender, valerian, iris, day lilies, Mexican heather, and other flowers. Ornamental grasses, dogwood trees, and shrubs back up the flowers. Along the periodic waterway created by an underground spring, swamp hibiscus, helenium, hosta, and umbrella plants display their colorful and seasonal blooms. The flower beds are outlined by large rocks dug up by a pickax. Blistered hands are worth the effort when people stop by to view the mountainside beauty.

38. This essay can be described as being

(A) speculative.
(B) argumentative.
(C) narrative.
(D) expository.

39. New research (Goodman) and alternative views (Flores) about all children—including the at-risk—challenge the status quo and ask teachers to revalue their habitudes and practices related to traditional ways of teaching. These assumptions for math teachers and language arts teachers indicate

(A) that at-risk children bring very few experiences to the classroom.
(B) that many children cannot be successful in a regular classroom program.
(C) that observing children and their language in authentic settings is not as helpful as standardized testing to determine literacy.
(D) that families of at-risk children are interested in their children and in their school experiences.

Use the figure below and the following facts to answer question 40:

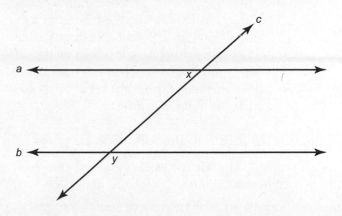

Lines *a* and *b* are parallel,

c is a line, and

the measure of angle *x* is 50°.

40. What is the measure of angle *y*?

    (A) 50°
    (B) 100°
    (C) 130°
    (D) 80°

41. In the given figure, assume that AD is a line. What is the measure of angle AXB?

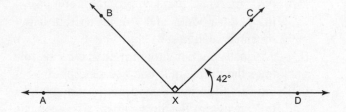

    (A) 48°
    (B) 90°
    (C) 42°
    (D) There is not enough information given to answer the question.

42. Which formula can be used to find the area of the triangle shown below?

    (A) $A = (l \times h)/2$
    (B) $A = (l + h)/2$
    (C) $A = 2(l + h)$
    (D) $A = 2(l \times h)$

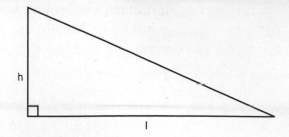

43. Which formula can be used to find the area of the figure below? (Assume the curve is *half* of a circle.)

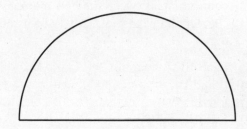

    (A) $A = \pi r$
    (B) $A = 2\pi r^2$
    (C) $A = \pi r^2$
    (D) $A = \pi r^2/2$

Use the figure below to answer question 44. Assume the following:

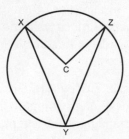

Point C is the center of the circle.

Angles XYZ and XCZ intercept minor arc XZ.

The measure of angle XYZ is 40°.

44. What is the measure of the major arc XYZ?

    (A) 140°
    (B) 280°
    (C) 160°
    (D) 320°

45. Why should children be encouraged to figure out the structure and the features of the text they are attempting to comprehend and remember?

    I. It helps the students to understand the way the author organized the material to be presented.
    II. It helps the students to look at the features of the text.
    III. Talking about the structure of the text provides an opportunity for the teacher to point out the most salient features to the students.
    IV. The discussions may help the child make connections between the new material in the chapter and what is already known about the topic.

    (A) I and III
    (B) II and IV
    (C) I and IV
    (D) I, II, III, and IV

46. Ms. Smith decided to stage three different versions of *Cinderella* with her students. Knowing that this is one of the world's most famous fairy tales, she located Chinese, Native American, and Russian versions of the story. She found age-appropriate plays of each that could be staged in her classroom. In addition to acting in these plays, her students are creating scenery, costumes, and props to use in their performances. Which of the following best describes what Ms. Smith primarily expects her students to achieve through these activities?

    I. Understanding cultural similarities and differences through dramatic literature
    II. Understanding theatrical practices
    III. Gaining experience with creative drama practices
    IV. Gaining experience with adapting stories into plays

    (A) I only
    (B) I and II
    (C) III and IV
    (D) I, II, and IV

47. In order to extend the literacy of others, teachers must engage in some self-reflection to meet the needs of the learners. Teachers will find that

    (A) comparing their own literacy history to that of their students is futile.
    (B) considering how a school setting helped them and making such comparisons with the students they teach is probably inapplicable.
    (C) school experiences have no effect on the self identity of most of the diverse learners.
    (D) self-evaluation of their own values, attitudes, and dispositions is helpful.

Question 48 refers to the following passage.

Mrs. Gettler teaches 26 third graders in a large inner city school. About one-third of her students participate in the ESL program at the school. Mrs. Gettler suspects that some of the students' parents are unable to read or write in English. Four of the students receive services from the learning resource teacher. At the beginning of the year, none of the students read above 2.0 grade level, and some of the students did not know all the letters of the alphabet.

48. Which of the following describes the instructional strategy that is most likely to improve the reading levels of Mrs. Gettler's students?

    (A) An intensive phonics program that includes drill and practice work on basic sight words.
    (B) An emergent literacy program emphasizing pattern books and journal writing using invented spelling.
    (C) An instructional program that closely follows the third-grade basal reader.
    (D) Participation by all students in the school's ESL program so they can receive services from the learning resource center.

The following scenario is to be used for questions 49 through 52.

Mrs. Doe began planning a two-week unit of study of the Native Americans for her fifth-grade class. To begin the unit, she chose a movie on the twenty-first century Native Americans. As Mrs. Doe reflectively listened, the students asked key questions.

The following day, Mrs. Doe reviewed the use of encyclopedias, indexes, and atlases. She then divided the students into groups and took them to the library. Each group was responsible for locating information on a particular topic. The topics wcrc maps showing the topography of the land, charts illustrating the climate, plants and animals, a map showing migration routes, and a map showing the general areas where the Native Americans settled.

49. The students' involvement in the unit of study is a result of

   I. the teacher's reflective listening during the discussion.
   II. the available resources and materials.
   III. careful planning and its relationship to success in the classroom.
   IV. the students' personal acquaintance with Native Americans.

   (A) I only
   (B) I and II only
   (C) II and III only
   (D) I and IV only

50. Days 3 and 4 of this unit were spent with each group being involved in library research. They wrote information on index cards. Each group prepared a presentation that included a written explanation of an assigned topic, a shadow box, and a sawdust map or models of Native American clothing. A pictograph was to be used in the telling of a legend or folk story. The presentation concluded with a collage depicting the Native American way of life. Multiple strategies and techniques were used for

   I. motivation of the group and its effects on individual behavior and learning.
   II. allowing each student regardless of ability to participate in the project.
   III. integrating the project with other subjects.
   IV. developing a foundation for teaching American history.

   (A) I, II, and III only
   (B) I and II only
   (C) III only
   (D) IV only

51. Day 10 of the unit was Field Trip Day, which involved visiting museums. The students were given a choice of museums. Each student was expected to take notes of what was seen, heard, and experienced to share with the remainder of the class on the following day. Field Trip Day and its experiences

   I. allowed the students to make connections between their current skills and those that were new to them.
   II. allowed external factors to create a learning environment that would take advantage of positive factors.
   III. allowed a sense of community to be nurtured.
   IV. allowed the students to take responsibility for their own learning.

   (A) I and II only
   (B) III only
   (C) IV only
   (D) III and IV only

52. Giving the students a choice of field trip locations

   I. was meant to enhance the students' self-concept.
   II. was meant to respect differences and enhance the students' understanding of the society in which they live.
   III. was meant to foster the view of learning as a purposeful pursuit.
   IV. was meant as an example of using an array of instructional strategies.

   (A) II only
   (B) II and IV only
   (C) I and II only
   (D) III only

53. Troubled by what seems to be an increase in gang-type activity among younger children, Mr. Billings wants to find out what his students think and know about gangs. He wants to learn the most he can about the students' thinking about this topic in the least amount of time. Additionally, he wants to give all students the chance to share what they think and know while maximizing interaction among students. The students will spend the entire morning reading, talking, and writing a group

report about this subject. Which of the following seating arrangements would best help Mr. Billings meet his objectives?

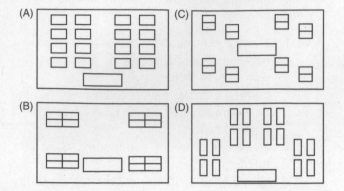

54. The strength of requiring a cognitive objective and a performance objective is that

   (A) some students are not test takers and do poorly on paper and pencil tests.
   (B) the score for one objective could offset the score for the other objective.
   (C) the developmental level in one domain may affect performance in another domain.
   (D) the teacher is matching the students' learning styles to her teaching style.

55. When developing a unit about the Erie Canal for elementary-age students, how would you handle assessment of the students?

   (A) Explain to the students that the unit will cover a variety of projects; therefore, you will be using different assessment tools.
   (B) Explain to the students each project in the unit, then describe what they will be asked to do.
   (C) Give to the students a list of new vocabulary words that they will need to know for the final test.
   (D) Explain to the students that they will need to hand in their notebooks at the end of the unit.

56. Rubrics are used by many teachers in elementary schools for the purposes of assessment. What criteria should be used when creating a rubric?

   I. Set clearly defined criteria for each assessment.

   II. Include a rating scale.
   III. Use only one idea at a time so that students are not confused.
   IV. Tell students that they can rate themselves.

   (A) IV and III
   (B) III and II
   (C) I and II
   (D) None of these

57. Mr. O'Brien ends class by telling students that over the next few weeks they will be required to keep a communications journal. Every time they have an eventful exchange—either positive or negative, they are to record the details of the exchange in their journal. This assignment is given as

   (A) a way to help students improve their composition and rhetorical skills.
   (B) a way of understanding individual students, monitoring instructional effectiveness, and shaping instruction.
   (C) a way of helping students become more accountable for the way they manage their time.
   (D) the basis for giving daily grades to students.

Scenario: It is the first day of class. Ms. Johnson, the language arts teacher, tells the students a little bit about herself. She tells them that she wants to know about each individual in the class. She asks them to write about themselves and hand their papers to her as they leave the class to go to lunch.

58. By requiring that students write about themselves, Ms. Johnson is

   (A) fulfilling her responsibilities as an English teacher.
   (B) preparing her class to create autobiographies.
   (C) relying on the Language-Experience-Approach (LEA) for instruction.
   (D) preparing her class to read biographies about great Americans from diverse cultural backgrounds.

59. Ms. Johnson collects the students' papers at the end of class. As she reads the papers, she decides

that the best way to give her students positive feed-back is

(A) not to mark errors on the paper so as not to discourage or inhibit their creativity.

(B) to make at least one positive comment about each paragraph.

(C) begin with one or two positive comments about the paper and then suggest how students could improve their writing.

(D) give everyone a high grade on the paper for participating in the assignment.

60. After Ms. Johnson finishes reading all the students' papers, she observes that some of the students had difficulty identifying and describing their strengths, whether in class or outside class. She believes that all of her students have strengths and she wants to help them see the assets they possess. She decides that in the next class, students will

(A) take a learning style assessment to uncover their particular learning strengths and characteristics.

(B) listen to a lecture about how everyone possesses special skills and strengths.

(C) read a chapter from a book about Guilford's Structure of Intellect, as a precursor to a discussion about how intelligence is specialized and diverse.

(D) rewrite their papers, correcting their errors and revising their paragraphs to name at least two additional classroom strengths they possess and at least two additional interpersonal skills they possess.

61. Mr. Swenson teaches mathematics in high school. He is planning a unit for his advanced math students on fractal geometry, using the computer lab for demonstrations and exploration. The students have used various computer programs to solve algebra and calculus problems. As Mr. Swenson plans a unit of study, he determines that a cognitive outcome will be that students will design and produce fractals by using a computer program. An effective outcome is that students will become excited about investigating a new field of mathematics and will show this interest by choosing to develop a math project relating to fractals. The most appropriate strategy to use first would be

(A) explaining the exciting development of fractal geometry over the past 10 to 15 years.

(B) demonstrating on the computer the way to input values into formulas to produce fractal designs.

(C) giving students a few simple fractal designs and asking them to figure out the formulas for producing them.

(D) showing students color pictures of complex fractals and asking them for ideas about how they could be drawn mathematically.

62. Which teacher action works best to reduce racial problems in a classroom? A teacher should

(A) work to make all students think, talk, and act as he or she does to foster harmony.

(B) seek to be conscious of differences among students.

(C) treat all students in the same way.

(D) seek to be color blind.

63. The characteristics of fascism include all of the following EXCEPT:

(A) totalitarianism.
(B) democracy.
(C) romanticism.
(D) militarism.

64. The industrial economy of the nineteenth century was based upon all of the following EXCEPT:

(A) the availability of raw materials.
(B) an equitable distribution of profits among those involved in production.
(C) the availability of capital.
(D) a distribution system to market finished products.

65. "Jim Crow" laws were laws that

(A) effectively prohibited blacks from voting in state and local elections.

(B) restricted American Indians to U.S. government reservations.

(C) restricted open-range ranching in the Great Plains.

(D) established separate segregated facilities for blacks and whites.

66. Which of the following is used to effect the release of a person from improper imprisonment?

    (A) A writ of mandamus.
    (B) A writ of habeas corpus.
    (C) The Fourth Amendment requirement that police have probable cause in order to obtain a search warrant.
    (D) The Supreme Court's decision in *Roe v Wade*.

67. Which of the following defines a salt?

    (A) One of the reactant products of an acid and base.
    (B) One of the reactant products of a base and water.
    (C) One of the reactant products of an acid and water.
    (D) A reactant product of a phase transformation.

68. The atomic number for neutral (unionized) atoms as listed in the periodic table refers to

    (A) the number of neutrons in an atom.
    (B) the number of protons in an atom.
    (C) the number of electrons in an atom.
    (D) Both (B) and (C).

69. Which of the following is a phenomenon involving the physical properties of a substance?

    (A) Corrosion of iron
    (B) Burning of wood
    (C) Rocket engine ignition
    (D) Melting of ice

70. Isotopes of a given element contain

    (A) more electrons than protons with equal numbers of neutrons.
    (B) more protons than electrons with equal numbers of neutrons.
    (C) equal numbers of protons and electrons with differing numbers of neutrons.
    (D) unequal numbers of protons and electrons with differing numbers of neutrons.

71. Newton's second law of motion states that "the net force acting on a body is equal to the product of its mass and its acceleration." Which of the following is a good example of the law's application?

    (A) Decreased friction between surfaces by means of lubrication.
    (B) Potential energy stored in a compressed spring.
    (C) A rocket lifting off at Cape Canaveral with increasing speed.
    (D) Using a claw hammer to pull a nail out with multiplied force.

72. Which of the following is most likely to contain the greatest thermal energy?

    (A) The Pacific Ocean with an average temperature of ~5°F.
    (B) A 1 g sample of molten metal at 2,000°F.
    (C) A bucket of water at 75°F.
    (D) Lake Michigan at an average temperature of ~5°F.

73. Which cellular component is responsible for the regulation of exchanges of substances between a cell and its environment?

    (A) The endoplasmic reticulum
    (B) The cell nucleus
    (C) The cytoplasm
    (D) The cell membrane

74. Humans have 46 chromosomes in their body cells. How many chromosomes are found in the zygote?

    (A) 2
    (B) 10
    (C) 23
    (D) 46

75. Human body temperature regulation via the skin involves

    (A) respiration.
    (B) transpiration.
    (C) perspiration.
    (D) sensation.

76. Darwin's original theory of natural selection asserts that

    (A) all organisms have descended with modification from a common ancestor.
    (B) random genetic drift plays a major role in speciation.

(C) species characteristics are inherited by means of genes.

(D) speciation is usually due to gradual accumulation of small genetic changes.

77. The lunar period is nearest in length to

(A) 24 hours.
(B) 30 days.
(C) 365 days.
(D) 1 week.

78. A supernova normally occurs when

(A) a star first initiates fusion.
(B) galaxies collide.
(C) the end of a star's lifetime nears, with its nuclear fuel exhausted.
(D) a wandering comet plunges into the a star's interior.

79. The most important factor in Earth's seasonal patterns is the

(A) distance from the Sun to Earth.
(B) Earth's rotation period of 24 hours.
(C) tilting of the Earth's axis.
(D) the Moon and associated tides.

80. Metamorphic rocks are

(A) derived from igneous rocks.
(B) unrelated to igneous rocks.
(C) a type of sedimentary rock.
(D) a type of rock not found on this planet.

81. Which of the following is considered to be evidence for plate tectonics?

(A) Continental coastline "fit"
(B) Identical fossil evidence at "fit" locations
(C) Intense geological activity in mountainous regions
(D) All of the above

82. Seafloor spreading is characterized as

(A) plate spreading with upwelling magma forming ridges.
(B) plate collisions with associated ridge formation.
(C) plate spreading with no ridge formation.
(D) plate collisions with no ridge formation.

83. Igneous rocks are formed by

(A) magma cooling in underground cells and pockets.
(B) magma ejected aboveground as lava, which cools.
(C) layers of sediment collecting and compacting at the bottom of lakes and seas.
(D) both (A) and (B).

84. In descending order of abundance, what is the composition of the Earth's atmosphere?

(A) Oxygen, nitrogen, carbon dioxide, trace gases
(B) Nitrogen, oxygen, carbon dioxide, trace gases
(C) Nitrogen, carbon dioxide, oxygen, trace gases
(D) Carbon dioxide, oxygen, nitrogen, trace gases

85. What is the greatest common divisor of 120 and 252?

(A) 2
(B) 3
(C) 6
(D) 12

86. How many odd prime numbers are there between 1 and 20?

(A) 7
(B) 8
(C) 9
(D) 10

87. Round the following number to the nearest hundredths place: 287.416.

(A) 300
(B) 290
(C) 287.42
(D) 287.4139

88. Teacher should seek to bridge cultural gaps between home and school. To bridge home-school gaps when cultural differences exist, teachers

(A) should avoid home visits since the visits may increase misunderstanding, particularly if a language barrier exists.
(B) should avoid the use of a translator at a parent-teacher conference since this might involve a breach of confidentiality.

(C) should keep the same school routines but should encourage the student to adapt to the new situation.

(D) should observe the student in situations involving others on the playground or in work situations in the classroom.

89. When maintaining a running reading record, a teacher is

(A) tape recording while a student reads aloud.
(B) writing what a student reads aloud.
(C) testing for comprehension.
(D) noting what books have been read.

90. There are certain attributes which characterize thematic learning and the integration of instruction. Which of the following is an attribute of thematic teaching and the integration of instruction? Thematic learning and the integration of instruction

(A) promote fragmentation of the curriculum.
(B) emphasize the acquisition of isolated facts.
(C) are new features of the 21st Century.
(D) resemble the way many students learn.

91. Children under the age of eight

(A) are unable to answer questions.
(B) process information more slowly than older children.
(C) can answer the same questions as slightly older children.
(D) cannot learn in a cooperative environment.

92. It is the end of the school year, and the achievement test scores have not arrived. All the parents are eager to find out how their children did on the tests. Mrs. Brown is getting telephone calls nightly to find out what these scores are. What should Mrs. Brown do?

(A) Mrs. Brown should volunteer to call each parent of students in her class and give them the scores over the phone during the summer.
(B) Mrs. Brown should not bother the principal with the problem. She should simply tell the parents that she will post the scores on her classroom door. Because the school will be open for painting for the next two weeks, the

parents will have no trouble getting into the building. They can find the scores in alphabetical order by the last name of the student.
(C) Mrs. Brown should talk to the principal to find out the policy for sharing these scores with parents—especially because the next day school will be over for that school year.
(D) Mrs. Brown can at last tell the parents she is no longer the students' teacher, so she is no longer responsible for talking with them.

93. A teacher consistently returns graded papers to her students within three days of their turning their work in. She writes very complete comments on each paper to help students understand what they have done correctly or incorrectly on their assignments. Doing this is important to the teacher's instructional goals because

(A) it is easy to fall behind in grading if a teacher doesn't keep up with the workload.
(B) grading papers is an important part of a teacher's job performance.
(C) students have a responsibility to keep track of their graded work.
(D) providing students with information about their performance is one way to help them improve their performance.

94. Inquiry learning is most likely characterized by

(A) preplanned assignments by which the learner might elicit factual information from a textbook and complete a test for evaluation.
(B) problem-posing by learners or by teachers and problem solving; emphasis is on process—not just content.
(C) a learner's gaining meaning primarily through teacher lecture.
(D) a teacher's conducting short, purposeful, direct-teaching sessions with the class.

95. Writing programs may vary from situation to situation, but the most effective writing program for teaching multicultural students has a main characteristic. The characteristic is that the writing program

(A) connects students' lives to their classroom writing experience.

(B) is conducted by a teacher who engages the students in story starters, language games, and worksheets developed for the purpose of creative writing.

(C) presents the teacher as an authority figure diverse students can learn from and model.

(D) has a teacher who is confident, experienced, and willing to present the writing techniques to them systematically.

96. Two students always finish their assigned work before their classmates. Consequently, they are usually disruptive to the rest of the class, who are still working. An effective way to help the two students learn time-management skills and to keep them out of trouble would be for the teacher to

(A) send them to the principal's office for their horseplay.

(B) point out the careless errors they make on their assignments for not taking their time and for not giving more thought to their work.

(C) plan activities for students who finish their classwork early.

(D) count 10 points off their assignment for each time the teacher has to tell the students to quiet down.

97. Devices used to aid memorization using rhymes, acronyms, songs, or stories are called

(A) choral responses.
(B) repetitions.
(C) codings.
(D) mnemonics.

98. If a teacher asks, "Does everyone understand where to place the answers?" the teacher is probably

(A) using a transition between lessons.
(B) determining if the class understands the directions.
(C) assuming that the students were off-task.
(D) introducing a new skill.

99. The most effective time for students to retain information is for them to review or study

(A) within 8 hours of the material first being presented.

(B) 24 hours after the material is presented.

(C) more than 24 hours after the material is first presented but just before being tested.

(D) None of the above.

100. Inclusion is a way of treating diverse learners in a regular classroom. It is based primarily on

(A) the understanding that general education teachers can deal best with individual differences in their own classrooms without special education teachers or classes.

(B) the theory that special education teachers are the only ones who can deal effectively with diverse learners with individual differences.

(C) the supposition that parents want their children to work with a variety of people in the learning situation.

(D) the technique of having both the classroom teacher and the special education teacher deal with the diverse learners in the classroom.

101. What can be determined by behavioral observation?

(A) Concept comprehension
(B) Ability to organize concepts
(C) Amount of time spent on-task
(D) Verbal skills

102. If a student is usually quick to attempt answers to questions, but often blurts out wrong responses, the teacher's best response to the student is to

(A) say, "Wrong answer, but better luck next time."

(B) say, "Well, not exactly. But, you're close."

(C) say nothing, but smile and call on someone else.

(D) say, "Why don't I give you another minute to think about that answer?"

103. What is one benefit of practice activities?

(A) The teacher can observe where students need additional instruction.

(B) The students can develop their creative writing skills.

(C) Students can revisit previously learned skills.

(D) Students can learn new concepts.

104. A teacher ran out of copies of a worksheet before handing them out to the entire class, thus interrupting

    (A) materials.
    (B) class interest.
    (C) instructional momentum.
    (D) passing out the papers.

105. Two teachers have different views of what their students have accomplished in the computer lab. One teacher, who has had little experience in the computer lab and does not like using the lab, does not feel that students are making progress. In contrast, the second teacher, who has had extensive experience in the computer lab and who enjoys using the lab with students, feels that students are making good progress. To understand the difference in the teachers' perceptions, it is important to know that

    (A) teacher experience with technology has an impact on the effective use of technology.
    (B) the students in both classes enjoy working in the computer lab.
    (C) the students in both classes do not enjoy working in the computer lab.
    (D) some of the students in both classes enjoy working in the computer lab, and some of the students do not like it.

106. Benjamin Rodriguez teaches a fifth-period class of 20 academically gifted fifth-graders. Having recently read about the bell-shaped curve, Mr. Rodriguez tells his class that he will be using it for grading. "This means," he tells them, "that only about 2 percent will be making A's, 2 percent will fail the class, 13 percent will make D's, 13 percent will make B's, and the rest of you will be making C's." (Note that 2 percent of 20 is less than 1.) What is your professional opinion on his decision?

    (A) The decision on how to grade the class is the teacher's decision; if a teacher sets the standards high and gives only 2 percent A's, the students will all stretch to get the one A.
    (B) The students should make the decision on how the teacher should grade them and the grading scale; the teacher should hand the decision down to the students.

    (C) Mr. Rodriguez doesn't seem to understand the bell-shaped curve; because it is for use with the general population, it is not suitable for application to a group of above-average students.
    (D) Fifth-graders have no business knowing how the teacher will determine the grades; grading is a teacher's decision, and students are not a part of it.

107. James is having a problem remaining at his desk before lunch. His third-grade teacher wants to help him maintain a longer attention span and eventually to help him practice self-discipline. Which of the following items would be a part of the teacher's plan for James?

    (A) James would lose his music period (a favorite part of his week) if he does not stay in his seat for at least 30 minutes each day in the time before lunch.
    (B) James would have to stand for an hour in the corner if he fails to remain seated for the full 30 minutes before lunch.
    (C) The teacher will send a letter home to the parents to tell them that he will no longer agree to teach James if he cannot remain seated for half an hour, and James will have to have a new teacher—the teacher in the other third-grade class.
    (D) The teacher will set up incentives for James; for instance, he can receive a popsicle stick for each day he is able to remain seated for 30 minutes. When he collects 5 of these, he will be eligible to receive a free pass to the computer lab for 30 minutes to use the educational computer games he likes best.

108. While on after-school hall duty, Mrs. Dominguez notices a student showing a boy a shiny object. As she moves closer, she notices that it is a hunting knife. The best plan of action would be for her to

    (A) tell the boys that they must get on the bus immediately or leave the school grounds and ignore the knife because school is not in session and she is no longer in charge.
    (B) take the knife from the boy with the stipulation that his parents must contact her if he wants it back.

(C)   take the knife from the boy and escort him to the principal's office.

(D)   lecture to the boy the dangers of bringing a knife of any sort to school and warn him not to bring it again on penalty of losing the knife permanently.

109. A quiet classroom is

(A)   a good classroom.
(B)   a negative learning environment.
(C)   inappropriate for some learning activities.
(D)   the classroom of a teacher who has appropriate control of his/her students.

110. To encourage students to read more books on their own time, a teacher develops a reward system to give students tokens for the books they read depending on the difficulty and the length of the book. At the end of the semester, students will be able to use their tokens to purchase "rewards" from the school store (pens, pencils, erasers, notebooks, and so forth). This reward system appeals to students who are

(A)   intrinsically motivated.
(B)   extrinsically motivated.
(C)   reading below grade level.
(D)   able to purchase their own school supplies.

111. In the beginning of the year, David was a quiet child. However, in the middle of the year he has been starting to frequently shout out and cause disruptions. What should an effective teacher do first?

(A)   Send David to the office.
(B)   Talk to the school administration.
(C)   Use verbal and nonverbal cues to try to modify the behavior.
(D)   Contact David's parents.

112. A teacher observes two kindergarten students on the playground who are having a disagreement. The conflict appears to be escalating. Just as the teacher approaches the two students, they are beginning to hit and shove each other. The teacher should

(A)   yell at the students to "Stop!" and grab each by the arm, pulling them apart.

(B)   yell at the students to "Stop!" and send them to the principal's office.

(C)   step between the students to separate them and then ask each one, in turn, to tell what has happened, encouraging them to use their words to express their feelings instead of hitting each other.

(D)   continue to watch the students closely, hoping that they will be able to work out their differences.

113. Two children are fighting. The best approach for the teacher to take first is which of the following?

(A)   Send another person for an administrator, separate the two, turn the aggressor over to the administrator, and then deal personally with the victim.

(B)   Separate the two and take both to the guidance counselor for a conference.

(C)   Separate the two and attend first to the victim.

(D)   A teacher of young children should not attempt to separate the two unless an adult witness is present.

114. Which of the following punishments is probably LEAST effective in dealing with a second grader who constantly has tantrums at the smallest provocation?

(A)   The teacher might prohibit the child's participation in the situation that caused the child to have a tantrum; after discussion with the child indicates that the child is again ready to attempt, for example, a board game with the other members of his/her group, the teacher may allow the child to try again.

(B)   The child should have an opportunity to realize that the teacher has more power; the teacher might demonstrate this by staging a situation in which the teacher does not achieve the results he or she wants and the teacher can enter into a tirade or tantrum much worse than the child's to demonstrate the adult's power.

(C)   The teacher might continue with the class activities and ignore the pouting child.

(D)   The teacher might isolate the child from the rest of the class in a time-out room.

115. What is one important feature of classroom management?

    (A) Speaking in a loud voice.
    (B) Developing a conduct code during the first half of the year.
    (C) Carefully stating expectations at the beginning of the year.
    (D) Ignoring minor infractions.

116. Which of the following teacher responses more clearly provides student feedback that a response is incorrect?

    (A) "No, that is not the answer."
    (B) "Well, let's think about this further. Mary, do you want to add anything?"
    (C) "Good try, but . . . Kurt, what would you say?"
    (D) "Well, that's a good point you've made, but that's not the answer I was looking for."

117. A teacher tells her class that 1 meter equals 39.37 inches or 3.28 feet or 1.09 yard. The teacher has

    (A) taught her class the principle of cause-and-effect.
    (B) provided her class with a stated principle or law.
    (C) connected cause-and-effect principles.
    (D) provided applications of a law.

118. A major theme in the theoretical framework of many of today's educators is constructivist theory. Which of the following is true of this theory?

    (A) Constructivist theory recognizes that most new ideas and learnings cannot be based on current or past knowledge.

    (B) The task of the instructor is to learn along with the student.
    (C) Constructivist theory recognizes that it is more time-economical to "tell" rather than to have the student "discover."
    (D) None of the above.

119. Which of the following is NOT an example of a closed question?

    (A) Which bear's bed was too soft?
    (B) What was the name of the girl who went to the three bears' house?
    (C) Why did the girl go to the three bears' house?
    (D) What happened when the girl sat in little bear's chair?

120. The principal plans a meeting at which each teacher will allow the parents to visit the classroom. The meeting is scheduled for a Monday night, and the announcement has already aired on radio and television. Miss Jones, the new teacher, had signed up for dance lessons during the summer. The Monday night in question is the night of the final recital. Miss Jones

    (A) explains to the principal about the necessity of missing the meeting; she tells him she will send home a note to each parent to explain her absence.
    (B) explains to the dance instructor that her job and her students come first; she will not be at the recital.
    (C) sends home a note to each of her parents and schedules another night for meeting with them.
    (D) decides it is easier to get forgiveness than to ask permission; she decides not to "show."

Praxis II

Elementary Education
Test Code 0014

Answers: Practice Test 1

Answer Key

1. (B)	21. (C)	41. (A)	61. (D)	81. (D)	101. (C)
2. (C)	22. (A)	42. (A)	62. (B)	82. (A)	102. (D)
3. (A)	23. (A)	43. (D)	63. (B)	83. (D)	103. (A)
4. (C)	24. (C)	44. (B)	64. (B)	84. (B)	104. (C)
5. (A)	25. (D)	45. (D)	65. (D)	85. (D)	105. (A)
6. (D)	26. (C)	46. (B)	66. (B)	86. (A)	106. (C)
7. (B)	27. (D)	47. (D)	67. (A)	87. (C)	107. (D)
8. (D)	28. (C)	48. (B)	68. (D)	88. (D)	108. (C)
9. (C)	29. (C)	49. (C)	69. (D)	89. (D)	109. (C)
10. (A)	30. (D)	50. (B)	70. (C)	90. (D)	110. (B)
11. (C)	31. (D)	51. (A)	71. (C)	91. (B)	111. (C)
12. (C)	32. (C)	52. (B)	72. (A)	92. (C)	112. (C)
13. (D)	33. (C)	53. (B)	73. (D)	93. (D)	113. (C)
14. (D)	34. (D)	54. (C)	74. (D)	94. (B)	114. (B)
15. (D)	35. (C)	55. (B)	75. (C)	95. (A)	115. (C)
16. (D)	36. (B)	56. (C)	76. (A)	96. (C)	116. (A)
17. (B)	37. (B)	57. (B)	77. (B)	97. (D)	117. (B)
18. (C)	38. (C)	58. (C)	78. (C)	98. (B)	118. (D)
19. (B)	39. (D)	59. (C)	79. (C)	99. (A)	119. (C)
20. (A)	40. (C)	60. (A)	80. (A)	100. (D)	120. (B)

Elementary Education: Content Knowledge (0014) Practice Test 1

Detailed Explanations of Answers

1. (B)

Students are able to perform better on tests when their physical setting, which includes lighting, temperature, and seating, is favorable. When students feel anxious over a test (A), or when teachers threaten against poor performances (D), students do not perform as well. Outside disruptions (C) can break a student's concentration; this is especially true for younger children.

2. (C)

When a teacher sets a mastery level at a certain percentage, students who reach that percentage are considered to have mastered that skill and receive a grade of "A" for their efforts. Therefore, (A) and (B) are incorrect. Answering 75 percent of all of the skills correctly (D) is also incorrect because in order to master a particular skill, the student does not need to master all of the skills.

3. (A)

A redirect (A) occurs when a teacher asks one student to react to the response of another student. A corrective (B) occurs when a teacher responds to a student error by explaining why it is an error and then provides a correct answer. When teachers are redirecting, they are neither giving any feedback (C) nor directly responding (D) to the student comments.

4. (C)

Written academic feedback should contain specific comments on errors and how to improve them. It should also contain a positive remark that notes an aspect of the assignment that was done well. Therefore, delaying feedback by a day (A), specifying uniform guidelines (B), and presenting feedback in a vague manner (D) are not the correct answer choices.

5. (A)

As the decades change, so do the labels the school systems use to identify children who differ from the mainstream—and may have difficulty with mathematics and other subjects; the school systems of the 21st Century tend to label children who differ from the mainstream as "at-risk (A)," not "culturally different (C)," "slow learners (D)," "semi-lingual," "culturally deprived (B)," or "limited-English speaking."

6. (D)

Individual goals for a student should be developed after reviewing both the student's history and assessing the student's motivation. This will ensure that the goals can be met by the student. Goals should not be based solely on the student's academic record (A) or created only from individual observations (C). They should also not be the same for all students (B) because students learn at different levels and aim for different goals.

7. (B)

Research has shown that it is favorable to provide feedback in test situations when the feedback is delayed by a day or so, rather than giving immediate feedback (A). Delaying the feedback session for a few weeks is not beneficial to the students because too much time has elapsed (C). A class review of the test has been shown to be more beneficial in clearing up misunderstandings than handwritten notations (D).

8. (D)

Good and Gouws found that effective teachers conducted reviews as part of their daily, weekly, and monthly routines. Therefore, (A), (B), and (C) are incorrect because they were not findings in the Good and Gouws study.

9. (C)

Inclusion places the focus on ability and decreases the focus on disability and inability; A and B are incorrect. With inclusion, the neighborhood school accepts children as the first option and considers other educational placements only if that child, even with substantial support, cannot succeed in the class with age-appropriate peers. (C) is the best option. The neighborhood school should not be the last option; (D) is not the best choice.

10. (A)

Praise has been shown to be the most effective when it is authentic and low-key (A). It should be used frequently; therefore (B) is incorrect. It should consist of complex responses that provide information about the reasons for the quality of the student response; therefore, (C) is incorrect. It should be used to provide all students with positive experiences; therefore, (D) is incorrect.

11. (C)

If the teacher ignores the answer entirely (A) or moves on to another question (D), it devalues the student response. If the teacher responds immediately to the digression (B), the disruptive behavior has been rewarded. The correct answer is (C).

12. (C)

Teachers/tutors who have "pulled out" students from an inclusive classroom situation for short term

instruction have found that these diverse learners seem to learn best with increased positive reinforcement (C). Skills should be emphasized; A, therefore, is incorrect. The use of ONLY basic texts is not highly effective; (B) is not the best choice. Whole language instruction (D) does not work with everyone; (D) is not the best choice.

13. (D)

Teachers and students must clarify the purposes for reading. These purposes—which may vary from passage to passage, student to student, and situation to situation—include aesthetics, fact attainment (efference), and a combination of factual and aesthetic purposes. (D) is, therefore the best answer. Neither the factual aspects (A) nor what the words suggest (B) is important alone. Both factual information and aesthetic purposes are important; (C) is not an adequate answer.

14. (D)

To master a second language, one must participate. Those students who listen instead of participating are least successful. (D) is the correct choice. All students—successful and unsuccessful—will make many mistakes; (A) is not appropriate. The students who are going to be successful will take risks—not vice versa; (B) is a poor choice. Teachers and fellow classmates do not need to focus on mistakes ESL students make; reinforcement is crucial. (C) is not a good answer. The classroom should be a supportive classroom environment that allows English-as-Second-Language (ESL) students to take risks since 1) writing and reading develop through social interactions, not merely listening; 2) literacy develops through relationships between English learners and English speakers; 3) ESL students will risk interactions only if fully supported; and 4) mistakes often precede success.

15. (D)

Let x be the number of lambs in the barn. Then, because each person and lamb has only one head, the number of people must be $30 - x$. Since lambs have four legs, the number of lamb legs equals $4x$. Similarly, the number of human legs equals $2(30 - x)$. Thus, the equation for the total number of legs (104) is:

$$4x + 2(30 - x) = 104.$$

Use the distributive property, $a(b - c) = ab - ac$, to get

$$4x + 60 - 2x = 104,$$

which reduces to

$$2x + 60 = 104.$$

Subtract 60 from each side to get

$$2x = 44, \text{ or } x = 22.$$

So the number of lambs is 22, and the number of people is $30 - 22 = 8$.

16. (D)

According to the operant model in behavioral theory, negative reinforcement is removing a stimulus, which causes a behavior to increase. Reinforcement can be positive or negative in that is it applied or removed. All reinforcement, positive or negative, increases the likelihood that the behavior will occur again. Likewise, punishment can be positive or negative, but all punishment decreases the likelihood that the behavior will occur again.

17. (B)

Friedrich Wilhelm Froebel, a German philosopher and educator, was the founder of the modern kindergarten. Benjamin Franklin (A) was a political leader, philosopher, and scientist who developed the structure of the modern high school. Maria Montessori (C) was an Italian physician who developed an early childhood curriculum based on a structured environment. Johann Pestalozzi (D) established the first training schools for teachers in Prussia.

18. (C)

Black line spectra are formed when the continuous spectra of the Sun passes through the atmosphere. The elements in the atmosphere absorb wavelengths of light characteristic of their spectra (these are the same wavelengths given off when the element is excited; for example, the red color of a neon light). By examining the line spectral gaps scientists can deduce the elements that make up the distant atmosphere. Item (A) is true, but it explains the source of a line spectrum. Item (B) is true, but it explains why a blue shirt is blue when placed under a white or blue light source. Recall that a blue shirt under a red light source will appear black because there are no blue wavelengths to be reflected. Item (D) is a partial truth, black lights do give off ultraviolet light that the human eye cannot see.

19. (B)

Grouping patterns affect a student's perceptions of self-esteem and competence. Maintaining the same groups throughout the year encourages students in the average group to view themselves as average, students in the above average group to view themselves as above average, and students in the below average group to view themselves as below average. Choice (A) is incorrect because most students do not like unpredictable teacher behavior. Response (C) is incorrect because changes in the classroom often create an atmosphere of mistrust and uneasiness, and do not cause students to be more alert. Choice (D) is incorrect because although the explanation is correct, it is incomplete when compared to the answer (B).

20. (A)

A needs assessment will help students make the connection between their current skills and those that will be new to them. (B) is wrong because a needs assessment focuses on the skills a student currently possesses. (C) is incorrect because the needs assessment is designed to determine what needs to be taught that is not currently in the curriculum. (D) is a false statement. A needs assessment is not designed to motivate students.

21. (C)

A positive environment must be created to minimize the effects of negative external factors. (A) is inappropriate because changing the text but allowing the environment to remain the same only results in maintaining the status quo. (B) is incorrect because relating the students' personal interests to the new material is only a part of creating a positive environment. (D) is wrong because, again, it is only a small part of maximizing the effects of a positive learning environment.

22. (A)

When students are allowed to select their own problems for study, they become self-directed problem-solvers. As such, they have the opportunity to structure their own learning experiences. Assessing students' needs in a naturalistic setting (B) is highly time-consuming and not an important benefit of having students select their own problem to investigate. There may not be a wide variety of instructional materials available to the students (C) as they engage in studying the temperature problem, so this is not likely to be a major benefit. Learning to appreciate opposing viewpoints (D) is a competency that would be better addressed in social studies and language arts rather than in an activity that deals with a natural empirical science.

23. (A)

People are more highly motivated to solve problems that they choose, rather than problems that are chosen for them. Choosing a problem for investigation does not increase student diversity (B). Problem selection has nothing to do with the structure of student groups (C). Although students may engage in more self-assessment, this is not the most important force at work (D).

24. (C)

The teacher would be fostering strong home relationships that support student achievement of desired outcomes. Choice (A) is the result of (C). As the teacher interacts with professionals in the community, her own professional growth is promoted. (B) is also the result of (C). All teachers are expected to interact with the community to help meet the expectations associated with teaching. (D) is incomplete because strong home relationships are developed through the principles of conferences, trust, and cooperation.

25. (D)

This question relates to enabling teachers to document their teaching and to be aware of students' efforts, progress, and achievements. A portfolio is a purposeful collection of work that exhibits efforts, progress, and achievement of students and enables teachers to document teaching in an authentic setting. Standardized tests are commercially developed and are used for specific events (A). A teacher-made test is used to evaluate specific objectives of the course, so (B) is not the best choice. Observation is used only to explain what students do in classrooms and to indicate some of their capabilities; therefore, (C) is incorrect.

26. (C)

This question relates to evaluating specific objectives and content. Teacher-made tests are designed to evaluate the specific objectives and specific content of a course. (A) is incorrect because self and peer evaluation utilizes students' knowledge according to evaluation criteria that is understood by the students. A portfolio (B) is a purposeful collection of work that exhibits effort, progress, and achievement of students and enables teachers to document teaching in an authentic setting. Observation (D) is used to explain what students do in classrooms and to indicate to some degree their capabilities.

27. (D)

Standardized tests rate student performance against the performance of other students and report the scores in terms of percentiles, stanines, and scaled scores. A portfolio (A) is a collection of student effort, progress, and achievement. Teacher-made tests evaluate specific objectives and content, so (B) is incorrect. Students' classroom behaviors and capabilities are evaluated through observation, making (C) incorrect.

28. (C)

Self and peer assessment requires that the students be aware of and understand the evaluation criteria. A collection of work that exhibits students' success and enables teachers to document teaching is a portfolio

(A). A teacher-made test (B) evaluates specific objectives and content. Observation (D) is used to indicate capabilities and actions of students.

29. (C)

Mrs. Ratu's lack of competency is exhibited in her lack of understanding of her students and in her teaching at the elementary level. Mrs. Ratu was not teaching her students at the appropriate level (A). Although she may have desired to make reading easy for her students (B), she was not going about it correctly. When appropriate techniques are used, teaching ninth graders to read is no more difficult than teaching third graders to read.

30. (D)

Students who speak English as a Second Language are a challenge to educators. Guidelines, however, are available to help both specialized and mainstream teachers who have not worked with ESL students in the past. (D) is the best answer. Language-minority students have the right and the responsibility to learn to read and write in English. (B), which indicates that ESL students do not have the right to speak their native language, is incorrect and should not be a selection. ESL students do not have the obligation to speak their native language; (C) is not a good choice. ESL students do have the right in our country to speak their native language; (A) is not, therefore, a good choice.

31. (D)

Activities that tend to combine reading, writing, listening, and speaking are more likely to enhance literacy and the development of orality for the language-minority student. (D) suggests that this integration is advantageous. (D) is the best answer. (A), (B), and (C) indicate a sequence in literacy instruction; none of these answers is appropriate.

32. (C)

The most efficient way to gain information about a new setting is to speak with someone who is familiar with the circumstances. Orienting oneself with the physical layout (A) would be helpful but cannot tell her about the student population or materials. Although communication with the principal (B) is always a good idea, the principal usually will have little time to have an in-depth discussion and will not be able to tell specifically which books are available. Eventually, Ms. Woods will need to match curriculum guidelines to the material available (D), but sitting in a closet will not introduce her to staff and student characteristics.

33. (C)

All known living things are grouped in categories according to shared physical traits. The process of grouping organisms is called classification. Carl Linné, also known as Linnaeus, devised the classification system used in biology today. In the Linnaean system (A), all organisms are given a two-word name (binomial). The name consists of a genus (e.g., *Canis*) and a species (e.g., *lupus*) designation. The DNA holds the genetic materials of a cell, so (B) could not be the correct answer. Because there is a correct answer, (D) is not a correct choice.

When the genetic type of parents is known, the probability of the offspring showing particular traits can be predicted by using the Punnett Square (C). A Punnett Square is a large square divided into four small boxes. The genetic symbol of each parent for a particular trait is written alongside the square, for one parent along the top and for the other parent along the left side, as shown in the figure.

	Parent Aa	
	(A)	(a)
Parent Aa (A)	AA	Aa
(a)	Aa	aa

Each gene symbol is written in the boxes below or to the right of it. This results in each box having two gene symbols in it. The genetic symbols in the boxes are all the possible genetic combinations for a particular trait of the offspring of these parents. Each box has a 25 percent probability of being the actual genetic representation for a given child.

34. (D)

"Acid" and "base" are terms used to describe solutions of differing pH. The concentration of hydrogen ions in a solution determines its pH. Solutions having a pH of 0 to 7 are called acids and have hydrogen ions (H+) present. Common acids include lemon juice, vinegar, and battery acid; acids are corrosive and taste sour. Solutions having a pH of 7 to 14 are called bases (or alkaline) and have hydroxide ions (OH–) present; bases are caustic and feel slippery in solution. Common bases include baking soda and lye. Solutions of pH 7 are called neutral and have both ions present in equal but small amounts. Coice (D) is the correct answer because 5 is the only number between 0 and 7 (acids).

35. (C)

A liquid has a definite volume, but it molds to the shape of the container holding it. Titanium (A) is a solid (D), and solids have a definite shape and volume, so (A) and (D) are not the best answers. A gas will expand to fit the container in both volume and shape, so (B) is not the correct answer.

36. (B)

The instrument for measuring the intensity of an earthquake is a seismograph. A thermograph (A) measures temperature, a telegraph (C) is a communication device, and an odometer (D) measures distance traveled, so (A), (C), and (D) are not correct.

37. (B)

Energy is defined as the ability to do work. Work occurs when a force (push or pull) is applied to an object, resulting in movement. Work = force × distance. The greater the force (A) applied, or the longer the distance traveled (D), or interval between two points, the greater the work done, but they are not the ability to do the work. Speed is rate of movement, so (C) is not the best answer.

38. (C)

Essays fall into four rough categories: speculative, argumentative, narrative, and expository. The purpose of this essay is narrative (C). The narrative essay may recount an incident or a series of incidents and is almost always autobiographical, in order to make a point. The informality of the storytelling makes the narrative essay less insistent than the argumentative essay, but more directed than the speculative essay. But the thesis may not be as obvious or clear-cut as that in an expository or argumentative essay. This essay is not speculative (A).

The speculative essay (A) is so named because, as its Latin root suggests, it looks at ideas and explores them rather than explains them. The purposes of the argumentative essay (B) are always clear: to present a point and provide evidence, which may be factual or anecdotal, and to support it. The structure is usually very formal, as in a debate, with counterpositions and counterarguments. An expository essay (D) may have narrative elements, but that aspect is minor and subservient to that of explanation.

39. (D)

New research (K. Goodman) challenges the status quo literacy and asks teachers to revalue their habitudes and practices related to the traditional way of teaching language and literacy. Flores, Cousin, and Diaz propose alternative views about <u>all</u> children. These assumptions show that even the at-risk are proficient in some communication skills; bring many experiences into the classroom; need opportunities to learn language in rich, integrated settings; can be successful in regular classroom programs; can be monitored by observing their language use in authentic settings; and the at-risk, also, have families interested in the school setting and are potential partners in the educational experience. For these reasons, it is evident that (D) is the right answer; families of at-risk students still have an interest in their children and are potential partners. Because at-risk children can bring many experiences to the classroom and can be successful in a classroom, (A) and (B) are incorrect. Standardized literacy tests may not be as helpful to a teacher as observing the students in authentic settings; (C) is incorrect.

40. (C)

When two parallel lines are crossed by another line (called a transversal), eight angles are formed. However, there are only two angle measures among the eight angles, and the sum of the two measures is 180°. All the smaller angles will have the same measure, and all the larger angles will have the same measure. In this case, the smaller angles all measure 50°, so the larger angles (including angle *y*) all measure 130°.

read the text critically, as part of the conversation can address the issue of what is missing in the text.

41. (A)

One must know two things to answer the question. One is the meaning of the small square at the vertex of angle BXC. That symbol means that angle BXC is a *right angle* (one with 90°). The second is that a straight line, such as AXD, can be thought of as a *straight angle*, which measures 180°. Therefore, since the sum of the angles DXC (42°) and BXC (90°) is 132°, the remaining angle on the line must measure 48° (= 180° − 132°).

42. (A)

The area of any rectangle is equal to the measure of its length times the measure of its width (or, to say it differently, the measure of its base times the measure of its height). A right triangle can be seen as half of a rectance (sliced diagonally). Answer (A) represents, in effect, half of a rectangle's area (i.e., the area divided by 2).

43. (D)

The formula for finding the area of any circle is $A = \pi r^2$ (about 3.14 times the length of the radius times itself). In this case, take half of πr^2; hence, answer (D) is correct.

44. (B)

Angle XYZ is an inscribed angle (its vertex is on the circle). Angle XCZ is a central angle (its vertex is at the circle's center). When two such angles intercept (or cut off) the same arc of the circle, there exists a specific size relationship between the two angles. The measure of the central angle will always be double the measure of the inscribed angle. In this case, that means that the measure of angle XCZ must be 80°. That means that minor arc XZ also has measure 80°. Every circle (considered an arc) has measure 360°. That means that major arc XYZ has measure 280° (360°−80°).

45. (D)

Children learn more from a text if the teacher helps them figure out how the book was put together. It makes the text more understandable. It also helps them

46. (B)

In using three different versions of this well-known story. Ms. Smith is creating an opportunity to bring a multicultural perspective to the drama activity (I). In versions of Cinderella from around the world, the story of the mistreated but kindhearted protagonist is basically the same, but the characters, settings, and ways in which the plot unfolds are culturally centered. Furthermore, because Ms. Smith is using scripted versions of the story and staging these plays with costumes, scenery, and props, she is making theatrical elements integral to the performances (II). The students are engaging in formal dramatic activity that will reslt in a theatrical product, rather than informal, process-centered drama, so III is incorrect. Choicc IV is incorrect because the students are not the ones who have adapted the storied and, therefore, they are not having firsthand experience with that process. So the correct answer is (B), which includes only I and II.

47. (D)

Teachers must engage in ongoing self-evaluation of their own values, attitudes, disposition, and belief systems to teach diverse learners effectively and to invite and extend literacy forms, skills, and interests; these teachers must reflect on how their 1) literacy histories compare to those of other teachers and students; 2) peer experiences may have been privileged in school settings, and 3) literacy experiences are tied to their identities in order to extend literacy. (D) is the best answer. For this reason choice (A) is incorrect because remembering one's past can help. Thinking back on one's school setting may be applicable—not inapplicable; (B) is a poor choice. Answer (C) suggests that school experiences have no effect on the learner's self identity; this is false and (C) is not a correct answer.

Formative assessment is continuous and intended to serve as a guide to future learning and instruction. Summative evaluation (A) and summative assessment (B) are both used to put a final critique or grade on an activity or assignment with no real link to the future. Peer assessment would require students to critique each other (D).

48. (B)

The best way to teach children to read, regardless of grade level, is to use a program of emergent literacy that includes pattern books and journal writing with invented spelling. Although an intensive phonics program that includes drill and practice work may be effective with some students, it is not the most effective way to teach all students to read, so (A) is incorrect. Choice (C) is clearly incorrect because none of the students read above 2.0 grade level. An ESL program is intended to provide assistance to only those students who are learning English as a second language, so (D) is incorrect. Additionally, the learning resource teacher should provide assistance to only those students who have been identified as having a learning disability that qualifies them to receive services.

49. (C)

Careful planning (III), which includes checking on the availability of resources and materials (II) resulted in student involvement in the unit (I). Mrs. Doe did reflective thinking during the discussion; however, reflective thinking is only one component of communication and is included in careful planning and its correlation to success in the classroom. Resources and materials were available, but this is a result of careful planning. Personal acquaintance with a Native American (IV) would have helped shape the students' attitudes, but it is not necessary for student involvement. So the correct answer (C) includes II and III only.

50. (B)

Multiple strategies were planned for the motivation of the students (I), but a result of the strategies was that each student participated in some way regardless of ability (II) and the unit was integrated into other subjects (III) (e.g., reading, writing) through library assignments. Ultimately, the unit will be integrated with the other subjects; however, this is not the only goal, so (A) and (C) are incorrect. Developing a foundation for teaching American history (IV) is not even a long-range goal, although the attitudes and beliefs developed in the project may become the foundation upon which the stu-

dents will build their philosophy of American history. Therefore, (D) is incorrect.

51. (A)

The external factors of the field trip could create a positive motivation and would allow the students to make the connection between their old skills and the new skills they were learning (I). The external factors involved in a field trip are positive; however, Mrs. Doe gave instructions that each student was to take notes on what he or she saw, heard, and experienced (II). The skill of note taking was founded upon the library assignment that had preceded the field trip, and the students were to make the connection. No mention is made of community involvement in the field trip; the statement III is not relevant. The students did not take responsibility for their own learning (IV); they were given instructions concerning what they were to do before they left for the field trip. Choices (B), (C), and (D), which include incorrect statements (III and IV), are therefore incorrect.

52. (B)

Respect was shown to the children by allowing them a choice of field trips (II). It is an example of the array of instructional strategies (IV) used by Mrs. Doe. (A) is incomplete and therefore incorrect. Enhancing students' self-concept and fostering the view of learning as a purposeful pursuit [(C) and (D)] are both incorporated in II, respecting differences and understanding the society in which we live.

53. (B)

Placing the students in small groups in which they meet face to face will allow Mr. Billings to maximize the students' interaction while giving each student the maximum opportunity to speak. Placing students in the traditional rows facing the front (A) discourages student interaction and minimizes each student's opportunities to speak. Although placing students in pairs (C) maximizes each student's opportunity to speak, it limits the sources of interaction because each student may share thoughts with only one other student. In contrast, a group of four allows the student to interact as part of three dyads, two triads, and a quad. When placing the students in cooperative groups, it is wise to arrange the desks within the physical space of the classroom in such a way that each group's talking does not distract the members of other groups, as it does in (D).

54. (C)

Requiring both a cognitive and a performance objective makes the student show that he or she not only had the knowledge but could apply that knowledge to a life situation, so (C) is the correct response. Although statement (A) is true, it is not the foundation for developing specific objectives. Statement (B), again, is an assumption and not relevant to the setting of certain objectives. Teaching style and learning styles (D) are not relevant to the behavioral objectives.

55. (B)

This question is designed to demonstrate an understanding that the performance objective should directly tie into the assessment. Students need to know what the expectation is for them to complete the necessary assignments. Students do not understand what assessment tools are; they need clear directions and a list of explanations, so (A) is incorrect. Although the unit may have many new vocabulary words, students need to learn them within the context of the unit rather than from a random list; they should not feel threatened when learning to prepare for a test, so (C) is incorrect. There is no connection between notebooks and learning, so (D) is incorrect.

56. (C)

Rubrics are designed to help teachers assess each student's achievement and the quality of his/her responses (I). Therefore, each criterion needs to have quality points (II), such as outstanding (5–4), good (3–2), and/or fair (1–0). Rubrics need to cover a number of subject areas to allow for a fair assessment of the student's work, in contrast to option III. Students may rate themselves (IV); however, the teacher needs to work with them as they complete the ratings. Therefore, only I and II, or option (C) is correct.

57. (B)

Students often disclose more personal information in journals than when speaking in class. The teacher can also check for comprehension of content and the success or failure of class objectives. Journals typically are not graded with consideration to standard usage or grammatical constructions; therefore, (A) is incorrect. The assignment has no direct bearing on time-management skills; therefore, (C) is incorrect. Choice (D) is irrelevant: no mention is made of giving daily grades on the journal writing.

58. (C)

The Language-Experience-Approach (LEA) is a proven method of increasing students' reading and writing proficiency and their overall language competency. It requires that students write about what they know. Choices (A), (B), and (D) are irrelevant. Choice (A) superficially addresses that Ms. Johnson is an English teacher and choice (B) refers to autobiographies, something that is not mentioned in the preceding information. Choice (D) foreshadows the library project, but it has not yet been introduced into the context of these questions.

59. (C)

A basic principle in providing students with appropriate feedback is to first note the student's strengths (or positive aspects of the student's work and/or performance) and then to note specific ways the student can improve his or her work and/or performance. Therefore, the best approach for a teacher to take in providing students with feedback on written work is to first note the good things about students' writing and then to suggest ways to improve. Choices (A) and (B) are in essence the same; both choices indicate that only students' strengths would be acknowledged, omitting the important aspect of addressing ways students can improve. Neither action would enhance students' cognitive skills or their metacognitive skills (or self-awareness). Choice (D) is unacceptable because it denigrates the teacher's responsibility to evaluate students' performance on the basis of individual merit against the standards established by particular disciplines.

60. (A)

Option (A) is the best answer of the four options for the following reasons. First, learning style information acknowledges that although learners acquire knowledge in different ways, those differences can lead to effective learning when students are taught cognitive strategies that complement their natural learning tendencies; basically, teaching students about learning styles (and especially about their own learning styles) is a recognition of human diversity. Second, beyond mere recognition of human diversity is the legitimacy of different approaches to learning. Every student can perform at a level of proficiency, although not every student will attain that level in the same manner; in other words, learning styles validate students as learners and promote high standards for academic achievement. Third, when students are taught not only about learning styles in general, but specifically about their own learning styles, they are empowered to take responsibility for their own learning. Fourth, of the four options, only choices (A) and (D) are tasks actively engaging the student. Choices (B) and (C) are both passive activities, and are therefore poor choices. Choice (D) requires that students perform a task without any help (direct instruction) for accomplishing the task; simply asking students to name additional strengths without giving them an opportunity to self-examine, to self-assess, and to explore their strengths will not produce the desired outcome. Only choice (A) gives students the information they need to accomplish the task the teacher has identified as being important.

61. (D)

The question relates to appropriate sequencing of activities. Choice (D) is the best introductory activity in order to generate student interest in this new field of mathematics and to get students thinking about how to produce fractals. It would stimulate students to use higher-level thinking skills to make predictions by drawing on their knowledge of how to solve problems mathematically. Choice (A) would be the least appropriate to begin the study. Students who want to learn more could research this topic after they have developed an interest in fractals. Choice (B) would be appropriate as a later step, after students are interested in the process and are ready to learn how to produce fractals. Choice (C) would be appropriate as a subsequent step in the process of learning how to produce fractals. Choice (B) requires students to use preplanned formulas; Choice (C) allows them to develop their own formulas, a very high-level activity.

62. (B)

Teachers can contribute to racial problems if they (C) treat all students the same, (D) ignore individual differences, and (A) work to make students act as the teacher does. Instead, teachers must be aware of individual differences in the classroom (B) to improve relations.

63. (B)

Democracy is the correct response because it is the antithesis of the authoritarianism of fascism. Indeed, the totalitarian, romantic, militaristic, and nationalistic characteristics were, in large part, a reaction against the perceived inadequacies of democracy.

64. (B)

The industrial economy of the nineteenth century was not based upon an equitable distribution of profits among all those who were involved in production. Marxists and other critics of capitalism condemned the creed of capitalists and the abhorrent conditions of the industrial proletariat. Raw materials, a constant labor supply, capital, and an expanding marketplace were critical elements in the development of the industrial economy.

65. (D)

In the 1880s and 1890s, the U.S. Supreme Court struck down desegregation laws and upheld the doctrine of segregated "separate but equal" facilities for blacks and whites. These laws became known as "Jim Crow" laws. Their impact was to allow racist governments in the South to set up "separate but unequal" facilities in which blacks were forced to sit in the rear of streetcars and buses and to eat in the back rooms of restaurants, were excluded completely from white businesses, and had to use separate and usually inferior public restroom facilities. These laws allowed white supremacists to "put blacks in their place" and effectively kept blacks from achieving anything near equal status. It wasn't until the 1950s and 1960s that new Supreme Court decisions finally forced the repeal of these laws.

66. (B)

A writ of habeas corpus (B) is a court order that directs an official who is detaining someone to produce the person before the court so that the legality of the detention may be determined. The primary function of the writ is to effect the release of someone who has been imprisoned without due process of law. For example, if the police detained a suspect for an unreasonable time without officially charging the person with a crime, the person could seek relief from a court in the form of a writ of habeas corpus. (A) is incorrect because a writ of mandamus is a court order commanding an official to perform a legal duty of his or her office. It is not used to prevent persons from being improperly imprisoned. The Fourth Amendment requirement that police have probable cause in order to obtain a search warrant regulates police procedure. It is not itself a mechanism for affecting release of a person for improper imprisonment, so (C) is incorrect. Answer (D) is incorrect because the decision in *Roe v Wade* dealt with a woman's right to have an abortion; it had nothing to do with improper imprisonment.

67. (A)

By definition, acids and bases combine to produce a salt and water. An example would be HCl (hydrochloric acid) and NaOH (sodium hydroxide) reacting to form NaCl (salt) and water.

68. (D)

Atoms are neutral, so the net charge must be zero, requiring that the number of negative particles (electrons) equals the number of positive particles (protons).

69. (D)

(A), (B), and (C) all involve chemical changes in which iron, wood, and rocket fuel, respectively, are reacted with other substances to produce a reactant product with different chemical properties. Melted ice in the form of water still has the same chemical formula, so the correct answer is (D).

70. (C)

Isotopes for a given element all have the same chemical properties, differing only in their atomic weight, or number of neutrons.

71. (C)

Newton's second law states that an unbalanced force acting on a mass will cause the mass to accelerate. In equation form, $F = ma$, where F is force, m is mass, and a is acceleration. Only (C) involves a mass that is being accelerated by an unbalanced force.

72. (A)

Thermal energy is the total amount of internal energy of a given body, whereas temperature is a measure of the vibrational activity of atoms or molecules within the material. Therefore, thermal energy involves both the mass and temperature of a given body. Thus, (A) is the most likely answer, as its mass far exceeds 1 g, a bucket of water, and Lake Michigan. (B) is ruled out because even though its temperature is very high, its mass is extremely small.

73. (D)

The cell membrane (D) is a selectively permeable barrier that permits some substances to pass through while forming a barrier for others. None of the other choices have this property.

74. (D)

(D) is correct because the zygote of a human is a cell derived from a sperm containing 23 chromosomes and an egg containing 23 chromosomes. (A) cannot be the correct answer because it represents too few chromosome for either a haploid sex cell or a diploid body cell. (B) cannot be the correct answer because it also represents too few chromosome for either a haploid sex cell or a diploid body cell. (C) cannot be the correct answer because it represents the number of chromosomes in a sperm or an egg.

75. (C)

The body regulates water and heat through perspiration. Transpiration describes a process not involving humans; thus (B) is not correct. Respiration (A) is breathing in humans and will cause some water loss, but the question asks how the body regulates substances through the skin. (D), sensation, is the ability to process or perceive. Although the skin does have nerve endings that can sense, this does not involve temperature or water regulation.

76. (A)

Choices (B), (C), and (D) are ruled out because Darwin was unaware of the genetic work that was later done by Mendel. Darwin and most other nineteenth-century biologists never knew of Mendel and his research. It was not until the beginning of the twentieth century that Mendel's pioneer research into genetic inheritance was rediscovered.

77. (B)

The lunar period is about 30 days, or one month, which is the time it takes for the Moon to orbit Earth one time.

78. (C)

A star "going nova" is presumed to be at the end of its life. As hydrogen (or sometimes helium) is depleted, the fusion reaction becomes incapable of sustaining the pressures required to push the star's mass outward against the pull of gravity. The star then collapses, resulting in a gigantic explosion known as a supernova. Choice (A) is neither observed nor possible; (B) is not observed; and (D), although occasionally observed, does not trigger nova-sized explosions.

79. (C)

The tilting of Earth's axis causes the Northern Hemisphere to point more sunward in the summer months and more antisunward in the winter months (with the reverse being true for the Southern Hemisphere), so (C) is the correct answer. (B) is ruled out because the rotation period is the same from season to season. (A) is ruled out because Earth is actually somewhat closer to the sun in December through January than it is in June through July, which is winter for the Northern Hemisphere. (D) is ruled out because this is a daily, not seasonal, phenomenon.

80. (A)

Igneous rocks are transformed or "metamorphed" into metamorphic rocks. Thus, they are related to igneous, not sedimentary, and are found on this planet.

81. (D)

The east coast of South America and the west coast of Africa fit together like pieces of a jig-saw puzzle. Fossil remains in locations where "fit" is observed are too well matched to be coincidental. Earthquakes and volcanism are more prevalent in mountainous regions, where plates collided, than in other regions. Thus, all support the theory of plate tectonics.

82. (A)

According to the theory of plate tectonics, plate spreading is associated with magma upwelling to fill the vacated space, which forms ridges at these locations. This is true also under the oceans.

83. (D)

The raw material for igneous rock formation is magma, which—when cooled either above or below ground—becomes igneous rock.

84. (B)

Multiple investigators have confirmed the order given in (B): Nitrogen, oxygen, carbon dioxide, trace gases.

85. (D)

To find the greatest common divisor (GCD), factor both numbers and look for common factors. The product of these common factors is the GCD. The GCD here is the greatest integer that divides both 120 and 252.

$$120 = 2^3 \times 3 \times 5 \text{ and } 252 = 2^2 \times 3^2 \times 7,$$

so the GCD = $2^2 \times 3 = 12$.

86. (A)

A prime number is an integer that is greater than one and that has no integer divisors other than 1 and itself. So, the prime numbers between 1 and 20 (not including 1 and 20) are: 2, 3, 5, 7, 11, 13, 17, 19. But 2 is not an odd number, so the odd primes between 1 and 20 are: 3, 5, 7, 11, 13, 17, 19. Hence, there are seven odd primes between 1 and 20.

87. (C)

The 1 is in the hundredths place. If the number to the immediate right of the 1 (i.e., the number in the thousandths place) is greater than or equal to 5, we increase 1 to 2; otherwise, do not change the 1. Then we leave off all the numbers to the right of the 1. In our problem, a 6 is in the thousandths place, so we change the 1 to a 2 to get 287.42 as our answer.

88. (D)

Teachers should address home and school cultural incongruencies; possible ways include 1) changing aspects of the school routines to make the routine more compatible with patterns with which the children are familiar (so C is incorrect); 2) explaining to the parents and children the rules of classroom interaction, the teaching methods, and reasons for the rules with a translator if needed (so B is incorrect); 3) bridging the gap between home and school by home visits, class meetings with parents, and drop-in visits (so A is incorrect); and 4) observing the child at work or play with peers.

89. (D)

A teacher keeps a running reading record by writing down what the student actually reads aloud. This helps the teacher in identifying and addressing what the student may need to do to increase reading skills. The record does not necessarily involve a tape recorder (A), oral reading (B), or testing (C).

90. (D)

Thematic instruction resembles the way that many students learn; (D) is the best answer. Thematic teaching and the integration of instruction provide learning experiences 1) that resemble the way many students learn, 2) that promote higher order thinking skills, 3) that avoid fragmentation of the curriculum, and 4) that downplay acquisition of isolated facts. Thematic teaching does not promote curriculum fragmentation; (A) is incorrect. Thematic teaching is not a new feature; it was particularly popular in the 1920s and 1930s. (C) is, therefore, not an appropriate answer. Acquiring isolated facts is not a feature of thematic instruction; (B) is not a good answer.

91. (B)

When designing learning activities, teachers should be aware that younger students process information more slowly than their older counterparts. Activities for younger children should be simple and short in duration. Young children can answer questions, so (A) is inappropriate. They cannot answer the same questions as older children, but they can learn cooperatively, so (C) and (D) are incorrect.

92. (C)

A professional teacher will recognize that due to the confidentiality laws, the school will have procedures for sharing the scores. She should find out what these rules are. It surely will be illegal to post the names (B). Most schools do not allow teachers to share scores by telephone (A) because it would be impossible to interpret the scores to parents if they are not present, and it would be difficult to know if the voice is that of the correct person. Answer (D)—which allows the teacher to say she is no longer in charge—is not a satisfactory one.

93. (D)

The outcome or product of an instructional activity is to help students improve their work. Answers (A), (B), and (C) may be true statements, but they describe a teacher's priorities or expectations, rather than an instructional goal.

94. (B)

Focusing on process—not just content—is an important feature of inquiry learning. Inquiry learning creates a questioning environment; includes conferences; responds to issues; promotes individual and small group inquiry; and is facilitated by guiding and encouraging teachers. Getting information mainly from a textbooks (A), teacher lecture (C), and direct-teaching are not required components of inquiry learning.

95. (A)

Teaching multicultural students effectively should enable them to connect the curriculum to their own lives. Such teaching may not result in a standardized approach to the curriculum (B) but rather varying instructional approaches. Ideally, teachers may continue to examine their own beliefs and those of their students; (C) and (D) are not the best answers.

96. (C)

The best teachers should plan activities for students who finish their classroom work before their peers. Answers (A) and (D) are merely punitive measures, which are not instructive regarding time management. Although answer (B) may imply a need for better time management, it does not provide the students with a remedy for staying out of trouble.

97. (D)

Mnemonics are devices used to aid memorization, such as using ROY G. BIV to remember the colors of the rainbow (Red, Orange, Yellow, Green, Blue, Indigo, and Violet). Choral responses (A) are the oral repetition (B) of skills or words, and codings (C) are making marks or taking shorthand.

98. (B)

It is important to make sure that students understand directions so as to limit any factors that may prevent a successful lesson. This question is not a transition between lessons (A) and does not assume that the students were off-task (C). It is a way of monitoring something that has already been explained. Answer (D) is incorrect because the teacher is not introducing a new skill.

99. (A)

The best time to study for memory retention is within 8 hours of information first being presented.

Twenty-four hours later (B), the average learner will recall less than 50 percent of the information. If the material is not studied for more than 24 hours, memory will deteriorate even further, diminishing to around 20-25 percent within 48 hours. Even if there is a short review before the test (C), memory will not be as strong as it is shortly after the material is first presented.

100. (D)

Inclusion is based on the understanding that both special education teachers and general education teachers have expertise about models and theories, characteristics of learners, assessment, learning styles, learning environments, strategies and techniques, curriculum, classroom management, and child development; ideally, both special education and general education teachers will work together to improve the instruction so that all the students will benefit from the arrangement. (D) is the best answer. It is better for the general education teachers to work with special education teachers or classes; (A) is not a correct choice. Because special education teachers are not the only ones who can deal effectively with diverse learners with individual differences, (B) is a poor selection. Many parents may not understand the importance of trained teachers—not just a variety of people—working with their children; (C) is not a good choice.

The teacher is asking the student questions to allow the student to correct a spelling error. Spelling does not allow for divergent or creative thinking (A). Although the teacher reminds the student of a mnemonic, the teacher is not teaching the mnemonic (B); finally, applying spelling rules or guides to improve spelling would be an example of deductive reasoning, not inductive reasoning (D).

101. (C)

Behavioral observation is the examination of what the student does during class time. A teacher should be interested in how much time a student spends on-task and how much time is spent off-task. Teachers generally observe a student for a limited period of time and mark the activities in which the student is engaged. If a particular activity, such as talking, appears frequently, the teacher notes it. Behavioral observation alone is not the best way to determine comprehension (A, B) or verbal skills (D).

102. (D)

Many times, teachers fail to give students enough time to think about their answers, especially if their first response is incorrect. Answers (A) and (C), although technically correct, are not as good as (D) because they fail to provide the student with any feedback or chance to self-correct the answer. Answer (B) gives the student a false impression that the answer was almost correct.

103. (A)

Practice activities provide an opportunity for teachers to monitor students to see if additional instruction is needed after a lesson (A). Practice activities are used for any subject matter just featured in the class lesson, not only creative writing; therefore, (B) is incorrect. Practice activities reinforce skills that the students have just learned, rather than reviewing old material (C) or introducing new concepts (D).

104. (C)

To keep students on-task, it is very important to keep any distractions to a minimum, or the instructional momentum will be lost. The teacher should always be sure to have enough copies of materials, as well as to check to see whether audiovisual equipment is working properly.

105. (A)

The question provides information about the teachers' attitudes and backgrounds with computers. Research shows that teacher experience is positively related to students' achievement using computers. The other answers (B), (C), (D) contain irrelevant information that in itself would not affect student progress in a differential manner.

106. (C)

The bell-shaped curve is for application to the general population. Teachers of academically gifted groups (and likewise, teachers of resource classes) should not use the bell-shaped curve because they are not working with the general population. Choice (C) implies all of this. (A) is not a satisfactory answer because it is not acceptable for a teacher to predetermine that in the gifted class, there will be only one grade of A. If the students achieve the grade, most teachers would say that they should receive it. (B) is not a good answer because it is usually not acceptable for the students to dispense their own grades; the teacher is responsible for the grading, and the students can conceivably meet the criteria that the teacher—perhaps with their input—set. Fifth-graders do need to know the manner in which the teacher determines grades; therefore, (D) is not an acceptable answer.

107. (D)

Offering reinforcements for desirable behavior will be preferable to punishment—particularly those listed here. Neither James nor any other student should ever be prevented from attending music (or physical education or art) classes; these subjects also are part of the school curriculum. Therefore, (A) is not a correct answer. Having James stand in the corner (B) is not an acceptable answer because it may involve embarrassing a child in front of the group. Teachers do not normally have the option of choosing their students, so (C) is not an acceptable answer and, incidentally, would not normally be a viable alternative.

108. (C)

It is against school policy to bring any sort of weapon to school. The only choice the teacher has if he or she wants to follow the school rules is to turn the knife and the student over to the principal. Ignoring the incident (A), taking the weapon away and not reporting it (B), or letting the weapon remain in the possession of the boy (D) would be a violation of school policy.

109. (C)

A quiet classroom may be appropriate for some learning activities and inappropriate for others. It is not necessarily a good or bad learning environment, nor does it demonstrate that the teacher has appropriate control of the students (e.g., the students might all be asleep).

110. (B)

Providing external rewards (such as tokens and prizes) for reading appeals to students who are extrinsically motivated. Intrinsically motivated students (A) read for the pleasure and self-satisfaction of reading. Students who read below, at, and above grade level may be motivated extrinsically or intrinsically, so (C) is too exclusive. Some students may not be interested in earning tokens to acquire school supplies, whether or not they are able to purchase their own supplies (D).

111. (C)

A teacher should first try to modify the behavior in the classroom with management techniques. However, if the behavior continues to persist, the teacher should discuss the matter with the student's parents (D). The teacher should not send David to the office (A) without prior notice. Talking to the school administration (B) may not be a necessary part of the teacher's strategy.

112. (C)

The teacher must intervene in the situation and attempt to help the two students resolve their differences by communicating with each other. Answer (A) resorts to physical coercion, and answer (B) escalates the situation by involving the principal. Answer (D) is negligent, failing to take action and letting the situation deteriorate further.

113. (C)

After separating the two, the teacher should attend first to the victim and, if possible, deal with the situation; the guidance counselor may be consulted (B) if it is a school rule, but the teacher may handle the situation more easily himself/herself. If the teacher responds first to the aggressor, it conveys that he/she is more important. The teacher should not wait for a witness before separating the two children (D) because harm could come to either or both. Separating the two by having the aggressor dealt with by the administrator and the victim dealt with by the teacher is not the best approach.

114. (B)

Having the teacher enter into a temper tantrum would hardly be beneficial to the child who has tantrums or to the other children in the classroom. (B) is probably the least effective choice. Prohibiting the child's participation in the activity that caused the tantrum until the child is ready to attempt the activity again (A) might be a reasonable course to follow. Ignoring the pouting child (C) might be a reasonable policy to follow—particularly if behavior modification is being employed. Using a time-out room for a tantrum (D) also seems a logical procedure to follow.

115. (C)

It has been shown that it is very important for a teacher to carefully explain the objectives and procedures of the classroom from the beginning. These objectives and procedures should then be consistently enforced throughout the year. Speaking in a loud voice (A) may intimidate the students and is not an effective method of classroom management. Developing a conduct code during the first half of the year (B) is not effective because students need to know what is expected of them from the beginning. Ignoring minor infractions (D) is not a feature of class-room management.

116. (A)

This is clear and unequivocal feedback. The other responses (B, C, D) send unclear and/or mixed messages.

117. (B)

By telling her students about equivalent measurements, she has stated a principle or law. She has not taught cause-and-effect (A, C) or provided applications of the principle (D).

118. (D)

(D) is the best answer because all of the other answers are incorrect, according to Jerome Bruner's constructivist theory. Bruner stresses that teachers must base new learnings/ideas/concepts on the current/past knowledge of the learners, so (A) is incorrect. Bruner believes that the instructor should try to encourage students to discover principles on their own and to translate this new information into a format that is appropriate to the learner, so (B) is incorrect because Bruner does not stress that the instructor must learn with the students. A major theme in Bruner's theoretical framework is that learning is an active (not a passive) process; because the students discover (ideally) on their own, (C) is incorrect.

119. (C)

This is not a closed question, but an open question, requiring some thoughtful reflecting and speculation to answer. Answers (A), (B), and (D) are examples of closed questions, requiring a simple statement of recall as an answer.

120. (B)

The meeting with parents is a crucial way to achieve cooperation with the home. Miss Jones's responsibility is at the school, so she should not try to make an excuse for the meeting (A) nor should she merely "cut" the meeting (D). Miss Jones does not have the right to open the school at night nor to send notes to the parents to come on a different night (C). Although the principal should have talked with the teachers prior to the scheduling, Miss Jones must attend as a professional.

Praxis II

Elementary Education
Test Code 0014

Practice Test 2

This test is also on CD-ROM in our special interactive Praxis Elementary Education (0014) TEST*ware*®. It is highly recommended that you first take this exam on computer. You will then have the additional study features and benefits of enforced timed conditions and instantaneous, accurate scoring. See page 3 for guidance on how to get the most out of our Praxis Elementary Education software.

Answer Sheet

1. Ⓐ Ⓑ Ⓒ Ⓓ	31. Ⓐ Ⓑ Ⓒ Ⓓ	61. Ⓐ Ⓑ Ⓒ Ⓓ	91. Ⓐ Ⓑ Ⓒ Ⓓ
2. Ⓐ Ⓑ Ⓒ Ⓓ	32. Ⓐ Ⓑ Ⓒ Ⓓ	62. Ⓐ Ⓑ Ⓒ Ⓓ	92. Ⓐ Ⓑ Ⓒ Ⓓ
3. Ⓐ Ⓑ Ⓒ Ⓓ	33. Ⓐ Ⓑ Ⓒ Ⓓ	63. Ⓐ Ⓑ Ⓒ Ⓓ	93. Ⓐ Ⓑ Ⓒ Ⓓ
4. Ⓐ Ⓑ Ⓒ Ⓓ	34. Ⓐ Ⓑ Ⓒ Ⓓ	64. Ⓐ Ⓑ Ⓒ Ⓓ	94. Ⓐ Ⓑ Ⓒ Ⓓ
5. Ⓐ Ⓑ Ⓒ Ⓓ	35. Ⓐ Ⓑ Ⓒ Ⓓ	65. Ⓐ Ⓑ Ⓒ Ⓓ	95. Ⓐ Ⓑ Ⓒ Ⓓ
6. Ⓐ Ⓑ Ⓒ Ⓓ	36. Ⓐ Ⓑ Ⓒ Ⓓ	66. Ⓐ Ⓑ Ⓒ Ⓓ	96. Ⓐ Ⓑ Ⓒ Ⓓ
7. Ⓐ Ⓑ Ⓒ Ⓓ	37. Ⓐ Ⓑ Ⓒ Ⓓ	67. Ⓐ Ⓑ Ⓒ Ⓓ	97. Ⓐ Ⓑ Ⓒ Ⓓ
8. Ⓐ Ⓑ Ⓒ Ⓓ	38. Ⓐ Ⓑ Ⓒ Ⓓ	68. Ⓐ Ⓑ Ⓒ Ⓓ	98. Ⓐ Ⓑ Ⓒ Ⓓ
9. Ⓐ Ⓑ Ⓒ Ⓓ	39. Ⓐ Ⓑ Ⓒ Ⓓ	69. Ⓐ Ⓑ Ⓒ Ⓓ	99. Ⓐ Ⓑ Ⓒ Ⓓ
10. Ⓐ Ⓑ Ⓒ Ⓓ	40. Ⓐ Ⓑ Ⓒ Ⓓ	70. Ⓐ Ⓑ Ⓒ Ⓓ	100. Ⓐ Ⓑ Ⓒ Ⓓ
11. Ⓐ Ⓑ Ⓒ Ⓓ	41. Ⓐ Ⓑ Ⓒ Ⓓ	71. Ⓐ Ⓑ Ⓒ Ⓓ	101. Ⓐ Ⓑ Ⓒ Ⓓ
12. Ⓐ Ⓑ Ⓒ Ⓓ	42. Ⓐ Ⓑ Ⓒ Ⓓ	72. Ⓐ Ⓑ Ⓒ Ⓓ	102. Ⓐ Ⓑ Ⓒ Ⓓ
13. Ⓐ Ⓑ Ⓒ Ⓓ	43. Ⓐ Ⓑ Ⓒ Ⓓ	73. Ⓐ Ⓑ Ⓒ Ⓓ	103. Ⓐ Ⓑ Ⓒ Ⓓ
14. Ⓐ Ⓑ Ⓒ Ⓓ	44. Ⓐ Ⓑ Ⓒ Ⓓ	74. Ⓐ Ⓑ Ⓒ Ⓓ	104. Ⓐ Ⓑ Ⓒ Ⓓ
15. Ⓐ Ⓑ Ⓒ Ⓓ	45. Ⓐ Ⓑ Ⓒ Ⓓ	75. Ⓐ Ⓑ Ⓒ Ⓓ	105. Ⓐ Ⓑ Ⓒ Ⓓ
16. Ⓐ Ⓑ Ⓒ Ⓓ	46. Ⓐ Ⓑ Ⓒ Ⓓ	76. Ⓐ Ⓑ Ⓒ Ⓓ	106. Ⓐ Ⓑ Ⓒ Ⓓ
17. Ⓐ Ⓑ Ⓒ Ⓓ	47. Ⓐ Ⓑ Ⓒ Ⓓ	77. Ⓐ Ⓑ Ⓒ Ⓓ	107. Ⓐ Ⓑ Ⓒ Ⓓ
18. Ⓐ Ⓑ Ⓒ Ⓓ	48. Ⓐ Ⓑ Ⓒ Ⓓ	78. Ⓐ Ⓑ Ⓒ Ⓓ	108. Ⓐ Ⓑ Ⓒ Ⓓ
19. Ⓐ Ⓑ Ⓒ Ⓓ	49. Ⓐ Ⓑ Ⓒ Ⓓ	79. Ⓐ Ⓑ Ⓒ Ⓓ	109. Ⓐ Ⓑ Ⓒ Ⓓ
20. Ⓐ Ⓑ Ⓒ Ⓓ	50. Ⓐ Ⓑ Ⓒ Ⓓ	80. Ⓐ Ⓑ Ⓒ Ⓓ	110. Ⓐ Ⓑ Ⓒ Ⓓ
21. Ⓐ Ⓑ Ⓒ Ⓓ	51. Ⓐ Ⓑ Ⓒ Ⓓ	81. Ⓐ Ⓑ Ⓒ Ⓓ	111. Ⓐ Ⓑ Ⓒ Ⓓ
22. Ⓐ Ⓑ Ⓒ Ⓓ	52. Ⓐ Ⓑ Ⓒ Ⓓ	82. Ⓐ Ⓑ Ⓒ Ⓓ	112. Ⓐ Ⓑ Ⓒ Ⓓ
23. Ⓐ Ⓑ Ⓒ Ⓓ	53. Ⓐ Ⓑ Ⓒ Ⓓ	83. Ⓐ Ⓑ Ⓒ Ⓓ	113. Ⓐ Ⓑ Ⓒ Ⓓ
24. Ⓐ Ⓑ Ⓒ Ⓓ	54. Ⓐ Ⓑ Ⓒ Ⓓ	84. Ⓐ Ⓑ Ⓒ Ⓓ	114. Ⓐ Ⓑ Ⓒ Ⓓ
25. Ⓐ Ⓑ Ⓒ Ⓓ	55. Ⓐ Ⓑ Ⓒ Ⓓ	85. Ⓐ Ⓑ Ⓒ Ⓓ	115. Ⓐ Ⓑ Ⓒ Ⓓ
26. Ⓐ Ⓑ Ⓒ Ⓓ	56. Ⓐ Ⓑ Ⓒ Ⓓ	86. Ⓐ Ⓑ Ⓒ Ⓓ	116. Ⓐ Ⓑ Ⓒ Ⓓ
27. Ⓐ Ⓑ Ⓒ Ⓓ	57. Ⓐ Ⓑ Ⓒ Ⓓ	87. Ⓐ Ⓑ Ⓒ Ⓓ	117. Ⓐ Ⓑ Ⓒ Ⓓ
28. Ⓐ Ⓑ Ⓒ Ⓓ	58. Ⓐ Ⓑ Ⓒ Ⓓ	88. Ⓐ Ⓑ Ⓒ Ⓓ	118. Ⓐ Ⓑ Ⓒ Ⓓ
29. Ⓐ Ⓑ Ⓒ Ⓓ	59. Ⓐ Ⓑ Ⓒ Ⓓ	89. Ⓐ Ⓑ Ⓒ Ⓓ	119. Ⓐ Ⓑ Ⓒ Ⓓ
30. Ⓐ Ⓑ Ⓒ Ⓓ	60. Ⓐ Ⓑ Ⓒ Ⓓ	90. Ⓐ Ⓑ Ⓒ Ⓓ	120. Ⓐ Ⓑ Ⓒ Ⓓ

Elementary Education: Content Knowledge (0014) Practice Test 2

TIME: 120 Minutes
120 Questions

> **Four-Function or Scientific Calculator Permitted**

1. Before working with mathematical word problems, a teacher needs to determine that

   (A) the student can complete the math unit.
   (B) the student is at a high enough reading level to understand the problems.
   (C) the math textbook mirrors the skills used in the word problems.
   (D) the class will be on-task for the problems.

2. A student describes an analysis of a recent presidential address for the class. The teacher replies, "You have provided us with a most interesting way of looking at this issue!" The teacher is using

   (A) simple positive response.
   (B) negative response.
   (C) redirect.
   (D) academic praise.

3. When a teacher leads choral chants, the teacher is

   (A) practicing aural skills.
   (B) practicing vocal exercises.
   (C) having students repeat basic skills orally.
   (D) repeating what the students answer.

4. A lesson for which students are given a tankful of water and various objects and are asked to order the objects by weight would be considered a(n)

   (A) science lesson.
   (B) discovery-learning lesson.
   (C) inductive-reasoning lesson.
   (D) eg-rule lesson.

5. Mr. Drake is a first-grade teacher who is using the whole language method while teaching about animals. Before reading a story to the students, Mr. Drake tells the students what he is expecting them to learn from reading the story. What is his reason for doing this?

   (A) The students should know why the instructor chose this text over any other.
   (B) It is important for teachers to share personal ideas with their students in order to foster an environment of confidence and understanding.
   (C) Mr. Drake wants to verify that all students are on-task before he begins the story.
   (D) Mr. Drake is modeling a vital prereading skill in order to teach it to the young readers.

6. Mr. Drake wants to ensure that the class will have a quality discussion on the needs of house pets. In response to a student who said that her family abandoned their cat in a field because it ate too much, Mr. Drake asks: "What is one way to save pets that are no longer wanted?" This exercise involves what level of questioning?

   (A) Evaluation
   (B) Analysis
   (C) Comprehension
   (D) Synthesis

7. Mr. Drake has a heterogeneously grouped reading class. He has placed the students in groups of two—one skilled reader and one remedial reader—and asked that they read the selected story and question each other until they feel that they both understand the story. By planning the lesson this way, Mr. Drake has

   (A) set a goal for his students.
   (B) condensed the number of observations necessary, thereby creating more time for class instruction.
   (C) made it possible for another teacher to utilize the limited materials.
   (D) utilized the students' strengths and weaknesses to maximize time, materials, and the learning environment.

8. Mr. Drake is continuing his lesson on the animal kingdom. He wants to ensure that the students learn as much as they can about animals, so he incorporates information familiar to the students into the new information. Knowing that these are first-grade learners, what should Mr. Drake consider when contemplating their learning experience?

   (A) The students will know how much information they can retrieve from memory.
   (B) The students will overestimate how much information they can retrieve from memory.
   (C) The students will be able to pick out the information they need to study and the information they do not need to study due to prior mastery.
   (D) The students will estimate how much they can learn in one time period.

9. Before reading a story about a veterinary hospital, Mr. Drake constructs a semantic map of related words and terms using the students' input. What is his main intention for doing this?

   (A) To demonstrate a meaningful relationship between the concepts of the story and the prior knowledge of the students
   (B) To serve as a visual means of learning
   (C) To determine the level of understanding the students will have at the conclusion of the topic being covered
   (D) To model proper writing using whole words

10. Student data such as scores on tests and assignments would be the best criteria for determining which of the following?

    (A) Only the students' academic grades
    (B) Behavior assessment
    (C) Student grades and the teacher's quality of instruction
    (D) Student grades and behavior assessment

11. Results of a standardized test indicate that a teacher's students did poorly on the mathematics problem-solving section; students in another classroom in the same school did much better. What would be the best action to take for the teacher of the students who did poorly?

    (A) Look at the students' scores from last year to justify their poor achievement.
    (B) Tell future students to study more because that section is more difficult.
    (C) Suggest that parents hire a math tutor.
    (D) Ask the other teacher to share the strategies used to help make the other students successful.

12. Mr. Joseph is a fifth-grade math and science teacher working in a large suburban middle school. At the beginning of each of his classes, he stands outside of his classroom and greets his students as they walk into his classroom. Mr. Joseph notices students coming into his class who appear upset or angry and show signs of poor self-esteem. Sometimes he overhears his students arguing with other students before class. Often, these students seem to "shut down" during class and do not follow along with the work. He knows this is a problem, but he is not

sure what he should do to solve it. He wants to keep these students from getting behind in their learning. To reduce this problem, Mr. Joseph should

(A) inform the school counselor of the problem and send each student with these symptoms to see the counselor as soon as class starts.
(B) call the parents of students who seem upset or angry and try to persuade them to fix the problem.
(C) send students with these kinds of problems out in the hall so they can get themselves together and learn.
(D) create an environment in his classroom where students feel safe and let them know he is aware of their problems and will do all he can to help them learn.

13. The question, "What was the name of Hamlet's father?" is

(A) a high-order question of evaluation.
(B) a low-order question that can be used to begin a discussion.
(C) a transition.
(D) questioning a skill.

14. Mr. Owen, a third-grade teacher, has been teaching in a small rural district for three years. He enjoys the slow pace of the community and the fact that he knows most of his students' families relatively well. He is a member of the Evening Lions Club, plays on the church basketball team, and volunteers at the animal shelter.

His class this year is made up of 21 eight- and nine-year-olds. Most of the students are of average ability, two receive special services for learning disabilities, and one receives speech therapy. Mr. Owen works hard at making his classroom an exciting place to learn, with lots of hands-on, problem-based cooperative group projects. In the past, students have had difficulty grasping relationships between math concepts and economics. Mr. Owen has decided to offer a savings program with the help of local banks. Once a week, students will make deposits into their savings accounts. Periodically, they will use their accounts to figure interest at different rates, class totals saved, etc. As part of the social studies curriculum, he encourages them to do chores at

home and in their neighborhoods to earn the money for their savings. This approach is evidence that Mr. Owen understands the importance of

(A) the relevance and authenticity in planning instructional activities for students.
(B) integrating curriculum concepts across disciplines that support learning.
(C) saving money.
(D) all of the above.

15. Students are presented with the following problem: "Bill is taller than Ann, but Ann is taller than Grace. Is Ann the tallest child or is Bill the tallest?" This question requires students to use

(A) inductive reasoning.
(B) deductive reasoning.
(C) hypothesis formation.
(D) pattern identification.

16. Which of the following is the correct chronological order for the events in history listed below?

I. Puritans arrive in New England.
II. Protestant Reformation begins.
III. Columbus sets sail across the Atlantic.
IV. Magna Carta is signed in England.

(A) IV, III, II, I
(B) IV, III, I, II
(C) III, IV, II, I
(D) III, II, I, IV

17. The intellectual movement that encouraged the use of reason and science and that anticipated human progress was called the

(A) American System.
(B) Mercantilism.
(C) Enlightenment.
(D) Age of Belief.

18. In the U.S. government, the function of "checks and balances" is meant to

(A) regulate the amount of control each branch of government would have.
(B) make each branch of government independent from one another.
(C) give the president control.
(D) give the Supreme Court control.

19. Which of the following groups did not play a role in the settlement of the English colonies in America?

    (A) Roman Catholics.
    (B) Puritans.
    (C) Mormons
    (D) Quakers.

20. On the following map, which letter represents the Philippines?

    (A) K
    (B) D
    (C) I
    (D) M

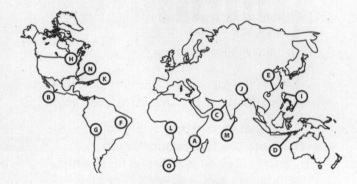

21. The Bill of Rights

    (A) listed the grievances of the colonists against the British.
    (B) forbade the federal government from encroaching on the rights of citizens.
    (C) gave all white males the right to vote.
    (D) specified the rights of slaves.

22. A teacher asks her eighth-grade English students to select a career they would enjoy when they grow up and then to find three sources on the Internet with information about that career. She tells the students that they must find out how much education is required for this career. If the career requires postsecondary education, then the student must find a school or college that provides this education and find out how long it will take to be educated or trained for this career. Through this assignment, the teacher is helping her students to

    (A) explore short-term personal and academic goals.
    (B) explore long-term personal and academic goals.
    (C) evaluate short-term personal and academic goals.
    (D) synthesize long-term personal and academic goals.

23. A teacher asks a student, "When you were studying for your spelling test, did you remember a mnemonic we talked about in class for spelling *principal* that 'a principal is your pal'?" The teacher is

    (A) leading the student in a divergent thinking exercise.
    (B) teaching the student mnemonics, or memory devices.
    (C) asking a question to guide the student in correcting an error.
    (D) modeling inductive reasoning skills for the student.

24. When working with ESL students, the teacher should be aware that

    (A) students should speak only English in class.
    (B) an accepting classroom and encouraging lessons will foster learning.
    (C) such students should be referred to a specialist.
    (D) limiting the number of resources available is beneficial to the students.

25. Ms. Borders, a second-year third-grade teacher, is preparing a theme study on water and the related concepts of conservation, ecology, and human needs. One of her instructional outcomes deals with students' abilities to demonstrate their new learning in a variety of ways. As she plans her unit of study, Ms. Borders first needs to consider

    (A) the strengths and needs of the diverse learners in her classroom.
    (B) the amount of reading material she assigns.
    (C) how the theme connects to other academic disciplines.
    (D) inviting guest speakers to the classroom.

26. Sequential language acquisition occurs when students

   (A) learn a second language after mastery of the first.
   (B) learn a second language at the same time as the first.
   (C) learn two languages in parts.
   (D) develop language skills.

27. Teachers should provide a variety of experiences and concrete examples for children with reading difficulties because some children

   (A) come from environments with limited language exposure.
   (B) have poor learning habits.
   (C) have trouble distinguishing letters.
   (D) can speak well but have difficulty reading.

28. A teacher writes "All men are created equal" on the board and asks each student to explain the meaning of the statement. One student says that it means that all people are equal, but another student says that it just applies to men. A third student says that it is a lie because not all people are equally good at all things, and that, for example, some people can run faster than others and some can sing better than others. The teacher's instructional aim is to

   (A) see whether students can reach consensus on the meaning of the statement.
   (B) see how well students can defend their beliefs.
   (C) provoke the students to disagree with the statement.
   (D) engage the students in critical thinking and to allow them to express their opinions.

29. If the other students laugh when a first-grade girl says, "I want to be a truck driver when I grow up," and tell her, "Girls can't drive big trucks," what should the teacher do?

   (A) Tell the class to quiet down, that the student can be whatever she wants to be when she grows up.
   (B) Tell the class that most truck drivers are men.
   (C) Tell the class that both women and men can be truck drivers, depending on their skills.

   (D) Ask the class to vote on whether women should be truck drivers.

Use the bar graph titled "Unemployment, 1929–1945" to answer the two questions that follow.

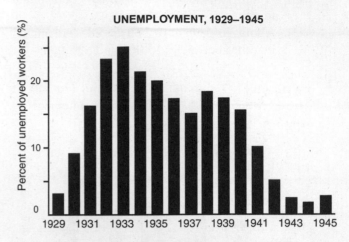

UNEMPLOYMENT, 1929–1945

30. According to the bar graph, the unemployment rate was highest in

   (A) 1929.
   (B) 1933.
   (C) 1938.
   (D) 1944.

31. According to the graph, the unemployment rate was lowest in

   (A) 1929.
   (B) 1933.
   (C) 1938.
   (D) 1944.

32. According to the graph titled "Households by Income Class," which one of the following statements is true?

Households by Income Class

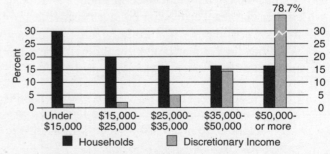

Percentage Distribution of Households and Discretionary Income (Total U.S. = 100 percent)

(A) About 50 percent of households had annual incomes of less than $15,000.

(B) Almost 75 percent of households had annual incomes of $50,000 or more.

(C) About 78 percent of households had annual incomes of $50,000 or more.

(D) About 20 percent of households had annual incomes between $15,000 and $25,000.

33. According to the graph titled "Age of Household Head," which one of the following statements is true?

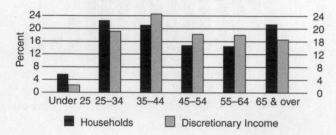

Age of Household Head

Percentage Distribution of Households and Discretionary Income (Total U.S. = 100%)

(A) Middle-aged households tend to have greater discretionary income.

(B) The youngest have the most discretionary income.

(C) The oldest have the most discretionary income.

(D) The older people get, the less discretionary income they have.

34. An ESOL student is proficient in oral language; however, he continues to experience difficulty with academic language used in science and social studies classes. The teacher believes academic proficiency correlates with oral language proficiency. What has the teacher failed to acknowledge in her analysis of the student's language proficiency?

(A) Both basic interpersonal communication skills and cognitive academic language proficiency are needed for successful academic performance.

(B) Basic interpersonal communication skills develop equally with cognitive academic language proficiency.

(C) Basic interpersonal communication skills are criteria for successful academic performance.

(D) Cognitive academic language proficiency is primary to basic interpersonal communication skills.

35. A student making top grades in class has received a percentile score of 63 on a nationally standardized math test. The best explanation of the student's score is

(A) a percentile score of 63 means that on a scale of 1–100, the student is 37 points from the top.

(B) a percentile score of 63 means that out of a group of 100 students, 37 would score higher and 62 would score lower, and the student has done well by scoring in the top half of all students taking the test.

(C) a percentile score of 63 is just like a grade of 63 on a test; it means that the student made a low D on the test.

(D) a percentile score of 63 means that out of a group of 100 students, 37 would score higher and 62 would score lower, showing a big difference between the student's performance on the standardized test and in class.

36. The launching of *Sputnik* by the Soviet Union in 1957 triggered increased emphasis on all of the following areas of study EXCEPT

(A) world history.
(B) math.
(C) science.
(D) foreign language.

37. Rueben Stein is a middle-school teacher who wants to teach his class about the classification system in the animal kingdom. He decides to introduce this unit to his class by having the students engage in general classification activities. He brings to class a paper bag filled with 30 household items. He dumps the contents of the bag onto a table and then asks the students, in groups of three or four, to put like items into piles and then to justify or explain why they placed certain items into a particular pile. By assigning this task to his students, Mr. Stein is

providing his students with a developmentally appropriate task because

(A) middle-school students like to work in groups.

(B) the items in the bag are household items with which most students will be familiar.

(C) the assignment gives students the opportunity to practice their skills at categorizing.

(D) the assignment will give students a task to perform while the teacher finishes grading papers.

38. Maria Smith is a sixth-grade teacher who is concerned about a student who is failing English class. The student has not turned in any outside assignments, and Ms. Smith has noticed a definite decline in the quality of work the student completes in class. Ms. Smith also has observed that the student has great difficulty staying awake in class and that she seems irritable and distracted most of the time. In her efforts to help the student, Ms. Smith decides to ask the student

(A) if she has been having family problems.

(B) if she realizes that the quality of her classwork is suffering and if she knows of any reasons for the decline.

(C) to work on better time-management skills.

(D) to start coming in early or to stay after class to receive extra help with her work.

39. Elva Rodriguez teaches fourth grade. She has structured her class so that students can spend 30 minutes daily, after lunch, in sustained silent reading activities with books and reading materials of their own choosing. In order to maximize this reading opportunity and to recognize differences among learners, Ms. Rodriguez

(A) allows some students to sit quietly at their desks while others are allowed to move to a reading area where they sit on floor cushions or recline on floor mats.

(B) makes sure that all students have selected appropriate reading materials.

(C) plays classical music on a tape player to enhance student learning.

(D) dims the lights in the classroom in order to increase students' reading comprehension.

40. Karla Dixon is a second-grade teacher who has selected a book to read to her class after lunch. She shows the students the picture on the cover of the book and reads the title of the book to them. She then asks, "What do you think this book is about?" By asking this question, Ms. Dixon is

(A) learning which students are interested in reading strategies.

(B) trying to keep the students awake because she knows they usually get sleepy after lunch.

(C) encouraging students to make a prediction, a precursor of hypothetical thinking.

(D) finding out which students are good readers.

41. Mrs. Johnson teaches sixth-grade reading. She teaches reading skills and comprehension through workbooks and through reading and class discussion of specific plays, short stories, and novels. She also allows students to make some selections according to their own interests. Because she believes there is a strong connection between reading and writing, her students write their responses to literature in a variety of ways. Some of her students have heard their high school brothers and sisters discuss portfolios, and they have asked Mrs. Johnson if they can use them also.

Which of the following statements are appropriate for Mrs. Johnson to consider in deciding whether to agree to the students' request?

I. Portfolios will develop skills her students can use in high school.

II. Portfolios will make Mrs. Johnson's students feel more mature because they would be making the same product as their older brothers and sisters.

III. Portfolios will assist her students in meeting course outcomes relating to reading and writing.

IV. Portfolios will make grading easier because there will be fewer papers and projects to evaluate.

(A) I, II, and IV

(B) I and III only

(C) II and III only

(D) II and IV only

42. The diagram below shows a path for electric flow. As the electrically charged particle flow moves through one complete circuit, it would NOT have to go through

    (A) V to get to W.
    (B) W to get to M.
    (C) Q to get to T.
    (D) T to get to S.

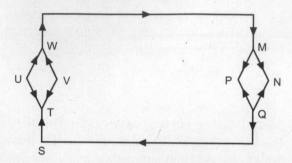

43. The floor of a 9′ × 12′ rectangular room depicted in the diagram is to be covered in two different types of material. The total cost of covering the entire room is $136.00. The cost of covering the inner rectangle is $80.00. The cost of covering the shaded area is $56.00. To compute the cost of material per square foot used to cover the shaded area, which of the following pieces of information is (are) NOT necessary?

    I.   The total cost of covering the entire room
    II. The cost of covering the inner rectangle
    III. The cost of covering the shaded area

    (A) I only
    (B) II only
    (C) I and II
    (D) I and III

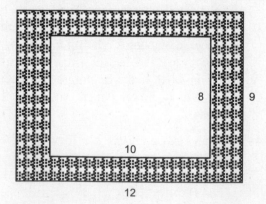

44. The drop in temperature that occurs when sugar is added to coffee is the result of

    I.   sugar passing from a solid to a liquid state.
    II. sugar absorbing calories from the water.
    III. heat becoming latent when it was sensible.

    (A) I only
    (B) I and II
    (C) I, II, and III
    (D) I and III

45. Ms. Thompson wants to teach her students about methods of collecting data in science. This is an important skill for first-graders. Which of the following describes the most appropriate method of teaching students about collecting data in science?

    (A) Ms. Thompson should arrange the students into groups of four. She should then have each group observe the class's pet mouse while she gently touches it with a feather. The students should record how many times out of 10 the pet mouse moves away from the feather. Then, she should gently touch the class's philodendron 10 times with a feather. The students should record how many out of 10 times the philodendron moves away from the feather.
    (B) Ms. Thompson should arrange the students into groups of four. She should give each group five solid balls made of materials that will float and five solid balls made of materials that will not float. She should have the students drop the balls into a bowl of water and record how many float and how many do not.
    (C) Ms. Thompson should show the students a video about scientific methods of gathering data.
    (D) Ms. Thompson should have a scientist come and talk to the class about methods of collecting data. If she cannot get a scientist, she should have a science teacher from the high school come and speak about scientific methods of data collection.

46. A positive condition depending on the absence of cold is

    (A) Fahrenheit.
    (B) intense artificial cold.
    (C) heat.
    (D) Celsius.

Questions 47–49 refer to the following short passages.

(A)   Once upon a time and a very good time it was, there was a moocow coming down along the road and this moocow that was coming down along the road met a nicens little boy named baby tuckoo . . .

(B)   And thus have these naked Nantucketers, these sea hermits, issuing from their anthill in the sea, overrun and conquered the watery world like so many Alexanders . . .

(C)   A large rose tree stood near the entrance of the garden: the roses growing on it were white, but there were three gardeners at it, busily painting them red. Alice thought this a very curious thing, and she went nearer to watch them, and, just as she came up to them, she heard one of them say "Look out now, Five!"

(D)   Emma was not required, by any subsequent discovery, to retract her ill opinion of Mrs. Elton. Her observation had been pretty correct. Such as Mrs. Elton appeared to her on this second interview, such she appeared whenever they met again: self-important, presuming, familiar, ignorant, and ill-bred. She had a little beauty and a little accomplishment, but so little judgment that she thought herself coming with superior knowledge of the world, to enliven and improve a country neighborhood . . .

47.   Which passage makes use of allusion?

(A)
(B)
(C)
(D)

48.   Which passage employs a distinct voice to imitate the speech of a character?

(A)
(B)
(C)
(D)

49.   Which passage is most likely taken from a nineteenth-century novel of manners?

(A)
(B)
(C)
(D)

Questions 50–53 refer to the following passage.

The issue of adult literacy has finally received recognition in the media as a major social problem. It is more important that the politicians themselves recognize the seriousness of the problem and support increased funding for literacy programs.

Literacy education programs need to be directed at two different groups of people with very different needs. The first group is composed of people who have very limited reading and writing skills. These people are complete illiterates. A second group is composed of people who can read and write but whose skills are not sufficient to meet their needs. This second group is called functionally illiterate. Successful literacy programs must meet the needs of both groups.

Instructors in literacy programs have three main responsibilities. First, the educational needs of the illiterates and functional illiterates must be met. Second, the instructors must approach the participants in the program with empathy, not sympathy. Third, all participants must experience success in the program and must perceive their efforts as worthwhile.

50.   What is the difference between illiteracy and functional illiteracy?

(A)   There is no difference.
(B)   A functional illiterate is enrolled in a literacy education program, but an illiterate is not.
(C)   An illiterate cannot read or write, and a functional illiterate can read and write but not at a very high skill level.
(D)   There are more illiterates than functional illiterates in the United States today.

51.   What is the purpose of the passage?

(A)   To discuss the characteristics of successful literacy programs
(B)   To discuss the manner in which literacy programs are viewed by the media

(C) To discuss some of the reasons for increased attention to literacy as a social issue

(D) All of the above

52. According to the passage, which of the following is NOT a characteristic of successful literacy programs?

(A) Participants should receive free transportation.

(B) Participants should experience success in the program.

(C) Instructors must have empathy, not sympathy.

(D) Programs must meet the educational needs of illiterates.

53. What is the author's opinion of the funding for literacy programs?

(A) Too much

(B) Too little

(C) About right

(D) Too much for illiterates and not enough for functional illiterates

Questions 54 and 55 refer to the following passage.

Mr. Dobson teaches fifth-grade mathematics at Valverde Elementary. He encourages students to work in groups of two or three as they begin homework assignments so they can answer questions for each other. Mr. Dobson notices immediately that some of his students choose to work alone even though they had been asked to work in groups. He also notices that some students are easily distracted even though the other members of their group are working on the assignment as directed.

54. Which of the following is the most likely explanation for the students' different types of behavior?

(A) Fifth-grade students are not physically or mentally capable of working in small groups; small groups are more suitable for older students.

(B) Fifth-grade students vary greatly in their physical development and maturity; this

variance influences the students' interests and attitudes.

(C) Fifth-grade students lack the ability for internal control and therefore learn best in structured settings. It is usually best to seat fifth graders in single rows.

(D) Mr. Dobson needs to be more specific in his expectations for student behavior.

55. Mr. Dobson wants to encourage all of his students to participate in discussions related to the use of math in the real world. Five students in one class are very shy and introverted. Which of the following would most likely be the best way to encourage these students to participate in the discussion?

(A) Mr. Dobson should call on these students by name at least once each day and give participation grades.

(B) Mr. Dobson should not be concerned about these students because they will become less shy and introverted as they mature during the year.

(C) Mr. Dobson should divide the class into small groups for discussion so these students will not be overwhelmed by speaking in front of the whole class.

(D) Mr. Dobson should speak with these students individually and encourage them to participate more in class discussions.

Question 56 refers to the following passage.

Mrs. Kresmeier teaches sixth-grade language arts classes. One of her curriculum goals is to help students improve their spelling. As one of her techniques, she has developed a number of special mnemonic devices that she uses with the students, getting the idea from the old teaching rhymes like "I before E except after C or when sounding like A as in neighbor or weigh." Her own memory tricks—"The moose can't get loose from the noose" or "Spell rhyme? Why me?"—have caught the interest of her students. Now, besides Mrs. Kresmeier's memory tricks for better spelling, her students are developing and sharing their own creative ways to memorize more effectively.

56. To improve her students' spelling, Mrs. Kresmeier's method has been successful primarily because of which of the following factors related to student achievement?

    (A) The students are not relying on phonics or sight words to spell difficult words.
    (B) Mrs. Kresmeier has impressed her students with the need to learn to spell.
    (C) The ideas are effective with many students and help to create a learning environment that is open to student interaction.
    (D) Mrs. Kresmeier teaches spelling using only words that can be adapted to mnemonic clues.

Questions 57–59 refer to the following passage.

> Mr. Freeman is preparing a year-long unit on process writing for his fifth-grade class. He plans for each student to write about a series of topics over each six-week grading period. At the end of each grading period, students will select three completed writing assignments that reflect their best work. Mr. Freeman will review the assignments and conference with each student. During the conference, Mr. Freeman will assist the students with preparing a list of writing goals for the next grading term.

57. Which of the following best describes Mr. Freeman's plan for reviewing student writing assignments, conferencing with each student, and helping each student set specific goals for writing to be accomplished during the next grading period?

    (A) Summative evaluation.
    (B) Summative assessment.
    (C) Formative assessment.
    (D) Peer evaluation.

58. Mr. Freeman's goal in planning to conference with each student about the student's writing could be described as

    (A) creating a climate of trust and encouraging a positive attitude toward writing.
    (B) an efficient process for grading student writing assignments.

    (C) an opportunity to stress the importance of careful editing of completed writing assignments.
    (D) an opportunity to stress the value of prewriting in producing a final product.

59. Philip, a student in Mr. Freeman's class, receives services from a resource teacher for a learning disability that affects his reading and writing. Which of the following is the most appropriate request that Mr. Freeman should make of the resource teacher to help Philip complete the writing unit?

    (A) Mr. Freeman should ask the resource teacher to provide writing instruction for Philip.
    (B) Mr. Freeman should excuse Philip from writing assignments.
    (C) Mr. Freeman should ask the resource teacher for help in modifying the writing unit to match Philip's needs.
    (D) Mr. Freeman should ask the resource teacher to schedule extra tutoring sessions to help Philip with the writing assignments.

60. Mr. Liu and Mr. Lowery, a science teacher, are planning a celebration of Galileo's birthday. The students will research Galileo's discoveries, draw posters of those discoveries, and prepare short plays depicting important events in his life. They will present the plays and display the posters for grades 1–4. This is an example of

    (A) an end-of-the-year project.
    (B) problem solving and inquiry teaching.
    (C) working with other teachers to plan instructions.
    (D) teachers preparing to ask the PTA for science lab equipment.

61. The principal asks Mr. Liu and Ms. Gonzalez, another fifth-grade math teacher in the school, to visit the math classes and the computer lab in the middle school that most of the students at Valverde Elementary will attend. By asking Mr. Liu and Ms. Gonzalez to visit the middle school, the principal is most likely encouraging

    (A) collaboration among the math teachers at Valverde and the middle school.
    (B) Mr. Liu and Ms. Gonzalez to consider applying for a job at the middle school.

(C) the use of computers in math classes at Valverde.

(D) the use of the middle school math curriculum in the fifth-grade classes.

62. Use the Pythagorean theorem to answer this question: Which of the following comes closest to the actual length of side *x* in the triangle below?

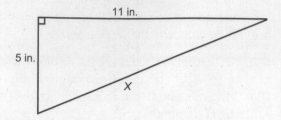

(A) 14 in.
(B) 12 in.
(C) 11 in.
(D) 13 in.

63. If the two triangles, ABC and DEF, shown below are similar, what is the length of side DF?

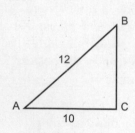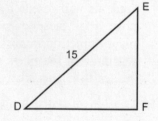

(A) 12.5 units
(B) 13 units
(C) 12 units
(D) 13.5 units

64. Which of the following types of pollution or atmospheric phenomena are correctly matched with their underlying causes?

I. global warming – carbon dioxide and methane

II. acid rain – sulfur dioxide and nitrogen dioxide

III. ozone depletion – chlorofluorocarbons and sunlight

IV. aurora borealis – solar flares and magnetism

(A) I and II only
(B) II and III only
(C) I and IV only
(D) I, II, III, and IV

65. Which of the following observations best describes the "Ring of Fire"?

(A) Similarities in rock formations and continental coastlines created the "Ring of Fire."

(B) Earth's plates collide at convergent margins, separate at divergent margins, and move laterally at transform-fault boundaries.

(C) Earthquakes produced waves that continue to travel through the Earth in all directions and created the "Ring of Fire."

(D) Volcanoes form when lava accumulates and hardens.

66. Use the pie chart below to answer the following question. If the total number of people voting was 600, which of the following statements are true?

Votes for City Council

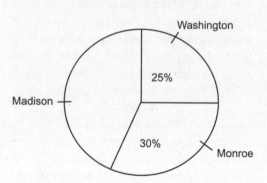

I. Madison received more votes than Monroe and Washington combined.

II. Madison received 45 percent of the votes.

III. Monroe received 180 votes.

IV. Madison received 180 votes.

(A) I and III only
(B) I and IV only
(C) II and III only
(D) II and IV only

67. Which of the following scenarios could be represented by the graph shown below?

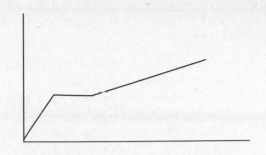

(A) Mr. Cain mowed grass at a steady rate for a while, took a short break, and then finished the job at a steady but slower rate.

(B) Mr. Cain mowed grass at a steady rate for a while, mowed at a steady but slower rate and then took a break.

(C) Mr. Cain mowed grass at a variable rate for a while, took a short break, and then finished the job at a variable rate.

(D) Mr. Cain mowed grass at a steady rate for a while, took a short brcak, and then finished the job at a steady but faster pace.

68. Only one of the statements below is necessarily true according to the bar graph below. Which one?

Ms. Patton's Earnings, 1998–2002

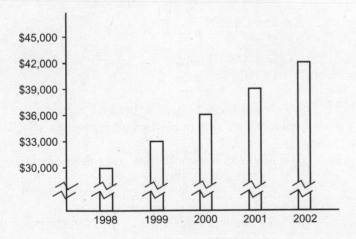

(A) The range of Ms. Patton's earnings for the years shown is $15,000.

(B) Ms. Patton's annual pay increases were consistent over the years shown.

(C) Ms. Patton earned $45,000 in 2003.

(D) Ms. Patton's average income for the years shown was $38,000.

69. Which equation best describes the following graph?

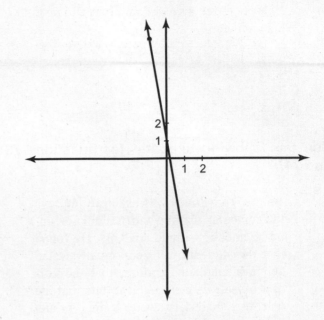

(A) $y = 0x$

(B) $y = x + 0$

(C) $y = -8x$

(D) $y = 8x$

70. What is the solution to the equation $x/3 - 9 = 15$?

(A) 18

(B) 8

(C) 36

(D) 72

71. Translate this problem into a one-variable equation, then solve the equation. What is the solution?

"There are ten vehicles parked in a parking lot. Each is either a car with four tires or a motorcycle with two tires. (Do not count any spare tires.) There are 26 wheels in the lot. How many cars are there in the lot?"

(A) 8

(B) 6

(C) 5

(D) 3

72. Which equation could be used to solve the following problem?

"Three consecutive odd numbers add up to 117. What are they?"

(A) $x + (x + 2) + (x + 4) = 117$
(B) $1x + 3x + 5x = 117$
(C) $x + x + x = 117$
(D) $x + (x + 1) + (x + 3) = 177$

Use the following scenario for questions 73 and 74.

Tom Jones was asked to improve the remedial reading curriculum for upper elementary-grade students. He found that the students were continually tested and evaluated on reading, that the current objectives were unclear, and that the teaching materials were inappropriate. Following a lengthy observation of Mrs. Ratu's teaching strategies, Mr. Jones concluded that she was teaching basic reading skills in the same manner as did the lower elementary teachers. The teaching materials used a controlled vocabulary and simple sentences. The students were being taught to rely heavily upon pictures and illustrations for the story. Most of the material was fictional in genre. Rote was Mrs. Ratu's preference for learning. Mr. Jones analyzed the test results and found that many of the students in Mrs. Ratu's class had average scores in the areas of art, math, and music. He concluded that, with the exception of reading, most were normal students and would be successful when their remediation was complete. Mr. Jones made several decisions: (1) the students would be evaluated annually with an achievement test; (2) reading materials of interest to upper elementary students would be substituted for elementary materials; (3) each student would be encouraged to read about the subject of his or her choice; and (4) roundtable discussions would be developed for each "favorite subject."

73. Mrs. Ratu's method of teaching remedial reading focused upon

I. the level at which the students should have learned the basic reading skills.
II. her own minimal competency in instructional design and evaluation.
III. her lack of understanding of the learners in her class.
IV. her desire to make remedial reading easy for the students.

(A) I only
(B) I and IV only
(C) II and III only
(D) II only

74. Mr. Jones, having reviewed the students' scores in other classes, knew

I. that development in one area would lead to development in another area.
II. how to use a variety of techniques for creating intrinsic and extrinsic motivation.
III. that allowing students to have choices in their learning would create camaraderie.
IV. that roundtable discussions would make class more enjoyable but have no effect on students' grades.

(A) I and II only
(B) II only
(C) I, II, and III only
(D) IV only

75. How can a teacher elicit a high-order response from a student who provides simple responses?

(A) Ask follow-up questions.
(B) Repeat the questions.
(C) Ask the same questions of a different student.
(D) Ask another student to elaborate on the original response.

76. According to the Socratic method, teachers should

(A) impart all of their knowledge to their students in ways they deem most appropriate.
(B) ask questions to get students to think about universal truths.

(C) ask questions so that students can show how much they know.

(D) encourage students to ask questions which will enable them to learn.

77. All of the following were true of education in the Southern colonies EXCEPT:

(A) private tutors were used to educate the sons of wealthy plantation owners.

(B) the education of girls was limited to the knowledge of how to manage a household.

(C) slaves were taught to read so that they could study the Bible.

(D) teaching a slave to read or write was a criminal act.

78. The ruling of the Supreme Court in *Brown v Board of Education of Topeka, Kansas* (1954) found that

(A) separate educational facilities could offer equal educational opportunities to students.

(B) students could be placed in segregated tracks within desegregated schools.

(C) segregated schools resulted in unequal educational opportunity but caused no psychological effects.

(D) separate educational facilities were inherently unequal and violated the Fourteenth Amendment.

79. President Lyndon B. Johnson's "War on Poverty" resulted in all of the following EXCEPT

(A) the Peace Corps.
(B) Head Start.
(C) Elementary and Secondary Education Act.
(D) VISTA.

80. The Education for All Handicapped Children Act of 1975 mandates that schools provide free and appropriate education for all of the following EXCEPT

(A) mentally handicapped.
(B) physically handicapped.
(C) socially–emotionally handicapped.
(D) learning disabled.

81. Miss Bailey teaches fifth-grade social studies in a self-contained classroom with 25 students of various achievement levels. She is starting a unit on the history of their local community and wants to stimulate the students' thinking. She also wants to encourage students to develop a project as a result of their study. Which type of project would encourage the highest level of thinking by the students?

(A) Giving students a list of questions about people, dates, and events, then having them put the answers on a poster, with appropriate pictures, to display in class.

(B) Giving students questions to use to interview older members of the community, then having them write articles based on the interviews and publish them in a booklet.

(C) Discussing the influence of the past on the present community, then asking students to project what the community might be like in 100 years.

(D) Using archived newspapers to collect data, then having them draw a timeline that includes the major events of the community from its beginning to the current date.

82. Mr. Roberts' sixth-grade social studies class has developed a research project to survey student use of various types of video games. They designed a questionnaire and then administered it to all fourth-, fifth-, and sixth-grade students on their campus. The students plan to analyze their data, then develop a presentation to show at the next parent-teacher meeting. Which types of computer software would be helpful during this class project?

I. Word processing.
II. Database.
III. Simulation.
IV. Graph/chart.

(A) I, II, III, and IV
(B) I, II, and IV
(C) I and III only
(D) III and IV only

83. What might Mrs. Walker, a sixth-grade teacher of world history, include in her planning to keep gifted students challenged?

(A) An extra report on the history of the Greeks.
(B) Let them tutor the students who are unmotivated.

(C) Encourage students to plan learning activities of their own.

(D) Create for the student a tightly organized and well-designed unit.

84. Ms. Carter is a second-grade social studies teacher at a small rural school. Several times during the semester, she has found herself in conversations with colleagues in the school and various community members regarding concerns about a program initiated by the school librarian who is active in the wildlife refuge program in the county. The librarian often brings hurt or orphaned animals to the library to care for them during the day. Several parents are concerned about issues of hygiene and students with allergies. As a member of the site-based decision-making (SBDM) committee, Ms. Carter's best course of action is to

(A) tell the librarian to remove the animals at once.

(B) submit an agenda item to the principal to discuss the concerns at the next meeting.

(C) call the Health Department for a surprise inspection.

(D) support the librarian and praise her efforts to expose students to the issues of wildlife preservation.

85. When a member of the House of Representatives helps a citizen from his or her district receive federal aid to which that citizen is entitled, the representative's action is referred to as

(A) casework.
(B) pork barrel legislation.
(C) lobbying.
(D) logrolling.

86. The term "Trail of Tears" refers to

(A) the Mormon migration from Nauvoo, Illinois, to what is now Utah.

(B) the forced migration of the Cherokee tribe from the southern Appalachians to what is now Oklahoma.

(C) the westward migration along the Oregon Trail.

(D) the migration into Kentucky along the Wilderness Road.

87. Earth's Moon is

(A) generally closer to the Sun than it is to Earth.

(B) generally closer to Earth than it is to the Sun.

(C) generally equidistant between Earth and the Sun.

(D) closer to Earth during part of the year, and closer to the Sun for the rest of the year.

88. Which of the following statements is NOT true?

(A) Infectious diseases are caused by viruses, bacteria, or protests.

(B) Cancers and hereditary diseases can be infectious.

(C) Environmental hazards can cause disease.

(D) The immune system protects the body from disease.

89. Which equation could be used to solve the following problem? "Here is how Acme Taxicab Company computes fares for riders: People are charged three dollars for just getting into the cab, then they are charged two dollars more for every mile or fraction of a mile of the ride. What would be the fare for a ride of 10.2 miles?"

(A) $3 \times (2 \times 10.2) = y$
(B) $3 + (2 + 11) = y$
(C) $3 \times (2 + 10.2) = y$
(D) $3 + (2 \times 11) = y$

90. What does it mean that multiplication and division are *inverse operations*?

(A) Multiplication is commutative, whereas division is not. For example: 4×2 gives the same product as 2×4, but $4 \div 2$ is not the same as $2 \div 4$.

(B) Whether multiplying or dividing a value by 1, the value remains the same. For example, 9×1 equals 9; $9 \div 1$ also equals 9.

(C) When performing complex calculations involving several operations, all multiplication must be completed before completing any division, such as in $8 \div 2 \times 4 + 7 - 1$.

(D) The operations "undo" each other. For example, multiplying 11 by 3 gives 33. Dividing 33 by 3 then takes you back to 11.

91. Which of the following statements correctly describes each group of vertebrates?

    I. Amphibians are cold-blooded and spend part of their life cycle in water and part on land.

    II. Reptiles are generally warm-blooded and have scales that cover their skin.

    III. Fish are cold-blooded, breath with gills, and are covered by scales.

    IV. Mammals are warm-blooded and have milk glands and hair.

(A) I and IV only
(B) I, III, and IV only
(C) IV only
(D) I, II, III, and IV

92. Mrs. Fisher notices that one of her female sixth-grade students, Lisa, always asks to go to the restroom during class, which is immediately following lunch. Lisa typically makes good grades, and she is active in extracurricular activities. Mrs. Fisher also notices that Lisa has been more conscious of her weight lately, making comments such as "if I weren't so fat" and "if I were skinny." Mrs. Fisher suspects that Lisa has an eating disorder and is going to the restroom in order to purge. Based on this suspicion, Mrs. Fisher should

(A) share her concerns with the school counselor.
(B) send another student to check on Lisa the next time she is in the restroom.
(C) call Lisa's parents to express her concerns.
(D) confront Lisa with her suspicions in order to find out the truth.

Questions 93 refers to the following passage:

    Mr. Shahid wants his students to understand how water is formed from the two elements of hydrogen and oxygen. He uses a manipulative of two blue balls labeled hydrogen and one white ball labeled oxygen. The balls are connected with wooden rods. Mr. Shahid briefly uses this manipulative, but then continues his explanation with an in-depth description of how water is formed and the theoretical underpinnings for this scientific discovery.

93. In order for students to understand this science lesson, they must be at which one of Piaget's stages of development?

(A) Concrete operational
(B) Formal operational
(C) Preoperational
(D) Sensorimotor

94. In the number 72104.58, what is the place value of the 2?

(A) Thousands
(B) Millions
(C) Ten thousands
(D) Tenths

95. The daily high temperatures in Frostbite, Minnesota, for one week in January were as follows:

Sunday: –2°F

Monday: 3°F

Tuesday: 0°F

Wednesday: –4°F

Thursday: –5°F

Friday: –1°F

Saturday: 2°F

What was the mean daily high temperature for that week?

(A) 7
(B) –7
(C) –1
(D) 1

Questions 96–98 are based on the following passage:

    The social studies teachers of an inner city school wanted to change to a more relevant curriculum, with units on economics throughout the world instead of only regions of the United States. Ms. Dunn was asked to submit a proposal for the new curriculum, related activities, sequencing, themes, and materials. In consultation with the other teachers in the department, a needs assessment was planned.

96. The teachers believed that the needs assessment would

   (A) help the students make a connection between their current skills and those that will be new to them.
   (B) reveal community problems that may affect the students' lives and their performance in school.
   (C) foster a view of learning as a purposeful pursuit, promoting a sense of responsibility for one's own learning.
   (D) engage students in learning activities and help them to develop the motivation to achieve.

97. When the needs assessment was evaluated, it revealed an ethnically diverse community. Student interests and parental expectations varied, different language backgrounds existed, student exceptionalities were common, and academic motivation was low. The question confronting the teachers was how to bridge the gap from where the students were to where they should have been. The available choices were to

   (A) change the textbook only.
   (B) relate the lessons to the students' personal interests.
   (C) create a positive environment to minimize the effects of the negative external factors.
   (D) help students to learn and to monitor their own performance.

98. At the end of a question-and-answer period, the group of teachers, headed by Ms. Dunn, set a goal of having the students gain an awareness of the correlation between their skills or lack of skills and their expected salaries. A parent/guardian support group would be established to enhance the students' motivation to master new skills. Strategies to use at home and in the classroom would be developed. Ms. Dunn felt that, with the aid of parents, this plan would enable her to

   (A) promote her own professional growth as she worked cooperatively with professionals to create a school culture that would enhance learning and result in positive change.
   (B) meet the expectations associated with teaching.
   (C) foster strong home relationships that support student achievement of desired outcomes.
   (D) exhibit her understanding of the principles of conducting parent–teacher conferences and working cooperatively with parents.

99. During a period of field experiences in the community, Ms. Parks continually directs her students' attention to science as a way of solving problems. Following the period of field experiences, Ms. Parks asks her students to identify a problem in their school and to devise a scientific way of studying and solving that problem. The students work in groups for two class periods and select the following problem for investigation: It is late spring, and the classroom gets so hot during the afternoon that most students are uncomfortable. Their research questions are, "Why is it hotter in our classroom than in the music room, art room, or library?" and "How can we make our classroom cooler?" Which of the following is the most important benefit of allowing the students to select their own problem to investigate rather than having the teacher assign a problem?

   (A) Students become self-directed problem solvers who can structure their own learning experiences.
   (B) The teacher can best assess each student's academic and affective needs in a naturalistic setting.
   (C) Students will have the opportunity to work with a wide variety of instructional materials.
   (D) Students will learn to appreciate opposing viewpoints.

Questions 100–104 are based on the following passage:

Frederick Douglass was born Frederick Augustus Washington Bailey in 1817 to a white father and a slave mother. Frederick was raised by his grandmother on a Maryland plantation until he was eight. Then he was sent to Baltimore by his owner to be a servant to the Auld family. Mrs. Auld recognized Frederick's intellectual acumen and defied the law of the state by teaching him to read and write. When Mr. Auld warned that education would make the boy unfit for slavery, Frederick sought to continue his education in the streets. When his master died, Frederick, who was only 16 years of age, was returned to the plantation to work in the fields. Later, he was hired out to work in the shipyards in Baltimore as a ship caulker. He plotted an escape, but was discovered before he could get away. It took five years before he made his way to New York City and then to New Bedford, Massachusetts. He managed to elude slave hunters by changing his name to Douglass.

At an 1841 anti-slavery meeting in Massachusetts, Douglass was invited to give a talk about his experiences under slavery. His impromptu speech was so powerful and so eloquent that it thrust him into a career as an agent for the Massachusetts Anti-Slavery Society. To counter those who doubted his authenticity as a former slave, Douglass wrote his autobiography in 1845. This work became a classic in American literature and a primary source about slavery from the point of view of a slave. Douglass went on a two-year speaking tour abroad to avoid recapture by his former owner and to win new friends for the abolition movement. He returned with funds to purchase his freedom and to start his own anti-slavery newspaper. Douglass became a consultant to Abraham Lincoln, and throughout the Reconstruction period he fought doggedly for full civil rights for freedmen; he also supported the women's rights movement.

100. According to the passage, Douglass's writing of his autobiography was motivated by

(A) the desire to make money for the anti-slavery movement.
(B) his desire to become a publisher.
(C) his interest in authenticating his life as a slave.
(D) his desire to educate people about the horrors of slavery.

101. The central idea of the passage is that Douglass

(A) was instrumental in changing the laws regarding the education of slaves.
(B) was one of the most eminent human rights leaders of the nineteenth century.
(C) was a personal friend and confidant to a president.
(D) wrote a classic in American literature.

102. According to the author of this passage, Mrs. Auld taught Douglass to read because

(A) Douglass wanted to go to school like the other children.
(B) she recognized his natural ability.
(C) she wanted to comply with the laws of the state.
(D) he needed to be able to read so that he might work in the home.

103. The title that best expresses the ideas of this passage is

(A) The History of the Anti-Slavery Movement in America.
(B) The Outlaw Frederick Douglass.
(C) Reading: A Window to the World of Abolition.
(D) Frederick Douglass's Contributions to Freedom.

104. In the context of the passage, *impromptu* is the closest in meaning to

(A) unprepared.
(B) nervous.
(C) angry.
(D) loud.

105. Which formula can be used to find the area of the figure shown below? (Assume the curve is *half* of a circle.)

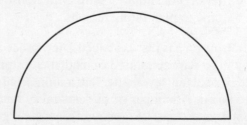

(A) $A = \pi r$
(B) $A = 2\pi r^2$
(C) $A = \pi r^2$
(D) $A = \pi r^2/2$

106. In the figure below, assume that:

Point *C* is the center of the circle.

Angles *XYZ* and *XCZ* intercept minor arc *XZ*.

The measure of angle *XYZ* is 40°.

What is the measure of major arc *XYZ*?

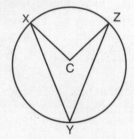

(A) 140°.
(B) 280°.
(C) 160°.
(D) 320°.

107. Mr. Dobson plans mathematics lessons so that all students will experience at least 70 percent success during independent practice. Considering student success during independent practice reflects Mr. Dobson's understanding that

(A) a student's academic success influences overall achievements and contributes to positive self-esteem.
(B) students who are academically successful have happy parents.
(C) if students are successful when working alone they can finish their homework independently.
(D) if the students are successful they will ask fewer questions, giving Mr. Dobson more time to plan future lessons.

108. Mr. Dobson has just explained a new procedure for solving a particular kind of mathematics problem. He has solved several demonstration problems on the board. A number of students raise their hands to ask questions. If a student's question requires more than two or three minutes to answer, then Mr. Dobson knows that

(A) the original explanation was faulty.
(B) the students were not paying attention.
(C) the students are below average in listening skills.
(D) the students have a very poor background in mathematics.

109. Mr. Dobson wants his fifth-grade students to serve as tutors for the first-graders who are learning addition and subtraction. The main advantage for the fifth graders who participate is

(A) they will develop proficiency and self-esteem.
(B) they will be encouraged to view teaching as a possible career.
(C) they will learn specific tutoring techniques.
(D) they will have an opportunity to become friends with younger children.

110. Mr. Stephens, a science teacher, has the students in Ms. Allen's second-period social studies class during first-period physical science. He tells Ms. Allen and Mr. Ramirez, the other social studies teacher, that he would like to collaborate with them by integrating some science topics into their unit on the American Revolution. This will most likely

(A) frustrate Ms. Allen and Mr. Ramirez because they will now have to discuss science.
(B) cause the students to develop a broader view of the Revolutionary time period.
(C) irritate the school librarian who must put all the books related to the American Revolution on reserve.
(D) cause the students to do English homework in science class and science homework in history class.

111. In his science class, Mr. Ivarez has two students who are overly talkative. These two students volunteer to answer every question. Which of the following is the best way to deal with these students?

(A) Mr. Ivarez should call on the overly talkative students only once during each class.
(B) Mr. Ivarez should ask these students to be the observers in small group discussions and

take notes about participation and topics discussed.

(C) Mr. Ivarez should place these students in a group by themselves so they can discuss all they want and not disturb the other students.

(D) Mr. Ivarez should recognize that overly talkative students need lots of attention and should be called on to participate throughout the class period.

112. A hot-air balloon rises when propane burners in the basket are used to heat the air inside the balloon. Which of the following statements correctly identifies the explanation for this phenomenon?

(A) Heated gas molecules move faster inside the balloon, their force striking the inside causes the balloon to rise.

(B) Hot gas molecules are themselves larger than cool gas molecules, resulting in the expansion of the gas.

(C) The amount of empty space between gas molecules increases as the temperature of the gas in-creases, resulting in the expansion of the gas.

(D) The combustion of propane releases product gases that are lighter than air and that are trapped in the balloon causing it to rise.

113. Using student ideas and interests in a lesson

(A) takes students off-task.

(B) detracts from the subject content.

(C) does not allow for evaluation of students' prior knowledge.

(D) increases learning and student motivation.

114. The atmospheres of the Moon and other planets were studied by using telescopes and spectrophotometers long before the deployment of interplanetary space probes. In these studies, scientists studied the spectral patterns of sunlight that passed through the atmosphere of distant objects to learn what elements make up those atmospheres. Which of the following explains the source of the black-line spectral patterns?

(A) When an element is excited, it gives off light in a characteristic spectral pattern.

(B) When light strikes an object, some wavelengths of light are absorbed by the surface

and others are reflected to give the object its color.

(C) When light passes through a gas, light is absorbed at wavelengths characteristic of the elements in the gas.

(D) The black lines are the spectra of ultraviolet light, which is called black light because it cannot be seen by human eyes.

115. A marble and a feather are both released at the same time inside a tube that is held at very low pressure (a near vacuum). Which of the following correctly links the observation to explanation?

(A) The marble falls faster because it is heavier.

(B) The marble falls faster because it has less air resistance.

(C) Both fall at the same rate because there is no air resistance in a vacuum.

(D) Both fall at the same rate because the forces of gravity are different in a vacuum.

116. Propelling a large projectile requires a massive force. An initial force of 12,000 yards per second is really a reference to the projectile's initial speed. The calculation of force required to move an object with a mass of 20,000 pounds from rest to a speed of 12,000 yards per second in a time span of 0.05 seconds is reflected in which of the following:

(A) $20,000 \times (12,000 / 0.05)$

(B) $20,000 \times 12,000 \times 0.05$

(C) $(20,000 \times 9.8) / (20,000 \times 0.05)$

(D) $(20,000 / 9.8) \times (12,000 / 0.05)$

Questions 117 and 118 are based on the following passage.

America's national bird, the mighty bald eagle, is being threatened by a new menace. Once decimated by hunters and loss of habitat, the bald eagle is facing a new danger, suspected to be intentional poisoning by livestock ranchers. Authorities have found animal carcasses injected with restricted pesticides. These carcasses allegedly are placed to attract and kill predators such as the bald eagle in an effort to preserve young grazing animals. It appears that the eagle is being threatened again by the consummate predator, humans.

117. One can conclude from this passage that

   (A) the pesticides used are beneficial to the environment.
   (B) ranchers believe that killing the eagles will protect their ranches.
   (C) ranchers must obtain licenses to use illegal pesticides.
   (D) poisoning eagles is good for livestock.

118. The author's attitude is one of

   (A) uncaring observation.
   (B) concerned interest.
   (C) uniformed acceptance.
   (D) suspicion.

Question 119 is based on the following passage.

   Water is a most unusual substance because it exists on the surface of Earth in its three physical states: ice, water, and water vapor. Other substances exist in a solid and liquid or gaseous state at temperatures normally found at Earth's surface, but water is the only pure substance to occur in all three states on Earth.

   Water is odorless, tasteless, and colorless. It is a universal solvent. Water does not corrode, rust, burn, or separate into its components easily. It is chemically indestructible. It can, however, corrode almost any metal and erode the most solid rock. A unique property of water is that, when frozen in its solid state, it expands and floats on liquid water. Water has a freezing point of 0 °C and a boiling point of 100 °C. Water has the capacity to absorb great quantities of heat with relatively little increase in temperature. In addition, *distilled* water is a poor conductor of electricity, but when salt is added, it is a good conductor of electricity.

119. According to the passage, what is the most unique property of water?

   (A) Water is odorless, tasteless, and colorless.
   (B) Water exists on the surface of the Earth in three physical states.
   (C) Water is chemically indestructible.
   (D) Water is a poor conductor of electricity.

120. Before Ms. Chin's class goes to the library, she asks her students to predict how they will find the information they will need for the assignment. By doing this, Ms. Chin is

   (A) engaging the students in hypothetical thinking and inductive reasoning.
   (B) saving time so that the students will be able to go straight to work once they get to the library.
   (C) helping her students acquire good self-management skills.
   (D) assisting the librarian by covering important information in class.

Praxis II

Elementary Education
Test Code 0014

Answers: Practice Test 2

Answer Key

1. (B)	21. (B)	41. (B)	61. (A)	81. (C)	101. (B)
2. (D)	22. (B)	42. (A)	62. (B)	82. (B)	102. (B)
3. (C)	23. (C)	43. (C)	63. (A)	83. (C)	103. (D)
4. (B)	24. (B)	44. (C)	64. (D)	84. (B)	104. (A)
5. (D)	25. (A)	45. (B)	65. (B)	85. (A)	105. (D)
6. (D)	26. (A)	46. (C)	66. (C)	86. (B)	106. (B)
7. (D)	27. (A)	47. (B)	67. (A)	87. (B)	107. (A)
8. (B)	28. (D)	48. (A)	68. (B)	88. (B)	108. (A)
9. (A)	29. (C)	49. (D)	69. (C)	89. (D)	109. (A)
10. (C)	30. (B)	50. (C)	70. (D)	90. (D)	110. (B)
11. (D)	31. (D)	51. (D)	71. (D)	91. (B)	111. (B)
12. (D)	32. (D)	52. (A)	72. (A)	92. (A)	112. (C)
13. (B)	33. (A)	53. (B)	73. (C)	93. (B)	113. (D)
14. (D)	34. (D)	54. (B)	74. (C)	94. (A)	114. (C)
15. (B)	35. (D)	55. (C)	75. (A)	95. (C)	115. (C)
16. (A)	36. (A)	56. (C)	76. (B)	96. (A)	116. (A)
17. (C)	37. (C)	57. (C)	77. (C)	97. (C)	117. (B)
18. (A)	38. (B)	58. (A)	78. (D)	98. (C)	118. (B)
19. (C)	39. (A)	59. (C)	79. (A)	99. (A)	119. (B)
20. (C)	40. (C)	60. (C)	80. (C)	100. (C)	120. (A)

Elementary Education: Content Knowledge (0014) Practice Test 2

Detailed Explanations of Answers

1. (B)

It is important to ensure that the word problems given to students are at their reading level; otherwise, a teacher will be unable to evaluate their successes with these problems accurately. (A), (C), and (D) are not the best answers to the question.

2. (D)

Academic praise comprises specific statements that give information about the value of the object or about its implications. A simple positive response, such as, "That's a good answer!" (A), does not provide any information other than the praise. There is nothing negative (B) about the teacher's response. A redirect (C) occurs when a teacher asks a student to react to the response of another student.

3. (C)

Choral chant is the term used for students' repeating basic facts, spellings, and laws.

4. (B)

A discovery-learning lesson is one in which the class is organized to learn through the students' own active involvement in the lesson. In inductive-reasoning lessons (C), the students are provided with examples and non-examples and are expected to derive definitions from this information. The eg-rule method (D) moves from specific examples to general rules or definitions. Even though the lesson may take place in a science class (A), the type of learning is discovery.

5. (D)

Comprehension is shown when the reader questions his or her intent for reading. For example, one may be reading a story to find out what terrible things may befall the main character. The rationale for choosing a book may be an interesting bit of information (A), but it is not a major topic of discussion with the students. Sharing personal information (B) creates a certain bond, but this is not directly relevant to the question. It is also important that all students are on-task before the beginning of a lesson (C), but this is a smaller part of the skill modeled in response (D).

6. (D)

A question testing whether a student can synthesize information will include the need to make predictions or solve problems. An evaluation question (A) will require a judgment of the quality of an idea or solution. In order to be real analysis (B), the question would have to ask students to analyze given information to draw a conclusion or find support for a given idea. Comprehension questions (C) may require the rephrasing of an idea in the students' own words, and then using this for comparison.

7. (D)

By having a mixed, level pair read together, the remedial student receives instruction and the skilled student receives reinforcement. This method uses alternate teaching resources, the students themselves, to enhance the learning environment. A certain goal, comprehension, has been set (A), but this is not the most important outcome. The teacher will need to observe fewer groups (B), but it is unlikely that this will change the time needed to work with all groups as long as quality is to be maintained. Even though they are reading in pairs, each student should have a book, and it would be impractical to permit another teacher to utilize the books while one teacher is using them.

8. (B)

Students at this age do not have the cognitive skills to realize how much they have actually learned or how much they will actually be able to retain. For this reason, (A) must be incorrect. At this stage in their intellectual development, students cannot differentiate material that is completely understood from material they have not completely comprehended (C). Students will generally feel that they are capable of learning much more than they will actually retain (D).

9. (A)

By mapping out previous knowledge, information already known can be transferred to support new information. Although words on the board are visual (B), this is not the underlying motive. Semantic mapping done at the beginning of a story tests how much knowledge the students have about the topic at the outset, not the conclusion (C). Although this method does model proper use of words (D), this is not the main intent of the exercise.

10. (C)

Data gathered within the learning environment resulting from day-to-day activities could also provide a means for reflection and discussion. This includes using student scores in class not only for their most recognized use, student academic grades, (A), but also using the success of students to guide a teacher's professional development plan. Looking for inconsistencies in grading can be a basis for teachers to explore their teaching practices while looking for new and more effective methods. In considering answers (B) and (D), student academic grades should never be used in behavior assessment.

11. (D)

All teachers have different strengths and weaknesses. By working collaboratively, they can share their abilities to create more strengths and fewer weaknesses. If a teacher has found a method of teaching a concept that is successful, it is worth trying. Viewing the students' scores from the previous year would assist in seeing if they had made any progress since their last test (omit comma) but should not be used to justify their poor scores (A). This does nothing to assist students in improving their academic achievement. Telling future students to study more (B) or suggesting math tutors (C) may be good advice omit comma but should not be the only course of helping students improve in a certain area.

12. (D)

During late childhood and early adolescence, students often exhibit problems with self-image, physical appearance, eating disorders, feelings of rebelliousness, and other similar problems. Teachers should be aware of these developmental problems and do all they can to minimize them in the classroom. By providing a safe learning environment and letting students know that the teacher is aware of these issues, the teacher can assist in keeping these students on-task. (A) is incorrect. Many students at this age exhibit these kinds of problems. This reaction would cause a major disruption in the learning process, and generally counselors do not have time to address all of the students' problems. (B) is incorrect. Although parents can sometimes help, solution (B) should be used only for the most severe cases. (C) is incorrect because calling other students' attention to any student's problems in this way often only makes the problems worse by isolating and ostracizing individuals.

13. (B)

The question presented here is a low-order question (B) that ensures that a student is focused on the task at hand; it can be used to develop into higher questioning. A high-order question (A) tests the student's ability to apply information, evaluate information, create new information, and so on, rather than to recall simple content. Transitions (C) are used to connect different ideas and tasks. The information that the question is looking for is one of content, not skill (D).

14. (D)

The integrated, real-life nature of this project builds deeper understandings of the economic concept of work and wages, saving versus spending, and banking. While providing the authentic experience of working and saving, the project also builds the class's capacity to complete mathematical functions such as figuring interest rates and compounding interest. In addition, the idea of the value of saving money has been communicated.

15. (B)

The example illustrates a deductive reasoning task (B). Inductive reasoning (A) would be giving the class some information and asking them to form a rule or generalization. Choices (C) and (D) are simply examples of inductive tasks.

16. (A)

The Magna Carta was signed in 1215. Columbus's voyages began in the fifteenth century. The Protestant Reformation occurred in the sixteenth century. The Puritans came to America in the seventeenth century. Therefore, the best choice is (A).

17. (C)

Choice (A), as conceived by Henry Clay, referred to the nationalist policy of uniting the three economic sections of the United States following the War of 1812. Choice (B) is an economic theory whose principal doctrine was the belief that the wealth of nations was based on the possession of gold. Choice (D) is tied to tradition and emotion. Choice (C) is the best possible answer.

18. (A)

Choice (A) is correct; checks and balances provide each of the branches with the ability to limit the actions of the other branches. (B) is incorrect; branches of the federal government do not achieve independence from each other because of checks and balances. Choices (C) and (D) are also incorrect because they deal with only one branch, whereas the system of checks and balances involves the manner in which the three branches are interrelated.

19. (C)

Choices (A), (B), and (D) all played a role in the early settlements of the English colonies in America. The correct response is item (C); Mormonism was founded at Fayette, New York, in 1830, by Joseph Smith. The Book of Mormon was published in 1830; it describes the establishment of an American colony from the Tower of Babel.

20. (C)

The letter K represents Cuba, letter D represents Indonesia, and letter M represents Sri Lanka. The correct answer is (C) because letter I represents the Philippine Islands.

21. (B)

The Bill of Rights clearly states that Congress may not make laws abridging citizens' rights and liberties. Choices (C) and (D) are incorrect because the Bill of Rights does not talk about voting rights or slaves. A list of grievances (A) is contained in the Declaration of Independence.

22. (B)

This assignment asks students to gather information or explore long-term goals—goals many years in the future. Short-term goals (A, C) are those that can be achieved in days, weeks, or maybe months. Answer (D), synthesize, is a more complicated process than merely gathering information.

23. (C)

The teacher is asking the student questions to allow the student to correct a spelling error. Spelling does not allow for divergent or creative thinking (A). Although the teacher reminds the student of a mnemonic, the teacher is not teaching the mnemonic (B). Finally, applying spelling rules or guides to improve spelling would be an example of deductive reasoning, not inductive reasoning (D).

24. (B)

It is very important that all students feel welcome, but it is especially effective for ESL students to feel comfortable and welcomed in the classroom. Students should be able to use many resources to help them so (D) is incorrect. Most schools will not have a specialist to whom the teacher can refer the student; (C) is not an acceptable choice. A teacher should never deprive a student of the student's language or culture; (A) is not an appropriate answer.

25. (A)

Ms. Borders must consider the learning preferences and emotional factors of her learners as she constructs learning activities for the study. To consider cooperative group projects versus independent work is one aspect of her preparation. Another would be the range of products deemed acceptable as demonstrations of knowledge (written or spoken, visual or performed art, technology-based, etc.). Choices (B), (C), and (D) might be considered once she plans the study, but they are unrelated to the issue of preparing for the stated instructional outcomes.

26. (A)

Students learn to speak two languages in one of two ways: sequentially, in which one language is mastered before the study of the second language has begun (A), or simultaneously, in which both languages are learned concurrently (B). Sequential language acquisition does not mean a student learns two languages in parts (C) or that the student develops language skills (D).

27. (A)

Some students may not speak English at home or may have limited exposure to the vocabulary of the classroom. It is important to be aware of these factors and provide the materials appropriate to help guide mastery. Answers that say negative things about the students are never the best choice; for that reason, one should not choose answer (B), (C), or (D).

28. (D)

The teacher hopes to engage the students in critical thinking by allowing them to express their opinions; the teacher realizes that students will have different interpretations of the statement. (A), (B), and (C) are possible outcomes, but (D) is the best answer because it relates specifically to the teacher's aim.

29. (C)

The best response (C) is to emphasize that occupations are open to both men and women and that most people make career choices based on their abilities and their preferences. (A) and (B) fail to take advantage of the opportunity to teach the class about equal opportunity in career choices, and (D) implies that popular opinion determines career choices.

30. (B)

The 1933 bar is highest, and the graph measures the percent of unemployment by the height of the bars. The bars for 1929 (A), 1938 (C), and 1944 (D) are all lower than the bar for 1933, the year in which unemployment was the highest.

31. (D)

1944 (the bar between 1943 and 1945) is the lowest bar on the graph. As previously mentioned, the graph measures the percentage of unemployment on the length of the bars. The bars for 1929 (A), 1933 (B), and 1938 (C) are all higher than the bar for 1944.

32. (D)

Choice (A) is wrong because about 30%, not 50%, of households had under $15,000. Choices (B) and (C) are also incorrect because slightly more than 15% fell into this category.

33. (A)

Graph reading and interpretation is the primary focus of this question. Choice (B) is obviously wrong because the youngest have the least discretionary income. The oldest group has less discretionary income than those between 25 and 65; therefore, item (C) is wrong. The discretionary income for all ages over 25 is more than for those under 25; (D) is incorrect.

34. (D)

In general, teachers believe that oral language proficiency correlates with academic proficiency. Research indicates, however, that oral language proficiency is easily acquired through daily living experiences, whereas academic language proficiency requires an academic setting with context-related activities.

35. (D)

Choice (D) is the best answer because it contains information that is technically correct and expresses a concern about the difference in the student's standardized test score and about the usual performance in math

class. (A) is technically correct; however, it does not really provide as complete an answer as (D). (B) tends to provide the student with a false impression; although the student scored in the top half, as one of the best students in class, the student could have been expected to have scored perhaps in the top 10 percent or at least the top quartile. (C) is simply a false statement.

36. (A)

The United States was shocked by the launching of Sputnik by the Soviet Union in 1957. Comparisons between Soviet education and the education available in the public schools of the United States indicated a need to emphasize math (B), science (C), and foreign language (D) for the United States to compete with other countries and to remain a world power.

37. (C)

According to Piaget's theory of cognitive development, students in middle school would be at the stage of concrete operational thought. Students at this stage of cognitive development would be able to categorize items. Choice (A) is a false statement. Although some students do like to work in groups, other students prefer to work alone—at this and at any age group or cognitive stage. Preferring to learn in groups (or socially) or to learn alone (or independently) is a characteristic of learning style or preference, not a characteristic of cognitive or affective development. Choice (B) is irrelevant to the teacher's intent in assigning the task. Students could just as easily work with unfamiliar items, grouping them by observable features independent of their use or function. Choice (D) is not a good choice under any circumstances. Teachers should assiduously avoid giving students any assignments merely to keep them busy while they do something else. All assignments should have an instructional purpose.

38. (B)

This question opens the door for dialogue with the student about a range of possible problems. This response shows that the teacher is concerned about the student and her welfare without making assumptions, jumping to conclusions, and/or intruding into the private affairs of the student. Choice (A) presumes that the source of all problems lies with the family. Although the student may be having family-related difficulties, there are other possibilities to consider as well. The student may have taken on an extra-curricular activity that is taking too much of her time away from her studies, or the student may be having health problems. It is unwise for the teacher to conclude that the student is having family problems. Choice (C) is inappropriate because it too narrowly identifies one possible coping mechanism as the solution to the student's problem. Although the student may benefit from acquiring better time-management skills, it also is possible that the student's present problems have little or nothing to do with time management. Choice (D) is equally inappropriate in that it demands that the student devote even more time to school, even though she currently is having trouble with present demands. If the student is unwell, then certainly spending more time at school is not the solution to her problem. Clearly, choice (B) is the best choice for helping the student identify her problem(s) and find a solution.

39. (A)

Only choice (A) takes into account differences among learners by giving them options as to how and where they will read. Choice (B) violates the students' freedom to select reading materials they find interesting and wish to read. When students are allowed to choose their own reading materials, it may seem that some students select materials beyond their present reading comprehension. However, reading research indicates that students can comprehend more difficult material when their interest level is high. Therefore, any efforts by the teacher to interfere with students' selection of their own reading material would be ill advised (D). Choices (C) and (D) are equally poor in that they both describe a concession to only one group of learners. For example, with choice (C), even though some students may prefer to read with music playing in the background, other students may find the music distracting. The best action for the teacher to take would be to allow some students to listen to music on earphones while others read in quiet. In regard to choice (D), some students will prefer bright illumination just as some students will read better with the lights dimmed. Ms. Rodriguez would do well to

attempt to accommodate various learner needs by having one area of the room more brightly illuminated than the other.

40. (C)

The teacher is encouraging students to become engaged in the learning process by making a prediction based on limited information given in the book title and cover illustration. When students can generate their own predictions or formulate hypotheses about possible outcomes on the basis of available (although limited) data, they are gaining preparatory skills for formal operations (or abstract thinking). Although second-grade students would not be expected to be at the level of cognitive development characterized by formal operations, Piagetian theory would indicate that teachers who model appropriate behaviors and who give students opportunities to reach or stretch for new cognitive skills are fostering students' cognitive growth. Choice (A) is a poor choice because students' responses to this one question posed by the teacher cannot be used to assess adequately their interest in reading activities. Choice (B), likewise, is a poor choice in that it implies no instructional intent for asking the question. Choice (D) is incorrect because students' responses to a single question cannot allow the instructor to determine which students are good readers and which ones are not.

41. (B)

The question asks for appropriate statements for Mrs. Johnson to consider in making an instructional decision. Option I is a valid reason for teaching students how to develop portfolios. Teachers teach students skills that will be useful in school and in their careers. Although Option II may produce positive affective results, feeling mature because students are imitating older siblings is not a sufficient reason to choose portfolios. Option III is the most appropriate reason for using portfolios. Most activities and projects that promote achievement of course outcomes would be considered appropriate strategies. Option IV is not necessarily true; portfolio assessment can result in more written work, which can be more time consuming. Even if option IV were true, emphasizing student achievement is more important than easing the workload of teachers. Options I and III (choice (B)) are appropriate.

42. (A)

Note that the particle flow divides at two points, T and M. At these points the flow has two paths to reach either point W or point Q. Thus, the correct choice is (A). Particle flow can reach point W by going through point U, rather than V. It would have to flow through all other points listed in order to make a complete circuit or total clockwise path.

43. (C)

To find the cost per square foot of material to cover the shaded area, one divides the total cost of covering the shaded area (III) by the square footage of the shaded area. Only option III is necessary; I and II are *not* necessary. The answer is, therefore, (C). The problem would be solved as follows: The total area of the larger rectangle is the base times the height, 12 ft × 9 ft, which equals 108 sq ft. Therefore, the area of the shaded portion surrounding the inner rectangle is

$$108 \text{ sq ft} - 80 \text{ sq ft} = 28 \text{ sq ft}$$

If the total cost of material is $56 to cover the shaded area of 28 sq ft, the cost per square foot is $56/28 sq ft = $2/sq ft.

44. (C)

The best answer is (C) because it includes three correct statements. The sugar does pass from a solid to a liquid state (I), the sugar does absorb calories from the water (II), and the heat does become latent when it is sensible (III). Since I, II, and III are all causes of the drop of temperature when sugar is added to coffee, *all three* must be included when choosing an answer. Although choices (A), (B), and (D) each contain one or more of these causes, none contains all three; subsequently, each of these choices is incorrect.

45. (B)

A hands-on activity will best help the students learn about data collection. (B) is the only choice that employs a hands-on activity, so this is the best answer. The students would learn about direct observation by watching Ms. Thompson tickle the mouse and the philodendron (A); however, this method would not be as effective as allowing the students to conduct their own data collection. Research suggests that viewing a video (C) is an inefficient method of learning. Having a guest speaker tell the students about data collection (D) is not a good choice for first-graders.

46. (C)

Because heat is a positive condition depending on the absence of cold, (C) is the correct answer. Fahrenheit and Celsius are measures of temperature, not conditions; therefore, (A) and (D) are incorrect choices. Heat is the opposite of intense artificial cold; (B) is not acceptable.

47. (B)

This passage from Melville's *Moby-Dick* contains an allusion in the phrase, "like so many Alexanders." Melville is illustrating the strength and power of whalers ("naked Nantucketers") by alluding and comparing them to Alexander the Great, the famous conqueror who died in 323 BCE.

48. (A)

This passage, which opens James Joyce's *A Portrait of the Artist as a Young Man*, is written in "baby talk" ("moocow," "nicens," "baby tuckoo") to convey to readers the age, speech, and mental state of the narrator.

49. (D)

Nineteenth-century novels of manners employed such themes as the importance (or unimportance) of "good breeding," the elation (and suffocation) caused by society, and the interaction of individuals within the confines of a closed country community, to name just a few. This passage, taken from Jane Austen's *Emma*, mentions "opinions" of other characters, the importance of "beauty" and "accomplishment" (note how Emma sees them as almost saving graces for Mrs. Elton), and the "improvement" of a "country neighborhood."

50. (C)

Choice (C) is the definition of illiterate and functional illiterate stated in the second paragraph. Choice (A) cannot be correct because the passage clearly distinguishes between illiterates and functional illiterates. Choice (B) is not correct because the definition stated is not related to participation in a program. The relative number of illiterates and functional illiterates is not discussed,; choice (D) is incorrect.

51. (D)

This passage has several purposes. First, the author presents some complaints concerning the way literacy issues are presented in the media (B). The author also discusses the increased attention given to literacy by society (C). Third, the author discusses many aspects of successful literacy programs (A). Therefore, choice (D), which includes all of these purposes, is correct.

52. (A)

This question must be answered using the process of elimination. You are asked to select a statement that names a possible program component that is *not* characteristic of successful literacy programs. Choice (A) is correct because choices (B), (C), and (D) are specifically mentioned in the passage.

53. (B)

Choice (B) is correct because the author specifically states that politicians should support increased funding for literacy programs. Choices (A) and (C) are incorrect because the author states that funding should be increased. There is no discussion of funding for different programs, so choice (D) is incorrect.

54. (B)

The variance in fifth graders' physical size and development has a direct influence on their interests and attitudes, including their willingness to work with others and a possible preference for working alone. (A) is incorrect because fifth graders do have the physical and mental maturity to work in small groups. (C) is incorrect because not all fifth-grade students lack the ability for internal control. (D) is incorrect; although Mr. Dobson might need to be more specific in his directions to the students, this is not the main reason for their behavior.

55. (C)

Students who are shy are usually more willing to participate in small groups than in discussions involving the entire class. (A) is incorrect because calling on each student once per day will not necessarily assist shy students to participate in class discussions, even if participation grades are assigned. (B) is incorrect because although students may become less shy as the year progresses, the teacher still has a responsibility to encourage students to participate. Choice (D) is incorrect because although speaking to students individually may help some to participate, it is likely more students will participate if the procedure outlined in choice (C) is implemented.

56. (C)

Mrs. Kresmeier uses effective communication strategies to teach students and encourages them to interact for the same purposes. Mnemonic devices are apparently a new technique for most of the students; in addition, the teacher's own creative spelling clues are often new ones matching the age level, interests, and patterns of humor enjoyed by her students. The most success is probably derived from her encouragement to examine the words to find a feature that can be turned into a mnemonic device. (A) is incorrect because there has been no attempt to rule out other techniques of learning to spell. (B) is incorrect because certainly other teachers have also impressed upon the students that spelling is important. The creative methodology is probably the major difference between Mrs. Kresmeier's method and those that students have encountered in the past. (D) is incorrect because no evidence exists to show that Mrs. Kresmeier is especially selective in choosing her spelling lessons.

57. (C)

Formative assessment (C) is continuous and is intended to serve as a guide to future learning and instruction. Summative evaluation (A) and summative assessment (B) are both used to put a final critique or grade on an activity or assignment with no real link to the future. Peer assessment would require students to critique each other (D).

58. (A)

Meeting one-to-one to discuss a student's strengths and weaknesses creates a feeling of trust and confidence between the student and the teacher. Grading papers solely on the content of a conference (B) is not an efficient means of grading. The student/teacher conference should not focus on only one part of the writing process, such as careful editing (C) or pre-writing (D).

59. (C)

The role of the resource teacher is to provide individual instruction for students who qualify for services and, through collaborative consultation, work with the classroom teacher to adapt instruction to match each student's needs. A resource teacher should not be entirely responsible for teaching a learning-disabled student (A) and is also not responsible for tutoring outside of the scheduled class meetings (D). A learning-disabled student should not be totally excused from assignments (B).

60. (C)

This is an example of working with other teachers to plan instruction. Response (A) is incorrect because it is incomplete. This activity may complete the school year, but this activity is not necessarily an end-of-the-year project. (B) is incorrect because problem solving and inquiry teaching are only small components of the activity. Choice (D) is incorrect because asking students to research Galileo and asking the PTA to buy science equipment are not necessarily related.

61. (A)

Visiting other teachers in other schools will promote collaboration and cooperation. Choice (B) is incorrect because there is no reason to believe that the principal is encouraging these teachers to apply for a job in the middle school. Choice (C) is incorrect because, although using computers in science classes may be a topic on which teachers choose to collaborate, choice (A) is more complete. Choice (D) is incorrect because the middle school math curriculum is not intended for use in the fifth grade.

62. (B)

Use the Pythagorean theorem to compute the length of any side of any right triangle, as long as the lengths of the other two sides are known. For any right triangle with side lengths a, b, and c, where c is the length of the hypotenuse (the longest side, and the one opposite the right angle), $a^2 + b^2 = c^2$. Substituting the real values for a and b from the problem gives

$$c^2 = 11^2 + 5^2$$

or

$$c^2 = 146.$$

To complete the work, take the (positive) square root of 146, which is slightly more than 12 ($12 \times 12 = 144$).

63. (A)

If two triangles are similar, they have the exact same shape (although not necessarily the same size). This means that the corresponding angles of the two triangles have the same measure and the corresponding sides are proportional. To find the missing side (side DF) set up the proportion:

$$AB/AC = DE/DF$$

or, by substituting the given values,

$$12/10 = 15/x$$

where x is the length of side DF. This can be read as "12 is to 10 as 15 is to x." The problem can be solved by using cross-multiplication. Thus, $12x = 150$, or $x = 12.5$.

64. (D)

All are correctly matched.

65. (B)

Expansion occurring on the ocean floor creates pressure around the edges of the Pacific Plate and produces geologic instability where the Pacific Plate collides with the continental plates on all sides. Neither earthquakes (C), hardened lava (D), or rock similarities (A) alone are sufficient to account for the "Ring of Fire."

66. (C)

Washington and Monroe together received 55% of the votes. Everyone else voted for Madison; Madison must have received 45% of the votes. (All of the candidates' percents must add up to 100%.) Statement I cannot be true and statement II must be true. Monroe received 30% of the 600 votes. 0.30 times 600 is 180, so statement III is true. Madison received 45% of the vote, and 45% of 600 is 270, so statement IV is false. Therefore, only II and III are true, and the correct answer is (C).

67. (A)

The somewhat steep straight line to the left tells you that Mr. Cain worked at a steady rate for a while. The completely flat line in the middle tells you he stopped for a while—the line does not go up because Mr. Cain did not cut grass then. Finally, the line continues upward (after his break) less steeply (therefore more flatly), indicating that he was working at a slower rate.

68. (B)

Because Ms. Patton's increases were constant ($3,000 annually), and because the directions tell you that only one statement is true, choice (B) must be the correct answer. To be more confident, however, you can

examine the other statements. The range of Ms. Patton's earnings is $12,000 (the jump from $30,000 to $42,000), not $15,000, so choice (A) cannot be correct. Although Ms. Patton may have earned $45,000 in 2003, you do not know that because the graph goes only to 2002; choice (C) cannot be correct. Choice (D) gives the incorrect earnings average; it was $36,000, not $38,000.

69. (C)

There are several ways to determine which equation best matches the line. An easy way is to decide first whether the line has a positive or negative slope. Because the line moves from the upper left to the lower right, it has a negative slope. In a linear equation of the form $y = mx + b$ (where y is isolated on the left side of the equation), the coefficient of x is the slope of the line. The only equation with a negative slope (-8) is choice (C), so that is the correct answer. Another clue that choice (C) is correct is that the line appears fairly steep, and a slope of -8 (or 8) is considered fairly steep, too.

70. (D)

Using the rules for solving one-variable equations, the original equation is transformed as follows:

$$x/3 - 9 = 15.$$

Adding 9 to each side of the equation gives

$$x/3 = 24.$$

Multiplying both sides by 3 gives

$$x = 72.$$

71. (D)

One way to solve the problem is by writing a one-variable equation that matches the information given:

$$4x + 2(10 - x) = 26$$

The $4x$ represents four tires for each car. Use x for the number of cars because at first you do not know how many cars there are. Then $(10 - x)$ represents the number of motorcycles in the lot. (If there are 10 vehicles total, and x of them are cars, subtract x from 10 to get the number of "leftover" motorcycles.) Then $2(10 - x)$ stands for the number of motorcycle tires in the lot. The sum of the values $4x$ and $2(10 - x)$ is 26, which gives the equation above. Using the standard rules for solving a one-variable equation, x (the number of cars in the lot) equals 3. Another approach to answering a multiple-choice question is to try substituting each choice for the unknown variable in the problem to see which one makes sense.

72. (A)

The correct equation must show three consecutive odd numbers being added to give 117. Odd numbers (just like even numbers) are each two units apart. Only the three values (x, $x + 2$, $x + 4$) given in choice (A) are each two units apart. Because the numbers being sought are odd, one might be tempted to choose (D). However, the second value in choice (D), ($x + 1$), is not two units apart from the first value (x); it is different by only one.

73. (C)

Mrs. Ratu's lack of competency is exhibited in her lack of understanding of her students and in her teaching at the elementary level. Mrs. Ratu was not teaching her students at the appropriate level (A). Although she may have desired to make reading easy for her students (D), she was not going about it correctly. When appropriate techniques are used, teaching ninth graders to read is no more difficult than teaching third graders to read.

74. (C)

Mr. Jones knew that development in one area leads to development in other areas. He also knew that using a variety of instructional techniques could lead to inquiry, motivation, and even further development in certain areas. Allowing students to have choices in their learning leads to a positive self-concept and can lead to camaraderie. Roundtable discussions lead to questions and often to the solving of problems and, therefore, to the improvement of grades (D).

75. (A)

A teacher can guide a student to a higher-level answer through questioning. Repeating the question (B) would probably elicit the same response, and asking a different student (C, D) would not help the student who provided the simple response.

76. (B)

According to the Socratic method, teachers should ask questions that allow students to find the truth within themselves.

77. (C)

The general public believed that the slaves would be more submissive if they remained illiterate; therefore, most slaves were never taught to read or write. Teaching a slave to read or write was, in fact, a criminal act.

78. (D)

In handing down its decision in *Brown v Board of Education of Topeka, Kansas* in 1954, the Supreme Court stated that "Separate but equal has no place … Separate educational facilities are inherently unequal and violate the equal protection clause of the Fourteenth Amendment."

79. (A)

The Peace Corps (A) was established by President John F. Kennedy. Johnson's VISTA (D) was modeled after the Peace Corps. Head Start (B) and the Elementary and Secondary Education Act (C) were also put into effect as part of Johnson's "War on Poverty."

80. (C)

The Education for All Handicapped Children Act of 1975 provides for mentally (A) and physically (B) handicapped as well as learning disabled children (D). It does not include socially-emotionally handicapped youngsters.

81. (C)

Project (C) calls for work involving analysis, synthesis, and evaluation levels. Choice (C) is the best choice because it asks the students to analyze how past causes have produced current effects, then to predict what future effects might be based on what they have learned about cause–effect relationships. It requires students to put information together in a new way. Choice (A) may involve some creativity in putting the information on a poster, but in general, answering factual questions calls for lower-level (knowledge or comprehension) thinking. Choice (B) may involve some degree of creativity, but giving students prepared questions requires thinking at a lower level than having students develop their own questions, and then determining which answers to write about. Choice (D) also is a lower-level activity, although there may be a great deal of research for factual information. All options may be good learning activities, but (A), (B), and (D) do not require as much deep thinking as choice (C). Depending on the depth of the study, a teacher may want to include several of these activities.

82. (B)

This question asks for an evaluation of which software programs will help the students achieve their goals of analyzing data and presenting the results. Item I, word processing, would be used in developing and printing the questionnaire, as well as writing a report on the results. Item II, a database, would be used to sort and print out information in various categories so students could organize and analyze their data. Item III, a simulation, would not be appropriate here because the students' basic purpose is to collect data and analyze it. The project does not call for a program to simulate a situation or event. Item IV, graph or chart, would be very useful in analyzing information and in presenting it to others.

83. (C)

People are more highly motivated to solve problems that they choose, rather than problems that are chosen for them. Assigning an additional report (A) may seem like punishment. Although some students

may enjoy teaching the unmotivated students (B) and may learn from the experience, the gifted students must always increase their level and must never take over the role of the teacher. Worksheets and many tasks (busy-work activities?) are not the best way to help students; (D) is not the best answer.

84. (B)

Choice B describes the procedure in place at the campus level to deal with this type of issue. It respects the processes and oversight authority of the committee while addressing the concern of faculty and community. Choice A is incorrect because Ms. Carter does not have the authority to enforce the removal of the animals. Choice C is incorrect because the issue should remain at the campus until the committee and the principal have an opportunity to consider the concerns. Choice D is incorrect because even though Ms. Carter may appreciate the librarian's efforts, the health concerns are legitimate. Ms. Carter should remain neutral until the campus can act on the issue.

85. (A)

The term "casework" (A) is used by political scientists to describe the activities of members of congress on behalf of individual constituents. These activities might include helping an elderly person secure social security benefits or helping a veteran obtain medical services. Most casework is actually done by congressional staff and may take as much as a third of the staff's time. Representatives supply this type of assistance for the good public relations it provides. Pork barrel legislation (B) is rarely, if ever, intended to help individual citizens. Pork barrel legislation authorizes federal spending for special projects, such as airports, roads, or dams, in the home state or district of the representative. It is meant to help the entire district or state. Also, there is no legal entitlement on the part of a citizen to a pork barrel project, such as there is with social security benefits. (C) is not the answer because lobbying is an activity directed toward the representative, not one done by the member of congress. A lobbyist attempts to get members of congress to support legislation that will benefit the group that the lobbyist represents. Logrolling (D) is incorrect because it does not refer to a congressional service for constituents. It refers instead to the congressional practice of trading votes on different bills. Representative X will vote for Representative Z's pork barrel project, and in return Z will vote for X's pork barrel project.

86. (B)

The term "Trail of Tears" is used to describe the forced relocation of the Cherokee tribe from the southern Appalachians to what is now Oklahoma (B). The migration of Mormons from Nauvoo, Illinois, to the Great Salt Lake in Utah (A), the westward movements along the Oregon Trail (C), and, much earlier, the Wilderness Road (D), all took place and could at times be as unpleasant as the Cherokees' trek. They were, however, more voluntary than the Cherokee migration and therefore did not earn such sad titles as the "Trail of Tears."

87. (B)

The Moon is much closer to Earth than to any other celetial body or the Sun.

88. (B)

Cancers and hereditary diseases (B) are *not* infectious. Diseases caused by viruses, bacteria, or protists (A) that invade the body are called infectious diseases. These disease-causing organisms are collectively referred to as germs. Despite the fact that the immune system protects the body from disease (D), environmental hazards can still cause disease (C). (B) is the only answer that is false and is, therefore, the answer to this question.

89. (D)

All riders must pay at least three dollars, so 3 will be added to something else in the correct equation. Only choices (B) and (D) meet that requirement. The additional fare of two dollars "for every mile or fraction of a mile" tells you that you will need to multiply the number of miles driven (use 11 because of the extra fraction of a mile) by 2, leading to the correct answer, (D).

90. (D)

It is true that multiplication is commutative and division is not (A), but that is not relevant to their being inverse operations. Choice (B) also contains a true statement, but, again, the statement is not about inverse operations. Choice (C) gives a false statement; in the example shown, the order of operations tells you to compute $8 \div 2$ before any multiplication. As noted in choice (D), two operations being inverse indeed depends on their ability to undo each other.

91. (B)

Reptiles are not generally warm blooded; all other statements are correct.

92. (A)

Mrs. Fisher's best option is to express her concerns and the reasons for these concerns to the school counselor, who is trained to help in matters such as this. Involving another student (B) is a poor choice in this instance because it places a large emotional burden on the second student. In addition, it makes the teacher's concern public rather than keeping it confidential among school officials. As choice (C) suggests, Lisa's parents do need to be notified soon. However, this decision should be made by the counselor, who is a professional trained to deal with these types of concerns. Confronting Lisa directly (D) could cause her to be defensive about her actions and, if there is indeed an eating disorder, could cause her to hide her symptoms to avoid further detection.

93. (B)

Students at the formal operational stage can understand complex theoretical descriptions with little or no direct observation. Students at the concrete observational stage (A) must have direct observation to reach understanding and generally have trouble with complex theoretical descriptions. The sensorimotor stage (D) applies to infants, and the preoperational stage (C) applies to children ages two to seven.

94. (A)

72104.58 is read "seventy-two thousand, one hundred four and fifty-eight hundredths."

95. (C)

To find the average (mean) of a set of values, first add them together. In this case, the negative and the positive integers should be added together separately. Those two sums are –12 and 5. (The zero can be ignored; it does not affect either sum.) Then –12 and 5 should be added together for a sum of –7. To complete the work, the sum of –7 must be divided by the number of values (7), giving –1.

96. (A)

A needs assessment will help students make the connection between their current skills and those that will be new to them. Choice B is incorrect because a needs assessment focuses on the skills a student currently possesses. Choice C is incorrect because the needs assessment is designed to determine what needs to be taught that is not currently in the curriculum. Choice D is a false statement; a needs assessment is not designed to motivate students.

97. (C)

A positive environment must be created to minimize the effects of negative external factors. Choice A is inappropriate because changing the textbook but allowing the environment to remain the same only results in maintaining the status quo. Choice B is incorrect because relating the students' personal interests to the new material is only part of creating a positive environment. Choice D is incorrect because, again, it is only a small part of maximizing the effects of a positive learning environment.

98. (C)

The teacher would be fostering strong home relationships that support student achievement of desired outcomes. Choice A is a result of choice C; as the teacher interacts with professionals in the community, her own professional growth would be promoted. Choice B is also the result of choice C; all teachers are expected to interact with the community to help meet the expectations associated with teaching. Choice D is incomplete, because strong home relationships are developed through the principles of conferences, trust, and cooperation.

99. (A)

When students are allowed to select their own problems for study, they become self-directed problem solvers. As such, they have the opportunity to structure their own learning experiences. Assessing students' needs in a naturalistic setting is highly time consuming and not an important benefit of having students select their own problems to investigate (B). There may or may not be a wide variety of instructional materials available to the students as they engage in studying the temperature problem (C); this is not likely to be a major benefit. Learning to appreciate opposing viewpoints is a competency that would be better addressed in social studies and language arts rather than in an activity that deals with a natural empirical science (D).

100. (C)

The passage suggests that Douglass was concerned with raising social consciousness about slavery. His interest in refuting those who doubted his claims was for the sake of authenticity.

101. (B)

Douglass was one of the eminent human rights leaders of the nineteenth century. All the other choices, while true, are irrelevant to the question and are not supported by the text.

102. (B)

The passage states "Mrs. Auld recognized Frederick's intellectual acumen." A synonym for "acumen" is "intelligence," "insight," or "natural ability." The other choices are inaccurate.

103. (D)

Choices A, B, and C are too vague or ill-defined. Thus, choice D is correct.

104. (A)

An "impromptu" speech is one given extemporaneously, without prior preparation, or "off the cuff."

105. (D)

The formula for finding the area of any circle is $A = \pi r^2$ (about 3.14 times the length of the radius times itself). In this case, the figure is half of that area, so the correct choice is D.

106. (B)

Angle XYZ is an inscribed angle (its vertex is on the circle). Angle XCZ is a central angle. (Its vertex is at the circle's center.) When two such angles intercept (or "cut off") the same arc of the circle, a special size relationship exists between the two angles: The measure of the central angle will always be double the measure of the inscribed angle. In this case, that means that the measure of angle XCZ must be 80°. This, in turn, means that the minor arc XZ also has a measure of 80°. Every circle (considered as an arc) has a measure of 360°. Therefore, major arc XYZ has a measure of 280° ($= 360° - 80°$).

107. (A)

Planning lessons that will enable students to experience a high rate of success during the majority of their practice attempts is directly related to enhanced student achievement and heightened self-esteem. Choice (B) is incorrect because although parents are often happy as a result of a student's academic success, this is the result of structuring lessons so students will be successful. Choice (C) is incorrect because, although students are more likely to complete homework if they are successful in early practice attempts, this is only part of

answer (A). Choice (D) is incorrect because students who are successful in independent practice may or may not ask more questions.

108. (A)

As a general rule, if student questions require lengthy responses, then the initial explanation was probably faulty. Choices (B) and (C) are incorrect because there is insufficient information to suggest that the students were not paying attention, or that they have below average listening skills. Choice (D) is incorrect because a teacher should direct all explanations of new information to the level of the students. Even if students did have poor backgrounds in mathematics, the teacher should have taken that into account when explaining new information.

109. (A)

Students who tutor peers or younger students develop their own proficiency as a result of assisting other students. Choice (B) is incorrect because, although some students may view teaching as a possible career, this is not the intended purpose of the tutoring. Choice (C) is incorrect because the goal is helping first graders learn addition and subtraction facts, not teaching fifth graders specific tutoring techniques. Choice (D) is incorrect because, although becoming friends with younger children may occur as a result of tutoring, it is not the main goal of the activity.

110. (B)

Integrating another content area into the students' study of the American Revolution will develop a broader view of that period in history. (A) is incorrect because even though the teachers are integrating their lessons, they are each responsible for their own subject area. (C) is incorrect because librarians are usually pleased when books are used by teachers and students. (D) is incorrect because teaching integrated units does not mean that students will be doing homework for one subject during another subject's class period.

111. (B)

Students who are overly talkative are usually flattered to be asked to take a leadership role. Asking these students to take notes also assigns them a task that allows the other students to voice their opinions uninterrupted. Choice (A) is incorrect because calling on these students only once during the class period will most likely frustrate them and create problems. Choice (C) is incorrect because placing overly talkative students in a group by themselves does not teach them to listen to other students' opinions. Choice (D) is incorrect because, although overly talkative students usually need attention, they must learn to recognize that other students also have opinions, even though they may not be assertive in voicing them.

112. (C)

The gas molecules themselves do not expand in size when heated, but the spaces between them increases as the molecules move faster. The expanding hot air leaves the balloon body through the opening at the bottom. With less air in the balloon casing, the balloon is lighter. The combustion products of propane are carbon dioxide (molar mass 44 g/mol), which is heavier than air, and water (molar mass 18 g/mol), which is lighter.

113. (D)

Students are more likely to be more enthusiastic when something that they enjoy are is the subject or focus of a lesson, which, in turn, helps to build the academic success of the lesson.

114. (C)

All of the choices are true, but only choice (C) addresses the exercise. Black line spectra are formed when the continuous spectra of the Sun passes through the atmosphere. The elements in the atmosphere absorb wavelengths of light characteristic of their spectra (these are the same wavelengths given off when the element is excited—for example, the red color of a neon light). By examining the line spectral gaps, scientists can deduce the elements that make up the distant atmosphere. Choice

(A) is true, but it explains the source of a line spectrum. Choice (B) is true, and it explains why a blue shirt is blue when placed under a white or blue light source. Recall that a blue shirt under a red light source will appear black because there are no blue wavelengths to be reflected. Choice (D) is partially true because black lights do give off ultraviolet light that the human eye cannot see.

115. (C)

The upward force of air resistance partially counteracts the force of gravity when a feather falls in air. In a vacuum, or near vacuum, this force is dramatically reduced for the feather and both objects will fall at the same rate. The effect can be modeled without a vacuum pump by comparing the falling of two papers, one crumpled to reduce air resistance and the other flat.

116. (A)

Force is equal to mass multiplied by acceleration ($F=ma$). The force needed is the product of the objects mass (20,000 lbs.) and the acceleration. Acceleration is the change in speed per unit time. The projectile's acceleration is thus (12,000 yards/second – 0 yards/second) / 0.05 seconds). Therefore, the correct equation is (A) $20,000 \times (12,000 / 0.05)$.

117. (B)

The ranchers believe that killing the eagles will protect their ranches. This is understood by the implication that "attract[ing] and kill[ing] predators . . . in an effort to preserve young grazing animals" will protect their ranches.

118. (B)

The author's use of words such as "mighty bald eagle" and "threatened by a new menace" supports concern for the topic. For the most part, the author appears objective; thus, choice (B), concerned interest, is the correct answer.

119. (B)

The first paragraph states that this is the reason that water is a most unusual substance. Choices (A) and (C) list unusual properties of water, but they are not developed in the same manner as the property stated in choice (B). Choice (D) is not correct under any circumstances.

120. (A)

Only choice (A) recognizes the cognitive principle underlying the teacher's assignment. Choices (B) and (D) are essentially the same; although the assignment may result in these time saving features, they are not the instructional principle guiding the teacher's practice. Choice (C) is irrelevant. Asking students to hypothesize is not directly related to inculcating self-management skills in learners.

INSTALLING REA's TEST*ware*®

SYSTEM REQUIREMENTS

Pentium 75 MHz (300 MHz recommended) or a higher or compatible processor; Microsoft Windows 98 or later; 64 MB available RAM; Internet Explorer 5.5 or higher.

INSTALLATION

1. Insert the PRAXIS Elementary Education CD-ROM into the CD-ROM drive.

2. If the installation doesn't begin automatically, from the Start Menu choose the RUN command. When the RUN dialog box appears, type d:\setup (where d is the letter of your CD-ROM drive) at the prompt and click OK.

3. The installation process will begin. A dialog box proposing the directory "C:\ProgramFiles\ REA\Praxis_ElEd" will appear. If the name and location are suitable, click OK. If you wish to specify a different name or location, type it in and click OK.

4. Start the PRAXIS Elementary Education TEST*ware*® application by double-clicking on the icon.

REA's PRAXIS Elementary Education TEST*ware*® is **EASY** to **LEARN AND USE**. To achieve maximum benefits, we recommend that you take a few minutes to go through the on-screen tutorial on your computer. The "screen buttons" are also explained there to familiarize you with the program.

TECHNICAL SUPPORT

REA's TEST*ware*® is backed by customer and technical support. For questions about **installation or operation of your software**, contact us at:

> **Research & Education Association**
> **Phone: (732) 819-8880 (9 a.m. to 5 p.m. ET, Monday–Friday)**
> **Fax: (732) 819-8808**
> **Website: *www.rea.com***
> **E-mail: info@rea.com**

Note to Windows XP Users: In order for the TEST*ware*® to function properly, please install and run the application under the same computer administrator-level user account. Installing the TEST*ware*® as one user and running it as another could cause file-access path conflicts.

Index

H

I